Yrs. very truly,
Mary A. Livermore.

ENGRAVED FROM A PHOTOGRAPH EXPRESSLY FOR THIS WORK.
A.D. WORTHINGTON & CO., PUBLISHERS, HARTFORD, CONN.

# MY STORY OF THE WAR:

## A Woman's Narrative

OF

# FOUR YEARS PERSONAL EXPERIENCE

AS NURSE IN THE UNION ARMY, AND IN RELIEF WORK AT HOME,
IN HOSPITALS, CAMPS, AND AT THE FRONT, DURING
THE WAR OF THE REBELLION.

WITH

### Anecdotes, Pathetic Incidents, and Thrilling Reminiscences

PORTRAYING

THE LIGHTS AND SHADOWS OF HOSPITAL LIFE

AND

THE SANITARY SERVICE OF THE WAR.

BY

## MARY A. LIVERMORE.
New introduction by Nina Silber.

---

### Superbly Illustrated

*WITH PORTRAITS AND NUMEROUS FULL-PAGE ENGRAVINGS ON
STEEL, AND FINE CHROMO-LITHOGRAPH PLATES.*

---

DA CAPO PRESS • NEW YORK

Library of Congress Cataloging in Publication Data

Livermore, Mary Ashton Rice, 1820–1905.
  My story of the war: the Civil War memoirs of the famous nurse, relief or-
ganizer, and suffragette / by Mary A. Livermore; new introduction by Nina
Silber.
     p.    cm.
  Previously published: New York, Arno Press, 1972.
  ISBN 0-306-80658-4
  1. Livermore, Mary Ashton Rice, 1820–1905. 2. United States—History—
Civil War, 1861–1865—War work. 3. United States Sanitary Commission. 4.
Flags—United States. 5. United States—History—Civil War, 1861–1865—
Flags. 6. United States—History—Civil War, 1861–1865—Personal narratives.
7. United States—History—Civil War, 1861–1865—Women. 8. Nurses—
United States—Biography. I. Title.
E621.L79   1995
                                                                    95-21082
                                                                         CIP

First Da Capo Press edition 1995

This Da Capo Press paperback edition of *My Story of the War* is an
unabridged republication of the edition originally published in
Hartford, Connecticut in 1887, with the addition of a new
introduction by Nina Silber.

Published by Da Capo Press, Inc.
A Subsidiary of Plenum Publishing Corporation
233 Spring Street, New York, N.Y. 10013

TO

## THE VICTORIOUS SOLDIERS OF THE UNION ARMY,

HOWEVER CIRCUMSTANCED AND WHEREVER LIVING;

TO

### The Honored Memory of the Heroic Dead,

WHO MADE THE SOIL OF THE SOUTH BILLOWY
WITH THEIR GRAVES;

AND TO

MY SURVIVING CO-WORKERS IN THAT NOBLE ORGANIZATION,

THE UNITED STATES SANITARY COMMISSION,

*THIS WORK IS DEDICATED.*

# INTRODUCTION

I ABHOR war," wrote Mary Livermore towards the end of her life, "yet believe . . . that there are times when 'war is God's missionary.'" Certainly few were more qualified than she to discuss the abhorrent side of war. Mary Livermore had seen more human suffering and misery in the four years of the Civil War than most people would see in a lifetime. Yet, hardly a pacifist, Livermore also saw the war, and everything connected to it, as a righteous struggle to destroy "the last stronghold of human slavery." Indeed, she herself became one of the most prominent missionaries on behalf of the Union and its soldiers during the four years of sectional conflict; and in her unflagging efforts for the United States Sanitary Commission, Mary Livermore emerged as one of the most visibly active women of the nineteenth century. When she composed her wartime reminiscences in 1887, her words were read by tens of thousands of nineteenth-century Americans. Yet, in the late twentieth century, few recall this influential figure or her writings. This reissue of Mary Livermore's wartime memoirs resurrects a long-neglected classic in Civil War literature.[1]

Mary Ashton Rice was nurtured in an atmosphere that was at once both stifling and inspiring. Born on December 19, 1820, she was the first child to survive infancy in the family of Timothy Rice, a laborer of Welsh background, and Zebiah

---

[1] Livermore quoted in Lilian Whiting, *Women Who Have Ennobled Life* (Philadelphia, 1915), p. 83; Phillip Paludan, *"A People's Contest": The Union and Civil War, 1861-1865* (New York, 1988), pp. 386-388.

Ashton, the Boston-born daughter of an English sea captain. Mary recalled her childhood in Boston as one which was "steeped" in "the Calvinistic faith in its entirety and severity," especially as it was administered under the stern authority of her father. Mary was apparently awed by her father's powerful religious vision, but somewhat resentful of its gloomier and pessimistic side. In her autobiography she wrote of her constant search for something that would free her from the haunting specter of eternal damnation.[2]

Education, to some extent, offered Mary Rice an expressive outlet. As a young woman of the early nineteenth century, she seems to have been favored with a considerable amount of schooling. Despite a two-year hiatus while her family tried farming in western New York State, she attended school fairly regularly until the age of sixteen. After graduating from a female seminary in Charlestown, Massachusetts, she remained on the staff as a teacher. In 1839, at the age of nineteen, she moved to a southern Virginia plantation where she was employed as a tutor for several children.

"This residence at the South," Livermore explained in her autobiography, "was to change and shape my future career." Life on the Henderson plantation exposed her to numerous influences which had not been permitted in the Rice household. She deeply appreciated the chance to learn more about literature and history from the cultivated Mr. Henderson. Yet she was also deeply disturbed by the strange combination of Southern refinement and barbarity, especially what she saw of the brutality and misery connected with slavery. After three years, she returned to New England "a pronounced abolitionist."[3]

While employed as the headmistress of a coeducational school in Duxbury, Massachusetts, she met Daniel Parker Livermore, a young minister in the Universalist Church. Livermore's relig-

---

[2] Mary Livermore, *The Story of My Life* (Hartford, CT, 1897), pp. 40-41.

[3] Livermore, *Ibid.*, pp. 146-364.

ion of love and hope again offered Mary Rice an outlet from her father's stern and pessimistic philosophy. Over Timothy Rice's objections, Mary and Daniel married in 1845. For the next several years they moved throughout New England and western New York as Daniel was called to different pastorates. During this time she gave birth to three girls, one of whom died in childhood. By 1858 the Livermores had moved to Chicago where Daniel owned and edited a Universalist journal; Mary served as associate editor. In May 1860 Livermore's journalist credentials gained her admittance as the only female reporter to the Chicago convention which nominated Abraham Lincoln as the Republican Party's candidate for President. She recalled the incident in *My Story of the War*, describing how her presence provoked a confrontation on the convention floor. Supported by her fellow journalists, Livermore stayed and observed Lincoln's triumph. In the months that followed, she watched as the national apocalypse approached.[4]

"It is not possible for any one who did not live at the time to understand the mental condition of the North during the winter of 1860-61," Livermore recalled. "As state after state rushed from the national constellation, it seemed to the states that remained faithful as if the nation were lapsing into chaos." That wartime chaos thrust Mary Livermore into a position of prominence and influence; it also changed her life immeasurably. Hiring a housekeeper and governess to oversee her domestic duties, she immediately became a volunteer for the Chicago (later the Northwestern) Sanitary Commission. For the next four years the Commission and the well-being of the Union soldiers became her principle concern.[5]

Although initially resisted by Abraham Lincoln as an unnec-

---

[4]Robert E. Riegel, "Mary Livermore," in Edward T. James, ed., *Notable American Women* (Cambridge, MA, 1971), Vol. II, p. 411; Whiting, *Women Who Have Ennobled Life*, p. 62.

[5]Whiting, *Ibid.*, pp. 62-63.

essary appendage to the Union war machine, the United States Sanitary Commission eventually became a highly effective vehicle, mobilizing the voluntary efforts of tens of thousands of Union women. As the Commission's rank and file, the women worked tirelessly to send clothing, food, bandages, and nurses to the men in the field. Most of the Commission's officers were men. But by the second year of the war Mary Livermore and Jane C. Hoge became two of just a handful of women who rose from the ranks of the Commission network to positions of leadership. In December 1862 Livermore and Hoge were placed in charge of the Chicago operations.[6]

For four years Livermore and Hoge devoted themselves wholeheartedly to their relief efforts. Occasionally they nursed sick and wounded soldiers on the battlefront; more often, their work revolved around fundraising and organizing efforts throughout the Northwest. Within this latter sphere they had no peers; few traveled so widely, spoke so frequently, or canvassed so effectively on the soldiers' behalf. Indeed, so thorough were their efforts that one contemporary believed their names had become "household words."[7]

When she did visit the camps and hospitals on or near the Western battlefronts, Livermore positioned herself as an arbiter of honest and effective relief work. She personally oversaw the delivery of food and medical relief items and frequently intervened in the care and management of patients, even, on one occasion, appealing to General Grant to win the release of 21 suffering soldiers. Perhaps the culmination of her war work came in October 1863 when she planned and organized what became the first of many Sanitary Fairs. Her work for the Chicago fair inspired thousands of women in several Northern cities to hold their own fairs which eventually raised more than a million dollars for relief work.

[6]James McPherson, *Battle Cry of Freedom* (New York, 1988), p. 481.
[7]Mary Elizabeth Massey, *Bonnet Brigades* (New York, 1966), p. 49.

First published in 1887, *My Story of the War* presents Mary Livermore's recollections of her own remarkable war experiences as well as the larger story about women's contributions to the Union effort. Indeed, the book offers a catalog of women's vast and various wartime activities, including their work as nurses, their arduous agricultural labor in Midwestern fields, their military contributions, even their assistance as military strategists. Livermore explicitly intended, in writing the book, to trumpet the triumphs of women and to use that as a basis for demanding greater public recognition for her sex. Given her postwar dedication to the women's suffrage campaign, she undoubtedly sought to use Northern women's war work as an argument for women's political power.

This was not simply an argument based on hindsight. As Livermore suggests, her own wartime efforts convinced her of the need for women's legal and political equality. She recalled her experience during the planning of the Chicago Sanitary Fair when she was informed by "an illiterate builder" that her husband would have to give his consent so she could spend her own money in enlisting the builder's services. At that point, she observed, "I registered a vow that when the war was over I would take up a new work—the work of making law and justice synonymous for women" (p. 436). As Livermore was keenly aware, the war had propelled women into public life but had simultaneously brought them up against the social, legal, and economic restrictions of Victorian America.

Commission workers like Livermore repeatedly confronted those restrictions in their daily struggles with the war machine and Union bureaucracy. She recalled, for example, an overwhelming "prejudice against Protestant women nurses," especially on the part of medical directors and surgeons who found them far less compliant than the Catholic "Sisters." Even women within the bureaucracy threw up obstacles. Livermore thus described, somewhat unenthusiastically, her impressions of

Dorothea Dix and her decision to exclude young and attractive women from the Army Medical Bureau's nursing service. Finally, Livermore provided some of the most dramatic examples of female suffering and dependency in the several accounts of poor women who became utterly bereft of economic resources when they were deprived of a man's earning power.

Yet *My Story of the War* is by no means a record of repeated roadblocks for Commission and other Northern women. In many ways, it provides a remarkable testament to women's power and their ability to carve out an impressive sphere of influence in wartime. More than anything, Livermore compels even the late twentieth-century reader to marvel at women's ability to wage successful battles with the staunchest bureaucrats and most unenlightened medical professionals. In part, the women's success stemmed from the very same stereotypes which sought to confine them to the domestic sphere. Union women drew on a tradition of female moral authority when they confronted drunken or corrupt doctors and army officials. And they used their domestic skills—especially their commitment to personal hygiene and wholesome food preparation—to uplift the health and morale of the sick and wounded. Indeed, the women's very presence seemed to inspire the soldiers who longed for a reminder of home and domestic comfort. As Ann Douglas reminds us, the majority of Union soldiers were boys who really did miss their mothers and who thoroughly welcomed the maternal presence of the Commission ladies. Livermore herself was keenly aware of this relationship and remarked on it in her description of one boat trip to Memphis when ailing soldiers came on board and the women "fell into maternal relations with them, as women instinctively do when brought into juxtaposition with weakness" (p. 345).[8]

Thus, as Livermore suggests, a unique bond was formed be-

[8]Ann Douglas Wood, "The War Within a War: Women Nurses in the Union Army," *Civil War History* XVIII (September 1972), pp. 197-212.

tween the youthful soldiers of the rank and file and the slightly older (although usually not elderly) women of the Commission and the nursing corps. The women aided, assisted, and championed "their boys," even to the point of battling army officialdom, especially a wide array of "middle managers" who seemed preoccupied with army rules and bureaucratic red tape. Because they were outside the bureaucracy and official reigns of power, and because they often served as volunteers, women like Jane Hoge, Mary Livermore, and "Mother" Bickerdyke could challenge authority without risking their own careers. The ultimate success of these women was registered in the general welcome and approval they received from the Union high command—including such distinguished figures as Generals Sherman and Grant, and Abraham Lincoln. In effect, women's lack of power became a source of strength, enabling them to circumvent the usual chain of command. By positioning themselves as mothers who could marshal a power higher than that of mundane rules and regulations, these women earned a unique reputation, summed up in the curious phrase which Livermore often heard, that "women could do anything they desired with army officers" (p. 313).

*My Story of the War* was one of many reminiscences written in the postwar years that recounted women's wartime activities and experiences. As Livermore explained in the preface, she briefly considered writing her war memoirs soon after the fighting had ceased but decided, instead, to attend to numerous literary and philanthropic pursuits. By the time Livermore's volume did appear, the author had established herself as a prominent figure on the lecture circuit and in reform circles, devoting herself especially to talks and campaigns on behalf of women's rights. Her impressive presence on the lyceum stage led some to refer to her as "the Queen of the Platform." Such prominence undoubtedly boosted book sales; the memoirs apparently sold between 60,000 and 100,000 copies. Her subsequent autobiography—*The Story of My Life* (1897)—sold equally well. Nonetheless, it seems likely that Livermore's publisher had some initial trepidations about publishing a woman's war memoirs—and so included numerous illustrations of Northern and Southern battle flags in order to enhance sales. But, interesting as those illustrations are, her reading public were no doubt more enthralled by the author's vivid recollections of the home-front and the warfront from 1861 to 1865. In those reflections Livermore presents us with her singular view of a war that, although abhorrent, was certainly one of the most transformative experiences for men and women in American history.[9]

NINA SILBER
Boston University
April 1995

---

[9]Riegel, "Mary Livermore," p. 412; Riegel's piece places sales for *My Story of the War* at around 60,000; in *Women Who Have Ennobled Life*, Lilian Whiting quotes from a letter by Mary Livermore in which she maintains that sales came closer to 100,000 copies. In the same letter Livermore also claimed that a fire at the publisher's office had destroyed the plates and the remaining volumes (pp. 82-83). For more on other women's wartime memoirs see Mary Massey, *Bonnet Brigades*, pp. 185-196.

## PREFACE.

A T the close of the war, I was importuned to publish my
experiences and reminiscences in connection with the
hospitals and the relief work of the Sanitary Commission.
But I declined to do so. A horror of the war still en-
wrapped the country. The salvation of the nation had been
purchased with the blood of her sons, and she was still in
the throes of anguish because of her bereavement. The
people had turned with relief to the employments of peaceful life, eager to forget the fearful years of battle and carnage. I put away all mementoes of the exceptional life I
had led, and re-entered with gladness upon the duties connected with my home and family, giving my leisure, as
before the war, to charitable work and literary pursuits.
I expected this quiet and happy order of things would continue to the end.

It has been otherwise ordered. The twenty-odd years
that have passed since the bells rang in the long prayer for
peace have been unlike any of which I had ever dreamed.
They have been packed with work, have brought me in contact with people and events of national importance, have
afforded me extended opportunities of travel in my own
country and Europe, and have given me a largeness and

7

variety of experience not often gained by a woman. The
sun of my life is now sloping swiftly to the west, the years
that I have travelled lie stretching in long array behind me,
and I am approaching the time when one lives much in
memory. I have again been asked to write for publication
my story of the war and its relief work, and this time the
request has found me favorably disposed to the undertaking.

The public ear has listened eagerly to the stories of the
great battles of the war of the rebellion, told by the master
spirits who conducted them, and who led the hosts of freedom to victory. The plan of the campaigns, the division
of the forces, and the parts assigned to the various officers
in command, the topography of the battle-fields, the personal
prowess and heroism developed in the hotly contested
struggle, and the jubilant victory which resulted, whose
pæans of joy drowned the cries of the wounded and the
wails of bereavement — of these histories the people have not
grown weary. Every detail of Fort Donelson and Vicksburg, Antietam and Gettysburg, and the surrender of
Appomattox is eagerly sought and devoured with zest.
Millions of readers bend over the thrilling autobiographies
of Grant, Sherman, Logan, and other great captains of the
memorable war, when, on the top wave of a nation's righteous wrath with slavery, four million of slaves were lifted
to the level of freemen.

But there is a paucity of histories of the private soldier,
of sketches of the rank and file. These have not been
written, partly because of the modesty of the men whose
experiences were worth narrating, and partly because they
were not favorably circumstanced for extensive observation.
There is a whole world of thrilling and heroic deed and
endeavor, of lofty patience, silent endurance and sacrifice,
connected with the soldiers of the army, of which the world

will always remain ignorant. It cannot be told. Neither can the deeds of nobleness performed by the people who remained at home, and who stood loyally by the government in its every hour of extremity. They measured their ready aid by the nation's need, and, in their consecration to the cause of national unity and freedom, outran all outward demands made upon them.

The patriotism of men, the solemn joyfulness with which they gave of their possessions and of themselves, the unfaltering faith which no disaster could shake and no treachery enfeeble, who has told us of these, in detail? Who has fully narrated the consecrated and organized work of women, who strengthened the sinews of the nation with their unflagging enthusiasm, and bridged over the chasm between civil and military life, by infusing homogeneousness of feeling into the army and the people, "keeping the men in the field civilians, and making the people at home, of both sexes, half soldiers"? It can never be understood save by those who lived through that period, when one year counted more in the history of noble development than a half-score of ordinary years of buying and selling, building and furnishing, visiting and feasting. If this book shall in any way help to supply the deficiency I have indicated, my purpose will be accomplished.

I am largely indebted to my husband and friends for the materials from which this book has been made. My own tendency is to destroy the records of my past, as soon as an event or experience has ended. I have had little taste for preserving records, journals, memoranda, and letters, and am never hampered with this sort of *impedimenta*. "Let the dead past bury its dead!" has been one of my cherished mottoes. The duty of the hour, the work of the "living present," has enthralled me, rather than contemplation of the past. But, in this instance, what I have been careless of preserving, my kindred and friends have held in trust for me.

For more than a dozen years, covering the entire period of the war, I was associated with my husband in the editorship of his paper, published in Chicago. For its columns I wrote sketches of all events, that were interesting or inspiring, in connection with the Sanitary Commission. Its readers were informed of every phase of its relief work, as soon as it was undertaken, and of its special calls for aid. And when I went to the hospitals on errands connected with the sick, wounded and dying, or made trips into the army in charge of sanitary stores, for whose disbursement I was held responsible, I always corresponded for the press. And no issue of my husband's paper appeared, when I was thus engaged, that did not contain long letters from the front, packed with narrations of facts and events, for which I knew its readers were eagerly looking.

I sent similar letters to other periodicals in the Northwest, wrote war sketches for magazines struggling for existence, edited the monthly bulletins of the Chicago Branch of the Commission, which were its means of communication with its four thousand Aid Societies, wrote its circular letters appealing for specific and immediate aid, wrote for its contributors a detailed history of the first great Sanitary Fair, which proved the inspiration and model of those which followed it, dictated and penned letters by the thousand from the rooms of the Commission, which were inspired by the emergencies of the time, and which have been largely preserved by the individuals and societies to whom they were addressed, answered every soldier's letter that I received, whether I had ever heard of him or not, wrote letters by the hundred to their friends at home, by the bedside of sick, wounded and dying soldiers, and in behalf of those who had died — in short, notwithstanding the herculean work imposed on me, as on all women at the head of the Branch Commissions, I accomplished more with my pen during the four years of the war than during any similar period of time before or since.

Whatever of mine was published, or whatever related to my work during the war, my husband preserved in chronological order, as he did all memoranda or diaries made by me. And whatever letters came to me from the army, or from civilians working in the interest of the country, he saved from destruction. When to these were added my personal letters to friends, which after twenty years were returned, in response to an appeal for them, copies of circulars, bulletins, reports, crude magazine sketches, synopses of addresses, all inspired by the one absorbing topic of the time — the war for the Union, and its brave soldiers, with their anxious and suffering families,— I was embarrassed by the enormous bulk of the collection. It was no small task to collate and arrange the appalling mass of documents, and to decide what would be of present interest, and what had been made valueless by the lapse of years.

At last the book is completed, and is now presented to the public. In no sense does it purport to be a history. It is a collection of experiences and reminiscences, more interesting to me in the retrospect than at the time of their occurrence. For then all who loved their native land, and strove to save it from disintegration, carried its woes on their hearts like a personal bereavement, and only lived through the awful anguish by the help of the mighty panacea of absorbing work for others. No one is more keenly alive than I to the defects of this volume. But any farther attempt at improvement would result, I fear, in its entire withdrawal. And as I have something to say in behalf of the common soldiers, most of them veritable Philip Sidneys in their heroism and unselfishness, and of that noble army of women who worked untiringly for the right, while the war lasted, "exerting a greater moral force on the nation than the army that carried loaded muskets," I hasten to save my work from destruction, by placing it beyond my reach, in the hands of the publisher.

May it receive a warm welcome from the " Boys in Blue," whose thinning ranks can never know an increase, and from my surviving co-workers in the Sanitary Commission, whose beloved comradeship is one of the priceless possessions of which the covetous years have not wholly bereft me.

*Mary A. Livermore*

# LIST OF ILLUSTRATIONS.

## Finely Engraved on Steel

From Photographs, and from Original Designs drawn expressly for this work by Mr. F. O. C. Darley and Mr. Wm. L. Sheppard.

## PORTRAITS.

1. PORTRAIT OF THE AUTHOR . . . . . . . . *Frontispiece*

> From a photograph taken expressly for this work. Engraved on steel in pure line, by Mr. CHARLES SCHLECHT.

2. MRS. JANE C. HOGE . . . . .
3. MRS. MARY A. BICKERDYKE .
   ("MOTHER BICKERDYKE")
4. MISS MARY J. SAFFORD. . . .
5. MRS. CORDELIA A. P. HARVEY,

PAGE

} WOMEN OF THE WAR. — FAMOUS NURSES OF UNION SOLDIERS . *To face* 160

> Engraved from photographs expressly for this work by Mr. S. HOLLYER.

## FIGURE ILLUSTRATIONS.

Engraved on steel in pure line and stipple, by Mr. JOHN J. CADE.

1. A WOMAN IN BATTLE.—"MICHIGAN BRIDGET" CARRYING THE FLAG. DESIGNED BY F. O. C. DARLEY . . *To face* 116

> "Sometimes when a soldier fell she took his place, fighting in his stead with unquailing courage — always fearless and daring, always doing good service as a soldier."

2. THE DYING SOLDIER. — THE LAST LETTER FROM
   HOME. DESIGNED BY F. O. C. DARLEY . . . . . *To face* 210

  "He drew from an inside pocket a letter inclosing a photograph of a
most lovely woman, and feebly whispered, 'My wife.' I spoke to him, but
he seemed not to hear, and there was a far-away look in the gaze, as if his
vision reached beyond my ken. The wardmaster approached, and laid his
finger on the wrist. 'He is dead!' he whispered."

3. PRAYER-MEETING IN A CONTRABAND CAMP. — WASH-
   INGTON, 1862. DESIGNED BY WM. L. SHEPPARD . . *To face* 262

  "Oh, I'm gwine home to glory — won't yer go along wid me,
   Whar de blessed angels beckon, an' de Lor' my Savior be?"

4. FLEEING FROM THE LAND OF BONDAGE. — ON THE
   MISSISSIPPI RIVER IN 1863. DESIGNED BY F. O. C. DAR-
   LEY . . . . . . . . . . . . . . . . . *To face* 342

  "Mothers carried their babes on one arm, and led little woolly-headed
toddlers by the other. Old men and women, gray, nearly blind, some of
them bent almost double, bore on their heads and backs the small 'plunder' they had 'toted' from their homes. They were all going forth, like
the Israelites, 'from the land of bondage to a land they knew not.'"

5. "OUR BATTERY" AT THE FRONT. — REVEILLE AFTER
   AN ANXIOUS NIGHT. DESIGNED BY WM. L. SHEPPARD.
                 *To face* 380

  "They stood ready to aid in an immediate attack for three days and
nights."

6. DEATH OF SERGEANT DYER WHILE SPIKING HIS GUN.
   DESIGNED BY F. O. C. DARLEY . . . . . . . . *To face* 394

  "Our boys tried to save their guns, but, finding that impossible, they
endeavored to spike them. Sergeant Dyer, whom I have before mentioned
as a rare nurse in sickness, was shot through the lungs, and mortally
wounded, while in the act of spiking his gun. Of one hundred and ten
horses, they took off the field but forty-five."

7. MIDNIGHT ON THE BATTLE-FIELD. DESIGNED BY F. O.
   C. DARLEY . . . . . . . . . . . . . . . *To face* 484

  "It was Mother Bickerdyke, with a lantern, still groping among the
dead. Stooping down and turning their cold faces towards her, she scrutinized them searchingly, uneasy lest some might be left to die uncared for.
She could not rest while she thought any were overlooked who were yet
living."

8. A REBEL SHELL BURSTING IN A UNION HOSPITAL.
   DESIGNED BY F. O. C. DARLEY . . . . . . . *To face* 494

  "On the second day of the fight (Corinth), to her horror, her hospital
came within range of the enemy's artillery, and the fearful missiles of death
fell with fatal precision among her helpless men."

## ARRANGED BY STATES.

### MAINE.

|  | PLATE | PAGE |
|---|---|---|
| 1ST MAINE HEAVY ARTILLERY | ii. | 239 |

### NEW HAMPSHIRE.

| 5TH REGIMENT INFANTRY | vi. | 597 |
|---|---|---|

### VERMONT.

| HEADQUARTERS GUIDON OF THE OLD VERMONT BRIGADE, | i. | 93 |
|---|---|---|
| 1ST VERMONT CAVALRY | vi. | 597 |

### MASSACHUSETTS.

| 20TH REGIMENT INFANTRY | vi. | 597 |
|---|---|---|
| 21ST REGIMENT INFANTRY | ii. | 239 |
| 24TH REGIMENT INFANTRY | ii. | 239 |
| 54TH REGIMENT INFANTRY | vi. | 597 |

### RHODE ISLAND.

| 1ST RHODE ISLAND CAVALRY | vi. | 597 |
|---|---|---|

### CONNECTICUT.

| 1ST CONNECTICUT HEAVY ARTILLERY | ii. | 239 |
|---|---|---|
| 11TH REGIMENT INFANTRY | i. | 93 |
| 14TH REGIMENT INFANTRY | ii. | 239 |
| 16TH REGIMENT INFANTRY | vi. | 597 |

### NEW YORK.

| 7TH NEW YORK HEAVY ARTILLERY | iii. | 329 |
|---|---|---|
| 18TH NEW YORK CAVALRY | viii. | 657 |
| 40TH REGIMENT INFANTRY | ii. | 239 |
| 48TH REGIMENT INFANTRY | v. | 443 |
| 105TH REGIMENT INFANTRY | v. | 443 |

### NEW JERSEY.

| 1ST NEW JERSEY CAVALRY | v. | 443 |
|---|---|---|
| 9TH REGIMENT INFANTRY | v. | 443 |

### PENNSYLVANIA.

| 78TH REGIMENT INFANTRY | viii. | 657 |
|---|---|---|
| 83D REGIMENT INFANTRY | v. | 443 |
| 150TH REGIMENT INFANTRY | v. | 443 |

### OHIO.

| | PLATE | PAGE |
|---|---|---|
| McMULLEN'S 1ST INDEPENDENT OHIO BATTERY | vii. | 625 |
| 78TH REGIMENT INFANTRY | viii. | 657 |

### INDIANA.

| | | |
|---|---|---|
| 32D REGIMENT INFANTRY | viii. | 657 |

### KENTUCKY.

| | | |
|---|---|---|
| 9TH REGIMENT INFANTRY | viii. | 657 |

### ILLINOIS.

| | | |
|---|---|---|
| 13TH REGIMENT INFANTRY | iii. | 329 |
| 129TH REGIMENT INFANTRY | viii. | 657 |

### MICHIGAN.

| | | |
|---|---|---|
| 2D REGIMENT INFANTRY | iii. | 329 |
| 24TH REGIMENT INFANTRY | iii. | 329 |

### WISCONSIN.

| | | |
|---|---|---|
| "OLD ABE," WISCONSIN'S WAR EAGLE | vii. | 625 |
| 2D REGIMENT INFANTRY | vii. | 625 |

### MINNESOTA.

| | | |
|---|---|---|
| 1ST MINNESOTA ARTILLERY | iii. | 329 |

### IOWA.

| | | |
|---|---|---|
| 9TH REGIMENT INFANTRY | vii. | 625 |

### MISSOURI.

| | | |
|---|---|---|
| 7TH REGIMENT INFANTRY | vii. | 625 |
| 8TH REGIMENT INFANTRY | iii. | 329 |

### KANSAS.

| | | |
|---|---|---|
| 2D REGIMENT INFANTRY | vii. | 625 |
| 2D KANSAS BATTERY | vii. | 625 |

| | | |
|---|---|---|
| HEADQUARTERS GUIDON OF THE 6TH ARMY CORPS | i. | 93 |

## CONFEDERATE BATTLE–FLAGS.

| | | |
|---|---|---|
| BATTLE-FLAG CAPTURED FROM GENERAL BRAGG | iv. | 421 |
| BATTLE-FLAG OF THE 42D MISSISSIPPI REGIMENT | iv. | 421 |
| BATTLE-FLAG OF THE 12TH MISSISSIPPI CAVALRY | iv. | 421 |
| BLOOD-STAINED SILK FLAG OF THE 9TH TEXAS REGIMENT, | iv. | 421 |
| BATTLE-FLAG OF AUSTIN'S BATTERY | iv. | 421 |
| BATTLE-FLAG OF A SOUTH CAROLINA REGIMENT | iv. | 421 |
| BATTLE-FLAG, BLACK (NO QUARTER), SUPPOSED TO HAVE BELONGED TO A TEXAS REGIMENT | iv. | 421 |
| SILK BATTLE-FLAG | iv. | 421 |

PUBLISHERS' INTRODUCTION TO THE FLAGS.

THE Publishers deem a few words of explanation necessary respecting the colored battle-flag plates which occupy so prominent a place in this volume. No patriot eye can look upon these battle-stained mementos of the war without mingled feelings of admiration, pride, and sadness. They have been wafted by the sighs and prayers of a struggling people, and hallowed by the blood of patriot sons. They have a peculiar fitness and place in this record of a woman's work for and among private soldiers, for they were the men who proudly and bravely carried them. Private soldiers were the true heroes of the war. Their bravery was as great, their judgment often as good, and their capacity for commanding often equal to those under whom they were content to fight without distinction or reward.

It was no part of the original plan to introduce in this volume so many of these flags. It was at first thought that a single frontispiece page, composed of two or three flags in *fac-simile*, would be a novel and appropriate feature, and lend additional interest to the work. But it proved a difficult and delicate matter to select only two or three from many thousand flags entitled to representation; for the Publishers wished to act with strict impartiality and without rendering themselves open to the criticism of exalting one flag, regiment, or state over others entitled to equal praise. In this dilemma it became apparent that if flags were introduced as illustrations at all, the North ought to be generally represented.

To this end an artist and a photographer were sent to the capital of each northern state, to make photographs and color sketches of the flags. Serious and unexpected obstacles met them at the very outset, for nearly every state had provided a permanent place for its tattered banners, and rightfully guarded them with tender care. In several states legislative enactments made it seemingly impossible to obtain permission to disturb the flags in the least, — no hand was even permitted to touch them — much less to remove them from their glass cases for any purpose whatever. And yet it was absolutely necessary to take them out of the cases and arrange them properly before they could be photographed and color sketches made. One by one all obstacles were surmounted, and the Publishers are at last enabled to show the flags with exact fidelity to the originals, both in appearance and color.

In selecting the flags the Publishers endeavored to exercise a wise and careful discrimination. Their artists photographed a number of flags in each state capital, selecting those that were represented as possessing the most interesting history. From these the Publishers made a final choice, and they were guided in this by first obtaining from reliable sources a history of each flag, finally selecting those that appeared to have the greatest interest attached to them. They cannot hope that they have been completely successful in making this selection, but they acted wholly from the best information they could obtain, and carefully weighed every fact and incident, and the authority for them, before making their decision. If one color-bearer or regiment performed more conspicuous service than another, it was only because of better opportunity. All were brave men, and the Publishers regret that every Union battle-flag could not find a place in this book. If all the heroic deeds of those who died under their folds, and of those who took their places and kept the colors flying, could be gathered, they would fill a volume.

The most difficult task of all was to obtain the story of each flag and establish its truth. Many of the men who so proudly carried them in battle sleep in unknown graves on southern battle-fields, far away from their northern homes. " Southern dews will weep above them as gently as though they lay in their northern village church-yards; grass and grain will cover them; winter will decorate their resting-places as with monumental marble, and summer will spread over them its flowers of red, white and blue ; the labors of the husbandmen may obliterate these hillocks of the dead, but the power of their sacrifice will forever circulate in the life of the nation." * Of the survivors many have died since the close of the war, and twenty-five years have made the memory of those who are left much less reliable than they think. Conflicting statements have arisen even from those who were eye-witnesses of some of the scenes described, but these differences were generally respecting minor details. Even official statements do not always agree. In one state capitol is exhibited a flag on which is pinned a piece of paper purporting to give its history. The story is very thrilling, but only a small part of it is true. The writer of it (unknown) simply got the story of two flags mixed and attached his " history " to a single flag, which is daily gazed upon by visitors, who naturally regard this par-

* Rev. Dr. E. H. Chapin on presentation of New York battle-flags, at Albany, N. Y.

ticular flag as the most interesting of them all. To get at the truth under such circumstances was by no means easy. A vast amount of correspondence, too, was necessary. Veterans of the war are widely scattered. One comrade would refer to another, and he to another, often in a distant state, and frequently after long and patient search information was returned that the man sought for died many years ago. Sometimes the most meagre data came in response to repeated appeals, and where the most was expected the least was obtained. Many letters were returned marked "unknown" or "uncalled for." It is much to be regretted that a full history could not be obtained of all the flags. Earnest and patient effort was made in every case.

It will be seen from the above statement that the labor and care involved in producing these illustrations have necessarily made this part of the work both difficult and slow, and in consequence the publication of the volume has been delayed nearly two years.

One page is devoted to a few of the many hundred Confederate battle-flags captured by Union soldiers. With two exceptions these are from photographs and color sketches made from the original flags, in the keeping of the War Department at Washington. The statements pertaining to these flags are taken from Government Record and presumably are correct.

The Publishers invite further information from any source respecting the flags shown in this volume, so that in future editions of the work a still fuller history of each one may be given. Despite the greatest care, inaccuracies may have crept into the narratives, and the Publishers will gladly correct any misstatements.

Finally, the Publishers return their sincere thanks to all — and their name is Legion — who have in any way helped them in this undertaking. The uniform courtesy of governors and state officials made it possible to obtain photographs and color sketches of the flags; and veterans of the war, and others, have imparted valuable information, without which the story of these flags could not have been written.

# THE FLAG OF OUR UNION.

Flag of the brave! thy folds shall fly,
The sign of hope and triumph high!
When speaks the signal-trumpet tone,
And the long line comes glistening on
(Ere yet the life-blood, warm and wet,
Hath dimmed the glistening bayonet),
Each soldier's eye shall brightly turn
To where thy sky-born glories burn;
And as his springing steps advance,
Catch war and vengeance from the glance.
And when the cannon mouthings loud
Heave in wild wreaths the battle-shroud,
And gory sabres rise and fall
Like shoots of flame on midnight's pall—
There shall thy meteor-glances glow,
And cowering foes shall sink beneath
Each gallant arm that strikes below
That lovely messenger of death.

   .     .     .     .     .

Flag of the free heart's hope and home—
By angel hands to valor given!
Thy stars have lit the welkin dome,
And all thy hues were born in heaven.
Forever float that standard sheet!
Where breathes the foe that falls before us,
With Freedom's soil beneath our feet,
And Freedom's banner streaming o'er us!

J. RODMAN DRAKE

WITH

## 𝔇𝔢𝔰𝔠𝔯𝔦𝔭𝔱𝔦𝔬𝔫𝔰 𝔞𝔫𝔡 𝔈𝔵𝔭𝔩𝔞𝔫𝔞𝔱𝔦𝔬𝔫𝔰.

NOTE BY THE PUBLISHERS. — No expense or pains have been spared to make these chromo-lithograph plates accurate in drawing and coloring. The flags were first photographed, thus insuring fulness of detail, and a color-sketch was then made of each flag, by a skilful artist, directly from the flag itself. The photographs were then transferred to stone, from which the plates herewith presented were printed. Each plate requires no less than sixteen printings to produce the various colors and tints necessary to a faithful representation of the flags, thus requiring *one hundred and twenty-eight* engraved stones to produce these eight plates. The engraving and printing were done by Messrs. Wm. H. Dodd & Co., Hartford, Conn.

## PLATE I.    PAGE 93.

## NO. 1. — FLAG OF THE ELEVENTH REGIMENT CONNECTICUT VOLUNTEERS.

THIS regiment saw over four years' service, and took an active part in many of the most noted battles of the war, including Newbern, South Mountain, Antietam, Fredericksburg, Drury's Bluff, Cold Harbor, Petersburg, etc. The national color carried by the regiment, and which is now deposited in the state capitol at Hartford, consists of the remnants of two flags. One of these flags was presented by the Sons of Connecticut residing in New York, when the regiment passed through that city *en route* for the war, in 1861. In time it became so badly worn and shot-riddled that it could hardly be unfurled, and a new flag was presented to the regiment March 1, 1863, by Miss Julia A. Beach of Wallingford, Conn., through its colonel, Griffin A. Stedman, to whom she was engaged.* The new flag, and what remained of the old one, were tied to the original staff, and were in this manner carried by the regiment till the close of the war.

* General Stedman was killed in front of Petersburg in 1864.

The first color-sergeant was George E. Bailey, Jr., of Deep River, Conn., a large, fine-looking man, who was killed at the storming of the stone bridge at Antietam. The 11th led the charge, and lost one hundred and eighty-one men in this battle. The state flag was carried in this battle by Sergeant David Kittler, who refused to go forward in the charge because the color was not supported by a full color-guard. Kittler was immediately wounded by an officer, who slashed him across the arm with his sword for refusing to advance. At this moment Corporal Henry A. Eastman of Ashford stepped forth and said, "Give me the colors!" and, taking them from Kittler, went forward amid the cheers of his comrades. Eastman carried the colors for some time, and was finally promoted captain.

At the battle of Drury's Bluff the flag was carried by Sergeant Orrin Wilson. Four of the color-guard were wounded. At the battle of Cold Harbor one of the color-guard was killed, and Color-Sergeant Metzger and two members of the color-guard were wounded. In that short, terrible and unsuccessful charge, nearly one-half the regiment were killed or wounded in the short space of five minutes. In this battle the flag was struck by many bullets, and the flag-staff was shot completely in two. The staff was then bound together with pieces of a harness belonging to the horses of a battery near by.

July 30, 1864, at the "Crater" in front of Petersburg, a rebel shell burst among the color-guard, killing one and wounding six. The one killed was literally blown to pieces, and his brains were spattered on the flag and staff.

While in front of Petersburg the camp of the regiment was in a ravine, through which flowed a small stream of water. One day a violent storm quickly made the stream a roaring torrent, and the camp was suddenly under water. The men hardly had time to reach high ground before the camp was swept away. Corporal Reisel of the color-guard tried to save the colors, but was borne down by the *débris* in the water and drowned. The colors were carried down the stream some distance before they were recovered. This flag was among the very first to enter Richmond, April 3, 1865.

## No. 2. — Headquarters Guidon of the Old Vermont Brigade.

This was the oldest brigade in the service from Vermont, and had mustered on its rolls, in all, almost ten thousand men. At one time hard fighting had reduced its numbers to eleven hundred.

The Vermont Brigade was composed of the 2d, 3d, 4th, 5th, and 6th Vermont regiments, to which was subsequently added the 11th. It was a portion of the 6th Corps, and General Sedgwick proudly spoke of it as " the best brigade in the Army of the Potomac." Its history is written on every page of that of the Army of the Potomac, and no brigade in that gallant army performed more brilliant service or received greater honor.

## No. 3. — Major-General John Sedgwick's Sixth Corps Headquarters Flag.

No corps in the Union army was better known or more honored than the old 6th; and no corps commander was better loved than Major-General John Sedgwick, — " Uncle John," as he was called by " the boys." At the close of the war this headquarters flag came into the possession of Colonel James H. Platt, a member of General Sedgwick's staff and Judge-Advocate-General of the army. In 1868 Colonel Platt presented the flag to the Association of Vermont Officers, and in a letter to the association said : —

" This flag should be especially dear and sacred to the old Vermont brigade, as it is the *only one* that our beloved Sedgwick ever used while he commanded the immortal 6th Corps. *It was his headquarters battle-flag.* Always carried near his person in every action in which he commanded the corps, it will be recognized by every soldier of the Old Brigade at once, and must awaken in their hearts vivid memories of the numerous fields upon which, under its folds, they achieved so much of their imperishable renown. It will recall the noble Sedgwick, who loved them so well and was so well loved in return, who was at once the brave soldier, the able commander, the sincere friend; the best soldier and the noblest man it was ever our good fortune to serve under. It will also recall our brave comrades who sealed their devotion to their country by their heroic deaths upon the field of battle under its folds. I have regarded it as a precious and sacred relic; and, believing I had no right to retain it all to myself, have long contemplated presenting it to this association. I respectfully request my old comrades, through you, to accept it as a valuable addition to their store of relics; that they will permit it to grace the hall at their annual reunions, and cherish it as a memento of our beloved Sedgwick and the old Corps."

General Sedgwick was killed May 9, 1864, at Spottsylvania. He was at the most advanced point of the Union line of battle, near a section of artillery at a fatal angle in the works, accompanied by members of his staff, and was directing the movements of the men then occupying the rifle-pits. His manner, attitude and gesture as he stood communicated to the enemy that he was an officer of rank and authority, though he wore no uniform, not even a sword.    From across the little valley which separated the Union forces from the enemy's line, from one of their sharpshooters concealed in the woods, came the swift messenger of death, which pierced his left eye and killed him instantly.

His body, immediately after death, was placed under a bower of evergreens, hastily constructed to receive it, among the pine woods, and was laid out upon a rough bier made for him by soldiers' hands, and this, his old headquarters flag, was thrown over his face.    All day long, as he lay upon this bier, there came from all parts of the army the old and the young, the well and the wounded, officers and men, to take their last look at the beloved chieftain.

## PLATE II.    PAGE 239.

### No. 1.—FLAG OF THE TWENTY-FIRST REGIMENT MASSACHUSETTS VOLUNTEERS.

THE national flag of this regiment is reddened with the blood of the brave Sergeant Thomas Plunkett, shed while the 21st was charging upon the enemy's works in front of Petersburg, December 12, 1862. The regiment was met by a terrible storm of shot and shell, and when within about sixty rods of the enemy's line Color-Sergeant Collins, who had carried the flag through five battles, was struck by a shot, and fell. Sergeant Plunkett instantly seized the flag, and bore it onward to the farthest point reached by the Union troops during the battle, when a shell, coming with fatal accuracy from the rebel works, burst over the flag, and brought it to the ground wet with Plunkett's blood. Both of his arms were shot completely off. Plunkett died in Worcester, Mass., in 1884, and in honor of his memory this flag was taken from the State House in Boston and placed beside his coffin, a mute but eloquent reminder of his great sacrifice.

### No. 2.—FLAG OF THE FORTIETH REGIMENT NEW YORK VOLUNTEERS.

This regiment was organized in the city of New York, and left for the seat of war July 4, 1861, with one thousand men, splendidly armed and equipped. Its national flag was presented by Hon. Fernando Wood, mayor of New York, on behalf of the Union Defence Committee. It was one of the fighting regiments of the war, and sealed its devotion to the nation whose emblem it carried by the loss of nine hundred and thirty-six men in battle. Of its color-bearers five were killed in battle, four were wounded, and two died of disease.

Color-Sergeant Joseph Conroy carried this flag into action at Fair Oaks, and was killed on that field. Color-Corporal Charles Boyle then took the colors, was wounded and ordered to the rear, refused to go, and was killed soon after. Color-

Corporal George Miller bore it at Robinson's Field, Glendale, Malvern Hill, Haymarket, Bull Run, and Chantilly. He died of disease. Color-Corporal Alfred Conklin carried it at Williamsburg, Fair Oaks and Malvern Hill. He died of disease, at Harrison's Landing. Color-Corporal Edwin Howard carried it at Bull Run and Chantilly; was distinguished in all the battles of the regiment, and wounded at Fredericksburg. Color-Corporal Oliver P. Bisbing carried it at Williamsburg and Fair Oaks, and was killed in the last named battle. Color-Corporal John Brundage carried it at Williamsburg, Fair Oaks, Glendale, Malvern Hill, and Bull Run, and was killed in the latter battle. Private Joseph Browne carried it at Haymarket, Bull Run, and Chantilly; was distinguished in eight engagements, and was promoted Color-Sergeant. Color-Corporal Robert Grieves carried it at Williamsburg, Fair Oaks, and Malvern Hill; was wounded and promoted at Fair Oaks. Color-Corporal Thomas Read carried it at Williamsburg, Fair Oaks, Malvern Hill, Bull Run, and Chantilly; was always distinguished, and was afterwards killed at Fredericksburg. Color-Corporal Thomas Braslin carried it at Fair Oaks, and was dangerously wounded. Color-Corporal Horatio N. Shepherd carried it at Malvern Hill, Bull Run, and Chantilly. Color-Corporal Jacob D. Bennett carried it at Williamsburg. Color-Corporal William Moyne carried it at Williamsburg, Fair Oaks, and Malvern Hill; and Color-Corporal Joel Slattery carried it at Malvern Hill, Bull Run, and Chantilly; was afterwards badly wounded at Fredericksburg.

## No. 3. — Flag of the Fourteenth Regiment Connecticut Volunteers.

To tell the story of this flag is to write the history of the Army of the Potomac. The regiment saw long and severe service, and was everywhere known as the "Fighting Fourteenth." It participated in thirty-three battles and skirmishes, besides the long siege of Richmond. This list includes all the great battles of the Army of the Potomac from Antietam to the close of the war. Its casualties were seven hundred and eighty-eight.

All through Grant's campaign, from the Wilderness to Appomattox, the 14th had its full share of work, glory, and losses. Its colors are so torn by shot, shell and bullet that they cannot be safely unfurled without being supported by ribbons. Ninety-one different soldiers held commissions in the 14th during its term of service. Three of its field officers were brevetted to be brigadier-generals, and several to colonelcies. It was a familiar saying that "he who joins the 14th will be a captain or a dead man in a year's time." Its colors were proudly borne in the battle of Antietam, and were passed from hand to hand as their brave bearers fell. In this battle the staff of the national flag was shot in two by a bullet, and the eagle's head knocked off with a piece of shell. Color-Sergeant Thomas J. Mills of New London was mortally wounded, and dropped the flag as he fell. Sergeant George A. Foote, Jr., of Guilford, instantly volunteered to take it, and carried it the rest of the day.

At the battle of Fredericksburg, as the regiment charged up into the jaws of death on Marye's Heights, Sergeant Charles E. Dart of Rockville carried the flag, and fell mortally wounded. Again Sergeant Foote attempted to carry it, but was shot in the leg and fell. Sergeant Foote was a brother of the late Mrs. Gen. Joseph R. Hawley, and was one of the most gallant soldiers of the war. Of her brother's part in this battle Mrs. Hawley writes : —

" The color-sergeant fell, terribly wounded, just as the regiment had been ordered to fall back. Foote stooped, and tried to pick up the flag ; the brave old sergeant held on to it, saying, ' I will take care of it,' and suddenly rose to his feet, but instantly fell back dead. As Foote stooped to pick it up, he was shot in the leg and fell. After lying on the field a short time, he tried to rise, but was instantly fired upon by the rebels, wounding him slightly in the head and hip. All the rest of that awful day he lay still where he had fallen ; three times our men charged over him, of course trampling on his wounded leg, while he, half-delirious, begged them to kill him to end his sufferings, — but none had time then to attend to one poor wounded fellow.

"That night he managed to crawl off to a little hut near the field, where some other wounded men had hung out a yellow flag. Here they lay, with a little hardtack and still less water, till the third day after the fight, when they were visited by a rebel officer with a few men, who spoke roughly to them, asking them what they were here for. Foote coolly lifted his head, and said, ' I came to fight rebels, and I have found them ; and if ever I get well I'll come back and fight them again.' ' Bully for you ! ' said the officer ; 'you are a boy I like ! ' and at once gave him some water out of his own canteen, sent one of his men for more, washed his leg and foot, and bound it up as well as he could, paroled him, and helped him across the river to the Lacy House hospital. In fact, he and his men gave him a blanket, and cheered him as the wagon drove off. Foote said afterward, ' I didn't know but he would blow my brains out, but I didn't mean he should think we were sneaks.'

" The poor fellow's leg had to be amputated ; and, although he was commissioned a lieutenant for his gallantry, he was never able to be mustered in, nor did he recover strength to survive the war but a few years, dying in 1869."

After Foote was wounded, the state flag was picked up by Private William B. Hincks (afterwards major) and Captain Doten, both of Bridgeport, and by them brought safely off the field.

At Chancellorsville Sergeant Samuel Webster, while carrying the national flag, was wounded in the wrist, and afterwards transferred to the Invalid Corps. At Morton's Ford battle, in 1864, Sergeant Amory Allen of Hartford, while carrying the national flag, and Corporal Chadwick of Lyme, of the color-guard, were killed in a charge upon the enemy across the Rapidan. Corporal John Hirst of Rockville picked up the flag as Allen fell, and bore it the rest of the day. At the battle of Hatcher's Run, Henry Hospodsky of Rockville, of the color-guard, was wounded.

Of the battle of the Wilderness, in 1864, Major Hincks writes : —

" On the morning of the second day's fight the brigade to which the 14th belonged drove back the rebel outposts for upwards of half a mile. It being almost impossible to hear an order in the horrible din, the adjutant took the color-bearer by the shoulder, and, pointing to the trunk of a fallen tree, shouted for him to kneel by it. Many officers and men of the 14th then rallied around the colors, together with a handful from the other regiments, other members of the 14th extending the line by deploying as skirmishers, and fighting from behind trees, Indian fashion. Corporal Charles W. Norton of Berlin was severely wounded at this time, while carrying the flag. Later in the day, during an attack by Longstreet's corps, Corporal Henry K. Lyon of New London, a brave soldier who carried the national flag, was mortally wounded. Handing the flag to Lieutenant-Colonel Moore, the dying soldier said, ' Take it, Colonel; I have done my best!' Colonel Moore gave it to John Hirst of Rockville. The regiment at this time was almost surrounded, and in danger of being captured, but Sergeant Hirst brought the flag safely from the field, and carried it from that time through every battle until the close of the war."

Corporal Robert Wolfe of Waterbury, a member of the color-guard, was wounded in this engagement, and subsequently at the battle of Ream's Station.

At the battle of Gettysburg, the 14th held one of the most important positions in the line of the Second Corps, on which line the rebel charge spent itself in vain. In this battle the 14th charged upon the enemy and captured the colors belonging to the 14th Tennessee, 1st Tennessee, 16th North Carolina, and 4th Virginia, besides capturing many prisoners.

At the close of the war the flag was carried, amid the plaudits of thousands, before the President, at the grand review in Washington; thence it was borne back to old Connecticut, to be deposited in its final resting-place at the Capitol.

## No. 4.—Flag of the Twenty-Fourth Regiment Massachusetts Volunteers.

The flag of this gallant regiment is inscribed with the names of twenty-three battles in which it participated. Further than this its history cannot be learned.

## No. 5.— Flag of the First Maine Heavy Artillery.

The 1st Maine Heavy Artillery was in service three years, but served in the field only the last year of the war, joining the Army of the Potomac near Spottsylvania Court-House in May, 1864. The colors were then in charge of Sergeant James M. Smith of Ellsworth. He, with eight other noncommissioned officers, composed the color-guard. On May 19, 1864, out of the nine three were killed and four wounded, leaving the sergeant and one corporal unhurt. Seven men immediately filled their places, and on June 18 following, while storming the enemy's works near Petersburg, two were killed, and Sergeant Smith with five others wounded, leaving only Corporal Ames, who thus twice passed through the furnace of fire, only to be taken prisoner four days later. On the above named 18th of June the regiment advanced over a level field about seven hundred yards. Sergeant Smith fell near the rebel works, with a leg shattered. Under cover of the smoke from the batteries, he quickly rolled up the flag, and, drawing the case from his pocket, slipped it over the colors; then, with the help of the staff, he worked himself off the field. Major-General Robert McAllister, who witnessed this charge, wrote of it as follows: "In all my army experience no scene of carnage and suffering is so impressed on my mind as that fatal charge made by your regiment on the 18th of June, 1864. . . . The brigade moved off, your fine regiment handsomely in the front. You went gallantly, not to meet success. That was impossible, . . . you were a *forlorn hope.* In a few minutes out of your regiment, which advanced nine hundred strong, six hundred and thirty-two were laid low on the battle-field."

Four days later this regiment formed a part of the 3d Division, 2d Corps, which was flanked by the enemy. Intently engaged in front, it was suddenly attacked in the rear. The line faced about, and immediately, among the thick undergrowth, the blue and the gray became mixed, lines broken, and men fighting in squads; prisoners were taken and retaken, flags were captured and again yielded up to a superior force, the regiment all the while working itself out of the thicket. Nobly the color-guard defended their flag, one of their number being snatched from the squad a prisoner, until they gained a more open space, where they planted their standard, around which the regiment rallied and held their ground against further attack.

April 6, 1865, the regiment formed the skirmish line of the vanguard of the 2d Army Corps, following General Lee's retreating columns. It made seven distinct charges on the hastily constructed works of the enemy. Their captures during the day amounted to forty-seven wagons, three pieces of artillery, two battle-flags, and three hundred and fifty prisoners. Sergeant Woodcock, who carried the flag at this time, showed such reckless bravery in displaying his colors, always a little in advance of the skirmish-line, that the colonel sent an orderly bidding him to be more cautious lest the flag fall into the enemy's hands. During the war five from the color-guard were killed, eleven wounded, and one taken prisoner.

## No 6. — Flag of the First Connecticut Heavy Artillery.

The 1st Connecticut Heavy Artillery was one of the largest and most efficient organizations sent to the war from Connecticut, and was ranked by military judges as the best volunteer regiment of heavy artillery in the field. It left Hartford for the seat of war in June, 1861, and soon after, by special orders from the War Department, its organization was changed to consist of twelve companies of one hundred and fifty men each. It now numbered eighteen hundred officers and men, under a high state of discipline. It was in service four years and four months, and was splendidly equipped with a siege train of seventy-one pieces of artillery, many of them very heavy guns. It took a prominent part in the siege of Yorktown, and in the series of battles at Hanover Court-House, Gaines' Mill, Chickahominy, Golden Hill, Malvern Hill, siege of Fredericksburg, Kelly's Ford, Orange Court-House, siege of Petersburg, siege of Richmond, Fort Fisher, etc.

At Malvern Hill, during the night of June 30, fourteen heavy guns were dragged up the steep ascent and occupied the highest ground on that battle-field. The guns were served with great rapidity and caused tremendous havoc amid the enemy's advancing column.

General McClellan had great confidence in the Connecticut Heavy Artillery, and Major-General W. F. ("Baldy") Smith writes: "I saw much of the 1st Connecticut Artillery during the campaign of 1862, and was surprised at the skill and gallantry of its officers and men. During the time I commanded the 18th Corps before Petersburg, I called heavily upon it for siege guns, and never before during the war have I witnessed such artillery practice as I saw with that regiment, which has not its equal in artillery firing."

Its great services were recognized by an order directing the names of its battles to be emblazoned on its flag.

---

## PLATE III.    PAGE 329.

### No. 1.—FLAG OF THE THIRTEENTH REGIMENT IL-LINOIS VOLUNTEERS.

THIS flag is stained by the life-blood of Patrick Reilly, color-sergeant, who was killed at Ringgold Gap, November 27, 1863. He was shot through the breast and fell in such manner as to be rolled up in the flag.

## No. 2.—NATIONAL FLAG OF THE TWENTY-FOURTH REGIMENT MICHIGAN VOLUNTEERS.

The fatality that attended the color-bearers, officers, and men of this regiment at the battle of Gettysburg was very great. It had in its ranks on the morning of this memorable fight four hundred and ninety-six officers and men. It lost in killed and wounded three hundred and sixteen. The 24th was a part of the Iron Brigade, which was the first infantry engaged at Gettysburg. It carried into this battle only a state flag, which was presented to the regiment by the citizens of Detroit. This was carried by Color-Bearer Abel G. Peck, a tall, straight, handsome man, and as brave a soldier as ever gave up his life for his country. He was instantly killed almost at the beginning of the famous charge of the Iron Brigade. The flag was then seized by Private Thomas B. Ballou, who was desperately wounded immediately after, and died a few weeks later. The flag was then carried by Private August Ernst, who was instantly killed. Corporal Andrew Wagner then took the colors and carried them until shot through the breast, from the effects of which he died about a year after the close of the war.

When Corporal Wagner fell, Colonel Henry A. Morrill took the flag, and gallantly attempted to rally the few survivors of the regiment. But Private William Kelly insisted on carrying it, saying to Colonel Morrill, "You shall not carry the flag while I am alive." The gallant fellow held it aloft and almost instantly fell, shot through the heart. Private L. Spaulding then took the flag from the hands of Kelly, and carried it until he was himself badly wounded. Colonel Morrill again seized the flag, and was soon after shot in the head and carried from the field.

After the fall of Colonel Morrill, the flag was carried by a soldier whose name has never been ascertained. He was seen by Captain Edwards — who was now in command of the regiment — lying upon the ground badly wounded, grasping the flag in his hands. Captain Edwards took the flag from him and carried it himself until the few men left of the regiment fell back and reached Culp's Hill. Captain Edwards is the only man who is known to have carried the flag that day, who was not killed or wounded.

This grand old flag is no longer in existence. It was so riddled and torn with shot and shell that scarcely a square foot of it remained intact. The staff was shot and broken in pieces also. The men had great affection for the old flag, and after the battle of Gettysburg they agreed to cut it up and distribute the pieces to the survivors. This was done, and to-day in many a Michigan household a small piece of faded blue silk is cherished as one of the sacred mementoes of the war. The flag shown in the illustration is the national color carried by the regiment.

### No. 3.—Flag of the Eighth Regiment Missouri Volunteers.

This was the first flag on the parapets of Forts Henry and Donelson. It was riddled at Shiloh; was carried up to the breastworks in the charge at Vicksburg; was upon the breastworks at Kenesaw, where the regiment went over the works, and changed sides with the rebels, and fought hand-to-hand. It led the way in the march to the sea; waved over Fort McAllister, and on the flag-staff at Columbia, S. C., and Raleigh. It was carried in many battles and skirmishes.

### No. 4.—Flag of the First Minnesota Artillery.

History unknown.

### No. 5.—Flag of the Second Regiment Michigan Volunteers.

This flag was presented to the regiment by the ladies of Niles, Mich., and during the war was followed by no less than two thousand one hundred and fifty-one men. Of that number three hundred and twenty-one lie buried on southern soil. If this old flag, that so many brave men followed to the death, could only tell its own story, what a tale it would tell of love of country, of patriotism, of glory, of suffering, disease, wounds, and death. It was carried through forty-four battles and skirmishes, and was the first Union flag to enter Petersburg. It was carried in Burnside's "Geography Class," from Virginia to Maryland, Kentucky to Mississippi, back to Kentucky and Tennessee, and finally back to Virginia, there to participate in the closing scenes of the rebellion.

## No. 6.—Flag of the Seventh New York Heavy Artillery.

This flag and that of the 5th New Hampshire were the only ones that went over the rebel works at Cold Harbor. An officer of the 5th New Hampshire Regiment writes: "The 7th New York Heavy Artillery was a very gallant regiment. At Cold Harbor both regiments went over the rebel works together, and no other colors but those of these two regiments were anywhere near that point." Both regiments, however, were driven out with great loss, but, before falling back, captured and sent to their rear about two hundred and fifty prisoners. The 7th New York Heavy Artillery also performed splendid service at Ream's Station, and covered itself with glory. In this engagement it was reduced to a mere handful.

---

## Plate IV.
Page 421.

### CONFEDERATE BATTLE—FLAGS.

### No. 1.—Confederate Battle-Flag Captured from General Bragg's Rebel Army at Lookout Mountain.

This flag was captured by Sergeant F. N. Potter of the 149th Regiment New York Volunteers, November 24, 1863, in a desperate hand-to-hand fight, from a rebel sergeant, who was disarmed and taken prisoner by Sergeant Potter. The latter was soon afterwards wounded. (Now in the keeping of the War Department, at Washington, D.C.)

## NO. 2. — CONFEDERATE BATTLE-FLAG OF THE FORTY-SECOND MISSISSIPPI REGIMENT.

Captured before Petersburg, in a hand-to-hand fight, by Corporal Charles H. Dolloff of the 11th Regiment Vermont Volunteers. Seeing the furious charge of the Union troops, the rebel color-bearer tore the flag from its staff and attempted to destroy it, but was prevented by the quick movements of Corporal Dolloff, who captured the flag and its bearer. (Now in the keeping of the War Department, at Washington, D.C.)

## NO. 3. — CONFEDERATE BATTLE-FLAG OF THE TWELFTH MISSISSIPPI CAVALRY.

This flag was captured with its bearer, at Selma, Ala., April 2, 1865, by Private James P. Miller of the 4th Iowa Cavalry. (Now in the keeping of the War Department, at Washington, D.C.)

## NO. 4. — CONFEDERATE BLOOD-STAINED SILK BAT-TLE-FLAG OF THE NINTH TEXAS REGIMENT.

Captured in battle by Private Orrin B. Gould of the 27th Regiment Ohio Volunteers. The 9th Texas Regiment, with this flag at their head, charged upon the 27th Ohio. Private Gould of the 27th shot down the rebel color-bearer and rushed forward for the colors. A rebel officer shouted, "Save the colors, men," and at the same time shot and wounded Gould in the breast. Gould, with the flag in his hands and a bullet in his breast, rushed back to his regiment, waving the flag defiantly in the face of the enemy. (Now the property of the state of Ohio.)

## No. 5. — Confederate Battle-Flag of Austin's Battery.

Captured at Columbus, Ga., April 16, 1865, with its color-bearer, inside the rebel line of works, by Private Andrew W. Tibbetts of the 3d Iowa Cavalry. (Now in the keeping of the War Department, at Washington, D.C.)

## No. 6. — Confederate Battle-Flag Captured at Malvern Hill.

Captured July 1, 1862, by Sergeant W. J. Whittrick of the 83d Regiment Pennsylvania Volunteers. It was taken from a South Carolina regiment, who piled up their dead to resist the attack of the Union Brigade. (Now in the keeping of the War Department, at Washington, D.C.)

## No. 7. — Confederate Battle-Flag, Black (No Quarter), Probably from Texas.

Captured within the rebel lines near North Mountain, Maryland, August 1, 1864. The "Lone Star" in the centre of the flag no doubt indicates that it belonged to a Texas regiment. (Now in the keeping of the War Department, at Washington, D.C.)

## No. 8. — Confederate Silk Battle-Flag.

Very handsome, and one of the first Confederate flags captured in Virginia. It contains the words "For Liberty We Strike" in gold letters on the centre stripe. (Now the property of Post No. 2, G. A. R., Philadelphia, Pa.)

## PLATE V.     PAGE 443.

### No. 1. — FLAG OF THE FIRST NEW JERSEY CAVALRY.

THIS was one of the first regiments of volunteer cavalry that entered the field in the war of the rebellion, and was one of the last to leave it. According to the official report of the Adjutant-General, this gallant regiment was engaged in no less than ninety-seven actions, including many of the most noted battles of the war, and this flag was carried through ninety-two of them. The regiment was recruited three times to the full maximum, and as often melted away before the enemy's fire. The flag of a regiment that performed continuous service, and whose record is one of brilliant achievements, must have a thrilling story; but all efforts to obtain it have proved fruitless.

In the preface to the "History of the First New Jersey Cavalry," written by the chaplain of the regiment and published soon after the war, the following reference is made to the flag: — "Though soiled and tattered, it has a glory that belongs alone to itself and the men who carried and followed it so bravely." Notwithstanding this suggestive statement, not a single incident pertaining to the flag is given in the book.

### No. 2. — FLAG OF THE FORTY-EIGHTH REGIMENT NEW YORK VOLUNTEERS.

This flag was presented to the regiment by Mrs. General Viele, October, 1861, at Annapolis, Md. Part of the staff was shot away at Fort Wagner. It was borne in action at Port Royal Ferry, Pocotaligo, Morris Island, and Fort Wagner. The regiment was also engaged in the battles of Drury's Bluff, Cold Harbor, Petersburg, Chapin's Farm, Fort Fisher, and several minor engagements. Of the bearers of this flag, Sergeant George G. Sparks was wounded and transferred to the invalid corps; Corporal G. Vredenberg was wounded and discharged; Corporal James W.

Dunn was wounded, promoted Captain, and killed at Fort Fisher; and Corporals Alonzo Hilliker, Alexander Hyers, and Sidney Wadhams were killed.

At the battle of Cold Harbor, the 48th lost one flag, not through cowardice, but sheer bravery. The color-bearer was shot down, and another seized the fallen standard only to perish beneath its folds. Then a third man, Color-Sergeant William H. Porch, lifted its proud challenge to the foe and planted it upon the parapet, in the very midst of the rebel host, where he too died, pierced with bullets, and flag and bearer fell together over the parapet, into the arms of the enemy. The flag was never recovered.

Of the death of Sergeant Porch, Rev. A. J. Palmer, D.D., who served three years as a private in this regiment, says: — "It may be doubted if in the whole history of the Forty-eighth a more gallant deed will be chronicled than that of the death of Porch. He had been falsely twitted with cowardice at Drury's Bluff because he had taken the colors to the rear, when ordered to do so, when our force retired; some one, who did not know that he was but obeying orders, had accused him of showing the white feather. No charge could have stung his noble soul more keenly. Porch was a gentleman and a hero. He had been a student at Pennington Seminary, New Jersey, and was the first to write his name on the roll of Company D. He was an educated, well-to-do boy from New Jersey, and his death was a spectacle which his comrades ought never to forget. Sergeant John M. Tantum * was his bosom friend, and, just as our men reached that second line of rifle-pits that bristled with bayonets and swarmed with rebels, Tantum cried to Porch, 'Now, Billy, show them that you are no coward!' To mount that bank was instant death, and yet without hesitancy and without a single word Porch leaped up the bank alone. He was shot by a score of bullets, and, throwing his arms around his flag, fell with it into the midst of the foe. Not another man followed him — he was left alone there in the keeping of his flag and of glory."

* Sergeant Tantum was afterwards killed at Strawberry Plains.

For a regiment to lose its colors in battle is esteemed a reproach. In this case it was, on the contrary, a high honor, which was recognized at headquarters; for, although an order had been issued that a regiment losing its colors should not carry them again for three months, a special order was issued permitting the 48th to carry colors immediately.

## No. 3.—Flag of the 150th ("Bucktail") Regiment Pennsylvania Volunteers.

This regiment was recruited in the mountain region of Pennsylvania, where the deer range, and where every member, before he could be mustered in, was obliged to produce the evidence that he had shot a buck, which was the tail of the animal. This he wore in the front of his cap when he went into battle. The regiment was always designated as the "Bucktails." They were known as expert marksmen, and were correspondingly feared.

At the battle of Gettysburg the regiment was posted in an orchard, between the Chambersburg pike and the woods where General Reynolds was killed. The rebels attacked the regiment in great force, but the rapid and accurate fire of the "Bucktails," followed by a gallant charge, threw the enemy into confusion, and caused them to beat a hasty retreat. But the rebels soon renewed their attack with a greatly increased force and with desperate fury, and poured a destructive cross-fire from the woods into the regiment, inflicting great loss among the "Bucktails," particularly in the vicinity of the colors, causing the line to waver. The regimental flag was borne by Sergeant Samuel Phifer, than whom no braver soldier ever lived. Colonel Huidekoper ordered him to stand fast, and, in tones which rang like a bugle-call, cried, "'Bucktails,' rally on your colors!" The regiment instantly reformed, and, in spite of the fact that they now numbered less than two hundred men, they checked the rebel advance, and held the position until they were nearly surrounded, when, to escape capture, they fell back to Seminary Ridge. In this last desperate struggle Sergeant Phifer gave up his life at almost the last moment before the regiment retired, dying with his face towards the enemy, his hand waving the flag, while his life-blood flowed from numerous wounds. His gallantry had attracted the attention of the rebel General Hill, as the following extract from the diary of Colonel Freemantle, published in *Blackwood's Magazine* for September, 1863, will show : —

" General Hill soon came up. He said that the Yankees had fought with unusual determination. He pointed out a field in the centre of which he had seen a man plant the regimental color, around which the regiment had fought for some time with great obstinacy, and when at last· it was obliged to retreat, the color-bearer retired last of all, turning around every now and then to shake his fist at the advancing rebels. General Hill said he felt quite sorry when he saw this gallant Yankee meet his doom."

Corporal Gutelins, who was now the only member of the color-guard unwounded, seized and carried the flag. The regiment finally abandoned its position on Seminary Ridge, and fell back into the town of Gettysburg. Up to this time — about four P. M. — the flag was safe, although every member of the color-guard, excepting Corporal Gutelins, had been killed or wounded. Gutelins had nearly reached the town when he too was struck by a ball. He still insisted upon carrying the flag, but in passing through Gettysburg became confused, and was separated from the regiment. Becoming weak from loss of blood, he sat down for a moment on a step to rest, in company with a wounded comrade. Instantly the rebels were upon them, and Gutelins was shot dead, with the colors clasped in his arms. Before his comrade could release the flag-staff from Gutelins' dying grasp, the rebels had cut off his retreat, and the flag thus fell into the hands of the enemy.

The flag was soon afterwards presented by the rebels, with a grand flourish of trumpets, to Jefferson Davis, and was found with his effects when he was captured in Georgia, in the spring of 1865. At the close of the war, repeated efforts were made by Colonel Huidekoper and General Simon Cameron to secure the return of the flag to the state of Pennsylvania, and it was finally transmitted by the Secretary of War to the Adjutant-General of Pennsylvania, October 25, 1869, with a letter, in which the Secretary says: " I am directed by the President to send herewith the flag of the 150th Pennsylvania Volunteers, said to have been captured at Gettysburg, and recaptured with the baggage of Jefferson Davis." The flag is now deposited, with the other tattered ensigns of the state, in the Capitol at Harrisburg.

## No. 4.—Flag of the Eighty-Third Regiment Pennsylvania Volunteers.

In May, 1861, Governor Curtin addressed a message to the Legislature of Pennsylvania, informing that body that the " Society of the Cincinnati of Pennsylvania " had presented to him the sum of five hundred dollars, to be used towards arming and equipping Pennsylvania soldiers. The governor asked that the manner of its use should be directed by statute.

The " Society of the Cincinnati " was originally composed of surviving soldiers of the Revolution, who pledged lasting friendship and aid to each other. Washington was at its head, and Mifflin, Wayne, Reed, and Cadwalader were members of it. The gift thus tendered to the state of Pennsylvania was accepted by the Legislature for the state, and was devoted to the purchase of a battle-flag to be carried at the head of one of the Pennsylvania regiments.

The flag thus acquired was presented to the 83d Regiment Pennsylvania Volunteers, and was presented to them while in camp at Hall's Hill, Va., by Hon. Edgar Cowan, United States senator from Pennsylvania, who represented Governor Curtin on this occasion.

This flag was borne in the most desperate fighting at Gaines' Mill, where the commander of the regiment was killed. A few days later, at Malvern Hill, the 83d held a vital point in the line, and lost one hundred and forty-four men in the struggle. Corporal Ames, the color-bearer, was killed by a bullet, which at the same time pierced and splintered the flag-staff.  The flag fell, and he fell upon it.  It was picked up by Sergeant Alexander Rogers, who waved it over his head and gallantly advanced to the front of the regiment.  During the most desperate fighting Sergeant William Wittich of the 83d, seeing one of the enemy's battle-flags lying upon the field, in advance of our lines, dashed out and secured the flag.  For this act of heroism he was promoted to a lieutenancy, by order of General Porter, commanding the corps.

Sergeant Rogers bore the old flag gloriously through a dozen bloody fights, and was finally killed in the first day's battle in the Wilderness, on the 5th of May, 1864.  Finally, a new staff, and eventually a new flag, took the place of the old.  It was still, however, the same valor-inspiring emblem, and wherever its star-lit folds could be discerned amid the smoke and carnage of the fray there gathered the true and tried hearts, whose every beat was responsive to its safety and honor.

In the battle of Laurel Hill, on the 8th of May, 1864, the 83d was ordered to storm intrenched works strongly held by the enemy.  The charge was fearlessly made, and some of the men succeeded in crossing the enemy's works, where they fell to bayoneting the foe; but the odds were too great, and the regiment was forced to fall back, with a loss of over one hundred and fifty in killed and wounded — some of the bravest and most daring going down in this ill-advised charge.  The flag on this occasion was carried by Corporal Vogus, who had rescued it when Sergeant Rogers fell at the Wilderness, three days before.  While the regiment was charging up to the breastworks, he received a severe wound in the side, and fell with the flag.  Corporal John Lillibridge of the color-guard immediately seized it, and was about to carry it forward when Vogus recovered and, again taking the flag, pressed forward and planted it on the breastworks of the enemy.  In a few moments afterwards he was shot through the breast.  Fearing that the flag might be captured, and more careful for it than for him-

self, he seized it while he was in the act of falling, and
hurled it to the rear, where it was caught by Corporal Dan
Jones.  Jones was shortly after wounded himself, and, while
getting off the field, handed the flag to a soldier of the 44th
New York, and it was soon afterwards returned to the regiment.

The number of battles in which this flag was carried, as
published in orders and recorded in the Official Army Register of 1885, is twenty-five.


## No. 5. — Flag of the Ninth Regiment New Jersey Volunteers.

Color-Sergeant George Myers carried this tattered flag
at Roanoke Island, Newbern, Southwest Creek, Kingston,
Goldsboro, Walthall, Drury's Bluff, Cold Harbor, Petersburg, and in every campaign and battle in which the 9th
New Jersey participated.  Myers was a brave soldier, and
this flag always waved in the thickest of the fray.

In the unequal battle at Drury's Bluff, Va., May 16, 1864,
Myers had a narrow escape.  Under cover of a dense fog a
division of rebels suddenly burst upon the Union line, and,
although they met with a withering fire from the New Jersey Riflemen, and were four times hurled back in confusion
and dismay by the terrific volleys thrown among them, it
was at last evident that the Union line must give way.  The
9th New Jersey had lost most of its officers and men, when
suddenly the exultant rebels burst in upon the survivors
with redoubled fury, determined to be avenged for the terrible injuries inflicted upon them.  Sergeant Myers, undis-
mayed, and calm and collected as if on parade, seeing himself and a few comrades surrounded by the enemy, with
scarcely a hope of escape, stripped from the staff the silken
shred, which had been his inseparable companion for years,
and, hastily buttoning it within the folds of his blouse,
grasped a rifle, and, calling upon those near him to follow,
dashed through the advancing line of rebels, dealing heavy
blows for life and liberty, and thus escaped capture and
saved the flag.  His clothing was perforated with bullets.

## NO. 6.—FLAG OF THE 105TH REGIMENT NEW YORK VOLUNTEERS.

This flag was presented to the regiment by the ladies of Le Roy, Genesee County, N. Y., and was carried in many battles. Seven color-bearers were killed or wounded while carrying it. It bears the marks of many bullets and a piece of shell, and its staff was cut in two by a ball. The regiment was engaged in nine battles before it had been in the field nine months.

---

## PLATE VI.    PAGE 597.

## NO. 1.—FLAG OF THE FIFTH REGIMENT NEW HAMPSHIRE VOLUNTEERS.

OVER two thousand two hundred men were enrolled in this regiment during its three years' service. It lost over half the command in six different engagements. At Gettysburg, every fifth man of the number engaged was killed or mortally wounded. Its casualties in action, during its term of service, were appalling. Its first flag — which had upon it the blood-stains of three men, one a captain — was worn out at Fredericksburg. In this battle the regiment was first in line, and its dead were found nearer the enemy's position than those of any other troops. The flag was carried in this battle by Color-Sergeant Reuel G. Austin, who was wounded, and it was then carried by Sergeant George S. Gove, who was also wounded. The flag was then seized by Sergeant John R. McCrillis, who carried it off the field at the close of the day.

During the battle Captain James B. Perry, a most gallant officer, was shot in the breast and mortally wounded. It was impossible to take him to the rear under the terrific fire then raging, so he was cared for by his comrades where he lay. Turning to a brother-officer, the wounded soldier said, "I know I shall not recover from this wound, but I am content if I can see the old flag once more." The flag was brought to him, but his sight had failed and he could not see it. Its folds were put in his hands, and, pressing the banner to his lips, he murmured his farewell to it and to his comrades at the same time, and died with the flag in his grasp. The flag carried by the fifth at Gettysburg was one of a second set presented to it. In this battle seven men were killed or wounded with this flag in their hands.

No regiment fought more valiantly, and few, if any, were in a greater number of desperate battles. Its history is sad but glorious. Wherever the Army of the Potomac met the enemy, there lie the bones of the 5th New Hampshire.

## No. 2.—Flag of the First Rhode Island Cavalry.

Rev. Frederick Denison, chaplain of the 1st Regiment Rhode Island Cavalry, relates the following story of this flag : —

"Color-Sergeant G. A. Robbins (Troop I., 1st Cavalry R. I.), finding that capture was inevitable, stripped the regimental standard from the staff, broke the staff and threw it away. Opening his bosom, he wrapped the colors about his body, and so concealed them. He was captured, but on his way to Richmond, after a number of days, escaped and found his way back into our lines. Finding at length the headquarters of the broken but brave and honored regiment, he reported for duty, and then drew from his breast the loved and precious flag — an act that drew tears of gratitude and admiration from all beholders, and shouts of applause from his brave comrades, and won instantly for him a lieutenant's commission."

## No. 3.— Flag of the Sixteenth Regiment Connecticut Volunteers.

The 16th Connecticut Infantry Regiment was thrown into the hottest of the battle at Antietam, a brave but undisciplined and undrilled body of men, but twenty days from home. The regiment came out of this battle with a loss of two hundred and thirty-eight in killed, wounded, and missing. Subsequently it followed the fortunes of the Army of the Potomac, and saw service at Fredericksburg under Burnside, and participated in other engagements, finally being ordered to Plymouth, N. C.

Plymouth was a fortified post defended by a line of earthworks and by a fleet of Union gun-boats anchored in the river. Sunday evening, April 17, 1864, the picket line of the regiment was driven in by the rebels, and this attack was followed by a heavy artillery fire and an unsuccessful assault upon the earthworks. During the night the rebels brought their troops into position, and the light of morning showed they had completely invested the place with an overwhelming force. The Union troops consisted all told of only sixteen hundred men fit for duty. This force was surrounded by three brigades of rebel infantry — Hoke's, Ransom's and Kemper's — sixteen regiments in all, with eleven batteries of field artillery and two companies of cavalry, the entire force amounting to over thirteen thousand men, the choicest troops of Lee's army. They were aided by the rebel ram Albemarle, which drove off and sunk the fleet of wooden gun-boats in the river and poured a destructive fire into the Union camps. For three days the federal troops defended the garrison with the utmost gallantry, but one redoubt after another was carried by the rebels, until on Wednesday morning, April 20, it was evident that the Union troops could hold out but a few hours longer. All demands for surrender had thus far been met with refusal. After the last flag of truce from the enemy had returned to their lines bearing a refusal to surrender, a tremendous fire of musketry and artillery was opened on the Union line ; the rebels fairly swarmed over the last line of breastworks, and poured into the Union camps with the confidence of victory near at hand. At an angle in the breastworks they captured a portion of the artillery and turned the guns on the Union forces, by this act cutting the 16th Connecticut in two, part of the men, with the color-guard, being on one side, and a part, with some of the field officers, on the other. At this juncture, with every hope of escape destroyed, surrounded by nearly ten times their number, Lieutenant-Colonel Burnham shouted to the color-guard: "Strip the flags from their staffs and bring them here." To tear each flag from its staff was the work of a moment; but who should carry them across a field five hundred feet, through that merciless hail of grape and canister? It required brave men, and they were not wanting. Color-Sergeant Francis Latimer took the national color, Color-Corporal Ira E. Forbes the state flag, and, crossing the most exposed part of the field, safely delivered them to Colonel Burnham. Corporal Forbes then returned and brought back the flag of the 101st Pennsylvania Regiment. The only thought now was to save the colors from capture. An attempt was made to burn them, and was partially successful. What was left was torn into small pieces and distributed among members of the regiment near at hand, who at once concealed them on their persons.

Hardly had the flags been disposed of and the last pieces distributed, ere the defenders of the garrison found themselves prisoners of war. The rebels demanded the colors and were greatly chagrined at not obtaining them. Believing them to be concealed, they made a thorough but unsuccessful search for them.

The Union soldiers captured in this engagement were incarcerated in various southern prisons, most of them at Andersonville, where they suffered untold horrors. The 16th lost more men at Andersonville and other rebel prisons than any other Connecticut regiment. Nearly two hundred of this regiment alone — or nearly one-half of the entire number captured — died in Andersonville. No words can describe their terrible sufferings. A large number of the survivors died soon after the war, of disease contracted in those fearful pens. Few if any of those now living are free from the life-long effects of horrible starvation and exposure. All through the terrible days of their imprisonment the little patches of the old flag were carefully guarded and preserved by those to whom they were in-trusted.

After the war a beautiful white silk flag was procured for the regimental organization. A meeting of the survivors was held, and the little shreds of the old flag were assembled from widely scattered sources and sewed together in the form of a shield and scroll, and these were sewed on the centre of the new white silk flag.

A year after the close of the war the rebels were so determined to find the missing colors that they ploughed up the ground covered by the camps of the Union forces and levelled the breastworks at that end of the town, believing the flags had been buried by our men. They found nothing to reward them but the flag-staffs, which had been thrust into a hole under the breastworks.

One of the flags of the 16th was an elegant state flag which was presented to the regiment by the Sharps Rifle Manufacturing Company, Hartford, and had an inscribed silver shield on its staff, with the name of the donors. After the flag was stripped from its staff, torn up and passed around, this silver shield was removed by Color-Sergeant Latimer and hastily secreted in the lining of his dress-coat.

All through his long imprisonment Sergeant Latimer carefully guarded this cherished relic; but when exchanged and presented with clean clothes at Annapolis, in his delight at getting rid of his dirty, vermin-filled rags, he threw them on the lively pile accumulated from those ahead of him in line, utterly forgetful of the silver shield sewn into the lapel of his old coat. His grief was great when he discovered his loss; but it was too late, and the shield was forever lost.

## No. 4. — Flag of the Fifty-Fourth (Colored) Infantry Regiment Massachusetts Volunteers.

The 54th Massachusetts was a brave regiment of colored troops, commanded by Colonel Robert G. Shaw, a man of refinement and gentle manners, and brave as a lion. The national flag carried by this regiment was the gift of certain young colored ladies of Boston, and was presented to the regiment by the great war governor, John A. Andrew, after a speech full of eloquence and deep feeling, and passed from his hand to that of Colonel Shaw. It was the only national flag carried by the regiment during its term of service, and was borne in the following actions: — James Island, July 16, '63; assault of Fort Wagner, July 18, '63; siege of Fort Wagner, July 18, Sept. 7, '63; siege of Charleston, 1863, '64, '65; battle of Olustee, Feb. 20, '64; James Island, July 2, '64; Honey Hill, Nov. 30, '64; Devaux's Neck, Dec. 9, '64; and Boynkins Mills, April 18, '65.

The 54th led in the terribly fatal assault upon Fort Wagner, on the night of July 18, 1863, and the flag of the regiment was the object of the most determined bravery. The attack, although a failure, was signalized by unsurpassed daring, and thousands of men were sacrificed. The fort was surrounded by a moat filled waist-deep with water. Behind this rose a great bank twenty-five feet in height. Before the assaulting columns were formed, a storm arose, and it grew suddenly dark. It was about eight o'clock when the word of command was given to the 54th, who led the charge six hundred and fifty strong, commanded throughout by white officers. Colonel Shaw's last words as the regiment moved forward on the double-quick were, " We shall take the fort or die there." The charge was made with magnificent courage. As the troops approached the ditch, they met a withering fire. The garrison outnumbered them two to one. Before that murderous fire of grape, shrapnel, and musketry, the intrepid regiment of black men wavered, broke, and fled. Some followed their brave colonel through the ditch, and up the bank behind it, among them Color-Sergeant William H. Carney, who planted the flag in the most gallant manner upon the ramparts, and there maintained it until all hope of taking the stronghold was abandoned. There Colonel Shaw was shot through the heart, and fell back dead in the ditch, and many of his brave colored soldiers died by his side.

Most of the color-guard were killed or wounded. Finally Carney retired through the ditch, filled with dead and wounded, in the darkness, toward the federal lines, amid the storm of bullets and cannon-shot, and was wounded while doing so in the breast, both legs, and the right arm; but he struggled on, crawling on hands and knees, with the flag, until some distance from the fort. Here, at a point where Captain Luis F. Emilio was engaged in rallying the 54th, — he having succeeded by casualties to the command of the regiment on the field of battle, — the flag was brought to him, and, as it would serve no purpose in the darkness as a rallying-point, he directed the gallant Carney to take it to the rear.

A more ghastly scene was never witnessed than that on the slope and around the ditch of Fort Wagner the next morning. The dead and dying were piled on one another three feet deep, and the rebels claim to have buried over one thousand Union soldiers on the beach the next day. Colonel Shaw was buried "in a pit, under a heap of his niggers," but it was not in the power of the rebels to dishonor him.

At the battle of Olustee this flag was borne with conspicuous gallantry by Acting Sergeant James H. Wilkins, who escaped miraculously, though more than half the color-guard were killed or wounded, and the color-corporal (with the state flag) was mortally wounded at Wilkins' side.

Ever after this flag was carried with bravery and devotion by Sergeant Charles W. Lenox, who escaped severe wounds, but was frequently struck by spent balls or shot through his clothing.

## No. 5. — Flag of the First Vermont Cavalry.

It is to be regretted that no history of this flag is at hand. Its tattered and smoke-stained folds are eloquent with the names of glorious battles, from Mount Jackson to Cedar Creek. No soldiers performed more valiant service in the war of the rebellion than did the Green Mountain boys. Not a single flag did they surrender to the enemy during the four years of the rebellion.

## No. 6. — Flag of the Twentieth Regiment Massachusetts Volunteers.

The most diligent inquiry has failed to discover the story of this flag. It is inscribed with the names of no less than twenty-six battles.

---

## Plate VII.    Page 625.

## Old Abe, the Famous War Eagle of the Eighth Regiment Wisconsin Volunteers.

This famous bird was captured in Upper Wisconsin in 1861 by a Chippewa Indian, and was presented to the 8th Wisconsin when that regiment left for the seat of war. One of the tallest men of the regiment was detailed to carry and take care of him, with the understanding that at the end of the war he was to convey him to Washington and present him to President Lincoln. He was usually carried on a war shield, mounted at the top of a staff, and above this shield a perch was made to which Old Abe was tied by a cord. For three years he was carried beside the colors of this regiment, and during that time he was in twenty-two battles and thirty skirmishes, and was wounded in three of them. At the battle of Corinth, it is said, the rebel General Price ordered his men to capture or kill him at any hazard, saying that he would rather have them capture the eagle of the 8th Wisconsin than a dozen battle-flags; and that if they succeeded he would give his troops "free pillage in Corinth." During this battle the cord that confined him to his perch was severed by a ball, and Old Abe soared far above the sulphurous smoke. The rebels sought in vain to shoot him. Suddenly he caught sight of his regiment and flag, and, sweeping down, alighted on his perch. During a battle he was sometimes on the ground, then on his perch, uttering wild and terrific screams, and the fiercer and louder the storm of battle the more excited was he. He would stand by a cannon, which was being served with the greatest rapidity, without flinching, and the rattle of musketry had no terrors for him.

With the close of the regiment's period of service, Old Abe's fighting days were over, and he became the ward of the state of Wisconsin, to be "well and carefully taken care of as long as he lived," and his remarkable civil career was then begun. He made numerous triumphant journeys through the country, always proving a great attraction. His feathers were eagerly sought for at $10.00 each. Thousands of children throughout the North — from Maine to Oregon — were organized into a society, called "The Army of the American Eagle," for the purpose of selling a little pamphlet history of Old Abe's career, with his photograph, and their labors netted to the fund for sick and disabled soldiers the sum of $16,308.93. More than twelve thousand letters were received from boys and girls interested in this ingenious device for raising money for the soldiers. At this time a western gentleman offered $10,000 for him, and P. T. Barnum offered $20,000; but money could not buy him. A distinguished sculptor made a marble statue of him; and while Old Abe was on exhibition in Boston a celebrated artist painted his picture in oil, which still hangs on the walls of the Old South Church in that city.

On all his journeys he received a constant ovation. During the Centennial Exhibition, the Wisconsin legislature authorized the governor to detail a veteran soldier at state expense to take Old Abe to Philadelphia and care for him during the exposition. He was constantly surrounded by throngs of visitors, and his photographs were sold by the thousand. His fame had long before spread over Europe, and foreigners were greatly interested in him. Some of his feathers are now owned and prized by eminent persons, many of whom purchased them at round figures. A New York gentleman has one mounted in gold, and many important documents have been signed with pens made from Old Abe's quills. No other bird ever achieved such fame or reached such a distinguished place in history.

Old Abe died in 1881, and his preserved and stuffed body may now be seen in the War Museum at the state capitol in Madison, Wis.

## No. 1.—Flag of the Ninth Regiment Iowa Volunteers.

The 9th Iowa Regiment entered the service in August, 1861. At the battle of Pea Ridge, Ark., March 7, 1862, after a most extraordinary march of *forty-two miles*, the regiment displayed great valor and was engaged for ten hours in stubborn fighting, losing two hundred and thirty-seven men killed and wounded. But they held their ground against fearful odds, and that night they slept upon their arms, ready to re-form their lines at a moment's warning.

Five months after this battle the regiment received a handsome silk flag from some ladies of Boston, Mass., and the following comments on the presentation of this flag to the regiment are taken from Lieutenant-Colonel Abernethy's journal:—

"Camp 9th Iowa, near Helena, Ark., Sunday, August 3, 1862.—The regiment was formed at 2 P.M. to receive the stand of beautiful colors sent by a committee of ladies of Boston, Mass., as a testimonial of their appreciation of our conduct at Pea Ridge. Colonel Vandever delivered a short speech at the presentation and seemed much affected, as did many others present, at the respect and honor thus manifested by the noble women of a distant state, and at the associations connected with the occasion."

This flag was guarded and cherished with religious care, and was borne over many a field of blood.

On the 22d of May, at Vicksburg, in line with the whole Army of the Tennessee, the regiment led the assault. Its flag went down a few feet from the rebel works after the last one of the color-guard had fallen, either killed or wounded. In the few terrible moments of this assault the regiment lost seventy-nine killed and wounded, or nearly one-third of their number, in action. The assault failed, and the Union soldiers found themselves lying in ravines, behind logs, close up to and partly under the protection of the rebel earthworks. There they were compelled to lie until darkness gave them a cover under which to escape. Sergeant Elson had fallen, frightfully wounded, upon the flag. Captain George Granger drew its dripping folds from under the bleeding body of its prostrate bearer, and after dark brought it safely off the field, concealed beneath his blouse.

Eight other brave boys followed up the flag as color-guard in that memorable assault, namely : — Corporals Otis Crawford, Lewis D. Curtis, Zadoc Moore, Albert D. Strunk, James H. Gipe, Jasper N. Moulton, John Logue, and James Smith.

Though covered with blood, and riddled by both shot and shell, the flag was afterwards safely carried through the second siege of Jackson, and the battles of Brandon, Cherokee Station, Tuscumbie, Lookout Mountain, Missionary Ridge, and Ringgold, besides more than a score of lesser engagements. It travelled two thousand miles of Confederate soil, traversed six states in rebellion, went up to the cannon's mouth at the heights of Vicksburg, clambered up the rocky steep of Lookout Mountain, stood on the brow of Missionary Ridge on that bleak November night after the great battle of Chattanooga, in the midst of those shivering, hungry, and tired soldiers, and at last was no longer fit for service.

At this time the members of the regiment re-enlisted in a body for another "three years or during the war," and by unanimous vote the old flag was placed on the retired list and returned to the original donors in Massachusetts.

One month later, while the regiment halted for a day at Nashville on its way home on a thirty days' veteran furlough, another silk flag was received from the same committee of Massachusetts ladies, to take the place of the old one.

In connection with the extract previously quoted from Lieutenant-Colonel Abernethy's journal, the following interesting story, by Miss Phebe Adam, explains how it happened that a committee of Massachusetts ladies presented flags to the 9th Iowa Regiment. In a recent letter she says : —

"It seems to me that I ought to explain how it happened that Massachusetts women were interested in sending flags to an Iowa regiment. My brother, McG. Gordon Adam, who went from Massachusetts and was engaged in the practice of law at Decorah, Iowa, when the war of secession began, enlisted as a private soldier in Company H, 9th Iowa Infantry. In a home letter, shortly after the battle of Pea Ridge, he wrote to us that the regiment had not in that battle a flag to rally round, and added, 'Will not some of my Massachusetts friends send us one?'

"As soon as this was known among his Boston friends, they determined to supply the want, and the money to procure one came in so abundantly that not only a flag but a standard was sent to the regiment, reaching it while stationed at Helena, Ark. Colonel Vandever was asked by the donors to permit Private Adam to unfurl and present the colors on behalf of his Massachusetts friends; but my brother was too ill with fever, at the time, even to witness the presentation. The box was, however, opened by the side of his sick-cot, and the colors were unfurled for him to see them. This brief account of the flags will show that, although carried out in Massachusetts, the idea of our sending them was suggested by Private McG. Gordon Adam, and his name rather than that of his sister should be forever connected with them.

"In a letter written during convalescence with regard to the presentation of the flag, my brother writes: —

"'How disappointed you and my friends at home will be that I could not unfurl the colors and address the regiment in your behalf. I was not able to sit up when the flag arrived, and shall not be strong enough to go through with such an affair for a month, perhaps. I wrote a line to Colonel Vandever, telling him that I was too ill to comply with the kind wish of the ladies. He wrote me that he would delay the presentation if I wished it, but I wrote him not to wait as the time of my recovery was very uncertain, and I did not wish to deprive the regiment for so long a time. Colonel Vandever then sent me word that he would send through me a formal written acknowledgment of its reception. I have talked with a great many officers and men of the regiment, who came to see me while I was ill, and I will tell you what I have heard through them of the presentation, as I know how anxious you will be about it. As soon as the flags were unfurled and the address of the donors was read by the adjutant, Colonel Vandever read a printed reply, copies of which were delivered to the regiment. When he got to the last paragraph he choked for several moments, and three-fourths of the regiment were in tears. Not a single cheer was given for the flag at this time. What with the address and the reply, and the surprise at so splendid a testimonial from far-off Massachusetts, the men and officers were so affected that an attempt to cheer would have been a total failure. But when the colors were planted near the colonel's tent, the boys collected round them and cheered like madmen. Nothing could have a better effect on the regiment than this gift. The men were dispirited by their continued privations, because many of them, like myself, have never seen a paper in which their conduct at Pea Ridge received anything but the ordinary newspaper praise bestowed on the whole army. The poor fellows were surprised and delighted to find that they are understood and appreciated away off in old Massachusetts.

"'Your gift has infused a fresh spirit into the men. They look brighter and happier, and would die to the last man before the colors should fall into the hands of the rebels. I should like to write more, but am too weak to do so.'

" On the 29th of August, 1863, the flag was returned to us, accompanied by a letter from Colonel Carskaddon, then in command of the regiment. It showed the hard service it had been through, for it was torn and blood-stained, or, I should say, *is* torn and blood-stained, as it is preserved in our own home as a precious relic of the war.

" Colonel Carskaddon says at the close of his letter: 'We return this flag to you, because it has fulfilled the mission on which you sent it. Beneath it many a martyr to constitutional liberty has gone to his last rest. It is to us, and we trust it will be to you, the emblem of an eternal union cemented by the best blood of patriots.'

"When the regiment returned to Iowa on its veterans' furlough, the flag created a perfect furor in Dubuque. People hurrahed and cried over it. It was very difficult to preserve it from destruction, as everybody was trying to obtain a little piece of it as a relic of the fight in which some father, son, or brother served, perhaps was wounded or killed. Only one old lady got a piece. She begged the colonel, with tears in her eyes, to give her a small piece, as her two sons had fallen under it.

"After the battle of Vicksburg, my brother wrote to me as follows: 'The poor old 9th has been put in the front again at Vicksburg and suffered dreadfully. Your flag has been baptized by the blood of many a brave fellow. I had hoped that it would be the first to be planted on the hills of Vicksburg, for the 9th went farther than any other regiment and stood for two hours within twenty feet of the enemy's guns, but they were not sustained, and the remnant of the brave little band was at last compelled to fall back. During the assault, which was so bloodily repulsed, our color-bearer got on top of the enemy's works, and, being a little ahead of the boys who were clambering up the acclivity, he stuck the flag-staff firmly into the ground and cheered the men on to protect it. The brave fellow was shot down, and our charging party was almost annihilated and driven back. The color-sergeant had fallen on the flag, with a bullet through his thigh; his blood is on it. Afterwards each of the color-guard successively, excepting one, was shot down. We were obliged to lie close until dark, and, when the retreat commenced, Captain Granger took the flag along. It is riddled with balls and stained with blood, and unfit for further use. The boys are discussing whether to send it back to you, or to the governor of Iowa.' "

## No. 2.—Flag of the Second Kansas Battery.

History unknown.

### No. 3.—Flag of the Second Regiment Wisconsin Volunteers.

The 2d Wisconsin Regiment was a portion of the Iron Brigade of the West, of which General McClellan said, " They are equal to the best troops in any army in the world."

In the battle of Antietam the entire color-guard of this regiment was killed or wounded; but the flag was safely brought off the field.

At the battle of Gettysburg the first volley received from the rebel line cut down nearly thirty per cent of the regiment, and out of thirty-three men in the color company twenty-three were killed or wounded in thirty minutes. When the last color-bearer was killed, Private R. E. Davison picked up the colors and rushed to the front with them, and bore them in advance of the regiment in the charge of the Iron Brigade, shouting to the boys to " come on." For gallantry on this occasion he was made sergeant. The regiment went into this battle with three hundred men and in half an hour lost one hundred and sixteen in killed and wounded. That night there were but fifty of the three hundred men left to answer roll-call. In these and subsequent battles the flag was riddled and torn by bullets, the flag-staff was often shot and was once cut entirely in two. At Gettysburg it was so badly rent and torn that it was sent home and placed in the state capitol, and a new one was provided by the state.

The following interesting statement is taken from a letter recently received from Private R. E. Davison: —

" At the battle of Antietam we had a full color-guard; they were all killed or wounded. When the last one fell, I picked up the national colors and carried them. I did not have them more than five minutes before I was wounded by a minie-ball in my right shoulder, that put an end to my operations on that day. After I was wounded, I turned the flag over to a man belonging to Company C, who already

had the state colors. He told me afterwards that he carried
both flags the rest of the day, and was not wounded. The
next time the flag came into my hands was at the battle of
Gettysburg. Our color-guard was not full at this time. We
had one sergeant and one corporal as color-bearers, and two
corporals as guards. In the first of the fight the color-sergeant and guards were killed or wounded, and as the flag
went down I sprang forward and caught it, and carried it
through the rest of the fight. Captain Rollins made me a
sergeant on the field, and I was complimented in general
orders. I carried the flag from that day until the regiment
was discharged, in 1864. In the seven days' fight in the
Wilderness the flag-staff had two or three bullet-holes put
through it while in my hands, and I know not how many
holes through the flag."

## No. 4.—Flag of the Seventh Regiment Missouri Volunteers.

The 7th Missouri Regiment carried an American and an
Irish flag side by side. The Irish flag (shown in the illustration) was a beautiful silk one, and was presented to the
regiment by Surgeon P. S. O'Reilly and a few other friends.
It was carried through many battles, including Corinth and
the siege of Vicksburg.

The first two boats that ran the gauntlet of the rebel bat-
teries at Vicksburg carried the 7th Missouri Regiment.
While these boats were passing the batteries, Color-Sergeant
Fitz-Gerald defiantly waved the flag at the enemy. On the
22d of May the regiment stormed the rebel fortifications at
Vicksburg, making a most gallant charge. It reached the
rebel works (Fort Hill), when Private Patrick Driscoll
raised a scaling-ladder and held it while Color-Sergeant Fitz-
Gerald, with the Irish flag in his hands, bravely ascended.
Fitz-Gerald reached the top of the works, and triumphantly
waved the flag, but was instantly shot dead. Another soldier seized the flag and ascended the ladder only to suffer
the fate of his predecessor. Eight men were killed in a few

minutes under this flag, during this memorable assault. The regiment finally fell back, bringing its flag with it.

### No. 5. — Flag of the Second Regiment Kansas Volunteers.

" This was the only Federal flag on the battle-field of Wilson's Creek, when General Lyon was killed. Three color-bearers were killed or wounded while carrying it. It was finally carried from the field blood-stained, bullet-marked, tattered and torn."

This statement, pinned to the flag, is perhaps the only history that will ever be written of it, for the reason that the men who carried it were killed, and most of the officers and men who supported it are either dead or cannot be found. The flag is made of bunting, and the blood-stains are plainly discernible upon it. It is now deposited in the state capitol at Topeka.

### No. 6. — Flag of McMullen's First Independent Ohio Battery.

History unknown.

---

## Plate VIII. Page 657.

### No. 1. — Flag of the Seventy-Eighth Regiment Ohio Volunteers.

Thirteen members of the color-guard who defended or carried the regimental colors during the period of service of the 78th were killed or wounded. In the battle of Atlanta, July 22, 1864, Color-Sergeant John Spring, who held aloft the flag, was shot dead. He fell in the road in front of the line of battle, with the flag tightly clasped in his arms. Sergeant John F. Kennedy, and his comrade Joe Brown, seeing the flag about to be taken by the enemy charging the line, rushed out of the ranks, and, rolling the dead body of Spring off the flag, safely returned with the standard to the regiment. Sergeant W. Sutton then carried the flag, and was wounded in both thighs, and died shortly after. Sergeant James C. Aerick then took the flag, and was mortally wounded. Later in the same battle, while the flag lay on the ground by the side of its dead defender, a rebel rushed forward and had nearly succeeded in capturing it, and was stooping over for the purpose, when Captain John Orr completely decapitated him with his sword. For saving the flag on this occasion he received a gold medal from the Board of Honor of the Army of the Tennessee. The flag was carried through the rest of the battle by Sergeant Russell Bethel, who was slightly wounded.

### No. 2.—Flag of the Seventy-Eighth Regiment Pennsylvania Volunteers.

This flag was carried through the campaigns of the Army of the Cumberland, including the battles of Stone River, Chickamauga, the Atlanta campaign of 1862, battle of Nashville, etc. At the battle of New Hope Church, Georgia, May 27, 1864, while the regiment was under a heavy fire, a soldier of the 19th Ohio became separated from his regiment and attached himself to the 78th. While gallantly performing his duty a shell completely decapitated him, and dashed his head against the flag of the 78th, staining it with his blood.

### No. 3.—Flag of the Thirty-Second Regiment Indiana Volunteers.

This flag was carried through many battles, including Shiloh, Stone River, Chickamauga, Mission Ridge, the Atlanta Campaign, Resaca, Peach-Tree Creek, Siege of Corinth, and many minor engagements and skirmishes. It is part of the regimental history that the first four color-bearers were killed while carrying the flag at the head of the regiment, each man being shot through the head. The 32d Indiana was composed of Germans, and this flag was presented by German ladies of Indianapolis. The staff has two bullet-holes in it.

### No. 4.— FLAG OF THE NINTH REGIMENT KENTUCKY VOLUNTEERS.

In the battle of Stone River the color-bearer of this flag was instantly killed, and the flag fell to the ground. Moses Roark, a mere boy, instantly picked it up, and bravely carried it through the battle. He was promoted to color-sergeant, and carried the flag through every engagement in which the regiment afterwards participated.

### No. 5.— FLAG OF THE 129TH REGIMENT ILLINOIS VOLUNTEERS.

Color-Bearer Frederic D. Hess carried this flag in the charge upon the rebel works at Resaca, and was one of the first upon the enemy's breastworks, where he stood erect amid the rain of shot and shell, and waved the flag to cheer his comrades on. While holding it in his right hand a ball shattered the arm, but he immediately raised the falling colors with his left, which soon shared the fate of his right arm; but with his bleeding stumps he still clung to the flag, staining it with his life-blood.

### No. 6.— FLAG OF THE EIGHTEENTH NEW YORK CAVALRY,

Known as the "CORNING LIGHT CAVALRY." History unknown.

1. The Mississippi Steamer "Fanny Ogden" on her way with Relief for Sick and Wounded Soldiers.

2. On the Way to Antietam with Hospital Supplies.

# CONTENTS.

## CHAPTER I.

THE BEGINNING OF THE WAR—THE SPIRIT OF 1861—FIRST
CALL FOR VOLUNTEERS—UPRISING OF THE NORTH—EX-
CITING SCENES AND INCIDENTS.

In Boston with my dying Father—His early History—Surrender of Fort
Sumter—Uprising of the North—President Lincoln's Call for
Seventy-five Thousand Troops—Their Rendezvous in Faneuil Hall
—Departure of the Massachusetts Sixth for Washington—Scenes
at the Boston and Albany Station—Interview with Mr. Garrison
and Wendell Phillips—The Massachusetts Sixth attacked in Balti-
more—War Scenes in Auburn, N. Y.—My Return to Chicago—
Impressive Scenes in the Republican Wigwam—Cairo, Ill., a
strategic Point—North and South hasten to seize it—Chicago
Troops arrive first and take Possession—Increased Preparations for
War—Washington carefully guarded—Defeat at Bull Run—The
North nerved to Power and Purpose—The South exultant in Self-
Confidence—Lines now sharply drawn between loyal and disloyal
States . . . . . . . . . . . . . . . . . . . . . . . . 85

## CHAPTER II.

LOYAL WOMEN OF THE NORTH—THEIR PATRIOTISM AND
DEVOTION — HEROINES OF THE BATTLE-FIELD — HOME-
WORK AND RELIEF SOCIETIES—SCRAPING LINT AND
ROLLING BANDAGES.

The Patriotism of Men paralleled by that of Women—Notable Exam-
ples—Testimony of President Lincoln—Blunders of Inexperience
—The Havelock Mania—A Woman Soldier in the Nineteenth Illi-
nois—Sent out of Camp, she attempts Suicide—Is rescued and
joins her Husband—Madame Turchin, Wife of the Colonel—Her
Bravery and military Skill—Her Ability as a Nurse—She defeats a
Court-Martial—Other military Heroines—Annie Etheridge of the
Third Michigan—Bridget Devens of the First Michigan Cavalry—

Kady Brownell of the Fifth Rhode Island — Georgianna Peterman,
the Wisconsin Drummer-Girl — Army Stories of military Women —
Bandage and Lint Craze — Local Relief Societies — Queer Assort-
ment of Supplies — Cars flooded with fermenting Goodies — Great
Waste and Loss — Liberality of the People continues — Wiser
Methods are devised  .  .  .  .  .  .  .  .  .  .  .  .  .  .  .  .  .  . 109

## CHAPTER III.

### AT THE FRONT—WRETCHED HOSPITAL ARRANGEMENTS— THE SANITARY COMMISSION — ITS OBJECT, METHODS, AND WORK—BATTLE-FIELD RELIEF.

Early Ignorance and Inefficiency of Officers — The Cause of Sickness
and Death in Camp — Letters from the Front in Proof — Fearful
Mortality of British Soldiers in the Crimea, in 1855 — Occasioned by
similar Causes — Local Relief Societies organized — New York
Women show practical Wisdom — The Sanitary Commission evolved
from their Methods — Plan of Organization drawn up by Dr. Bel-
lows — Sanctioned by the President and Secretary of War — The
Commission soon conquers all Prejudice — Its Work very extensive
— Inspectors sent to Camps and Hospitals — Monographs prepared
on the Hygiene of the Army — Portable " Soup-Kettles " — " Hos-
pital Cars " — Forty Soldiers' Homes — Claim, Pension, and Back
Pay Agency — " Hospital Directory " — " Battle-field Relief Service "
— Ten " Branch Commissions " — Relief rendered at Shiloh and
Antietam — The Supplies, or Money for their Purchase, Made or
Collected by Women  .  .  .  .  .  .  .  .  .  .  .  .  .  .  .  .  .  . 123

## CHAPTER IV.

### MY FIRST CONNECTION WITH THE SANITARY COMMISSION— HOME SUPPLIES FOR THE SOLDIERS— A PEEP INTO THE BOXES — LETTERS FOUND INSIDE— ODD CONTRIBUTIONS.

Local Societies merged in the Commission — Become identified with the
Chicago Branch — The Secrets of the Boxes of Supplies — Notes
packed in with the Clothing — They are tender, pathetic, heroic,
and comic — A letter-writing Army — " Consecrated Chicken, be
jabers! " — " Butter an' *Chase*, bedad! " — " Comfort-bags " —
" Benedictions " in the Murfreesboro' and Vicksburg Boxes — " One
Box a Month " — Ingenious Wisconsin Farmers' Wives — Women
in the Harvest-field — A Talk with them — Generosity of a " Tail-

oress" — The "five-dollar gold Piece" — "Matches! Matches!" —
Afraid of a Kiss — Children's sanitary Fairs — Gift of a five-year
old Boy . . . . . . . . . . . . . . . . . . . . . 135

## CHAPTER V.

AT THE ROOMS OF THE SANITARY COMMISSION — ITS WORK-
ERS AND ITS VISITORS — HEART-RENDING SCENES AND
INCIDENTS — THE RECORD OF A DAY.

Rooms of the Chicago Commission — The Din of Draymen and Packers
— Sewing-Rooms for Soldiers' Families — "The Perfume of the
Sanitary" — The dingy little Office — Immense Work performed in
it — Judge Skinner, the President — Mr. Blatchford, Treasurer —
The "Quartette" of the Office — John Freeman, the "Man of all
Work" — William Goodsmith, our "Sheet-Anchor" — Mrs. Hoge,
my Friend and Co-Worker — Volunteer and transient Help —
Women, Girls, and Soldiers — Drayloads of Boxes — Ladies seeking
Information — Express Messengers — The Morning Mail — The aged
Father and his dead Son — "What ails the little Fellow?" — A
Bevy of Nurses — A sorrow-stricken Mother — Soldiers from the
City Hospitals — More loaded Drays — More Men and Women come
and go — The Day declines — Return to my Home — "A Suburb of
Heaven" . . . . . . . . . . . . . . . . . . . . . 155

## CHAPTER VI.

A CAMPAIGN PLANNED BY A WOMAN — DESPERATE BATTLES
— TERRIBLE SCENES ON THE BATTLE-FIELD — TERRIFIC
FIGHTING AND APPALLING SUFFERING — THE AGONIES
OF WAR.

General McClellan supersedes General Scott — Missouri becomes the
Field of Battle — General Grant wins a Victory at Belmont — Fleet
of "Ironclads" for Service on Southern Rivers — The "Tennessee
Campaign" planned by Anna Ella Carroll, of Maryland — Plan
adopted by President Lincoln and Secretary Stanton — Carried out
by General Grant — The "Court of Claims," in 1885, decides in her
Favor — Fort Henry on the Tennessee captured by Gunboats — They
fail to take Fort Donelson on the Cumberland — General Grant
attacks by Land — The Fort surrenders, after Three Days' Fighting
— "Unconditional Surrender Grant!" — Joy of the Northwest —
Frightful Suffering of the Wounded — Many frozen to Death on
both Sides — The People move to succor the Wounded — Immense
Quantities of Supplies forwarded — Seven thousand Prisoners sent
to Camp Douglas — Five hundred die . . . . . . . . . . 171

## CHAPTER VII.

AFTER THE BATTLE — MY FIRST EXPERIENCE IN A MILITARY HOSPITAL — A DEATHLY FAINTNESS COMES OVER ME — NERVING MYSELF FOR THE WORK — TOUCHING SCENES.

Mrs. Hoge and myself visit the Hospitals of St. Louis — Our first Experience — Boisterousness of new Recruits — The grim Silence of Men who had "been under fire" — Our remarkable Hostess — Conspicuous and unflinching Loyalty — Her "Hospital Kitchen" and "Hospital Wagon" — "Eleven Hundred Soldiers' Letters!" — The Donelson Wards — Their sickening Odor and ghastly Sights — Horrible Mutilation of the Men — A deathly Faintness came over me — The Wounded and Dead robbed on the Field of Battle — Plucky Fellow — "They couldn't be bothering with us" — "Afraid to die!" — "Send for a Methodist Minister!" — The Magic of Song — The mental Conflict of the Night that followed — St. Louis sitting in Gloom — Sad Wedding in the Hospital — Death of the Bridegroom . 184

## CHAPTER VIII.

I BECOME ACCUSTOMED TO HOSPITAL WORK — FILTH AND DISCOMFORT, NEGLECT AND SUFFERING — LEAVES FROM MY EXPERIENCE — MESSAGES FROM THE DYING TO LOVED ONES AT HOME.

Cairo an immense Basin, partially filled — Skilful Pilotage needed — Comfortless Hospitals — "My Wife came this Morning" — "Bring me a drink from the Spring" — The "Brick Hospital" a Marvel of Excellence — "Sisters of the Holy Cross" its Nurses — The young rebel Prisoner — Longing for his Mother — "Philip Sidneys" in every Hospital — Mary Safford my Companion the second Time — Her Method of Work — Her Memorandum Book and Baskets — Something for every one — "You are the good Fairy of the Hospitals" — Men crying for Milk — Mourning the Loss of "Mother Bickerdyke" — Wounded Soldier from "Island No. Ten" — Noble Letter from his Wife — "The Children needed him more than I" — Eulogy of Mary Safford — Her Career since the War — Professor in the Boston University School of Medicine . 201

## CHAPTER IX.

AWAITING THE BATTLE OF SHILOH — PREPARATIONS FOR THE WOUNDED — AWFUL SLAUGHTER — VARIED PHASES OF HOSPITAL LIFE — "MISSING."

A Perfect Military Hospital — "Mother Angela," the Lady "Supérieure" — "White-winged Sun-bonnets" — Battle of Shiloh — Appalling Slaughter on both Sides — Rebel Prisoners' Ward — " You-uns is very good to we-uns!" — The Rebel Surgeon's Fear — Meet an Old Acquaintance among the Rebel Wounded — The Valiant Eleventh Illinois — Great Prejudice against Protestant Nurses — The "Sisters" preferred — "They never see anything, nor hear anything, and tell no Tales!" — Good General Strong, Post Commander at Cairo — Am sent to St. Louis for Invalid Soldiers — Turner's "Descriptive List" Missing — Found in the Clerk's Office — General Curtis discharges him — He also furloughs young Brackett — Great Jollification in the Ward — They accompany me to Chicago . . . . . . . . . . . . . . . . . . . . . . . 217

## CHAPTER X.

THE DARKEST PERIOD OF THE WAR — MY VISIT TO WASHINGTON IN 1862 — STRANGE EXPERIENCES ON THE JOURNEY — PITIFUL SCENES IN A CONVALESCENT CAMP.

Woman's Council called in Washington — Mrs. Hoge and myself the Chicago Delegates — Darkest Period of the War — Am detained at Suspension Bridge — A Restless Crowd in the Waiting-room — A blind Vocalist Charms them to Quietness — Homeward-bound Invalid Soldiers on the Trains — Repulsive Instrument of Slave Torture — Trains going North from Washington packed with furloughed Soldiers — President Lincoln's Explanation — "The War to be ended by Strategy!" — We take in our Charge a sick Soldier — New Experience in Baltimore — Visit to Dorothea Dix — Her extensive Work — Superintendent of Women Nurses — Washington Soldiers' Home — Amy Bradley the Matron — "Solid Chunks of Sunshine" — Visit Alexandria — "Camp Misery" — "A perfect Golgotha" — Great Indignation of Visitors — Amy Bradley takes up her Abode in the Camp — Great Improvement follows — "The Soldiers' Journal" — We visit President Lincoln . . . . . . . 232

## CHAPTER XI.

LIFE IN A CONTRABAND CAMP — WASHINGTON IN 1865 — A CONTRABAND PRAYER MEETING — MY INTERVIEW WITH SECRETARY STANTON — THE DRUMMER-BOY OF THE EIGHTH MICHIGAN.

Fugitive Slaves rejoicing in Freedom — Prayer-meeting in Camp — Meet old "Aunt Aggy" — An Episode of Slavery — "Thar's a Day a-comin'!" — Lively Praying — Tempestuous Singing — Intense Sectarians — A Boy Philosopher — Visit Washington in 1865 — Great Changes — Deserters from the Enemy — Runaway Negro with a

Six-Mule Team — Courtesy and Kindness of Secretary Stanton — Meet Admiral and Mrs. Farragut — Their Simplicity and Geniality — Lieutenant Cushing, the Hero of the Ram Albemarle — Other Eminent Notabilities — The Drummer Boy of the Eighth Michigan — Enlists with his Teacher — Charlie petted by all — His Teacher and Captain shot at James Island — Fierce Life of the Eighth Michigan — Charlie shares it All — Struck by a chance Shot — Fatal Result . . . . . . . . . . . . . . . . . . . 257

## CHAPTER XII.

A TRIP DOWN THE MISSISSIPPI — AMONG THE SICK AND DYING — OUR MISSION AND STORES — LOVING MESSAGES FROM HOME — A BRIDE'S SONG FOR A DYING SOLDIER.

The Army encamped at Young's Point — They cut the Levees — Great Sickness results — Special Relief Corps sent down —Mrs. Colt, of Milwaukee, and myself attached to the Corps — Our Programme — Outfit — Some of the Messages entrusted me — Our wheezy Boat — Disloyal Officers — Musical Talent on Board — Singing in the Hospitals — Touching Episode — Scene in a Memphis Hospital — "Mother, don't you know your Boy?" — Our Headquarters in Memphis, at Gayoso House — Women Secessionists — To be sent within Confederate Lines — A stormy Interview — "*Allows* me to be at large!" — We embark on the Tigress for the lower Mississippi — A dreary Journey . . . . . . . . . . . . . . . . . . 280

## CHAPTER XIII.

ALONG THE DREARY RIVER—SAD SIGHTS IN A REGIMENTAL HOSPITAL — JOLLY BATTERY BOYS — I AM WELCOMED TO CAMP BY OLD FRIENDS.

Perils of the lower River — The Tigress and its disloyal Officers — The Stewardess a Virago — " I could throw you overboard as if you were a Cat!" — Lake Providence and its fathomless Mud — " The Sanitary Commission's got mired!" — Go down to Milliken's Bend — Distribute Supplies to Hospitals — Sorry Plight of a Wisconsin Regimental Hospital — Surgeon-General Wolcott, of Wisconsin, breaks it up — In the Camp of the Chicago Mercantile Battery — "What a Hubbub! What a Jubilee!" — Evening Prayers in Camp — The Boys get Breakfast — " The Victuals will taste better if you don't see the Cooking!" — Leave for Young's Point — General Grant's Despatch Boat Fanny Ogden gives me Passage . . . . . . . . . . . . . . . . . . . . 295

## CHAPTER XIV.

OPPOSITE VICKSBURG — ARRIVAL AT GENERAL GRANT'S HEADQUARTERS — MY INTERVIEW WITH HIM — MY PETITION — A TOUCHING STORY.

We call on General Grant — Reticent, patient, and persistent — We put ourselves on "short Rations" of Talk with him — Stories of his Intemperance foul Calumnies — His chivalric Defence of General Sherman — Am entrusted with a Variety of Errands to him — My Decision concerning them — Second call alone on General Grant — "The Gibraltar of America" — The General is very accessible — Not hedged about by Formalities — The most bashful Man I had ever encountered — "I will let you know To-morrow" — Discharges twenty-one invalid Soldiers, and gives me Transportation for them — One dies in Memphis — Another dies in Chicago, almost Home .   308

## CHAPTER XV.

I AM INSTALLED HEAD COOK IN A FIELD HOSPITAL — CHEERING UP THE "BOYS" — CAPRICIOUS APPETITES — MY RIDE WITH BLACK SOCRATES — VICKSBURG.

Large Field Hospital at Young's Point — Am put in Charge — Cater to the capricious Appetites — "Tea and Toast" for a forty-five-year-old "Boy" — "Tea! tea! tea! from the homespun Teapot" — Lemonade under Difficulties — Men transferred to Hospital Steamer City of Memphis — Visit to the Thirteenth Illinois — "Socrates" and his Six-Mule Team — "Mules is dat mean dey has ter be licked!" — Accomplishments of the Thirteenth Illinois — "The stealing Regiment" — Accompany the Engineer Corps down the Levee — Peep into Vicksburg with a powerful Glass — No sign of Home-Life — Rams Lancaster and Switzerland run the Blockade — One destroyed, the other disabled . . . . . . . .   319

## CHAPTER XVI.

COMING UP THE RIVER — A FREIGHT OF LIVING MISERY — GOING OUT FROM THE LAND OF BONDAGE — AMONG SICK SOLDIERS, CONTRABANDS AND REFUGEES.

A forward Movement — Gunboats run the Vicksburg Batteries — They convey Transports down the River — Troops cross and beleaguer

Vicksburg — We take Passage in the Maria Denning for Cairo — The Boat packed with human and animal Misery — Sick Soldiers comforted by our Presence — Johnny, the Virginia Refugee, given to my Care — His History — The tempestuous "Praise-meetings" of the Contrabands tabooed — Refugees encamped on the River Bank — Signal the Boat to stop — The Captain dares not — Fears Treachery — Meet Ford Douglas at Lake Providence — Agree to take a slave Boy to Chicago, despite Illinois "Black Laws" . . . 339

## CHAPTER XVII.

THE STORY OF THREE LITTLE ORPHANS — SMUGGLING A PLANTATION WAIF THROUGH "EGYPT" — THE UNDERGROUND RAILROAD — SAFE AT LAST — AFFECTING MEETING.

We find three Orphan Refugees in Camp Convalescent, Fort Pickering — Their pitiful History — We take them to the Chicago Home of the Friendless — Adopted by an Iowa Family — Cairo makes Addition to our Cares — Lizzie the Orphan Refugee from Missouri — Go aboard the Chicago Sleeper, with Johnny and the black Lad — The stuttering Porter hides the black Boy — " D-d-d-dat Woman's slep' mighty little fo' mos' s-s-s-six Weeks " — " She's d-d-d-done got monst'ous sick " — We defy "Egypt" and the " Black Laws " — Reach Chicago at Midnight — Sunday Morning, hunt up the black Lad's Mother — Affecting Meeting — Sarah Morris tells her Story — Johnny and Lizzie cared for . . . . . . . . . . . . . 356

## CHAPTER XVIII.

OUR BATTERY BOYS — A SECRET DRILL — THE DISCOVERY — OFF TO THE FRONT — GOD-SPEED AND FAREWELL TO MY SUNDAY-SCHOOL BOYS — EXTRACTS FROM THEIR DIARIES.

Our Church in Chicago — The *Morale* of its young Men — Memories of the Past — A loyal Congregation — What happened at Evening Service — Sudden Disappearance of our young Men — A peculiar Sound from the Sunday-School Room — Tramp ! Tramp ! Tramp ! — We stealthily open the Door and peep in — Our Discovery — " We have all decided to enlist " — An unspoken Prayer — All but two of our young Men are mustered into the Chicago Mercantile Battery — The Grief of Parting — Solemn Consecration — An affecting Farewell — Extracts from their Diaries — A jolly set — Roughing it without Whining — The Art of Frying Cakes — " Sweet Times here " — The Siege of Vicksburg — Awaiting the Battle — Army

Life at the Front — " Spoiling for a Fight " — Ordered into Action — We keep up Communication with our Boys — A Country devastated by War — An unexpected Visitor . . . . . . . . . . 369

## CHAPTER XIX.

THE STORY OF OUR BATTERY BOYS CONTINUED — A DISASTROUS EXPEDITION — A TRAP OF DEATH AND DESTRUCTION — SCENES OF HORROR — THRILLING ACTS OF BRAVERY AND DEVOTION.

Changes among our Boys — Breaking down under the Hardships of War — The Battery constantly shifts its Encampment — Working hard to kill Time — The Humorous Side of Life in Camp — History of "Doggie Doggett," the Canine Member of the Battery — His Exploits and Unknown Fate — Lost in the Service — Unfortunate Expedition — Up the Red River — Charging the Enemy with a Baggage-Train — Our Boys fall into a Trap of Death and Destruction — A terrific Charge by ten thousand Rebels — Overpowered by superior Numbers — Retreat or Surrender the only Alternative — The Guns of the Battery captured — Death of Lieutenant Throop — Sergeant Dyer shot while spiking his Gun — Many of our Boys are taken Prisoners — Hugh Wilson's Devotion — Only eight of our Boys return at the Close of the War . . . . . . . . . . 387

## CHAPTER XX.

THE FIRST GREAT SANITARY FAIR — RAISING MONEY FOR HOSPITAL RELIEF — A GREAT AND MEMORABLE DAY — A MOTLEY PROCESSION THREE MILES LONG.

Continued Needs of the Hospitals lead to a great Sanitary Fair — A Woman's Enterprise from the Beginning — Large Preparations — Seventeen Bushels of Fair Circulars and Letters sent at one Mail — Mrs. Hoge obtains Help from Pittsburg and Philadelphia — Potter Palmer from New York — Boston and Connecticut contribute — The whole Northwest ransacked for Attractions — At last, Men catch the Fair Mania — Their varied Gifts — Opening Inaugural Procession — Captured rebel Flags borne along — School Children in Carriages and Omnibuses — Convalescent Soldiers from Hospitals — Procession of Farm Wagons, with Vegetables — Procession halts on the Court House Lawn — Firing of thirty-four Guns announces the Opening of the Fair . . . . . . . . . . . . . . . 409

## CHAPTER XXI.

STORY OF THE GREAT FAIR CONTINUED — ITS SIX HALLS — PRESIDENT LINCOLN'S DONATION — UNEXAMPLED EN- THUSIASM — "GOD BLESS THE FARMERS."

Profusion of Wares and rapid Sales — Daily Excursion Trains — Presi- dent Lincoln donates the Manuscript of the Proclamation of Eman- cipation — Large Quantities of Food sent from the Country to the Dining-Hall — How Dubuque furnished her Quota of Supplies — Picturesque Scene — Hall erected for Donations of Machinery — Our Bargain with the Builder — A Revelation and its Results — County Court Room transformed into a "Curiosity Shop" — Rebel Flags, and Battle Trophies — Slave Shackles and Collars — Large Loan Collection of Art Works — Anna Dickinson's Lectures — Dinner to Northwestern Governors, Congressmen, and other Digni- taries — Gift of Live Stock — Auction Sales on the Sidewalk  .  . 427

## CHAPTER XXII.

LAST DAYS OF THE GREAT FAIR — SOLDIERS' DAY — TOTAL RECEIPTS NEARLY ONE HUNDRED THOUSAND DOLLARS — INTERESTING ITEMS AND INCIDENTS.

Dinner given by the Ladies to eight hundred invalid Soldiers in Hos- pitals — Lady Managers dined by Gentlemen, who serve the Feast — Mighty Frolic — "Completely tuckered out!" — Items and Inci- dents — Afghan made with Money found in a dead Soldier's Pocket — Contraband's Gift — Donation of Octogenarians — Mite of the German Woman — The Luck of the Chickamauga Soldier — Major- General Herron of Iowa in the Fair — Letters of Gratitude from Soldiers in Hospitals — "Must see that Fair" — "All I have" — Safe place of Retreat — Pleasant Greetings — "A Soldier's Psalm of Woman" — Cheers for Lincoln — Cheers for the Soldiers — Cheers for the Ladies of the Sanitary Commission — Specimen of the Soldiers' Battle-cry — The Dead .  .  .  .  .  .  .  .  .  .  . 450

## CHAPTER XXIII.

SHERMAN'S MARCH TO THE SEA — DEATH-BLOW TO THE RE- BELLION — SURRENDER OF LEE — ASSASSINATION OF PRES- IDENT LINCOLN — THE MARCH OF EVENTS.

The End draws near — Sherman's March to the Sea — He finds the Southern Confederacy a Shell to be easily crushed — Much Anxiety

felt at the North for the Result — He takes Savannah, with its
immense Stores, and informs the President of his Gift — The
South surprised — English Journals prophesy Failure — Reaches
the Atlantic Coast — Co-operates with Grant and Lincoln — Richmond evacuated — Lee surrenders — Delirious Joy of the Nation —
Characteristic Procession improvised in Chicago — Lincoln assassinated — Joy swallowed up in passionate Sorrow — Disbanding of
the Army — Motley Treasures brought Home by Soldiers — Eager
to reach Home — Gladness of the Nation at the Return of Peace . 463

## CHAPTER XXIV.

MOTHER BICKERDYKE — STORY OF A REMARKABLE WOMAN —
HER MOTHERLY CARE OF THE "BOYS IN BLUE" — HOS-
PITAL SIGHTS AND SCENES — ON THE BATTLE-FIELD AT
NIGHT.

A remarkable Woman — Sent into the Service at Cairo by Ladies of
Galesburg, Ill. — Improvises a sick-diet Kitchen — Stratagem to
detect the Thieves who steal her Delicacies — " Peaches don't seem
to agree with you, eh ? " — Colonel (now General) Grant removes
the dishonest Officials — Mother Bickerdyke after the Battle of
Donelson — A Surgeon's Testimony — She extemporizes a Laundry
— Is associated with Mrs. Porter of Chicago — After the Battle of
Shiloh — " I get my Authority from the Lord God Almighty; have
you anything that ranks higher ? " — Her System of foraging — Her
" Night-Gowns " as hospital Shirts — " Say you jerked them from
the Secesh, Boys ! " — Experiences at Corinth — Finds a dying
Soldier left in a Tent . . . . . . . . . . . . . . . . 476

## CHAPTER XXV.

THRILLING INCIDENTS IN THE LIFE OF MOTHER BICKER-
DYKE — HER HOSPITAL EXPERIENCES — HER FIRST FUR-
LOUGH — RETURN TO THE FRONT — FIGHTING THE DOC-
TORS — A COW-AND-HEN EXPEDITION.

She is much worn down — Extremely Perilous to remain longer with-
out Rest — Her Health demands a Respite from her Labors for a
Time — Comes to my House on her Furlough — Attends a Wed-
ding — " Have enjoyed your Wedding as if it were a Prayer-
Meeting ! " — Calls Meetings to raise Supplies — Returns to the
Front, organizes and regenerates Hospitals — Re-organizes her
Laundries in Memphis — Quarrels with the Medical Director — Out-
generals him — " One of us two goes to the Wall, and 'taint never
me ! " — The Storm finally ends in Sunshine — They become
Friends — He sends her North on a Cow-and-Hen Expedition —

Returns with a hundred Cows, and a thousand Hens — Improved
Condition of the Hospitals — Confided in everywhere — Impatient
of Red Tape — Cared little for Sect, but much for the Comfort of
the Soldiers . . . . . . . . . . . . . . . . . . . . .   499

## CHAPTER XXVI.

MOTHER BICKERDYKE AND GENERAL SHERMAN — A NIGHT
OF HORROR — HEROIC EFFORTS TO SAVE THE WOUNDED
FROM FREEZING — HEART-RENDING SCENES AND TERRI-
BLE SUFFERING.

Mother Bickerdyke's Idolatry of General Sherman — She becomes an
*Attachée* of his Corps — Comes to Chicago and does good Work
for Soldiers' Families — Goes to Chattanooga after the Battle, and
establishes a Hospital — Incredible Exertion to save her Patients
from Freezing — Orders Breastworks torn down for Fuel — " All
right, Major, I'm arrested! Only don't meddle with me till the
Weather moderates!" — General Burnside beleaguered in Knoxville, Tenn. — Sherman marches to his Relief — Fearful Suffering
from Cold and short Rations — Horrors of the Return Route to
Chattanooga — Railroad from Nashville completed at last — Joyful
Welcome of the first Train — All Night in the icy Gale — She ran
from Tent to Tent — She encouraged the shivering Soldiers — Her
Name mentioned only with Tears . . . . . . . . . . . .   515

## CHAPTER XXVII.

STORY OF MOTHER BICKERDYKE CONCLUDED — FOLLOWING
THE FLAG IN THE ATLANTA CAMPAIGN — HER MOTH-
ERLY MINISTRATIONS IN THE MIDST OF BATTLE — HER
LIFE AND CAREER SINCE THE WAR.

Mother Bickerdyke makes an eloquent Speech — Disregards Sherman's
Orders, and calls on him. Obtains the Favor she seeks — Six
Months in the Rear of Battles — Death of General McPherson —
Sherman begins his March to the Sea — Mother Bickerdyke packs
all Hospital Supplies, and sends to Nashville — Goes to meet Sherman, with a Steamer loaded with Supplies, as he directed — They
are not needed, and she cares for the Andersonville Prisoners —
The War ends, and she returns to Louisville — Her Life since the
War — The Government grants a pension to her — The Soldiers do
not forget her — Her Effort to keep a Hotel in Kansas not a Success — Unsectarian, but Christian — Her present Home  . . . .   530

## CHAPTER XXVIII.

MY REMINISCENCES OF PRESIDENT LINCOLN — EXPERIENCES IN THE "WIGWAM" — EXCITING SCENES — MY INTERVIEWS WITH THE PRESIDENT AT THE WHITE HOUSE.

Early Life of President Lincoln — My first Knowledge of him, in 1858 — "The Battle of the Giants" — He is nominated in 1860 for the Presidency — My Experience in the "Wigwam" as a Reporter — The memorable Scenes attending the Nomination — My Visit to Washington in 1862 — Gloomy Period of the War — Call on the President — His Depression — Discouraging Statements — Wholesale Desertions from the Army — "To undertake to fill up the Army is like shovelling Fleas!" — Mrs. Hoge and I see the President alone — His Suffering during the War — He contributes the manuscript Proclamation of Emancipation to the Chicago Sanitary Fair — A Premium sent him as the largest Contributor  . . . . 547

## CHAPTER XXIX.

REMINISCENCES OF PRESIDENT LINCOLN CONTINUED — SCENES AT THE WHITE HOUSE — A WIFE'S SAD STORY AND AFFECTING PETITION — I INTERCEDE WITH THE PRESIDENT — HIS SYMPATHY AND MERCY.

The President refuses to pardon a Virginia Spy — Wife of the condemned Illinois Major — Her sad Story — She is too much broken down to plead for her Husband's Life — "Beg the President not to allow my Husband to be shot!" — I tell her Story — The President's Sympathy — "These Cases kill me" — He had already commuted the Major's Sentence — His Delight at the Discovery — "I know all about it now" — The grateful Woman fainted — She is told to go and visit her Husband — The broken-hearted Wife goes away imploring Blessings on the President — Beautiful Reception of Miss Elizabeth Peabody — Touching Letter to Mrs. Bixby — Her five Sons were killed in Battle — Humorous Reply to his Advisers — "Keep Silence, and we'll get you safe across"  . . . . . . . 566

## CHAPTER XXX.

MY LAST INTERVIEW WITH PRESIDENT LINCOLN — SCENES AT HIS RECEPTIONS — HIS INEXHAUSTIBLE HUMOR — HIS ASSASSINATION — A NATION IN TEARS.

Chicago projects a second mammoth Sanitary Fair — Attendance of President and Mrs. Lincoln solicited — His comical Narration of

his Experiences at the Philadelphia Fair—"I couldn't stand
another big Fair"—A humorous Inducement—Both promise
Attendance—Mrs. Lincoln's Reception—The President's Manner
of Receiving—Crowds in Attendance—Love for Children—
"Stop, my little Man"—"You expect to be President sometime"—An unexpected Reply—The Humble welcomed—Love
universally manifested for him—The Remains of the martyred
President are received in Chicago—The unfeigned Grief of the
Northwest—The Body lies in State at the Court House—"All is
well with him forever!" . . . . . . . . . . . . . . . 578

## CHAPTER XXXI.

### HEROISM OF SOLDIERS' WIVES—WHAT THEY ENDURED AT HOME—A SUNDAY MORNING VISIT TO THEIR FAMILIES— LEAVES FROM MY JOURNAL—PATHETIC INCIDENTS.

Petition of four hundred and eighty Soldiers in Southern Hospitals
—"Ignore us, but look after our suffering Families!"—Heroism
of Wives and Mothers—Visit Soldiers' Families with Chaplain
McCabe—Children fierce and wild with Hunger—An underground Room, and great Wretchedness—The Soldier's Widow dies
in the Night—Her Mother, in the Darkness, defends the Body
from Rats—The Baby falls from the Chamber Window, while the
Mother is away washing—A colored Woman turned out on the
Sidewalk, with her dying Child, for unpaid Rent—Her Husband
fighting under Colonel Shaw, in the Fifty-fourth Massachusetts—
Governor Andrew sends me *Carte blanche* in the way of Relief
for Families of that Regiment—The Historian should remember
the Heroism of the Hearthstone . . . . . . . . . . . . 586

## CHAPTER XXXII.

### MY FIRST PUBLIC SPEECH—CROSSING THE MISSISSIPPI IN A ROW-BOAT—"A VOICE FROM THE FRONT"—FACING AN AUDIENCE FOR THE FIRST TIME—AN EVENTFUL NIGHT.

Return from the Front—Accept Invitation from Dubuque to address
the Ladies—Ferry-boat detained by moving Ice in the Mississippi
—Cross in a Row-boat—The Trip attended with much Danger—
The Risk assumed—Many prophesied evil Results—They proved
false Prophets—Crossed the River safely—"All Iowa will hear you
to-night"—Appalled at the Prospect—Am advertised for a Lecture,
without being consulted—"A Voice from the Front!"—Fear to
attempt a public Speech—Hesitation overcome by Colonel Stone's

Argument — The Results that followed — An Iowa Sanitary Fair is planned and carried out — Aggregates nearly $60,000 . . . . . 601

## CHAPTER XXXIII.

REMINISCENCES OF THE WAR — TOUCHING STORY OF A RING — THE MAJOR WHO CRIED FOR MILK — CAPTURE OF GENERAL GRANT — "OLD ABE," THE WISCONSIN WAR EAGLE, AND HIS WONDERFUL CAREER.

Confronted by one of my own Letters — The widowed Mother tells her Story — Puts her dead Daughter's Ring on my Finger — Officers' Hospital at Memphis — Its wretched Condition — Is made comfortable by the Commission — Incident at the Fabyan House, White Mountains — "Do you remember the Major who cried for Milk?" — Second Sanitary Fair in Chicago — Held after the War ended — Regiments, Soldiers, and Officers received there — An Ovation to General Grant — Executes a flank Movement on the People — Is captured by young Ladies — "This beats Vicksburg all out of Sight!" — "Old Abe," the Eagle of the Eighth Wisconsin — His military Behavior — Children sell his Pictures for the Soldiers' Fair — Make $16,308.93 by the Sales . . . . . . . . 613

## CHAPTER XXXIV.

SOLDIERS' LETTERS FROM THE FRONT DURING THE FIRST YEAR OF THE WAR — VIVID PICTURES OF LIFE IN CAMP — DESOLATION — AMUSEMENTS — MARCHING — FORAGING — PICKET DUTY — LETTERS FROM HOME.

Authors of the Letters — Life in Camp — Exploits of the First Iowa — "A bully Boy" — Hardships of a Chaplain — Fight at Conrad's Ferry — The Desolation of War — Impatient to be led into Action — "Little Mack" — President's Reception — The Picture of Weariness and Despair — Amusements — Morals — Without the Comforts of Civilization — Secession Literature — Hutchinsons sing in Camp — Soldiers wild with Delight — Dying from Camp Diseases — The poor Horses — Depression of the Men — Picturesque Scenes — Breaking up Camp, and starting off — Going into Camp for the Night — Foraging — Difficulty of Moving a large Army — Longing for Letters from Home — Their blessed Influence — "The musty Crackers and rusty Bacon are better" — Fatigues of Picket Duty — In Pursuit of Something to eat — "Somebody had been frying

Chickens " — Battle of Pea Ridge — As good as Dead the last half
of the Battle . . . . . . . . . . . . . . . . . . . 620

## CHAPTER XXXV.

SOLDIERS' LETTERS FROM THE FRONT DURING THE SECOND
YEAR OF THE WAR — HOW A SOLDIER FEELS IN BATTLE
— SWAMPS OF THE CHICKAHOMINY — A BABY ON THE
BATTLE-FIELD — "OLD ROSY."

Letter from a Nurse on a Hospital Boat — After the Battle of Shiloh
— Battle Scenes — "Marching all Day, and fighting all Night " —
Fearful Condition of the Sick and Wounded — Intimidating Effect
of the howling Shells — Burning commissary Stores — "It is all
over! I am to be killed!" — Hard Lot of the Sick — Wading through
the villanous Mud of Virginia — General Howard wounded —
"Hereafter let's buy our Gloves together!" — Letters from Home
— "A Means of Grace" — Negro Friendliness — Splendid Foraging
— Surprised at the good-looking Yankees — Life in a Rebel Prison
— The Counterpart of Jeffreys and Haynau — Putrid Mule-Beef —
Soup swarming with Bugs and Maggots — "A Baby on the Battle-
Field " — The Army of the Cumberland — "Old Rosy " — Nation-
alities represented in the Army — "Schpike dem new Guns! No,
Sheneral, it vould schpoil dem!" . . . . . . . . . . . . 650

## CHAPTER XXXVI.

SOLDIERS' LETTERS FROM THE FRONT DURING THE THIRD
YEAR OF THE WAR — HOUSEKEEPING IN CAMP — RIDING
"CRITTER-BACK" — DARING DEEDS — REBEL PICKETS.

Battle of Chickamauga — Remarkable Presentiment — Housekeeping in
Camp — Ignorance of the Enemy — "The walking Regiments " —
"Cannon Soldiers " — Wept over his lifeless Body — Ignorance of
secesh Soldiers — Yet they fight bravely — Have plenty of Hay, but
no Impunity — Greater Loss by Sickness than on Fields of Battle
— Evidence that the Enemy are near — "Riding Critter-back " —
After the Battle of the Wilderness — "Any Commander but Grant
would have retreated " — Recklessness of the Cavalry — Daring of
the Soldiers — "Divide is the word, or you are a dead Johnny!" —
Ten thousand Men sing "Rally round the Flag, Boys!" — "One
vast, exultant Roar!" — Talking with rebel Pickets . . . . . . 672

## CHAPTER XXXVII.

SOLDIERS' LETTERS FROM THE FRONT DURING THE LAST
YEAR OF THE WAR—LIFE IN REBEL PRISONS—DREAD-
FUL SCENES—HORRORS OF ANDERSONVILLE—LAST DAYS
OF THE GREAT REBELLION—PEACE.

A Hospital Picnic—"The Stump Squad"—Strawberries for the Army
—"Virginia a vast Blackberry Field"—"Old Hundred" in Camp
—Hunting Bloodhounds—Letter from a Hospital Nurse in Annap-
olis—Thirty thousand Prisoners cooped up at Andersonville, in
ten Acres—Their Hands and Feet rot off—Swarming with Vermin
—Bones protrude through the Flesh—The Men become Idiots and
Lunatics—Different Treatment of Southern Prisoners by the North
—"The Yankees take good Care of us"—Last Days of Sherman's
"March to the Sea"—The Army reaches the Atlantic Coast—
Columbia, S. C., is burned—Destitution of the South—"At the
Mercy of a General more powerful than Grant or Sherman, Gen-
eral Starvation" . . . . . . . . . . . . . . . . . . . . 682

AFTER THE BATTLE.

# CHAPTER I.

THE BEGINNING OF THE WAR—THE SPIRIT OF 1861—FIRST
CALL FOR VOLUNTEERS—UPRISING OF THE NORTH—EX-
CITING SCENES AND INCIDENTS.

In Boston with my dying Father — His early History — Surrender of Fort
Sumter — Uprising of the North — President Lincoln's Call for Seventy-
five Thousand Troops — Their Rendezvous in Faneuil Hall — Departure
of the Masachusetts Sixth for Washington — Scenes at the Boston and
Albany Station — Interview with Mr. Garrison and Wendell Phillips —
The Massachusetts Sixth attacked in Baltimore — War Scenes in
Auburn, N. Y. — My Return to Chicago — Impressive Scenes in the
Republican Wigwam — Cairo, Ill., a strategic Point — North and South
hasten to seize it — Chicago Troops arrive first and take Possession —
Increased Preparations for War — Washington carefully guarded —
Defeat at Bull Run — The North nerved to Power and Purpose —
The South exultant in Self-Confidence — Lines now sharply drawn
between loyal and disloyal States.

HE opening of the War of the Rebellion
found me in Boston, my native city. My
own home had been in Chicago for years,
but my aged father was thought to be
dying, and the stern speech of the telegram had
summoned me to his bedside. It was a time of
extreme and unconcealed anxiety. The daily papers
teemed with the dreary records of secession. The
Southern press blazed with hatred of the North,
and with fierce contempt for her patience and her
avowed desire for peace. Northern men and women
were driven from Southern homes, leaving behind all
their possessions, and thankful to escape with life.

Every one was asking his neighbor, "What will be the end?" but there was no answer, for over the whole North the paralysis of death seemed to have settled.

The day after my arrival, came the news that Fort Sumter was attacked, which increased the feverish anxiety. The threats of its bombardment had been discredited, for the North believed the South to be as deeply rooted in attachment to the Union as it knew itself to be. All its high-sounding talk of war was obstinately regarded as empty gasconade, and its military preparations, as the idle bluster of angry disappointment. When, therefore, the telegraph, which had registered for the astounded nation the hourly progress of the bombardment, announced the lowering of the stars and stripes, and the surrender of the beleaguered garrison, the news fell on the land like a thunderbolt.

During those never-to-be-forgotten days of Sumter's bombardment, I vibrated between my father's sick-room and the bulletin-board. With his anxious eyes asking speechless questions, he challenged every one who entered his apartment. When the speedy end came, and he was told that "Sumter had fallen!" he turned his face to the wall with an exceedingly bitter cry: "My God! now let me die, for I cannot survive the ruin of my country!" His illness was occasioned by mental suffering, and not by bodily ailment. The pending calamities of the nation, and the threatened disruption of the Union, had smitten him with sore anguish of heart. And mistaking the patience of the North, which hoped to avoid a collision with the excited South, as acquiescence in its rebellion, he believed the Republic rent in twain. For him, every fibre of whose being was intertwined with an almost ecstatic love of country, all joy in life was over.

Born just at the close of the War of the Revolution, in which his father and his kindred had served, my father was reared in a home where the memories of that war were sacredly cherished. Its great underlying moral cause — the defence of "inalienable human rights," — its hardships, heroism, and undying glory, — these were burned into him in his boyhood by constant recital, and he grew to manhood an enthusiast in his love for the young Republic. When, in 1812, war was declared by the United States against Great Britain, my father was more than a willing volunteer, and he entered the naval service.

The persistent claim of Great Britain that she had a right to search American vessels for deserters from her navy, — a right which she exercised in the most offensive manner, until she had "impressed" thousands of American-born seamen into her unwilling service, — was the cause of the war. My father had been a victim of the British "press-gang," and, although born in Massachusetts, among the Berkshire hills, he was arrested on board an American trading-vessel, as an English deserter, and was forced to do duty on a British man-of-war.

I have listened, spell-bound, in childhood, to his graphic narration of the indignities and cruelties to which he was there subjected. Suspected of a purpose to escape, he was degraded to menial service; and when he refused to fight against his own countrymen in time of an engagement, he was put in irons and threatened with death. When unexpectedly restored to menial service, he watched his opportunity, and, running fearful risks, succeeded in escaping from the detested British war-vessel while it was lying at Copenhagen. After weary weeks of hiding and watching and waiting, with experiences of danger that afterwards were woven into many a terrible dream of the night, a chance of return to his own country was given him, and was gladly accepted.

Hostilities had already commenced between the two belligerent nations, and, fired with a desire to avenge his wrongs, he enlisted on the frigate "Constitution" and served under Commodores Hull and Bainbridge until the end of the war. Now, fighting under the flag of his country, he coveted hardship and rejoiced in peril, for his early patriotism had become a devouring flame, only equalled in its intensity by his burning hatred of Great Britain. Ever after, love of country and pride of American citizenship were a vital part of his nature, dominating his speech and his life. The dreary winter of secession, when the nation seemed slowly disintegrating, had brought low his pride, and consumed both life and hope, and it seemed doubtful if he would survive the shock of Fort Sumter's reduction.

The next day, April 14, was Sunday. The pulpits thundered with denunciations of the rebellion. Congregations applauded sermons such as were never before heard in Boston, not even from radical preachers. Many of the clergy saw with clear vision, at the very outset, that the real contest was between slavery and freedom; and, with the prophetic instinct of the seer, they predicted the death of slavery as the outcome of the war. Some of the ministers counselled war rather than longer submission to the imperious South. Better that the land should be drenched with fraternal blood than that any further concessions should be made to the slaveocracy. For they were willing to disrupt the Union rather than yield their hated purpose to extend slavery throughout the Republic. The same vigorous speech was heard on the streets, through which surged hosts of excited men. There was an end of patience, and in its stead was aroused a determination to avenge the insult offered the nation. Conservative and peaceful counsel was shrivelled in a blaze of belligerent excitement.

Monday dawned, April 15. Who that saw that day will ever forget it! For now, drowning the exultations of the triumphant South, louder than their boom of cannon, heard above their clang of bells and blare of trumpets, there rang out the voice of Abraham Lincoln calling for seventy-five thousand volunteers for three months. They were for the protection of Washington and the property of the government. All who were in arms against the country were commanded to return home in twenty days, and Congress was summoned to meet on the 4th of July.

This proclamation was like the first peal of a surcharged thunder-cloud, clearing the murky air. The South received it as a declaration of war, the North as a confession that civil war had begun; and the whole North arose as one man. The Union was not to be destroyed without a struggle that would deluge the land with blood. The calls of the governors of the loyal states were met with a response so generous, that ten times seventy-five thousand volunteers could have been furnished had they been asked. All the large cities and towns raised money for the volunteers and their families, and it was believed

that abundant means were placed at the disposal of
the general government for a speedy quelling of the
rebellion.

Everywhere the drum and fife thrilled the air with
their stirring call. Recruiting offices were opened
in every city, town, and village. No stimulus was
needed. The plough was left in the furrow; the
carpenter turned from the bench; the student closed
his books; the clerk abandoned the counting-room;
the lawyer forsook his clients; and even the clergyman exchanged his pulpit for the camp and the tented
field, preaching no longer the gospel of peace, but
the duty of war. Hastily formed companies marched
to camps of rendezvous, the sunlight flashing from
gun-barrel and bayonet, and the streets echoing the
measured tread of soldiers. Flags floated from the
roofs of houses, were flung to the breeze from cham-
bers of commerce and boards of trade, spanned the
surging streets, decorated the private parlor, glorified
the school-room, festooned the church walls and
pulpit, and blossomed everywhere. All normal habits
of life were suspended, and business and pleasure
alike were forgotten.

To my father this uprising of the country was the
very elixir of life. The blood came again to his
cheek, and vigor to his system. And when, on the
morning of Tuesday, volunteers began to arrive in
Boston, and Faneuil Hall, the old "Cradle of Liberty," was opened for their accommodation, he insisted on being lifted into a carriage, and on going to
witness their arrival and reception. As they marched
from the railroad stations, they were escorted by
crowds cheering vociferously. Merchants and clerks
rushed out from stores, bareheaded, saluting them as

they passed. Windows were flung up; and women leaned out into the rain, waving flags and handkerchiefs. Horse-cars and omnibuses halted for the passage of the soldiers, and cheer upon cheer leaped forth from the thronged doors and windows. The multitudes that followed after, and surged along on either side, and ran before in dense and palpitating masses, rent the air with prolonged acclamations.

As the men filed into Faneuil Hall, in solid columns, the enthusiasm knew no bounds. Men, women, and children seethed in a fervid excitement. "God bless it!" uttered my father in tender and devout tone, as he sat beside me in the carriage, leaning heavily forward on his staff with clasped hands. And following the direction of his streaming eyes, and those of the thousands surrounding us, I saw the dear banner of my country, rising higher and higher to the top of the flagstaff, fling out fold after fold to the damp air, and float proudly over the hallowed edifice. Oh, the roar that rang out from ten thousand throats! Old men, with white hair and tearful faces, lifted their hats to the national ensign, and reverently saluted it. Young men greeted it with fierce and wild hurrahs, talking the while in terse Saxon of the traitors of the Confederate States, who had dragged in the dirt this flag of their country, never before dishonored.

I had never seen anything like this before. I had never dreamed that New England, slow to wrath, could be fired with so warlike a spirit. Never before had the national flag signified anything to me. But as I saw it now, kissing the skies, all that it symbolized as representative of government and emblematic of national majesty became clear to my

mental vision. It was honored on all seas — it afforded sanctuary in all lands — it represented the
authority and protection of a united people. It
signified an advance in human government, for it
had been adopted by millions of men, who stepped
out before the on-looking world, and wrote out a
declaration of human rights as the basis of national
life, pledging to its maintenance "life, fortune, and
sacred honor" — a pledge they kept so nobly that
the world learned a new meaning to the word, consecration. It was this holy flag that had been insulted
— it was this mother country, the grandest on earth,
with all its faults, that the South were determined to
slay — it was this nationality of which they would
bereave us. And all in the interest of human
slavery! I knew the full meaning of slavery, for I
had lived two years on a plantation in Southern
Virginia, twenty years before, and had seen its woe
and shame. "If it be a question of the supremacy
of freedom or slavery underlying this war," was my
mental ejaculation, "then I pray God it may be settled now, by us, and not be left to our children.
And oh that I may be a hand, a foot, an eye, a
voice, an influence, on the side of freedom and my
country!" I was weak with the new tides of feeling
coursing through my being.

That day cartridges were made for the regiments
by the hundred thousand. Army rifles were ordered
from the Springfield Armory. Fifteen hundred
workmen were engaged for the Charlestown Navy
Yard. Enlistments of hardy-looking men went on
vigorously, and hundreds of wealthy citizens pledged
pecuniary aid to the families of the soldiers. Military and professional men tendered their services to

PLATE I

FAMOUS UNION BATTLE-FLAGS.

1. Eleventh Reg't. Conn. Volunteers.
2. Headquaters Guidon Old Vermont Brigade.  3. Gen. Sedgwick's 6th. Corps Headquaters Flag.
*For Descriptions see pages  23 - 26.*

PHOTOGRAPHED AND PAINTED FROM THE ORIGINAL FLAGS EXPRESSLY FOR THIS WORK.
A.D. WORTHINGTON & CO. PUPLISHERS, HARTFORD, CONN.

the government in its present emergency. The Boston banks offered to loan the state three million six hundred thousand dollars without security, while banks outside the city, throughout the state, were equally generous in their offers. By six o'clock on the afternoon of Tuesday, April 16, three regiments were ready to start for Washington, and new companies were being raised in all parts of the state. On the afternoon of the next day, the Sixth Massachusetts, a full regiment one thousand strong, started from Boston by rail, leaving the Fourth Massachusetts to follow.

An immense concourse of people gathered in the neighborhood of the Boston and Albany railroad station to witness their departure. The great crowd was evidently under the influence of deep feeling, but it was repressed, and the demonstrations were not noisy. In all hands were evening editions of the daily papers; and as the record of the disloyal behavior of Maryland and Virginia was read aloud, the comments were emphatic in disapproval. With the arrival of the uniformed troops, the excitement burst out into a frenzy of shouts, cheers, and ringing acclamation. Tears ran down not only the cheeks of women, but those of men; but there was no faltering. A clergyman mounted an extemporized platform, to offer prayer, where he could be seen and heard by all, and a solemn hush fell on the excited multitude, as if we were inside a church. His voice rang out to the remotest auditor. The long train backed down where the soldiers were scattered among mothers, wives, sweethearts, and friends uttering last words of farewell.

"Fall into line!" was the unfamiliar order that rang

out, clear and distinct, with a tone of authority. The
blue-coated soldiers released themselves tenderly
from the clinging arms of affection, kissed again,
and again, and again, the faces upturned to theirs,
white with the agony of parting, formed in long lines,
company by company, and were marched into the
cars. The two locomotives, drawing the long train
slowly out of the station, whistled a shrill "good-
bye "— every engine in the neighborhood shrieked
back an answering farewell — from the crowded
streets, the densely packed station, the roofs of
houses, the thronged windows, and the solid mass of
human beings lining both sides of the track, further
than the eye could see, there rang out a roar of good
wishes, and parting words, accompanied with tears
and sobs, and the waving of hats and handkerchiefs
— and the Sixth Massachusetts was on its way to
Washington. Ah, how little they, or we, foresaw the
reception awaiting them in the streets of Baltimore!

As I turned to leave the station, my attention was
attracted by little groups, in the centre of which
were sad men and weeping women. A woman had
fainted, and I waited till restoratives and kind offices had brought her back to life. She apologized
for her "weakness," saying she was not very well,
and her son's departure was sudden. One of the
company added that "Mrs. —— didn't know that
Andrew had enlisted till to-day noon, and she hadn't
got over the bad news received a week ago; for
Clement, her only other child — and a good boy he
was, too — was drowned last week in the Bay of San
Francisco." My heart went out to the poor woman,
and I tried to say something comforting to her.

" He has only gone for three months, you know,"

I said, " and probably will not be called to do more than police duty. I hardly think there will be any fighting — certainly nothing more than skirmishing." My speech took counsel of my wishes, for I did not believe what I said. But there was a general feeling that the rebellion would be suppressed speedily, and that the determined attitude of the North would end very shortly the hostile bluster of the South.

The pallid middle-aged mother was weak in body only. " If the country needs my boy for three months, or three years, I am not the woman to hinder him," was her answer. " He's all I've got, now that Clement is drowned; but when he told me he'd enlisted, I gave him my blessing, and told him to go — for if we lose our country what is there to live for?"

My father's condition was so improved that there was no longer any need of my remaining in Boston. He lived, active and vigorous, and with perfect mental clearness, until within a few weeks of the surrender of Lee, in April, 1865 — always admonishing me, whenever we met, that " the severest years of a war are the twenty-five that succeed it, when the demoralization which it has engendered is found in every department of business, society, and government." He had had experience in war and its demoralizing influence.

My husband's letters from Chicago were full of the war excitement of the West. The more than doubtful position of Missouri, and the fact that the lower tiers of counties of Illinois and Indiana were allied to the South by kinship, trade, and political sympathy, caused great anxiety. The banks of Illinois were based on Southern state bonds, and secession had caused suspension, failure, and financial distress. My husband was editor and proprietor of a prosperous weekly paper, whose subscribers were scattered throughout the Northwest, and I was associated with him. I knew that a large proportion of them sympathized with the secessionists, and would immediately discontinue the paper, and become its active, open enemies, if its editors came out decidedly loyal to the Union, as he had written me we must do in the very next issue. I must hasten home to Chicago. But, before leaving, I coveted an interview with Mr. Garrison or Wendell Phillips. For many years they had been to me prophet and king, and I now sought them, as, of old, the oracles were consulted.

I found Mr. Garrison in his office on Washington Street, with composing-stick in hand, setting up matter for the next week's *Liberator*. He was as calm and serene as a summer morning. No one could have divined, from his passionless face and manner, that a hurricane of feeling was raging in the moral and political world.

"Mr. Garrison," I inquired, "what is your opinion of this Southern rebellion? Will it be a 'sixty days' flurry,' as Secretary Seward prophesies, or are we to have war?"

"We are to have war — a bloody, merciless war — a civil war, always more to be dreaded than one with a foreign nation."

"Do you think it will be a long war?"

"No one can tell. It *may* last as long as the War of the Revolution. The North underrates the power, purpose, and ability of the South, over which it expects an easy triumph. Instead of this, it will be plunged into a desperate struggle, of which it does not dream."

" What will be the result?   How will the war end
— in dissolution of the Union? "

"No one can answer that question.   Of one thing
only am I certain— the war will result in the death
of slavery! "

"Do you believe that, Mr. Garrison?   Theodore
Parker has predicted that slavery would go down in
blood, but it has never seemed possible that his
prophecy would be verified."

At that moment Mr. Phillips entered, with the
morning paper in hand, glowing with the account
it gave of the magnificent ovation accorded the Sixth
Massachusetts in its passage through New York.
How impassioned he was, and yet how self-poised!
If Mr. Garrison appeared the incarnation of serenity,
Mr. Phillips seemed aglow with sacred fire.   In the
first pause of the conversation between the two men,
I interrogated Mr. Phillips as I had Mr. Garrison.

"Mr. Garrison tells me that he is confident the
war will result in the destruction of slavery.   Do
you share this confidence with him, Mr. Phillips? "

"Yes; slavery has taken the sword, and it will
perish by the sword.   Five years hence not a slave
will be found on American soil! "

The next morning I left for Chicago.   All along
the route were excited groups of people, eager for
news from Washington, and everywhere was displayed the national flag.   At Albany, where we
halted for dinner, we learned the reception given the
Massachusetts Sixth in their passage through Baltimore the day before.   A vast and angry crowd had
opposed their progress, showers of stones and other
missiles were hurled at them from the streets and
house-tops, the soldiers had defended themselves and

fired into the mob, and the dead, dying, and wounded lay in the streets. So read the telegram. It was startling news, and blanched the cheeks of those who listened while the exaggerated accounts of the papers were being read. The war had indeed begun. The dead silence was broken by a tall, stern, sinewy, and grizzled Yankee, who had listened standing with both hands deeply plunged in his pockets.

"Waal, now, them Southern fire-eaters *have* gone and done it — that's a fact!"

The quaintness of the speech, with the peculiar tone and manner, spoke volumes. The breach between the North and South was fast becoming irreparable. War had begun in Baltimore, and its streets were reddened with fratricidal blood. The bodies of the Massachusetts fallen were "tenderly sent forward" to Governor Andrew, in obedience to his telegram. The whole city joined in the obsequies of these first martyrs of the new revolution, and, linking their memories with those of the early patriots who fell at Concord and Lexington, the drums that had done service at the battles of Lexington and Bunker Hill, were beaten at the head of the funeral escort.

I was detained *en route* over Sunday in Auburn, N. Y. The war spirit was rampant there, as everywhere. A newly recruited company of volunteers were to leave on Monday morning for New York, and they were honored with a public leave-taking in one of the churches that evening. The spacious church was crowded to suffocation, — as large an audience waiting outside as was packed within. The pulpit was decked with the national colors. Bunting festooned the walls and the sides of the gallery. The great audience rose, clapping and applauding, as the soldiers filed into the pews reserved for them. The very air was electric with patriotic feeling. The sermon stirred the pulses like the blast of a bugle. It was a radical discourse, and recognized slavery as the underlying cause of the outbreak, which, it predicted, would result in the freedom of the Southern serfs.

The choir sang patriotic odes, the audience joining with one voice in the exultant refrain, " It is sweet, it is sweet, for one's country to die! " The great congregation without caught it, thrilling the evening air with the spirit of the hour, " It is sweet, it is sweet, for one's country to die! " So intense was the feeling that when an appeal was made from the pulpit — transformed by the excitement into a recruiting office — for volunteers to defend the country, some half dozen rose, who were afterwards mustered into the service.

In Chicago there was more stir and excitement than I had seen elsewhere. The war spirit, war news, and war preparations engrossed everybody. The day presented scenes of din and bustle, and the night was scarcely less tranquil. The streets were thronged with eager men and women rushing here and there as incidents called them.

On the evening of the very day that Fort Sumter capitulated, an immense meeting of citizens was held in the great " Republican Wigwam," erected especially for the accommodation of the convention which nominated Abraham Lincoln to the presidency, less than a year before. It was now re-baptized, and called " National Hall," and was consecrated afresh, not to " party," but to " patriotism." Every inch of standing room was utilized on the ground floor, and the gallery was packed to the ceiling. Men of all religious creeds and party affiliations came together — a unit now — to deliberate on the crisis of the hour.

The gentleman chosen to preside had voted against President Lincoln. "But," he said, "the Administration, which I did not help elect, shall have my support now to the last, for this is a just and holy war on which we are entering."

Hon. George Mannière, eminent and popular, administered to the assemblage the oath of fealty to the government. Never was there a more impressive scene. The vast multitude rose, numbering nearly ten thousand, and, reverently baring the head, and raising the right hand, — old men and youths, matrons and maidens, and even young children, — they repeated solemnly after Judge Mannière the words of the following oath :

"I do solemnly swear, in the presence of Almighty God, that I will faithfully support the Constitution of the United States, and of the State of Illinois. So help me God."

All the speeches of the evening were short and to the point. The time for harangue was over — the time for action had begun.

"I did not vote for Abraham Lincoln," said Hon. John Van Armen, "but I will sustain him to the last drop of my blood."

"As long as this war lasts," said E. W. McComas, of the Chicago *Times*, a Democratic journal, "I will stand by the flag of my country. Intimations have been thrown out that I shall not be true to my country, because I am of Southern birth. I came here of my own free will. Your allegiance is my allegiance. I am no longer a Virginian, but a citizen of Illinois and of the United States."

On Sunday night, eight days after the fall of Sumter, troops were despatched from Chicago to Cairo, the southern terminus of the state, and a point of great strategic importance. At that time a muddy little town, it is situated at the confluence of the Ohio and Mississippi rivers, and is the key to the navigation of both. It is also the southern terminus of the Illinois Central railroad, whose northern termini are Dubuque and Chicago. Its importance as a military post at that time could not be over-estimated. Had the South seized it, it could have controlled the railway combinations of the Northwest, and closed the navigation of the Ohio and Mississippi. Southern leaders were well aware of its value as a railway and river centre, and were hurrying preparations to take possession of it.

They were forestalled in their action by Chicago. In less than forty-eight hours a force of infantry and a company of artillery were ready to march from that city. It was a citizen-corps, made up mainly of young men, most of them belonging to the best families of the state. Not only were these youths surrendered to the service of the country, but, aided by requisitions on the stores of Chicago, they were equipped with such munitions of war as they carried. They left in haste, little time being accorded to leave-taking or indulgence in grief. The long train of twenty-six cars stood waiting them at the station, with two powerful engines attached, which panted and puffed and shrieked as if eager to be off. As the precious train moved slowly out along the pier, the tens of thousands who lined the lake-shore bade them farewell with deafening cheers. Round after round rang out over the Prairie City, and were seconded by the prolonged shrill shrieks of all the locomotives waiting at the numerous railway stations.

They were none too soon in their occupation of Cairo. Many of the inhabitants were credited with a leaning towards secession, and would have been glad to welcome Southern instead of Northern troops. But they found the arguments of four brass six-pounders, accompanied by men with power and authority to use them, quite irresistible, and the town stiffened into undoubted loyalty immediately. "Them brass missionaries converted a heap o' folks that was on the anxious seat, now I tell ye!" said a plain, loyal man of the town, with a knowing wink of the eye, when narrating these events.

If the North had been skeptical as to the probability of war with the South, it was swiftly undeceived. For the President of the Southern Confederacy had also called for volunteers, and for persons to take out letters of marque as privateers, to destroy the commerce of the North, and his proclamation was received with an enthusiastic response. To meet this, President Lincoln declared all Southern ports blockaded, and denounced as pirates the commissioned privateers. Nothing daunted by the dreary prospect before them, the Southern leaders sent messengers to Europe, to obtain a recognition of their government as an equal nation contending with the North, and to get the blockade broken by promising England free trade and an ample supply of cotton. The South was in earnest, and the North began to believe it.

On the 3d of May, President Lincoln issued another proclamation, calling for forty-two thousand and thirty-four volunteers, at the same time increasing the regular army. In six weeks from the fall of Sumter, over half a million of men had volunteered to support the Union, nearly two hundred thousand of whom had been accepted, or were on the march, or were drilling preparatory to active service. More than one hundred thousand were organized by the different states, who were not accepted.

The two hostile armies were rapidly nearing each other on the Potomac, for the South was intent on capturing and holding Washington, and boastingly proclaimed its determination to do this. This would give the Confederacy prestige in the eyes of the world; and when once in occupation of the capital city of the nation, it could demand the recognition of foreign powers with a probability of success. Now its position was anomalous. Its seat of government was at Montgomery, Alabama, " a capital without a capitol. It had a Secretary of Treasury without any treasury; a Secretary of Navy without any navy; a Secretary of the Interior without any interior; a Secretary of Foreign Affairs without any foreign affairs; a Postmaster-General without any post-office; a Judiciary without any judgment, — in short, an Administration with nothing to administer."

To protect Washington was the one agony of the Northern people. Regiments were hurried forward without proper preparations for their care, which caused them great privation and suffering. They were quartered in the Capitol; they camped in the public squares; they were even accommodated in the house of the President. Arms were stacked in the rotunda of the Capitol, the stately edifice became a fortification. Zouaves lounged in the cushioned seats of members of Congress; and a military hospital was made of the Washington Infirmary, located on the site of the present Judiciary Square Hospital. Washington looked like a besieged city; and the nation breathed freely, for its seat of government was safe. There were constant collisions between small bodies of troops, and an incessant skirmishing between pickets, in which the Union soldiers were generally victorious. This kept the war excitement at fever heat, and confirmed the North in its confidence of crushing the rebellion at an early day.

The defeat at Bull Run extricated the nation from this condition of perilous self-confidence, and lea it to measure more accurately the mighty work on which it had entered. Our soldiers, enlisted only for three months, most of them unskilled, and commanded by officers who had never "smelt gunpowder," marched into Virginia to attack the rebels with a gay *sang froid*, as if bound on a military picnic. They plundered as they marched, riotous with fun and frolic, accompanied by Congressmen, reporters, civilians — all who could muster passes from the government — and who followed on in carriages, omnibuses, and on horseback. They were going to witness an easy victory.

From a combination of causes the battle of Bull Run was lost to the Union army, composed mostly of raw troops fresh from the counting-room, farm, and workshop, who had been marching and fighting for thirteen hours without any respite. Wearied and famished, and agonizing with thirst, ten thou-

sand fresh troops of the enemy were thrown suddenly upon them, and a panic ensued. Back they
fled to Washington, a headlong, disorderly mob;
men in regiments and men in groups, army wagons
and sutlers' teams, riderless horses, and the thunder-
ous artillery, crushing all that came in their way
— a routed host, confused, terror-stricken, and
choked with dust, that no authority could halt, and
no military skill re-organize. The rain came down in
torrents, deepening the gloom, as the drenched fugitives poured over Long Bridge into the capital,
cumbering the roads behind them with abandoned
cannon, arms, and equipments, leaving their dead
and dying uncared for. They filled the public ear
with exaggerated accounts of surprise, slaughter,
and pursuit, which could not be corrected, when
later they were followed by orderly regiments and
solid battalions, that unbroken and with military
discipline marched back to their old encampments.

As the story of this disaster was carried by the
telegraph into the homes of the people, the North
was stunned and temporarily paralyzed. Its dream
of invincibility was over. It was a gigantic war
into which it was precipitated, and a gigantic army
must be collected, equipped, and organized to meet it.
Lifting itself out of the despair which for the moment prostrated it, the nation girt itself anew with
power and purpose. Its army of seventy-five thousand
three months' men melted away as soon as its brief
term of service was ended. In its place the government now proceeded to raise, equip, drill, and prepare for the field an army of half a million ; and the
North rose in majesty to aid the administration in
its herculean task.

But if the North was sobered by this disaster, and nerved to a firmer grapple with her foes, the South was intoxicated with her easy success. Her forces were strengthened and consolidated by this victory. She had little doubt but the independence of the Southern confederacy was now achieved. Whoever throughout the South had hesitated to swear allegiance to the cause of secession delayed no longer. Tennessee now voted to leave the Union. A great army of rebels suddenly made their appearance in Missouri, which was now rent with the ravages of civil war. And Fort Fillmore, in New Mexico, with seven hundred men, surrendered to a body of Texans without firing a gun. And now at last matters had sharply defined themselves ; the lines were drawn between the States that were loyal and disloyal, and the millions of the United States were ranged on one side or the other of a long and desperate struggle.

Meantime, what did the women of the North?

# CHAPTER II.

LOYAL WOMEN OF THE NORTH — THEIR PATRIOTISM AND DEVOTION — HEROINES OF THE BATTLE-FIELD — HOME-WORK AND RELIEF SOCIETIES — SCRAPING LINT AND ROLLING BANDAGES.

The Patriotism of Men paralleled by that of Women — Notable Examples — Testimony of President Lincoln — Blunders of Inexperience — The Havelock Mania — A Woman Soldier in the Nineteenth Illinois — Sent out of Camp, she attempts Suicide — Is rescued and joins her Husband — Madame Turchin, Wife of the Colonel — Her Bravery and military Skill — Her Ability as a Nurse — She defeats a Court-Martial — Other military Heroines — Annie Etheridge of the Third Michigan — Bridget Devens of the First Michigan Cavalry — Kady Brownell of the Fifth Rhode Island — Georgianna Peterman, the Wisconsin Drummer-Girl — Army Stories of military Women — Bandage and Lint Craze — Local Relief Societies — Queer Assortment of Supplies — Cars flooded with fermenting Goodies — Great Waste and Loss — Liberality of the People continues — Wiser Methods are devised.

THE great uprising among men, who ignored party and politics, and forgot sect and trade, in the fervor of their quickened love of country, was paralleled by a similar uprising among women. The patriotic speech and song, which fired the blood of men, and led them to enter the lists as soldiers, nourished the self-sacrifice of women, and stimulated them to the collection of hospital supplies, and to brave the horrors and hardships of hospital life.

If men responded to the call of the country when it demanded soldiers by the hundred thousand, women planned money-making enterprises, whose

vastness of conception, and good business management, yielded millions of dollars to be expended in
the interest of sick and wounded soldiers.  If men
faltered not, and went gayly to death, that slavery
might be exterminated, and that the United States
might remain intact and undivided, women strengthened them by accepting the policy of the government uncomplainingly.  When  the  telegraph
recorded for the country, " defeat " instead of " victory," and for their beloved, " death " instead of
" life," women continued to give the government
their faith, and patiently worked and waited.

It is easy to understand how men catch the
contagion of war, especially when they feel their
quarrel to be just.  One can comprehend how, fired
with enthusiasm, and inspired by martial music, they
march to the cannon's mouth, where the iron hail
rains heaviest, and the ranks are mowed down like
grain in harvest.  But for women to send forth their
husbands, sons, brothers and lovers to the fearful
chances of the battle-field, knowing well the risks
they run, — this involves exquisite suffering, and
calls for another kind of heroism.  This women did
throughout the country, forcing their white lips to
utter a cheerful " good-bye," when their hearts were
nigh breaking with the fierce struggle.

The transition of the country from peace to the
tumult and waste of war, was appalling and swift —
but the regeneration of its women kept pace with it.
They lopped off superfluities, retrenched in expendi-
tures, became deaf to the calls of pleasure, and
heeded not the mandates of fashion.  The incoming
patriotism of the hour swept them to the loftiest
height of devotion, and they were eager to do, to

bear, or to suffer, for the beloved country. The fetters of caste and conventionalism dropped at their feet, and they sat together, patrician and plebeian, Protestant and Catholic, and scraped lint, and rolled bandages, or made garments for the poorly clad soldiery.

An order was sent to Boston for five thousand. shirts for the Massachusetts troops at the South. Every church in the city sent a delegation of needle-women to " Union Hall," heretofore used as a ball-room. The Catholic priests detailed five hundred sewing-girls to the pious work. Suburban towns rang the bells of the town hall to muster the seam-stresses. The plebeian Irish Catholic of South Boston ran the sewing-machine, while the patrician Protestant of Beacon Street basted, — and the shirts were made at the rate of a thousand a day. On Thursday, Dorothea Dix sent an order for five hundred shirts for her hospital in Washington. On Friday, they were cut, made, and packed — and were sent on their way that night. Similar events were of constant occurrence in every other city. The zeal and devotion of women no more flagged through the war than did that of the army in the field. They rose to the height of every emergency, and through all discouragements and reverses maintained a sympathetic unity between the soldiers and themselves, that gave to the former a marvellous heroism.

At a meeting in Washington during the war, called in the interest of the Sanitary Commission, President Lincoln said: " I am not accustomed to use the lan-guage of eulogy. I have never studied the art of paying compliments to women. But I must say that if all that has been said by orators and poets since the creation of the world in praise of women, was applied to the women of America, it would not do them justice for their conduct during this war. I will close by saying, God bless the women of America!"

Entirely unacquainted with the requirements of war and the needs of soldiers, it was inevitable that the first movements of women for army relief should be misdirected. They could not manifest more ignorance, however, nor blunder more absurdly, than did the government in its early attempts to build up an effective and disciplined army. Both learned by blundering.

It was summer; and the army was to move southward, to be exposed to the torrid heats of the season and climate. A newspaper reminiscence of the good service rendered British troops in India by General Havelock set the ball in motion. He had devised a white linen head-dress to be worn over the caps of his men, which defended them from sunstroke, and in his honor it was named the "Havelock." Our men must, of course, be equipped with this protection, and forthwith inexperienced women, and equally inexperienced men in the army, gave orders for the manufacture of Havelocks. What a furor there was over them! Women who could not attend the "sewing-meeting" where the "Havelocks" were being manufactured, ordered the work sent to their homes, and ran the sewing-machines day and night till the nondescript headgear was completed. "Havelocks" were turned out by thousands, of all patterns and sizes, and of every conceivable material.

In the early inexperience of that time, whenever

regiments were in camp awaiting marching orders, it was the custom of many women to pay them visits, laden with indigestible dainties. These they furnished in such profusion, that the "boys" were rarely without the means of obtaining a "permit" to the hospital until they broke up camp. While the Havelock fever was at its height, the Nineteenth Illinois, commanded by Colonel Turchin, was mustered in, and was ordered to rendezvous at Camp Douglas. A detachment of the "cake and pie brigade," as the rollicking fellows called them, paid the regiment an early visit, and were received by the men who were not under drill, *en Havelock*. As the sturdy fellows emerged from their tents, all wearing "the white nightcaps," as they had irreverently christened the ugly head-dress, their appearance was so ludicrous that a shout went up from officers, soldiers, and lady visitors. They were worn in every imaginable fashion, — as nightcaps, turbans, sunbonnets, bandages, sunshades, — and the fate of the "Havelock" was sealed. No more time nor money was wasted in their useless manufacture.

*En passant*, I remember another occurrence of that afternoon when we visited the camp of the Nineteenth Illinois. I was watching companies that were drilling, a good deal amused at their awkwardness and their slow comprehension of the orders given them. One of the captains came to me, with an apology for intrusion, and begged to know if I noticed anything peculiar in the appearance of one of the men, whom he indicated. It was evident at a glance that the "man" was a young woman in male attire, and I said so. "That is the rumor, and that is my suspicion," was his reply. The seeming soldier was called from the ranks and informed of the suspicions afloat, and asked the truth of them. There was a scene in an instant. Clutching the officer by the arm, and speaking in tones of passion· ate entreaty, she begged him not to expose her, but to allow her to retain her disguise. Her husband had enlisted in his company, she said, and it would kill her if he marched without her. "Let me go with you!" I heard her plead. "Oh, sir, let me go with you!" She was quietly conducted outside the camp, when I took her in charge. I wished to take her to my home; but she leaped suddenly from the carriage before we were half way from the camp, and in a moment was lost amid the crowds hastening home from their day's work.

That night she leaped into the Chicago river, but was rescued by a policeman, who took her to the Home of the Friendless. Here I found her, a few days later, when I made an official visit to the institution. She was extremely dejected, and could not be comforted. It was impossible to turn her from her purpose to follow her husband. "I have only my husband in all the world," she said, "and when he enlisted he promised that I should go with him; and that was why I put on his clothes and enlisted in the same regiment. And go with him I will, in spite of everybody." The regiment was ordered to Cairo, and the poor woman disappeared from the Home the same night. None of us doubted but she left to carry out her purpose.

Madame Turchin, the wife of the Colonel of the Nineteenth Illinois, was the daughter of a Russian officer, and was born and reared in foreign camps, a favorite with the men of her father's command.

She followed the fortunes of her husband in the War of the Rebellion, and accompanied him to the field. I met her at Springfield, Ill., where her husband's regiment was waiting marching orders. Fine-looking, but unmistakably foreign in appearance and manner, she was intensely loyal to the Union, and thoroughly American in her sympathies and interests. She was as popular with the men of her husband's regiment as she had been with the Russian soldiers commanded by her father. They went to her with their illnesses and troubles, and she received them with kindness, a good deal of playful badinage, and very careful nursing when it was needed.

In the spring of 1862, when the Nineteenth Illinois was actively engaged in Tennessee, Colonel Turchin was taken seriously ill, and was carried for days in an ambulance. Madame Turchin not only nursed her husband most tenderly, but took his place at the head of the regiment — the men in the ranks, and the subordinate officers, according her implicit and cheerful obedience. She was not one whit behind her husband in courage or military skill. Utterly devoid of fear, and manifesting perfect indifference to shot or shell, or minie-balls, even when they fell thickly around her, she led the troops into action, facing the hottest fire, and fought bravely at their head. When her husband was able to resume his command, she gave herself again to the care of the sick and wounded, in the field hospital.

An attempt was made to drive Colonel Turchin from the army, and on some pretext, ill or well founded, he was court-martialed. His plucky wife hastened to Washington, and not only obtained an order to set aside the court-martial, but her husband's promo-

tion to the rank of Brigadier-General. Dashing back
to Tennessee, she entered the court-room triumphantly, just as her husband was being declared
"guilty," with the order to abandon his trial in one
hand, and his commission in the other. If the young
woman who was mustered into her husband's regiment, disguised as a man, appealed to Madame Turchin for permission to accompany her young soldier
husband, I know she was not denied. No captain
would be allowed to conduct her out of camp a
second time. Madame Turchin's permission for her
to serve as a soldier would be as effective as one from
the Secretary of War.

The number of women who actually bore arms
and served in the ranks during the war was greater
than is supposed. Sometimes they followed the
army as nurses, and divided their services between
the battle-field and hospital. I remember Annie
Etheridge, of Michigan, who was with the Third
Michigan in every battle in which it was engaged.
When their three years' service was ended, the re-
enlisted veterans joined the Fifth Michigan, and
Annie went with them. Through the whole four
years of the war she was found in the field, often in
the thickest of the fight, always inspiring the men to
deeds of valor, always respected for her correctness
of life. Soldiers and officers vied with one another
in their devotion to her.

Bridget Devens, known as "Michigan Bridget,"
went to the field with the First Michigan Cavalry,
in which her husband was a private, and served
through the war. Sometimes when a soldier fell
she took his place, fighting in his stead with unquailing courage. Sometimes she rallied retreating

Engraved by J.J Cade, New York.

## A WOMAN IN BATTLE.—"MICHIGAN BRIDGET" CARRYING THE FLAG.

"Sometimes when a soldier fell she took his place, fighting in his stead with unquailing courage—always fearless and daring, always doing good service as a soldier."

A. D. Worthington & Co. Publishers, Hartford, Conn.

troops — sometimes she brought off the wounded from the field — always fearless and daring, always doing good service as a soldier. Her love of army life continued after the war ended, and with her husband she joined a regiment of the regular army, stationed on the Plains.

Mrs. Kady Brownell was, like Madame Turchin, born in camp, her father being attached to the British army. She accompanied the Fifth Rhode Island Infantry to the war, of which regiment her husband was a non-commissioned officer. She was the color-bearer of the regiment, and was a skilful sharp-shooter and expert swordsman. She marched with the men, and asked no favors as a woman, but bore the brunt of the battle, on occasion, as fearlessly as her comrades. She was in General Burnside's expedition to Roanoke Island and Newbern, where her husband was severely wounded. When he was pronounced unfit for further service, and discharged, she also sought a discharge, and retired with him to private life and domestic duty.

The Plattville, Wis., *Witness*, of March, 1864, records, as if it were nothing unusual, "the return from the army of Miss Georgianna Peterman." Says the local paragrapher, "Miss Peterman has been for two years a drummer in the Seventh Wisconsin. She lives in Ellenboro', Wis., is about twenty years old, wears soldier clothes, and is quiet and reserved." Similar paragraphs appeared occasionally in other Western papers all through the war. These half-soldier heroines generally adopted a semi-military dress, and became expert in the use of the rifle, and skilful shots.

Some one has stated the number of women soldiers

known to the service as little less than four hundred. I cannot vouch for the correctness of this
estimate, but I am convinced that a larger number
of women disguised themselves and enlisted in the
service, for one cause or other, than was dreamed of.
Entrenched in secrecy, and regarded as men, they
were sometimes revealed as women, by accident or
casualty. Some startling histories of these military women were current in the gossip of army life;
and extravagant and unreal as were many of the
narrations, one always felt that they had a foun-
dation in fact.

Such service was not the noblest that women rendered the country during its four years' struggle for
life, and no one can regret that these soldier women
were exceptional and rare. It is better to heal a
wound than to make one. And it is to the honor of
American women, not that they led hosts to the
deadly charge, and battled amid contending armies,
but that they confronted the horrid aspects of war
with mighty love and earnestness. They kept up
their own courage and that of their households.
They became ministering angels to their countrymen
who perilled health and life for the nation. They
sent the love and impulses of home into the extended
ranks of the army, through the unceasing correspondence they maintained with "the boys in blue."
They planned largely, and toiled untiringly, and
with steady persistence to the end, that the horrors
of the battle-field might be mitigated, and the hospitals abound in needed comforts. The men at the
front were sure of sympathy from the homes, and
knew that the women remembered them with sleepless interest. "This put heroic fibre into their

souls," said Dr. Bellows, " and restored us our
soldiers with their citizen hearts beating normally
under their uniforms, as they dropped them off at
the last drum-tap."

The decline of the Havelock fever was followed
by a " lint and bandage " mania, which set in with
great fury. For a time it was the all-absorbing
topic. Knowing now how insignificant in value
these items of relief proved in the actual experience
of the war, one cannot forbear a smile when reading
the sapient discussions of the time. " What is the
best material for lint ? " " How is it best scraped
and prepared ? " " By what means can it be best
gathered, in the largest quantities ? " These were
the questions of the hour, discussed gravely by professional men. And the " New York Medical Association for furnishing Hospital Supplies," actually
held meetings to discuss " the lint question," and
finally opened a " lint and bandage depot." Thus
stimulated, every household gave its leisure time to
scraping lint and rolling bandages, till the mighty
accumulations compelled the ordering of a halt. A
little later, the making of lint by machine relieved
women of any further effort in this direction.

So determined were the people that their citizen
soldiers should be well cared for, that " Relief Societies" were frequently organized in the interest of
regiments, as soon as they were mustered into the
service. They proposed to follow the volunteers of
their neighborhoods with their benefactions —" to provide them with home comforts when well, and with
hospital supplies and nurses when wounded or sick."
It would have been an admirable plan if it could
have been carried out. But numerous difficulties

and failures soon brought these methods into disrepute. The accumulation of perishable freight for the soldiers became fearful. It demanded instant transportation, and the managers of freight trains and expresses were in despair.

Women rifled their store-rooms and preserve-closets of canned fruits and pots of jam and marmalade, which they packed with clothing and blankets, books and stationery, photographs and " comfort-bags." Baggage cars were soon flooded with fermenting sweetmeats, and broken pots of jelly, that ought never to have been sent. Decaying fruit and vegetables, pastry and cake in a demoralized condition, badly canned meats and soups, whose fragrance was not that of " Araby the blest," were necessarily thrown away *en route*. And with them went the clothing and stationery saturated with the effervescing and putrefying compounds which they enfolded.

Added to this discouragement was the frequent loss of the packages. For the constant movements of troops rendered it impossible for express agents to forward boxes to special regiments. For a time there was great waste of the lavish outpouring of the people. It did not, however, check their liberality, but compelled wiser methods. For out of this chaos of individual benevolence and abounding patriotism the Sanitary Commission finally emerged, with its carefully elaborated plans, and its marvellous system.

# CHAPTER III.

AT THE FRONT—WRETCHED HOSPITAL ARRANGEMENTS—
THE SANITARY COMMISSION — ITS OBJECT, METHODS,
AND WORK—BATTLE-FIELD RELIEF.

Early Ignorance and Inefficiency of Officers — The Cause of Sickness and
Death in Camp — Letters from the Front in Proof — Fearful Mortality of
British Soldiers in the Crimea, in 1855 — Occasioned by similar Causes
— Local Relief Societies organized — New York Women show practical
Wisdom — The Sanitary Commission evolved from their Methods — Plan
of Organization drawn up by Dr. Bellows — Sanctioned by the President
and Secretary of War — The Commission soon conquers all Prejudice —
Its Work very extensive — Inspectors sent to Camps and Hospitals —
Monographs prepared on the Hygiene of the Army — Portable "Soup-
Kettles" — "Hospital Cars" — Forty Soldiers' Homes — Claim, Pension,
and Back Pay Agency — "Hospital Directory" — "Battle-field Relief
Service" — Ten "Branch Commissions" — Relief rendered at Shiloh
and Antietam — The Supplies, or Money for their Purchase, Made or
Collected by Women.

THE work of sanitary relief was very soon outlined by the necessities and sufferings of the men at the front. In the early period of the war, the troops reached their destinations generally in a very unsatisfactory condition. They were crowded into cattle cars as if they were beasts, frequently with empty haversacks, and with no provision for their comfort on the road. Prompted by generous impulse, men and women boarded the trains as they halted at the stations in cities, and served to the men hot coffee and such food as could most readily be provided. But it was only by accident, or through tireless and

123

patient watching, that they were enabled to render this small service to their country's defenders; for no telegram announced the coming of the hungry men, nor for long and weary months was a system devised for the comfort and solace of the soldiers, as they passed to and from the battle-field. Many became ill or exhausted from exposure, but no relief was furnished.

Rarely were preparations made for their reception. "Men stood for hours in a broiling sun, or drenching rain, waiting for rations and shelter, while their ignorant and inexperienced Commissaries and Quartermasters were slowly and painfully learning the duties of their positions. At last, utterly worn out and disgusted, they reached their camps, where they received rations as unwholesome as distasteful, and endeavored to recruit their wasted energies while lying upon rotten straw, wrapped in a shoddy blanket." Such fearful misery contrasted sadly with the cheerful scenes they had left, and if it did not cool their enthusiasm for the national cause, it developed an alarming prevalence of camp diseases, which might have been prevented, if efficient military discipline had prevailed.

The hospital arrangements, in the early part of the war, were as pitiful and inadequate as were the facilities for transportation. Any building was considered fit for a hospital; and the suffering endured by army patients, in the unsuitable buildings into which they were crowded during the first year of the war can never be estimated. Before the war there was no such establishment as a General Hospital in the army. All military hospitals were post hospitals, and the largest contained but forty beds. There was no trained, efficient medical staff. There were no well-instructed nurses, no sick-diet kitchens, no prompt supply of proper medicines, and no means of humanely transporting the sick and wounded. Our entire military and medical systems, which seemed well nigh perfect at last, were created in the very midst of the war.

All this was the more keenly felt by our volunteer soldiers, because they were, in the beginning, men of remarkable character and spirit. They were not reared in dissolute camps, nor raked from the slums of the cities. They were the flower of our youth, young men who not unfrequently had been tenderly reared by mothers, to whom young wives had surrendered the keeping of their happiness, and who had faithfully discharged their duties in time of peace. They sprang, at the call of their country, from the workshop, the counting-room, the farm, the college, the profession, the church, the Sunday-school and Bible-class, ready to lay down their lives for their country, if it were necessary. All the more sensitive were such men to the neglect of government and the incapacity of officers.

I maintained a somewhat extensive correspondence with many of these young citizen soldiers throughout the war. Their letters lie before me. One of the volunteers of the Chicago Light Artillery, writing from "Camp Smith, near Cairo, Ill.," June 2, 1861, says: —

My departure from Chicago was very unceremonious. I had not time to say "good-bye" to my father and mother, to say nothing of my friends; but I resolved, when the first gun was fired at Sumter, if the government should call for men to sustain the honor of the country, not to be the last to offer. A young man cannot sacrifice too much in this cause; and every man in my company is of this mind. Not a man among us but has left a lucrative situation, and is undergoing many privations for the country's service. Not a man here knows as yet, or is anxious to know, what pay he is to receive for his services. To know that we have done our duty will be sufficient pay for most of us.

The government has done very little for us yet. My friends at home gave me a capital outfit, and I am prepared for all kinds of weather. Many of our men are not so fortunate. Many are sick from exposure and lack of proper protection. For these we need very badly, beds, blankets, pillows, socks, and something in the way of food besides "hardtack and salt junk." But nobody complains; for we know the administration is heavily burdened, and has everything to do, and that all has been done for us that could be done, during the time that we have been in camp. We are eaten up by mosquitoes, and maintain a constant warfare with every kind of insect and " creeping thing."

Another, belonging to the Fifth Wisconsin, writing from " Camp Griffen, near Washington, D. C.," Nov. 12, 1861, tells a similar story: —

I suppose you would like to hear what we are doing in Virginia in the way of bringing the rebels to subjection. As yet we have done little fighting, but have lost a large number of men. They are dying daily in the camps and hospitals, from pneumonia, dysentery, and camp diseases, caused by severe colds, exposure, and lack of proper food when ill. We have taken very heavy colds lying on our arms in line of battle, long frosty nights. For two days and nights there was a very severe storm, to which we were exposed all the time, wearing shoddy uniforms and protected only by shoddy blankets, and the result was a frightful amount of sickness. We have about thirty in our regimental hospital who will never again be good for anything, if they live.

Our hospitals are so bad that the men fight against being sent to them. They will not go until they are compelled, and many brave it out and die in camp. I really believe they are more comfortable and better cared for in camp, with their comrades, than in hospital. The food is the same in both places, and the medical treatment the same when there is any. In the hospital the sick men lie on rotten straw; in the camp we provide clean hemlock or pine boughs, with the stems cut out, or husks, when we can " jerk " them from a " secesh " cornfield.

In the hospital the nurses are "convalescent soldiers," so nearly sick themselves that they ought to be in the wards, and from their very feebleness they are selfish and sometimes inhuman in their treatment of the patients. In the camp we stout hearty fellows take care of the sick, — rough in our management, I doubt not, but we do not fail for lack of strength or interest. If we could be sure of being half-way well cared for when we get sick or wounded, it would take immensely from the horrors of army life.

We need beds and bedding, hospital clothing and sick-diet, proper medicines, surgical instruments, and good nurses, — and then a decent building or a good hospital tent for the accommodation of our sick. I suppose we shall have them when the government can get round to it, and in the meantime we try to be patient.

One of the writers of these letters was a teacher, and the other was in his sophomore year in college, when the war began. Similar letters, from equally intelligent sources were written to parties throughout the country, and they quickly found their way into print.

The same lack of sanitary care and proper food complained of in these letters had wrought fearful havoc in the British army, in the war of the Crimea, in 1855, only six years before, and the American people remembered it. Out of twenty-four thousand troops sent to the Crimea, eighteen thousand had died in less than nine months, — a mortality, it has been said, "never equalled since the hosts of Sennacherib fell in a single night." They died from lack of care, proper sanitary regulations, and the diet necessary to the sick. With their slowly dimming eyes they could see the vessels anchored in the harbor, freighted with the food and medicine, clothing and tenting, sanitary supplies and preventives, for want of which they were perishing.

All were tied up with the red tape of official

formalism until Florence Nightingale, with her corps
of trained nurses, and full power to do and command,
as well as advise, landed at Scutari, and ordered the
storehouses opened.    Then want gave place to
abundance, and, through her executive skill and
knowledge of nursing and hospital management, the
frightful mortality was arrested.

There was a resolute determination in the hearts
of the people, that neither inexperience nor dogged
adherence to routine should cause such wholesale
slaughter of their beloved citizen soldiers.    Whether
sick or well, they should receive such care as the
soldiers of no nation had ever known before.    No
failure of their plans of relief abated their ardor, and
no discouragement stayed the stream of their beneficence.    Especially did women refuse to release their
hold on the men of their households, even when the
government had organized them into an army.
They followed them with letters of inquiry, with
tender anxiety and intelligent prevision, which eventually put them *en rapport* with the government, and
developed a wonderful system of sanitary prevention
and relief.    For the outcome of their patriotism and
zeal, their loyalty and love, was the Sanitary Commission.

"The Woman's Central Association of Relief"
was the name of a large and remarkable organization, formed in the city of New York, very early in
the war.    In connection with other similar organizations, they decided to send a committee to Washington, to learn, from the highest authorities, "in what
way the voluntary offerings of the people could best
be made available for the relief of the army."

Dr. Bellows was chairman of this committee, and

before he returned from Washington, a plan of organization for the U. S. Sanitary Commission, drawn up by himself, received the sanction of the President and the Secretary of War. Not heartily, however, for the very highest officials of the government regarded the whole plan as quixotic, and consented to it only because " it could do no harm." President Lincoln himself failed at first to comprehend the large humanity of the organization, and described it as " a fifth wheel to the coach." But for the zeal, intelligence and earnestness of his numerous women constituents, it is more than probable that Dr. Bellows would have retreated before the rebuffs and hindrances opposed to his humane efforts.

The object of the Sanitary Commission was to do what the government could not. The government undertook, of course, to provide all that was necessary for the soldier, whether sick or in health; whether in the army or hospital. But, from the very nature of things, this was not possible, and it failed in its purpose, at times, as all governments do, from occasional and accidental causes. The methods of the Commission were so elastic, and so arranged to meet any emergency, that it was able to make provision for any need, seeking always to supplement, and never to supplant, the government. It never forgot that " it must be subordinate to army rules and regulations, and in no way break down the essential military discipline, on the observance of which everything depended."

In a few months, the baseless prejudice against the Commission melted away. The army surgeons, at first opposed, became enthusiastic in its praise. And the people, who were, in the outset, bent on dispensing their charities only to the companies and regiments organized in their neighborhoods, came finally to accept the larger methods of the Commission, which disbursed the sanitary supplies it received to any hospitals or soldiers that needed them, without regard to sectional limits. The government accorded to the Commission increased facilities for performing its work. The railroads transported all its freight free of charge — the express companies carried its packages at half price — and the telegraph companies remitted the usual charges on its messages.

The Commission did a more extensive work than was at first contemplated, or is to-day generally known. It sent inspectors, who were always medical men, to the army, to report on the " quality of rations and water — the method of camp cooking — ventilation of tents and quarters — the drainage of the camp itself — the healthfulness of its site — the administration of the hospital — the police of the camp — the quality of the tents, and the material used for flooring them — the quality of the clothing, and the personal cleanliness of the men "—and other points of importance tò the health and efficiency of the army.

It also caused to be prepared, by the best medical talent in the country, eighteen concise treatises on the best means of preserving health in camp, and on the treatment of the sick and wounded in hospital and on the battle-field. These were acknowledged by the surgeons to be of great value.

It put nurses into the hospitals who had been trained for the work, and who, in addition to having aptitudes for the care of the sick, were attracted to it by large humanity and patriotic zeal.

It established a series of kettles on wheels, with small portable furnaces attached, in which soup was quickly made in the rear of battle-fields, for the faint and wounded, even while the battle was in progress.

It invented hospital cars, for the humane transportation of the wounded, in which the ordinary hospital bed was suspended by stout tugs of india rubber, preventing jolting.

It maintained forty " Soldiers' Homes," or " Lodges," scattered all along the route of the army, and over the whole field of war, which were free hotels for destitute soldiers, separated from their regiments, or passing back and forth, with neither money, rations, nor transportation. Over eight hundred thousand soldiers were entertained in them, and four and a half million meals, and a million nights' lodgings were gratuitously furnished.

It established a " Claim Agency," to secure the bounty of the soldiers, when, by some neglect or informality, it had been kept back. It opened a " Pension Agency," whose name explains its office. It arranged a " Back Pay Agency," which took the defective papers of the soldiers, on which they could not draw their pay, regulated them, and in a few hours drew the money due them, sometimes securing twenty thousand dollars back pay in one day.

It maintained a " Hospital Directory," through which information could be officially obtained concerning the invalids in the two hundred and thirty-three general hospitals of the army, and concerning others, reported as " missing," and " fate unknown." In the four offices of the Directory, at Washington, Philadelphia, New York, and Louisville, there were recorded the names of more than six hundred thousand men, with the latest information procurable in regard to them.

The Commission also methodized a system of " Battle-Field Relief," which did much to mitigate the horrors inevitable to battles. Its agents were always on the field during an engagement, with surgeons, ambulances, and store wagons, with anæsthetics, surgical instruments, and every species of relief. They rendered invaluable aid, and were sometimes in advance of the government in their ministrations on the field of conflict. There were over six hundred pitched battles between the two hostile forces during the War of the Rebellion. History will record only a very few of them as " great battles." The suffering and horror incident to those were so immeasurable, that they could be only partially relieved ; and had the ability of the government and of all the volunteer agencies of the country been tenfold greater than they were, they would have been inadequate to the awful necessities of those titanic conflicts.

After the battle of Antietam, where ten thousand of our own wounded were left on the field, besides a large number of the enemy, the Commission distributed " 28,763 pieces of dry goods, shirts, towels, bed-ticks, pillows, etc.; 30 barrels of old linen, bandages, and lint; 3,188 pounds of farina; 2,620 pounds of condensed milk; 5,000 pounds of beef-stock and canned meats; 3,000 bottles of wine and cordials; 4,000 sets of hospital clothing; several tons of lemons and other fruit; crackers, tea, sugar, rubber cloth, tin cups, chloroform, opiates, surgical instruments, and other hospital conveniences."

After the battle of Shiloh, in the West, where

nearly as many wounded men were left on the field as at Antietam, the Commission distributed " 11,448 shirts; 3,686 pairs of drawers; 3,592 pairs of socks; 2,777 bed-sacks; 543 pillows; 1,045 bottles of brandy, whiskey, and wine; 799 bottles of porter; 941 lemons; 20,316 pounds of dried fruit; 7,577 cans of fruit; and 15,323 pounds of farinaceous food."

Whence came these hospital supplies, or the money for their purchase? They were gathered by the loyal women of the North, who organized over ten thousand "aid societies" during the war, and who never flagged in their constancy to the cause of the sick and wounded soldier. As rapidly as possible, "branches" of the United States Sanitary Commission were established in Boston, New York, Philadelphia, Cincinnati, Chicago, and other cities — ten in all. Here sub-depots of sanitary stores were maintained, and into these the soldiers' aid societies poured their never-ceasing contributions. The supplies sent to these ten sub-depots were assorted, repacked, stamped with the mark of the Commission, only one kind of supplies being packed in a box, and then a list of the contents was marked on the outside. The boxes were then stored, subject to the requisitions of the great central distributing depots, established at Washington and Louisville. Through these two cities, all supplies of every kind passed to the troops at the front, who were contending with the enemy.

A most rigid system was observed in the reception, care, and disbursement of these hospital supplies; for the methods of the Sanitary Commission, through its entire system of agencies, were those of the best business houses. It was easy to trace the

packages sent to hospitals back to their original contributors, vouchers being taken of those who received them, at every stage of their progress to their
ultimate destination.   Only a very insignificant frac-
tion of them was lost or misused.

Through all the branches of the Commission there
was the same wisdom in planning, ability in execut-
ing, and joyfulness in sacrifice.   Into them all, were
borne the suffering and patience of the soldier in the
hospital, and the sorrow and anxiety of his family at
home.   Men *en route* to the front, full of manly
strength and courage, and men *en route* from the
camp or battle-field going home to die, invaded the
busy "headquarters."   People of all conditions and
circumstances, wise and unwise, rich and poor,
women and men, went thither for inspiration and direction.   Scenes were there enacted and deeds performed which transfigured human nature, and made
it divine.   It was there that one felt the pulse of the
country, and measured its heart-beats.

My own experience was with the Chicago Branch
of the Sanitary Commission.   And the brief résumé
of the varied phases of life that flowed and ebbed
through its unpretentious rooms, which follows in
the next chapter, will give the reader some idea of
the patriotic zeal, the noble self-denial, and organized
work of the women of the war, in which they were
grandly assisted by men.

# CHAPTER IV.

MY FIRST CONNECTION WITH THE SANITARY COMMISSION —
HOME SUPPLIES FOR THE SOLDIERS — A PEEP INTO THE
BOXES — LETTERS FOUND INSIDE — ODD CONTRIBUTIONS.

Local Societies merged in the Commission — Become identified with the
Chicago Branch — The Secrets of the Boxes of Supplies — Notes packed
in with the Clothing — They are tender, pathetic, heroic, and comic —
A letter-writing Army — " Consecrated Chicken, be jabers!"— " Butter
an' *Chase*, bedad!" — " Comfort-bags" — "Benedictions" in the Mur-
freesboro' and Vicksburg Boxes — " One Box a Month " — Ingenious
Wisconsin Farmers' Wives — Women in the Harvest-field — A Talk with
them — Generosity of a " Tailoress" — The "five-dollar gold Piece" —
"Matches! Matches!" — Afraid of a Kiss — Children's sanitary Fairs
— Gift of a five-year old Boy.

RGANIZATIONS of women for the relief
of sick and wounded soldiers, and for the
care of soldiers' families, were formed with
great spontaneity at the very beginning of
the war. There were a dozen or more of
them in Chicago, in less than a month after
Cairo was occupied by Northern troops. They
raised money, prepared and forwarded supplies of
whatever was demanded, every shipment being accompanied by some one who was held responsible
for the proper disbursement of the stores. Sometimes
these local societies affiliated with, or became parts of,
more comprehensive organizations. Most of them

135

worked independently during the first year of the war, the Sanitary Commission of Chicago being only one of the relief agencies. But the Commission gradually grew in public confidence, and gained in scope and power; and all the local societies were eventually merged in it, or became auxiliary to it. As in Chicago, so throughout the country. The Sanitary Commission became the great channel, through which the patriotic beneficence of the nation flowed to the army.

When the local aid society of which I was president, merged its existence in that of the Sanitary Commission, I also became identified with it. Thenceforth, until the bells rang in the joyful news of peace, my time and energy were given to its varied work. In its busy rooms I was occupied most of the time when not in the hospitals, or engaged with some of the Northwestern soldiers' aid societies.

Here, day after day, the drayman left boxes of supplies sent from aid societies in Iowa, Minnesota, Wisconsin, Michigan, Illinois, and Indiana. Every box contained an assortment of articles, a list of which was tacked on the inside of the lid. These were taken out, stamped in indelible ink with the name of the "CHICAGO SANITARY COMMISSION," the stamp as broad as your hand, and the letters so large as to be easily read across a room. For the convenience of the hospitals they were repacked, — shirts by themselves, drawers by themselves, and so on. Then they awaited orders from the hospitals.

One day I went into the packing-room to learn the secrets of these boxes, — every one an argosy of love, — and took notes during the unpacking. A capacious box, filled with beautifully made shirts, drawers, towels, socks, and handkerchiefs, with "comfort-bags" containing combs, pins, needles, court-plaster, and black sewing-cotton, and with a quantity of carefully dried berries and peaches, contained the following unsealed note, lying on top: —

DEAR SOLDIERS, — The little girls of —— send this box to you. They hear that thirteen thousand of you are sick, and have been wounded in battle. They are very sorry, and want to do something for you. They cannot do much, for they are all small; but they have bought with their own money, and made what is in here. They hope it will do some good, and that you will all get well and come home. We all pray to God for you night and morning.

The box was carefully unpacked, each article stamped with the mark of the Commission, as a preventive to theft, and then carefully repacked just as it was received. That sacred offering of childhood was sent intact to the hospital.

Another mammoth packing-case was opened, and here were folded in blessings and messages of love with almost every garment. On a pillow was pinned the following note, unsealed, for sealed notes were never broken: —

MY DEAR FRIEND, — You are not *my* husband nor son; but you are the husband or son of some woman who undoubtedly loves you as I love mine. I have made these garments for you with a heart that aches for your sufferings, and with a longing to come to you to assist in taking care of you. It is a great comfort to me that God loves and pities you, pining and lonely in a far-off hospital; and if you believe in God, it will also be a comfort to *you*. Are you near death, and soon to cross the dark river? Oh, then, may God soothe your last hours, and lead you up "the shining shore," where there is no war, no sickness, no death. Call on Him, for He is an ever-present helper.

Large packages of socks, carefully folded in pairs in the same box, contained each a note, beautifully written, and signed with the name and address of the writer. They were as various as the authors. Here is one: —

DEAR SOLDIER, — If these socks had language they would tell you that many a kind wish for you has been knit into them, and many a tear of pity for you has bedewed them. We all think of you, and want to do everything we can for you; for we feel that we owe you unlimited love and gratitude, and that you deserve the very best at our hands.

Here is another, of a different character: —

MY DEAR BOY, — I have knit these socks expressly for *you.* How do you like them? How do you look, and where do you live when you are at home? I am nineteen years old, of medium height, of slight build, with blue eyes, fair complexion, light hair, and a good deal of it. Write and tell me all about yourself, and how you get on in the hospitals. Direct to ——.

P. S. If the recipient of these socks has a wife, will he please exchange socks with some poor fellow not so fortunate?

And here is yet another: —

MY BRAVE FRIEND, — I have learned to knit on purpose to knit socks for the soldiers. This is my fourth pair. My name is ——, and I live in ——. Write to me, and tell me how you like the foot-gear and what we can do for you. Keep up good courage, and by and by you will come home to us. Won't that be a grand time, though? And won't we all turn out to meet you, with flowers and music, and cheers and embraces? " There's a good time coming, boys! "

Very many of these notes were answered by the soldiers who received them, and a correspondence ensued, which sometimes ended in lifelong friendship, and, in some instances which came to my knowledge, in marriage.

A nicely made dressing-gown, taken from one of the boxes, of dimensions sufficiently capacious for Daniel Lambert, had one huge pocket filled with hickory nuts, and the other with ginger-snaps. The pockets were sewed across to prevent the contents from dropping out, and the following note was pinned on the outside : —

My Dear Fellow, — Just take your ease in this dressing gown. Don't mope and have the blues, if you *are* sick. Moping never cured anybody yet. Eat your nuts and cakes, if you are well enough, and snap your fingers at dull care. I wish I could do more for you, and if I were a man I would come and fight with you. Woman though I am, I'd like to help hang Jeff Davis higher than Haman — yes, and all who aid and abet him, too, whether North or South!

There was exhumed from one box a bushel of cookies, tied in a pillow-case, with this benevolent wish tacked on the outside : —

These cookies are expressly for the sick soldiers, and if anybody else eats them, *I hope they will choke him!*

A very neatly arranged package of second-hand clothing, but little worn, was laid by itself. Every article was superior in quality and in manufacture. Attached to it was a card with the following explanation, in most exquisite chirography : —

The accompanying articles were worn for the last time by one very dear to the writer, who lost his life at Shiloh. They are sent to our wounded soldiers as the most fitting disposition that can be made of them, by one who has laid the husband of her youth — her all — on the altar of her country.

Rarely was a box opened that did not contain notes to soldiers, accompanying the goods. In the pocket of one dressing-gown, a baby's tin rattle was found — in another, a small china doll, tastefully dressed — in another, a baby's photograph — in yet another, a comic almanac. In every box was a good supply of stoutly made " comfort-bags." A " comfort-bag " usually contained a small needle-book, with a dozen stout needles in it, a well-filled pin-

ball, black and white thread, buttons, etc. These
" little usefuls," as the boys called them, were invaluable to the handy fellows, who very often became
skilful extempore tailors.

As whittling and wood-carving were among the
prime amusements of the hospital, a jack-knife was
added, and generally a pair of scissors. Sometimes
a square piece of tobacco was included among the
miscellanies, nor was the " comfort-bag " considered
less valuable in consequence. Often a small Testament increased the value of the little bag, with the
name and residence of the donor on the fly-leaf.

And if the comfort-bag contained no letter, with a
stamped envelope, and blank sheet of paper added,
its recipient was a little crestfallen. The stationery was rarely forgotten. Folded in the sleeves
of shirts, tucked in pockets, wrapped in handkerchiefs, and rolled in socks, were envelopes with
stamps affixed, containing blank sheets of note
paper, and usually a pencil was added. The soldiers expressed their need of stationery in almost
every letter they wrote. Most of the letters sent
to the army contained stamped envelopes, and
paper, for the men were without money so much
of the time, that when the sutlers had stationery for
sale at exorbitant prices, the soldiers were unable to
buy it.

There never was an army so intent on correspond-
ing with the kindred and friends left behind. If
you went into any camp at any time, you would see
dozens, and sometimes hundreds, of soldiers writing
letters. Some would be stretched at full length on
the ground, with a book or a knapsack for a table —
some sitting upright against the trunks of trees, with

the paper resting on their drawn-up knees — others would stand and write. The average number of letters sent to the army on the Atlantic coast was forty-five thousand daily. An equally large number was sent through the mails by the soldiers, making an aggregate of ninety thousand daily letters that passed through the post-office at Washington. About the same number were carried by the mails to and from Louisville, these two cities being the gateways to the army during the war. One hundred and eighty thousand daily letters received and answered, created a demand for stationery, which in the army it was not always easy to supply. On one day of the week preceding the battle of Pittsburg Landing, or Shiloh, there were sold to the soldiers, from the Pittsburg post-office, seven hundred dollars worth of postage-stamps. Who wonders that our army fought like heroes?

Over and over again, with unnecessary emphasis and cruel frequency, officers, surgeons, and nurses were adjured, through notes in the boxes, to bestow on the sick and wounded the comforts and delicacies contained in the cases. There was more honesty in the hospitals, and much less stealing by the officials, than was popularly believed.

"For the love of God, give these articles to the sick and wounded, to whom they are sent!"

"He that would steal from a sick or wounded man would rob hen-roosts, or filch pennies from the eyes of a corpse!"

"Surgeons and nurses, hands off! These things are not for you, but for your patients,— our sick and wounded boys!"

"Don't gobble up these delicacies, nurses! They are for the boys in hospital!"

Similar injunctions were found tacked on the inside lid of many boxes, or stared us in the face in startling colored capitals, when the cover was hammered off.

Occasionally the opening of a box revealed an unwise selection of donations, or a careless preparation of them. A packing-case was opened one morning, smooth and polished without and neatly jointed, when an overpowering odor smote the olfactories, that drove every one from the room. It was as if a charnel-house had been opened. Windows and doors were flung wide to let in the fresh air, and a second attempt was made to examine the odoriferous box. The intolerable stench proceeded from " concentrated chicken," which had been badly prepared. The box had been some time on the journey, and the nicely cooked chicken had become a mass of corruption. " Be jabers ! " said Irish Jimmy, the drayman, as he wheeled the box back into the " receiving-room," " I hope the leddies — God bless 'em ! — won't send enny more of their *consecrated* chicken this way, for it smells too loud intirely."

Another box came from the depot completely besmeared with honey, leaking from within. Irish Jimmy pronounced it " grease," and, always ready with an opinion, declared that " the leddies were gittin' no sinse at all, to be afther sindin' grease in a box, loose like that, and the weather jist hot enough to cook ye ! " When told that the Sanitary Commission called for no " grease," he ventured the sagacious opinion that it was " butter and *chase* inside, bedad ! and by the howly Moses ! they'd a jist melted in the great heat and run together. And shure ! that was grease, and nobody could deny it." Two large boxes of honey in the comb had been packed with hospital clothing. In transportation the honey had drained from the comb, leaving it empty and broken, and had saturated the contents of the box.

Many of the boxes for the wounded at Murfreesboro' and Vicksburg, and packed for them especially, contained indications of the deepest feeling. "We send these supplies to the noble boys that beat back Bragg's army! We are proud of them!" "Three cheers for Rosecrans' army!" "Dear wounded soldiers! we shall never forget your gallant conduct at Murfreesboro' and Stone River!" "May God place his everlasting arms of love underneath you, my dear wounded brothers!" These and like benedictions were affixed to almost every article.

In looking over the contents of the boxes as they were unpacked, one realized the passionate interest in the war felt by the women of the North. They toiled, economized, and retrenched to furnish the necessary supplies to the hospitals, and then hallowed them with a patriotic and religious spirit. They flung heart and soul into the labor of their willing hands, until the articles of their manufacture were redolent of blessings and affection. Then, pouring out their souls in written ejaculations of love and in tender benedictions, they forwarded these to the soldiers with the material comforts.

The aid societies were asked to contribute one box of hospital supplies a month, and this was the standard of efficiency upheld throughout the war. Some did much more than this, and some less; but the standard was never lowered. As there were nearly four thousand aid societies in existence in the Northwest, auxiliary to the Chicago Branch of the Sanitary Commission, and as over seventy thousand boxes were received, or were packed and forwarded from our rooms to Southern hospitals, it is evident that the women in the newly settled and sparsely populated states did not shirk the duties which the war imposed on them. They rifled their houses of whatever bed-linen could be spared; denied their families canned and dried fruit; retrenched in the use of butter and eggs, that they might have more to take to market, and so more money to bestow on the soldiers; held festivals and dime parties; gave concerts; got up fairs, — in short, their ingenuity was as limitless as their patriotism.

Some farmers' wives in the north of Wisconsin, eighteen miles from a railroad, had donated to the hospitals of their bed and table linen, of their husbands' shirts, drawers, and socks, until they had exhausted their ability in this direction. While the need lasted, they could not be satisfied to remain inactive, and so cast about to see what could be done by new and untried methods. They were the wives of small farmers, lately moved to the West, and living in log cabins, — where one room sufficed for kitchen, parlor, laundry, nursery, and bedroom, — doing their own housework, sewing, baby-tending, and dairy-work. What *could* women do so burdened, hampered, and straitened? "Where there's a will, there's a way."

They resolved to beg wheat of the neighboring farmers, and turn it into money. Sometimes on foot, sometimes with a team, amid the snows and mud of early spring, they canvassed the country for twenty and thirty miles around, everywhere eloquently pleading the needs of the blue-coated boys in the hospitals, — their earnest speech proving an *open sesame* to the granaries. Now they obtained a little from a rich man, then a large quantity from a poor man — deeds of benevolence are half the time in an inverse ratio to the ability of the benefactors — till they had accumulated nearly five hundred bushels of wheat. This they sent to market, when they could obtain the highest market price, and forwarded the money to me, to be given the Sanitary Commission. Knowing the history of their contribution, their bank-check had a sacredness in my eyes.

During the war I was called into the country on frequent errands. Sometimes it was to organize aid societies — sometimes to attend mass conventions, called for inspiration and instruction in the work to be done. The attendance was increased by a natural desire for social enjoyment, which the necessities of the times greatly abridged. Sometimes a meeting would be called in a large town for the double purpose of stimulating hospital supplies and enlistments — sometimes I went in charge of soldiers, too ill or enfeebled from wounds to be sent alone. On these trips I noticed a great increase of women engaged in outdoor work, and especially during the times of planting, cultivating, and harvesting.

In the early summer of 1863, frequent calls of business took me through the extensive farming districts of Wisconsin, and Eastern Iowa, when the farmers were the busiest, gathering the wheat harvest. As we dashed along the railway, let our course lead in whatever direction it might, it took us through what seemed a continuous wheat-field. The yellow grain was waving everywhere; and two-horse reapers were cutting it down in a wholesale fashion that would have astonished Eastern farmers. Hun-

dreds of reapers could be counted in a ride of half a
dozen hours.    The crops were generally good, and
in some instances heavy, and every man and boy was
pressed into service to secure the abundant harvest
while the weather was fine.

Women were in the field everywhere, driving the
reapers, binding and shocking, and loading grain,
until then an unusual sight.    At first, it displeased
me, and I turned away in aversion.    By and by, I
observed how skilfully they drove the horses round
and round the wheat-field, diminishing more and
more its periphery at every circuit, the glittering
blades of the reaper cutting wide swaths with a
rapid, clicking sound, that was pleasant to hear.
Then I saw that when they followed the reapers,
binding and shocking, although they did not keep
up with the men, their work was done with more
precision and nicety, and their sheaves had an artistic finish that those lacked made by the men.    So I
said to myself, "They are worthy women, and deserve
praise: their husbands are probably too poor to hire
help, and, like the 'helpmeets' God designed them
to be, they have girt themselves to this work — and
they are doing it superbly.    Good wives! good
women!"

One day my route took me off the railway, some
twenty miles across the country.    But we drove
through the same golden fields of grain, and between
great stretches of green waving corn.    Now a river
shimmered like silver through the gold of the wheat
and oats, and now a growth of young timber made a
dark green background for the harvest fields.    Here,
as everywhere, women were busy at the harvesting.

"I've got to hold up a spell, and rig up this 'ere

harness," said my driver; "something's got out o' kilter." And the carriage halted opposite a field where half a dozen women and two men were harvesting. Not a little curious to know what these women reapers were like, I walked over and accosted them.

"And so you are helping gather the harvest!" I said to a woman of forty-five or fifty, who sat on the reaper to drive, as she stopped her horses for a brief breathing spell. Her face was pleasant and comely, although sunburned, with honest, straightforward eyes, a broad brow, and a mouth that indicated firmness and tenderness. Her dress, a strong calico, was worn without hoops, then thought essential on all occasions, and she was shod with stout boots, and wore a shaker bonnet.

" Yes, ma'am," she said; "the men have all gone to the war, so that my man can't hire help at any price, and I told my girls we must turn to and give him a lift with the harvestin'."

" You are not German? You are surely one of my own countrywomen — American ? "

"Yes, ma'am; we moved here from Cattaraugus county, New York state, and we've done very well since we came."

" Have you sons in the army? "

" Yes," and a shadow fell over the motherly face, and the honest eyes looked out mournfully into vacancy. "All three of 'em 'listed, and Neddy, the youngest, was killed at the battle of Stone River, the last day of last year. My man, he went down to get his body, but he came back without it. There were nine thousand of our men left dead on the field there, and our Neddy's body couldn't be found among so many. It came very hard on us to let the boys go, but we felt we'd no right to hinder 'em. The country needed 'em more'n we. We've money enough to hire help if it could be had; and my man don't like to have me and the girls a-workin' outdoors; but there don't seem no help for it now."

I stepped over where the girls were binding the fallen grain. They were fine, well-built lasses, with the honest eyes and firm mouth of the mother, brown like her, and clad in the same sensible costume.

" Well, you are like your mother, not afraid to lend a hand at the harvesting, it seems! " was my opening remark.

" No, we're willing to help outdoors in these times. Harvesting isn't any harder, if it's as hard as cooking, washing, and ironing, over a red-hot stove in July and August — only we have to do both now. My three brothers went into the army, all my cousins, most of the young men about here, and the men we used to hire. So there's no help to be got but women, and the crops must be got in all the same, you know."

"One of our German women," said another of the girls, " tells us we don't know anything about war yet. For during the last war in Germany men were so scarce that she had to work three years in a blacksmith's shop. You wouldn't think it, though, if you should see her. That would be rather tough, but I tell Annie we can do anything to help along while the country's in such trouble."

" I tell mother," said the Annie referred to, standing very erect, with flashing eyes, " that as long as the country can't get along without grain, nor the army fight without food, we're serving the country just as much here in the harvest-field as our boys are on the battle-field — and that sort o' takes the edge off from this business of doing men's work, you know." And a hearty laugh followed this statement.

Another one of the women was the wife of one of the soldier sons, with a three-year-old boy toddling beside her, tumbling among the sheaves, and getting into mischief every five minutes. His mother declared that he was "more plague than profit." From her came the same hearty assent to the work which the distress of the country had imposed on her. And she added, with a kind of homely pride, that she was considered "as good a binder as a man, and could keep up with the best of 'em."

Further conversation disclosed the fact that amid their double labor in the house and field, these women found time for the manufacture of hospital supplies, and had helped to fill box after box with shirts and drawers, dried apples and pickles, currant wine and blackberry jam, to be forwarded to the poor fellows languishing in far-off Southern hospitals. My eyes were unsealed. The women in the harvest-field were invested with a new and heroic interest, and each hard-handed, brown, toiling woman was a heroine. When the driver called to me that he had mended the broken harness, I bade the noble harvesters "good-bye," assuring them that they were the "peers of the women of the Revolution."

A poor girl, who called herself a "tailoress," came one day to the rooms of the Commission.

"I do not feel right," she said, "that I am doing nothing for our soldiers in the hospitals. I must do something immediately. Which do you prefer — that

I should give money, or buy material and manufacture it into hospital clothing?"

"You must be governed by your circumstances," was the answer made her. "We need both money and supplies, and you must do that which is most convenient for you."

"I prefer to give money, if it will do as much good."

"Very well, then, give money. We need it badly, and without it cannot do what is most necessary for our brave men."

"I will give the Commission my net earnings for the next two weeks. I would give more, but my mother is an invalid, and I help support her. Usually I make but one vest a day, as I do 'custom work,' and am well paid for it. But these next two weeks, which belong to the soldiers, I shall work earlier and later."

In two weeks she came again, the poor sewing girl, with a radiant face. Opening her porte-monnaie, she counted out *nineteen dollars and thirty-seven cents*. She had stitched into the hours of midnight on every one of the working days of those two weeks.

A little girl, not nine years old, with sweet and timid grace, entered one afternoon, and laid a five-dollar gold piece on my desk. Half-frightened, she told its story. "My uncle gave me that before the war, and I was going to keep it always. But he's got killed in the army, and now mother says I may give it to the soldiers if I want to — and I'd like to. Will it buy much for them?"

I led the child to the store-room, and pointed out to her what it would buy — so many cans of condensed milk, or so many bottles of ale, or so many pounds of tea or codfish, etc. Her face brightened with pleasure. But when I explained that her five-dollar gold piece was equal then to seven and a half dollars in greenbacks, and told her how much comfort could be carried into a hospital with the amount of stores it would purchase, she fairly danced for joy. "Why, my five dollars will do lots of good, won't it?"

Folding her hands before her in a charmingly earnest way, she begged me to tell her something that I had seen in the hospitals. A narration of a few touching events, such as would not too severely shock the child, but which showed the necessity of continued benevolence to the hospitals, brought tears to her eyes, and the resolution to her lips, to "get all the girls to save their money to buy things for the wounded soldiers." And away she ran, happy in the luxury of doing good.

A little urchin who often thrust his unkempt pate into the room, with the shrill cry of "Matches! Matches!" had stood a little apart, watching the girl, and listening to the conversation. As she disappeared, he fumbled in his pockets, and drew out a small handful of crumpled fractional currency, such as was then in use. "Here," said he, "I'll give yer suthin' for them are sick fellers!" And he put fifty-five cents in my hand, all in five-cent currency. I was surprised, and hesitated.

"No, my boy, don't give it. I am afraid you cannot afford it. You're a noble little fellow, but that is more than you ought to give. You keep it, and I'll give fifty-five cents for you — or somebody else will."

"Git eout!" was his disgusted commentary on my

proposal. "Yer take it, now. P'raps I ain't so poor as yer think. My father, he saws wood, and my mother, she takes in washin', and I sells matches, and Tom, he sells papers, and p'raps we've got more money than yer think. Our Bob, he'd a gone to the war hisself, but he got his leg cut off on the railroad, in a smash-up. He was a brakeman, yer see. You take this, now!"

I took the crumpled currency. I forgot the boy's dirty face and tattered cap; I forgot that I had called the little tatterdemalion a "nuisance" every day for months, when he had caused me to jump from my seat with his shrill, unexpected cry of "Matches!" and I actually stooped to kiss him.

He divined my intention and darted out on the sidewalk as if he had been shot.

"No, yer don't!" he said, shaking his tangled head at me, and looking as if he had escaped a great danger. "I ain't one o' that kissin' sort!"

Ever after, when he met me, he gave me a wide berth, and walked off the sidewalk into the gutter, eyeing me with a suspicious, sidelong glance, as though he suspected I still thought of kissing him. If I spoke to him, he looked at me shyly and made no reply. But if I passed him without speaking, he challenged me with a hearty "Hullo, yer!" that brought me to an instant halt.

During the July and August vacation of 1863, the little folks of Chicago were seized with a veritable sanitary-fair mania,— a blessed form of craze, which had had an extensive run among their elders during the winter and spring. These juvenile fairs were held on the lawns of private houses, or, if it rained, in the large parlors, and they became immensely popular among the little people. They were planned and carried on exclusively by children from nine to sixteen years of age, who manifested no little shrewdness in their calculations, and ingenuity in their devices. In one fortnight these fairs netted the Commission about three hundred dollars in money — a handsome sum for children to make during the torrid holidays.

I accepted a pressing invitation to one of these mimic bazars. A boy of eleven stood at the gate as custodian, gravely exacting and receiving the five cents admission fee. Another little chap, of ten, perambulated the sidewalks for a block or two, carrying a banner inscribed, "SANITARY FAIR FOR THE SOLDIERS!" and drumming up customers for his sisters under the trees. "Here's your Sanitary Fair for sick and wounded soldiers!" he shouted, imitating the candy vender who was licensed to sell his wares from a stand just around the corner. "All kinds of fancy goods, in the newest style, and cheap as dirt, and all for the soldiers! Walk up and buy, ladies and gentlemen, walk up!"

The fair tables were spread under the trees, with an assortment of toilet-mats, cushions, needle-books, pen-wipers, patriotic book-marks, dolls, and confectionery. The national colors floated over the little saleswomen, some of the very smallest sitting in high dinner-chairs, and all conducting their business with a dignity that provoked laughter. Big brothers and sisters stood behind them, ostensibly to assist in making change, but in reality because they enjoyed the affair. The mimic traders stoutly resented their interference, declaring "they could make change themselves." One of the little gypsies shook back her yellow curls, and, lifting her sunny face to the assembled buyers, announced that "they'd *dot* twenty-*free* dollars already, and the fair hadn't but just begun."

The fair mania extended into the country, and children's letters were daily received containing various sums of money netted by their little enterprises. A carriage stopped at the door of the Commission one day, and landed a black-eyed and rosy-cheeked boy at the office. He ran into the room with a two-dollar greenback in his extended hand. "I'm five years old to-day, and my *dranpa div* me this to buy some nuts and *tandy*. But *tandy* makes me sick, and I don't want none, and mamma says *div* it to the soldiers what gets shot." And back he ran, clambering into the carriage without waiting to give his name or to be kissed.

It was from these and similar sources, multiplied thousands of times, that the stream of supplies for the sick and weary of the army maintained its vast and constant proportions to the very close of the war. The supplies varied according to the needs of the men at the front. But whatever was the need as to quality, quantity, or cost, it was soon apparent that in the zeal and intense nationality of the women of the North there was a certainty of its being supplied systematically and bountifully. No rebuffs could chill their zeal; no reverses repress their ardor; no discouragements weaken their devotion. The women had enlisted for the war.

# CHAPTER V.

AT THE ROOMS OF THE SANITARY COMMISSION — ITS WORK-
ERS AND ITS VISITORS — HEART-RENDING SCENES AND
INCIDENTS — THE RECORD OF A DAY.

Rooms of the Chicago Commission — The Din of Draymen and Packers —
Sewing-Rooms for Soldiers' Families — " The Perfume of the Sanitary "
— The dingy little Office — Immense Work performed in it — Judge
Skinner, the President — Mr. Blatchford, Treasurer — The "Quartette "
of the Office — John Freeman, the " Man of all Work " — William
Goodsmith, our "Sheet-Anchor " — Mrs. Hoge, my Friend and Co-
Worker — Volunteer and transient Help — Women, Girls, and Soldiers
— Drayloads of Boxes — Ladies seeking Information — Express Mes-
sengers — The Morning Mail — The aged Father and his dead Son —
" What ails the little Fellow ? " — A Bevy of Nurses — A sorrow-
stricken Mother — Soldiers from the City Hospitals — More loaded
Drays — More Men and Women come and go — The Day declines —
Return to my Home — "A Suburb of Heaven."

HE headquarters of the Chicago, or
"Northwestern Sanitary Commission," as
it was correctly re-christened — for all the
Northwestern states became its auxiliaries
— were the least attractive rooms in the city.
Except during a brief period of its early existence, it occupied the large rooms under McVicker's Theatre, then, as now, on Madison Street. They
seemed smaller than they were, because they were
generally crowded with boxes and packages, huddled
together to suit the convenience of those who
opened, unpacked, assorted, stamped, and repacked
their contents. Drays were continually unloading

and re-loading with a furious racket; and the draymen were not possessors of " soft, low voices." The
din was further increased by incessant hammering
and pounding within, caused by opening and nailing
up boxes. Horse-cars passed to and fro every minute, and heavily laden teams, omnibuses, carriages,
carts and wagons of all descriptions, rolled by with
intermitting thunder.

The sewing-rooms of the Commission were located
on the floor above us, where between thirty and
forty sewing-machines ran all day. Upstairs, and
downstairs, and over our heads, the women of the
soldiers' families maintained a ceaseless tramp from
morning till night, coming to sew, to receive or return work, or to get their greatly needed pay. Add
to this a steady stream of callers, on every imaginable errand, in every known mental mood — grieved,
angry, stupid, astonished, incredulous, delighted,
agonized — all talking in the tones of voice in which
these various moods betray themselves — was there
an element of distraction omitted?

The odors of the place were villanous and a perpetual torment. Codfish and sauer-kraut, pickles and
ale, onions and potatoes, smoked salmon and halibut,
ginger and whiskey, salt mackerel and tobacco, kerosene for the lamps, benzine for cleansing purposes,
black paint to mark the boxes, flannel and unbleached
cotton for clothing, — these all concentrated their
exhalations in one pungent aroma, that smote the
olfactories when one entered, and clung tenaciously
to the folds of one's garments when one departed.
We called it " the perfume of the sanitary," and at
last got used to it, as we did to the noise.

From one corner of this room an office was partitioned, so economical in dimensions that ten people crowded it. One large window lighted it, the lower half of ground glass. The upper half of the partition was also of glass, for the double purpose of light, and of keeping easily in communication with our co-workers in the outer room. The floor was carpeted with ingrain, and desks of the simplest pattern and chairs of the hardest wood completed the furnishing.

In these uninviting quarters the work of the Northwestern Sanitary Commission was outlined or performed. Here were packed and shipped to the hospitals or battle-field 77,660 packages of sanitary supplies, whose cash value was $1,056,192.16. Here were written and mailed letters by the ten thousand, circulars by the hundred thousand, monthly bulletins and reports. Here were planned visits to the aid societies, trips to the army, methods of raising money and supplies, systems of relief for soldiers' families and white refugees, Homes and Rests for destitute and enfeebled soldiers, and the details of mammoth sanitary fairs.

Hon. Mark Skinner of Chicago was president of the Commission through the darkest and most arduous days of its existence. Just as its work had become so organized and systematized that anxiety concerning it was at an end, and the machinery ran with very little friction, Judge Skinner was compelled to resign because of ill-health, and Mr. E. B. McCagg of Chicago succeeded to the office. It was indeed a bereavement to lose Judge Skinner from the board. The weight of his name and character, and his worth as an adviser, greatly strengthened the organization with the outside community; while the charm of his manner, and the subtle humor that

brightened his speech, rendered his almost daily visits
to the rooms a pleasure that was keenly anticipated.

Mr. E. W. Blatchford of Chicago was treasurer
till the Commission disbanded. His office was no
sinecure, for he not only received the money, but expended it. No language can describe the promptness, accuracy, and conscientiousness, which he
carried into this work. Nor is it possible to measure
in words the courtesy, patience, kindness, and fine-
ness of spirit, which all felt who were brought into
relations with him. I shall always congratulate
myself that the work of the Sanitary Commission
brought me into association with Mr. Blatchford.
For I learned of him an exactness and promptness,
and a careful attention to detail in matters of business,
that, as a woman, I should have learned nowhere
else. Both Judge Skinner and Mr. Blatchford had
large business and professional engagements of their
own, demanding all their time and attention, which
rendered their devotion to the cause of hospital relief
more noteworthy.

The constant habitues of the little office were four.
Mr. John Freeman was nominally the shipping clerk;
but if there was any kind of work connected with the
rooms at which he did not lend a hand, I have yet to
learn what it was. He attended to the boxes, to the
packing, to the shipping; helped soldiers to obtain
transportation back to their regiments, or assisted
them, when feeble and wounded, to reach their homes;
went on the most surprising and unheard-of missions,
and accomplished them, — in short, did anything and
everything, whether in the line of his duty or not,
and always did it well. He was a man of remarkable
good-nature, which no *contretemps* could disturb, and

this made him a universal favorite.  He possessed
that "tact which is almost talent," and a discretion
which bore him safely through many peculiar experiences where another would have blundered.  Not
the least valuable of his accomplishments was his
keen sense of the ludicrous.  Rarely did he return
from one of his many expeditions — sorrowful though
they sometimes were — without a comic story to narrate, or a funny incident to describe.  Seasoning both
with a spice of native waggery, he would cause the
rooms to resound with laughter, and render us all
oblivious for a moment to both work and care.  We
regarded him at such times as a benefactor.

Mr. William Goodsmith was a man of different
temperament.  Care did not sit lightly on his shoulders.  Under Mr. Blatchford's directions he made
purchases of supplies, which were always selected
with care, paid bills, transacted business with banks,
and all difficult and delicate matters were entrusted
to his management.  All relied implicitly on his
judgment, good sense, and honor.  So careful was he
in all transactions, so absolutely faithful and pains-
taking in everything, that limitless confidence was
reposed in him.  I have never known a more trustworthy person.  His ideal of excellence was very
lofty, and his spirit so unselfish that at times he was
unjust to himself.  With all his recognized abilities,
there was a hint of reserved power in his speech and
manner, that made one sure he would be equal to the
duties of a much higher position than he held.  The
Commission was very fortunate to command his services.  We sometimes called him our " sheet-anchor."

Mrs. Jane C. Hoge and myself completed the quartette of the office.  Rarely were we both absent at

the same time. We were personal friends, and had long been associated in the charitable work of the city. She was a practical woman, and her executive ability was very marked. Her power of patient, persistent work was seemingly limitless. Her force of character was irresistible, and bore down all opposition. Her energy was simply tremendous. She excelled in conducting a public meeting, and was a very forceful and attractive public speaker. The inspiration of the war developed in her capabilities of whose possession she was not aware, and she surprised herself, as she did others, by the exercise of hitherto unsuspected gifts. Of how many women workers of the war could the same be said!

A devoted Presbyterian from childhood, Mrs. Hoge was very catholic in spirit. Her largeness of heart included the race, and, united to her keen sense of justice, led her into the charitable and reform work of the time. She was concerned for the public welfare, and gravitated instinctively towards public work. It was impossible for her to do otherwise than identify herself with the interests of the country. And when two of her sons entered the service, she gave herself unreservedly to the work of relieving our sick and wounded soldiers.

My friend still lives in Chicago, where the calm evening of her days is brightened by the society of her husband, with whom she has spent more than half a century of happy wedded life, and by the encompassing tenderness of her children, seven of whom are settled around her. By her grand, good life she has earned a long sojourn in the "Land of Beulah," while awaiting the summons to the "Celestial City."

Mrs. JANE C. HOGE.

Mrs. MARY A. BICKERDYKE
"MOTHER BICKERDYKE"

MISS MARY J. SAFFORD.

Mrs. CORDELIA A. P. HARVEY.

*Engby. L. Holtzer, Guttenberg, N. J.*

# WOMEN OF THE WAR

## FAMOUS NURSES OF UNION SOLDIERS.

A. D. WORTHINGTON & CO. PUBLISHERS HARTFORD, CONN.

There was always more or less volunteer and transient help in the rooms. Sometimes companies of
ladies, who gave their services on certain days; sometimes young girls, who caught the patriotic spirit of
the time, and craved a share in the work; sometimes detailed soldiers from Camp Douglas, doing
guard duty over rebel prisoners; sometimes convalescent soldiers from the hospitals, who sought to
dispose of the lagging hours while awaiting transportation to their regiments. There was never any
lack of employment. The rush of business lasted all
day and ran over into the midnight. We frequently
took letters to our homes requiring immediate answer,
and in the stillness of the night overtook the work
that outran our most diligent efforts during the day.
Not even could we control the hours of Sunday
during those busy years. The work of hospital
relief ran over into them, and busy scenes were sometimes enacted at the " rooms," of which the closed
doors gave no hint to the thronging church-goers.
" It is lawful to do good on the Sabbath day."

A description of " A DAY AT THE ROOMS OF THE
SANITARY COMMISSION," which I wrote at the time
for the columns of my husband's paper, gives a
vivid idea of the routine of daily life in the busy
office, and so I transcribe it here: —

" It is early morning, — not nine o'clock, for the
children are flocking in merry droves to school. The
air is resonant with their joyous treble and musical
laughter, as with clustering heads and interlacing
arms they recount their varied experiences since they
parted the night before, and rapturously expatiate on
the delights of a coming excursion or promised picnic. With a good-bye kiss, I launch my own little

ones, bonneted, sacqued, and ballasted with books, like the rest, into the stream of childhood that is setting in a strong, full current towards the school-room. I then catch the first street-car and hasten to the rooms of the 'Northwestern Sanitary Commission.'

"Early as is my arrival, a dray is already ahead of me, unloading its big boxes and little boxes, its barrels and firkins, its baskets and bundles. The sidewalk is barricaded with the nondescript and multiform packages, which John, the faithful porter, with his inseparable truck, is endeavoring to stow away in the crowded 'receiving-room.' Here, hammers and hatchets, wedges and chisels are in requisition, compelling the crammed boxes to disgorge their heterogeneous contents, which are rapidly assorted, stamped, repacked, and reshipped, their stay in the room rarely exceeding a few hours.

" I enter the office. Ladies are in waiting, desirous of information. The aid society in another state, of which they are officers, has raised at a Fourth of July festival some six hundred dollars, and they wish to know how to dispose of it, so as to afford the greatest amount of relief to the sick and wounded of our army. They were also instructed to investigate the means and methods of the Commission, so as to carry conviction to a few obstinate skeptics, who persist in doubting if the Sanitary Commission, after all, be the best means of communication with the hospitals. Patiently and courteously the history, methods, means, views, and successes of the Commission are lucidly explained for the hundredth time in a month, and all needed advice and instruction imparted; and the enlightened women leave.

"An express messenger enters. He presents a package, obtains his fee, gets a receipt for the package, and without a word departs.

"Next comes a budget of letters — the morning's mail. One announces the shipment of a box of hospital stores which will arrive to-day. Another scolds roundly because an important letter sent a week ago has not been answered, while a copy of the answer in the copying-book is indisputable proof that it has received attention, but has in some way miscarried. A third narrates a bugaboo story of surgeons and nurses in a distant hospital, with gluttonous habits, who are mainly occupied in 'seeking what they can devour' of the hospital delicacies, so that little is saved for their patients. A fourth pleads passionately that the writer may be sent as a nurse to the sad, cheerless, most poorly furnished and far-away hospitals. A fifth is the agonized letter of a mother and widow, blistered with tears, begging piteously that the Commission will search out and send to her tidings of her only son, —

> ' Scarce more than a boy, with unshaven face,
> Who marched away with a star on his breast,'

and has not been heard from since the battle of Grand Gulf. A sixth asks assistance in organizing the women of a distant town, who have just awaked to their duty to their brothers in the field. A seventh is a letter from two nine-year-old girls, who have between them earned five dollars, and wish to spend it for 'the poor sick soldiers.' God bless the dear children! An eighth begs that one of the ladies of the Commission will visit the aid society of the town in which the writer lives, and rekindle the flagging zeal of the tired workers. They propose to cease work during the hot weather, forgetting that our brave men halt not on their marches, and postpone not their battles, because of the heat or of weariness. A ninth announces the death of one of our heroic nurses, who was sent by the Commission a few months ago to Tennessee—a serious, comely girl, with heart as true as steel, and soul on fire with patriotic desire to do something for her country, and who has now given her life. And so on through a package of twenty, thirty, forty, sometimes fifty letters; and this is but one mail of the day — usually the heaviest, however.

"Now begins the task of replying to these multitudinous epistles — a work which is interrupted every five minutes by some new comer. A venerable man enters, walking slowly, and my heart warms towards him. I remember my aged father, a thousand miles away, who is, like him, white-haired and feeble. He has been here before, and I immediately recognize him.

"'Have you heard anything yet from my son in Van Buren Hospital, at Milliken's Bend?'

"'Not yet, sir; you know it is only nine days since I wrote to inquire for him. I will telegraph if you think best.'

"'No matter;' and the old man's lip quivers, his figure trembles violently, a sob chokes him, his eyes fill with tears, as with a deprecating wave of the hand he says, 'No matter now!'

"I understand it all. It is all over with his boy, and the cruel tidings have reached him. I rise and offer my hand. He encloses it convulsively in his, leans his head against the iron column near my desk, and his tears drip, drip steadily.

"'Your son has only gone a little before you,' I venture to say; 'only a hand's breadth of time between you now.'

"'Yes,' adds the poor old father; 'and he gave his life for a good cause — a cause worthy of it if he had been a thousand times dearer to me than he was.'

"'And your boy's mother — how does she bear this grief?'

"The tears rain down his cheeks now.

"'It will kill her; she is very feeble.'

"What shall assuage the sorrow of these aged parents, bereft of the son of their old age by the cruel war that slavery has invoked? Sympathy and comfort are proffered the poor father, and after a little the sorrowing man turns again to his desolate home.

"A childish figure drags itself into the room, shuffles heavily along, drops into a chair, and offers a letter. What ails the little fellow, whose face is bright and beautiful, and yet is shaded by sadness? I open the letter and read. He is a messenger-boy from Admiral Porter's gunboats, who is sent North with the request that the child be properly cared for. Not thirteen years old, and yet he has been in many battles, and has run the gauntlet of the Vicksburg batteries, which for ten miles belched forth red-hot and steel-pointed shot and shell, in fruitless efforts to sink the invulnerable ironclads. Fever, too much medicine, neglect, and exposure, have done their worst for the little fellow, who has come North, homeless and friendless, with the right side paralyzed. He is taken to the exquisite tenderness of the 'Soldiers' Home,' and for the present is consigned to the motherly care of the good ladies who preside there.

"Who next ?    A bevy of nurses enter with carpet-bags, shawls, and bundles.    A telegram from the Commission has summoned them, for the hospitals at Memphis need them, and straightway they have girded themselves to the work.    One is a widow, whose husband fell at Shiloh ; another is the wife of a lieutenant at Vicksburg ; a third lost her brother at Chancellorsville ; a fourth has no family ties, and there is no one to miss her while absent, or to mourn her if she never returns.    They receive their instructions, commissions, and transportation, and hurry onward.    God guide you, brave, noble women !

"Ah ! that white, anxious face, whiter than ever, is again framed in the doorway.    Is there no possible escape from it ?    One, two, three, four days she has haunted these rooms, waiting the answer to the telegram despatched to Gettysburg, where her son was wounded ten days ago.    The answer to the telegram is this moment in my pocket — how shall I repeat its stern message to the white-faced, sorrow-stricken mother ?    I involuntarily leave my desk, and bustle about, as if in search of something, trying to think how to break the news.    I am spared the effort, for the morning papers have announced her bereavement, and she has only come to secure the help of the Commission in obtaining possession of her dead. There are no tears, no words of grief ; only a still agony, a repressed anguish, which it is painful to witness.    Mr. Freeman accompanies her to the rail-road officials, where his pleading story wins the charity of a free pass for the poor woman to the 'military line.'    There she must win her way, aided by the letters of endorsement and recommendation we give her.    Bowing under her great sorrow, she goes forth on her sacred pilgrimage. Alas! how many thousand mothers have been bereft at Vicksburg and Gettysburg, refusing to be comforted, because their children are not!

"Soldiers from the city hospitals visit us, to beg a shirt, a pair of slippers, a comb, or a well-filled pin-cushion, 'something interesting to read,' or 'paper, envelopes, and stamps,' to answer letters from wives, mothers, and sweethearts. They tarry to talk over their trials, sufferings, and privations, and their anxiety to get well and join their regiments, 'which is better than being cooped up in a hospital, even when it is a good one.' They are praised heartily, petted in motherly fashion as if they were children, which most sick men become, urged to come again, and sent back altogether lighter-hearted than when they came.

"And so the day wears away. More loaded drays drive to the door with barrels of crackers, ale, pickles, sauer-kraut, and potatoes, with boxes of shirts, drawers, condensed milk and beef, with bales of cotton and flannel for the sewing-room, all of which are speedily disposed of, to make room for the arrivals of the morrow. Men and women come and go — to visit, to make inquiries, to ask favors, to offer services, to criticise and find fault, to bring news from the hospitals at Vicksburg, Memphis, Murfreesboro' and Nashville, to make inquiries for missing men through the 'Hospital Directory' of the Commission, to make donations of money, always needed, to retail their sorrows, and sometimes to idle away an hour in the midst of the hurrying, writing, copying, mailing, packing and shipping of this busy place.

" The sun declines westward, its fervent heat is abating, and the hands of the clock point to the hour of six, and sometimes to seven. Wearied in body, exhausted mentally, and saturated with the passing streams of others' sorrows, I select the letters which must be answered by to-morrow morning's mail, replies to which have been delayed by the interruptions of the day, and again hail the street-car, which takes me to my home. Its pleasant order and quiet, its welcome rest, its cheerful companionship, its gayety, which comes from the prattle and merriment of children, who have a thousand adventures to narrate,—all seem strange and unnatural after the experiences of the day. It is as if I had left the world for a time, to refresh myself in a suburb of heaven. And only by a mental effort do I shut out the scenes I have left, and drop back for a time into my normal life — the life of a wife, mother, and housekeeper. I try to forget the narratives of gunshot wounds, sabre strokes, battle and death, that have rained on me all day. This hour with my husband and children shall not be saddened by sketches of the suffering men and women who have defiled before my vision during the hours of daylight. There is a bright side even to these dark pictures; and there comes to me like a tonic the grand solace of the poet: —

" ' Above, or underneath,
What matters, brothers, if we keep our post
At truth's and duty's side! As sword to sheath,
Dust turns to grave — but souls find place in Heaven ! ' "

# CHAPTER VI.

A CAMPAIGN PLANNED BY A WOMAN — DESPERATE BATTLES — TERRIBLE SCENES ON THE BATTLE-FIELD — TERRIFIC FIGHTING AND APPALLING SUFFERING — THE AGONIES OF WAR.

General McClellan supersedes General Scott — Missouri becomes the Field of Battle — General Grant wins a Victory at Belmont — Fleet of " Ironclads " for Service on Southern Rivers — The " Tennessee Campaign " planned by Anna Ella Carroll, of Maryland — Plan adopted by President Lincoln and Secretary Stanton — Carried out by General Grant — The " Court of Claims," in 1885, decides in her Favor — Fort Henry on the Tennessee captured by Gunboats — They fail to take Fort Donelson on the Cumberland — General Grant attacks by Land — The Fort surrenders, after three Days' Fighting — " Unconditional Surrender Grant!" — Joy of the Northwest — Frightful Suffering of the Wounded — Many frozen to Death on both Sides — The People move to succor the Wounded — Immense Quantities of Supplies forwarded — Seven thousand Prisoners sent to Camp Douglas — Five hundred die.

AFTER the battle of Bull Run had been fought and lost, there was a lull in the storm of war on the Atlantic Coast. " All is quiet on the Potomac! " was daily bulletined from the army for months, until the people became depressed and exasperated. They could not understand the strange inactivity of the land forces, nor the timidity and weakness of the government.

In November, 1861, Major-General Scott, weighted with age and infirmities, resigned his position, and young General McClellan was installed in his place as commander-in-chief of the army. The heart of the nation went out to him in trust and affection, and it bent its ear southward, to catch the first sound of the forward movement of the mighty host under his leadership. The government had now in its service for the suppression of the rebellion six hundred and eighty-two thousand soldiers and sailors, and a larger force was at its disposal whenever it was demanded. But the mild weeks of the autumn dragged away, now and then a fierce storm presaged the coming winter; and yet the dreary bulletin was daily repeated, "All is quiet on the Potomac!"

In the meantime all eyes were turned to the West, for Missouri had become the great field of battle. General Fremont had returned from Europe in June with arms for the government, and had been assigned to the Department of the West. He reached St. Louis in July, and took command. Before he had had time to acquaint himself with the condition of affairs, to organize an army, or decide on a plan of action, the battle of Wilson's Creek occurred, in which General Lyon was killed, and a large portion of Missouri was left in the hands of the rebels. Then came the battle of Lexington, in which the enemy was again victorious, and Missouri was now the scene of widespread devastation and blood. Small bodies of troops kept the field, and there were incessant skirmishes and combats. Remote towns were occupied alternately by the Unionists and the enemy. Railroads and bridges were destroyed, houses and barns fired, families scattered, neighborhoods desolated, and murders were of constant occurrence.

Later, in November, an expedition was sent from Cairo, under General Grant, to break up a camp of the enemy in Belmont. It was not only done, but more was accomplished than was proposed, which toned up the troops engaged in the fight to great confidence and fortitude. Almost simultaneously with the battle of Belmont, Major-General Halleck superseded Fremont.

During the first two years of the war, the naval forces took a very prominent part in all Western operations. The blockade of the Mississippi and the breaking out of hostilities had thrown large numbers of the river steamers out of occupation. When these were sheathed with iron, they could defy the heaviest artillery of the enemy; and, as they were of light draught, they could steam up shallow streams into the interior of the country, and make their way in rivers at the lowest stage of water. When these "ironclads" carried heavy guns, as most of them did, they were especially dreaded by the enemy.

Early in the year 1862 a fleet of these dreaded ironclads moved down the Southern rivers, and began the long-talked-of advance into the Confederate States. No decisive blow had yet been struck at the rebellion, but there seemed now to be a purpose to wrest the valley of the Mississippi from the control of the enemy. It was seen that the strategic key of the war of the Southwest was not the Mississippi, but the Tennessee. It was determined to break the line of defences along the Tennessee and Cumberland rivers by taking Forts Henry and Donelson, both of them strong fortifications. Fort Henry was on the Tennessee and Fort Donelson on the Cumberland, only twelve miles apart, in Tennessee, near the state line.

This change of plan—which transferred the national armies from Cairo and Northern Kentucky to a new base, in Northern Mississippi and Alabama, and which

made the fall of the Confederacy inevitable — has a
remarkable history. It was planned by a woman,
Anna Ella Carroll, of Maryland, a descendant of
Charles Carroll, of Carrollton, of Revolutionary times,
and whose father was governor of the state in 1829.
Belonging to one of the first families of the country,
of brilliant intellect, and intensely loyal to the Union,
she comprehended state and military questions with
wonderful clearness. She wrote and published papers and pamphlets on some of the debated important
topics of the time, that attracted the attention of leading members of Congress, and made her one of the
advisers of President Lincoln. She was admitted to
his presence at all times, and " he reserved a special
file for her communications."

By advice of the War Department she went to St.
Louis in the fall of 1861, and there studied and
planned the Tennessee campaign, which was adopted
by the administration, and carried out by General
Grant. By this campaign the Confederacy was cut
in twain, the Mississippi was opened to Young's
Point, opposite Vicksburg, European intervention
with the United States was averted, the national
credit was revived, the heart of the country strengthened, and its drooping courage toned up to firm
resolution.

Not only did President Lincoln acknowledge Miss
Carroll to be the author of the plan of the Tennessee
campaign, but Secretary Stanton gave her the same
credit. So also did Hon. Henry Wilson, Chairman
of the Senate Military Committee of the Forty-
Second Congress, in a report on the memorial of
Miss Carroll, asking for compensation for her services, as she had become an invalid and was in want.

Hon. B. F. Wade, Chairman of the Committee on the Conduct of the War, was most emphatic in testifying to Miss Carroll's authorship of the plan of the campaign, as was Hon. L. D. Evans, of the Supreme Court of Texas. Their letters and statements have been published again and again, and have now passed into history.

At last the Court of Claims, which decides all cases on their merits, has, after careful consideration, decided in her favor. It has " substantiated the claim to recompense she long ago made before Congress for services performed during the civil war." That she has been obliged to wait until the present time for recognition is pitiful. But the delay has arisen from two formidable obstacles, as was stated before the Court of Claims: first, the unfavorable attitude of the military mind towards what emanates from outside circles; and, secondly, the fact that the claimant is a woman — a fact for which she is not responsible — has operated against her through all these years in a powerful manner.

In pursuance of this plan of the Tennessee campaign, Fort Henry was first attacked. Commodore Foote, with seven gunboats, engaged the batteries on the river front ; and before General Grant had arrived with his troops from Cairo, the main force of the enemy retreated to Fort Donelson, and the remainder surrendered.

Fort Donelson was next attacked, lying nearly opposite Fort Henry, a stronger and more important position, garrisoned by twenty-one thousand troops General Grant moved his forces across the country, and invested the place, while waiting for Commodore Foote with his gunboats, which were to engage the river batteries, as at Fort Henry. The three days of the fight, the thirteenth, fourteenth, and fifteenth of February, were days of intense anxiety in the West, especially in Chicago. It was known that the attack by water, which had been so easily successful at Fort Henry, had failed at Donelson through the disabling of Commodore Foote's gunboats; and the heart of the Northwest was sick with forebodings of failure.

When, therefore, on Sunday, the sixteenth, the telegraph flashed to the nation the news of Grant's victory, — that nearly fifteen thousand troops, sixty-five guns, some of them of the largest calibre, and seventeen thousand six hundred small arms, had fallen into the hands of the victor,— the delight of the West was boundless. " The whole of Kentucky and Tennessee fell at once into the hands of the national forces. The Tennessee and Cumberland rivers were opened to national vessels for hundreds of miles. Nashville, the capital of Tennessee, and a place of immense strategic importance, fell. And the Mississippi was left free of the rebel flag from St. Louis to Arkansas." All this was the legitimate result of the capture of Fort Donelson. It was a great victory, and the first of any importance since the beginning of the war. Great as were its military results, its happy effect on the spirits of the soldiers and the people was even greater.

No one of the later or larger victories of the war, not even the fall of Richmond, awoke the enthusiastic delight of the Northwest like the fall of Fort Donelson. Bells rang; cannon thundered the general joy; bands perambulated the streets of the cities, playing the national airs, deafening cheers often drowning their music; flags were flung out from almost every house, and where there was any reluctance to give this manifestation of loyal delight, from sympathy with secession, the overjoyed people took possession and compelled the display of the national colors. Many a disloyal wretch who had assisted to plot the rebellion, and had contributed money and arms to the enemy, was compelled to enter his house under the flag of the stars and stripes, which he had been forced to purchase. Men rushed from their stores, offices, counting-rooms, shops, and work-benches, to congratulate one another. They met on the streets and threw their hats in air, embraced one another, wept, and shouted.

The public schools of Chicago had each purchased a flag by joint subscription, and a flagstaff had been planted on the roof of every one of the handsome brick schoolhouses for just such occasions as this. So the boys ran up their flags amid immense cheering, and, under the direction of the teachers, the day was given up to patriotic dissipation. National songs were sung, patriotic scraps of speeches found in the reading-books were recited, and the location and importance of Fort Donelson were explained to the young people. When the hour of dismissal came, they added to the joyful confusion of the streets by shooting out of the schoolhouses like bombs from mortars, with shrill and prolonged hurrahs leaping from their lips as they rushed through every part of the city. Night came, and the people crowded the churches to return thanks to God. Meetings were held to raise funds for the relief of the wounded. The streets blazed with bonfires, and the glare of the flames was like that of a great conflagration. Nor did the rejoicings cease until physical exhaustion compelled an end of them.

With the news of the victory the telegraph flashed the terrible needs of the wounded men. During the first day of the fight a cold, heavy rain fell ceaselessly, converting the roads into rivers of mud, through which the troops painfully toiled. During the night the rain changed to sleet and snow, and the wind blew in fierce, wintry gusts, the weather became intensely cold, and the thermometer dropped to zero. Our brave fellows were mostly young, and not yet inured to the hardships of war. With the improvidence of inexperience, they had thrown away their blankets on the march, and had only the insufficient rations they had brought in their haversacks, of which they had been very careless. They had no tents; were obliged to bivouac in line of battle, lying on their arms; and as the rebel pickets were out in strong force, no fires could be kindled, as their position would be revealed.

The enemy were in much worse plight, as, in addition to their foodless, fireless and tentless condition, they were poorly clad. All through the long winter night both armies were pelted by the driving, pitiless snow and hail. Many of the soldiers on both sides were frozen to death before morning. "An incessant firing was kept up by the pickets; and the groans of the wounded, who lay shivering between the two armies, calling for help and water, were heard all through the night." Meantime the muffled sounds that came from the front during the pauses of the storm told them that the enemy were receiving heavy re-enforcements. The next two days were equally bleak and cold; and the men bivouacked each night on their arms, in the snow, and on the frozen ground. In the morning they were roused from their icy couches, and stumbled stiff and shivering into their places in the ranks.

The very topography of the battle-field added to the miseries of the fight. It was made up of hills and valleys, stretched across ravines and broken ground, and extended through dense forests. Every commanding height bristled with cannon, constantly sending shot and shell among our men massed below. Every position of the enemy on the precipitous heights was carried by storm. Our brave men, in regiments, swept up the steep sides of the hills, in the face of sheets of fire, and amid tempests of balls. The gaps in their ascending ranks were instantly closed, and, stepping over the dead and wounded, they pressed resistlessly on, silent as death, reserving their fire till they reached the crest of the heights. Then, with exultant shouts, they poured in their volleys of shot, and flung themselves like an avalanche on the enemy, driving them at the point of the bayonet. All through the three days of the struggle, the roar of the contending hosts was like that of a tornado, as they surged back and forth through the forest, strewing it with dead and wounded.

But few of the wounded could be removed from the field while the fight lasted. There they lay, some two and three nights and days, uncared for, many freezing to death. Hundreds who fell in the beginning of the battle, when the ground was soft and muddy, were frozen into the earth; and it was necessary to cut them out of the ground, when attention could be given them, and in this deplorable plight they were taken to the extemporized and unready hospitals. Their removal was horrible torture; for there were few ambulances, and the wagons and carts impressed into the service were of the rudest construction, and generally lacked springs. In these the poor fellows were jolted and pitched down the precipitous heights, where they had lain for two or three days and nights, encased in bloody and frozen uniforms. Any convenient shed, barn, house, or church received them. They were laid on the bare floor, their wounds undressed, their frozen clothing unchanged, faint from loss of blood and extreme bodily anguish, and hundreds died miserably before relief came to them.

The surgeons of the government were few in number, and its medical supplies utterly inadequate to the occasion. But the people moved to the succor of the wounded, with a royal generosity. The Chicago Board of Trade immediately raised three thousand dollars, needed supplies were purchased, and a committee of citizens started for the scene of suffering. Seventeen physicians were sent down on the first train that left Chicago after the fall of Donelson was known. The Chicago Sanitary Commission had been sending supplies to its depot in Cairo for weeks, at the rate of a thousand dollars' worth daily, and it continued to do this for weeks afterward. These were drawn upon *ad libitum* for the occasion.

Floating hospitals, or "Hospital Steamers," as they were called, which after this were always in the near neighborhood of the gunboats as they advanced down the Southern rivers, were rapidly fitted up and loaded with supplies by the Chicago and St. Louis Commissions, and sent on their errands of mercy. Merchants, lawyers, clergymen, women, — ten times as many as were needed, — volunteered as nurses. Spontaneous contributions of sheets, pillows, shirts, lint, bandages, jellies, canned fruits, and other stores of the housewife, were poured into the recently opened rooms of the Commission in magnificent abundance. There was but one heart in the community, an eager and determined purpose to alleviate the sufferings of the heroes of Donelson. Every day's fuller report of their bravery and indescribable endurance only intensified the compassion and gratitude of the great Northwest, — not then as rich and powerful as now,— and there was no withholding anywhere.

The elation of the country was boundless. After so many delays and defeats, this victory cheered the nation and inspired the army. General Grant had won national fame. His memorable answer to General Buckner, the rebel commander, who proposed "the appointment of commissioners to settle terms of capitulation," gave him the hearts of his countrymen. "No terms except immediate and unconditional surrender can be accepted. I propose to move immediately on your works." The speech and the deed, of the not yet recognized leader, were indications of character. The enthusiasm of the Western army was enkindled. They dubbed their commander "Unconditional Surrender Grant," declaring this to be the name indicated by the initials "U. S."

There was a great lack of hospital clothing, and one of the largest halls of Chicago was loaned to the women for its manufacture. To this hall they flocked in such numbers, that it was necessary to apportion the days of the week to the various districts of the city, so as to accommodate all the willing workers.

Every sewing-machine office in the city put its rooms, machines and operators to the same service, to the entire suspension of its own business. Never was clothing manufactured more rapidly; for the machines were run into the small hours of the morning, and there was no slacking of effort while the urgent demand lasted. It was the same all over the West. The facts of the desperate battle, the severe exposure of the wounded, the incomplete preparations for their removal and care, the great destitution of surgeons, instruments, supplies, of everything that was needed, — as these became known to the people, their patriotic generosity was stimulated to fever heat.

Seven thousand of the enemy taken at Fort Donelson were sent to Chicago as prisoners of war, and were given accommodations at Camp Douglas. They were quartered in the same barracks, and were furnished with the same rations, both as to quality and quantity, as were accorded our own troops that had occupied the camp a few months before. It was amusing, as well as pathetic, to listen to their openly expressed satisfaction. "You-uns got better grub than we-uns down South; better barracks, too." A more motley looking crowd was never seen in Chicago. They were mostly un-uniformed, and shivering with cold, wrapped in tattered bedquilts, pieces of old carpets, hearth rugs, horse blankets, ragged shawls,— anything that would serve to keep out the cold and hide their tatterdemalion condition.

They had evidently suffered severely in the terrible three days' fight at Donelson, not only from the arctic weather, but from insufficient food and clothing. If their own pitiful stories were true, they had failed to receive good care from the time they entered the Confederate service. They seemed a poorly nourished and uncared-for company of men, and their hopeless and indescribable ignorance intensified their general forlornness. Despite good medical attendance in camp and hospital, and notwithstanding the sick lacked for nothing in the matter of nursing and sick-diet — so well managed was the hospital, and so constant the ministrations of the women of Chicago — more than five hundred of them died at Camp Douglas before they were exchanged. It was pitiful to see how easily they gave up all struggle for life, and how readily they adjusted themselves to the inevitable. Not less uncomplainingly than the camel, which silently succumbs to the heavy load, did these ignorant, unfed and unclad fellows turn their faces to the wall, and breathe out their lives, without a regret, or a murmur.

# CHAPTER VII.

AFTER THE BATTLE — MY FIRST EXPERIENCE IN A MILITARY
HOSPITAL — A DEATHLY FAINTNESS COMES OVER ME —
NERVING MYSELF FOR THE WORK — TOUCHING SCENES.

Mrs. Hoge and myself visit the Hospitals of St. Louis — Our first Experience — Boisterousness of new Recruits — The grim Silence of Men
who had "been under Fire" — Our remarkable Hostess — Conspicuous
and unflinching Loyalty — Her "Hospital Kitchen" and "Hospital
Wagon" — "Eleven Hundred Soldiers' Letters!"—The Donelson Wards
— Their sickening Odor and ghastly Sights — Horrible Mutilation of the
Men — A deathly Faintness came over me — The Wounded and Dead
robbed on the Field of Battle — Plucky Fellow — "They couldn't be
bothering with us" — "Afraid to die!" — "Send for a Methodist Minister!" — The Magic of Song — The mental Conflict of the Night that
followed — St. Louis sitting in Gloom — Sad Wedding in the Hospital —
Death of the Bridegroom.

WHILE the demand for "battle supplies"
continued, Mrs. Hoge — my co-worker —
and myself, assisted in collecting, purchasing, cutting, making, and packing whatever was in demand. But it became
evident that the tide of war was setting towards
other large battles; and, as soon as there was a lull in
the demand for sanitary stores, Mrs. Hoge and myself
were sent to the hospitals and to medical headquarters at the front, with instructions to obtain any
possible information, that would lead to better preparation for the wounded of another great battle.

The great proportion of the wounded of Fort

Donelson had been taken to the excellent general hospitals established at St. Louis, and our first visit was to this city. We stopped at Springfield, Ill., *en route*, to obtain the endorsement of Governor Yates, and letters of recommendation from him. They were heartily given. From Chicago to Springfield, we went in company with recently formed regiments of soldiers, who, with the boisterous enthusiasm that always characterized the newly enlisted, made the night hideous with their shouts and songs. We soon learned that we could easily distinguish soldiers who had "been under fire" from the new recruits. Boatloads of the former would steam past us, going up or down the Mississippi, in a grim silence that was most oppressive; while men fresh from their first camp would deafen us with their throat-splitting yells and shouts. The former had had experience of war; and the first rollicking enthusiasm of ignorance had given place to a grimness of manner that impressed one with a sense of desperate purpose.

During our stay in St. Louis, we were the invited guests of one of the few wealthy families of the city which had remained loyal. The mistress of the household was a New England woman, whose ancestors had borne an honorable part in the war of the Revolution. Her husband, who had died just before the outbreak of the rebellion, was allied by blood and friendship with the foremost leaders of the Southern Confederacy, and was himself, during his life, a slaveholder, a stout defender of slavery, and intensely Southern in his feelings. At his death, his widow manumitted all the slaves bequeathed her, and then hired them all at fair wages. Eight of them were connected with the household in some capacity, and held their mistress in idolatrous estimation. The noble woman hesitated not an instant as to her line of conduct, when the rebellion was inaugurated. She clung to the loyal party of the state of Missouri, with a Roman firmness, and an uncompromising fidelity that never wavered.

Those of her children who had grown to manhood and womanhood sided with the South, as the younger ones would have done but for her all-compelling will, that held them true to their country. She overbore the purpose of the older sons to enter the Confederate army, and persuaded them to go to the south of Europe with a delicate sister, in quest of her health. Two of her children, a son and daughter, never returned, but died before the war ended, as much from chagrin and disappointment at the failure of the South, and grief over the death of kindred lost in the war, as from disease. The younger sons, who were terribly demoralized by the disloyal and defiant atmosphere of St. Louis, were sent to New England, to school and to college. Then, with one loyal daughter, she gave herself, her wealth, her elegant home, her skilled and trained servants, her influence, her speech, all that she was or had, unreservedly to the service of the country. That household was representative of many in the border states.

Some three of the wounded officers of Fort Donelson, one of whom had lost an arm, another a leg, and the third had a broken shoulder, and had been shot through the lungs, were taken to her stately home, where they were nursed as tenderly as if they had been her sons. There we found them in her charge, a hired, trained nurse being installed over them, and her own family physician entrusted with the duty of restoring them to health.' Her whole time and labor were given to the hospitals.

In her house, a kitchen had been fitted up expressly for the preparation of such delicate articles of sick-food as were not at that time easily cooked in the hospitals. It was called the " hospital kitchen," and her best cook was installed in it, with such assistants as she required. A light covered wagon, called by the coachman the "hospital wagon," was fitted up expressly for the transportation of these delicacies to the wards or invalids for whom they were designed. More than half the day was given by Mrs. —— to visiting the hospitals, to which her social position, her wealth, and her noted loyalty, always gave her admission, even under the most stringent medical administration. The evenings were devoted to writing letters for the soldiers, from memoranda she had gathered during the day — and into this work she impressed all who were under her roof. Mrs. Hoge and myself took our share of it every evening during our stay with her. Over eleven hundred letters for soldiers were written in this house in one year alone.

In company with this lady I made my first visit to a military hospital. We drove to the "Fifth Street Hospital," and passed directly into a ward of the wounded from Fort Donelson. The sickening odor of blood and healing wounds almost overpowered me. In the nearest bed lay a young man whose entire lower jaw had been shot away, and his tongue cut off. A surgeon came to dress the poor fellow's wounds, and I was directed to render him what assistance he required. The process of healing had drawn down the upper part of the face, so that when the ghastly wound was concealed by plasters and bandages, the exposed portion of the face was sadly distorted. But when the bandages were removed by the surgeon for examination of the wound, its horrible nature became apparent. A deathly faintness came over me, and I was hurried from the ward to the outer air for recovery.

Three times I returned, and each time some new horror smote my vision, some more sickening odor nauseated me, and I was led out fainting. The horrors of that long ward, containing over eighty of the most fearfully wounded men, were worse than anything I had imagined; but not worse than scenes in which I afterwards spent weeks and weeks without a tremor of the nerves or a flutter of the pulse. This was my first experience.

" A great many people cannot stay in hospitals, or render any service in them, they are so affected by the sights and smells," said the surgeon. " I would not try to do anything here were I in your place."

But was I to shrink from the sight of misery which these brave men were so nobly enduring? The thought was a tonic, and despising my weakness, I forced myself to remain in the ward without nausea or faintness. Never again were my nerves disturbed by any sight or sound of horror. I was careful to hold myself in iron control, until I had become habituated to the manifold shocking sights that are the outcome of the wicked business men call war.

In the second bed, a mere boy, a rebel prisoner, was dying. Both mutilated legs had been amputated above the knee, inflammation and fever had set in, the brain had become involved, and he was wild with delirium — singing, gesticulating, and babbling. Occasional paroxysms of fear seized him, when his shrieks would resound through the ward, and but for the attendants he would have leaped from the bed, struggling and wrestling with some phantom of his diseased brain, calling piteously all the while, "Mother! Mother! Mother!"

Another form of horror occupied a bed adjoining. He was one of the wounded who had fallen in the first of the battle, sinking into the mud, into which he was afterwards frozen, and from which he could not extricate himself. He had been cut out from the congealed earth ; but his feet had been so badly frozen as to render amputation necessary. The flesh in places had sloughed off his frozen back and thighs, and his lower limbs were paralyzed.

"How long were you left on the field?" I inquired.

"Two days and nights," was the answer.

"If you had been a rebel you could not have been used worse!" I replied, with indignation; for the dire necessities of war were then new to me. "Who was to blame for such neglect?"

"Oh, they couldn't be bothering with us," said the patient sufferer ; "they had to take the fort, and we didn't expect anybody to stop to see after us, till that was done."

"Did you think of that while you lay there freezing those long nights?"

"Of course!" was his nonchalant answer. "We knew we should be taken care of as soon as the fort surrendered. We were as anxious for that — we who were wounded — as were the troops who were fighting. We fellows on the ground all cheered, I tell you, when the fort showed the white flag, and we knew the rebs had surrendered. I had dropped into a drowse, when I heard the boys cheering enough to stun you. I couldn't cheer myself, for I was most gone. I guess I shouldn't have held out much longer. But Jerry, over in that bed," nodding across to a bed opposite, "his left arm was gone, and his right hand shot away; but he threw up his right stump of an arm, and hurrahed enough to split his throat." He gave this account feebly and disconnectedly — and not rapidly and coherently, as I have written it. He was yet in a low condition; but the surgeon thought he would ultimately recover, maimed as he was.

As the tide of battle flowed and ebbed around the fort during the three days' conflict, our wounded men on the field were sometimes brought within the lines of the enemy, by the surging back and forth of the combatants. They were well clad, and had money; for they had been paid only a few days before. The rebels were very insufficiently clothed; and, when the opportunity offered, they rifled the pockets of our helpless fellows, robbed them of their watches, and stripped them of any clothing they coveted. Wounded though they were, our men, in some instances, fought like tigers against this robbery, two or three lying together uniting against the rebel thief. They were overpowered by the robbers; and some who resisted were clubbed to death with their own muskets, and others were pinned to the earth with their own bayonets. Incredible as it seems, some of these latter were in this ward of the badly wounded, and in every instance were recovering.

"Well, boys," I said to some of them, "you got more than you bargained for this time. Don't you wish you had remained at home?"

"Not a bit of it!" was the plucky answer. "We enlisted as folks marry, for better or worse; and if it's for the worse, we oughtn't complain."

I had nearly completed the tour of this ward, making memoranda for letters which the men desired written, or of some want to be gratified or some errand done, — every bed being occupied by a very severely wounded man, — when I halted beside one on whose handsome face the unmistakable look of death was settling. He labored painfully for breath, and large drops of perspiration stood out on his forehead.

"You are suffering a great deal," I said.

"Oh, yes! oh, yes!" he gasped, "I am, I am! but not in body. I can bear that. I don't mind pain — I can bear anything — but I can't die! *I can't die!*"

"But perhaps you may not die. It is not certain but you may recover. While there is life there is hope, you know."

"Oh, no, I can't live — I know it — there's no chance for me. I've got to die — and I *can't* die! *I am afraid to die!*"

I went to the surgeon, still in the ward, and inquired about the man. The poor fellow was right; there was no chance for him. "He was horribly cut up," the surgeon said. One leg had been amputated, the other had suffered two amputations, the last one taking off the leg between the knee and hip; the right arm had been broken, a caisson had crushed the lower left arm, and he had been shot twice through the abdomen. "There had been no expec-

tation of his life when he was first brought in," said
the surgeon; "and it seemed an utterly hopeless
case.  But he has pulled along from day to day, as
if in defiance of death, and at last there seemed a
ghost of a chance for his recovery; but gangrene
has set in, and defies medical treatment, and it will be
over with him in a few hours.  All you can do is to
help him die easy."  I returned to the poor fellow,
whose anxious eyes were following me.

"What does the doctor say?" he asked.  "Oh, I
know I must die!  I can't!  I can't!  *I can't!*"  And
he almost shrieked in his mental distress, and trembled so violently as to shake the bed.

"Why are you afraid to die?" I inquired.  "Tell
me, my poor boy."

"I ain't fit to die.  I have lived an awful life, and
I'm afraid to die.  I shall go to hell."

I drew a camp-stool to his bedside, and, sitting
down, put my hands on his shoulders, and spoke in
commanding tones, as to an excited child: "Stop
screaming.  Be quiet.  This excitement is shorten-
ing your life.  If you *must* die, die like a man, and
not like a coward.  Be still, and listen to me."  And
I proceeded to combat his fear of death and his sense
of guilt with assurances of God's willingness to pardon.  I told him of Christ's mission on earth, and
assured him that however great had been his sins
they would be forgiven of God, since he was penitent,
and sought forgiveness.  And I bade him repeat
after me the words of a prayer, which he did with
tearful earnestness.  I backed up my assurances by
quotations from the Bible and illustrations from the
life of Christ; but I made little impression on the
dying man.

"Can't you get a Methodist minister?" he asked. "I used to belong to the Methodist church, but I fell away. Oh, send for a Methodist minister!"

One of the attendants remembered that the hospital steward was also a Methodist minister, and hastened to find him. To him I communicated the particulars of the case, and besought him to assist in allaying the anguish of the dying man, which was distressing to witness. Whatever was done for him must be done speedily, as he was fast sinking.

The announcement that the steward was a Methodist minister was beneficial to the sufferer. To him he listened eagerly. "The love of Christ," was the chaplain's theme. "He had only to trust in the Saviour, only to ask for forgiveness, and God, who was always ready to pardon, would grant his prayer. Christ had died to save just such conscience-smitten, stricken, penitent souls as he" — thus ran the chaplain's talk. And then he prayed, earnestly, feelingly, tenderly — the dying man frequently taking up the prayer, and joining in it.

"Can't you sing, chaplain?" I inquired. For it seemed to me the poor fellow, in this last hour of life, needed soothing more than argument or entreaty.

Immediately, in a rich, full, clear tenor, whose melody floated through the ward, and charmed every groan and wail into silence, he sang hymn after hymn, all of them familiar to most of his audience.

> " Come, humble sinner, in whose breast
>   A thousand thoughts revolve ; "—

> " Love divine, all love excelling,
>   Joy of heaven, to earth come down ; " —

"Jesus, lover of my soul,
    Let me to thy bosom fly;"—

"My days are gliding swiftly by,
    And I, a pilgrim stranger;"—

all of them hymns so well known to his dying
auditor, that I saw he followed the singer, verse after
verse. The music affected him as I had hoped.
The burden rolled from the poor boy's heart, and in
feeble, tender tones he said, "It's all right with me,
chaplain! I will trust in Christ! God will forgive
me! I can die, now!"

"Sing on, chaplain!" I suggested, as he was about
to pause, to make reply. "God is sending peace
and light into the troubled soul of this poor boy,
through these divine hymns, and your heavenly
voice. Sing on! Don't stop!"

He continued to sing, but now chose a different
style of hymn and tune, and burst forth into a most
rapturous strain: —

"Come, sing to me of heaven,
    For I'm about to die:
Sing songs of holy ecstasy,
    To waft my soul on high.
        There'll be no sorrow there,
        There'll be no sorrow there,
    In heaven above, where all is love,
        There'll be no sorrow there."

I looked down the ward, and saw that the wan
faces of the men, contracted with pain, were bright-
ening. I looked at the dying man beside me, and
saw, underneath the deepening pallor of death, an
almost radiant gleam.

With folded hands, and upturned gaze, almost

entranced with his own music, the chaplain continued
to sing: —

> " When cold, the hand of death
>   Lies on my marble brow,
> Break forth in songs of joyfulness,
>   Let heaven begin below.
>     There'll be no sorrow there," etc.

> " Then to my raptured ear
>   Let one sweet song be given;
> Let music charm me last on earth,
>   And greet me first in Heaven.
>     There'll be no sorrow there," etc.

A second and a third time he repeated the song,
the exultant air suiting well the triumphant words.
Patients, attendants, surgeons, all in the ward, glowed
under the soaring melody, and the dying man's
face grew rapturous. Then the chaplain was summoned away, by a call from his office. It was getting
late in the afternoon, for I had tarried a couple of
hours at this bedside, when my friends came from
other wards of the hospital, to say that it was time
to return.

"Don't go! stay!" whispered the fast sinking
man. The words rushed to my memory, " Inasmuch
as ye have done it unto one of the least of these, ye
have done it unto me," and I promised to remain
with him to the end. The end came sooner than
any one thought. Before the sun went down, he
had drifted to the immortal shore. The mutilated,
lifeless corpse was carried to the dreary " dead-
house," and preparations made for burial next day.

I reached my friend's house, with my nervous system at its highest tension. I could not
talk, eat, sleep, nor sit. All night I paced my

room, living over and over the experiences of the day. And this was only my *entrée* into hospital life and work. I was not equal to it — I would withdraw — I could not live in the midst of the agonies of war. And then I remembered that what I had witnessed in that ward of eighty men, was but a small segment of the physical anguish wrought by the battle of Fort Donelson, — that two thousand of our men were wounded, and twenty-five hundred of the enemy, — and that this battle might be multiplied by hundreds before the war ended.

And this war was but one of countless thousands which men had waged with one another, in which hundreds of millions had been slain — transfixed with lances, hewn in pieces with battle-axes, torn in fragments with plunging shot, or deadly canister, or fiendish bombs, mowed down with raking fires of leaden sleet, engulfed in the explosion of subterranean mines, impaled on gleaming bayonets, dying on the field, of wounds, fever, neglect, — forgotten, uncared for, a prey to the vulture, and devoured by the jackal and wild beast. While the mothers who bore these men, and the wives who loved them, lived on, suffering a prolonged death, finding the sweetness of life changed to cruel bitterness because of their bereavement. Never before had I attained a comprehension of what was meant by that one word " war."

Let me say that this instance which I have narrated, was the only case of fear of death I met in my visits to the hospitals. I often found men reluctant to die, because of families dependent on them — or because of a natural tenacity to life — or because, as they phrased it, " they did not want to be mustered out till the end of the war." But this man was the only one I ever met who was afraid to die. Over and over again I have listened to public narrations of horrible dying scenes in hospitals and on battle-fields — but I knew personally of but this one instance.

We spent some two or three weeks in the different hospitals of the city, visiting every ward, and communicating with every patient, doing for him whatever we could. I cannot recall a single cheerful or humorous event connected with the visit. There was gloom everywhere. St. Louis itself was under a cloud. The spirit of rebellion within it was intimidated, but not subdued. Business was depressed, stores were closed, and of its old-time sociality and hospitableness there was no sign. The guns of the fortifications were pointed at the city, holding it to compulsory neutrality, if not loyalty.

Fifteen thousand troops marched out of Benton Barracks, the great camp of rendezvous, and from other encampments while we were in St. Louis, and went down the river, on their way to the front. Many of them were without muskets, drill, or military experience. Some of the regiments had no surgeon, not a surgical instrument, nor a particle of medicine with them, while their officers were fresh from the plough, the shop, the counting-room, or office, ignorant of military tactics, knowing nothing of military hygiene or sanitary laws. In this wholly unprepared condition, these raw, undisciplined soldiers were, in a few weeks, precipitated into the battle of " Pittsburg Landing," or " Shiloh " — one of the most desperate, hotly contested, and sanguinary fights of the whole

war, when the two armies, for two days, stood up
and fought, without intrenchments on either side.

Through whole long streets these regiments
marched, on their way to the boats, with colors flying,
and bands playing, in their first enthusiasm rending
the air with their shouts; and not a face appeared at
a door or window with a " Godspeed" in its look,
not a woman waved her handkerchief in welcome,
not a child shouted its pleasure.  The closed houses
frowned down on them, as if untenanted; and the
few men who passed on the sidewalks drew their hats
over their eyes, and slouched by sullenly.  St. Louis,
at that time, had no heart in the gigantic preparations of the government to conquer the rebellion.

To add to the general depression, the city was full
of the relatives of the dead or wounded, waiting for
their bodies to be given them for burial, or striving to
nurse them back into health.  Fathers and mothers,
wives and sisters, were in the wards beside the men
they loved, and who had passed through the hell of
battle alive, but mangled and mutilated.  How they
fought death, inch by inch, for possession of these
remnants of humanity!  In every ward were dying
men; in every dead-house were the coffined dead, and
the ambulance, standing near, was ready to take the
cold sleepers to their last resting-places.  The men
whom no home friends visited looked with hungry
eyes at the manifestations of affectionate interest bestowed on their comrades, and, after a few preliminaries, were included in the petting, soothing, and
praising, that were always helpful to the poor fellows.

In one hospital I found a patient, feeble and
ghastly, packing a valise with the help of a convalescing comrade.  He had received a furlough, and

was going home for a month, and, despite his low physical condition, was full of courage. Three days later, I had occasion to pass through the same ward, and the man was just breathing his last.

"What has happened?" I inquired. "Wasn't the poor fellow able to make the journey after all?"

"His furlough was revoked for some reason; and he immediately fell back on the bed in a faint, and hasn't rallied yet."

He never rallied, but died from the removal of the stimulus of the promised visit home.

A young captain in the officers' ward interested me greatly, and I went daily to visit him. A refined and delicate fellow, with a very sensitive nervous organization, he had suffered severely. He had endured two amputations of the arm, which still refused to heal, and a third was ordered. He had become so reduced that the surgeon feared the result, and so informed his patient. Then the young officer telegraphed the girl who was to be his wife, and who had only delayed coming to him because of his earnest entreaty that she would not encounter the horrors of a hospital unless he sent for her. She came as fast as the lightning express could bring her; and, at her own desire, before he submitted to another operation, they were married by the chaplain. The arm was removed to the shoulder. For a day or two there was hope of him, and then he sank rapidly.

I entered the ward about two hours before his death, and found his three days' bride ministering to him with inexpressible tenderness. There were no tears on her cheek, no lamentations on her lip, but her face shone with unnatural brightness, and she seemed to be lifted above the depression of her surroundings. Mrs. —— and myself were about to pass them by, not thinking best to intrude on the sacredness of their privacy or sorrow. But the look in the husband's eyes invited us, and we moved softly towards the couch of death. He was conscious and understood what was said, but could only speak in occasional whispers.

"You are ready to go?" asked Mrs. ——, my hostess, who had seen much of him, and whom he welcomed with a smile.

For answer, he looked at his young wife, who was gazing in his face. She understood him, and answered:

"Yes, we are both ready — he, to go, and I, to stay." And, turning to us, she added, "When he enlisted, I gave him to God and the country. I expected this, and am prepared for it."

The next morning I met her embarking for home with the body of her beloved. Her own relatives were a married sister, and a brother in the Army of the Potomac. She was taking the coffined remains to the widowed mother of the dead man, who lived near Centralia, Ill., and who had two other sons in the army, and a son-in-law. The exaltation of her spirit still upbore her, and I saw that nature would not assert itself till her duties to the dead were over.

# CHAPTER VIII.

I BECOME ACCUSTOMED TO HOSPITAL WORK — FILTH AND
DISCOMFORT, NEGLECT AND SUFFERING — LEAVES FROM
MY EXPERIENCE — MESSAGES FROM THE DYING TO LOVED
ONES AT HOME.

Cairo an immense Basin, partially filled — Skilful Pilotage needed — Comfortless Hospitals — "My Wife came this Morning" — "Bring me a
drink from the Spring" — The "Brick Hospital" a Marvel of Excellence — "Sisters of the Holy Cross" its Nurses — The young rebel
Prisoner — Longing for his Mother — "Philip Sidneys" in every Hospital — Mary Safford my Companion the second Time — Her Method of
Work — Her Memorandum Book and Baskets — Something for every
one — "You are the good Fairy of the Hospitals" — Men crying for Milk
— Mourning the Loss of "Mother Bickerdyke" — Wounded Soldier from
"Island No. Ten" — Noble Letter from his Wife — "The Children needed
him more than I" — Eulogy of Mary Safford — Her Career since the
War — Professor in the Boston University School of Medicine.

ROM St. Louis we went to Cairo, Ill., where
were other hospitals overflowing with the
sick and wounded. It was by no means a
lovely place at that time. Every one visiting it bestowed on it a passing anathema.
A levee built up around the south and west
protected it from the overflow of the Mississippi
and Ohio. From the levee the town looked like an
immense basin, of which the levee formed the sides
and rim. It was partially filled with water; and the
incessant activity of the steam-pumps alone saved it
from inundation. Vile odors assailed the olfactories,
as one walked the streets. If it chanced to rain, one

was in a condition to obey the New Testament injunction, to "be steadfast and immovable"; for the glutinous, tenacious mud held one by both feet, making locomotion anything but agreeable. How to find my way to any given point was a problem; for the paths were fearfully circuitous, and skilful pilotage was necessary.

Go where I would, this was "the order of exercises." I went down a flight of crazy stairs, across a bit of plank walk, around a slough of unknown depth, behind somebody's barn, across somebody's back yard, over an extempore bridge of scantling that bent with my weight, then into mud, at the risk of losing rubbers, boots, and I sometimes feared for my feet, and, at last, ferried over a miniature lake in a skiff, I reached my destination. "Living in Cairo converts us soldiers into sailors," said the soldier who rowed me from the "Brick Hospital." "Yes," said another, "the children born in this town are web-footed." They certainly ought to be.

My object in visiting Cairo was to see the hospitals — not the town. I first visited the regimental hospitals, never very attractive institutions. There were some half-dozen of them, established in small dwelling-houses, carriage-houses, sheds, or other accessible places. Were I to describe them as I saw them, the account would be discredited. Compressed within their narrow limits were more filth and discomfort, neglect and suffering, than would have sufficed to defile and demoralize ten times as much space. The fetid odor of typhoid fever, erysipelas, dysentery, measles, and healing wounds, was rendered more nauseating by unclean beds and unwashed bodies; while from the kitchen, which

opened into the hospital wards, came the smell of
boiling meat and coffee, befouling still more the air
of the unventilated apartments.

The nurses were convalescent soldiers, wan, thin,
weak, and requiring nursing themselves; and, though
they were kind to their comrades, they were wholly
worthless as nurses. I saw no signs of a surgeon in
these poor hospitals, although the patients told me a
doctor had visited them one, two, or three days before, the statements varying in the different hospitals. Nor were there any signs of woman's presence, save in one instance, where a poor fellow, with
mingled tears and laughter, told me that "his wife
had come that morning, and now he believed he
*should* get well, although the night before he had
utterly given up hope."

And, to be sure, I soon met his wife — a cheery,
active little woman, under whose vigorous sweeping,
and scrubbing, and purifying, a dingy corner chamber
was growing sweet and clean. And when she
opened her trunk for my inspection, and showed the
coarse, but clean sheets, shirts, drawers, and socks,
she had brought, with "a new horse blanket for a
rug, when *he* put his feet on the floor," I could easily
believe her assurance that, "with the cleanliness, and
the sun shining through the clear window-panes, and
her to make his tea and gruel, he'd a'most think himself at home in a day or two."

It gave me the heartache to see the patient sufferers in these hospitals, for they seemed left to their
fate. They were very young, homesick, and ready
to break down into a flood of weeping at the first
word of sympathy. The sick men were always more
despondent than those who were wounded. For

under the wasting of camp diseases they became mentally as weak as children; while the men wounded in battle were heroes, and were toned up to fortitude. One fine fellow, not yet twenty, was raving in the delirium of brain fever. He fancied himself at home with his mother, to whom he incessantly appealed for " a drink of water right from the spring at the back of the house, the coldest and clearest in all Illinois."

He was sponged with tepid water, his tangled hair smoothed, his burning head bathed, and his stiff, filthy clothing changed for clean garments from the depot of the Chicago Sanitary Commission located in the town. He dropped off into a quiet sleep immediately, which lasted for several hours. Similar beneficial results followed similar small ministrations in all these wretched hospitals. Residents of Cairo were so tortured with the neglect and suffering of these hospitals that they were finally broken up, at their instance, and the patients transferred to the excellent " General Hospitals." The men always rebelled at being sent away from their regiments, and preferred to risk the chances of suffering and neglect with their comrades to any promise of better care, and wiser nursing, separated from them.

There was one General Hospital in Cairo, called by the people the " Brick Hospital." Here the " Sisters of the Holy Cross " were employed as nurses, one or more to each ward. Here were order, comfort, cleanliness, and good nursing. The food was cooked in a kitchen outside the hospital. Surgeons were detailed to every ward, who visited their patients twice daily, and more frequently if necessary. The apothecary's room was supplied with an ample store of medicines and surgical appliances, and the store-room possessed an abundance of clothing and delicacies for the sick.

It was a sad sight to pass through the wards and see row after row of narrow beds, with white, worn, still faces pressed against the white pillows. And it gave one a heartache to take each man by the hand, and listen to his simple story, and to hear his anxieties for wife and children, of whom he received no tidings, or for the dear mother, whom he could hardly name without tears.

A young man from West Virginia, a rebel prisoner, must have possessed the highest type of manly beauty, in health. He was battling for life, for he hoped to see his mother once more, who was on her way to him. There was something very winning in the lad's manner and spirit; and surgeons, nurses, and sick comrades, were deeply interested in him. Oh, how he longed for his mother's presence! "*Do* you really believe she will get here before I die?" he inquired anxiously, giving the date of her leaving home and her distance from him. I sought to buoy up his sinking spirits, and, sitting beside him, talked to him as if he were my own son. "If I had been home in Western Virginia I shouldn't have got into this hospital. My mother is a Union woman; but my uncle in Tennessee, for whom I was clerking, was a secessionist, and I had to go into the Confederate service."

In every ward the men greeted me gladly. They stretched out their hands to take mine; they talked freely of their homes, their friends, and regiments. Over and over again, with indescribable pathos, I was told by the poor fellows: "I've got a good mother at home, one of the best of mothers. She'd

come to me if she knew I was in the hospital; but I
dont want to worry her, and I'll write her when I get
well." The Christ-like patience of the men surprised
me. I had been accustomed, as are most women, to
think men more impatient in sickness, more exacting,
and less manageable than women. But this was not
true of these soldiers in hospital. They complained
little, endured much, were grateful for the least kindness, and as a rule were very unselfish. There were
Philip Sidneys in every hospital, who refused comforts and ministrations offered them, in behalf of
some more suffering comrade.

My second visit to the Cairo hospitals, was made
in company with Miss Mary Safford, then a resident
of Cairo. She commenced her labors immediately
when Cairo was occupied by our troops. If she was
not the first woman in the country to enter upon hospital and camp relief, she was certainly the first in
the West. There was no system, no organization,
no knowledge what to do, and no means with which
to work. As far as possible she brought order out
of chaos, systematized the first rude hospitals, and
with her own means, aided by a wealthy brother, furnished necessaries, when they could be obtained in
no other way.

Surgeons and officers everywhere opposed her,
but she disarmed them by the sweetness of her manner and her speech; and she did what she pleased.
She was very frail, *petite* in figure as a girl of twelve
summers, and utterly unaccustomed to hardship.
She threw herself into hospital work with such energy, and forgetfulness of self, that she broke down
utterly before the end of the second year of the war.
Had not her friends sent her out of the country, till

the war was over, she would have fallen a martyr to her patriotic devotion. She was in a Paris hospital for months, under the care of the most eminent surgeons of the world, receiving surgical treatment for injuries incurred in those two years of over-work.

Every sick and wounded soldier in Cairo, or on the hospital boats, at the time of my visit, knew her and loved her. With a memorandum book in one hand, and a large basket of delicacies in the other, while a porter followed with a still larger basket, we entered the wards. They had a vastly more comfortable appearance than on the occasion of my first visit. The vigorous complaints entered against them, and, more than all, a realistic description of them that found its way into the Chicago papers, had wrought reforms. The baskets were packed with articles of sick-diet, prepared by Miss Safford and labelled with the name of the hospital and number of the ward and bed.

The effect of her presence was magical. It was like a breath of spring borne into the bare, whitewashed rooms — like a burst of sunlight. Every face brightened, and every man who was able, half raised himself from his bed or chair, as in homage, or expectation. It would be difficult to imagine a more cheery vision than her kindly presence, or a sweeter sound than her educated, tender voice, as she moved from bed to bed, speaking to each one. Now she addressed one in German, a blue-eyed boy from Holland — and then she chattered in French to another, made superlatively happy by being addressed in his native tongue.

The baskets were unpacked. One received the plain rice pudding which the surgeon had allowed;

there was currant jelly for an acid drink, for the
fevered thirst of another ; a bit of nicely broiled
salt codfish for a third; plain molasses gingerbread
for a fourth; a cup of boiled custard for a fifth;
half a dozen delicious soda crackers for a sixth ;
"gum-drops" for the irritating cough of a seventh;
baked apples for an eighth; cans of oysters to be
divided among several, and so on, as each one's
appetite or caprice had suggested.  One man wished
to make horse-nets, while his amputated limb was
healing, and she had brought him the materials.
Another had informed her of his skill in wood-carving, but he had no tools to work with, and she had
brought them in the basket.

From the same capacious depths she drew forth
paper, envelopes, postage stamps, pencils, ink, Atlantic Monthlies, Chicago Tribunes, checkers and a
folding checker-board, a jack-knife, needles, thread,
scissors, buttons, music books, for the musically inclined, of whom there were many in every hospital;
a "waxed end" and a shoemaker's awl, for one to
sew up rents in his boots; knitting-needles and red
yarn, for one who wished to knit his boy some
"reins" for play, — every promise was remembered
by Miss Safford.

"Oh, Miss Safford!" said one bright young fellow, "you are the good fairy of this hospital! Can't
you bring me the invisible seven-leagued boots when
you come again, so that I can just step into Milwaukee and see what a certain little woman and her
baby are doing, in whom I am interested?"

One hospital thoroughly visited, Miss Safford departed, leaving it full of sunshine, despite its rude-
ness and discomforts, and hastened home, rejoining

me in a short time in "Hospital No 2," with a fresh instalment of baskets and goodies — and so on through the whole number. The visiting done for that day, she hurried home with her filled memorandum book, in which had been noted the wants and wishes for the next day, and began anew the marketing, purchasing, cooking, packing, and arranging. Was it wonderful the delicate little woman broke down, almost hopelessly, at the end of two years?

In one ward, two men were weeping bitterly; and when she inquired the cause, it appeared that the surgeon had given them permission to drink a tumbler of milk, night and morning. But the hospital funds were lacking for its purchase, and "French Maria," the milk-woman, who had just passed through the ward, had refused to let them have it on credit. This was too much for the fortitude of the feeble sufferers, and they were weeping like children. Miss Safford hurried out, and, recalling the milkmaiden, obtained the milk for the day, directing her to leave the same quantity every day, and come to her for payment. In another hospital, the men were all in the dumps. Every one looked sad. "What has happened?" inquired Miss Safford. "Mother Bickerdyke went down the river this morning, and we shall all die now," was the disconsolate answer. No wonder they mourned the loss of "Mother Bickerdyke," who more than any other person, in the beginning, assisted in the regeneration of the badly managed hospitals of Cairo.

As we were making the tour of the hospitals, a tall and stalwart man was brought in on a stretcher, who had been shot the night before on one of the gunboats stationed at Island Number Ten. It was not a dangerous wound apparently — only a little hole in the left side, that I could more than cover with the tip of my smallest finger — but the grand-looking man was dying.

"Can we do anything for you?" one of us inquired, after the surgeon had examined him, and he had been placed in bed.

"Too late! too late!" was his only reply, slightly shaking his head.

"Have you no friends to whom you wish me to write?"

He drew from an inside vest pocket — for his clothing was not removed — a letter, enclosing a photograph of a most lovely woman. "You wish me to write to the person who has sent you this letter?"

He nodded slightly, and feebly whispered, "My wife."

Bowing her head, and folding her hands, Miss Safford offered a brief touching prayer in behalf of the dying man, bending low over him that he might hear her softly spoken words. Her voice faltered a little, as she remembered in her prayer the far-absent wife, so near bereavement: "Amen!" responded the dying man, in a distinct voice, and then we left him with the attendant, to minister to others. Lifting the photograph, he gazed at it earnestly for a few moments, pressed it to his lips, and then clasped it in both hands. When I returned to his bed, some twenty minutes later, he was still looking upward, his hands still clasping the photograph, and his face was irradiated with the most heavenly smile I have ever seen on any face. I spoke to him, but he seemed not to hear, and there was a far-away look in the gaze, as though his vision reached beyond my ken.

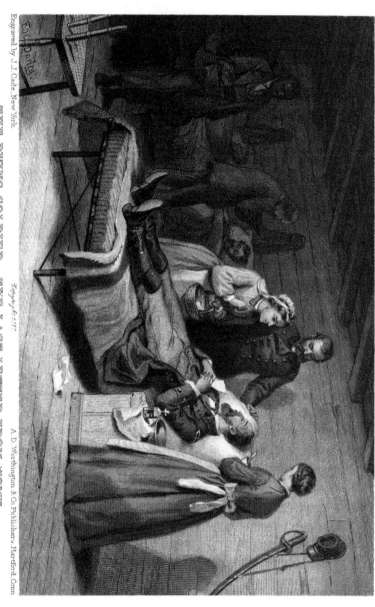

Engraved by J.J. Cade, New York.

Copyright 1837.

A. D. Worthington & Co. Publishers, Hartford, Conn.

# THE DYING SOLDIER.—THE LAST LETTER FROM HOME.

"He drew from an inside pocket a letter inclosing a photograph of a most lovely woman, and feebly whispered, "My wife."
I spoke to him but he seemed, not to hear; and there was a far-away look in the gaze, as if his vision reached beyond my
ken. The wardmaster approached, and laid his finger on the wrist. 'He is dead!' he whispered."

I stood still, awestruck. The wardmaster approached, and laid his finger on the wrist. "He is dead!" he whispered.

The duty of writing the widowed wife was assigned me, and I took the letter and photograph. Ah, what a letter was that which the dying man had placed in my hands! He had evidently not replied to it, for it had been only just received, and had not the worn look of having been carried long in the pocket. It was from his wife, informing her husband of the death, on the same day, of their two children, three and five years old. It was the letter of a superior woman, who wrote nobly and tenderly, hiding her own grief, in her desire to comfort her husband.

"I do not feel that we have lost our children," thus she wrote; "they are ours still, and will be ours forever. Their brief life was all sunshine, and by their early departure they are spared all experience of sorrow and wrong. They can never know the keen heartache that you and I must suffer at their loss. It *must* be well with them. Their change of being must be an advance, a continuance of existence on a higher plane. And some time, my dear Harry, we shall rejoin them. I sometimes fear, my darling, that you may meet them before I shall. Their death has taken from me all the fear of dying, which, you know, has so greatly distressed me. I can never fear to follow where my children have led. I have an interest in that other life, whatever it may be, an attraction towards it, of which I knew nothing before. Oh, my dear Harry, do not mourn too much! I wish I were with you, to share with you, not alone my hope, but the great conceptions of that other life which have come to me."

I enclosed to the bereaved wife her own letter and photograph taken from the dead hands of her husband, and told her all I knew of his death. A correspondence ensued, which stretched itself along the next three years. In the depth of her triple bereavement, the saddened woman found comfort in the belief that her children and husband were united. "I sometimes believe the children needed him more than I," was her frequent assertion.

While writing of Miss Safford, let me add the testimony of one of the captains of the Fifty-Seventh Illinois Volunteers, which regiment was badly cut up, a few days later, at the battle of Shiloh.

"God bless Mary Safford!" he writes. "She saved my life. When I was wounded at Shiloh I was carried on board the hospital boat, where she was in attendance. My wound got to bleeding, and, though I was faint from loss of blood, I did not know what was the matter. She found it out, for she slipped in a pool of blood beside my bed, and called a surgeon to me, just in time to save my life. Gracious! how that little woman worked! She was everywhere, doing everything, straightening out affairs, soothing and comforting, and sometimes praying, dressing wounds, cooking and nursing, and keeping the laggards at their work. For herself, she seemed to live on air.

"And she had grit, too, I tell you. They brought Sam Houston's son aboard, wounded, a rebel officer, wearing the Confederate uniform, and ordered one of the privates removed from a comfortable berth he had, to make room for this young traitor. You should have seen Miss Safford! She straightened up, as if she were ten feet tall, and declared, in a grand way, that 'the humblest Union soldier should not be removed to make room for a rebel officer, not if that officer were General Lee himself!' She stood by the berth, and looked so resolute that they were glad to find another berth for Sam Houston's son. I do not wonder that all the boys called her 'the Cairo angel!' She did as she pleased everywhere, and the biggest sort of men obeyed her. She was the only one that seemed to know what to do on that boat."

Many another Union soldier in the West owes his life to Mary Safford, and is proud to acknowledge it. After the battle of Belmont, she was the first to go on the field, in the face of the enemy's guns, which ploughed the ground around her with their plunging shot. Tying her handkerchief to a stick, she waved it above her head, as a flag of truce, and continued her ministrations to the wounded, whose sufferings were aggravated by a keen wintry wind sweeping over them. When war broke out in Italy, she was in Florence, and, at the invitation of Madame Mario, immediately joined the Italian ladies in their preparations for sick and wounded soldiers. So ingrained is her inclination to help the needy, that in Norway, Switzerland, and Germany, I heard of her devising ways and means for the assistance of poor girls who desired to emigrate to America, where they could find employment, and had relatives.

Her experiences during the war undoubtedly decided her future career. Returning from Europe with improved health, she determined to fit herself for medical practice. Graduating from a medical college in the city of New York, she returned to Europe, enlarging her knowledge in studies at Zurich and Vienna, where she had especial advantages in clinics. She is to-day one of the Professors in the Boston University School of Medicine, where she takes high rank as lecturer, physician, and surgeon. Her home life is as charming as though she were not a professional woman. Her residence is in a delightful part of the city of Boston, where she passes the brief leisure of her busy life, with the children of her love and adoption. But neither the charm of her home and family, nor her literary and professional labors, render her oblivious to the demands of the poor and friendless, who are sure to find in her "a present help in time of trouble." She listens patiently and tenderly to all who need her assistance, and the humblest have reason to bless God for the life of this grand, good woman.

# CHAPTER IX.

AWAITING THE BATTLE OF SHILOH — PREPARATIONS FOR THE WOUNDED — AWFUL SLAUGHTER — VARIED PHASES OF HOSPITAL LIFE — "MISSING."

A Perfect Military Hospital — "Mother Angela," the Lady "Supérieure" — " White-winged Sun-bonnets " —Battle of Shiloh — Appalling Slaughter on Both Sides — Rebel Prisoners' Ward — "You-uns is very good to we-uns!" — The Rebel Surgeon's Fear — Meet an Old Acquaintance among the Rebel Wounded — The Valiant Eleventh Illinois — Great Prejudice against Protestant Nurses — The " Sisters " preferred —" They never see anything, nor hear anything, and tell no Tales! "—Good General Strong, Post Commander at Cairo — Am sent to St. Louis for Invalid Soldiers — Turner's "Descriptive List" Missing — Found in the Clerk's Office — General Curtis discharges him — He also Furloughs young Brackett — Great Jollification in the Ward — They accompany me to Chicago.

ROM Cairo we proceeded to Mound City, Paducah, Bird's Point, and other places where hospitals were established. Except in Mound City, everything was in a chaotic condition, compared with the completer arrangements afterwards made. The hospital at Mound City occupied a block of brick stores, built before the war, to accommodate the prospective commerce of the town. They had not been occupied, and, as the blockade of the Mississippi rendered it uncertain when they would be needed for their legitimate use, they were turned over to the Medical Department for hospital use. At the time of my

visit, the Mound City Hospital was considered the
best military hospital in the United States. This
was due to the administrative talent of Dr. E. S.
Franklin, of Dubuque, Iowa, who, despite paucity of
means and material, transformed the rough block of
stores into a superb hospital accommodating one
thousand patients. Fifteen hundred had been
crowded into it by dint of close packing.

The most thorough system was maintained in every
department. There were an exact time and place for
everything. Every person was assigned to a particular department of work, and held responsible for
its perfect performance. If any one proved a shirk,
incompetent, or insubordinate, he was sent off on the
next boat. A Shaker-like cleanliness and sweetness
of atmosphere pervaded the various wards, the sheets
and pillows were of immaculate whiteness, and the
patients who were convalescing were cheerful and
contented. The "Sisters of the Holy Cross" were
employed as nurses, and by their skill, quietness,
gentleness, and tenderness, were invaluable in the
sick-wards. Every patient gave hearty testimony to
the kindness and skill of the "Sisters."

"Mother Angela" was the matron, the "*Supérieure*," of these "Sisters"—a gifted lady, of rare cultivation and executive ability, with winning sweetness of manner. She was a member of the Ewing
family, and a cousin of Mrs. and General Sherman.
The "Sisters" had nearly broken up their famous
schools at South Bend, Ind., to answer the demand
for nurses. If I had ever felt prejudice against these
"Sisters" as nurses, my experience with them during
the war would have dissipated it entirely. The
world has known no nobler and no more heroic

women than those found in the ranks of the Catholic Sisterhoods. But I often sympathized with some of the sick men, who frequently expressed a wish for a reform in the "headgear" of the "Sisters." "Why can't they take off those white-winged sun-bonnets in the ward?" asked one. "Sun-bonnets!" sneered another of the irreverent critics; "they're a cross between a white sun-bonnet and a broken-down umbrella; and there's no name that describes them."

It was very evident from preparations that another great battle was impending. Indeed, the surgeons admitted this. During the previous week the hospital beds had been emptied of all who were well enough to be furloughed, or sent back to their regiments. Over six hundred beds were awaiting occupancy by the wounded of the next battle, and another hospital was being fitted up rapidly with accommodations for five hundred more. Orders had been received at the rooms of the Commission in Cairo for supplies to be in readiness for twenty thousand wounded men; and shipments of battle-relief stores were arriving from Chicago in unprecedented quantities.

The battle came off at Shiloh before I reached home. The enemy, seventy thousand strong, swept down on the Union forces, greatly inferior in numbers, in an unbroken, overwhelming rush. It surprised them, and put them to flight like a flock of sheep, before they had time to form in line of battle. General Grant was at Savannah, several miles down the Tennessee river, when the fight began. But General Johnston, Commander of the rebel forces, was on the field, directing the movements of his army, and hurling it against the flying and disorderly

masses of the North.   Step by step, the Union army
was driven towards the river; and General Beaure-
gard's promise to " drive the whole Northern army
into the Tennessee " seemed sure of fulfilment.   The
close of the first day's conflict, a balmy, beautiful
Sunday in April, found the Union forces broken, despondent, and exhausted; while the enemy were
confident, and waited for the morning to complete
their triumph.

The next day, with General Grant in command, our
men retrieved their losses of the day before.   Guns
were recaptured, lost ground was won again, and the
batteries of the enemy, wrested from their possession, were turned on them with murderous fire.
Contesting the ground, inch by inch, fighting valiantly and with desperation, the enemy were driven
from the field, and moved off towards Corinth, where
the next struggle was to be made for possession of
the valley of the Mississippi.   The close of the
second day reversed the decision of the day before,
and the costly victory remained with our troops.
Ten thousand dead lay on the field, " the blue " and
" the gray " sleeping together, for the enemy had left
their dead for our men to bury.   Among them lay
dead horses in harness, broken caissons, abandoned
blankets and muskets, scattered drums and haversacks.   Trees, whose branches had been wrenched
off by bursting shells, looked as if Titans had been
hurling thunderbolts among them.   The air was
heavy with the sulphurous breath of gunpowder, and
tainted with the smell of blood.

The loss on each side was fourteen thousand in
killed, wounded, and missing, — a mighty slaughter,
and an appalling amount of suffering, for which no

adequate preparation could be made. All the means of relief of the Northwest were called into active service, and yet there were unavoidable neglect and suffering. Following so quickly on the carnage of Donelson, there was scarcely a hamlet in the whole Northwest that was not in mourning for its dead. And the notes of rejoicing for the severely won victory were mingled with the sound of the tolling bell, and muffled drum, heard everywhere.

I hastened to Chicago to assist in the work which the battle of Shiloh precipitated on the Commission. But I remained at Mound City long enough to visit every ward of the hospitals, and to converse with every patient. Without an exception, all testified to the excellence of the care they received, and to the kindness of their treatment. One ward was devoted entirely to wounded rebel prisoners, taken at Fort Donelson. Most of them were unlettered farmers' sons, innocent even of the alphabet. Their speech was almost unintelligible at times; for they talked a *patois*, made up in part of negro gibberish and in part of barbarous English.

" You-uns is very good to we-uns," said one of the convalescents, clad in a uniform of butternut jean. " How much furderer Norf do you-uns come from? "

" 'Spect I've got to tote a crutch round in ole Mississip' the balance o' my life,—*I* do," said another, *àpropos* to nothing.

" This 'ere grub's better'n th' ole woman's bacon and hominy," was the eulogium of a third, as he tasted his soup.

Two of the boys, who were superior to the others in bearing and intelligence, were but sixteen and eighteen years of age. They were from Mississippi.

Each had a fearfully crushed and mutilated leg.
Dr. Franklin had saved both from amputation, and
had patched and pieced and fitted together the
broken bones, and torn ligaments, as one would
mend a damaged specimen of bric-à-brac or rare
china. The boys were very grateful, and delighted
to recount, to any who would listen, the story of Dr.
Franklin's skill. Although the lads were more
intelligent than their comrades, they had no adequate conception of the magnitude of the war, nor
of the circumstances that led to it. They drifted
along with the current, and enlisted because the
rest did.

Dr. Hall, the surgeon of their regiment, had
allowed himself to be captured that he might take
care of "the boys." He frankly confessed that he
never imagined rebel prisoners would fare as well
as our own wounded men, and "he feared things
might be different in a reverse of circumstances."
Ah, the poor fellows in Libby Prison and at
Andersonville "found things" very "different!"
Dr. Hall was from Mississippi, a gentlemanly and
cultivated man. He declared himself opposed to secession in the abstract, and sought to hinder his state
from rushing out of the federal compact, "but when
Mississippi went out of the Union, honor compelled
him to go with her." He spoke mournfully of this
fratricidal war, but avowed himself ready to fight
for the South as long as the war lasted.

A young captain, wearing the Confederate gray,
kept his dark eyes upon me, following me, as I went
hither and thither, with intense scrutiny. Wondering why I was an object of interest, I commenced a
conversation with him.

"I have met you before," he said, after a little preliminary conversation. "You do not remember me? It is not strange," he continued, "for it is twenty years since I saw you on St. Leon plantation, in Mecklenburg county, Va., and then I was a boy ten years old." He had enlisted in Mississippi, as had most of the men in the ward. I recalled him as a bright little playmate of one of my pupils in southern Virginia, whose home was on a neighboring plantation. He was a rabid secessionist, and did not hesitate to avow his convictions in the most defiant manner.

Two boys belonging to the valiant Eleventh Illinois were in another ward, still suffering from the terrible wounds of the Fort Donelson battle. There were eighty-five in their company when they went into battle, but only seven came out alive and unharmed. They were shot down the day before the surrender, having been beaten back nearly two miles, fighting all the way, and were thought to be mortally wounded. Their uniforms, new the day before the battle, were stripped off by their inhuman enemies, whom they saw pillaging, and plundering the dead and dying. Nearly naked, the poor fellows managed to creep under both their blankets, lying as closely as possible to each other for warmth, and in this way lay neglected for forty-eight hours.

"What will you do when you get well?" I inquired.

"*Going back to our regiment to fight!*" was the plucky answer. "Hiram and I went in for three years, but I think we'll stay through the war. We've got an account to settle with these rebs now. We sha'n't forget in a hurry how the Eleventh Illi-

nois was cut up at Donelson." Never were there
greater loyalty and bravery than were shown by our
young soldiers. It was to me a perpetual wonder,
while their Titanic endurance of suffering compelled
my admiration.

I found everywhere, at this time, the greatest
prejudice against Protestant women nurses. Medical directors, surgeons, and even wardmasters, openly
declared they would not have them in the service,
and that only the "Sisters" of the Catholic Church
should receive appointments. I sought for the cause
of this decision. "Your Protestant nurses are
always finding some mare's-nest or other," said one
of the surgeons, "that they can't let alone. They
all write for the papers, and the story finds its way
into print, and directly we are in hot water. Now,
the 'Sisters' never see anything they ought not to
see, nor hear anything they ought not to hear, and
they never write for the papers — and the result
is we get along very comfortably with them." It
was futile to combat their prejudices, or to attempt
to show them that they lacked the power to enforce
their decisions. I contented myself with declining
to take any part in filling the hospitals and boats
with Catholic Sisters, as I was entreated, nor would
I consent to do anything to discourage the detail-
ing of Protestant nurses.

On my way home, I met at Centralia more than a
dozen Protestant nurses, *en route* for the hospitals.
They were women of nearly middle age, serious,
practical women, sensibly dressed, with no other
baggage than a necessary change of clothing in a
valise. All were women of experience, had been
carefully examined and properly detailed. They

bore with them letters of recommendation, and written assignments to their respective posts, signed in due form by Dorothea Dix, who was authorized to detail women nurses by the Secretary of War.

I told them the little chance they had for employment, and assured them they would be unwelcome, and would undoubtedly be sent back. They listened as though they heard not.

"Our husbands, sons, and brothers need us, and want us, if the surgeons do not. If we are sent from one post, we shall go to another. And if the medical authorities are determined to employ Catholic Sisters, to the exclusion of Protestant nurses, we shall appeal to the Secretary of War."

The Protestant nurses carried the day, chiefly because of their good sense and worth, and hundreds went to the front before the end of the war, welcomed by both surgeons and patients, and rendering invaluable service.

General Strong was the post commander at Cairo, and I met him there, when returning home. I shall always retain a tender memory of him, for, though not a man of military genius, he sympathized with the soldiers, whether in the field, in camp, or in hospital. I was indebted to him for many favors, which he granted for the sake of humanity — for the sympathy he felt for suffering everywhere. The last time I met him was at St. Louis, about eighteen months before the close of the war, when he gave me his always ready help, and saved at that time the life of one of our Chicago boys.

Among the thirty-four young men who enlisted on the same day from the "Church of the Redeemer," in Chicago, was one, a universal favorite, who should have been rejected because of physical disability, but whose patriotism and ambition would not allow him to remain behind, when his companions enlisted. They all went into the Chicago Mercantile Battery. After many ups and downs, and much hard service, he broke down utterly, and was sent with a sick comrade to the "House of Refuge Hospital" in St. Louis. He could never again be well, sank rapidly, and was certain to die soon in the hospital, if not discharged and sent home. This was the message that came to his friends and acquaintances — and everybody loved him. Immediate steps were taken to procure his discharge from the service, and his return to his home.

Three or four gentlemen of standing went to St. Louis, one after another, but though it was conceded by all the medical authorities that young Turner ought to be discharged on account of hopeless invalidism, each in turn came back without him. There was something wrong with his papers, that forbade his release, and as an order had just been issued forbidding furloughs, they were unable to take him to his home, that he might have the privilege of dying with his kindred. Finally, I was besought to undertake his discharge, and though it seemed absurd for me to attempt what three or four influential men had failed to accomplish, the intercession in his behalf was so urgent, and my own interest in him so tender, that I went on the errand, although hopeless of success.

The hindrance to the discharge of the young man was occasioned by the loss of his "descriptive list." An order had been sent to his command for another, but as the battery was in the field, moving from place to place, it might be months before the order was answered. Young Turner denied the truth of this statement, as did Brackett, his sick comrade, and both declared the surgeon mistaken. They were young men of great intelligence and business training, and not likely to be in the wrong. They belonged in the same battery, had come together to the same hospital, were located in adjoining beds in the same ward, and asserted, again and again, that they surrendered their descriptive lists to the hospital clerk at the same time.

I was confident, from my long acquaintance with both, that they were correct, and that Turner's missing list must be found, if at all, in the hospital office. So I returned to the surgeon, and told my story, and expressed my belief that the lost list was somewhere in the office. The face of the young clerk flushed a little with annoyance, but he politely drew from a pigeonhole the lists of " Ward D," filed alphabetically, and, standing beside me, began to turn them over, while I read aloud the name endorsed on the back of each.

" Stop! " I cried, as a familiar name met my eye.

" No," said the clerk, " that name has cheated all Turner's friends who have been down here. His name is *Lowell* D. Turner, and this, you see, is *Loring* D. Turner."

" Open it; let's see the inside." He did, and there the name was correctly written, but inaccurately engrossed on the back. This was the long-looked-for list. I had had just such an experience before.

It was plain sailing now. The surgeon made out the certificate of disability, and sent a military messenger with me to the medical director. He promptly wrote an order for the discharge papers, which the messenger boy received, and then he and I moved on to the headquarters of the Department, where they were to be filled out, and the work would be done. There I was halted. A pert little lieutenant, who sat smoking in the office, with his heels higher than his head, fell back on his dignity and "red tape," and declared these papers could not be made out in precedence of others, which it would take two weeks to dispose of, unless General Curtis, now the Commander of the Department, gave an order for them to receive immediate attention. And with evident satisfaction he informed me that General Curtis was holding a meeting with his staff officers, and had given positive orders not to admit any one to his room until four in the afternoon. All the time, I knew that the bribe of a dollar would remove the scruples of the lieutenant, and procure for me the rapid filling out of my papers. I had had previous experience in this line also.

I went out of the room, into the hall, and was standing still, trying to think what next to do, when General Strong happened to pass. He immediately came to me with extended hands, and beaming face, with his oft-asked question on his lips,—

"My dear madam, what can I do for you?"

"General Strong, if you can obtain me an interview of five minutes with General Curtis, you will make me the most grateful woman in St. Louis."

"Come with me!" Up stairs, and down stairs, and through almost interminable halls,. he led the way, and I followed. Every guard saluted him courteously, and allowed us to pass, until we reached General Curtis' room. A word of explanation to the guard, and he opened the door, when General Strong led me in, where General Curtis was sitting in solemn conclave with the officers of his staff. I had met the General in Helena, Ark.; and to my great relief he remembered me, and rose to meet me, calling me by name. I made known my errand, and obtained a written permission from him to take poor Turner to Chicago that afternoon.

"Can I do anything more for you?" asked the General, so kindly that I ventured to ask a fifteen days' furlough for Brackett, the sick comrade, whose family also lived in Chicago, promising to take charge of both, and to see them safely delivered to their kindred. Happy woman was I, for that, too, was granted, and the furlough was placed in my hands.

"General Strong, you can never measure the good you have done!" I said to him, when we were outside General Curtis' room. "You have probably saved the life of a noble young fellow, and have made two households happy, by the great favor you have granted me."

"*I* am very happy, madam, to have served them and you. It will be something pleasant for me to remember on my death-bed." A very brief time afterwards, the good man came to his death-bed. If the memory of his humanities did not then lighten the dark valley, he surely heard the One Voice welcoming him to heaven — "Enter thou into the joy of thy Lord!"

I hurried back to "Ward D," in the "House of Refuge Hospital," at some distance from the heart of the city. It was past noon and the train left for Chicago at three o'clock. As I opened the door of the ward, every soldier who was sitting up looked at me scrutinizingly. They all knew my errand; all had come to love young Turner, and had buoyed him up, during my absence, with the prediction that he would certainly see his friends the next morning.

"Oh, I'm afraid you haven't got Lowell's discharge!" said young Brackett, at his usual post beside Turner, who sat propped in bed; "you look dreadful glum!"

"You know I told you not to indulge in any expectations of my success."

Poor Turner gasped, turned a deadlier white, and would have fallen over had I not caught him. "My dear boy, don't do so silly a thing as to faint — you are no longer a soldier! You are to go to Chicago with me this afternoon, and here is General Curtis' order. Your discharge papers and back pay will be sent to you!"

"Bully for you, Turner!" was the first unconventional congratulation from a neighboring bed, and in a moment there was a tempest of cheers and rejoicing surging about Turner's cot. Brackett was quiet, but very tender towards his feeble comrade, congratulating him with eyes full of tears.

"General Curtis was so kind as to grant you a furlough of fifteen days, Brackett: do you want to spend your time in St. Louis, or in Chicago? I have transportation for you, if you want to go."

*Now*, there was a commotion in the ward. Most of the men were convalescent, and in good spirits. Brackett looked at me as one dazed for a moment, and then threw his arms around my neck and kissed me, as if I were his mother. Two or three of the men turned somersaults on their beds — another called for three cheers, for me, General Curtis, and Turner, and Brackett. And half a dozen organized themselves into a band, and promenaded the ward, one playing a bugle, another a bagpipe, another a double bass drum, another a flute, all in admirable pantomime, and in mimicry of the tones of the various instruments.

The excitement was too much for Turner. He fainted several times before we left St. Louis, and I watched him through the night in the sleeping-car, hardly expecting he would live, to reach his friends. But he did, and was nursed by them into such tolerable health, that, after two years' residence in the Minnesota pineries, he ventured to propose to the girl whom he had long loved, and they were married. Ten years of blissful wedded life were theirs, when he succumbed to the pulmonary trouble which had so long menaced him — and his young wife followed him, two years later, dying of the same disease.

# CHAPTER X.

THE DARKEST PERIOD OF THE WAR — MY VISIT TO WASH-
INGTON IN 1862 — STRANGE EXPERIENCES ON THE JOUR-
NEY — PITIFUL SCENES IN A CONVALESCENT CAMP.

Woman's Council called in Washington — Mrs. Hoge and myself the Chicago
Delegates — Darkest Period of the War — Am detained at Suspension
Bridge — A Restless Crowd in the Waiting-room — A blind Vocalist
Charms them to Quietness — Homeward-bound Invalid Soldiers on the
Trains — Repulsive Instrument of Slave Torture — Trains going North
from Washington Packed with Furloughed Soldiers—President Lincoln's
Explanation — "The War to be ended by Strategy!" — We take in our
Charge a Sick Soldier — New Experience in Baltimore — Visit to Doro-
thea Dix — Her extensive Work — Superintendent of Women Nurses —
Washington Soldiers' Home — Amy Bradley the Matron — "Solid
Chunks of Sunshine" — Visit Alexandria — "Camp Misery" — "A perfect Golgotha" — Great Indignation of Visitors — Amy Bradley takes
up her Abode in the Camp — Great Improvement follows — "The Soldiers' Journal" — We visit President Lincoln.

IN November, 1862, the United States Sanitary Commission called a council of its
members at Washington, to which every
Branch of the Commission sent women representatives. Sanitary supplies were rapidly
on the decrease, while the increasing demand
for them was pitiful. The people lacked confidence
in the ability of the Commission to carry to the
suffering soldiers the supplies intrusted to its care.
They knew nothing of its system of inspection
and relief. They did not then comprehend the dire
necessities of the hospital and battle-field, which grew
out of the expansion of the army, and the increased

232

area of its operations; nor yet the inability of the government to meet these necessities, while it was taxed to the utmost in every other direction.

A more perfect organization of the system of relief was necessary; so also was a greater concert of action and a unification of methods, while the patriotism of the people, their loyalty to the Union, and their sympathy with the soldiers, needed to be quickened and fired with new zeal. Only in this way would it be possible for the Commission to provide assistance and consolation for the sick and suffering of the army "abundantly, persistently, and methodically." To the women of the country the Commission looked for the accomplishment of these great aims. Hence the call for the "Woman's Council."

It was a time of great depression and discouragement. In the East there were only reports of disaster to our armies. After the battle of Antietam, which resulted in no substantial advantage, General McClellan rested so long a time on the north side of the Potomac, that President Lincoln and his military advisers ordered an immediate advance of the army. But McClellan still delayed, and, while he halted, raids were made into Maryland and Pennsylvania by the enemy, who penetrated to Chambersburg, a score of miles in the rear of our army, and then speedily returned to Virginia, having entirely completed the circuit of the Federal forces. When, at length, McClellan began to cross the Potomac, with the design of engaging the enemy, he received a telegram from Washington relieving him of the command of the army, and ordering him to turn it over to General Burnside, who reluctantly and with many protests accepted it.

This announcement fell on the country like a thunderbolt, and a fierce partisan discussion sprang up concerning the wisdom of the removal and the merits of the retired commander, which created great bitterness. Following quickly on the heels of this change, Burnside made a rapid march to Fredericksburg, hoping to capture the place before Lee's army could reach it, and thus cut off his retreat towards Richmond. He was repulsed with frightful slaughter, and the wearied and bleeding, but heroic Army of the Potomac was driven from before Richmond.

At the West the military movements were not crowned with the success the public had expected from previous rapid victories. The triumphant fleet which had regained control of the Mississippi above and below Vicksburg, was baffled by this city, built on a high bluff, fortified like another Gibraltar, and bidding defiance to the gunboats. It had seemed to the people that the work of opening the great river was about ended, and now it appeared to them just begun. The enemy again invaded Missouri, and made alarming raids into Tennessee and Kentucky. Cincinnati was threatened and consternation sent among its citizens, who rallied for immediate defence, as did the people of other similarly situated towns. Instigated by the enemy, the Indians on the frontier began their depredations, and Minnesota became the theatre of a horrible massacre.

The question of giving recognition to the Southern Confederacy was openly discussed in England — by the press, at public meetings, and in both Houses of Parliament. The South became bold and confident, and its President appointed a day of thanksgiving throughout the Confederacy, because of its successes and hopeful prospects. Those who opposed the war at the North broke out into defiant demands for an immediate cessation of hostilities, and for "peace at any price." The loyal masses found themselves confronted by an enemy within their own territorial limits. Everywhere there were doubt, despondency, gloom, and forebodings. It was one of the darkest periods of the war.

It was with heavy hearts that Mrs. Hoge and myself started from Chicago at this time, on a mid-winter journey to Washington. On account of my honored father, who had been waiting his release from life through weary months of physical infirmity, I was obliged to go to Washington by way of Boston. I was detained at Suspension Bridge one entire night by a collision of freight trains, which tore up the tracks, blocked the road, and hindered all travel for twelve or fourteen hours. There were not even sitting accommodations for the great multitude emptied into the comfortless station-rooms, as several other trains were halted here besides our own. After the first three or four hours of waiting, as the night deepened and the time wore heavily on, our condition became more comfortless, and the great crowd became intolerably uneasy. Mothers were impatient, children fretting and crying, fathers persistently ill-natured. One or two games of fisticuffs were extemporized, by way of settling political differences, which most of the men were discussing in loud and heated language; and there were universal grumbling and growling over our uncomfortable situation, thus making a bad matter worse.

Among the few who possessed their souls in patience was a young lady, nearly blind, and her brother, who carried a violin in a case. Some one carelessly asked the lad to "play a tune," when the boy replied that he did not play, but that his sister was an excellent performer on the violin, and several other instruments, and that she also sang. An earnest entreaty from three or four of us brought the violin from its case, which the young girl lifted to her shoulder. Inclining her cheek caressingly to it, she tuned it, and then gave us melody after melody of exquisite sweetness, that gradually hushed the turbulence of the restless throng, and charmed the noisiest into silence. A song was besought of her — and without excuse, or apology, or delay, the almost sightless girl gave us the touching ballad, "Just before the battle, mother," in a voice whose sweetness, purity, and pathos, thrilled every heart. Song after song was now asked for and granted, until the unknown singer had exhausted her répertoire of patriotic and common songs, when she fell back on operatic airs, giving English translations of Italian gems, and proving herself as skilful in execution as she was gifted in voice.

Gradually the mood of the heterogeneous audience changed from curiosity to interest. And when our young vocalist sang the majestic Marseillaise, throwing herself into the spirit of the grand hymn, interest heightened into enthusiasm. Here and there, one and another joined in the chorus, until it was sung by many voices. Men threw up their hats and cheered, and women clapped and applauded. For two hours she sang and played in the dingy, crowded waiting-room, only stopping occasionally, to mend a string of the violin, or to put it in tune, until, towards daylight, the train came shrieking to the door. And for two hours she held the weary, impatient, and at times semi-brutal crowd spell-bound by the magic of her voice. It was the old story of Orpheus and his lyre, charming the beasts from their savageness and the mountains from their immobility. In the detention at which all had murmured all now rejoiced.

Some conscientious body, who believed in paying for what he received, passed round the hat, taking up a collection of nearly twenty dollars, which the girl was compelled to accept, as a testimonial of gratitude for the most acceptable concert ever given. Our singer was chary of information concerning herself, and reluctant to speak of her blindness. But we learned enough of her to know that her case was one of those where nature withholds one gift that she may double another. She was on her way to New York, her brother said, for better cultivation of her rare musical gifts.

All along the route furloughed or discharged soldiers were taken aboard, on their way home, most of them maimed, crippled, pale, thin, weary, and shabby. Unobtrusive, patient, and submissive, they took whatever accommodations chanced to fall to them. When we stopped to breakfast or dine, they bought lunches of bread and meat, or brought forth rations from their haversacks, that they might more carefully husband their slender means. When inquired of, they gayly replied that " they had plenty, their money and food were ample," and of their discomforts they made very light, in a lofty soldier fashion. They were on their way home, and this soothed every pain, and made the poorest fare delicious.

At Springfield, Mass., where we made connection

with a New York train for Boston, some twenty more
of the poor fellows were added to the company.
They belonged to Maine regiments, and were on
their way home from Port Hudson, recovering from
wounds, or convalescing from sickness. Poor fellows!
How different their return from their going forth
to the war! Then, they marched in solid columns,
gay in new uniforms, led by martial music, cheered
by admiring crowds, their breasts heaving with ambition and patriotism. Now, if the grave had yielded
its dead, their appearance could not have been ghast-
lier. Many of the Maine men were without money,
and knew not what to do on their arrival in Boston,
in their enfeebled condition, but were confident they
should find friends, as they had done all along
the route. All were provided for long before they
reached Boston; for the people on the train became
infected with generosity and patriotism, and freely
gave whatever money was needed.

While I was in Boston, an instrument of slave
torture was on exhibition, such as Northern people
had often heard described, but in whose existence
few believed. It was shown at the art rooms of
Williams and Everett, on Washington Street, and
seemed fearfully out of place amid the pictures, statuary, and bric-à-brac, of the handsome rooms. It was
a rough, heavy iron collar, weighing half a dozen
pounds, from which three curved prongs rose, with a
joint at the back, and closed in front with a rivet.

It was taken from the neck of a slave girl, near
New Orleans, by Captain S. T. Reed, of the Third
Massachusetts Cavalry. The girl was about eighteen
years of age, quite white, — an octoroon, — and very
beautiful. She had attempted to run away; and, as

PLATE II.

FAMOUS UNION BATTLE-FLAGS.

1. Twenty-first Mass. Reg't.  2. Fortieth N.Y. Reg't.  3. Fourteenth Conn. Reg't.
4. Twenty-fourth Mass. Reg't.  5. First Maine Heavy Art.  6. First Conn. Heavy Art.

*For Descriptions see pages 27-34.*

PHOTOGRAPHED AND PAINTED FROM THE ORIGINAL FLAGS EXPRESSLY FOR THIS WORK.

A. D. WORTHINGTON & CO. PUBLISHERS  HARTFORD, CONN.

the city was occupied by Federal troops, she was suspected of "sympathy with the Yankees." For this she was invested with this iron collar, — which had rusted into the neck, — and she had been chained in a dungeon and half starved for three months.

The girl was taken to the city, where the iron collar was removed from her neck by a blacksmith, and she was subsequently freed by military authority.

As we approached Washington, we were filled with amazement at the number of furloughed soldiers whom we met *en route* for the North. It seemed as if the army was being disbanded. They were not like those whom we had met in Massachusetts, for few of these were disabled, wounded, or invalid. They were bronzed and hardy, jolly and hearty, looking as if they had seen service but had been toughened by it. They filled the railway stations, packed the trains, crowded the platforms of the cars, and cheered our southward bound train as they passed us. We could not understand it. While in Washington we received an explanation of this phenomenon, from no less an authority than President Lincoln.

"The army is constantly depleted," he said, "by company officers who give their men leave of absence in the very face of the enemy, and on the eve of an engagement, which is almost as bad as desertion. At this very moment," he continued, "there are between seventy and a hundred thousand men absent on furlough from the Army of the Potomac. The army, like the nation, has become demoralized with the idea that the war is to be ended, the nation united, and peace restored, by *strategy*, and not by hard desperate fighting. Why, then, should not the soldiers have furloughs?"

As we were approaching Baltimore slowly, experiencing numerous delays, our train ran off the track and we were detained for hours. While we waited, the afternoon deepened into evening, and despite the continued tramping in and out of impatient men, who vented their distress at our slow progress in emphatic and not very reverent language, I fell asleep. I was awakened by a peculiar noise, like that of an animal in distress. The conductor just then passed through the train, and Mrs. Hoge asked of him an explanation of the distressing sounds.

"A drunken soldier on the platform of the rear car, Madam!" was the nonchalant answer.

It was snowing furiously. The cries of distress continued, rising at times into short, sharp shrieks. The conductor returned through the train, and Mrs. Hoge again accosted him; —

"Drunk or sober, conductor, that man is in distress. He is a soldier, and must not be left on the platform. Please bring him in here." He gruffly refused, declaring that "drunken soldiers were no company for ladies!" and rudely pushed ahead.

Mrs. Hoge rose and went to the door, and I followed her. A man lay coiled in a heap on the platform of the rear car, writhing in the fierce throes of convulsions. With assistance from bystanders, we brought him in, arranged a rough bed with the seats, unbuttoned his military overcoat, brushed off the snow that covered him, and then looked into the pale face of a delicate lad of eighteen. His staring eyes saw nothing; his limbs were rigid; he was as cold as if dead; and his mouth was flecked with bloody foam. In the terrible spasms, his teeth had bitten through tongue and lips.

There was no lack of interest now, and no withholding of assistance. Every one in the car was eager to help. Blanket shawls were heated and wrapped around the slender fellow's figure. Hot bricks, and heated sticks of wood, were applied to his feet and legs. His hands and pulseless wrists were vigorously chafed, and hot cloths were applied to the chest and abdomen. The train was searched for a physician, and at last one was found who added his remedial skill to our nursing. In about two hours we were rewarded for our efforts by seeing the young soldier relieved from pain, his muscles relaxed, his breathing became regular, and he was conscious. Gazing at us wonderingly for a few moments, he covered his face with his thin fingers, through which the tears trickled. "Excuse me, ladies! I thought I was at home with my mother." He was a convalescent soldier, going from the hospital to his regiment, and altogether too much of an invalid for the exchange. The cold, exposure, fatigue, and improper food of the journey had nearly bereft him of life, when we fortunately discovered him.

Just as we were entering Baltimore an officer with a captain's bars on his shoulders came into our coach, and accosted our patient, in amazement, —

"Why, William, what's the matter?"

Mrs. Hoge answered with much feeling. "He has been very near death, but is better now. Are you his captain, sir?"

"Not exactly," was the reply. "I was put in charge of one hundred convalescents to be taken back to their regiments. None of them are well enough to go, but they had to be sent away, the hospitals are so crowded, to make room for sicker men. Some of my men are as sick as this fellow."

"Do you know this young man personally?" inquired Mrs. Hoge.

"No," he replied, "but they requested me at the hospital to be careful of him, as he is delicate, and they gave him a good name for pluck and patience. I had him in the rear car with the rest, and went out, leaving him there. I have been in the smoker, and only missed him just now when I went back."

"I was sick, captain," said the lad; "I thought I was going to faint, and went to the platform for air, and that is all I know."

Mrs. Hoge's indignation had been steadily rising, and now burst forth. "And this is the way you discharge your obligations to sick soldiers, placed in your care! You leave them for hours to be neglected, abused, branded as drunkards, while you seek your own gratification! Four hours after this boy fell on the platform, and was left to die like an animal, you come to inquire after him. But for us, you would have found only a corpse; for the physician who has attended him declared that he could not have lived an hour longer, uncared for. This is not the way, sir, to treat the 'rank and file' of our army, made up of the very flower of American young manhood. No wonder soldiers desert, if this is a specimen of the treatment accorded them. Had this lad died, sir, you would have been responsible for his death." She spoke sternly, and with feeling.

The captain winced under her rebuke, and said he had not intended to be neglectful, and had not supposed William was so badly off. When we volunteered to stop over in Baltimore, and see him safely bestowed in a hospital, he turned him over to our care, and gave us a written order for this purpose. We reached Baltimore at midnight, and for two hours rode from hospital to hospital with our charge, before we succeeded in finding a place for him. At last, we met a surgeon, in charge of a smaller hospital, who was willing to cut the red tape that barred our sick soldier from the wards, so as to admit him. Neither William's captain nor ourselves, at that time, were acquainted with the multitudinous forms to be observed before admission could be secured to a military hospital. We left him in comfort, and heard from him daily when in Washington. On our return to Chicago, weeks later, we received a touching letter of thanks from his mother and sister in New Jersey, who spoke of their son and brother most tenderly, as good and true, faithful and obedient.

It was Sunday morning when we arrived in Washington; and, as the Sanitary Commission held no meeting that day, we decided, after breakfast, to pay a visit to Miss Dix. I had known this lady by reputation for years. I had heard of her deep interest in the condition of paupers, lunatics, and prisoners, and knew that she had spent her life in their service. She had visited poorhouses, prisons, and insane asylums, had accomplished reforms, corrected abuses, and secured favorable legislation for their relief. With a passion for justice, great energy of character, and wonderful executive talent, she was a very interesting personage. I anticipated great pleasure from the interview.

Miss Dix passed through Baltimore shortly after

the dire tragedy of April, 1861, when the Sixth Massachusetts regiment, on its way to the defence of the national capital, was mobbed in its streets. Some were left dead, and others wounded. Her first work, on reaching Washington, was to nurse to health these victims of the Baltimore mob. Washington, at that time, was a great camp. Hospitals were hastily organized, and filled with sick, while there were few to nurse them. Everywhere there were confusion and disorder, lack of discipline and executive ability. Miss Dix offered her services to the government in any department where she could be made useful. On the tenth of June, 1861, Secretary Cameron vested her with sole power to appoint women nurses in the hospitals. Secretary Stanton, on succeeding him, ratified the appointment; and she had already installed several hundred nurses in their noble work,— all of them Protestants and middle-aged. She personally examined the qualifications of every applicant. The women must be over thirty years of age, plain almost to repulsion in dress, and devoid of personal attractions, if they hoped to receive the approval of Miss Dix. She also insisted on good health and an unexceptionable moral character. Many of the women whom she rejected because they were too young and too beautiful entered the service under other auspices, and became eminently useful. Many women whom she accepted because they were sufficiently old and ugly proved unfit for the position, and a disgrace to their sex.

Fortunately we found Miss Dix at home, but just ready to start for the hospitals. She was slight and delicate looking, and seemed physically inadequate to the work she was engaged in. In her youth she must have possessed considerable beauty, much as she deprecated its possession by her nurses. She was still very comely, with a soft and musical voice, a graceful figure, and very winning manners when she chose to use them. Her whole soul was in her work. She rented two large houses as depots for the sanitary supplies sent to her care, and houses of rest and refreshment for nurses and convalescent soldiers. She employed two secretaries, owned ambulances, and kept them busily employed, printed and distributed circulars, went hither and thither from one remote point to another in her visitations of hospitals, adjusted disputes, settled difficulties where her nurses were concerned, undertook long journeys by land and by water, and paid all expenses incurred from her private purse. Her fortune, time, and strength were laid on the altar of her country in its hour of trial.

Unfortunately, many of the surgeons in the hospitals did not work harmoniously with Miss Dix. They were jealous of her power, impatient of her authority, condemned her nurses, and accused her of being arbitrary, opinionated, severe, and capricious. Many, to rid themselves of her entirely, obtained permission of Surgeon-General Hammond to employ Sisters of Charity only in their hospitals, a proceeding not at all to Miss Dix's liking. I knew, by observation, that many of the surgeons were unfit for their office; that too often they failed to carry skill, morality, or humanity, to their work; and I understood how this single-hearted friend of the sick and wounded soldier would come in collision with these laggards.

Miss Dix regarded her army work as only an episode of her life, and, when the war closed, returned to her early labors, working for the insane and the criminal, until increasing years and infirmities compelled a cessation of them. Since the close of the war she has resided in Trenton, N. J.

Of the prolonged meetings of the Sanitary Commission held during the week, no account need be given. They resulted in the formation of wise plans of work, which, faithfully carried out, soon swelled the amount of sanitary stores to an extent never anticipated. Special agents were appointed, and a thorough system of canvassing was adopted. Monthly bulletins were issued by the various branches to their tributary aid societies, containing latest accounts of actual work, compiled receipts of sanitary stores up to date, and a statement of the immediate necessities of the hospitals. Earnest and successful efforts were made all along the lines to induce all organizations working for the relief of the army to adopt the Sanitary Commission as the almoner of their bounty; and great quickening resulted immediately. Henceforth to the end of the war " an enthusiastic spirit of devotion to the soldier inspired the popular heart." The treasury of the Commission was kept full, and " its storehouses overflowed with plenteousness."

The sessions of the Sanitary Commission being ended, and the Woman's Council adjourned *sine die,* we remained a few days in Washington to visit hospitals, soldiers' homes, and other places of interest. The hospitals in Washington were, even then, marvels of order, comfort, and neatness. Among the nurses were some of the very noblest women of the East — women of culture, of family, and of rare nobleness of character. The Soldiers' Home in Washington had been established by the Commission for the comfort of the private soldier travelling to his regiment or home, who ran the risk, while awaiting transportation, of being entrapped by sharpers, always seeking to fleece every man connected with the army. It also received the sick men who could not go on immediately with their regiments, furnishing them with food, medicines, and care. It obtained the back pay of discharged soldiers, secured for them railroad tickets at reduced rates, sought to make them clean and comfortable before they left for home, and was in constant readiness with food or clothing, in large quantities, for soldiers who passed through Washington in any direction. Forty similar homes were established and maintained before the close of the war.

On Reverend Frederick N. Knapp, an agent of the Commission, whose name is imperishably associated with its grand work of special relief, devolved the duty of establishing this Home. He selected as matron, Miss Amy M. Bradley — an alert, executive little woman from Maine. She had been a successful teacher before the war, and had already achieved an enviable reputation in the hospital service of the Commission. For our men speedily fell victims to the malaria of the miasmatic swamps of the Chickahominy during the terrible Peninsular Campaign, in the spring and summer of 1862. The hospital transports of the Commission did heroic service in those dark days, in removing the poor fellows North, where they could have a chance to live, or at least to die amid their kindred. Amy Bradley had made herself a power on these transports by her skill in nursing, in preparing food for the sick and wounded, in dressing wounds, and in making herself generally useful to the wretched men temporarily placed in her care.

She was absent from the Home when we entered it, but the spirit of neatness, good order, and cheerfulness which characterized her was visible everywhere. There were three hundred and twenty exquisitely clean beds awaiting occupants. The pleasant reading-room was filled with quiet readers, every man of whom seemed comfortable. As we spoke to them, each one had his grateful story to tell of Miss Bradley's care and faithfulness.

" Miss Bradley obtained over one hundred dollars' worth of back pay for me, which I could not get myself," said one, " and I have forwarded it to my family in need of it."

"One hundred dollars!" interjected another. " She has obtained over one hundred thousand dollars' worth of back pay from government for soldiers, since she came to this Home."

" She nursed over nine hundred of us in the hospital," chimed in another, " and only let thirteen die. Bring on your doctor who can do better."

" You ought to see the letters she writes every week for the men in this Home," added an assistant. " The letters *she* writes haven't any blue streaks in them, but are solid chunks of sunshine."

In every department of the Home this panegyric of Miss Bradley was repeated. She returned just as we were departing, and we had the pleasure of an interview with the noble little woman, whose untiring work, begun with the war, for the soldiers, has been continued to this day among the poor white people of the South. She is still laboring among them at Wilmington, N. C. Erect and decisive, quick of comprehension and prompt in action, we were immediately won by her kindly face and winning manners. It was not strange that the soldiers loved and respected her.

The next day we went to Alexandria, across the Potomac, some nine or ten miles from Washington. Just outside the town there was a large encampment, significantly named by the soldiers, " Camp Misery." Here we were to pass the day. We took the carriage road rather than the boat. The road was through an almost continuous encampment. The country was nearly bare of trees, for many of them, umbrageous with the growth of centuries, had long ago been felled by the necessities of war. The fences also had vanished, and the numerous forts and groups of tents revealed themselves plainly as we rode on. I had driven over this same country many times in happier years, and the desolation visible everywhere touched me painfully.

We were "halted" at every bridge, and cross-road, were compelled to show our passes, and, hour after hour, rode past never-ending trains of heavily laden army wagons, rumbling slowly along. Soldiers were everywhere — drilling, cooking, cutting wood, washing clothes, writing letters, cleaning arms, mending clothes, playing games, working on forts, digging graves. Whichever way we turned we beheld United States soldiers.

We stopped a moment at the hotel in Alexandria, where the chivalric Ellsworth foolishly threw away his life. I saw him for the last time in Chicago, just before the war began, when he gave an exhibition drill of his wonderful Zouaves. They had just returned home from a triumphal tour through the prin-

cipal cities of the East.   At the very first call of the
country, the Zouaves, with their brave Colonel, entered the service.   Their loyalty to the Union created
a furor wherever they appeared.   The career of the
young and handsome commander was brief, and
ended in a tragic death.

Passing the hotel in Alexandria, from the roof of
which floated a rebel flag, he was so stung by this
insult to the government, offered within the very
sight of the capital, that he bounded up the stairway
and tore it down.   On the instant he was shot dead
by the proprietor of the hotel, who, in his turn, fell
beside his victim, slain by the avenging bullet of
Ellsworth's friend and comrade, who had accompanied him.   The hotel had been entirely remodelled,
as a protection from the visits of the curious.

In the large encampment at Alexandria were included four camps.   One was for "new recruits
awaiting orders to join regiments in the field."   Another was for paroled prisoners waiting exchange.
Another for stragglers and deserters, captured and
soon to be forwarded to their regiments.   And the
fourth was for convalescents from the Washington
and Maryland hospitals.   The first two were in anything but a good condition, there being great destitution of everything needful and convenient.   The
stragglers' camp was neglected and disorderly, as
might be expected; but the convalescent camp was a
perfect Golgotha.   The four camps were located on
a hillside, bare of grass, whose soil was so porous
that a heavy shower saturated the whole like a
sponge.   The convalescents were camped at the foot
of the slope, where it was forever damp, even in dry
weather, from the drainage of the camps above.

Here, ranged in streets named from the states to which they belonged, were fifteen thousand feeble men, all of them unfit for duty, and sent here to recover. "*Recover!*" — this was the governmental fiction which glossed over the worst condition of things I had ever beheld.

Most of the men were poorly clad, without blankets, straw, or money, though many had seven or eight months' pay due them. They were lodged, in the depth of a very severe winter, in wedge and Sibley tents of the smallest pattern, five or six to a tent, without floors or fires, or means of making any, amid deep mud or frozen clods. They were obliged to cook their own food and obtain their own fuel; and, as all the timber in the neighborhood had been cut, it was necessary for them to go a mile for even green wood.

They slept on the bare ground, or, when it rained, as it did while we were there, in the mud. Their food was the uninviting rations of the healthy men. There were but three surgeons for the four camps; and if the boys needed medicine, they must go to one of them. The surgeons only visited the hospital of the camp, which was full and running over, so that many were refused admission who were seriously sick, and who remained in their fireless and bedless tents. Such destitution, squalor, and helplessness, I had never beheld. Bowel diseases were very prevalent; throat and lung difficulties met us at every turn, and the incessant coughing made us all nervous.

In our party were representatives from most of the Northern states; and there was a simultaneous burst of indignation from the lips of all, as we saw the utter neglect of these invalids. In Illinois Street, two young men, connected with the Eighth Illinois Cavalry, accosted me by name. They came from Chicago, and had been my near neighbors. But the mother who bore them would never have recognized the skeletonized fellows. Feeble as they were, they overwhelmed me with an avalanche of questions about home. Women were rare visitors in these camps, for the Alexandrian ladies were indifferent to the welfare of Northern soldiers. As the lady visitors, therefore, sought out the soldiers of their various states, they were instantly surrounded by groups of wan and fleshless men, eager to see a woman from home who had interested herself to call on them. The inquiries made by them can be imagined, but not their sad faces and sadder stories.

We visited many of the miserable little tents, where the poor fellows were doomed to pass much of their time. They were cold and cheerless; and memories of the condition of their suffering inmates gave us the heartache for weeks after. When, on our return to Washington, I read in a morning paper that half a dozen of the feeblest of these convalescents had frozen to death in their tents during the previous cold night, I was not surprised. As we left, we were commissioned with affecting messages for friends at home. I filled pages of my memorandum book with these messages and errands. I was to call and see the mother and sisters of one; to assist a wife in getting the discharge of her hopelessly invalid husband; to convey to a young wife her own photograph and that of her child, with a half-finished letter taken from the pocket of her dead husband; and so on.

All of us had been accustomed to hospitals from

the beginning of the war, and were used to sad sights; but this convalescent camp, — where fifteen thousand brave men, who had lost health and heart in the service of the country, were huddled as no good farmer would pen up cattle, — outweighed in sadness anything we had previously seen. The apparent indifference of the authorities concerning them seemed almost brutal. An endless stream of protests had been sent to the Secretary of War and the Surgeon-General, to whom the horrible condition of this camp was made known; and still it was not broken up, nor was any apparent attempt made at its improvement.

Before we left, we found a gleam of light, for we heard again of Amy Bradley. She had been sent down to "Camp Misery" by the Sanitary Commission, as a special relief agent, and had taken up her quarters among the men. She had made frequent visits to the camp during the previous three months, always bringing supplies, which she personally distributed. Now she had come to stay with the convalescents; and the desponding men took heart as they heard the glad tidings. She had set up her tents, and arranged her little hospital cook-room, storeroom, wash-room, bath-room, and office. We were told that she had passed round with the officers that very morning, as the men were drawn up in line for inspection, and had supplied seventy-five almost naked men, who were very feeble, with woollen shirts.

We walked over to her hospital tents. She had forty patients in them, who were washed, made clean, had been warmed and fed. We breathed easier; we felt sure that at last light had dawned on the darkness. Nor were we mistaken; for, during the next six months, she conveyed more than two thousand soldiers from this camp, whose discharges she had obtained, and turned them over to the Soldiers' Home in Washington. Most of them were incurably ill, and would have perished but for her divine ministrations. In four months she had relieved " one hundred and thirty patients in her little hospital, fifteen of whom died." To the friends of the dead she sent full accounts of the last hours of their lost ones. Before the close of *six* months she had procured the re-instatement of one hundred and fifty soldiers, who had been dropped from the muster rolls unjustly as " deserters," had secured their back pay to them, amounting in all to eight thousand dollars.

There seemed to be no limit to this little woman's capacity for helpfulness. She was as cheery as a sunbeam, and infused health, hope, and courage into all with whom she came in contact. When, at last, the convalescent camp was broken up, and its inmates transferred to the " Rendezvous of Distribution " in Washington, she located herself among them there. She established a weekly paper at their headquarters, called the " Soldiers' Journal," a quarto sheet of eight pages, which was edited with remarkable ability, until the breaking up of the Rendezvous and disbanding of the hospital at the end of the war. " The profits of the paper were twenty-two hundred dollars, besides the value of the printing-press and materials. This amount was expended for the benefit of orphans, whose fathers had been connected with the camp, and was increased by generous contributions from other sources."

# CHAPTER XI.

LIFE IN A CONTRABAND CAMP — WASHINGTON IN 1865 — A CONTRABAND PRAYER MEETING — MY INTERVIEW WITH SECRETARY STANTON — THE DRUMMER-BOY OF THE EIGHTH MICHIGAN.

Fugitive Slaves rejoicing in Freedom —Prayer-meeting in Camp — Meet old "Aunt Aggy" — An Episode of Slavery — "Thar's a Day a-comin'!" — Lively Praying — Tempestuous Singing — Intense Sectarians — A Boy Philosopher — Visit Washington in 1865 — Great Changes — Deserters from the Enemy — Runaway Negro with a Six-Mule Team — Courtesy and Kindness of Secretary Stanton — Meet Admiral and Mrs. Farragut — Their Simplicity and Geniality — Lieutenant Cushing, the Hero of the Ram Albemarle — Other Eminent Notabilities — The Drummer Boy of the Eighth Michigan — Enlists with his Teacher — Charlie petted by all — His Teacher and Captain Shot at James Island — Fierce Life of the Eighth Michigan — Charlie Shares it All — Struck by a Chance Shot — Fatal Result.

CONTRABAND camp had been established at Washington, made up principally of fugitives from Maryland and Virginia, though we found numerous representatives of the "patriarchal institution" from North and South Carolina, and Georgia. There were three thousand of them in camp at the time of our visit, but the number varied from week to week. Rev. D. B. Nichols, a former superintendent of the Chicago Reform School, was in charge of this motley company of escaped slaves, and although there was evidence of a lack of administrative talent, the poor refugees from bondage had certainly, for the time, a happy home in their miserable quarters.

All ages, both sexes, every shade of complexion, and every variety of character, were found here. I had lived on a Southern plantation for two years, in my early life, and the people and scenes were not as novel to me as to my companions. They were overwhelmed with astonishment at the intelligence, good sense, and decorum manifested by all. They had expected to see a gathering of half-humanized baboons or gorillas, and were not certain that they ought not take with them an interpreter. All with whom we conversed gave an intelligent and graphic account of their escape from slavery, and their descriptions of "massa" and "missus" revealed a clear insight into character. They admitted that they were not in as good condition now as they had been "at home," but they expected to have better days by and by, and to earn money, and to keep house, and to "live like white folks." Not one regretted their change of circumstances.

"Why, missus," said a very intelligent mulatto woman, with considerable pretensions to beauty, who had come from Point Lookout, laying her right forefinger in the broad palm of her left hand to give emphasis to her speech, "we'd ruther be jes' as po' as we can be, if we's only free, than ter b'long to anybody, an' hab all de money ole massa's got, or is eber gwine ter hab."

Compared with white people at the North they were not industrious, but they compared favorably with the humbler classes of whites at the South, and were even ahead of them in intellect and industry. Every morning the men of the camp went into the city to get work for the day. So did the women who had not young children to care for. Few of them failed to find employment. Government employed the men — and the women found chance jobs of house-cleaning, washing, etc., for which they asked and received moderate compensation. Many had thriven so well that they had commenced housekeeping by themselves, an event to which all were aspiring. The contraband camp at Washington was therefore very nearly a self-sustaining institution.

Our first visit to the contrabands proved so interesting that we accepted an invitation from Mr. Nichols to attend their evening prayer-meeting. The prayer-meetings were held every evening as soon as supper was ended, and were the great staple of their enjoyment. In them they found never-failing satisfaction. They had all assembled when we arrived, but the advent of so large a company of white people had the effect to disband several minor meetings in the various huts, and to augment the larger one in Mr. Nichols' quarters. Room was made for us by the dense crowd with great courtesy. The utmost decorum prevailed, seriousness sat on all faces, and a hush settled over the sable assembly. The oppressive stillness was broken by a comely mulatto woman, far advanced in years, who rose, and came towards me.

" I 'clar to goodness," she said, in a subdued undertone, respectfully extending her hand, " you're Miss Lucy's and Miss Mary's and Massa Robert's teacher, down on de ole plantation! I knowed yer de minit I seed yer a-comin' in, a-walkin' so straight and so tall! I allers knowed yer on de ole place, 'clar way off furder'n I could see yer face, cos yer allers walked so oncommon straight."

It was " Aunt Aggy," the housekeeper on the

plantation where I had been governess in my early
womanhood. She was the nurse of my pupils, and
the foster-mother of two or three of them. A slave,
she was entirely trusted, and was always respectful
and obedient. Never garrulous, always grave and
taciturn, she carried herself in those days with a rare
dignity, and never became obsequious, as did the
other house-servants. I instantly recalled a drama
of those long gone years, in which she was both
spectator and actor.

Her daughter "Car'line" (Caroline), a pretty and
graceful mulatto, was a servant in the dining-room.
One morning when passing a cup of coffee to Mr.
——, her master and owner, by an unlucky movement of his hand he knocked it from the tray on
which she served it, to his knees. It was warm
weather; he was attired in linen, and the hot coffee
scalded him. Jumping up with an oath, he raised
his chair, and felled the girl to the floor, striking her
two or three times after she had fallen. She was
carried to the cottage of "Aunt Aggy," her mother,
who had witnessed the scene from an adjoining room,
— stunned, bruised, bleeding, and unconscious. I
left the table and withdrew to my own apartment,
shocked beyond expression at the brutal outrage of
the passionate master.

Later in the day "Aunt Aggy" came to my room
on some household errand, when I expressed my
indignation at the brutal treatment her daughter had
received, uttering myself with the frankness of a
New England girl of nineteen who had been trained
to be true to her convictions. I was astonished at
the change that came over the taciturn and dignified
woman. Turning squarely about and facing me,

with her large, lustrous eyes blazing with excitement, she spoke in a tone and manner that would have befitted a seer uttering a prophecy: —

"Thar's a day a-comin'! Thar's a day a-comin'!" she said, with right hand uplifted; "I hear de rumblin' ob de chariots! I see de flashin' ob de guns! White folks' blood is a-runnin' on de ground like a riber, an' de dead's heaped up dat high!" measuring to the level of her shoulder. "Oh, Lor'! hasten de day when de blows, an' de bruises, an' de aches, an' de pains, shall come to de white folks, an' de buzzards shall eat 'em as dey's dead in de streets. Oh, Lor'! roll on de chariots, an' gib de black people rest an' peace. Oh, Lor'! gib me de pleasure ob livin' till dat day, when I shall see white folks shot down like de wolves when dey come hongry out o' de woods!" And without another word she walked from the room, nor could I ever afterwards induce her to speak of the beating given Caroline. I reminded "Aunt Aggy" of the occurrence, at the close of the prayer-meeting, and found that it was photographed on her memory as distinctly as on mine.

"I allers knowed it was a-comin'," she said. "I allers heerd de rumblin' o' de wheels. I allers 'spected to see white folks heaped up dead. An' de Lor', He's keept His promise, an' 'venged His people, jes' as I knowed He would. I seed 'em dead on de field, Massa Linkum's sojers an' de Virginny sojers, all heaped togedder, wid de dead hosses, an' de smash-up waggins — all de fightin' done done for dis yer world foreber. Ole massa and missus bof done died afore de war, an' young Massa Robert, what you teached in de school-room, he done died in dese yer arms. Little Mass' Batt, what liked to say his prars

in yer room, he went to de war, an' was shot in ole
Car'lina, an' buried wid his sojers. Miss Lucy an'
little Courty bof done died when de war begin, an'
dey was buried in Liberty Hill. De ole place is all
done broke up, an' de colored folks go jes' whar dey
please — no passes now. Oh, de Lor' He do jes'
right, if you only gib Him time enough to turn
Hisself."

The meeting commenced by the singing of a
hymn. It was a song and chorus. The leader, a
good singer, stood in the centre of the room, and
sang alone the first two lines: —

> "I see de angels beck'nin' — I hear dem call me 'way,
>   I see de golden city, an' de eberlastin' day!"

And then the whole congregation rose to their feet,
and with a mighty rush of melody, and an astonishing enthusiasm, joined in the inspiring chorus: —

> "Oh, I'm gwine home to glory — won't yer go along wid me,
>   Whar de blessed angels beckon, an' de Lor' my Saviour be?"

The leader was a good improvisatore as well as
singer, and long after the stock of ready-made verses
was exhausted, he went on and on, adding impromptu
and rough rhymes, and the congregation came in,
promptly and with ever-rising enthusiasm, with the
oft-repeated chorus. All sang with closed eyes,
thus shutting out all external impressions, and abandoned themselves to the ecstasy of the hour. The
leader gesticulated violently, swinging his arms
around his head, uplifting his hands, and clasping
them tightly and pointing into space; while his companions swayed slowly to and fro, beating time to
the music with their feet.

At last the swaying became wild and dizzy gyra-

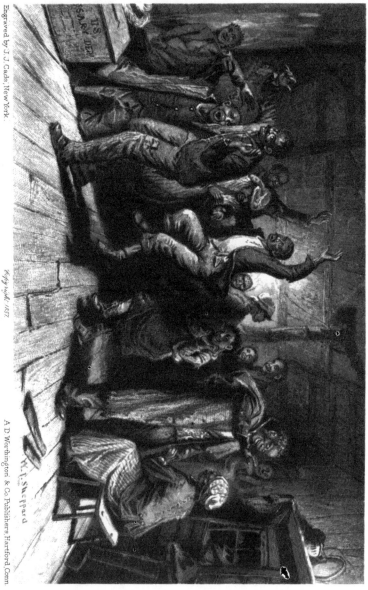

Engraved by J.J.Cade, New York.

Copyright 1887.

A.D.Worthington & Co. Publishers, Hartford, Conn.

**PRAYER MEETING IN A CONTRABAND CAMP.—WASHINGTON, 1862.**

"Oh I'm gwine home to glory—won't yer go 'long wid me,
Whar de blessed angels beckon, an' de Lor' my Saviour be!"

W.L.Sheppard

tions, which were interspersed with quick, convulsive leaps from the floor. Accompanying all this was a general hand-shaking, in which we white people were included. One powerful Maryland woman nearly toppled me from the elevated and precarious seat which I had selected, the better to look down on the congregation, so fervent was her hand-clasping. All of us were glad when this exercise was ended, for our hands ached.

After this followed a prayer. Never have I heard a prayer of more pathos and earnestness. It appealed to God, as Infinite Justice, and with confidence that the wrongs of the slave would be redressed.

"You know, O Lor' King," said the kneeling supplicant, "how many a time we've been hongry, and had noffin to eat,— how we've worked all day and night in de cotton and 'bacca fields, and had no time to sleep and take care of our chillen, and how we've bin kep' out in de frost and de snow, and suffered many persecutions. But now, O King, you've brought us up hyar under de shadder o' de Linkum army, and we 'pend on Thee for de rest. We're gwine to wait for Thee, O King, to show us de way." With the utmost fervor he prayed for the Union army — that "the Lor' would smother its enemies," — and for " Massa Linkum, who was doing de good Lor's will." And to both these petitions the whole audience added a tempest of supplicatory responses. Finally, after specifying every distressed class of which they had any knowledge, they begged the Lord to " pardon the damned out o' hell, if so be de good Lor' *could* do it."

During this prayer a dozen of half-grown mulatto

boys had entered the rear of the room, who were not imbued with the seriousness of the great congregation. After a few moments they became uneasy, and began to frolic. Once or twice one of the number made some comment to his companions, in an audible tone of voice, and several times they broke down in a suppressed giggle. They were remembered by a venerable negro who prayed next, in this ingenuous fashion: —

"O Lor', bress us all poor sinners. Bress dese yer boys, O Lor'; dey'se got so many blessin's, dey dunno what to do wid 'em; dey'se like de hogs under de 'simmons trees, eating 'simmons, — dey dunno whar dey come from. O Lor', bress us all poor sinners, an' bress my poor Jim," — who now laughed outright — "'case he's a berry bad boy, Lor'; he's a badder boy dan you know for; he swars; he swars more dan you know about; he swars more in de tent dan he does outdoors. Now, Lor', bress us all, an' stan' by me, an' I'll stan' by you, sartin."

A prolonged exhortation followed this prayer. It was mainly devoted to the case of one of their number who had died two nights before, who was a notorious thief, and who, the speaker unhesitatingly declared, "was in hell." "An' now, chillen, whar you 'spect uncle Jim done gone? Wednesday night, chillen, at half past ten o'clock," — the hour at which the man died, — "uncle Jim done gone to hell. Now he roll about on de red-hot sheet-iron floor thar, an' he clim' up de red-hot walls, an' fall back agin" — and so on. I confess I felt quite reconciled to uncle Jim's unpleasant predicament, in consideration of their prayer that God would pardon the damned. Other scenes, speeches, and prayers followed, but one was a sample of all. The meeting was of the liveliest character throughout. They were not only *hearers*, but in a very emphatic sense they were also *doers*, and with their gesticulations, beating of feet, shaking of hands, and unintermitted responses, they made busy and hard work of their prayer-meetings.

They were mostly Baptists, and were intensely sectarian. One Methodist brother ventured to start a hymn, but he had it all to himself. The Baptists sat still with folded hands and closed eyes, grim as sphinxes, and let him sing it through alone, without the aid of a single helping voice.

Mr. Nichols informed us that while the piety of these people was of the most orthodox character, their morality was not so satisfactory. The vices of slavery very naturally clung to them, and they were not truth-telling nor honest. All knew that the President had issued a Proclamation of Emancipation, and they expected to be free before the end of the war. When they sang their celebrated song, until then always sung stealthily and in secrecy, beginning,

> "Go tell Moses, go down into Egypt,
> An' tell King Pharaoh, let my people go,"

the leader improvised verses at the close suited to their circumstances, and the congregation changed the chorus, shouting with excitement, and gesticulating in a way that would have been terrific had they been less jubilant, " He *will* let my people go!"

Our return route to Chicago was by way of Philadelphia, as we wished to visit the Branch Commissions in Philadelphia and New York. Walking up Chestnut Street, I met a cheery-faced lad, wearing the blue uniform of the army, who had lost a leg, and was swinging along painfully on a crutch. I could not do otherwise than speak to him.

"My child, you have been very unfortunate."

"Yes, ma'am," he replied, as cheerfully as though I had simply remarked, "It is a pleasant day."

"Do you belong to the army?"

"Yes, ma'am — I am a drummer."

"Did you lose your leg in battle?"

"Yes, ma'am; I suppose it was partly my fault, though. I was told not to go down where the fight was, for I was not needed. But I wanted to see the fun, and went; and a piece of shell splintered my ankle so that I had to have my foot taken off."

"My poor boy! I am very sorry for you, and now you must be a cripple for life."

"Oh, well, 'taint so bad as it might be. I'm going to have an artificial leg, some time. I might have one now, but I should outgrow it in a year; and, as they cost fifty dollars, a fellow can't afford to have a new leg every spring, like he does a pair of trousers. But when I get grown I shall have one, and then I can go it as well as ever."

Blessings on the cheery-faced thirteen-year-old philosopher! In his sunny nature and hopeful spirit he had a greater fortune than the wealth of Vanderbilt would give him if he lacked these qualities.

I was compelled to visit Washington for the last time during the war, in 1865, about a month before Lee's army surrendered to General Grant at Appomattox. My visit then was in the interest of the last sanitary fair of the country. Washington was full, and running over. Congress was just at the close of the term, overcrowded with work, and holding sessions day and night to finish up the necessary business of the country. People were in the city, representing every taxable interest, entreating immunity from taxation for their particular industry, seeking appointments for themselves or friends, endeavoring to get real or fancied wrongs righted, eager to go to the front, — from curiosity or to aid sick and wounded friends, or awaiting the ceremonies of the approaching inauguration of President Lincoln for a second term, which promised to be more than ordinarily brilliant.

The city had changed during the war. More money had been spent on its streets during the four years of the war than in all its previous history. Horse-cars ran in every direction, the city was well lighted, and the sidewalks and crossings were in good condition. The city had taken on a business look, and its old dulness had disappeared. But it was even then what it had always been — one of the most unlovely cities of the Union. Ragged and straggling, with the oddest jumble of amazing houses on its spacious streets, whose depths of mud were immeasurable, the magnificent public buildings only emphasized the general meanness of the city, making it painful to behold.

The sights of war were not as numerous as in 1862. Then, all day and all night one heard the unceasing rumble of army wagons. Regiments were constantly passing through the city. Everywhere one caught the gleam of the bayonet, and heard the roll of the drum. Two great hostile armies were then encamped but a short distance from Washington, and one's spirits rose and fell with the rumors that hourly disturbed the public mind.

Now, one realized that the theatre of war was remote; and in the prophetic soul of every one dwelt the unshaken conviction that the end was near. The only unusual sight in the military line was the daily processions of deserters from the enemy, constantly arriving within the lines of our army. General Grant had promised, by proclamation, to buy of the deserters the teams and munitions of war they brought with them, and they came loaded, hundreds every night, squalid, ragged, dirty, and miserable. Two or three times a day I met them, under the escort of our soldiers, unkempt, almost barefooted, and generally bareheaded, as brown as berries, but jubilant, and often hilarious.

Whole picket lines deserted; and the rebel guards, who witnessed the transaction, and who remained behind because they had families in the Confederacy, refrained from firing on the deserters, or fired high, so as not to hit them. General Lee's army was melting away like snow in the spring sun; and to him every deserter was an irreparable loss, for he could not be replaced. Most of the men were unmarried, and some had families in the North. In conversation with them, they informed me that the married men deserted to their homes in the South, and in four times the numbers of the single men who escaped to the North.

One day, a negro, who was believed trustworthy, was sent out of the enemy's lines with a six-mule team for a big load of wood. He had got beyond the pickets, and seemed to think it worth while to venture a little farther, and so kept on towards "Uncle Sam's boys." The rebel pickets saw him going, and rushed after him. Our men saw him coming, and rushed towards him. The ebony teamster whipped up his mules, shouted, hurrahed, and urged them on. Guns were fired on both sides, and the yelling and excitement were tremendous for a few minutes. But the negro gained the day, and ran out of slavery into freedom. He was taken to the quartermaster, who gave him several hundred dollars for his team, so he not only got his liberty but a good start. He was sent up to Washington, at his desire; for his wife had worked her way to the city, and he wished to seek her. His story found its way into the papers, and for a brief day he was a small hero.

"Golly, missus!" was his comment, when I expressed my surprise that he had not been killed in the attempt to escape, "I was dat s'prised when I foun' myself alive and free in Massa Linkum's army, wid all dat money for my own, dat I couldn't b'lieve it. I was dat weak I couldn't stan' no more'n a broken-winded mule can run. It's a heap sight better up hyar, dan down on de ole place, and I 'spect me and de ole woman'll stay hyar when I'se found her."

Of my interview with President Lincoln, and its result, I have given an account elsewhere. I was commissioned to borrow the captured rebel flags, the battle-flags in the possession of the government, and the government bunting, for the use of the last great fair of the Sanitary Commission. For this purpose I went to the Secretary of War. I must confess that I never approached a human being more reluctantly than I did Secretary Stanton. I had heard fearful accounts of his porcine manners, discourtesy, and vulgar hauteur; and I dreaded to meet him. I did not then know that these charges were brought against him by cotton speculators, Southern traders in goods contraband of war, and other harpies, who had sought to prey on the government, and whose rapacious schemes he had thwarted.

A great crowd was in attendance, each waiting his turn, one standing behind the other in a long line that stretched far out into the hall. A hush like that of death pervaded the apartment. Each one in turn stepped forward to the Secretary, who stood to receive the applicants, and in a low tone proffered his request, or presented his papers. In the same subdued tone Mr. Stanton gave his advice or decision, and the interview ended.

My turn would not have come for two or three hours, and I had not the time to spare; so I sent by a page a brief letter of introduction given me by Mrs. Lyman C. Trumbull, long since deceased, one of the noblest women of the land, for whom Secretary Stanton had a great regard. It worked like the " open sesame " of the fairy tale. The page conducted me to the Secretary immediately, who greeted me very pleasantly, holding in his hand the open letter of our mutual friend. " Mrs. Trumbull sends no one to me on a trivial or doubtful errand! " was his only comment; and then he stood in an attitude of attention. There was no waste of words on either side. What I asked was granted, an order for the flags was written on the spot by the Secretary, who informed me how to obtain the bunting.

Finding this so easily accomplished, I grew bolder, and asked other favors of the same sort, and for the same use; and they were promised in black and white. At last, I invited the Secretary to honor our Chicago fair with his presence, as President and Mrs. Lincoln had promised to do, on the day of opening; and this he declined. "Your efforts, madam, are in the direction of mitigating the horrors of war. Mine are in the direction of finishing the war; and till that is accomplished, here is my place." I left the War Office with a very different impression of the Secretary from that with which I entered. Excepting President Lincoln, he was, by common consent, the hardest-working man of the administration. He had a grand head and a good face. He was fearfully industrious, laconic, and stern, when opposed to the enemies of the government, at home or abroad; but everywhere in Washington, among loyal people, he was known to be just, courteous, honest, and humane.

I accidentally fell in with Admiral and Mrs. Farragut on this occasion, whom it was a pleasure to meet — they were so simple and unaffected. The admiral was the most genial, social, simple-hearted, and jolly sailor imaginable. He seemed utterly oblivious to the fact that he was a great man; and I doubt if he ever comprehended that his deeds of loyalty and heroism were unusual. When I made some allusion to his being lashed to the mast while fighting the battle of New Orleans, he burst out in amazement: "I want to know if you have heard of that out in Chicago! That wasn't much of an affair, although the papers have made a great ado over it."

The admiral was living in Norfolk, Va., when that state seceded. He fought against secession with entreaty and argument; but it availed nothing, and he was notified by the authorities that he must leave Norfolk with his family in two hours. "I tell you," said the admiral, "we packed our trunks in a hurry, and brought off lots of plunder. There were four of us, and we packed sixteen large trunks among us, containing most of our valuables." In the course of the war he captured many of his old friends and neighbors. "They met me rather stiffly," said the admiral; "not a bit like they used to." Fond of the naval life he led, and proud of his profession, he liked to boast that "since his twentieth birthday, he had not been inland sixty miles from the ocean."

Lieutenant W. B. Cushing was another of the heroes whom I met in Washington. The whole country was at that time ringing with his praises, for he had performed one of the most daring and gallant deeds of the war, for which the Secretary of the Navy had thanked him, in a most complimentary letter. The rebel ram Albemarle had attacked the Union fleet, and destroyed some of our vessels. Lieutenant Cushing was charged with the perilous duty of destroying the ram. Constructing a torpedo boat, and selecting his officers and crew, thirteen in all, not one of whom expected to return alive, he set out on the expedition.

The Albemarle lay near the mouth of the Roanoke, defended by a stoutly built enclosure of logs, the banks of the river lined all the way with pickets. But with incredible daring the young lieutenant drove the torpedo under the ram, and exploded it, and the dreaded Albemarle sank at her moorings. Only one of the company besides Lieutenant Cushing returned from this exploit. The rest were never heard from, but were killed, captured, or drowned. No one would have imagined the boyish, rosycheeked lieutenant to be a hero. He was painfully modest, and any eulogistic allusion to his services dyed his face with crimson blushes to the roots of his hair.

There were other notable men and women to be seen in Washington at that time, some of whom will always be remembered by the country — General Hooker, the hero of Lookout Mountain, "the battle fought above the clouds," and who, despite the wear and tear of military life, was still one of the handsomest men of the day; Chief-Justice Chase, whose Jove-like head and kingly port made him the observed of all observers; Mrs. Stephen A. Douglas, who, it was said, had been more toasted and fêted than any other woman in America, because of her personal beauty; Mrs. General W. T. Sherman, who was intent on seeking attractions for the Catholic department of the forthcoming Sanitary Fair, of which she had been chosen superintendent; Captain Winslow, the brave commander of the Kearsarge, that crippled, and compelled the surrender of the Confederate Alabama, "which had made the ocean lurid with the flames of our burning merchantmen." There was no lack of eminent personages for the pursuit of the lion-hunter. But the nation was in no mood for lionizing its celebrities. It was watching the closing scenes of the mighty drama, now being played before Richmond. It was waiting in hushed expectancy for the news of the great surrender, which would bring an end of war, and restore peace to the weary people. In less than twenty days it came — and the lightning flashed the glad tidings to the farthest verge of the civilized world.

Just as I was leaving Washington, I received a telegram asking me to stop in Indianapolis to inquire the fate of a drummer boy, belonging to the

Eighth Michigan, whose family lived in my neighborhood. Charlie Gardner was a schoolboy, thirteen and a half years old, in the town of Flint, Mich., when the war began. Under the first call for seventy-five thousand troops, his father, who was connected with a military organization of long standing, left for the defence of the national capital. Soon there came a second call, for three hundred thousand more, when Charlie's teacher, an exemplary young man, resigned his position and entered the army. Between this teacher and the boy there existed a very ardent attachment, and Captain Guild seconded Charlie's earnest entreaties that he might go with him as a drummer. He had been famous from babyhood for his musical gifts, and had acquired a good deal of local notoriety for his skilful handling of the drumsticks.

"If I can go to the war with my drum, and take the place of a man who can carry a musket," was Charlie's persistent plea, "I think it my duty to go, especially as you, mother, do not greatly need me at home." At last, reluctantly, the poor mother, who had surrendered her husband, gave up her son, and he was mustered into the Eighth Michigan, with his teacher.

The regiment was ordered to Port Royal, and on their way thither Charlie met his father in Washington. As they were returning from the Navy Yard, where they had been to receive their arms, he saw his father at a distance, and, forgetful of military rule, he broke from the ranks, and ran with childish joy into his arms. It was their last meeting, as Mr. Gardner died the following November, at Alexandria, of typhoid fever. Charlie's letters to his mother, after this bereavement, were remarkably thoughtful for a boy of fourteen. "I am nearly broken-hearted," he writes. "I try to be cheerful, but it is of no use, for my mind continually runs towards home, and a fresh gush of tears comes to my eyes, and I have to weep. But, my dear mother, if this is so hard for me, what must it be for you? Do not take it too much to heart, for remember that you have me left, and I will do my best to help you. I shall send you all my money hereafter, for I really do not need money here." This promise he fulfilled to the letter.

By and by we heard of the fearless little fellow, small beyond his years, on the battle-field with the surgeon, where the grape and canister were crashing around him, pressing forward to the front during an engagement, with the hospital flag in his hand, to aid in the care of the wounded. A peremptory order from his superior officer sent him to the rear. When the wounded were brought in, he worked all night and the next day carrying water and bandages, and lighting up the sorrowfulness of the hour by his boyish but never-failing kindness. Never was the lad more serviceable than during a battle.

At the terrible battle of James Island, in an assault on the fort, his beloved captain, always foremost in a fight, had climbed the parapet, when a shot struck him, he fell backwards, and was seen no more. Now was Charlie indeed bereaved. His teacher, captain, friend, father, lover, dead on the battle-field, and the poor satisfaction denied him of burying his remains. His letters after this were one long wail of sorrow. He could not be comforted —

and yet, always thoughtful for others, he wrote, "Oh, how I pity Guild's poor mother!"

Months passed, and the Eighth Michigan was ordered to Vicksburg to re-enforce Grant, who had beleaguered that doomed city. Battle after battle followed — nineteen of them — in all of which Charlie participated, often escaping death as by a miracle. Something of the fierce life led by this regiment may be inferred from the fact that of fifteen hundred and sixty-three men whose names were on its muster-rolls, less than four hundred survived at the close of the war. On marches, on reconnoissances, and throughout campaigns, Charlie kept with the regiment. They crossed the mountains to Knoxville, Tenn., in General Burnside's corps, when they were compelled to subsist on three ears of corn a day. For weeks they were shut up in that city, besieged by Longstreet's forces, where they were put on quarter rations. Yet not one word of complaint ever came from the patient lad, — not one word of regret, only an earnest desire to remain in the service until the end of the war.

At last there came a letter from the surgeon. During the siege of Knoxville Charlie had been wounded for the first time. A chance shot entered the window of the house in which he was sitting, struck him on the shoulder, and, glancing, entered the left lung. "He *has* been in a very dangerous condition," wrote the surgeon; "but he is now fast recovering. He is a universal pet, and is well cared for in the officers' quarters." The next news was even more comforting. The regiment was on its way to Detroit on a thirty days' furlough, would re-cruit, return, and remain until the end of the war.

Now, a telegram announced that the regiment was in Louisville, then in Indianapolis, in Michigan City, at last in Detroit.

With a happy heart, the glad mother telegraphed her boy to come to her in Chicago, whither she had removed on her husband's death. Then she watched the arrival of the trains. "He will be here to-night! He will be here to-morrow!" she said; and answered every summons of the door-bell herself, expecting to greet her boy. Everything was in readiness for the lad — his room, his clothes, the supper-table spread with the delicacies he loved. Mother, sister, brother, all were waiting him.

A ring at the door. All start, all rush; now it is surely Charlie. No; only a telegram: " *The regiment has arrived in Detroit; but Charlie died in Indianapolis.*" God help the poor mother!

I obeyed the direction sent me to Washington, and went to Indianapolis in search of the lad's dead body. He had not been in that city. I went to Louisville, and consulted the hospital directory of the Sanitary Commission. He had died in Louisville, from hemorrhage of the lungs, occasioned by the chance shot which penetrated them. The lifeless corpse was exhumed from the soldiers' burying-ground, and forwarded to the mother. Ah, the war of the rebellion cost us dearly!

# CHAPTER XII.

A TRIP DOWN THE MISSISSIPPI — AMONG THE SICK AND
DYING — OUR MISSION AND STORES — LOVING MESSAGES
FROM HOME — A BRIDE'S SONG FOR A DYING SOLDIER.

The Army encamped at Young's Point — They cut the Levees — Great
Sickness results — Special Relief Corps sent down — Mrs. Colt, of Milwaukee, and myself attached to the Corps — Our Programme — Outfit —
Some of the Messages entrusted me — Our wheezy Boat — Disloyal Officers — Musical Talent on Board — Singing in the Hospitals — Touching
Episode — Scene in a Memphis Hospital — "Mother, don't you know
your Boy?" — Our Headquarters in Memphis, at Gayoso House — Women
Secessionists — To be sent within Confederate Lines — A stormy Interview — "*Allows* me to be at large!" — We embark on the Tigress for the
lower Mississippi — A dreary Journey.

HE grand passion of the West during the
first half of the war was to re-open the
Mississippi, which had been closed by the
enemy. This great water highway had
been wrested from the possession of the rebels
as far south as Vicksburg, which frowned down
from its unique eyrie, bristling with batteries, and
hurling shot and shell at our brave men encamped
at Young's Point, opposite. It seemed, from its
position, to be thundering forth the mandate, "Hitherto shalt thou come, but no farther."

General Sherman's attempt to take the fortifications and batteries which defended Vicksburg on the

north had failed, and, after a triumphant and conquering expedition up the White River into Arkansas, the whole Western army had been moved down
the Mississippi in transports. At that time the men
were living in boats, or were vainly seeking dry land
for their encampments, amid the swamps, lagoons,
bayous, and sloughs of the abominable portion of
that country, known as the "river-bottoms." The
levees of the river had been cut in many places, as a
"military necessity," or from sheer wantonness on
the part of the "boys," who gloried in any mischief
that brought trouble to the "secesh."

But cutting the levees in this case proved a two-
edged sword, not only injuring the enemy but
drowning out our own men. Those who could, took
to the crowded river-boats. The rest remained in
their wet encampments in the pestilential swamps
and bottom lands, drenched with the protracted
spring rains, almost buried in the unfathomable mud,
and drinking death from the crystal waters of the
Yazoo. Soon sickness and suffering stalked in
among them. The death which they had escaped on
Southern battle-fields sprang upon them here like a
tiger from the jungle. Twelve thousand men lay
sick at one time — about thirty-three and one-third
per cent of the army at that point — and the wail of
agony from the sick and dying was borne to the
listening ears of the tender-hearted Northwest.
Quick to hear, it was swift to relieve. Surgeons and
physicians who had acquired a national reputation
for skill in their profession, were despatched to the
scene of suffering, to battle with the miasmatic foe
which was conquering the conquerors.

Immense shipments of supplies were sent down on

the sanitary boats, with men and women of executive ability, who attended to their safe transmission and equitable distribution. Accompanying these were special corps of relief accustomed to the work in hospitals, and possessed of physical endurance, able to encounter any horror of army life without blenching.

It was with one of these shipments of sanitary stores, and as one of the relief corps, that I went down the Mississippi in March, 1863. Quartermasters, State Surgeon-Generals, members of the Legislature, representatives of the Chicago Chamber of Commerce, a company of nurses whom I was to locate in hospitals, and some two or three women who had been active in working for our invalid soldiers from the very first, made up the delegation. Two of us only — Mrs. Colt, of Milwaukee, and myself — were connected with the Sanitary Commission. Mrs. Colt was the executive woman at the head of the sanitary work in Wisconsin, whose enthusiasm infected the whole state with patriotism and generosity. The sanitary supplies, about thirty-five hundred boxes and packages in all, were sent by the Commission and Chicago Board of Trade.

The programme marked out for us was this. We were to visit every hospital from Cairo to Young's Point, opposite Vicksburg; relieve such needs as were pressing; make ourselves useful in any way among the sick and wounded, co-operating harmoniously as far as possible with medical and military authorities. From every point we were to report our movements, the result of our observations, what we had accomplished, and what we found needing attention, employing the Chicago Press and the bulletins of the Sanitary Commission as our mediums of communication.

Our assortment of stores comprised almost everything necessary in hospital relief; potatoes, onions, sauer-kraut, and vegetables — chiefly for the scorbutic patients, who constituted a majority of the sick — farina, corn starch, lemons, oranges, pearl-barley, tea, sugar, condensed milk, ale, canned fruits, condensed extract of beef, codfish, jellies, a small quantity of the best of brandy, with hospital shirts, drawers, sheets, socks, slippers, bandages, lint, rubber rings, and whatever else might be needed for wounded and sick men. We also took down about five hundred " private boxes," forwarded by private parties for particular companies, or squads, or individuals, and committed to our care for safe transmission and delivery. My own personal outfit consisted of a long pair of rubber boots, reaching to the knee, a teapot, a spirit-lamp to boil it, with a large quantity of Japan tea, condensed milk, sugar and crackers.

Through the daily papers, we volunteered to take letters, messages, or small packages, to parties on our route connected with the army, and to deliver them whenever it was possible. For a week before we started, my time was consumed by people who came to the rooms of the Sanitary Commission on these errands. I made memoranda of the verbal messages and inquiries, which were many and mostly from the poor and humble. My memorandum book lies before me. Here are samples of these messages: —

" Mercantile Battery, Milliken's Bend, George W——. His mother called. She is well; is not worrying about her son; has gained thirteen pounds

since the cold weather. Am to make particular inquiries about her son's habits; does he drink, swear,
or smoke? Tell him his mother would rather he
would be sent home dead, than that he should return
alive and dissipated."

"Young's Point, One Hundred and Thirteenth
Illinois, Peter R——. Wife called. She and the
six children are well; gets plenty of work, good pay,
and the county allowance of three dollars weekly.
He is not to worry about them at all — *at all*. *Must
never think of deserting.* Stand it like a man! All
the family pray daily to the Virgin for him."

"Lake Providence, Eighteenth Wisconsin, John
K——. Father and mother called. Brought four
letters for him. Tell him to take care of his health,
avoid liquor, *never be tempted to desert.* Brother
William, in Second Wisconsin, has got well of his
wound, and gone back to the Army of the Potomac."

"Try to learn something concerning Herbert
B——, of Fifteenth Wisconsin. Has not been heard
from since battle of Stone River." (He was never
heard from until the lists of the Andersonville dead
were published.)

"Try to get permission for James R—— to go to
Helena for his brother's dead body, and take it to
Chicago."

"Try to get discharge for Richard R——, dying
in Overton Hospital, Memphis, of consumption, and
bring him home to his parents."

Scores of pages were filled with similar memoranda.

Our stores, with ourselves, were passed over the
Illinois Central Railroad to Cairo, where we found
sanitary goods, — mostly for the relief of scorbutic

and fever patients, — pouring into the town from every point, all clamoring for immediate shipment. Government had impressed all the boats on the river into its service, and, as there were no troops to be hurried forward, these generous consignments were transhipped as rapidly as possible from the cars to the boats. The boat to which we were assigned was a little, rickety, wheezy, crowded, unsafe craft, which poked along down the river at about one-half the usual rate of speed. It towed along three or four barges of hay, which kept us in constant alarm, as they easily took fire from the sparks of the chimney.

One got loose and drifted away, nobody knew where, and nobody seemed to care, since it belonged to "Uncle Sam." We had no doubt it was purposely detached in the night, at a point agreed upon beforehand, where it could easily be secured by the rebels. The officers, like those of almost all the boats at that time, were secretly in sympathy with the rebellion; though, for the sake of the "greenbacks" of the government, they made a show of loyalty to it. They bore themselves very cavalierly towards us, treating us with scant politeness when they noticed us at all, and ignoring us altogether when it was possible to do so.

Several army officers were on board, who had been home on furloughs. Some of them were accompanied by their wives, who were going as far as Memphis, beyond which point no civilian could pass without special permission. The colonel of the Twelfth Michigan was accompanied by his bride, a beautiful young woman and an exquisite vocalist, whose voice had been carefully cultivated. There were also in the company flutists and violinists, and half a dozen members of a brass band attached to one of the regiments stationed down the river. The boat was ringing with patriotic music all the time. Wherever there were military posts or hospitals, the boat stopped for hours. As we steamed to the landings, all our musical force mustered on deck, and announced our arrival by a grand chorus of voices and instruments. They rendered "The Red, White, and Blue," "The Star-Spangled Banner," "Rally round the Flag, Boys!" and other national songs, in a ringing fashion, that brought every soldier from his tent, flying down the bluffs to welcome us. The vocalists always accompanied us to the hospitals, and made the tour of the wards with us, singing charmingly while they remained. It was a great delight to them to observe how the inspiring music brightened the weary, suffering men. Without any solicitation, they filled every moment of their stay with the cheeriest songs and most patriotic airs.

One poor lad, dying of consumption, too far gone to be sent to his home in Iowa, fixed his large, luminous eyes on the fair girl bride, whose voice was like that of an angel, and asked, " Can you sing something for a dying man? "

It was her first acquaintance with hospitals, her first contact with sickness and death. But without hesitation she moved to his bedside, seated herself on a campstool beside him, and, taking one of his thin hands in hers, sang, with great feeling, " Nearer, my God, to Thee." There was sobbing in the ward when she ended; but the boy to whom she sang only gazed at her with eyes of beseeching. " Can you sing ' The Sweet By and By?' " he inquired. That was given, with the chorus, in which all joined. And then, unasked, her tender, sympathetic voice floated again through the long ward, in the exquisite melody of "Sweet Home." Never have I heard it so feelingly rendered.

The scene that followed was alarming. Men buried their faces in the pillows, and wept aloud; and others, who were sitting up, in partial convalescence, threw themselves on the bed, face downward, in excess of emotion. This would not do. To change the current of feeling, I called for the stirring song, " Rally round the Flag, Boys!" which was given with a will. Then "America" rang out on the air; and, as the whistle of the boat was calling us to return, the choir took leave of the hospital, singing as they went, —

"There's a good time coming, boys,
Wait a little longer ! "

This visit to the hospital greatly affected our beautiful bride. She was to be separated from her husband at Memphis — he to go to his command, and she to return to her home in Detroit. She entreated her husband with tears to allow her to enter the hospitals as a nurse. " You are going to the front to serve your country, — let me be detailed to the hospitals in the same good cause." She was so thoroughly in earnest, and swept away his remonstrances with such passionate entreaty, that I went to his help with the assurance that her youth forbade her serving in the hospitals. I might have added, her beauty also — for Miss Dix detailed only those lacking personal attractions.

We distributed our sanitary stores with a lavish hand, wherever they were needed. Where women were acting as matrons in the hospitals, we committed our benefactions to their care. Where were suspicious looking stewards, or intemperate surgeons, we were less bountiful in our bestowments, and lingered to disburse our supplies to individual cases, as far as we could. At Memphis, there were eleven hospitals, containing nearly eight thousand patients, and this number was daily re-enforced by boatloads of sick men, sent up from points below. I went on board one of these newly arrived transports, and was appalled at the condition of the men. Not one in twenty could have been recognized by his kindred or friends, so disguised were the poor fellows by mud, squalor, vermin, rags, and the wasting sickness of scurvy and swamp fever.

I went with a woman, from central Illinois, to search for her son. We were informed that he had been taken to Jackson Hospital, and the record book of the clerk showed him to be in bed No. 15, ward C. We went to the bed indicated, but there lay an emaciated man of sixty or seventy apparently, sleeping. We did not wake him, but returned to the clerk of the hospital and assured him there was a mistake. The young man for whom we were looking was not there. He was sure his entry book was correct, and we returned for another examination. The mother gazed long and searchingly at the sleeping man in ward C, and then said: —

"No, that's not my boy. My son is but twenty-two."

Directly the sleeper opened his eyes, and stared vacantly at both of us.

"No," she repeated, "no, he is not my boy."

"Oh, mother!" cried the man, in sick, weak, quavering tones, quickly recognizing the dearly beloved face, and slowly uplifting his long bony arms toward her, " I *am* your boy! Don't you know your Willie?"

I went through every ward of every hospital in Memphis, and visited every patient, as I had promised when leaving Chicago. The most home-like and the best kept of them all was the " Gayoso," of which the well-known " Mother Bickerdyke " was matron, and which was called everywhere in Memphis, " Mother Bickerdyke's Hospital." I remember the names of many of the surgeons in charge of the other hospitals. But of " Mother Bickerdyke's " I only remember that she was matron, that " Handy-Andy," a detailed soldier, was her " right-hand man," working with her, and carrying out all her plans and purposes, as if there were but one mind and soul between them. I also remember that she had scores of " contrabands " detailed to her service. Who were her surgeons and stewards I never knew. They were really overshadowed by the matron.

There were nine hundred patients in the hospital. And, in addition to the work imposed on her by this immense charge, almost the entire laundry work of the hospitals in Memphis had drifted into her hands, and was being done by contrabands under her supervision. She was also virtually, though not nominally, matron of the " Small-pox Hospital " at Fort Pickering, two miles down the river, below Memphis. Once a week she went there, with her faithful " Andy," in an ambulance, ready to arouse a moral earthquake, or let loose a small tornado of wrath, if she discovered any cruelty or unkindness to the men, or found disorder and uncleanness in the hospital, or on the premises.

"I have to look after this hospital pretty sharp," she would say, "for small-pox patients are mighty apt not to be taken good care of." But I will not now expatiate on "Mother Bickerdyke," as I shall have something to say of this remarkable woman in another chapter.

Our headquarters while in Memphis were at the "Gayoso House," which had a great reputation for style, secession proclivities, and discomfort. The last two characteristics were pre-eminent. There were nightly drunken rows and fights in the house, sometimes in rooms adjoining ours, when the crash of glass, the ribald song, the fearful profanity, and the drunken mirth, drove sleep from our pillows. We were detained over two weeks in Memphis, so difficult was it to obtain transportation for ourselves and stores down the river. Strict military *surveillance* was kept over the boats bound for the South, and none were allowed to leave Memphis without a pass from the Commander of the Department. Our stores were piled on the levee, waiting reshipment, and a guard was placed over them to keep them from thieves. The Gayoso House was overflowing with *attachés* of the army, waiting a chance to go down the river, like ourselves.

A large company of women were also staying here, who made no secret of their sympathy with the South. Some half-dozen were waiting an opportunity to be passed within the enemy's lines, whither they had been ordered by our officers. They were acting as spies, and sending information to their husbands, fathers, and brothers, in the Confederate army. The officers were badgered beyond endurance by them, for they were continually clamoring to be sent to Vicksburg. Every loyal woman in the house was subjected to their insults, and that, too, while they were virtually prisoners of war. We who had just come from the North were specially obnoxious to them. In every petty way they manifested their aversion to us. They ran furiously against us in the halls and on the stairways, made a general stampede from the parlors whenever we entered them, held their handkerchiefs to their nostrils when in our neighborhood, withdrew their garments from the contamination of contact with ours as they passed us, uttering loud sneers against "Yankee soldiers," "Yankee women," and "Northern white trash."

One afternoon, while waiting for a chaplain, who was to drive me to some of the regimental hospitals outside of Memphis, two of these women came into the parlor and sat down. After we had measured each other with our eyes for a moment, one of them commenced a conversation. She was the wife of a member of the Confederate Congress, and her home was in Thibodeauxville, La.

"I am told you are going down below to look after sick Yankee soldiers," was her opening remark.

"I have been sent from Chicago with some thousands of boxes of hospital stores for the use of United States soldiers," I replied, putting a special emphasis on the words "United States," for I had heard her loudly express her disgust at the name.

"I think it is high time somebody went down to them, for they are dying like sheep, and have just no care at all."

"That is a mistake. They have the best of care, the best of nursing possible under the circumstances,

good surgeons, and delegations going down and
back all the while in their service."

" Well, anyhow, you're the first woman that has
come down here to look after them. This city is
full of Yankee women, wives of Yankee officers —
cold-blooded, white-faced, lank, lean women, decked
out in cotton lace, cheap silks, and bogus jewelry,
women who are their own servants at home, — what
do *they* care for Yankee soldiers, whether they live
or die? We have done wearing silks and jewels in
the South until the war is over. I sold my jewels
and gave the money to the hospitals; and I'd come
down to wearing ' nigger cloth,' and eating corn
bread mixed with water, and prepared with my own
hands, before the men in our hospitals should want
for anything."

" Madam, I honor your devotion to your soldiers,
and only regret the badness of your cause. At the
North we are equally solicitous for the welfare of our
men. But you make the mistake of supposing that
we at the North are as poor as you at the South.
The war is not impoverishing us as it is you. Our
women can afford to wear silks and jewelry, and yet
provide everything needful for the soldiers. Whenever it becomes necessary, we shall be ready to make
as great sacrifices as you."

" Ah, *we* have soldiers *worth* the sacrifice we
make! " she said, with a lofty air. " *Our* men are
the flower of our youth; they have the best blood of
the world in their veins — *gentlemen*, every one of
them. But your Yankee soldiers — ugh! " with a
shiver of disgust and a grimace of aversion; " they
are the dregs of your cities — gutter-snipes, drunken,
ignorant —! "

"Stop!" I interrupted; "stop! I won't hear such calumny. I know just what sort of 'gentlemen' your soldiers are; for we have had seven thousand of them at Camp Douglas in Chicago, taken prisoners at Fort Donelson; and if *they* were the 'flower of your youth,' you are worse off for men in the South than I had supposed."

"And I have seen *your* soldiers, too, to my sorrow and horror. They are barbarians, I tell you. They came to my husband's villa after he had gone to Congress, and I was left alone, with my servants in charge, and they destroyed everything — *everything!* My plate, china, pictures, carpets, even my furniture, were imported; and the wretches! they burned up everything!"

"If your manners were as unbearable as they have been during the two weeks I have seen you in this house, I only wonder you escaped cremation with your villa and furniture. It is astonishing clemency that allows you to be at large in this city, plotting against the government and insulting loyal people."

"*Allows me to be at large!*" she fiercely screamed, almost purple with rage. "Who dares imprison me, I'd like to know. You would like to put me in jail, and shut me up with murderers, and niggers, and thieves, would you? The tables will be turned by and by. England is going to help us; and we will have our feet on your accursed Yankee necks, before you are a year older or wickeder."

She was standing at her fullest height, her face aflame, her eyes on fire, her voice at its highest pitch. It was useless to talk further, so I rose and left the room, saying at the door, with a low bow, "Until that time, madam, I bid you farewell."

I learned afterwards that she went to the provost-marshal, and lodged a complaint against me, declaring that she had reason to believe I was taking contraband goods down the river to smuggle within the rebel lines, like morphine, quinine, chloroform, medicines in the package, and cotton cloth in the piece. Afterwards, at the dinner-table, she offered to lay a wager of a dozen pairs of gloves that not one of our party would go below Memphis, but that we would be sent North by the first boat. She would have lost her bet had any one taken it, as we left Memphis for Vicksburg that very night, on the Tigress.

I learned afterwards that this woman, with her friends and companions, was passed within the Confederate lines at Vicksburg a few days later, where they remained until the surrender of the city to General Grant, on the Fourth of July. They were as heroic in their endurance of the horrors of the long siege as the Confederate men, and evinced courage as unyielding, and tenacity of purpose as unflinching, as any officer who wore the Confederate gray.

# CHAPTER XIII.

ALONG THE DREARY RIVER — SAD SIGHTS IN A REGIMENTAL
HOSPITAL — JOLLY BATTERY BOYS — I AM WELCOMED TO
CAMP BY OLD FRIENDS.

Perils of the lower River — The Tigress and its disloyal Officers — The
Stewardess a Virago — " I could throw you overboard as if you were a
Cat!" — Lake Providence and its fathomless Mud — " The Sanitary Com-
mission's got mired!" — Go down to Milliken's Bend — Distribute
Supplies to Hospitals — Sorry Plight of a Wisconsin Regimental Hospital
— Surgeon-General Wolcott, of Wisconsin, breaks it up — In the Camp
of the Chicago Mercantile Battery — " What a Hubbub ! What a Jubi-
lee !" — Evening Prayers in Camp — The Boys get Breakfast — " The
Victuals will taste better if you don't see the Cooking !" — Leave for
Young's Point — General Grant's Despatch Boat Fanny Ogden gives
me Passage.

THE lower Mississippi was " on the rampage,"
and was all over its banks. It was shore-
less in some places, and stretched its dull,
turbid waste of waters as far as the eye
could reach. No river is as dreary as the lower
Mississippi. Day after day, there was but the
swollen, rushing stream before us. And when the
banks could be seen, only the skeleton cottonwood
trees greeted our eyes, hung with the funereal moss,
that shrouded them as in mourning drapery. The
swollen river was in our favor; for the enemy could
not plant batteries on the banks and fire into the passing boats until it subsided, especially as the steamers kept very near the centre of the stream. The

295

pilot-house of the Tigress was battened with thick oak plank, to protect the helmsman from the shots of the guerillas. Dozens of bullets were imbedded in it, which had been fired from the shore on the last trip up the river. And a six-pound shot had crashed through the steamer, not two months before, killing two or three passengers in the saloon, and badly shattering the boat.

The Tigress was a large, well-appointed boat, and had been handsome before it entered army service. The officers were understood to be disloyal at heart, but willing to work for the government because of its magnificent, prompt, and sure pay. The stewardess was a beautiful quadroon of thirty-five, with a cat-like grace and suppleness of figure, and was wonderfully attractive in her manners to those whom she liked. I have never seen a handsomer woman. But what a virulent, vulgar, foul-mouthed rebel she was! There was not a half-hour of the day that she did not grossly insult some one of our party. There was no redress; for we saw that she bore some relationship to the clerk, that she was a great favorite with all the officers, and that they enjoyed our discomfort under her insolence, which they abetted. She hung her mocking-bird, named "Jeffy Davis," at our door, and then talked *to* him by the hour, but *at* us, calling us by names with which I cannot befoul this page, and charging us with the vilest purposes in coming down to the army.

One day, while we were negotiating with the laundress of the boat concerning some work we wished done, Louisa, the stewardess, came along.

"Can I wash for these ladies to-day?" inquired the laundress of the quadroon virago.

"*Ladies!*" scornfully echoed the insolent creature. "*Ladies!* What's yer talkin' about, gal? Yer hasn't seen no *ladies* sence yer lef' N'Orleans. If yer means this ' white trash,' "— with a contemptuous toss of the head towards where we stood, — " yer may wash for 'em or the debil, if yer likes. But mind yer gits yer pay, gal, for Yankees are mighty mean cusses."

That day, after dinner, I went into the stern of our boat to read. We were opposite the mouth of the Yazoo, where a gunboat was standing guard, the river being miles wide, and rolling like a sea. Louisa followed, to hang up some wet linen to dry, and, as usual, commenced talking *at* me.

"Dere's dat Yankee gunboat agin! 'Pears like ebery Yankee dere 's done dead; for yer neber sees nobody. Bress de Lord if dey be! I'd like to see ebery boat gwine Norf, piled way up wid dead Yanks. *Ki!* Ebery boatload would make dis yere nigger grow one inch fat on de ribs."

She had approached very near, and was standing behind me, and we were alone. I turned sharply round, laid my hand heavily on her shoulder, and looked as terrible as possible. I spoke low, but in a very determined tone.

"You will please stop all this talk about ' dead Yankees,' and ' white trash,' and cease your insolent manners towards my friends and myself! We have had enough of it. If it is not stopped *immediately*, I will take the matter into my own hands. I shall not enter any complaints against you to the captain or clerk, but I will put you where we shall have no more of your impudence." I brought my other hand down heavily on her other shoulder, and spoke yet lower, and in a tone so tragically terrific that I half laughed to hear it. "I could throw you overboard as easily as if you were a cat, and I have a good mind to do it this minute!" — tightening my grasp on her arms and lifting her from her feet. "Go, take that cage down, and carry it to your room, and let me hear any more insolent talk if you dare, — that's all! You will see what *one* Yankee woman dares do, for I'll put you·where you'll be quiet, I promise you!"

She looked at me frightened, stammered something, and, evidently thinking I meditated mischief, hurried away from me into the saloon. She was completely cowed. Whenever we met afterwards, her eyes sought mine, with a "comest-thou-peaceably?" inquiry in them. She gave me a wide berth as she passed me, and treated me with a consideration that was born of vague fear. But there was a marked improvement in her behavior, so great, indeed, that it was the subject of general comment. I did not divulge my interview with her until after we had left the boat, when I informed the party of the moral suasion I had brought to bear on her.

We stopped at Lake Providence, Louisiana, and finding everything more than ordinarily comfortable in the hospitals, — the sickest of the men having been removed North, — we left a quantity of vegetables and needed stores for the convalescents, for there were no other invalids, and then visited the encampment. A canal had been cut from the Mississippi to Lake Providence, a quarter of a mile distant, in which was a fall of fifteen feet. It was hoped that the river would be turned from its natural channel, through the lake, — thence through two bayous connecting with it, and into the river Tensas, which empties into the Mississippi far below Vicksburg, making the circuit of the city. Thus it was believed a continuous waterway might be established in the rear of the defiant city, but this attempt at flanking Vicksburg by water failed, like all others before or afterwards. The swollen flood of the Mississippi rushed into the newly cut channel, broke away all confining levees, and deluged and nearly washed away eighteen or twenty of the richest counties of the state.

Everywhere we found our brown, busy, rollicking fellows seeking a dry place for their encampments. There was no limit to their ingenuity. For hours and hours we rode through sloughs, finally breaking down in one. Then a score of brawny fellows dropped their work of "shebang" building, as they called it, and rushed to our relief with rails, and planks, and whoops, and yells sufficient for a whole tribe of Indians. The two mules, that had sunk to their bellies, were extricated first. The men were devising ways to lift the ambulance to terra firma, when General Logan rode up, who was in command at this horrible place.

"What's the matter, boys?" asked the General, seeing the great commotion.

"Oh, the Sanitary Commission's got mired, that's all!"

The General peeped into the ambulance, where I was sitting on the floor, "holding on," as I had been directed. The forward wheels had broken through the rotten logs that formed a corduroy bridge over the slough. The ambulance had pitched forward,

and I was " holding on " as well as I could, considering I had laughed at the comical performances and
speeches around me until I was exhausted. The
whole thing was so ridiculous that the General
laughed too, but set himself to effect my release from
the imprisoning mud, and succeeded at the expense
of a soiled uniform. We left regiments and hospitals, fighting mud and water everywhere. We informed them of the vegetables sent them by the
Chicago Board of Trade, notified them of the private
boxes intended for different parties among them,
deposited at certain points, distributed the letters we
had brought, and then went to Milliken's Bend,
farther down the river.

When we arrived at the Bend, where some thirty
thousand men were encamped, we notified the Medical Director of our arrival with hospital stores.
He immediately despatched an " orderly " to every
hospital, sending to every surgeon in charge an
order on the sanitary boat for whatever he lacked or
needed, accompanying it with an order on the quartermaster for teams to remove the packages. In
many instances we followed the loads to the hospitals, and witnessed the joy of the poor fellows at this
tangible proof that they were not forgotten at home.
Here, as in Memphis, most of the patients were sick
with miasmatic diseases. There were comparatively
few, among the thousands and thousands whom we
saw, suffering from wounds. The dejection of sick
soldiers we always found greater than that of those
wounded. They needed more encouragement and
more cheerful talk. They were homesick, many of
them longing for mother, wife, sister, and friend.

Often as I bent over a sick man with a sympathetic word, he would burst into a passion of weeping, the more violent for long repression. If I found I had not time to go from bed to bed with a few words to each, I would take a central position, and endeavor to cheer the pale, sad, emaciated men, lying with white faces pressed against white pillows, their hearts travelling back to the homes they had left. I would tell them how they were remembered in loving pride by the loyal North; how all the women of the land were planning, and toiling, and sacrificing for them; of the loaded boats at the levee, sent them in care of a special delegation; of the certainty felt by all that our cause would triumph; of the glad welcome that awaited them when they returned conquerors; and of the dear God who was ever near, in sickness, in camp, on the battle-field, protecting and guiding, and from whose love they could never be separated by any depth of misery, suffering, degradation, or sin.

If any had messages to send home, or letters to write, or friends whom they wished me to visit, I took memoranda of what was desired, in my inseparable notebook. Many a dying message these books contained, from lips ·hushed a few hours after in death. Many an injunction was written in them to comfort friends at home, who still sit in the shadow of death, feeling that they cannot be comforted until they too pass over the river, to rejoin their lost ones.

From one of the hospitals at the Bend there came no surgeon and no requisition. I ordered the inevitable ambulance, with its pair of mules and colored driver, and rode two and a half miles to visit its surgeon. A sadder sight I never witnessed during the war. It was a regimental hospital — always a comfortless place. It contained about two hundred men, all of them very sick, all lying in their uniforms on the bare board floor, with their knapsacks for pillows, with no food but army rations, no nurses but convalescent soldiers, themselves too sick to move except on compulsion, the sick men covered with vermin, tormented by flies during the day, and devoured by mosquitoes at night, — and their surgeon dead-drunk in bed.

I went through the four large wards of the hospital, each one as horrible as the other. In all the wards men were dying, and in all they seemed hopeless and despairing. There was no complaint, no lamentation — only now and then some delirious fever patient would clamor for " ice water," or " cold water right from the well." I stooped down and took one man by the hand, who was regarding me with most beseeching looks. "My poor boy," I said, "I am very sad to see you in this dreadful condition." He pressed my hand on his eyes with both his own, and wept aloud.

Weeping is contagious, and in a few moments one half the men in the hospital were sobbing convulsively. I was afraid it would kill them, they were so excessively weak, but it was some time before they could be calmed. I had taken along in the ambulance, tea, sugar, condensed milk, and crackers. After I had made tea and distributed it with the crackers, I went back to medical headquarters to report the disgraceful condition of the hospital. I was fortunate, for I ran across Surgeon-General Wolcott, of Wisconsin, a very noble man. It was a Wisconsin regiment whose sick were left uncared for, to die like dogs — and he rested not until the hospital was broken up, the surgeon sent home in disgrace, and the men removed to the receiving-boat Nashville.

This was a hospital boat, built on a barge, three stories high, fitted up with cooking apparatus, bath-rooms, laundry, cots, and whatever else was neces-sary. It was towed from landing to landing, receiv-ing the sick temporarily, until they could be taken off by the hospital steamers, and carried farther North. Three weeks later, in passing through the wards of the Nashville, I was hailed from one of the beds in the following jolly fashion: "I say! We are going to live after all, spite of old G——" — the surgeon, — "maggots, flies, mosquitoes, and every-thing else. We are getting to be pretty *sassy* again." Here they were, sure enough, getting well and already full of fun, and jolly over their discom-forts.

The Chicago Mercantile Battery was encamped two miles from the landing, and, as it enrolled over thirty young men from the Sunday-school and society of my own church in Chicago, besides a great many others whom I knew, I determined to visit them, when the hospital work at Milliken's Bend was done. I had already sent them their private packages and letters, and notified them of my in-tended visit. The ambulance left me a mile from their camp, and in the fragrant twilight of a lovely spring day I walked inside the levee, towards its location. Soon I saw the dear fellows striding along the top of the levee to meet me, their figures stand-ing out clearly against the evening sky. I called to them, and down they rushed. Such a welcome! such a chorus of manly, familiar voices! such a shak-

ing of hands! such hearty embraces from the younger
members, sixteen of whom had been members of my
own Sunday-school class.   As I walked with them
into camp, the boys swarmed from tents and "shebangs," bronzed to the color of the Atlantic Monthly
covers, all shouting a hearty welcome, noisy, jolly,
and excited.   What a hubbub! What a jubilee!
Here was a guest from home, who had talked a few
days before with their fathers and mothers, sisters
and wives.   The best "shebang" of the encampment
was placed at my disposal, for I was to spend the
night with them.   I was too far from the boat to
return, had I desired it, and I had planned to be with
them two or three days.   There were unvisited hospitals in that neighborhood.

Everything in the way of shelter, in camp parlance,
that was not a tent, was a *shebang*.   Mine was a
rough hut made of boards, with a plank floor, roofed
with canvas, with a *bona fide* glass window at one
end, and a panelled door at the other.   The furniture
consisted of two bunks, one built over the other,
bedded with fresh hay.   A pair of blankets had
been shaken free from dust, and for my special use,
the officers' overcoats folded smoothly for pillows.
There was a rough pantry with shelves, holding rations, odd crockery and cutlery "jerked from the
secesh," a home-made rickety table, a bit of looking-
glass, sundry pails and camp-kettles, a three-legged
iron skillet, and a drop-light, extemporized from the
handle of a broken bayonet, and a candle, the whole
suspended from the ridge-pole by a wire.

We had a lively time in the "shebang" that evening.   It was packed with the boys, all eager to hear
from home, who put me through a course of cate-

chism concerning matters and persons in whom they were, interested, that soon exhausted my stock of information, and left me no resource but to draw on imagination. The tide of talk flowed over the night into the morning. The "tattoo" had been beaten for retiring, and still the boys were loath to go. At last I broke up the conference. But before withdrawing, George Throop, one of the young men, drew from his breast pocket a copy of the New Testament.

"You know," he said, "when Mr. T—— took public leave of us in church," — Mr. T—— was our pastor — "he gave each a Testament, and made us promise to read it, if possible, daily, while we were away. We haven't failed but once or twice, and then we were on a forced march. One reads aloud and the others listen; and if you are willing, we will read here to-night."

All heads were instantly uncovered, all hum of voices ceased, and a portion of the fifteenth chapter of Luke's Gospel was read, when Sergeant Dyer, a very noble man belonging to a Baptist church of Chicago, voluntarily offered a brief and appropriate prayer. Alas! I never saw again the young lieutenant who officiated as Bible reader, nor the sergeant who offered prayer. Both are sleeping under the sod on the banks of the Red River, where they fell in battle. One, the young, brave, and handsome lieutenant, was shot from his horse as he was urging his men on to the fight; and the other, the fatherly sergeant, was shot through the heart as he was spiking his gun, before joining in the retreat which was sounded.

I had a wakeful night. It was my first attempt to sleep in camp, and I did better afterwards, when I became used to it. I was in the enemy's country — I heard the steady footfall of the guard past my tent, and the incessant booming of the great guns at Vicksburg, fifteen miles away. I had lived in an atmosphere of suffering ever since I left home; and all the visions of horror I had witnessed now danced about my sleepless pillow. Long before the drums beat the réveillé, or the myriad birds had finished their matins, I had made my ablutions in the three-legged iron skillet, given me for that purpose, and completed my toilet before the little six-by-ten inch looking-glass. I hurried out at roll-call, and offered to assist in getting the breakfast.

But I was not allowed this gratification of my feminine desire, for the boys confessed that "they didn't do things woman fashion," and that I had better remain ignorant of their *modus operandi.* "The victuals would taste better if I didn't see the cooking!" I thought so too, after I got a glimpse of them making bread in the iron skillet in which I had bathed my face and hands. For breakfast, we had hot biscuit baked in ovens made of Louisiana mud; fried ham; good coffee, to which I added condensed milk and white sugar; potatoes, and pickles. Camp life gave me a good appetite, and I honored the *cuisine* of the boys by eating heartily. They challenged admiration of their ingenious housekeeping, and I gratified them by praising them *ad libitum.*

For two days and nights I remained with them. There was enough to do, as the Thirteenth Army Corps was stationed here. Then General Grant's despatch boat Fanny Ogden, the fastest boat on the river, steamed to the landing, and with the promise of repeating the visit before I returned home, I left for Young's Point. The Tigress had preceded me, and had transferred her remaining stores to the sanitary boat Omaha. Here I found them, the boat anchored beyond the range of the batteries, directly in front of beleaguered Vicksburg. Silent and dark as a dead city, it lay stealthily behind its defences, watching with Argus eyes the movements of the foe in front, belching defiance and protest from its monster guns, which bristled tier above tier, from the river brink to the top of the highest bluff. Not a sign of life was visible during the day, nor yet during the night, except when the heavy guns blazed out in fiery menace, accentuating their threat with a growl of thunder. Here too were moored the Black Hawk, the headquarters of Commodore Porter, and the Magnolia, headquarters of General Grant. My experiences here must form the subject of another chapter.

# CHAPTER XIV.

OPPOSITE VICKSBURG — ARRIVAL AT GENERAL GRANT'S
HEADQUARTERS—MY INTERVIEW WITH HIM—MY PETI-
TION—A TOUCHING STORY.

We call on General Grant—Reticent, patient, and persistent—We put ourselves on " short Rations" of Talk with him—Stories of his Intemperance foul Calumnies—His chivalric Defence of General Sherman—Am
entrusted with a Variety of Errands to him—My Decision concerning
them—Second call alone on General Grant—" The Gibraltar of America"—The General is very accessible—Not hedged about by Formalities—The most bashful Man I had ever encountered—" I will let you
know Tomorrow"—Discharges twenty-one invalid Soldiers, and gives me
Transportation for them—One dies in Memphis—Another dies in
Chicago, almost Home.

AVING reached Young's Point, our first
movement was to call on General Grant, to
present our letters of introduction and endorsement. Our letters of endorsement
were from the Secretary of War, the Governors
of Illinois and Wisconsin, and our letters of
introduction from Dr. Bellows, the President of the
United States Sanitary Commission. Two or three
of us, who had wished to be prepared for any special
emergency that might arise, had obtained letters of
recommendation from personal friends of General
Grant. His headquarters were on the Magnolia,
where we found him domiciled, unsurrounded by any

circumstance of pomp or state.  All of us who called upon him were as well bestowed in our sanitary boat Omaha, as he, and had in our quarters as much style and luxury.

Our interview was a brief one, and, on the part of the General, laconic.  *We* talked; *he* listened, and appeared to approve our errand.  For, as we rose to go, he inquired if he could aid us in our work.  Calling one of his staff officers, and presenting him to us, he requested him to see that any help we might require in the way of escort, passes, ambulances, transportation, etc., was promptly furnished.  He regretted, at the same time, that he had not a tug to put at our service, to take us from point to point on the river.  The Fanny Ogden, he continued, was his despatch boat, and the swiftest boat in the Western service.  It would be running back and forth continually, and whenever it went in a direction that corresponded with our movements we were heartily welcome to its transportation.

This interview decided two points which had been discussed among ourselves and others.  One was, that General Grant was not a garrulous man; and the other, *that he was not intemperate.*  All the way down from Chicago, we had heard continually of General Grant's sayings, as well as his doings.  We were told that he had said " he would take Vicksburg in so many days, if it cost him three fourths of his army"; that " he would turn the waters of the Mississippi, and leave Vicksburg high and dry, a mile and a half inland," with other like nonsense, which, at that time, did not seem nonsense to the anxious people at home, who neither understood Grant nor the colossal work on his hands.

Our faith in all this twaddle had been somewhat feeble, to be sure; but, as we went out from our first audience with the General, we utterly renounced all credence in its verity. In the first five minutes of our interview, we learned, by some sort of spiritual telegraphy, that reticence, patience, and persistence were the dominant traits of General Grant. We had had familiar and unconventional interviews with other officers we had met, had asked questions and given opinions, had gossiped and joked and "played the agreeable" with them. But we would as soon have undertaken a *tête-à-tête* with the Sphinx itself as with this quiet, repressed, reluctant, undemonstrative man; and we should have succeeded as well with one as with the other. We instinctively put ourselves on "short rations" of talk with him, and so compressed the porosities of language that no one of us will ever have to give account of "idle words" used on that occasion.

Neither was General Grant a drunkard, — that was immediately apparent to us. This conviction gave us such joy, that, had we been younger, we should all, men and women alike, have tossed our hats in air and hurrahed. As it was, we looked each other in the face, and said heartily, "Thank God!" and breathed more freely. We had seen enough, in our progress down the river, at the different headquarters where we had called, to render us anxious beyond measure lest our brave army should be jeopardized, if not our holy cause itself, by the intemperance of its commanders. But the clear eye, clean skin, firm flesh, and steady nerves of General Grant gave the lie to the universal calumnies, then current, concerning his intemperate habits and those of the oi,icers of his staff. Our eyes had become practised in reading the diagnosis of drunkenness.

There were ladies in our party who both played the piano, and sang, very charmingly. One evening, we accepted an invitation from General Grant's Chief-of-Staff to pass an hour or two on board the Magnolia. Our host informed us that " there was a very good piano at General Grant's headquarters, and that he was very fond of music." After an hour of music, we drifted into a conversation upon various topics, until finally General Sherman became the subject of discussion. I observed now that General Grant listened intently.

General Sherman, at that time, was under a cloud. With the right wing of the Army of the Tennessee, thirty thousand strong, he had passed down the Mississippi and up the Yazoo to Johnston's Landing, where he made an assault on the well-manned fortifications and batteries which defended Vicksburg on the north. Abundant and efficient co-operation was promised him, and he hoped to develop some weak point in the enemy's defences, which extended fifteen miles, from Haines' Bluff to Vicksburg. Then it was believed he could fight his way along the heights into the city.

But for various reasons he failed to receive the support which was promised, while the difficulties growing out of the topography of the abominable country were almost insurmountable. He was repulsed with great slaughter, losing over two thousand men, while the enemy reported a loss of only sixty-three killed. Burying his dead under a flag of truce, General Sherman re-embarked his men for Young's Point — and Secretary Halleck ordered

General John A. McClernand of Illinois to super-
sede him.

Immediately General Sherman fell in public estimation. The Northern press was very decided in condemnation of his generalship; and as we went down
the river, we had heard this condemnation reiterated and emphasized by men in all positions, many
of whom declared the General insane. Some of this
gossip was repeated in the conversation that took
place on the Magnolia, one of the company remark-
ing that " it was very evident that General Sherman
had been much overrated in the past."

This brought out General Grant. " You are mistaken, sir! " he said, very quietly. " General Sherman *cannot* be overrated. He is the greatest soldier
of the world; and if the Duke of Wellington were
alive, I would not rank him second even to him."

" The country will place you before General
Sherman in soldierly ability," replied some one
present. " It will never assent to the statement
that General Sherman is entitled to the first place,
not even when you make it."

" The country does General Sherman great injustice, at present," was General Grant's reply. " I am
not his superior as a soldier. If I surpass him anywhere, it may be in the planning of a campaign.
But of what value are the best planned campaigns,
if there are not great soldiers like General Sherman
to execute them? " And he spoke with the warmth
of friendship, and as one jealous of the honor of a
brother soldier. Subsequent events have justified
this estimate of General Sherman, and demonstrated
the impossibility of creating jealousy or antagonism
between these two great men.

I had been entrusted with a great variety of errands to General Grant, every military post and hospital at which we stopped adding to my budget. I received these commands, and took copious memoranda of facts, events and dates connected with them, not quite sure what I should do when the time came to act. Some presented requests to have wrongs righted. Others asked favors not easily obtained, or made a statement of grievances, or besought pardon for offences which were being punished with loss of position, — and so on. I was frequently told that my only hope of success, in some of these cases, lay in the fact that I was a woman, and that " women could do anything they desired with army officers."

I came to a very swift decision concerning these errands after I had been to General Grant's headquarters. Only one class of them was sufficiently important to challenge the attention of a commander whose whole soul was absorbed in the attempt to solve the problem how best and most speedily to conquer Vicksburg, the " Gibraltar of America," as Jefferson Davis had confidently declared it. There rose the impregnable city, strong in its natural position, bristling with batteries to its very highest pinnacle, and for fifteen miles along the river bank. And here sat the determined officer, defeated in his every attempt to flank the Mississippi, but still unfaltering in his resolve to subjugate this defiant citadel of the Confederacy, and revolving more daring schemes for the accomplishment of this never-to-be-yielded purpose. The only petition I could bring myself to present to such a man, at such a time, was one that involved the life of a score of his soldiers — my brothers.

In my visits to the hospitals there had been brought to my notice the cases of several sick soldiers — twenty-one in all — who were pronounced incurable by the surgeons. The poor fellows would speedily die, or their illnesses would become chronic, and they would drag on a few miserable years in confirmed invalidism. In any case they were worthless to the government, and should be discharged from its service. There were many such cases, but these were of peculiar hardship, because in every instance there was an absolute hindrance to their discharge, through irregularity, for which they were not responsible, and that could not be easily righted. They had lost their "descriptive lists"; or their regiments were on some remote expedition, beyond the reach of mails; or they were too ill to go home unaccompanied, and furloughs were just then a forbidden favor. All the details of these twenty-one cases were committed to me, with the endorsement of the surgeons in whose hospitals they were, and who certified that these men could render the government no further aid, and should be released from military service.

The request that these twenty-one dying soldiers should be discharged, and sent home, was the only one I felt willing to present to General Grant, for, as matters were, he alone could discharge them. Having "got the hang" of the General on the first interview, I resolved to see him again, alone, and urge my suit in behalf of the poor fellows. It was a somewhat irregular proceeding, and I knew it; but I also knew that he had the power to discharge them in the teeth of any informality, and I believed he would, when he knew all the facts. At any rate, I would not go back without making an effort for the helpless boys who had besought my aid, and had sent after me their prayers and anxious thoughts.

So a few mornings after, when breakfast was over, without informing any one on the sanitary boat of my purpose, I started alone for the Magnolia. How to get there was a question, for terra firma was nowhere. Where it was not mud, it was water; and where it was not water, it was mud; and the mud was so liquefied that you sank into it as though walking through porridge. There was substantial footing on the levees, but those did not run in the direction whither I was going. One of the boys of Colonel Bissell's Engineer Corps spied me standing ankle-deep in mud, and offered his help. I needed it, for the Magnolia had moved upstream nearly half a mile, and I had lost my reckoning. He piloted me over sloughs bridged by his corps, in which lay rotting carcasses of horses and mules, which had got "mired," and been left to die. I went up the gangway of the Magnolia, and there confronted the guard.

"I wish to see General Grant," I said to him. "I have letters of introduction — one from the Secretary of War — and I wish to put these papers in his hands."

"Pass up stairs into the saloon," was his reply. At the head of the stairway I was halted by another guard, to whom I told the same story.

"Pass round behind the screen," was the reply. The saloon of the Magnolia was partitioned into three apartments by movable green baize screens. I passed round in front of the first of these, as directed, and came upon the officers of General

Grant's staff, lounging and chatting. To them I repeated my story, and was directed to pass round behind the next screen. There sat a body of medical men, with reports and documents, and any quantity of budgets tied with red tape. One of them chanced to be a Chicago physician, and we recognized each other. To him I told my desire, and presented my papers, and was again directed to pass around behind the screen — the third one — where I should find the General alone.

I obeyed, and, through the blue haze of cigar smoke circling through the apartment, I saw General Grant, sitting at the table, wearing his hat, a cigar in his mouth, one foot on a chair, and buried to his chin in maps, letters, reports, and orders. Whatever *mauvaise honte* I may have felt in thus obtruding myself upon the modest General, was speedily banished by his discomposure. For a moment he seemed the most bashful man I had ever encountered. Rising, and placing a half-dozen chairs at my service, he begged me to be seated, removing his hat, and taking his cigar from his mouth, and then quickly and unconsciously replacing both. I remained standing, and, without any circumlocution whatever, announced my errand, and implored his aid. He heard me without interruption.

" But these are matters that should be laid before my Medical Director. I have put all these things out of my hands," were his first words.

Yes, I knew that, and told him so; and I also told him that it was necessary for some one to " cut red tape " boldly and promptly in behalf of these men; that no subordinate dared do it, but all said he could, and encouraged me to believe that he would.

And I besought him, with the earnestness that women felt in these sad cases during the war, to give me the pleasure of returning these boys to the mothers, sisters, and wives, who would lighten with love the dark valley of death into which they were fast descending. I promised, if he gave them discharge and transportation, to take every man to his friends, leaving no one of them until I saw him well cared for. The General briefly examined the documents I gave him, and then said "he would let me know to-morrow what could be done."

The next evening, an officer of his staff came to our boat, enlivening an hour with most charming and intelligent conversation. He made me supremely happy with the discharge of these twenty-one soldiers from the service of the country, who had been rewarded with loss of health, and, as it afterwards proved to some of them, with loss of life.

But if *I* was happy, what shall I say of the poor emaciated fellows, who looked for my return to them as one looks for a reprieve from sentence of death? Most of these men were brought North on our sanitary boat. One of them died on the way, and was buried at Memphis, and another died in Chicago. His home was in Wisconsin; and a ride of four hours more would have taken him to the arms of his mother, who was expecting him. But when we reached Chicago, Saturday evening, the train for his town had left, and he was compelled to remain in the city over Sunday. I took him to a hotel near the station from which he was to start on Monday; and, when I had seen him comfortable in bed, wished to leave him, to telegraph his mother of his nearness to her, and then to go to my own family. I promised

to send him a nurse in less than an hour, and to accompany him home to Wisconsin myself on Monday.
But he begged so wildly that I would return myself
and stay with him, that I consented, after I had informed my family of my return to the city.  He followed me to the door with his beseeching eyes, saying, "I hate to have you go, for it seems as if I
should not see you again."  I assured him that I
would not be absent above two hours at the furthest,
and, as he wished no one to remain in the room with
him, I left the door ajar, getting the promise of the
chambermaid to look in upon him occasionally.

In less than two hours I was back at his bedside.
"He has been sleeping quietly ever since you left,"
said the servant.  There he lay as I had left him,
with one hand under his head, his face turned
towards the door, that he might see any one who
entered the room.  Sleeping?  Yes — the sleep of
death.

Mothers will not think me weak when I confess
that I closed the door and locked it, and then wept
long and bitterly over the dead boy — not for him,
but for the mother whose youngest child he was.
He had so longed for his mother, this boyish, twenty-
year-old soldier!  Again and again had he said to
me: "I don't expect to get well — I know I must
die; but if I can only see my mother once more I
shall be willing to die."

On Monday she came for his coffined body.  As
she bent over him and wrestled with her mighty
grief, she seemed to find comfort in the oft-uttered
thought, that " he had given his life for his country."

# CHAPTER XV.

I AM INSTALLED HEAD COOK IN A FIELD HOSPITAL — CHEER-
ING UP THE "BOYS" — CAPRICIOUS APPETITES — MY RIDE
WITH BLACK SOCRATES — VICKSBURG.

Large Field Hospital at Young's Point — Am put in Charge — Cater to the
capricious Appetites — "Tea and Toast" for a forty-five-year-old "Boy"
— "Tea! tea! tea! from the homespun Teapot" — Lemonade under
Difficulties — Men transferred to Hospital Steamer City of Memphis
— Visit to the Thirteenth Illinois — "Socrates" and his Six-Mule
Team — "Mules is dat mean dey has ter be licked!" — Accomplish-
ments of the Thirteenth Illinois — "The stealing Regiment" — Ac-
company the Engineer Corps down the Levee — Peep into Vicksburg
with a powerful Glass — No sign of Home-Life — Rams Lancaster and
Switzerland run the Blockade — One destroyed, the other disabled.

OST of the hospitals at Young's Point were
regimental. There was one large field hospital, made by pitching tents lengthwise,
one beside the other, and one opening into
the other, but it was a comfortless place. In
this field hospital were one hundred and fifty or
two hundred men, all sick with diseases that had
assumed a chronic form, the surgeon said. A hospital steamer, the City of Memphis, was daily expected
at the Point, when this hospital was to be broken up,
and the patients removed to St. Louis. I received
permission to do anything I pleased for them within
certain specified limits; and the head surgeon seemed

319

much gratified that I manifested an interest in his
men. He evidently lacked force and vital sympathy
with his patients. He was a man of routine, a man
of prescriptions; but he was kind-hearted. He indicated what patients might have toast, tea, and soft-
boiled eggs; who could be treated to "egg nog,"
who to lemonade; who might have soup, and who
only gruel; and he plainly marked on the diet-book,
for my assistance, the food for each. There was
nothing for any of the patients in the hospital but
army rations.

"Moreover," said the surgeon, "if you really wish
to arrange special diet for these men yourself, I will
put at your service the most efficient colored help we
have, and our conveniences for cooking." *Conveniences!* The good man must certainly have meant
*in*conveniences; for there was no kitchen, no stove,
no cooking apparatus, — nothing except two or three
immense portable soup-kettles, or boilers, with a little
furnace and pipe attached. The cooking was performed in the open air, where rain, smoke, and ashes
saturated both the cook and the food. The colored
men speedily made a huge fire of cottonwood logs
sufficient to roast an ox; and, having seen water put
into the boilers to heat, I went into the hospital to
investigate the appetites of the men.

It was a miserable place, although, at that time, and
in that locality, the best probably that could be done.
The cots were placed inside the tents, on the un-
planked ground. The soil was so dropsical that
wherever one trod, it sank under one's weight, and
one immediately stood in a little pool of water. The
legs of the cots stood on small square pieces of board,
which alone kept them from sinking into the moist

earth.  The weather was warm as July in our climate, although it was April, and the atmosphere was
dense with gnats, small flies, and every other variety
of winged insect.  The hospital swarmed with large
green flies, and their buzzing was like that of a bee-
hive.  The men were hushed to the stillness of death.
They had been sick a long while, and had utterly
lost heart and hope.  Many of them did not even lift
their hands to brush away the flies that swarmed into
eyes, ears, noses, and mouths.

I walked through the oozy, muddy aisle to the end
of the connected tents; but not even the rare sight
of a woman among them induced a man to speak, few
even to turn their heads.  I wanted to break this
apathy, to see a little life kindled in these disheartened fellows.  I saw that I must create a little sensation among them.  So, taking a stand in the centre
of the tents, I called to them in a cheerful, hearty
tone, " Boys! do you know you are to be got ready
to go North in a day or two? "  This brought up a
few heads, and caused a little additional buzzing from
the flies, which were brushed away that the men
might hear better.  " This hospital is to be broken
up by day after to-morrow," I continued, " and you
are to go to St. Louis, and perhaps to the Chicago
hospitals.  The City of Memphis is on its way down
here for you.  By next Saturday at this time you
will be almost home.  Isn't this tiptop news? "

I had roused them now.  There was a general
waking up at the sound of the words "almost
home."  They had lost mental stamina in their protracted illness, and needed the tonic of a great hope,
or the influence of a stronger mind exerted upon
them.  After the first shock of surprise was over,

the men gathered their wits, and precipitated questions upon me, in a slow, sick, drawling, semi-articu-
late fashion, a dozen speaking at a time: "Where'd
— you — come — from?" "Who — told — you —
so?" "What — you — down — here — for?" I had
aroused their curiosity, and I hastened to answer
their questions as they had asked them — all at once.
I had gained an advantage, and hastened to follow
it up.

"Now, boys, I expect to stay here till this hospital
is broken up; and if you would like to have me, I
am going to stay here with you. I have lots of good
things for you. The folks at home have sent me
down here, and have given me everything that you
need; eggs, tea, crackers, white sugar, condensed
milk, lemons, ale, everything — and your surgeon
wants you to have them. He has told me what each
one of you can have. Now, my boy," turning to the
man nearest me, "if you could have just what you
wanted, what would you ask for?" He was a
married man, as old as myself, but at that time, in
his miserable weakness and discouragement, a mere
puling, weeping baby.

It was an effort for him to think or decide; but
finally he settled on a slice of toast, a poached egg,
and tea. I brought out my spirit lamp, bottle of
alcohol, and teapot, and made the tea before his eyes,
sweetening it with loaf sugar, and adding condensed
milk. One of the negro assistants toasted the bread
by the roaring, crackling fire outside, burning up
half a dozen slices by way of preliminaries, and
looking, when she brought the crispy cinders to me,
with her characteristic "It's done done, missis!" as
if she had strewn ashes on her head for her ill-luck.

I dropped an egg into boiling water, cooking it slightly, and laid it on the toast, buttering the whole economically for the sake of the sick man's stomach, and then took it to his cot.

A hundred pairs of eyes had been watching these preparations, and as I set the tin cup of tea and tin plate of toast on the campstool, I received a score of orders from neighboring beds for " some tea and toast, just like that 'ere." Crowding his knapsack and pillow behind him, I propped up the forty-five-year-old "boy" to whose uncertain appetite I was catering, and invited him to taste his "special diet." As he tasted, a sickly smile distorted his thin ghastly face, which was succeeded by a fit of weeping, his tears literally mingling with his drink. "Is it good?" I asked. "Oh, — *proper* — good! — jest — like — what — my — wife — makes!" with the drawl of long sickness and great weakness.

I had got into business. "Tea! tea! tea! with white sugar and milk in it!" — was the cry that came up from every bed. I undertook to make the tea by the wholesale, in the inevitable camp-kettle, in which soldiers make tea, coffee, soup, and cook everything. But no! they would have it from my "homespun teapot," as one of them called it. "Don't — let — that — 'ere — old — teapot — o' yourn — git — played — out — before — you — git — to — me!" entreated a Missourian at the farther end of the hospital. I explained to him that there was no "play out" to the teapot; that I had alcohol and tea enough to keep it in active operation for weeks, — and he then waited patiently for his turn.

For nearly three days I made tea for all who wanted it in that three-pint teapot, over an alcohol

lamp. It came out from this service as good as new.
And when a party of nine of us went from Chicago
across the Plains, four years after, all the tea necessary to our inspiriting was brewed in that same army
teapot. It still lives, and does duty at midnight,
when now and then a hard night's work cannot be
avoided.

I had with me the condensed extract of beef, and
desiccated vegetables, so that the soup-making was
an easy matter. Before dark, limited as were the
arrangements of my *cuisine*, every man was made
more comfortable, happier, and more hopeful, than
had seemed possible in these forlorn quarters. Except, alas! some seven who lay dying, their wide-
open eyes seeing only the invisible — slowly drifting,
drifting, drifting, out on the great ocean of eternity.
Three of them died before morning, and were buried
in the side of the levee before I got round to the
hospital the following day.

The next day and the day after were spent in
about the same way, varied with letter-writing for the
men, and in hearing the multiform versions of their
various troubles, which were mainly the troubles of
wives and children, and friends at home. As badly
off as they were themselves, covered with the mud
and filth of months of sickness, neglected, unnursed,
unwashed, uncared for as they needed to be, they had
little to say of themselves. It was of their dear ones
at home, some of whom, not thinking of the harm
they were doing, poured out their magnified little
sorrows into the letters they wrote their soldier relatives. These were read and re-read, and brooded
over, and then placed under the pillow to be read
again, until the sick man's fevered imagination peo-

pled his waking, as his sleeping hours, with phantoms of horror.

If our men were brave on the field, they were still braver in the hospital. I can conceive that it may be easy to face death on the battle-field, when the pulses are maddened by the superhuman desire for victory,— when the roar of artillery, the cheers of the officers, the call of the bugles, the shout and charge and rush impel to action, and deaden reflection. But to lie suffering in a hospital bed for months, cared for as a matter of routine and form, one's name dropped, and one only known as "Number Ten," "Number Twenty," or "Number Fifty"; with no companionship, no affection, none of the tender assiduities of home nursing, hearing from home irregularly and at rare intervals, utterly alone in the midst of hundreds; sick, in pain, sore-hearted and depressed, — I declare this requires more courage to endure, than to face the most tragic death.

Oh, the Christ-like patience I have seen in the hospitals! Oh, the uncomplaining endurance of soldiers who had been reared as tenderly as girls, and who were just from under their mothers' wing! In every hospital there were these silent heroes, whose gentle patience and uncomplaining fortitude glorified the rough wards. Every woman nurse, every matron, every "Sister of Mercy" who did duty beside the beds of our sick and wounded during the war, carries in her heart tender memories of them, which sanctify the otherwise horrible associations of army life.

On the third day the City of Memphis steamed to the landing, and as rapidly as possible the patients of this comfortless field-hospital were taken on board,

put in a warm bath, their hair cut, fresh, clean garments given them in exchange for the filthy ones
they wore, and then in sweet, clean beds they started
up the river for St. Louis. They had been transferred from one hospital to another, each as destitute
of proper accommodations as the one they had left;
so that most of them were rooted in the belief that
the transfer to this hospital steamer would prove
only another illustration of a change of place, and a
retention of discomfort. But a smile stole to their
faces as they were lifted into fresh beds, and from
scores of pallid lips came the outspoken satisfaction:
" Oh, this is good! this is like home!"

I went on board to bid them " good-bye," and
found them vastly improved by their change of condition. To some I had been more drawn than to
others, and in a few I had become specially interested. One of these had never recovered from an
attack of pneumonia, and was fearfully attenuated
and spectral. But his physical decay had not told
on his mental condition, and he was enduring mutely
and heroically, asking no sympathy, making no complaints, never parading his sufferings, never whining
or impatient, and always accepting the attentions
paid him with grateful courtesy. I went over to his
bed, and, offering my hand, said in a lower tone,
and less familiarly than to the others: " Good-bye,
my friend! I am glad you are going North. The
change of climate will set you up directly; I think
you will get well right away now."

He shook his head. " I am not concerned about
it. I gave myself to God when I entered the service,
and I have tried to do my duty. Whether I live or
die is His business."

" That is so; but for the sake of those who love you, I hope you will recover."

Without lifting his eyes again to my face, and withdrawing his hand from mine, he said in a lower voice, " There is nobody to care whether I live or die. I am obliged to you, though, for the interest you express." I never heard of him afterwards.

I had been requested before leaving home to visit the camp of the Thirteenth Illinois, if I should happen in their neighborhood; and I had been entrusted with various packages for individuals belonging to it. These I had sent forward, and had received acknowledgment of their receipt. They were encamped seven miles down the levee, and almost daily I had received a note from some man of the regiment charging me "not to forget to come to them," with other similar messages.

One pleasant day I started for their encampment. The only chance of riding was in an army wagon, drawn by six mules, and loaded with molasses, hardtack, salt pork, and coffee. A very black negro drove the team, who rejoiced in the name of " Socrates." He pronounced his name as if it were " Succotash." In this lumbering ark I took passage through the mud and water. We had gone but a little way when we stuck fast in the mud. Thereupon black Socrates fell into a passion worthy of Xantippe, and cudgelled the mules unmercifully. They kicked, and pulled, and floundered, and at last extricated themselves. We started again, rode slowly on a little farther, again got stuck in the mud, and again Socrates plied his cudgel, and beat and swore, and swore and beat, until I could endure it no longer.

" What *are* you beating the mules for?" I remonstrated. "Don't you see they are doing the best they can?"

"Lors, missis, dey orter be licked. Mules is dat mean dey allers won't pull a bit when dey knows yer's gwine som'whar in a hurry."

"Well, I won't have them beat any more. Now stop it. I cannot stand it. It hurts *me*."

Socrates threw back his head, showed all his gleaming teeth, and laughed immoderately. "Yer'd git hurt a heap, missis, if yer stayed hyar allers; for I 'clar to goodness, mules is dat mighty mean dat yer jes' has ter lick 'em!" and he flew to cudgelling again. It was too much. I could not endure it; and, crawling out from the molasses and pork, I picked my way to the top of the levee, thickly dotted with soldiers and tents.

For miles the inside of the levee was sown with graves, at the head and foot of which were rude wooden tablets, bearing the name and rank of the deceased, and sometimes other particulars. The soldiers spoke of their buried comrades in a nonchalant way, as "planted." In most cases the poor fellows had been wrapped in their blankets, and buried without coffins, or "overcoats," as the men called them. In places the levee was broken, or washed out by the waters, and the decaying dead were partially disinterred. This sickening sight did not move me then as it would now, for hospital and army life, after the first few weeks, mercifully bred a temporary stoicism, that enabled one to see and hear any form or tale of horror without deep emotion.

A young lieutenant became my guide and escort to the camp of the Thirteenth Illinois. We came upon it unexpectedly. I halted reverently, and laid

PLATE III.

## FAMOUS UNION BATTLE-FLAGS.

1. Thirteenth Ills. Reg't.  2. Twenty fourth Mich. Reg't.  3. Eighth Mo. Reg't.
4. First Minn. Art.  5. Second Mich. Reg't.  6. Seventh N.Y. Heavy Art.

*For Descriptions see pages 34-37.*

PHOTOGRAPHED AND PAINTED FROM THE ORIGINAL FLAGS EXPRESSLY FOR THIS WORK.

A. D. WORTHINGTON & CO. PUPLISHERS, HARTFORD, CONN.

my hand upon the lieutenant's arm, for some sort of
service was in progress in the camp. The men were
standing or sitting in a body, and a chaplain was
delivering an address, or preaching a sermon. As I
listened, he seemed to be setting the sins of his audience before them in a manner that savored more of
frankness than tact, and he was exhorting the men
to repentance. The boys, however, seemed to enjoy
the recital of their shortcomings and sins of commission, and frequently assisted the preacher's memory
to facts which he had forgotten, or did not know,
suggesting peculiar punishments for them, all of
which was immediately adopted into the discourse.
I thought the interruptions of the soldier audience
needless and profane. Little as I sympathized with
the queer exhortation of the chaplain, I tried to infuse into my manner an expression of reverence,
that would rebuke the wild fellows. The service
was brought to an abrupt close by one of the men
shouting out, "I say, Harry, you'd better wind up
your gospel yarn, and see who's behind you!"

There was a shout. The speaker turned toward
me, when lo, it was no chaplain, but the young
brother of one of my friends, an irrepressible wag
and mimic. His mimicry in this case, if reprehensi-
ble, was perfect. I found that this regiment had
made itself quite a reputation by its versatility.
There was nothing its men could not do. All the
arts, trades, professions, and mechanical employments were represented in it. In addition to their
other accomplishments they were such experts in
quizzical thefts, that they had earned the somewhat
equivocal *sobriquet* of "The Stealing Regiment."

The brigade surgeon walked back with me part of

the way, and gave me an amusing account of their
exploits in this line, some of which were very comical.  He told me afterwards, that while he was thus
engaged, the boys went to his tent, and while some
of them diverted the attention of his servant, others
stole his stove with all the pipe attached to it, the
fire in it burning all the while, all his kettles and
pans on it, and his supper cooking in them.  They
gave operatic concerts, theatrical performances, mock
trials, sham fights, exhibitions of gymnastics and
feats of legerdemain, were proficients in negro minstrelsy, gave medical lectures, and conducted religious services — in short, there was no performance
to which they were not equal.

As soon as we had recovered from the laughter
raised at the expense of the counterfeit chaplain, I
asked to be shown to the regimental hospital.

"Haven't got any!" was the answer in chorus.

"Why, what do you do with your sick men?"  I
inquired.

"Don't have any!" was the reply, again in chorus.
And indeed they rarely had sickness in their camp.
They were fortunate in the men to begin with, who
were strong, not too young, and mostly married.
Then almost all had resources in themselves, thanks
to their mental ability and early training.  They had
an inducement in their families to take care of themselves, and good influences were exerted over them
by the letters of wives and mothers.  Their officers
were men of intelligence, who knew how to take care
of their men, had become attached to their commands,
were humane and *not drunken*.  They had lost heavily at the battle of Chickasaw Bluffs, their colonel
being left among the dead.  But when it came to

sickness, they hooted at the idea. The regiments in their neighborhood were a little afraid of them, I found; they were so hearty and roistering, and so full of mad pranks. After dining with the adjutant, I left them, not quite satisfied with my visit, because, as that worthy explained, "I had unfortunately found them all well instead of sick."

On the way back I passed black Socrates, still ploughing through the mud, but evidently reconciled to the "mighty meanness" of his mules, as he was sitting aloft on the driver's seat, shouting in a sing-song recitative, —

> " An' I hope to gain de prommis' lan',
>    Glory, hallelujah !
> Lor', I hope to gain de prommis' lan',
>    Dat I do!
> Glory, glory, how I lub my Savior,
>    Dat I do! "

When I reached the sanitary boat Omaha, I found that a portion of our delegation, and some of the supplies, had been transferred to the Fanny Ogden, destined for a point up the river a few miles, where there were sick men in great destitution. I went on board the boat with them. But after dark we steamed down the river, below the point where a canal was being cut by Colonel Bissell's Engineer Corps, which, it was hoped, would divert the main current of the Mississippi, and leave Vicksburg on a bayou two or three miles inland. Backwards and forwards, up the river and down the river, the little boat darted most of the night, carrying orders and despatches for General Grant. Most of the time we were within range of the enemy's guns, which kept up an incessant firing of shot and shell at the dredging boats in the canal, whose locomotive headlights furnished an admirable mark.

We sat on deck through the night, watching the shells as they flew shrieking over our heads, which we could distinguish by the lighted fuse, and endeavoring to judge the size of the shot by the singing, howling, whizzing, or shrieking they made in their swift transit through the air. The Fanny Ogden did not go up the river at all, but returned to the landing by morning, out of the reach of the enemy's guns, where she lay until night. We were again informed she was bound up stream, again embarked on her, only to pass the second night like the first, steaming up and down the river, carrying General Grant's despatches.

During the day, a detachment of the Engineer Corps was sent down inside the levee, to plant a battery at the extreme point of land directly opposite Vicksburg, where the Mississippi is very narrow and deep. The levee at this place was nearly fifteen feet high, and the battery was to be built into the levee from the inside. Its object was to destroy the foundries and railroad and machine shops of Vicksburg, lying near the river, and which were in great activity day and night. The prospecting for the position of the battery, and the planning and marking out of the work, had been done in the night, not to attract the attention of the enemy. Now they were to work wholly inside the levee, and so were busy in the daytime.

Colonel Bissell himself was in command, and I accepted his invitation to accompany the squad, and take a nearer view of Vicksburg than it was possible to gain elsewhere. We steamed down near the mouth of the canal, took a rowboat through one of the creeks to the point of land opposite the city, and then walked behind the levee. While the men were working like Titans, the Colonel loaned me a powerful field-glass, and found for me a position where I could look over into the beleaguered city, without being seen by their pickets. Here the river was so very narrow that the pickets of the two armies could carry on conversation, when all was still — as they sometimes did.

At the right was the hospital, swarming with gray-uniformed Confederates. They were sitting in the windows, at the doors, on the piazzas, lying on the grass in the yard, coming and going, some on crutches, some led by assistants. A newsboy was selling papers among them, and I could distinguish between the large type of the headings and the smaller print of the columns. In the belfry of the court house, more than half-way up the hill, an officer was signaling with flags, of which he seemed to have an immense variety. Beside him stood two ladies, one wrapped in a cloak, and the other in a shawl. I could even see that the bonnet of one was blue in color. Two negresses, carrying baskets on their heads, which looked as if filled with clean clothes, set down their baskets, bowed and courtesied to one another, and then, with arms akimbo, stood and gossiped, laughing convulsively, if one could judge from the motions and gesticulations. Gray guards were pacing back and forth before the foundries. Officers were galloping to and fro; trains of freight cars were being loaded; new batteries were being placed in position; and other scenes of warlike activity were apparent. But nothing was visible that betokened pleasure or social life, or such proceedings as occupy the people of a city in time of peace. No children were on the streets, no women walking or shopping, no gay equipages, no sign of inhabited homes.

During the day I learned that the gunboats Lancaster and Switzerland were to run the Vicksburg batteries during the night, to co-operate with Admiral Farragut. He had steamed up the river from New Orleans, had fought his way past Fort Hudson, and was now moored nearly opposite the canal before spoken of, but on the other side of the bend, below Vicksburg. The Mississippi River was now open its entire length, save here at Vicksburg. The gunboats did not get started as soon as they were ordered, and it was daydawn before they came under the rebel fire. They were both rams; one, the Lancaster, being of wood, and every way frailer than its consort, the Switzerland.

As they rounded the peninsula, from which the trees had been cut, a signal rocket was sent up by the enemy, and then the heavy guns opened their iron throats and belched thunder and fire. All along the river bank, below, and above, flames seemed to leap out of the ground, as if the very bottomless pit had been uncapped, and then the earth and the water shook with the roar of the batteries. Louder and faster bellowed the cannon, and the whole opposite hillside seemed on fire. But on went the rams, not a living thing being visible about them, seeming to bear charmed lives, that could not be wrecked by shot or shell. "They will get by in safety!" we said, as we watched them through the portholes of the gunboat Lafayette, which hugged the west shore of the river: "Another quarter of an hour, and they are safe!"

Vain prediction! There came a plunging shot — a rush of steam — an explosion — the air was full of cinders and splinters, and then men could be seen leaping into the water, swimming and struggling for life. A shot from one of the upper batteries had exploded the boiler of the Lancaster, and then a shell, bursting in another part of the boat, completely wrecked her. The Confederate batteries continued to pour in upon her a tremendous fire. She was struck thirty times. Her entire bow was shot away, causing her to take water so rapidly that she sank almost instantly, turning a complete somersault as she went down.

The Switzerland was more fortunate, but was finally disabled by a sixty-pound ball penetrating her steam drum. She floated below Vicksburg, the batteries still keeping up their terrible fire upon her, and striking her repeatedly. At last, the Albatross, from Admiral Farragut's fleet, which had come up from New Orleans, steamed to her relief, fastened to her, and towed her to the lower mouth of the canal, where she lay helpless.

Those who were watching the contest, when the Lancaster was wrecked, and who knew the current of the river, climbed over the embankment of the Vicksburg and Shreveport Railroad, and threw out planks and limbs of trees, and aught else that the swimmers could seize, around whom, as they struggled in the water, the shot and shell were flying like hail. One after another they were drawn to land, some of them scalded, and all exhausted. As the engineer of the Lancaster clutched the hand of a man who drew him from the water, the skin of the scalded hand came off in that of his helper, almost as if it were a glove. It retained the creases of the knuckles, and the nails of the fingers. The poor fellow was scalded horribly, but as he stepped on shore he drew his revolver, and, turning upon his comrades, exclaimed: " Where's that coward that talked of surrendering? I'll shoot *him* before I die!" and discovering the man, who had said just before the explosion of the boiler, " It's of no use, we shall have to surrender!" he rushed upon him, and would have harmed him but for the bystanders.

The poor fellow, with one other as badly scalded, and several in less distress, was taken to the hospital, where he died that afternoon. I went over to see him, but he was free from pain and needed nothing, sinking rapidly away. He had no fear of death, and expressed regret only for one thing, that his boat, the Lancaster, had not run the batteries as well as the Switzerland, which got past the guns, and joined Farragut, although badly cut up. " But," he added, " I did my duty and never talked of surrendering. And I thank God I have no mother, wife, nor child to mourn for me." And so did I. " You may say a prayer for me," he said faintly; " a short one, for it's almost over." And the brave man's spirit went up, on the breath of the short, but heartfelt petition that was made for him.

# CHAPTER XVI.

COMING UP THE RIVER — A FREIGHT OF LIVING MISERY —
GOING OUT FROM THE LAND OF BONDAGE — AMONG SICK
SOLDIERS, CONTRABANDS AND REFUGEES.

A forward Movement — Gunboats run the Vicksburg Batteries — They con-
voy Transports down the River — Troops cross, and beleaguer Vicksburg
— We take Passage in the Maria Denning for Cairo — The Boat packed
with human and animal Misery — Sick Soldiers comforted by our Pres-
ence — Johnny, the Virginia Refugee, given to my Care — His History
— The tempestuous "Praise-meetings" of the Contrabands tabooed —
Refugees encamped on the River Bank — Signal the Boat to stop — The
Captain dares not — Fears Treachery — Meet Ford Douglas at Lake
Providence — Agree to take a slave Boy to Chicago, despite Illinois
"Black Laws."

T was the last week of April, 1863, when, having finished the work we were sent to do, we turned our faces homeward. There was no longer any need of our remaining "down the river." The troops at Lake Providence, and those sent to "flank the Mississippi" by the way of Yazoo Pass and Steele's Bayou, under Generals Sherman and McPherson, were brought down to Milliken's Bend. By the complete breaking up of all the hospitals, and the removing of all the sick to the North, as well as from the general note of preparation in the camp and among the fleet of gunboats, we understood that a "forward movement" of some kind was resolved on. We were not left to conjecture what it might be.

We were told frankly, by one of the officers, of the new line of operations marked out by General Grant. Vicksburg was to be assailed from the east; and the ironclads and gunboats, with the transports, were to run the batteries, and convey the army across the river at a point farther down. The Thirteenth Corps had already left Milliken's Bend, and marched down the west bank of the Mississippi. They were to be ready to cross in the transports when they should have run the gauntlet of the terrible batteries, and got safely below the defiant stronghold. So we now took passage in the Maria Denning, and prepared for our slow trip up the river.

While our boat was taking its heterogeneous freight on board, the last gunboat of the expedition returned, which had been seeking a way to the rear of the defences of Vicksburg via Yazoo Pass, on the east side of the Mississippi. Busy as everybody was, on land and on river, and *blasé* as the soldiers had become with continued excitement and adventure, the return of this gunboat created a decided sensation. It had been navigating narrow, tortuous streams, which, at that stage of high water, had a headlong current, bearing them through gigantic forests, which overarched and interlaced, sweeping away smoke-stacks, and scraping the deck clean of pilot-house and every other standing fixture.

Abrupt turns at almost every boat's length of the way down the Coldwater and Tallahatchie Rivers had broken her bow and damaged her sides, while snags and fallen trees, and now and then getting aground, had injured the rudder and wheels. They had been

halted at Greenwood, on the Tallahatchie, where the
rebels had erected defences, and, with the aid of
rifled Whitworth guns, had compelled the expedition
to return to the Mississippi by the same way it had
come. Some of the men had been killed; several
were badly wounded, and were brought on board our
boat to be taken to the Memphis hospitals. All were
exhausted by the protracted and excessive work, performed on half and quarter rations. And yet all
wanted to go forward with the new movement of the
forces to the east of Vicksburg. The wounded
brought on board the Maria Denning loudly lamented
their hard fate in being sent to the hospitals "just
when something was going to be done."

The Maria Denning was an uncouth and lumbering
three-decker, if so definite and dignified a name may
be applied to a nondescript river-boat. It was three
stories high, each of the upper two stories being more
contracted in dimensions than the one immediately
beneath it. The lowest deck, or story, was open, not
enclosed, and was devoted to the transportation of
condemned government mules and horses, sent to St.
Louis for sale. The second story was occupied by
contrabands who had come from the plantations
within the lines of our army, and who, like the mules
and horses, were bound for St. Louis. Here, also,
were sick and wounded soldiers, going home on furlough or discharge. The third story was for the
accommodation of the officers of the boat and passengers.

The dumb animals were driven from their corral,
some three or four hundred of them, with a vast deal
of whooping, shouting, and wild driving. They ran
in every direction but the one in which they ought,

and at every turn were met by fresh outbursts of shouts and yells and frantic gesticulations. For soldiers seemed to spring out of the ground, who joined in the unfeeling sport, until the poor, jaded, worn-out beasts were mad with fright. It was half a day before any of them were got on board. And several of them, in their terror, ran into an immense slough, sank slowly in the mire with but feeble struggle, and died before our eyes.

"When this war is over," said Mrs. Governor Harvey, of Wisconsin, who passed three years of the war in the hospitals, and at the front, in devoted labor for the soldiers, "I never want to see again a negro or a mule. Both of them are so abused in the army, and both are so dumbly patient, and uncomplaining, and receive so little sympathy, that I suffer a perpetual heartache on their account." To express pity for, or interest in, a suffering mule, or to interpose entreaties on its behalf, was to run the gauntlet of the most stinging ridicule. Everybody beat and neglected the unhandsome brutes; and when they fell into the hands of the ill-treated negroes, they fared worse than ever. From their own persecution and abuse, they seemed to have learned only lessons of brutality and tyranny, when they became mule-drivers.

As the half-imbruted contrabands came on board, under military *surveillance*, clad in the tattered gray and black "nigger cloth," and shod with the clouted brogans of the plantation, my heart went out to them. Subdued, impassive, solemn, hope and courage now and then lighting up their sable faces, they were a most interesting study. Mothers carried their piquant-faced babies on one arm, and led little

F.O.C. Darley

Engraved by J. J. Cade, New York.

Copyright 1877.

A.D. Worthington & Co., Publishers, Hartford, Conn.

## FLEEING FROM THE LAND OF BONDAGE.—On the Mississippi River in 1863.

"Mothers carried their babies on one arm, and led little woolly headed toddlers by the other. Old men and women, gray, nearly blind, some of them bent almost double, bore on their heads and backs the small 'plunder' they had 'toted' from their homes. They were all going forth, like the Israelites, from the land of bondage to a land they knew not'."

woolly-headed toddlers by the other. Old men and women, gray, nearly blind, some of them bent almost double, bore on their heads and backs the small "plunder" they had "toted" from their homes, on the plantation, or the "bread and meat" furnished them by some friendly authorities. They were all going forth, like the Israelites, "from the land of bondage to a land they knew not."

Like the Hebrews, they trusted implicitly in God to guide them, and their common speech, as we spoke with them, had an Old Testament flavor. Never before had I witnessed so impressive a spectacle. There were between three and four hundred of them. Half of the middle deck of the huge boat was assigned them, into which they filed, and began to arrange themselves in families and neighborhood groups.

The other half of this deck was used by sick and wounded soldiers, who were brought on board in great numbers. They were either furloughed or discharged. Some of them were brought on stretchers, and a comrade was detailed to accompany them, and assist them in their long journey. Others swung themselves painfully on crutches, or were led between their comrades, frequently falling from weakness; or they crept feebly and haltingly on board, without assistance.

We stationed ourselves — the women of the company — in this compartment of the boat, which we saw was going to be packed with misery and suffering. As the soldiers were brought in, we fell into maternal relations with them, as women instinctively do when brought into juxtaposition with weakness, and were soon addressing them individually as "my

son," "my boy," or "my child." They were all
greatly comforted to learn that we were going up
the river with them. Those who had had fears of
dying before they reached their homes, grew courageous and hopeful, as we assured them that we were
going to take care of them. Before the boat started
we were at work,— making tea for one, filling a canteen with fresh water for a second, bathing the soiled
face and hands of a third, sewing up rents in the
garments of a fourth, preparing hot applications for
the cure of earache for a fifth, and beseeching our
one physician on board to prepare immediately a
cough mixture for the whole company, who were
coughing in deafening chorus, but in the most in-
conceivable dissonance. The contrabands were also
coughing with might and main, and there were times
when this violent and irritating lung exercise was so
general, that conversation was as impossible as in the
midst of a brisk artillery fire.

Among the soldiers was one delicate boy of fifteen
— tall, slender, and frail. A chaplain accompanied
him, and gave me his history. He was the only child
of a wealthy Virginian, living near Petersburg, who
remained loyal to the old flag, and voted against
secession. When Virginia went out of the Union,
he was so fierce in his denunciation of its treason,
so active in his hostility to the new-fangled Confederacy, that he was arrested and sent to Libby Prison.
" Johnny," the son, sympathized with his father, and
after his arrest was more passionate and terrible in
his outspoken scorn and hate of the treachery of his
native state, than his father had dared to be.

Only the fact of his being a mere boy saved him
from his father's fate, or perhaps from assassination.

As it was, the overseer of one of his father's plantations, who loved the boy, secreted him for a few days;
for he had awakened such enmity towards himself,
that on one or two occasions he had been attacked
in the streets of Petersburg by a mob of boys of his
own age, and beaten half to death. The overseer
got him safely beyond the rebel lines, and gave him
a horse and two hundred dollars in gold, with the
name and residence of one of his father's brothers,
living somewhere in Missouri. He had also furnished
him with a letter of instruction as to the route he
was to take to reach his uncle.

Johnny got on very well as far as Louisville, Ky.
There he fell sick, and, when he recovered, found
himself in the " Refugees' Camp," his money gone,
his horse missing; even his letter of instruction had
been stolen. Strolling around, he came upon the
encampment of one of our regiments, into which he
was absorbed, notwithstanding his boyishness and
feebleness, and where he remained nearly a year.
He became the pet of the regiment, any of his
comrades being always ready to relieve Johnny of
any severe duty or rough work which fell to his lot,
or to share with him any delicacy or pleasure. He
was of the genuine metal, however, and asked no
favors, until the regiment came to live an amphibious
life at Young's Point. Then he succumbed to
swamp fever, and, after lying at the point of death
for days, had recovered partially. Thinking it sui-
cidal for the boy to remain in the army, young and
delicate as he was, one of the chaplains had procured
his discharge, and brought him on board the boat,
with transportation to St. Louis.

My heart went out to the poor child immediately.

He had never known his mother, as she had died at his birth; but of his father he spoke with eloquent and tearful affection. He was wholly unfitted to search for his uncle; and knowing, as he did not, what a complete overturning the war had made in Missouri, I proposed to him to go home with me, and stay until he became strong, when I would help him seek his relative, of whom he knew nothing save his name and address. The lad put his thin, tremulous hand in mine, lifted his large brown eyes to my face, and tried to say " Yes." But his lips moved only, without emitting any sound, and then he broke down in tearless sobs.

I hunted up the captain, and made friends with him, although he was a coarse, whiskey-drinking man, for I had a favor to ask of him. After some fifteen minutes of good-natured palaver, in which I played the rôle of the amiable woman to the utmost, I obtained permission to take Johnny into the upper saloon among the passengers, and also two or three others of the soldiers, who were very ill. They could be made more comfortable there than in the middle compartment of the boat, to which they were assigned, and I could more easily nurse them.

At last, after two or three days' delay, we started. It was a tedious journey home. We were impatient; for we had finished our work, and had been a long time from our families, who were eagerly looking for our return. The passengers, with whom we were closely shut up most of the time — for the weather had turned cold and stormy — were coarse, ruffianly, brutal fellows, with one or two exceptions. They smoked, chewed tobacco incessantly, and expectorated in so reckless a way as to make it dangerous to sit in their vicinity. Gambling, smoking, swearing, and berating the Union and its friends, were their unvaried pastimes.

The Maria Denning was a slow sailer, and puffed and snorted up the river against the rapid, headlong current at a snail's pace, compared with the speed at which we had descended the Mississippi. A terrific gale drove us against the east bank of the river, which was skirted with cottonwood trees, heavily shrouded from their roots to the topmost branches with the funereal moss which is a parasite, upon them. Here we remained immovable nearly twenty-four hours; not without anxiety, for we were in the enemy's country, and boats in similar stress had been burned by the rebels only a few days before, and their crews and passengers murdered or taken prisoners.

Now and then, as we kept the middle of the stream, still at a very high stage of water, we would be signalled by people on the banks, where was no sign of habitable life. With waving of white flags, and passionate gestures of entreaty, they begged us to take them on board. An inspection of them through the field-glass aroused our captain's suspicion, and, fearing a *ruse* to decoy us ashore to our own destruction, we went on our way, and left them behind.

One afternoon, as the sunset was deepening into twilight, we made a bend in the river, when we received a momentary fright from a huge fire blazing red, straight before us, close at the water's edge. A great crowd was hovering about it, waving flags, gesticulating, and signalling us. As we came nearer, we found they were negroes, of all sizes, and had their little bundles in their hands or on their heads and backs.

The captain dared not, or would not, stop. As the poor creatures saw us steaming directly by, they redoubled their exertions to attract our attention. Catching up blazing firebrands, they ran up the shore with them, waved them, threw them in air, and with the most frantic pantomime sought to convey to us a sense of their eagerness to be taken aboard. It seemed pitiful not to stop for them. They had made their way to the river, not doubting, probably, but any of " Massa Linkum's " boats would take them on board. Doubtless they had signalled other boats ahead of us; and still they were left on the river banks, amid the gray moss-draped cottonwoods, as far from the land of freedom as ever.

At Milliken's Bend another detachment of broken-down mules was received on the lower deck, but without the brutality attending the reception of the first lot. Our contrabands were increased by the addition of fifty or a hundred more; and a score or two of soldiers were taken aboard, all a little under the weather, going home on brief leave of absence, or permanently discharged from the service. One who undertook to come on the boat slipped, in his weakness, as he came up the plank, and his crutch flew out from his grasp into the river. He tried to catch it, lost his balance, and tumbled head foremost into the turbid, whirling stream. Once he came to the surface on the other side of the boat, whither he was carried by the current. Ropes, chains, and planks were thrown him, but he sank, and we saw him no more. Who he was, what was his name, where was his home, what was his regiment, no one couid tell us. Perhaps father and mother looked and longed vainly for his coming, until hope died out in despair. To all their inquiries they could only learn the one fact, that he started for home, and could be traced no farther. " Missing " was his only record.

At Lake Providence we stopped to take on cotton. Very little of the cotton on the deserted Providence plantations had been gathered; and the government let the job to contractors, who picked it on halves, delivering it in bales to the government. The contractors paid the negroes a penny a pound for picking, and the government furnished them rations. A large quantity being ready for transportation North, the Maria Denning agreed to carry it.

As I was standing on the upper deck, watching the negroes roll the bales up the plank, I espied in the crowd below Ford Douglas, a well-known colored man of Chicago, who had no inconsiderable local reputation as an anti-slavery lecturer. Like his great namesake, he was born in slavery, had run away from his master, and concealed his own name, assuming one which he liked better. Although prejudice against the black race was then at its highest pitch at the North, and especially in Illinois, and the offers of colored men to enlist in the service of the country were refused with scorn, Ford Douglas was enlisted in the Ninety-fifth Illinois, where his virtues, talents, and, above all, his fiery eloquence, gave him welcome. He was fraternized with as if he were a white man. Everybody respected him.

He uttered a little cry of joy as he saw me, accompanying his salute with a gesture of delight. We had known each other for some years, and he rushed on board to meet me. Grasping my hand warmly, he said: "The Lord has sent you this time, sure! I have been praying that He would send along somebody that I could trust; but I little thought He would answer by sending you. You will not refuse to do me a great favor?"

"Certainly not, Ford; you know that without asking."

"I have in my tent a little colored boy, six or eight years old, a slave child whom I have stolen. His mother was a slave living near New Orleans, but before the war she escaped to Chicago. Will you take the boy to his mother?"

"It will not be safe, Mrs. Livermore," immediately interposed one of our company, a member of the Illinois Legislature. "You will run great risk in undertaking to carry a negro boy through Illinois."

The infamous "Black Laws" of Illinois were then in force, and any one who took a negro into the state was liable, under these statutes, to heavy fine and imprisonment. Under the stimulus of a most senseless and rabid negrophobia, then at fever heat, the provost-marshal at Cairo searched every Northern-bound train for negroes, as well as deserters. Whenever they were found, they were arrested; the former were sent to the contraband camp, an abandoned, comfortless, God-forsaken place, and the latter to the guard-house.

"You cannot escape detection if you try to run this boy through Cairo," said the surgeon of our party. "You had better let the child alone."

I knew both of these objectors thoroughly. They felt it to be their duty to warn me of the risk I was inclined to run, and were unwilling that I should get into trouble. But they were the most reliable of anti-slavery men, and, when their feelings were touched, would run any gauntlet of danger to serve a distressed human creature. So I turned to Mr. Douglas, and pressing his arm significantly, to secure his silence, I replied, "Well, never mind about your slave boy, Ford, let me know what *you* are doing down here. Come to the after part of the boat, out of the way of this noise, where I can talk with you." And we went aside by ourselves, where I learned the little black boy's history.

Not long before the war, the boy's mother, then a slave on a Louisiana plantation, accompanied her master and mistress to Newport, R. I., leaving her only child behind her, a guaranty, in the opinion of her owners, that she would return. But the slave mother, following the example of several of her relatives, found her way to Chicago on the "underground railroad." After she had obtained her well-earned freedom, she made persistent efforts to get possession of her child, but without success. Once her uncle, himself a runaway slave, and from the same neighborhood, went down to the vicinity of the plantation to hunt for the lad. But after lurking around for weeks, and almost securing him, he returned without him.

When Mr. Douglas' regiment was ordered South, to Lake Providence, the mother begged him to search for her boy, and, if he was found, to forward him to her. Ford obtained leave of absence from his regiment, went directly to the plantation, found the child, and brought him away with him. For six weeks the boy had been concealed in his tent, and he had been watching an opportunity to send him to

Chicago. The opportunity had now arrived. Clad
in plantation clothes, the lad was stealthily brought
on board the Maria Denning, and placed among the
other contrabands, whom he resembled in appearance, in the *patois* he spoke, the rough clothing he
wore, and in manners. The colored stewardess, a
woman of elephantine proportions, whose heart must
have been as big as her body, judging from her
devotion to the forlorn people of her own color, took
my protégé under her special care. She fed him
bountifully whenever he was willing to eat, which
was about every hour of the twenty-four.

More sick soldiers were brought on board, and
given to our care. One, on a stretcher, was so very
low, that I ordered him carried immediately to the
upper saloon, and deposited beside my stateroom,
where I could attend him night and day. Then we
started again, after twenty-four hours delay at Lake
Providence.

What a freight of living misery our boat bore up
the river! I ventured once to the lower deck, given
up to the horses and mules. Some had slipped their
halters, and, in consequence of weakness, had fallen
under the feet of others, where they were stamped to
death. It was a horrible sight, which I wished I had
not seen. In the middle compartment of the boat
were the contrabands, always in great activity, in
consequence of the large number of children among
them. I could only think of a vast nest of angle-
worms, wriggling and twisting, when I went among
them. When they were awake, they were either
cooking, or eating, or holding " praise-meetings."
It would be difficult to say which they most enjoyed.

The " praise-meeting " was the usual occupation of

the evening.   Then they sang and prayed until their
enthusiasm became tempestuous.   They beat time
with their feet, they whirled in dizzy gyrations, or
vented their effervescence of spirit in quick convulsive leaps from the floor, accompanied by ear-splitting
shouts.

The sick soldiers, who shared one half of the middle compartment, dreaded these "praise-meetings"
inexpressibly.   The poor fellows were so feeble that
they had neither strength nor nerve to endure the
intolerable din, and it became necessary at last to
interfere with the negroes, and to prohibit the meetings altogether, since, once begun, they could not be
kept within bounds.

One of our sick men died before we reached Memphis.   Like most men in his circumstances, he was
possessed with but one desire — to see his home once
more — but it was apparent from the first that he
would be buried on the way.   In his delirium he
babbled incessantly of home and its occupations.
"Harness the horses to the reaper, and we will start
out for that twenty-acre piece of wheat!"   "We are
all going to the picnic to-morrow, so get your basket
ready, Sis!"

Sometimes in his lucid moments he would please
himself by instituting comparisons between his
mother and myself.   "You have just her eyes, and
her hair, and her way of talking and doing; and if
I didn't look, I should think she was here!"   I rarely
rendered any service to these poor fellows that they
did not assure me that I was like their mother, or
wife, or sister.

# CHAPTER XVII.

THE STORY OF THREE LITTLE ORPHANS — SMUGGLING A
PLANTATION WAIF THROUGH "EGYPT" — THE UNDER-
GROUND RAILROAD — SAFE AT LAST — AFFECTING MEET-
ING.

We find three Orphan Refugees in Camp Convalescent, Fort Pickering —
Their pitiful History — We take them to the Chicago Home of the
Friendless — Adopted by an Iowa Family — Cairo makes Addition to our
Cares — Lizzie the Orphan Refugee from Missouri — Go aboard the
Chicago Sleeper, with Johnny and the black Lad — The stuttering
Porter hides the black Boy — "D-d-d-dat Woman's slep' mighty little
fo' mos' s-s-s-six Weeks — She's d-d-d-done got monst'ous sick" — We
defy "Egypt" and the "Black Laws" — Reach Chicago at Midnight —
Sunday Morning, hunt up the black Lad's Mother — Affecting Meeting
— Sarah Morris tells her Story — Johnny and Lizzie cared for.

AT Fort Pickering, two miles below Memphis,
there was a convalescent camp, and, while
the boat stopped for coal, we went ashore
to pay it a brief visit. In one of the tents
we found three dark-haired, dark-eyed little
girls, whose ages ranged from two to nine
years. They seemed perfectly at home, climbing
upon the knees of the four convalescent soldiers
assigned to the tent, ransacking their pockets for
jack-knives, pencils, and other like treasures which
the soldiers stowed in them for the use of the children. And with juvenile restlessness they rushed
from one employment to another, asking the aid of

their military companions, with a confidence that showed they were not often repulsed. Whose children were these tangle-haired, bare-footed, unkempt, ragged little urchins? The soldiers told us.

Their father was a Union man of Memphis, and lost his life before our troops took possession of the city. Their mother, with these three children, the youngest then an infant in arms, came within our lines for protection, and made herself useful in the officers' quarters by washing, cooking, etc. Three months before, she had died from exposure, hard work, and heartsickness. There was no one to take the children, and so the soldiers had gathered them into their tents, and taken as good care of them as they knew how.

"But what's to become of them when you are ordered away?" we asked.

The soldiers shook their heads. "Don't know; they ought to be taken care of, for they are good, bright little things!" was their reply.

We could think of but one thing to do for them, and that was to take them to Chicago. But we were already burdened with as many dependants as we could take along at one time. While we were debating what to do — for to leave the children with so uncertain a future, and no one responsible for them, was not to be thought of — the chaplain of the post came along, and we learned that his wife was with him on a brief visit, and was to return North in a week. It was arranged that she should bring the children, and deliver them to my care in Chicago. This she did, and I took them to the "Chicago Home of the Friendless," of which institution I was a manager, and advertised in the daily papers for a

home for them, giving a brief account of their history
and appearance. After they were washed and dressed
in decent apparel, they were very pretty and promising.

An Iowa tradesman, from one of the growing inland cities of his state, came to the Home with his
wife, in quest of a baby for adoption. They had
buried five infant children in eight years, and had
decided to adopt an orphan child to fill the void in
their bereaved and childless home. They selected
the youngest of the three little refugees as the object
of their parental affection. But when they prepared
to take her away, a touching scene ensued. Jenny,
the eldest sister, clasped the little one in her arms,
and wildly and with tears protested.

"Oh, no, no, no!" she cried; "you mustn't have
my baby. I won't let you have her. You sha'n't
tote her away! You sha'n't have my baby! No, no,
no!" and they clung wildly to each other, hugging
each other with all their little might.

The Iowa couple sought to compromise the matter
by offering to take the middle sister. But to that
Jenny also opposed tears and resistance. "No, no,
no!" refused the child. "You sha'n't tote either of
them away; they shall stay with me!"

The more we sought to persuade the eldest sister,
the more fiercely she clung to the little ones, who
shrieked in terror, at they knew not what, until half
the children in the house were screaming in sympathy. So I pacified the motherly little Jenny, telling
her that nobody should take her "babies" away,—
for so she called her sisters,—unless she said so, and
dismissed the Iowa people.

The next morning the gentleman and his wife
came back, offering to take all three of the sisters,

and adopt them as their own. They had lain awake all night, talking it over, and, as the lady expressed it, they had concluded that God had emptied their hearts and home of their own children, to make room for these three orphans. We called Jenny and told her of the proposal. Half laughing and half crying, she put her hand on her adopted mother's shoulder, and sobbed out the question, " Then won't you tote us all right away to-day, before anybody comes to take sister and baby? "

Trembling with eagerness, delight, and fear lest something would yet intervene between them and their future home, she followed the two little ones into the carriage with the adopted parents, unwilling to go herself until the last, lest somebody should be left. In the last year of the war, the dear Jenny, who had grown close to the hearts of the adopted father and mother, died of scarlet fever. She was much the most promising of the three, and, had she lived, would have developed into a womanhood of unusual excellence.

At Cairo, where we left the boat and took the Illinois Central Railroad for Chicago, there was another accession to our cares. Dr. Taggart, the humane surgeon of the large General Hospital in Cairo, had picked up on the levee, some three months before, a girl of fourteen, whom he had first thought in a dying condition. She, too, was the daughter of Southern refugees. Her father was a Union man of southern Missouri, who was driven from his farm with his wife and two daughters. Escaping, with others, to St. Louis, he joined our troops, leaving his family behind him in the city, and was killed at Island Number Ten.

Shortly after he left them, his wife and younger daughter died of typhoid fever, induced by improper food and water, neglect, hunger, cold and exposure. Then Lizzie, the elder daughter, not knowing that her father was dead, sought to find him. Aided by the kindness of officials, and chance friends who started up in her path, she reached his regiment on the island, only to learn that she was an orphan. Not knowing where to go, she struggled back to Cairo. In the incessant rush and whirl of the then busy city, she was unnoticed, and left to live or die as might happen. For sixteen bitterly cold nights, she slept in outhouses, barns, underneath overturned boats, in sheds, or in any other place that offered shelter. Such food as she obtained, was given her at back doors, by servants, or by soldiers, who were continually crowding the levees. At last she succumbed to the hardships of her fate. Seeking an out-of-the-way corner, racked with pain, burning with fever, weak, sick, footsore, discouraged, she lay down to die, praying God for speedy release from suffering.

Here, Dr. Taggart stumbled upon her, and, immediately ordering an ambulance, he took her to his hospital, and devoted himself to her cure. Poor Lizzie always insisted that her mother came to her in her abandonment, and remained with her, only going back to heaven when her daughter was partially restored to health. Who can say that this was a mere sick-bed fancy? Not I, and I never gainsaid the poor child's assertion. To whom should the angels of heaven minister, if not to the homeless and friendless little ones of earth? I had agreed to receive her when she was able to go to Chicago, and it was thought best that she should be taken along now, when I could attend to her in person.

We bade adieu to the contrabands who were going to St. Louis, and to those of the sick men whose transportation papers took them by the same route. Then, taking the refugee boy, Johnny, by one hand, and Ford Douglas' charge, Ben Morris, the little slave boy, by the other, I walked directly to the train standing on the track. It was nearly midnight; the train was to start for Chicago at three in the morning, and the sleeping-car was then half full of sleeping passengers. Almost all our party had similar responsibilities on their hands as myself; and those who had not, agreed to assist our sick and wounded soldiers to re-embark on the Chicago-bound train. Entering the sleeping-car, to my great joy, I found the same colored porter who had been in charge whenever I had journeyed to and from Cairo.

He dropped the boots from which he was scraping deposits of Cairo mud, and gave me a glad welcome.

" I g-g-g-got jes' one lower b-b-b-berth lef' ! " he said. He was an inveterate stammerer.

" But, Henry, does the provost-marshal come in now to search the train for negroes and deserters? " I asked.

" Y-y-y-yes, jes' afore the t-t-t-train st-tarts; " and he glanced at the white boy on one side of me, and then at the colored boy on the other. So I gave him the boy's history, and asked him to help me hide the little fellow until we had safely passed through " Egypt," as the southern part of Illinois was called, and which at that time was aflame with intense hatred and persecution of negroes. He proposed at first that I should put the boy in the back of my berth, and cover him well with the blankets; but, as the child was swarming with vermin, I entreated him to think of some other plan. Looking under the berth, where was a large unoccupied space sufficient for a good-sized valise, for it was a sleeping-car of an old style, Henry said, —

"A p-p-p-plantation nig like dis yere ch-ch-ch-chile can sleep anywhar!" and forthwith he stowed him away under my berth, where no provost marshal would ever think of searching for him. In a few moments I heard him snoring as nonchalantly as though there were no provost-marshals or negro-haters in existence.

Henry was very uneasy when the provost-marshal came in to inspect the train; for, by the "Black Laws" of Illinois, whoever assisted in bringing a negro into the State, was liable to a year's imprisonment and a fine of one thousand dollars. So he walked up the aisle of the sleeper with the officer, past my berth, talking rapidly, asking needless questions, and stuttering at a fearful rate. Meanwhile, the little fellow underneath the berth was snoring as loudly as though he was under a contract to furnish nasal music for the entire train. But his hiding-place was not suspected, and we reached Centralia at nine the next morning, no one having discovered this waif of the plantation, who was enjoying a free ride through the great State of Illinois, in utter defiance of its "Black Laws."

It was arranged that I should not leave my berth until we reached Centralia, where we were to breakfast, and to change conductors, and where Henry left the train. The cars were crowded to overflowing, a large number of persons being obliged to stand. As I occupied in my section the room that would accommodate four when seated, there was naturally a very urgent desire among the standing passengers that I should be compelled to get up.

"Why don't you wake that woman up?" I heard one savagely inquire of Henry. "Is she going to lie abed all day?"

"D-d-d-dat woman's bin down to t-t-t-take keer ob de s-s-s-sick sojers!" stuttered Henry. "S-s-s-she's slep' mighty little f-f-f-fo' mos' six weeks, an' she's d-d-d-done got *monst'ous* sick! L-l-l-let her sleep!"

Henry was right. I was "monst'ous sick," and for the next ten days I could hardly lift my head from the pillow. Every other member of the party had been sick down the river. I was the only one who had not had a touch of swamp fever, and I had boasted of my exemption. But my time had come. It would not do to give up until we reached Chicago, and I compelled my will to triumph over my aching, fevered body until I was again at home.

At Centralia, I learned, from the wife of a Chicago physician, that the conductor who now took charge of our train had served a long apprenticeship on the "underground railroad," and so my black boy's perils were over. We reached Chicago at midnight on Saturday. Johnny and Lizzie went home with me, but the black lad was altogether too filthy to be taken into any decent house. One of the gentlemen left him in care of his barber until morning, and the little fellow dropped sound asleep on the floor, beside the stove, almost immediately.

The next morning, about church time, we instituted a search for the boy's mother. We only knew her name, and that she was a regular attendant at the African Baptist Church. To that church we wended our way, and in the vestibule met the sexton, to whom we told our errand. He proceeded to the pulpit and repeated the story to the minister. In his turn he rehearsed it to the congregation, and inquired if Sarah Morris, the boy's mother, was present. One of the assembly informed the minister that the mother was a Methodist, and not a Baptist; and so we turned our steps to the Methodist church, where the same programme was followed, eliciting the information that Sarah Morris was not at church, but lived at No. — —— Avenue.

We followed up our clew, accompanied by quite a procession that had joined us from both the Baptist and Methodist churches, and at last discovered the house where the mother lived as cook. She was not at home, however, but was sitting with a sick friend that day, and very confused directions to the house of the friend were given us, which we proceeded to follow. At last Sarah Morris was found. As the door was opened to us, we saw some eight or ten colored men and women sitting within, and, as my eye ran over the group, I recognized the mother, from her resemblance to her son. Before one word was spoken, she threw herself upon her boy with a joyful shriek of recognition, the child rushing towards her half-way, as if by filial instinct, and they wept in each other's arms, uncontrollably. In kisses and claspings, and endearing epithets, the defrauded love of the mother vented itself upon her child, whom she had mourned almost as one dead. All in the room dropped on their knees, and the air was vocal with thanksgivings and hallelujahs.

In a week or two the mother called on me with her

boy, to show me how cleanliness and decent dress had improved him, and to reiterate her gratitude for his recovery.

"But how could you run away from your baby, even to obtain your freedom?" I inquired.

"Well, missis," said the woman, "when I left Lou's'anny I didn't tink not to go back agin. I tole my ole man, and all de folks on de ole place dey'd see me back, sure, to my pickaninny. Ebery gal missis had done took Norf for tree year had done gone and run off; and dat's why she took me, an' lef' my chile on de place. When we'd got Norf, to a place dey call Newport, I didn't tink den to run away. But one Sabba' day massa and missis dey gone to ride on de beach, an' I set down on de doorstep an' tink o' my little chile; an' den I hear de Lor' speak to me out o' de stillness. He say, 'Sarah, go up stars, an' pack up your tings, an' go to Ch'cago!' But I say: 'Oh, no, Lor'! I want to go back to dat chile. What dat little chile do on dat big place widout his mammy? No, Lor', I don't want to go to Ch'cago.'

"An de Lor' He speak agin in de stillness, an' dis time wid a great voice, and say: 'Sarah, do as I tell yer! I'll take keer o' dat chile; you go to Ch'cago.' So I go up stars, an' pick up my duds, a-cryin' an' a-cryin' all de time. I tell de Lor' on my two knees two, tree time: 'If yer please, O Lor' King, lemme go back to my chile! I don't want to be free. What for shall I be free, an' my chile be lef' down on massa's ole place?' Ebery time de Lor' King He say loud, so it fill all de room, 'Go to Ch'cago!' So I go down to de cars, an' sot down on de seat, a-cryin' all de time in my heart, 'cos I was 'shamed to cry wid my eyes 'fore all de people. An' when de conductor gib de word, 'All aboard!' I was gwine to jump off, for I said: 'O Lor' King, I don't want noffin widout my chile! I don't want heben widout my pickaninny! I can't go to Ch'cago!' An' de Lor' King he ketched me back; an' he said, so loud and strong I 'spected all de folks would hear, 'DAT CHILE'S MY CHILE; I'LL TAKE KEER O' HIM!' So I gin up to de Lor' den, honey; and all de big storm in my heart stop, an' I was dat happy I could ha' sung an' shouted, like I was in a praise-meetin'.

" An' de Lor' He take all de trouble out o' my way, an He fix eberyting for me, 'fore I know it's got to be fixed; an' He send frien's at ebery place, to tell me whar to go, an' to gib me money, an' clo'es, an' grub, till I git to Ch'cago. An' he hab a place all ready for me hyar, an' I nebber hab a day idle 'cos thar was noffin to do, or 'cos I was sick. Sometimes, when I hab a great misery in my heart for my chile, den I go to de Lor', an' tell Him all about it. An' de Lor' He would take all de misery 'way; for He would 'clar dat chile was Hisn, an' dat He would tote him to me bimeby. An' de Lor' King is jes' as good as His word; an' He's sent de pickaninny, grown so peart an' so big dat nobody but his mammy would eber ha' known him. So now I prommis' de Lor' King I'll neber mistrust Him no more, an dat dis chile shall be His chile, for shure, sence He done took keer o' de little chap when he didn't hab no mammy, an' was too little to take keer o' hisself."

The earnestness, pathos, and solemnity of this narration cannot be described. To the mother, the voice of the Lord and His direct guidance were verities.

But what of Johnny and Lizzie? As soon as

possible, I published their histories in brief in the city papers, and applied to a loyal and generous people to compensate them for the suffering entailed on them by the loyalty of their parents. Most generous were the responses. Chaplain McCabe, known throughout the country, saw the published account of the refugee children, and came to my house to see them, suspecting that he knew something of Johnny's father. In conversation with the lad, his impressions deepened into certainty. Chaplain McCabe was taken prisoner at the first Bull Run battle, and was thrown into Libby Prison. Here he found a number of Virginians incarcerated for their hostility to secession.

One of them was in failing health, and solicited the chaplain's prayers and ministrations. Gradually the man told him his story. He proved to be Johnny's father. He had been informed of his son's departure for Missouri, and often begged the chaplain to seek the lad and the uncle in Missouri, whenever he regained his liberty. The chaplain had the address of the uncle, which was the same as that given to Johnny. "If I needed other proof of your being the son of my fellow-prisoner," said the chaplain, "I have it in your complete resemblance to him. You are his perfect fac-simile."

"Yes," said Johnny, "they always used to say I was exactly like my father. Did you leave him in Libby Prison when you were released?"

A shadow fell over the chaplain's fine face. Alas! alas! Johnny was an orphan. Chaplain McCabe had seen his father pass through the valley of death and had commended his departing spirit to the dear God, who rules, even in the midst of the inharmonies and strifes of our human existence. The boy could not be comforted. He went to his room, and, locking himself in, wept aloud. It was hours before I could obtain access to him. His father had been to him both father and mother, and until the war they had been inseparable. Now all was gone — he was alone.

After a time he was received into a family, that became deeply interested in him; and as there were only daughters in the home, they hoped to keep him always with them. For a year he attended school, and grew rapidly to the height of manhood, but was thin and frail. The iron had entered his soul deeply, and it was not possible for him to settle down into quiet life in the North. Despite the remonstrances of his adopted parents and sisters, who had become much attached to him, and in utter disregard of my entreaties and promises to aid in re-instating him in his home and property at the close of the war, he went again into the service, about six months before the conflict ended. He was in camp at Springfield, Ill., for some time, where he was attacked with pneumonia, and died in hospital, never reaching the field.

Lizzie was adopted by a Southern family driven from Mississippi for loyalty. Not brilliant, nor very quick of perception, she proved a good girl, and matured in the home of her adoption, under most favorable influences. There were no other children in the family, and she became the companion of the lady who stood to her in place of mother. I often saw her, and rejoiced that the habitually sad look on her face was gradually displaced by as heavenly a smile as ever irradiated a human countenance. She had a very happy temperament.

# CHAPTER XVIII.

OUR BATTERY BOYS — A SECRET DRILL — THE DISCOVERY —
OFF TO THE FRONT — GOD-SPEED AND FAREWELL TO MY
SUNDAY-SCHOOL BOYS — EXTRACTS FROM THEIR DIARIES.

Our Church in Chicago — The *Morale* of its young Men — Memories of the
Past — A loyal Congregation — What happened at Evening Service — Sud-
den Disappearance of our young Men — A peculiar Sound from the Sun-
day-School Room — Tramp ! Tramp ! Tramp ! — We stealthily open the
Door and peep in — Our Discovery — "We have all decided to enlist"
— An unspoken Prayer — All but two of our young Men are mustered
into the Chicago Mercantile Battery — The Grief of Parting — Solemn
Consecration — An affecting Farewell — Extracts from their Diaries —
A jolly set — Roughing it without Whining — The Art of Frying Cakes
— "Sweet Times here" — The Siege of Vicksburg — Awaiting the Bat-
tle — Army Life at the Front — "Spoiling for a Fight" — Ordered into
Action — We keep up Communication with our Boys — A Country
devastated by War — An unexpected Visitor.

HERE was an unusually large number of interesting young people in the —— —— Society, of Chicago, when the war of the rebellion began. The older members of the parish felt that the church had in itself more than ordinary strength and promise, because of the well-born, well-bred, well-educated, and consecrated young men and women who confessed loving allegiance to its faith and its interests. Especially were they proud of its young men; and they felt that the future of the church was very much in their keeping. Some were about to enter Harvard, Tufts, or Yale, and all were connected with good

369

families. In addition to their other excellences, they possessed that nameless ease and grace which are only acquired in the environments of homes presided over by pure, refined, affectionate mothers and sisters.

The Sunday-school was large, numbering more than five hundred teachers and scholars, who packed the vestries and parlors of the church every Sunday, regardless of weather or outside attractions. Into this school was harnessed our entire force of young men and maidens, who did duty as teachers, librarians, singers, or members of the Bible class. They did their work with wonderful heartiness and earnestness; and there was such genuine friendliness among them that one would have thought they were members of the same family.

What marvellous festivals and pleasure parties they extemporized in those days! Into what delightful rural fêtes and excursions were we older people enticed by these "young folks," who led us captive to their will! What continual surprises they planned for the bewilderment of the pastor, and the no less beloved pastor's wife! How they swarmed at the fortnightly church "sociables," and with their brightness and buoyancy, their contagious good-nature and overflowing hilarity, their wit and cleverness, their unselfishness and tact, made each of these small occasions more inviting than a grand banquet! I recall the memory of those days, removed into the past forever, not with pleasure alone, but with a sense of loss. Some of the grandest of our young men were brought from the battle-field, wrapped in the flag for which they had given their lives. Others are sleeping in sunny, but unknown graves in the far-away South, and all are scattered by land or by sea, never to be re-united until God "gathers in one, all the families of the earth."

There was not, from first to last, a disloyal person in the parish. It honored every draft upon its means with generous contributions of money, and almost every young man it numbered, old enough to bear arms, went into the service of the country, with the addition of several so young and some so old as to be legally exempted from military duty. First, one enlisted in the cavalry service; then two or three went into one of the Illinois regiments. Two or three others raised companies, and went to the front in command of them. Then the gunboat service took away a few more; until finally we found our large Bible class wholly depleted of its young men. But as they went singly, or in groups of two and three, with intervals of months between, we gradually became used to it, as to other sad events of the war. We had still a large number left, and, as their ranks were thinned, they closed up more solidly, increased their activity, became doubly useful to the parish, and doubly dear also.

One evening in the summer of 1862 there happened to be two meetings in the vestry — one of Sunday-school teachers, in the library-room, and another of some sort in the small Sunday-school room. We missed our young men teachers, but went on with the business of the evening without them. Something unusual must have detained them, we said, for they were rarely absent from meetings of this kind.

"What is going on in the large Sunday-school room?" was asked. No one knew. But all the

evening we heard a muffled, peculiar, regular sound
proceeding thence — tramp! tramp! tramp! — tramp!
tramp! tramp! — which we could not explain. It
continued with almost the regularity of the ticking
of a clock. Tramp! tramp! tramp! tramp! — and,
our meeting being ended, we stealthily opened the
door, and peeped in. There were our missing young
men, and they were drilling.

The settees were all moved to one side of the
room, so as to make a clear space for their rudimen-
tal drill. The drillmaster was the Superintendent
of the Sunday-school, who had organized it in the
beginning, and had brought it to its present efficiency
and size. He ceased the "left! left! left!" with
which he directed their steps, as we swarmed, curious and fascinated, into the room, and the young
men came to a halt. Before we could ask an explanation of this unusual proceeding, Mr. S—— had
vouchsafed it; —

"We have all decided to enlist in the Chicago
Mercantile Battery, now being formed, and shall
hand in our names to-morrow."

We scanned their faces earnestly for a moment,
and in silence. No! they were not jesting — they
were in dead earnest. An audible sigh ran through
the group of lookers-on, and some of us took in the
whole meaning of what Mr. S—— had said. To our
prophetic vision, the future loomed up clad with the
sorrow, anxiety, and grief it afterwards bore. "Let
this cup pass from us!" was the unspoken prayer of
every heart.

Could we give up Mr. S——, the idol of our
four hundred Sunday-school children, the leader
of the choir, whose cheerful words and presence

always toned us to hopefulness and courage? Must George Throop go, whom the loss of a finger legally exempted, when his enlistment would bereave his parents anew? They had just laid under the sod one of the noblest sons God ever gives to parents. Could not the Brackett brothers excuse themselves from obeying the call of the country, by pleading the necessity of parents declining in years, the invalidism of a brother, and the helpless condition of the little daughter, whose young mother had but just passed on to heaven?

Young Willard was a mere boy, preparing for Harvard, unfitted by constitution and mental training for the life of a soldier. Turner was delicate, alarming us continually by his oft-recurring illnesses, and he would be on the sick-list immediately. The almost girlish slightness and fragility of young Munn were a perpetual reminder of the insidious pulmonary weakness which had carried his mother to a premature grave. Pitts had just taken to his heart and home a beautiful bride, a fair young girl, who shrank in an agony of apprehension from the prospect of his leaving her for the dangers of the tented field. While Hugh Wilson, the youngest of them all, was still in the High School — a sixteen-year-old boy, the youngest of his own family — a sort of church Mercury, who ran hither and thither as with wingèd feet, distributing library books, carrying messages, doing errands, ubiquitous, almost omniscient. Surely they would never muster that child into the artillery service!

All this, and much more, I thought, faster than it has been written, but I did not say it then. Mr. T——, our minister, spoke first, with tremulous voice, and eyes glistening with tears. "It will be very hard to give you up, and we shall miss you inexpressibly; but if you feel it to be your duty, go, and God bless you!" Our lips acquiesced, but our hearts said, "Stay here!" Their resolution could not be shaken, although fathers, mothers, lovers, wives, sisters, and friends, pleaded for a reconsideration of their determination. They were all mustered into the Chicago Mercantile Battery, and ever after were known to us as "OUR BATTERY BOYS." This dismantled our society of the young strength and promise of which we had been so proud. All the young men of the parish, except two, were swallowed up in this battery, and they would have gone if the surgeons who examined them had not refused to accept them. It was a heavy blow to the parish, and for a time it was enshrouded in sadness. Almost every home had its individual share in the grief of parting, as, indeed, almost every family in the community had part in a like sorrow. For

> " The lines of every printed sheet
> Through their dark arteries reeked with running gore.
> Girls at the feast, and children in the street,
> Prattled of horrors."

But we were too patriotic and considerate of the feelings of the brave young fellows, who had made heroic sacrifices for their country, to manifest the depression we felt. Towards them we bore ourselves like Roman matrons and maidens, going often to their camp to witness their military drills, talking proudly of their future, and pledging to them our devotion and service to the uttermost. Picnics were planned almost daily for their benefit, and there was not a day while they were in camp that they were unvisited by some members of the parish. We made them waterproof needle-books, filled with needles, thread, scissors, and buttons, whose use they were skilful in learning. We made them portable waterproof writing-cases, and supplied them with abundant postage stamps. We provided those who would accept them with small cases of such medicines as were supposed to be indispensable in army life. It became a part of our religion to serve and to minister to their happiness.

Before they broke up camp, and went to the front, public leave was taken of them in church. It was a lovely Sunday in August, and the house was crowded to suffocation. The boys occupied front seats, wearing their artillery uniform; and the entire services were arranged with reference to their departure and their consecration to the cause of liberty. Instead of a sermon, Rev. Mr. T—— delivered an address to the newly made soldiers, in which he besought them to guard well their health and morals, not only for their own sakes, but for the sake of those who remained at home. They were entreated to return to us, if they came at all, as good and pure as they were leaving us. They were instructed that the war was caused by slavery, and would only end with the death of slavery, and the transformation of the slave to a free man; and they were cautioned not to side with the persecutors of this long downtrodden people.

To each one Mr. T—— presented a pocket Testament, with the request that it should be read daily, when unavoidable hindrances did not prevent. He asked the boys, as far as practicable, to maintain weekly religious services when on the march and in the camp. He pledged to them the public prayers of the church on every Sabbath until their return, or their relief from the service by death. He promised that their friends and families should be the special charge of the church, which would rejoice in their joy, and sorrow in their sorrow, and, when circumstances demanded it, would match their need with requisite aid. Nobly were these promises redeemed! The soldiers were never forgotten, and their friends at home were ever remembered.

The young artillerymen were consecrated to God in prayer, its solemnity and earnestness moving every heart; its tearful tenderness indicating the preciousness of the gift being laid on the altar of freedom. I wrote verses in those days, and, by request of the boys, furnished the following hymn, which was sung by the great congregation to "Auld Lang Syne": —

> So here we part! Our paths diverge —
>   Each leads a different way :
> You go to freedom's holy war;
>   We tarry here to pray.
> Our hands join brief in farewell now,
>   That ne'er so clasped before :
> Oh, brothers, in this parting hour,
>   Death's bitterness is o'er.
>
> Yet proudly, though with hearts that ache,
>   We give to you "Godspeed!"
> Haste! for our country gasps for life —
>   This is her hour of need.
> Her anguished cry comes on the breeze,
>   And smites the listening ear;
> The traitor's sword is at her heart —
>   And shall ye linger here?

Nay, brothers! haste, with blessings crowned,
  Engirded with our love;
Our hourly prayers, besieging heaven,
  Shall plead for you above.
Your dear ones left in lonely homes,
  Shall hence our lot divide;
We are but one blest household now,
  Whatever may betide.

We will not weep!   Be done with tears!
  Both paths lead home to heaven —
That marked for you through battle-fields,
  And that which God has given
To us, who, weary, watch afar
  The tide of battle swell —
Then, hearts, be brave, and, souls be strong!
  'Tis but a brief farewell!

The chorus of voices became less in volume as the song proceeded.   One after another ceased to sing, because they could not forbear to weep.   And by the time the last stanza was reached, our boys were singing alone, clear, strong, and unfaltering.

There were other excellent and very superior young men in the battery besides our boys, but my sketch does not deal with them.   Lockport, Ill., sent a contribution to the battery, from the flower of her youth — young men who had grown up in refined, cultivated homes, with no thought of the destiny Providence had in store for them.   There was a great variety of talent among them.   One was a noble fellow, born in Burmah, the son of a missionary.   Another had so good a knowledge of nursing, and so general an acquaintance with the milder forms of sickness, that he was nicknamed " Doctor," and was soon installed as the nurse of the battery.   There was another whose forte was cooking, and who was forever building ovens of Southern clay, and out of the crudest materials concocting some delicacy to tickle the palates of his companions. I can testify that he was specially skilful in the art of frying cakes, and baking corn bread.

The young men affiliated readily, regardless of sect or difference of opinion, reading, singing, playing baseball, and often holding religious meetings together, as if they had always been associated.

I have in my possession some of the diaries kept by them, from the time of enlistment to the expiration of their time of service. In looking them over, I am impressed anew with the evident cheerfulness that characterized them, as it did the men of our army generally. When well, they were a jolly set, roughing it without much whining, and inclined to make the best of their frequent grave discomforts. I give a few of the entries taken at random from two of the diaries: —

"Weather terribly cold. Rose at half-past eight o'clock. Sat on the ground in captain's tent, and wrote a long New Year's letter to mother. In the afternoon, put up tents, and got a warm meal. Had hardtack and raw pork for breakfast — oyster supper in the evening. A jolly time."

"Had funeral over Squad Six's horse. Doggie Doggett" — a dog they took with them — "principal mourner."

"Built a splendid 'shebang'; as convenient and handsome as a Yankee pigsty. Invited the squad, and had a pow-wow in the evening."

"Spent all the morning frying cakes; could not get ahead, boys ate them so fast. Don't like the business. Lewis died this morning. Body to be sent to Chicago. Had a jolly supper of oranges, soft bread, cold boiled beef, onion and cucumber pickles, and coffee. Wrote to father."

"Boys foraging freely. Plenty of turkeys and chickens. One of the Forty-Eighth Ohio, and one of the Twenty-First Iowa, captured by guerillas, while foraging, a mile from camp. They were tied together, and shot. One killed, the other wounded. They were brought into camp, and the wounded and dead were passed through on a horse, so that all saw them. There was great indignation. The Sixth Missouri Cavalry sent in pursuit. Boys found some hogsheads of molasses. Helped themselves. Got daubed from head to foot, and came into camp buzzing like beehives with flies. Had a bully game of base ball. Received letters from home."

"Boys all busy making molasses candy. Sweet times here."

"Face and lips parched with the wind, and covered with dust. Squad Two's men crossed the bayou, and caught sheep, but were ordered by the guard to leave them. After dark, Dick Powell swam over with a rope, and hitched the sheep to it; one of them was drawn over by the boys. Ordered to move at five o'clock in the morning."

"Thirtieth day of the siege of Vicksburg. Bullets flying over us day and night. Have had lively times. Shell from a twelve-pound howitzer struck a man belonging to Ninety-Sixth Ohio, while lying in bed, — tearing his jaw, and dislocating his shoulder. Read 'Bitter Sweet.' Took a bath. Held theological discussion with Higby, Mendsen, and others. Wrote to mother."

"Put up tent, just in time to escape a terrible

shower.  Turned in, and slept in the water all
night, but knew nothing of it till morning.  Hot
— hot — hot!  We're getting cooked down here, and
the rebs, knowing it, keep trying their hand at
peppering us.  Got nine letters from home to-day.
Other boys got more.  We talked, and sang low, a
great deal about home.  No sleep all night."

There is scarcely an entry in one of the diaries
that does not record some event with a touch of
humor in it, a frolic, or, at least, a gay social time
that enlivened the gloominess of army life.

They reached the army just in time to be incorporated with the troops whose efforts were directed to
the re-opening of the Mississippi, and first to the
reduction of Vicksburg, as the direct means to that
end.  They accompanied General Sherman on the
Tallahatchie march, which was "mere fun," as the
roads were good, the country new to them, and very
pleasant.  Then they went in his command to Chickasaw Bluffs, where they stood ready to aid in an
immediate attack, for three days and nights.  The
horses were ready harnessed, and standing, and
the men sleepless and expectant; the rain pouring,
the mud of the swamp-land where they were stationed deepening, the execrable bayous about them
becoming hourly more dangerous and impassable.
Baffled, beaten back, and repulsed with great slaughter, Sherman returned up the river to Milliken's
Bend, and our boys, incorporated into the Thirteenth Corps, in which they afterwards remained,
were ordered thither also.

Under command of General McClernand, they
next went on an expedition against Arkansas Post,
or Fort Hindman, up White River, fifty miles from

Engraved by J.J. Cade, New York.

Copyright 1887.

W.J. Sheppard Pinx

A.D. Worthington & Co. Publishers, Hartford, Conn.

"OUR BATTERY" AT THE FRONT.—REVEILLE AFTER AN ANXIOUS NIGHT.

"They stood ready to aid in an immediate attack for three days and nights."

the Mississippi, which fell into the hands of our troops, with five thousand prisoners. The following entries from two of the diaries briefly tell the story of their share in this engagement: —

"January 9, 1863. — Started up White River on steamer Louisiana, which received our men, horses, and guns. Left our sick men on the Adriatic, in charge of Corporal Dyer (the excellent nurse we have before mentioned), as we are bound on an expedition of some sort against the enemy. Sent two short notes to father and friends, not knowing what may happen. Men in excellent spirits, spoiling for a fight."

"Jan. 10. — Left the boat, and travelled three miles towards the Fort, against which we are proceeding. Received an accession of five men to our squad from the One Hundred Thirty-first Illinois Infantry. Horses remained harnessed to the guns all night. Passed a line of rebel rifle-pits. The gunboats shelled the woods and Fort all the evening."

"Jan. 11. — Our battery ordered into action. Started about nine o'clock. Passed the second line of rifle-pits, and halted near a grave-yard. At noon the ball opened. We were drawn up within three hundred yards of the Fort. Early in the engagement a shell exploded over and around us, giving Hugh Wilson a big scare, who, boy-like, had climbed a tree, standing right in the range of the enemy's guns, hoping to see what was being done in the Fort. He was covered with broken branches, cut off by the explosion of the shell, and came down in a hurry, uttering a prayer or an oath, he says he does not know which. The artillery thundered around the Fort in all directions. We fired about forty rounds from 'Old Abe,'"— for so they had named one of their guns,—" when the rebs ran up the white flag. Amid tremendous cheering, that seemed to rend the heavens, we swarmed into the Fort, and took possession. We camped on the field that night."

Our boys were highly complimented by their officers for their gallant behavior on this occasion. The papers trumpeted their praises, and on the next Sunday, when Mr. T—— thanked God for their preservation, in the prayers of the morning service, every heart uttered a voiceless but fervent and devout "Amen!"

Next came the siege of Vicksburg, when they marched from Milliken's Bend down the west bank of the Mississippi nearly seventy miles, to a point opposite Grand Gulf. Here they crossed with other troops, and, under the lead of General Grant, marched to the rear of that seemingly invincible city. Until its surrender, they were active in the various measures that led to its capitulation on that glorious Fourth, when the nation surrendered itself to a delirium of joy over the success of our armies at Gettysburg and Vicksburg.

Hitherto we had been able to keep up constant communication with the boys. There was an uninterrupted procession of boxes going down to them, filled with everything for which they asked and with many things for which they never thought of asking. Letters, papers, periodicals, clothing, writing materials, postage-stamps, photographs of persons, places, and scenes, everything which seemed likely to amuse, comfort, or assist, was sent on its way to their encampment. Very many of their friends obtained passes within the lines, and visited them, returning with such cheerful accounts of their daily life as greatly relieved their relatives of anxiety for them.

But from this time they passed beyond the reach of friends or packages from home, except at rare intervals. While they were in the rear of Vicksburg, there were weeks when we knew nothing of their condition or whereabouts. But through all the daily assaults and sallies of that memorable siege, although they were often in great danger, they were unharmed, except as the terribly hot weather, poor fare, and bad water caused sickness among them. Hardly had Vicksburg surrendered when they were sent with other troops to re-enforce Sherman on the Big Black, who had gone thither to oppose Johnston.

Over a region devastated by war, parched by the drought, both men and horses being maddened by thirst, suffocated by dust, and scorched by the July sun, they pressed on towards Jackson, Miss., only to learn that the city was evacuated by the rebels. They had hurried across Pearl River, burning the bridges behind them to prevent pursuit. They were ordered back to Vicksburg; and after the fall of Port Hudson the battery was transferred to General Banks' command in the Department of the Gulf. The surrender of Port Hudson completely removed the rebel embargo on the commerce of the Mississippi, and permitted its waters to flow unvexed to the sea.

In one of the diaries are the following entries: —

"July 10, 1863. — Glory to God in the Highest! Port Hudson surrendered four days after Vicksburg! The Mississippi has got back again into the Union! The Confederacy is cut in twain! General Gardner gave up his sword to General Banks, they ran up the stars and stripes on the top of the highest bluff, and then a sutler opened his shop down by the landing. The Mississippi is open to trade its whole length!"

"July 20, 1863.—Hartley suddenly dropped down in our camp to-day. Didn't know he had left Chicago, or thought of visiting us. A visit from the Sultan of Turkey wouldn't have surprised us more. He brought St. Louis papers of July 12, eight days after the fall of Vicksburg. Counted advertisements of *nineteen steamboats*, soliciting passengers and freight for the lower Mississippi, including Helena, Memphis, Vicksburg, and New Orleans. The old times are coming back to us! The Mississippi is once more open to commerce! Hurrah!"

# CHAPTER XIX.

THE STORY OF OUR BATTERY BOYS CONTINUED—A DISAS-
TROUS EXPEDITION—A TRAP OF DEATH AND DESTRUC-
TION—SCENES OF HORROR—THRILLING ACTS OF BRAVE-
RY AND DEVOTION.

Changes among our Boys — Breaking down under the Hardships of War —
The Battery constantly shifts its Encampment — Working hard to kill
Time — The Humorous Side of Life in Camp — History of "Doggie Doggett," the Canine Member of the Battery — His Exploits and Unknown
Fate — Lost in the Service — Unfortunate Expedition — Up the Red
River — Charging the Enemy with a Baggage-Train — Our Boys fall into
a Trap of Death and Destruction — A terrific Charge by ten thousand
Rebels — Overpowered by superior Numbers — Retreat or Surrender the
only Alternative — The Guns of the Battery captured — Death of Lieutenant Throop — Sergeant Dyer shot while spiking his Gun — Many of
our Boys are taken Prisoners — Hugh Wilson's Devotion — Only eight
of our Boys return at the Close of the War.

BY this time, a good many changes had occurred among the boys. Five of them had
broken down under the unaccustomed hardships to which they were subjected, and,
after suffering for a long time in hospitals,
were discharged from the service. One had
died, and his body had been sent home for burial.

Lieutenant S——, the original superintendent of
the Sunday-school, was forced to resign because of
circumstances that he could not control, and he had
returned to Chicago. His resignation caused deeper
despondency and discouragement than the sickness
and death of all the others. The remarkable manli-

ness, judgment, and good sense of the man, as well as the sterling integrity of his character, his cheerfulness, and affectionate nature, made him indispensable to our boys. We all felt that his association with them gave them a sort of immunity from many of the ills of a soldier's life. In a very large sense, the boys of the parish had been given to his keeping, as to that of a wise and good elder brother. But after a while we became accustomed to these changes, as to the other inevitable bereavements, disappointments, and griefs which the war had brought on us and on the dear country. We had counted the cost, and did not lose heart when it proved heavier than we anticipated.

Until the spring of 1864, our boys were stationed in Louisiana and Texas, shifting their encampments occasionally as the movements of the enemy compelled them. Now, we heard from them at Carrollton, some half-dozen miles from New Orleans. Then, at Franklin, Algiers, Brashear City, Opelousas, New Iberia, Baton Rouge, and other points. They were continually flitting hither and thither, now to protect a point which the enemy threatened; or, as an intimidation to guerillas; or, because a " reconnoissance in force " was proposed; or, as the boys themselves sometimes believed and openly declared, to render safe the cotton spoliations, in which not a few of our officers were at that time concerned. This sort of life was not to their liking, and they grumbled about it not a little.

Much of the time for the six or eight months succeeding the fall of Vicksburg, they were comparatively idle, save as they worked hard to kill time. The diaries kept during this period, show that this was dreary business. They gave concerts, extemporized theatrical performances, built shebangs, and painted over each some *outré* name, in the temporary absence of the occupants, which was intended as a joke on their peculiarities or history. If one was of a taciturn temperament, and had a shebang all to himself, he would find in the morning that his cabin had acquired during the night the painted cognomen of "Celibacy Hall." The shebang occupied by two dear friends rejoiced in the name of "Hotel de Siamese Twins." Three or four, more given to fault-finding than the rest, dwelt in "Grumblers' Den." A quartette of inveterate wags sported over their tent the staring announcement, "Pow-Wow Hall! Protracted meetings held here!" Two or three others, not very scrupulous, who had been detected in imposing on their best friends, the negroes, received their retribution in the unsolicited sign, painted in the night: "Legree House—Negroes for Sale Here!" And so on.

Sometimes a waggish squad, assisted by a neighboring infantry company, would arouse the whole encampment at midnight with a moonlight parade. The men would be attired fantastically in what they called "night uniforms," with wash-dishes for caps, and caisson shovels for swords, and every other ridiculous contrivance in the way of dress. They would have "cow-horn" music, by "Gideon's Band," a blast of which was strong enough to blow down the walls of any Jericho against which it was directed.

At Baton Rouge, where they were encamped some time, they found employment for themselves, and helped fill their empty pockets, by a public exhibition

of negro minstrelsy. They persuaded the provost-
marshal to give them the free use of the largest and
most elegant hall in the city for several nights.
There was a good deal of musical talent among the
boys. They could play several instruments finely,
and had often assisted us at home when we gave
exhibitions of tableaux, or held festivals, with the
music of an improvised band. Many of them were
excellent singers; so they arranged a programme,
blackened their faces, got up fantastic costumes, and
for a week gave nightly entertainments to crowded
houses, their audiences expressing their delight by
the most boisterous applause. This was so profita-
ble pecuniarily, that they would have repeated their
negro performance elsewhere had they been able to
command a hall.

Sometimes they went a-fishing, or, more frequently,
a-foraging, and "Doggie Doggett" always accompanied them. I find frequent mention of this canine
member of the battery. When our boys left Chicago
they took two dogs with them; one a large, noble
Newfoundland, which was lost on the Tallahatchie
march, and the other a miserable little shepherd
dog, that they christened "Doggie Doggett," and
which proved invaluable to them. He was a great
pet, and was instructed, and trained, and frolicked
with, and caressed, until he became a highly accomplished animal. His exploits would occupy
more space and time in recounting than would
those of "old Mother Hubbard's dog," whose
chronicles are to be found in the veritable nursery
books of Mother Goose. He paid no heed to
the stringent orders issued from time to time,
commanding respect for the rights of property in

the country through which he marched or where he encamped. If he saw a sheep or a pig at a distance, he immediately went for it, and held it until our boys could despatch it. Stimulated by the praise he received, he redoubled his efforts in the foraging line; and it was the boast of the battery that "Doggie Doggett could kill more sheep in one night than any other dog on record." He possessed so much of the *savoir faire*, that if he visited a flock, and was not discovered and called off, he left not one alive to tell of his dealings with them.

It was the intention of the boys to bring him North and make a hero of him; and this they promised the ugly little brute over and over, all through the war. His love of sheep would have cost him his life at an early day had they brought him home; and it is not therefore to be regretted that they lost him, just as the war ended, when they were on their way to the North. Amid the confusion of regiments hastening homeward, the dog became bewildered, and marched off with the wrong battery. That is the theory of the boys. So dear had he become to them, that they actually obtained a pass for a man to go to Brashear City to seek him, as he was supposed to have straggled off in that direction. But "Doggie Doggett" was not to be found, and to this day no one knows his fate; but his memory is honored in the records of the battery.

In the latter part of the winter of 1864, General Banks planned an ill-starred expedition, whose line of operations was Red River. Its object, was the capture of Shreveport, with the rout and dispersion of Kirby's army, culminating in the recovery of Texas, and a boundless supply of cotton for our mills and for export.  Admiral Porter was to take ten thousand of Sherman's old army, under General A. J. Smith, up Red River, with a strong fleet of ironclads.  At Alexandria he was to meet General Banks with fifteen thousand more, who were to march overland from the Atchafalaya.  At the same time General Steele, with fifteen thousand tried troops, was to move on Shreveport from Little Rock.  Our boys went on this badly planned expedition, with two thin divisions of the Thirteenth Corps, of which they were a part, under the immediate command of General Ransom, than whom the country had no nobler patriot and soldier.

The expedition proved a disastrous and mortifying failure.  General Banks' force was ten days behind time in effecting a junction at Alexandria with Admiral Porter.  There was not water enough to float the heavy ironclads as they proceeded up Red River, and the heaviest were left below Alexandria.  To make matters yet worse, a portion of General Smith's troops were recalled to protect the Mississippi from incessant and troublesome raids.  As General Steele could not render any assistance until the three divisions met at Shreveport, General Banks' force of forty thousand men was reduced, practically, to twenty thousand.  There was little pretence of secrecy on the part of our army, and the enemy knew, just as well as did our own commanders, what was the object of the expedition, where it was going, by what route, how many troops were engaged in it, and what were the character, calibre, and experience of the men who officered it.  Every rebel prisoner captured on the way was as well posted on these matters as our own men — sometimes even more so.

They met with no very obstinate resistance until they reached Natchitoches, although the enemy kept up a steady skirmishing with the van of our army all the eighty miles of the way from Alexandria. From Natchitoches to Shreveport was one hundred miles, through pine woods, barren, sandy, and uninhabitable. On they pushed, into the trap set for them, right into the jaws of death and destruction. They left Natchitoches on the 6th of April and pressed on, meeting larger bodies of the enemy, the skirmishing growing hotter, the fight assuming larger, sharper, and more serious proportions. On the morning of the 8th, when they had come within two miles of Mansfield, they were unexpectedly confronted by the rebel " Army of the Trans-Mississippi," twenty thousand strong, commanded by Kirby, Smith, Dick Taylor, and other able officers. The principal portion of the rebel troops lay in thick pine woods, with a hill between them and our forces; and across this hill lay the only road which our men could follow, as it was the only one leading to Shreveport.

The van of our army was mainly composed of the Thirteenth Corps, and the Mercantile Battery, to which our boys belonged, was in the extreme front. Just as they marched from a dense pine forest into a small clearing, they were attacked by the rebels in great force, on both flanks and in front. A line of battle was immediately formed. The guns of the battery were put in position, and, for a time, it seemed as though our men would make a successful defence. But suddenly there rose, as if out of the very ground, ten thousand rebel troops, who charged down on our panic-stricken men with terrific yells. They stood their ground bravely until they were overpowered by superior numbers. What availed two thousand cavalry, three thousand infantry, and twenty pieces of artillery, so placed as to be unable to act in concert, against a solid force of ten thousand men? An immense baggage and supply train of between three and four hundred huge army wagons was in the immediate rear of the advance, completely filling up the one narrow, winding forest road, and rendering it impossible for the main body of the army to give any support to the advance.

There was nothing left our men but to retreat or surrender. The officers of the battery, which was doing good service, cheered on the men; for it was not in their nature to give way, while there was a possibility of beating back the rebels. With uplifted sword, and words of cheer on his lips, George Throop, now a lieutenant of the battery, was struck in the pit of the stomach by the fragment of a shell. With the single exclamation, " My God, I am killed! " he fell back from his horse, was caught by his companions, and taken to the rear. But, heroically, he bade them return to the fight and leave him to die, since they could do him no good. A surgeon pronounced his wound mortal, and he was placed in an ambulance to be taken from the field.

Before it could get under headway, a retreat was sounded, and then a horrible rout ensued, of which General Franklin has said that " Bull Run was not a circumstance in comparison." He was on both battle-fields. Our boys tried to save their guns, but, finding that impossible, they endeavored to spike them. Sergeant Dyer, whom I have before mentioned as a rare nurse in sickness, was shot through the lungs, and mortally wounded, while in the act of spiking his

Engraved by J J Cade, New York.

Copyrighted 1867

A D Worthington & Co. Publishers, Hartford, Conn.

## DEATH OF SERGEANT DYER WHILE SPIKING HIS GUN.

"Our boys tried to save their guns, but, finding that impossible, they endeavored to spike them. Sergeant
Dyer whom I have before mentioned as a rare nurse in sickness, was shot through the lungs, and mortally
wounded, while in the act of spiking his gun. Of one hundred and ten horses, they took off the field but forty-five."

gun. The captain and two other commanding officers were taken prisoners, one of them was fatally wounded, and thirty-two of the men were killed or captured. Of one hundred and ten horses, they took off the field but forty-five. The rest were left wounded, dying, and dead. All their guns were captured, and fourteen others, belonging to other batteries.

"*Sauve qui peut!*" — Let whoever can, save himself — was the motto of the hour, and a wild and maddening flight ensued. The drivers of the army wagons, occupying the only road through the woods, turned to flee, upsetting the huge vehicles, when they cut the traces from the mules, and fled with them. Immediately the road was choked with overturned, crushed, entangled wagons, with struggling horses and mules, and half-crazed men. It was impossible to save the valuable wagon-train, and that, too, fell into the enemy's hands. There was no order, no heeding of commands, no thought of anything but safety, and only a headlong stampede.

Men on foot rushed precipitately to the rear. Bareheaded riders, with ashen faces, lashed their terrified beasts to more furious haste. Cavalry horses galloped riderless, at full speed, over the terrified infantry, the prostrate wounded and dying, and others on foot. Officers with drawn sabres, hoarse voices, and almost death-stricken faces, implored their unheeding men 'to stop, form again, and make a new stand. And in full pursuit of these routed fugitives the rebels followed pell-mell, yelling, shouting, and maintaining a continuous fire. The whistle of musket-balls filled the air in all directions. The crashing of trees, the breaking of fallen wood, the galloping

of horses and mules, the eddying whirlpool of maddened men,—all this made up a scene of horror that
beggars description.

For a full mile this terrible stampede continued;
and then the fugitives came upon the magnificent
Nineteenth Corps, formed in full line of battle, right
across their road. Even this could not halt the
panic-stricken men. So, opening their ranks, the
Nineteenth Corps permitted the disorderly retreating
forces to pass through. Then they closed up solidly
again, and waited the oncoming shock of the enemy,
flushed with victory, who anticipated no check. On
they came, with headlong impetuosity, shouting and
firing as they advanced, driving in the skirmishers
that had been thrown out, and charging on the intrepid lines of blue and glistening steel as though
they were the routed fugitives they had been driving.
On they galloped, rushing almost up to the very
muzzles of the guns, till they could look in the eyes
of their foes, our men standing like animated gran-
ite, reserving their fire till the word of command was
given. Then there came one blinding flash of flame,
one reverberating burst of thunder, from our gallant
hosts, one fierce rain of leaden hail on the ranks of
the enemy, and the rebels surged back in a great
wave, like the outgoing tide. Their pursuit was
checked, their lines broken, and they could not rally
again. It was now their turn to flee; and they fell
back in haste, leaving their dead and dying on the
field. The fight lasted but a few hours, but it brought
discomfiture and deep humiliation to our forces. It
cost the loss of three thousand men and twenty
pieces of artillery, and compelled the entire army to
turn sadly back to New Orleans.

But what of our boys? When George Throop fell, despite the battle raging around them, the boys all rushed to their fallen leader. But he commanded them to return to their duty, saying to each a tender "good-bye," as they turned away, and, dashing off the blinding tears, stood again manfully to their guns. "I am dying," were his words; "but I am not afraid to die. Tell my father and mother that I die willingly; my firm faith sustains me. I give my life for a glorious cause, and I do not regret it. So leave me, boys, for you can do nothing for me, but take care of yourselves." And so they left the brave young officer to die.

All but one; and he would *not* obey. He was Hugh Wilson. We had objected more seriously to his entering the service than to all the others. A mere schoolboy, a Sunday-school pet, the youngest child of his mother, he would be only the plague and the plaything of the battery. Why should he go? A larger license had always been permitted him than to any other of the battery boys, and so, instead of obeying the command of his officer to return to duty as the others did, he jumped into the ambulance, determined to save Lieutenant Throop if possible. The cry of retreat was sounded behind him, and the terrified driver immediately cut one mule from the traces, and, mounting it, sought his own safety. Hugh seized the reins, and with the remaining mule endeavored to pilot the ambulance through the labyrinthine maze of fleeing men, broken wagons, and galloping horses, to a place of safety. The road was rough, and the dying lieutenant was roused to consciousness. Again, with characteristic unselfishness, he remonstrated with the lad for running such risks to his own life and safety: "I am dying, Hugh, and you can do nothing for me. Save yourself; leave me, I entreat you!"

But the warm-hearted boy, loving his long-time friend more and more as he saw him drifting away forever, once more gathered up the reins, and urged the mule to greater speed. They came to a side road, and into this Hugh turned the ambulance. It looked as if it might lead to a less obstructed pathway. Alas! it led to a narrow stream of water, with steep banks and deep, swift current. It could not be forded. Again the lieutenant paused on the very threshold of heaven to beseech Hugh to seek his own safety. The iciness of death had already settled upon him. The unmistakable look of mortal pallor, that the human face never wears but once, was on his features. His speech was becoming inarticulate, and his pulse barely fluttered under the pressure of Hugh's finger. "Hugh, you *must* go! You will be taken prisoner. I am beyond the reach of the enemy; they cannot harm me. Put something under my head, and then go. Save yourself! Quick, Hugh!" At the same moment rebel troopers came dashing down the road, and, catching a glimpse of Hugh, called on him to "surrender!"

Quick as thought, Hugh stripped off his jacket, forgetting that it contained all his money (he had been paid off a few days before), the photographs of his father and mother, the little Testament his pastor had given him, and all the valuables he had in the world. Folding it under George Throop's head, he kissed his cold lips again and again, whispered a swift "good-bye," which the dying man had no voice to answer, leaped down the bank of the stream, and hid himself among the rank undergrowth, half in the water. They were parted now; one going back to the conflict, the other mounting heavenward.

The rebels rushed down to the bank, and, not seeing Hugh, fired into the clump of bushes where he was secreted, and then rode away. The balls whizzed around him, but did not harm him. Cautiously the poor lad felt his way out to the edge of the still retreating tide of Union soldiers, and, weeping silently, disheartened, and bereaved, commenced a search for his surviving comrades. He found them at last, such as were not left dead on the field, or prisoners in the hands of the enemy.

It was a gloomy hour. But one officer was left the battery, and of the missing they could not tell who was dead and who captured. Some time after, one of the battery boys who was left wounded on the field, and was taken to a rebel hospital, was paroled and came home. He brought with him a blouse which was known to be Lieutenant Throop's, as it bore his name marked by himself. He stated that he discovered one of the attendants at the hospital wearing it, and, on inquiry, learned that he took it from the dead body of a lieutenant of artillery, whom he had buried with other Union dead, after the battle of Mansfield. The grave of Lieutenant Throop is not known to this day, but his memory is green in the hearts of all who loved him, and they number all who knew him. It is no disparagement to the other members of the battery to say that his was the completest, most harmonious, and best developed character among them. To all the battery boys he was leader, and his influence was always for good. His superior officers respected him the more deeply in proportion as they were truly superior in the highest sense of the word. All trusted him.

His diary came into my hands, and its indications of filial and fraternal affection impressed me deeply. No one sought to comfort his father and mother, but all sat down and wept with them. "Oh," said one of his comrades, "how George Throop loved his mother! It would have been easy for him to die for her!" And by that token judge how the mother loved the son. She was the first to speak when the sad news was borne to the broken household. Lifting her white, tearless face, she said, "If it be true that all is over with George in this world, that he is dead, and not lingering in suffering, I rejoice for him! He will never have to suffer as his father and I are suffering now."

We gathered in the church on the following Sabbath, a sad and weeping congregation. We recalled the hour when from its altar we had dismissed the now glorified young leader to battle, to death, to Heaven. God had granted him a discharge from all earthly conflict, and for him there were no tears. We repressed our own lesser grief in the presence of the great bereavement of the parents. The choir sang of victory, and their voices swelled in a triumphant song of thanksgiving for the glorious hope of immortality that illumines our darkness. The prayers of the morning breathed resignation to the inscrutable order of Divine Providence, which had stricken us so severely, and implored the peace of Heaven to enter our souls. And the sermon lifted us out of the damps and fogs of our earthly atmosphere into the serene light of the happy hereafter. Time has softened the poignancy of grief felt during the months that followed, and memory and hope have done much to subdue the pain inflicted by that grievous wound.

> — "God keeps a niche
> In heaven to hold our idols! and albeit
> He brake them to our faces, and denied
> That our close kisses should impair their white, —
> I know we shall behold them raised, complete —
> The dust shook from their beauty — glorified
> New Memnons, singing in the great God-light!"

Those of our boys who were taken prisoners were carried to Camp Ford, in Tyler, Tex. Although they fared hard, and endured many privations, their lot was comfortable compared with that of the poor martyrs at Andersonville. They were placed in a camp of about ten acres, where seven thousand Union men were held as prisoners of war. It was inclosed by a stockade of oak timber, twelve feet high, and within its limits were five living springs of pure, clear water. These springs were ample for all the uses of the men, and, crowded as was the place, there was no excuse for personal uncleanness. No prisoner was allowed to come within ten feet of the stockade, and not unfrequently men who violated this rule, inadvertently or through ignorance, were shot down like dogs. When our boys first reached the rebel camp, there were but six axes for the entire seven thousand men, who were obliged to cut their own fuel and build their own cabins. But an exchange of prisoners was effected shortly after the arrival of the battery boys; and as some of the exchanged men were from Illinois, an appeal was sent to Governor Yates for axes and clothing. The appeal was munificently answered by an abundant supply of whatever was asked, sufficient for six or seven hundred men, which was faithfully distributed. With the arrival of the axes, the boys went to "shebang" building, in which they had had much experience. Permission was given them to cut timber in the woods, and very soon they had as good houses of their own as the Texans of the town, and commenced housekeeping under difficulties, and in a somewhat primitive way.

Many of the men were in a complete state of nudity, and their entire persons were browned to the color of Indians. Even their blankets were in rags; and on one occasion, when some were exchanged, they were sent to New Orleans, and marched through the streets in very nearly the simple costume of our first parents before they went into the manufacture of fig-leaf clothing. They also suffered from a lack of vegetables, and this induced scurvy. Some of the discharged men were so afflicted with scurvy that their teeth fell out, and they came home with them in their pockets instead of in their mouths. To obtain vegetables, our boys manifested no little ingenuity, assisted by others as energetic as themselves.

The prisoners had to slaughter their own cattle; and they were allowed the heads and hoofs as perquisites. From the hoofs the Yankee boys made glue. With this and the sinews of the cattle they manufactured violins of every size, and by and by organized a band, whose performances were greatly relished by their fellow-prisoners. They obtained files, and transformed the backs of their knives into saws, with which they sawed the horns of the cattle lengthwise, and then cut them into combs. These combs were very salable, and brought a good price in Confederate money. Not infrequently, rebels of high social position would come into camp, and order combs, stipulating in advance their size and the price to be paid. Some who bought of them had been without combs for a year. With the money thus earned, our boys bought sweet potatoes and other vegetables, which kept scurvy, the great foe of the camp and prison, at a distance. They bribed the guard to bring them chisels and files, and then manufactured from the horns that fell to their share complete sets of chessmen and checkers. For one set of chessmen they received from a rebel officer Confederate money equal in value to ten dollars of our currency.

There were frequent but always futile attempts to escape from the prison. The men dug tunnels, one of which was eight months in progress. But there were always rebel spies in camp, who were well informed of the plans for escape, and when, after eight months' patient subterranean labor, the tunneling party came out through it, one hundred and fifty yards beyond the camp, there stood the rebel jailers waiting to receive them. If, by good luck, a man made his escape for a time, he was soon caught, and in two or three weeks brought back to his old comrades, who received him with shouts of laughter and mocking jeers and jibes. Some escaped temporarily by hiding in the carts of refuse and offal that were daily hauled outside the camp. When the officers learned this, a cartload was never dumped outside until the guard had repeatedly plunged his bayonet through the mass, sometimes transfixing the secreted soldier, nearly suffocated under the refuse *débris* of the cabins. Fresh lots of prisoners were constantly added to the camp, and with them there was always smuggled in one or more of the rebels, disguised in Union uniform, who prowled about as spies.

The rebel regiments sent to guard the camp were repeatedly changed. The Union prisoners soon demoralized them; for the guards became completely fascinated with their conversation. This was understood in the camp, and, although conversation was prohibited between the guards and the prisoners, it was carried on constantly and without interruption. The former had sufficient intelligence to comprehend that their prisoners were better educated than themselves, better informed, and vastly their superiors in all matters of knowledge and skill. As they listened to their recital of the causes of the war, the overwhelming advantages of the North, and the inevitable and fast-hastening end of the conflict, the guards were won over to the side of loyalty, and fraternized with those whom they were to control.

At Marshall, Tex., where the boys were sent to the hospital for a time, they found an openly avowed sentiment of loyalty. The ladies of the town came to the wards and nursed them, fed them with food from their own tables, and attended personally to their wants, as if they were kindred instead of strangers. The mayor of the city and his son called on them, openly avowing Union sentiments, and denouncing the war and the Confederate government. Had they been in a Chicago hospital, among their own friends, they could not have received kinder or more generous treatment.

The boys were held as prisoners for fourteen months, and then the war ended. As soon as the news of the fall of Richmond reached the rebel guards, they left their posts without ceremony and went home. The prisoners saw their camp unguarded, and, understanding what it meant, made preparations to follow the example of their guards. With their usual good sense and foresight, they had been preparing to leave for some time, and, as they earned money, had bought supplies of crackers, and sewed them up in their clothing, against a day of need. It was well they did; for, though their jailers promised rations for the long march to Shreveport, and thence, hundreds of miles, to New Orleans, it was days before any were received, and then there was but a meagre supply. Nearly naked, not very well fed, they at last found their way within the Union lines, when each man was furnished transportation to his own command, where he could receive his pay, or be mustered out of service.

They found the wreck of the battery at New Orleans, where the men had been doing "fatigue duty," a part of the time at Camp Parapet. The powers that be had ordered them to take muskets and serve as infantry, and, I think, had sent the muskets for that purpose. But the boys indignantly refused them, or to perform any of the duties of infantry. They had enlisted in the artillery. Their decision brought them into bad odor with the resident military authorities. Some petty tyrannies and indignities were attempted towards them by officials, which waked up the Chicago Board of Trade, under whose auspices they were mustered into the service; and that organization took the matter in hand, and summarily redressed their wrongs.

At the close of the war the battery was mustered

out of the service, and our boys came back to Chicago. *There were but eight of them left.* All the others had died, or been killed in battle, or had dropped out of the service from invalidism; but two or three of them survive to-day. One died in Minnesota, of illness contracted in the service. Another graduated from Harvard, and practises law in Michigan. Another is connected with the silver mines of Colorado. And of the young and manly strength, and power, and beauty, which were our boast when the war commenced, there is scarcely a trace remaining. Our boys are not; and others have succeeded to their places. We have lost them; but some time we shall find them.

> " For as we hasten through these regions dim,
> Lo, how the white wings of the Seraphim
> Shine in the sunset! On that joyous shore,
> Our lighted hearts shall know
> The life of long ago:
> The sorrow-burdened Past shall fade —
> Forevermore!"

# CHAPTER XX.

THE FIRST GREAT SANITARY FAIR—RAISING MONEY FOR HOSPITAL RELIEF—A GREAT AND MEMORABLE DAY—A MOTLEY PROCESSION THREE MILES LONG.

Continued Needs of the Hospitals lead to a great Sanitary Fair — A Woman's Enterprise from the Beginning — Large Preparations — Seventeen Bushels of Fair Circulars and Letters sent at one Mail—Mrs. Hoge obtains Help from Pittsburg and Philadelphia — Potter Palmer from New York — Boston and Connecticut contribute — The whole Northwest ransacked for Attractions — At last, Men catch the Fair Mania — Their varied Gifts — Opening Inaugural Procession — Captured rebel Flags borne along — School Children in Carriages and Omnibuses — Convalescent Soldiers from Hospitals — Procession of Farm Wagons, with Vegetables — Procession halts on the Court House Lawn — Firing of thirty-four Guns announces the Opening of the Fair.

HE continued need of money for the purchase of comforts and necessaries for the sick and wounded of our army, had suggested to the loyal women of the Northwest many and various devices for the raising of funds. Every city, town, and village had had its fair, festival, party, picnic, excursion, concert, and regular subscription fund, which had netted more or less for the cause of hospital relief, according to the population, and the amount of energy and patriotism awakened. But the need of money for this sacred purpose still continued. Our brave men were still wrestling with the Southern rebellion, which,

though oft-times checked, was not conquered.  The
hospitals whose wards were vacated by death, or recovery of their patients, were speedily refilled by
new faces which disease had rendered pallid, and
new forms shattered by cannon-shot or sabre-stroke.
It was necessary to continue to pour down sanitary
supplies for the comfort and care of the suffering
soldiers, whose well-being, at that time, lay so near
the hearts of all loyal men and women.  Since the
most valuable sanitary supplies could only be obtained with money, the ingenuity of women was
taxed to the utmost to raise funds.

The expenses of the Northwestern Sanitary Commission had been very heavy through the summer of
1863, and every means of raising money had seemed
to be exhausted.  At last, Mrs. Hoge and myself
proposed a great Northwestern Fair.  We had been
to the front of the army ourselves, and had beheld
the practical working of the Sanitary Commission,
with which we were associated.  We knew its activity, its methods, its ubiquity, its harmony with military rules and customs, and we knew that it could be
relied on with certainty when other means of relief
failed.  We saw that an immense amount of supplies
was necessary for the comfort and healing of the
army of brave invalids, and wounded men, that filled
our military hospitals, and our hearts sank as we
realized the depleted condition of the treasury of the
Commission.

We were sure that a grand fair, in which the whole
Northwest would unite, would replenish the treasury
of the Commission, which, from the beginning, had
sent to battle-fields and hospitals thirty thousand
boxes of sanitary stores, worth, in the aggregate, a

million and a half of dollars. We knew, also, that it would develop a grateful demonstration of the loyalty of the Northwest to our beloved but struggling country. That it would encourage the worn veterans of many a hard-fought field, and strengthen them in their defence of our native land. That it would reveal the worth, and enforce the claims of the Sanitary Commission, upon those hitherto indifferent to them. That it would quicken the sacred workers into new life.

Accordingly, we consulted the gentlemen of the Commission, who languidly approved our plan, but laughed incredulously at our proposition to raise twenty-five thousand dollars for its treasury. By private correspondence, we were made certain of the support and co-operation of our affiliated Aid Societies, and our next step was to issue a printed circular, embodying a call for a woman's convention, to be held in Chicago on the 1st of September, 1863. Every Aid Society, every Union League, and every Lodge of Good Templars in the Northwest, were invited to be present, by representatives. Some ten thousand of these circulars were scattered through the Northwest. A copy was sent to the editor of every Northwestern paper, with the request that it might appear in his columns — a request generally granted — and clergymen were very generally invited by letter to interest their parishioners in the project.

Pursuant to this call, a convention of women delegates from the Northwestern states was held in Chicago on the 1st and 2d of September, at Bryan Hall. The convention was harmonious and enthusiastic. The fair was formally resolved on. The time and place for holding it were fixed. The delegates came instructed to pledge their respective towns for donations of every variety, and help to the utmost. The women delegates were remarkably efficient and earnest; for each society had sent its most energetic and executive members. This convention placed the success of the fair beyond a doubt, and Mrs. Hoge and myself saw clearly that it would surpass in interest and pecuniary profit all other fairs ever held in the country.

On. the evening of the first day, a grand social re-union was held in the parlors of the Tremont House. This gave the ladies who had gathered from all parts of the country an opportunity of forming each others' acquaintance, and of discussing socially the various topics of interest suggested by the convention. On the afternoon of the second day, a mass meeting of women was held in Bryan Hall, when addresses were delivered by Thomas B. Bryan, Esq., Hon. O. H. Lovejoy of Illinois, Hon. Z. Chandler of Michigan, and some of the city clergymen. Their utterances nerved those who were laboring in the arduous work of hospital relief, to renewed and deeper consecration. It was a fitting close to the two days' meeting, and kindled a flame in the hearts of the women who attended it. They returned to their homes glowing with enthusiastic interest in the forthcoming fair.

This first Sanitary fair, it must be remembered, was an experiment, and was pre-eminently an enterprise of women, receiving no assistance from men in its early beginnings. The city of Chicago regarded it with indifference, and the gentlemen members of the Commission barely tolerated it. The first did not understand it, and the latter were doubtful of its success.  The great fairs that followed this were the work of men as well as of women, from their very incipiency — but this fair was the work of women. Another circular was now issued, and this enumerated and classified the articles that were desired. It was a new experience to the Northwest, and advice and plans were necessary in every step taken.

Preparations now went on in good earnest.  Up to this point the efforts had been to create a public sentiment in its favor, and to induce the prominent organizations in the Northwest to pledge it their active support.  These ends being now attained, the work of gathering articles for the fair went on rapidly.  Twenty thousand copies of the second circular, specifying what articles were needed, when, where, and how they should be sent, were distributed over the Northwest.  The aid of the press was invoked, and it was granted in a most hearty and generous fashion.  An extensive correspondence was carried on with governors, congressmen, members of state legislatures, military men, postmasters, clergymen, and teachers.  The letters addressed to the women of the Northwest, explanatory, hortatory, laudatory, and earnest, were numbered by thousands. Some idea may be formed of the amount of machinery requisite to the creation of this first Northwestern fair — the pioneer of the great Sanitary fairs which afterwards followed, "the first-born among many brethren" — from the fact that on one occasion alone there were sent from the rooms of the Sanitary Commission, *seventeen bushels of mail matter*, all of it relating to the fair.

Nor was this all.  Mrs. Hoge went to Pittsburg, Pa., for a few days, and formed a society for the express purpose of aiding the fair. She had formerly resided in that city, and had scores of friends and relatives there. So successful were her appeals to the citizens of Pittsburg, that it was necessary to fit up a booth for the reception of the articles contributed. Manufacturers, artisans, and merchants sent choice specimens of value, skill, and taste, from a huge sheet of iron, worthy of Vulcan, and a breech-loading steel cannon of terrible beauty, to rich and rare fabrics of foreign looms, fit for the draping of a princess. Even the carbon oil, with which we have only unsightly and unsavory associations, was sent in hundreds of beautiful casks with painted staves and gilded hoops, bearing mottoes of undying loyalty.

From Pittsburg she proceeded to Philadelphia, the city of her birth and early girlhood. Although the remoteness of Philadelphia might have excused her from participating in the work of the fair, she caught the contagion of liberality, and sent substantial tokens of approval and interest.

Potter Palmer, the proprietor of the famous hotel that bears his name in Chicago, took the city of New York in hand, obtaining contributions from her importers, jobbers, and manufacturers, amounting to nearly six thousand dollars.

Boston was already astir with preparations for a grand soldiers' and sailors' fair, which proved a magnificent success. But she did not turn a deaf ear to my request for aid, but, with characteristic generosity, sent a large box filled with treasures abundant with her, but rare in the Northwest. The specimens of Chinese handiwork, of Fayal laces, of Sea Island algæ as delicate as vapor and arranged in sets, curious fans, slippers, pictures, and table ware in the highest style of Japanese art — these were rare at that time in the West, and when offered for sale at large prices vanished like dew before the sun. All sold quickly.

Connecticut sent a magnificent donation that realized thousands of dollars, and with it a deputation of Connecticut ladies, who superintended that department, and acted as saleswomen.

In every principal town of the Northwest "fair meetings" were held, which resulted in handsome pledges that were more than fulfilled. Towns and cities were canvassed for donations to the "Bazar" and "Dining Saloon." The whole Northwest was ransacked for articles, curious, unique, *bizarre*, or noteworthy, to add to the attractions of the "Curiosity Shop." Homes beautified with works of art, paintings, or statuary, were temporarily plundered of them for the "Art Gallery," and all who possessed artistic, dramatic, decorative or musical talent were pressed into the service of the "Evening Entertainments." Executive women were chosen in every state, who freighted the mails with rousing appeals from their pens, or with suggestions born of their experience, frequently visiting different sections to conduct meetings in the interest of the great and noble enterprise.

At last, even men became inoculated with the fair mania. They voluntarily came forward, pledging large donations in money or merchandise, or favoring the ladies with suggestions, and aiding in the work, which had now grown to huge proportions, and eclipsed all other interests. Mechanics offered their manufactures, one after another, — mowing machines, reapers, threshing-machines, corn-planters, pumps, drills for sowing wheat, cultivators, fanning-mills, — until a new building, a great storehouse, was erected to receive them. They gave ploughs, stoves, furnaces, millstones, and nails by the hundred kegs. Wagons and carriage-springs, plate glass, and huge plates of wrought iron, — one the largest ever rolled, at that time, in any rolling-mill in the world, — block tin, enamelled leather, hides, boxes of stationery, cases of boots, cologne by the barrel, native wine in casks, refined coal oil by the thousand gallons, a mounted howitzer, a steel breech-loading cannon, a steam-engine with boiler, pianos, organs, silver ware, crockery, trunks, pictures, boatloads of rubble-stone, loads of hay and grain and vegetables, stall-fed beeves, horses, colts, oxen, the gross receipts of the labor or business of certain days, — in short, whatever they had of goods or treasure.

During the last week of preparation, the men atoned for their early lack of interest, and their tardiness in giving, by a continued avalanche of gifts. The fate of Tarpeia seemed to threaten the women who were the committee of reception. Such a furor of benevolence had never before been known. Men, women, and children, corporations and business firms, religious societies, political organizations, — all vied with one another enthusiastically as to who should contribute the most to the great fair, whose proceeds were to be devoted to the sick and wounded of the Southwestern hospitals. As the Hebrews, in olden time, brought their free-will offerings to the altar of the Lord, so did the people of the Northwest, grateful to their brave defenders, lay their generous contributions on the altar of the country. The rich gave of their abundance, and the poor withheld not from giving because of their poverty.

An inaugural procession on the opening day of the fair was proposed, and the proposal crystallized into a glorious fact. The whole city was now interested. The opening day of the fair arrived. The courts adjourned; the post-office was closed; the public schools received a vacation; the banks were unopened; the Board of Trade remitted its sessions. Business of all kinds, whether in offices, courts, stores, shops, or manufactories, was suspended. All the varied machinery of the great city stood still for one day, that it might fitly honor the wounded soldiers' fair. Could a more eloquent tribute be paid our brave men, pining in far-off hospitals, who had jeopardized life and limb in the nation's cause?

No better description of this splendid inaugural pageant can be given than the following, taken from the Chicago *Tribune* of Oct. 28, 1863. It gives a graphic picture of the procession as it gathered up its forces and moved on under the bright October sun, three miles in length. But there can be no description given of the spontaneous patriotism, the infinite tenderness, the electric generosity, the moral earnestness, and the contagious enthusiasm, that transfused and glorified the occasion. One could as easily depict the shifting hues and lights of the Aurora: —

"Yesterday will never be forgotten, either in the city of Chicago or in the Northwest. It will remain forever memorable, as history and as patriotism. Such a sight was never before seen in the West upon any occasion, and we doubt whether a more impressive spectacle was ever presented in the streets of the Imperial City itself. The vast procession of yesterday, with its chariots and horsemen, its country wagons and vehicles, its civic orders and military companies, on horse and on foot, with their various designs, and mottoes, and brilliancy of color, converted Chicago, for the time being, into a vast spectacular drama.

"From the earliest dawn of day, the heart of the great city was awake. Long before eight o'clock the streets were thronged with people. Citizens in gala dress hurried excitedly to and fro. Country women, with their children, drove in early in the morning, with ribbons tied to their bridles, the national colors decorating their wagons, and miniature flags and banners at their horses' heads. From the housetops, from the churches, from the public buildings, was displayed the glorious flag of liberty. By nine o'clock, the city was in a roar. The vast hum of multitudinous voices filled the atmosphere. Drums beat everywhere, summoning the various processions, or accompanying them to the great central rendezvous. Bands of music playing patriotic airs, bands of young men and women singing patriotic songs, groups of children singing their cheerful and loyal school songs, enlivened the streets. Every pathway was jammed with human beings, so that it was with extreme difficulty any headway could be made.

"The procession was advertised to assemble at nine o'clock precisely, and was composed of nine divisions. As near ten as possible, it started — banners flying, drums beating, all manner of brazen instruments thrilling the listening ear, and stirring the hearts of the vast multitudes of people with exciting music. It was a mighty pageant. The enthusiasm that accompanied the procession, from first to last, has rarely been witnessed on any occasion. It was a grand, sublime protest, on behalf of the people, against the poltroons and traitors who were enemies to the government, and opposed to the war. Bursts of patriotic feeling came from many a loyal bosom on this never-to-be-forgotten day. The people were overflowing with loyalty, and could not contain themselves.

"For a long time they had been silent, keeping alive their love for the old flag, nursing their wrath against those that hated it — and who had so long fired upon it in the rear — finding nowhere any adequate utterance of their passionate feeling. Now the mighty eloquence of this majestic and sublime procession spoke for them. This was the thing which all along they had wanted to say, but could not. They were in themselves ciphers, mere units of the nation; but in all those thousands of men they saw themselves multiplied into an incalculable, irresistible host. They felt that their hour of triumphant speech had come at last. This was the answer which they thundered out in trumpet tones, to the miserable traitors who had so long torn the bleeding heart of their country."

"I always knew," said one old man at our elbow in the crowd, while we were watching the procession, "that the heart of the people was right; they did not know their danger for a long while; now they have found it out, and this is what they say about it."

In this remarkable pageant, the carriage containing the captured flags attracted much attention, and excited great enthusiasm. These were the flaunting rags which the rebels had borne on many a battle-field, and which our brave soldiers had torn from the hands of their standard-bearers. No longer were they flaunting in haughty defiance at the head of rebel armies, but as *bellorum exuviæ* — spoils of war — they were carried in triumph at the head of a civic procession in the peaceful streets of Chicago. They must have conjured up many a tearful memory in the minds of spectators there present, whose sons fought in the battles where these flags were captured, and whose graves make the soil of the South billowy.

No less attractive was the sixth division of the procession, consisting of omnibuses and carriages crowded with children, who rent the air with their song of "John Brown's body lies a-mouldering in the grave!" and whose tiny flags fluttered incessantly in the air, like the wings of gigantic butterflies. After them came, in carriages, the convalescent soldiers from the hospitals in the immediate vicinity; wan, thin, bronzed, haggard, maimed, crippled. One incessant roar greeted them in their progress. They were pelted with flowers. Ladies surrendered their parasols to them, to screen them from the sun. People rushed from the sidewalks to offer their hands. Handkerchiefs were waved, and shout followed shout throughout the long three miles.

But perhaps the most interesting spectacle of all was the "Lake County delegation." This was a procession of the farmers of Lake County, who came into the city at an early hour, and wheeled into line with the procession. There were hundreds of farm wagons, loaded to overflowing with vegetables. The staid farm-horses were decorated with little flags, larger flags floating over the wagons, and held by stout farmer hands. The first wagon of the pro-

PLATE. IV.

## CONFEDERATE BATTLE-FLAGS.

1. From Bragg's Army.  2. Forty-Second Miss. Reg't.  3. Twelfth Miss. Cavalry  4. Ninth Texas Reg't.
5. Austin's Battery.  6. So. Carolina Flag.  7. Texas Black Flag.  8. Virginia Flag.

*For Descriptions see pages 37-39.*

PHOTOGRAPHED AND PAINTED FROM THE ORIGINAL FLAGS EXPRESSLY FOR THIS WORK.

A. D. WORTHINGTON & CO. PUBLISHERS, HARTFORD, CONN.

cession bore a large banner, with this inscription:
" THE GIFT OF LAKE COUNTY TO OUR BRAVE BOYS
IN THE HOSPITALS, THROUGH THE GREAT NORTH-
WESTERN FAIR." It was a free-will offering from
hearts that beat true to freedom and the Union. No
part of the procession attracted more attention, and
no heartier cheers went up from the thousands who
thronged the streets, than those given, and thrice
repeated, for the splendid donation of the Lake
County farmers. There were no small loads here.
Every wagon was filled to overflowing with great
heaps of potatoes and silver-skinned onions, mammoth squashes, huge beets and turnips, monster cabbages, barrels of cider, and rosy apples — load after
load, with many a gray-haired farmer driving.

Many of the farmers were sunburned men, with
hard and rigid features, and a careless observer would
have said that there was nothing in these farm-wagons
and their drivers to awaken any sentiment. But
there was something in this farmers' procession that
brought tears to the eyes as the heavy loads toiled
by. On the sidewalk, among the spectators, was a
broad-shouldered Dutchman, with a stolid, inexpres-
sive face. He gazed at this singular procession as it
passed, — the sunburned farmers, the long narrow
wagons, and the endless variety of vegetables and
farm produce, the men with their sober faces and
homely gifts, — until, when the last wagon had passed,
he broke down in a flood of tears. He could do
nothing and say nothing; but he seized upon the
little child whom he held by the hand, and hugged
her to his heart, trying to hide his manly tears behind
her flowing curls.

Among the wagons was one peculiar for its look

of poverty. It was worn and mended, and was drawn by horses which had seen much of life, but little grain. The driver was a man past middle age, with the clothing and look of one who had toiled hard, but his face was thoughtful and kindly. By his side was his wife, a silent, worn woman, — for many of the farmers had their wives and daughters on the loads, — and in the rear was a seeming girl of fifteen and her sister, both dressed in black, and with them a baby.

Some one said to the man, "My friend, I am curious to know what you are bringing to the soldiers. What have you?" "Well," said he, "here are potatoes, and here are three boxes of onions; and there are some ruta-bagas, and there are a few turnips; and that is a small bag of meal; and then, you see, the cabbages fill in; that box with slats has ducks in it, which one of our folks sent."

"Oh, then this is not all your load alone, is it?"

"Why, no; our region where we live is rather poor soil, and we haven't any of us much to spare, anyway; yet for this business we could have raked up as much again as this, if we had had time. But we didn't get the notice that the wagons were going in until last night at eight o'clock, and it was dark and raining then. So my wife and I and the girls could only go round to five or six of the neighbors within a mile or so; but we did the best we could. We worked pretty much all the night, and loaded so as to be ready to get out to the main road and start with the rest of 'em this morning. It's little, but then it's something for the soldiers."

"Have you a son in the army?"

"Well, no," he answered slowly, turning round

and glancing stealthily at his wife. " No, we haven't
*now.* We had one there once. He was buried down
by Stone River. He was shot there. That's his
wife there with the baby," pointing over his shoulder
to the rear of the wagon without looking back; " but
I should not bring these things any quicker if he were
alive now and in the army. I don't know as I should
think so much as I do now about the boys way off
there. He was a good boy."

The goal of the procession was the spacious yard
of the Court House, where it halted for an address by
Thomas B. Bryan, the loyal and gifted nephew of
the rebel general Robert Lee.

The fair was opened at noon, and the firing of
thirty-four guns gave to the public the indication
that its managers were in readiness to receive guests,
and to put on the market its varied wares. As the
last gun boomed on the ears of the vast multitude,
they surged like a tidal wave towards Bryan Hall, —
the first of a series of six or seven, occupied by the
fair, to be entered.

The Lake County delegation of farmers proceeded
first to the rooms of the Sanitary Commission to
unload their freight of vegetables. The hundreds of
wagons drew up before the doors, and soon the sidewalks and streets were filled with boxes, barrels, and
sacks. Scores and scores of bystanders eagerly put
their shoulders to the work, proud to aid in unloading the farmers' produce. Madison Street, for a
whole square, was blockaded an hour, and the progress of the street-cars arrested, but nobody grumbled. The passengers alighted and increased the
crowd, cheering the farmers, shaking hands with
them, offering help, uttering congratulations and

benedictions. Many a rough fellow, who elbowed his way into the dense throng to lend a hand at the disburdening of the wagons, found his hitherto ever-ready words fail him, and turned to dash away, with the back of his hand, unwonted tears, of which he need not have been ashamed.

The back room of the Commission was speedily filled with wheat. Mr. McVicker, the well-known theatrical manager, tendered the use of his capacious cellar under the theatre for the vegetables, and that also was soon filled. While unloading, a messenger from the women managers approached the farmers with an invitation to Lower Bryan Hall, where a sumptuous dinner was awaiting them. The sturdy yeomen, accompanied by the marshals of the several divisions, marched to the hall, where the women warmly welcomed them.

A touching little episode occurred while the farmers were dining. In the neighborhood of their table were several soldiers, who had also ordered dinner. One of them chancing to give an order during a brief pause in the conversation, the tones caught the ear of one of the farmers, who turned quickly, and recognized in the bronzed and blue-coated soldier behind him his own son, whom he had not seen for two years and a half. He was now on his way home from Vicksburg on a short furlough. The discovery and recognition were mutual. Father and son started up at the same glad moment, and, in the touching language of Scripture, literally "fell on each other's necks and wept." This little occurrence gave new zest to the dinner, and added to the excitement of the hour.

# CHAPTER XXI.

STORY OF THE GREAT FAIR CONTINUED — ITS SIX HALLS —
PRESIDENT LINCOLN'S DONATION — UNEXAMPLED EN-
THUSIASM — "GOD BLESS THE FARMERS."

Profusion of Wares and rapid Sales — Daily Excursion Trains — President
Lincoln donates the Manuscript of the Proclamation of Emancipation —
Large Quantities of Food sent from the Country to the Dining-Hall —
How Dubuque furnished her Quota of Supplies — Picturesque Scene
— Hall erected for Donations of Machinery — Our Bargain with the
Builder — A Revelation and its Results — County Court Room trans-
formed into a "Curiosity Shop" — Rebel Flags, and Battle Trophies —
Slave Shackles and Collars—Large Loan Collection of Art Works—Anna
Dickinson's Lectures — Dinner to Northwestern Governors, Congress-
men, and other Dignitaries — Gift of Live Stock — Auction Sales on the
Sidewalk.

## BRYAN HALL BAZAR.

THE inaugural ceremonies being over, we will
follow the multitude to Bryan Hall, transferred for the nonce into a bazar, rivalling
those of the Orient in bewildering beauty.
A semi-circle of double booths followed the
curve of the gallery, and another semi-circle
was arranged against the wall, a broad aisle being
left between for a promenade. In the centre of the
hall, under the dome, a large octagonal pagoda was
erected, two stories high; the lower floor occupied
by fair saleswomen and brilliant wares, while in the
gallery, overhead, the band discoursed sweet music
through the afternoon and evening. The leading

427

architect of the city planned the interior arrangements of the halls, while their decoration was happily
entrusted to a committee of German artists. This
was eminently patriotic in character, and full of sig-
nificance in the history of the country at that time.

The national flag was festooned, and clustered in
all appropriate places. It floated overhead, it depended from arches, it entwined columns. It was
looped in silken folds over every door so that no one
could enter any of its departments without passing
under the flag. Soldiers from the battle-field, on
brief furloughs home, would glance around on the
beloved banner everywhere displayed. They had followed it to victory, and had endured, in its defence,
hardship, sickness, and mutilation. Tears, which
they could not repress, coursed down their brown
faces, as they beheld the exaltation of the national
ensign. Soldiers were welcomed to any department
of the fair, on all occasions, and the blue uniform of
the army or navy gave a free passport to all soldiers
and sailors.

If the goods and wares exhibited for sale were as
astonishing in profusion as in variety, there was no
lack of purchasers. From eight o'clock in the morning until ten at night, and sometimes until a later
hour, the six halls of the fair were densely packed
with eager and interested crowds. To judge from
the liberality of the purchasers, one would have supposed that each possessed the inexhaustible purse
which the fairy gave to Fortunatus, for there was no
haggling about prices, and no backwardness in buying. If the sales slackened, the fair traders had but
to utter the talismanic words, " Buy for the sake of
the soldiers!" and they proved the " *open sesame* "

to all purses and pockets. The affable saleswomen, who, at the opening of the fair, were dismayed at *les embarras des richesses*, that piled their counters, remembering the vast quantities that lay snugly packed in boxes underneath, saw their goods disappear like snow in the warm spring sunshine, and the second week found them exercising their woman's ingenuity to replenish their rapidly disappearing stock.

Arrangements had been made with the railroads to run excursion trains, at low prices, each day, from different parts of the country. This brought daily new crowds of large-hearted, whole-souled country people, who brought with them a fresh gush of national feeling and glowing patriotism, and before whose unselfishness and devotion to country, the disloyalty of the city shrank back abashed. The weather had no effect on the throngs — rain or shine, cold or warm, calm or blustering, the halls of the fair were so densely packed that at times it was impossible to cross them. Policemen were stationed at the doors of the halls, to enforce entrance by one door and exit by another. The sales of tickets were sometimes stopped for an hour or two at a time, to relieve the overcrowded halls. It was ascertained from the doorkeepers that the average daily attendance was six thousand.

It would not be possible to describe in detail the rare and beautiful articles that attracted throngs of people to this hall. The most noteworthy of all, and that in which the widest interest was felt, was the original manuscript of President Lincoln's " Proclamation of Emancipation," of the four million slaves of the South. This was the gift of the

President to the fair, who accompanied it with the following characteristic letter: —

EXECUTIVE MANSION, WASHINGTON, Oct. 26, 1863.

*To the Ladies having in charge the Northwestern*
*Fair for the Sanitary Commission, Chicago, Ill.: —*

According to the request made in your behalf, the original draft of the Emancipation Proclamation is herewith enclosed. The formal words at the top, and at the conclusion, except the signature, you perceive, are not in my handwriting. They were written at the State Department, by whom I know not. The printed part was cut from a copy of the preliminary Proclamation, and pasted on merely to save writing. I had some desire to retain the paper; but if it shall contribute to the relief or comfort of the soldiers, that is better.        Your obedient servant,

A. LINCOLN.

This manuscript was purchased for three thousand dollars, by Thomas B. Bryan, for the Chicago Soldiers' Home, of which association he was president. It was finely lithographed, and copies were sold by the Board of Managers for the benefit of a permanent Home for invalid Illinois soldiers, thousands of dollars accruing to the fund from their sale. The original manuscript was finally placed in the archives of the Chicago Historical Society for safe keeping, and was there burned at the time of the great conflagration.

### THE DINING-HALL.

While Upper Bryan Hall was occupied as a sales-room, Lower Bryan Hall was used throughout the fair as a dining and refreshment hall. The lady managers had promised to dine fifteen hundred people daily, with home comfort and elegance; and they amply fulfilled their pledge. The rush to this hall was as great as to the others, and hundreds went away every day to restaurants and hotels who could not be accommodated. The perfect system with which the dinners were managed, merits a passing notice.

The city was thoroughly canvassed for donations to the fair, every district being taken by a lady, and faithfully visited by her, or her subordinates. The names and residences of all who would contribute to the dinner-tables were taken, with the articles they would furnish, and the days on which they might be expected. The canvassing over, a meeting of the canvassers was held, and the aggregate supply for each day ascertained. Previous experience in these fair dinners had taught the ladies what quantities of each article were necessary for one dinner — so many turkeys, so many ducks, so many roasts, so many pies, so many puddings, so many gallons of milk, so many pounds of coffee, and so many cans of oysters, etc. If the amount pledged for each day was not sufficient, the dinner committee supplied deficiencies. These supplies thus pledged were sent to the dining-hall on the days they were promised, or to depots appointed in the various divisions of the city, whence express wagons ran daily, at specified and advertised hours.

In addition to this source of supply, large quantities of ready-cooked food were sent from various parts of the country. Notification of the time when it might be expected was previously mailed to the committee. Michigan sent immense quantities of the finest fruit, twenty times as much as was required by the exigencies of the refreshment tables. Hundreds of barrels of apples of late varieties were immediately despatched to the hospitals, whence in due time came grateful acknowledgment of the welcome donations. Grundy County, Ill., sent game exclusively, nicely cooked and carefully packed, and forwarded with such despatch that it hardly had time to cool before the express delivered it in the dining-hall. Elgin, Ill., from her abundant dairies, supplied a large proportion of the milk used during the fair, her " milkmen " calling regularly at the dinner hour with overflowing cans.

Dubuque, Iowa, came to the help of the dining-hall in a most generous manner. The Dubuque ladies who visited the fair during the first week learned that there was not enough of poultry pledged for certain days of the week following. They hastened home to make up the deficiency. Some half-dozen of their best " shots " were instantly sent off " gunning." A general raid was made on hencoops. Turkeys were bought or begged by the dozen. Ducks and chickens were soon obtained by the hundred. On the days when their contributions for edibles were due, they sent to Chicago over one hundred turkeys, two or three hundred ducks, and as many chickens, exquisitely cooked, which were carried piping hot from the Dubuque kitchens to the express car. Several of the ladies sat up all the previous night, and gave personal help and supervision to the work of dressing, baking, and packing these fowls. By some mystery of the *cuisine*, on their arrival in Chicago, they were brought to the table as hot as though they had just made their *début* from the bakepan.

Fourteen tables were set in the dining-hall, with accommodations for three hundred at one time. Every table was reset four or five times daily. Six ladies were appointed to take charge of each table throughout the fair. Two presided daily — one to pour coffee, the other to maintain general supervision. These ladies were the wives of congressmen, professional men, clergymen, editors, merchants, bankers, commissioners, — none were above serving at the Soldiers' Fair dinners. Each presiding lady furnished the table linen and silver for her table, and added any other decorations and delicacies that her taste and means suggested, or that her friends and acquaintances contributed. The table waiters were the young ladies of the city, deft-handed, swift-footed, bright-eyed, pleasant-voiced maidens, who, accustomed to being served in their own homes, transferred themselves for the nonce into servants. Both the matrons who presided, and the pretty girls who served, were neatly attired in a simple uniform of white caps and aprons, made, trimmed, and worn, to suit the varied tastes and styles of the wearers. In common with every lady who assisted at the fair in every capacity, they wore the national colors.

A more picturesque scene than the dining-hall offered, when dinner was in progress, cannot be imagined. The decorations were like those of the other halls, with the national flag waving over every table, and crowning the table ornaments. There was a profusion of flowers everywhere, mostly hothouse exotics; and a small bouquet was laid beside every plate. The gas was lighted day and night, giving additional brilliancy to the scene. The numerous tables, crowded with ladies and gentlemen who had come to dine; the long line of carvers, one for each variety of meats, who had closed the ledger, and laid

down the pen, to don the white apron, and take the
knife of this department; the graceful girls in their
pretty uniforms, gliding hither and thither in the discharge of their novel duties; the agreeable matrons,
who received all who came to their tables as though
they were honored guests in their own homes; the
crowds who stood round, determined to dine in this
hall, good-naturedly biding their turn, with many a *bon
mot* which provoked constant peals of laughter; the
continual incoming of fresh trays, baskets, and pails,
laden with viands for the dinner, — all this formed an
animated and unusual picture, that pen cannot por-
tray. There was no lack of sociality at these dinners.
Mirth and laughter were as abundant as the food.
Wit held high carnival. And a stranger, ignorant of
the occasion, would have believed this a new Babel,
where a second " confusion of tongues " had been
wrought.

The kitchen adjoined the dining-hall, where the
heavy work was done by servants; and into these
*penetralia* only a favored few were admitted. The
rule was inexorable; and woe to the curious wight
who ventured within its precincts without leave or
business! Little ceremony was employed in enforc-
ing his departure. Checks laid beside the plate
indicated to each his indebtedness, which was more
or less according to the bill of fare he had ordered.
These bills were settled at the table of the cashier,
who gave in return a receipt, in the form of another
check, on the presentation of which at the door the
party offering it was allowed to leave the hall. There
was no exit otherwise. No department of the fair
required more executive skill in management, and
none was more popular or successful.

## MANUFACTURERS' HALL.

A temporary hall was erected, adjoining Bryan Hall on the east, for the reception of the heavy and bulky machinery contributed. A hall on the ground floor was necessary for this purpose, and such a hall Chicago did not possess. Obtaining a permit from the authorities for the erection, within the fire limits, of the temporary wooden structure that was needed, Mrs. Hoge and myself sought a builder. A gift of lumber had been made for this use; and we desired to contract with him for the erection of the hall. The plan was drawn, the bargain made, the contract written, and we both signed it.

"Who underwrites for you?" asked the builder.

"What?" we inquired in concert.

"Who endorses for you?" he explained.

"We wish no endorsers. We have the money in bank, and will pay you in advance, if you will draw the contract accordingly. We have more faith in you than you manifest in us," we replied.

"It isn't a matter of faith at all," was his answer, "but of law. You are married women; and, by the laws of Illinois, your names are good for nothing, unless your husbands write their names after yours on the contract."

"Let us pay you then in advance," we said. "We have money of our own earning, and are able to settle your bill on the spot. Instead of a contract, give us a promissory note, like this: 'In consideration of —— dollars, I promise to build for Mrs. Hoge and Mrs. Livermore a hall of wood,' etc. Can't you do that?"

"The money of your earning belongs to your husbands, by the law. The wife's earnings are the property of the husband in this state. Until your husbands give their written consent to your spending your earnings, I cannot give you the promise you ask. The law must be respected."

Here was a revelation. We two women were able to enlist the whole Northwest in a great philanthropic, money-making enterprise in the teeth of great opposition, and had the executive ability to carry it forward to a successful termination. We had money of our own in bank, twice as much as was necessary to pay the builder. But by the laws of the state in which we lived, our individual names were not worth the paper on which they were written. Our earnings were not ours, but belonged to our husbands. Later in the conversation, we learned that we had no legal ownership in our minor children, whom we had won, in anguish, in the valley of death. They too were the property of our husbands.

We learned much of the laws made by men for women, in that conversation with an illiterate builder. It opened a new world to us. We thought rapidly, and felt intensely. I registered a vow that when the war was over I would take up a new work — the work of making law and justice synonymous for women. I have kept my vow religiously.

The signing of the contract was delayed till our husbands could give legality to it, by signing with us. And then the building was pushed rapidly forward to completion. When it was no longer needed, it was removed, and passed away forever. But the influence of the conversation with its builder still abides with me.

It was so constructed as to be entered from Bryan

Hall by a side door. The contributions to this department were amazingly liberal, embracing almost every article of farm and household use, and were sufficient in number and importance for a good-sized State Fair. As the articles were mostly manufactured by contributors especially for the fair, they were made of the best material, and in the highest style of workmanship. In some remote districts, where a knowledge of the fair penetrated at a late day, manufacturers donated orders for machinery not then made. One order of this kind from Decatur, Ill., was for nine hundred dollars' worth of machinery, and was available until the next July.

Of ploughs there were scores, embracing almost every patent. Nails were donated by hundreds of kegs. Stoves were contributed by dozens, no two being of the same pattern. Barrels of kerosene oil of every brand were piled on one another, no inconsiderable portion of the space being allotted them. There were a dozen sets of scales, four of them of the manufacture of the Messrs. Fairbanks, worth one hundred dollars each. Reapers and mowers were donated that had borne off the prizes at several State Fairs, and threshing machines which had received similar honors. There were corn-shellers and corn-planters, straw-cutters, and grain and grass seed drills, fanning-mills and non-freezing pumps, sugar-mills and marble mantels, nests of wash-tubs and stacks of pails, every conceivable style of washing and wringing-machines, millstones, knife and scissors sharpeners, cases of boots and shoes, Saratoga trunks, common-sense chairs, carriage-springs, axles, hub and buggy spokes — in short, there were specimens of every branch of Northwestern manufacture.

That which attracted the most attention was a beautiful ten-horse power upright engine made and presented by the generous employés of the Chicago Eagle Works — every member of the establishment contributing to it. It was a most thoroughly built piece of machinery, and was very handsome. A boiler was also contributed by the boiler shops of the city, so that the engine was run during the fair, exciting great admiration by its easy and almost noiseless movements. The mechanics of the Northwest manifested a noble interest in the fair. In several instances, the employés of manufactories clubbed together and worked " after hours " to build machines for the fair. When this was not possible, they contributed their money, and sent a generous cash donation to its treasury, or they gave the entire proceeds of certain days' work. Not only did they contribute articles of their manufacture, but in the evening they came and assisted the ladies to sell them, disposing of the heaviest by raffling, and finding purchasers among their own customers for others. God bless them! Whether in the workshop or on the battle-field, the mechanics of the Northwest at that time proved themselves brave, true, noble-hearted men.

### THE CURIOSITY SHOP.

The supervisor's hall in the Court House, occupied mostly by the sessions of the County Court, Judge Bradwell presiding, was surrendered to the ladies, to be occupied by them as a "Curiosity Shop." Not only did the obliging Judge adjourn his court for two weeks, but gave up his room to the fair, and, with his wife, Mrs. Myra Bradwell, he gave his services to

assist in arranging and superintending this department. More attractive than all else in this hall were
the battle-torn flags of our own regiments, and the
captured rebel flags. The fourteen rebel flags, which
were trophies of victory, were loaned for exhibition
by Secretary Stanton. In the history of each of
them there was material for volumes of narrative
and romance. One Union flag, blood-stained and
rent, had been selected by General Grant to be first
unfurled over the Court House at Vicksburg when
that city surrendered. Another had been captured
in the battle of Bull Run, and with it the color-
bearer. Both were in Libby Prison for more than a
year. A heartfelt and tearful interest clustered
around the flags; and, though rent in shreds, dis-
colored, soiled, and blood-stained, they lent a glory
to the walls upon which they hung. Nor was it forgotten that those who had fought under them had
laid down life in their defence, and were then sleeping
the "sleep that knows no waking," no more to be
saluted by friend or assaulted by foe.

A long table ran through the centre of the hall,
covered with a motley collection of trophies captured
from the enemy, including guns, cimeters, bowie-
knives of all shapes, butcher-knives of most ferocious
aspect, swords, balls, pistols, shells, camp-stools, etc.,
— every one of which had a history.

Among these trophies was a shackle taken from
the neck of a slave at Port Gibson by the "Walsh
Guards," Eleventh Wisconsin. It was made of bar
iron, three inches wide and half an inch thick, weighing between three and four pounds, and had been
worn eleven months. One trophy, which challenged
the attention and roused the indignation of all, was

called the "Southern necklace," and had the following
history: —

While our army was at Grand Gulf, Miss., an intelligent contraband gave much valuable information
as to the position of the enemy, and otherwise rendered himself useful to our forces. He finally fell
into the hands of the rebels, who administered one
hundred and fifty lashes, and placed an iron collar
around his neck, riveting it on very strongly. Afterwards the negro was captured from the rebels at
Baton Rouge, La., by Company F, Fourth Wisconsin, and was immediately released from the collar.
This collar was a round rod of iron, two inches in
circumference, riveted together before and behind
with two iron prongs one inch wide, three fourths of
an inch thick, and twelve inches long, rising from
each side directly outside the ears.

There were little keepsakes made from the old
historic frigate Constitution, better known as " Old
Ironsides," and fragments of the wrecks of the rebel
ram Merrimac, and the frigate Cumberland, which
the Merrimac had so murderously destroyed in
Hampton Roads a short time before. A silver band
and three silver bracelets, in perfect preservation,
taken from the brow and arm of a gigantic Indian
skeleton, were sent from Quincy, Ill., where it was
exhumed a few days previous to the fair. A young
lady from the Island of St. Helena visiting Chicago,
enriched the fair with a full collection of views of the
island, and a large number of relics associated with
Napoleon's life when held a prisoner there by Great
Britain. Senator Chandler of Michigan sent an
Alpine staff used by Napoleon when crossing the
Alps to make war on Italy. The assistants in this

department daily talked themselves hoarse and weary in reiterated explanations of their storied collection, to the never-ceasing crowds of curiosity-seekers. And probably this was the most interesting collection of articles and relics ever seen by Western people.

The best arranged and best lighted hall in the city was placed at the disposal of the fair for an Art Gallery. It was free of rent, and to be occupied as long as it might be needed for that purpose. Partitions were run up between the large windows, dividing the spacious hall into alcoves, both sides of which, as also the walls of the room, were covered with pictures. Lady canvassers waited upon the citizens of Chicago, and obtained the loan of their best works of art for exhibition. Very few declined, and the number collected was a surprise to all. Pictures were sent from New York, Wisconsin, Michigan, Iowa, and some from Pittsburg. The Chicago artists generously painted pictures which they donated, and which were sold at very liberal prices. Young as Chicago was at that time, over three hundred works of art were loaned from her homes.

Church was represented by two South American pictures, which reminded one of his "Heart of the Andes." There were pictures by Rossiter, Cranch, Angelica Kauffman, Durand, Cropsey, Gifford, and Kensett. Of works by the old masters, there were paintings by Rembrandt, Sassaferato, and Tintoretto. Many of Mr. Healy's best portraits were on the walls. He had just completed a portrait of Dr. Orestes A. Brownson, and another of the glorious head and face of Longfellow. They were classed among the masterpieces of this artist. Like all Healy's portraits, they were distinguished for their marvellous coloring,

their careful finish, and conscientiousness of detail.
The exhibition of statuary was small. A Mercury
and Venus by Thorwaldsen, with several bronzes and
medallions, made up all that was valuable in the collection. Above the gallery was another hall, devoted
to photographs, water-colors, and steel engravings;
and a very creditable collection was brought together.

The success of the Art Exposition may be inferred
from the fact that twenty-five thousand people visited
the gallery during the fair, and that it was necessary
to continue it two weeks after the other departments
closed, to satisfy the demands of the public. During
the first five days, seven thousand catalogues were
sold; and the profits from their sale alone were sufficient to defray all the expenses of the exhibition. On
one day alone, eighteen hundred and fifty tickets
were sold at the door, and eight hundred catalogues.

## EVENING ENTERTAINMENTS.

Metropolitan Hall was devoted exclusively to evening entertainments, and was not open during the day.
Its decoration was given to a company of German
artists, who transformed it into a scene of bewildering
beauty. Every iron column was fluted with the
white and the red. Festoons of red, white, and blue,
glittering with gold stars, depended from the gallery. Everywhere were mottoes expressive of faith
in God, devotion to the country, and undying interest in her brave defenders. The proscenium was
arranged with fluted decorations and festoons of the
national colors. Busts of Washington and Lincoln
were on either side of the stage; while over the curtain hovered the national eagle, resting on a shield,

Plate V.

Text visible on flags:

105th REGT N Y VOLS.

Cedar Mountain Aug 9th 1862.

RAPPAHANOCK STATION Aug 15th 1862

Thoroughfare Gap Aug 28th 18

2nd BULL RUN Aug

Chantilly Sept 18

EXCELSIOR

## FAMOUS UNION BATTLE-FLAGS.

1. First N.J. Cavalry.                     2. Forty-eighth N.Y. Reg't.
3. One hundred and fiftieth Penn. Reg't. ("Bucktails")
4. Eighty-third Penn. Reg't.     5. Ninth N.J. Reg't.     6. One hundred and fifth N.Y. Reg't.

*For Descriptions see pages 40–47.*

PHOTOGRAPHED AND PAINTED FROM THE ORIGINAL FLAGS EXPRESSLY FOR THIS WORK.

A. D. WORTHINGTON & CO. PUBLISHERS  HARTFORD  CONN.

grasping the stars and stripes in the talons of one foot, and the arrowy lightnings with the other.

In this hall the managers of the fair catered to the amusement of the crowd every evening of the fair. Every night the spacious hall was filled to its utmost capacity. Sometimes it was a children's concert. Then an exhibition of tableaux, allegorical, historical, patriotic, or classical, exhibited on a revolving platform. Chicago audiences never wearied of tableaux in those days. The ladies of Detroit gave an exhibition of tableaux, bearing all the expenses incident to preparation, — costumes, travelling expenses, hotel bills, — and giving to the fair the gross receipts of the entertainment. For magnificence of costume, artistic grouping, and startling effects, they could not be surpassed, even when arranged by professional artists. A monastic procession at midnight was a moving tableau. A company of nuns and priests, arrayed in the garb of their several orders, and bearing torches, filed slowly through the corridors and arches of the monastery, chanting clearly and sweetly the "Miserere" from "Il Trovatore."

Richard Storrs Willis, brother of N. P. Willis the poet, known then as one of the first composers and pianists of the country, with Mrs. Willis, accompanied the Detroit party to Chicago. In the closing tableau, Mrs. Willis personated the Goddess of Liberty, in a bodice formed of the Union, with a skirt of the stars and stripes, wearing the liberty cap, and holding the flag. At her left were army officers, and a group of jolly tars in naval uniform. In a semi-circle in the background were arranged the three graces, Faith, Hope, and Charity. Suddenly the goddess, Mrs. Willis, broke forth with the "Anthem

of Liberty," both music and words of which were
composed by Mr. Willis for the occasion: —

> "Anthem of Liberty, solemn and grand,
>   Wake in thy loftiness, sweep through the land!
>   Light in each breast anew, patriotic fires!
>   Pledge the old flag again, flag of our sires!
>   Fling all thy folds abroad, banner of light!
>     Onward, still onward, flag of our might!
>     Onward, victorious, God for the right!
>                                   Amen, amen!"

The chorus was sung by all the group, and was
most inspiring. The effect was electrical. The immense audience rose to its feet, and the curtain fell
amid tumultuous cheers and applause. Again it rose;
and again the Goddess of Liberty, as if inspired anew
with patriotic fervor, sang the "Star-Spangled Banner," the entire audience rising and joining in the
chorus, accompanied by the Light Guard Band.

Vocal and instrumental concerts filled up the evenings, with hops and pantomime and amateur theat-
ricals. Then came the novelty of two lectures,
delivered by

ANNA DICKINSON,

whose career as an eloquent and patriotic lecturer
was then attracting universal attention. It was her
first appearance in Chicago. The press had raised
the expectations of the people very high by the narration of her oratorical triumphs in the East. The
Republican party had acknowledged its indebtedness
to her eloquence for victories in Connecticut and
New Hampshire; and those who had been brought
under the spell of her speech were extravagant in
her praise. Every one was on the *qui vive* to see and

to hear her; and her audiences were limited only by the capacity of the hall.

Her addresses were not so remarkable for originality, logic, òr argument, as for the magnetic power with which they were delivered. With a fearful array of indisputable facts, she exposed the subterfuges of those who planned the rebellion at the South, and those who defended it at the North. With the majesty of a second Joan of Arc, she invoked the loyalty, patriotism, and religion of the North to aid in quelling it. It was a wonderful sight. She was a young girl, of twenty summers; but she held an immense audience spell-bound by her eloquence, now melting them to tears by the pathos of her voice and of her speech, and now rousing them to indignation as she denounced the enemies of the country, fighting against our armies at the South, or plotting treason at home.

Sandwiched between Miss Dickinson's lectures was a grand dinner, given by the lady managers to the dignitaries of the Northwest. Governors and ex-Governors, members of Congress, distinguished military men, at home on furlough, with such local magnates as could add *éclat* to the occasion, composed the guests. There were some two hundred in all. The most complete arrangements were made for their reception and entertainment. The hall was decorated for the occasion; and to add to the picturesque effect, the young lady waiters were attired in a costume of their own devising, which harmonized admirably with the patriotic surroundings. A blue peasant-cap, skirt of the stripes of the flag, and a jaunty little red cap, trimmed with gold braid and tassels, gave to some of the girls a stateliness of presence, and to others only added piquancy. " I do not find it easy to give orders for dinner to these young goddesses of liberty," said one of the Governors; and others experienced a like embarrassment. A large audience listened to the after - dinner speeches of the eminent guests, which were all aglow with lofty patriotism. It was the aim of the managers of the fair not only to make money, but to kindle anew the loyalty and devotion of the North-west.

A second farmers' procession of wagons loaded with vegetables came in to the fair at noon on the day of the Governors' dinner. One would have supposed that the fair had just commenced, the procession created so much excitement. The streets were again thronged with people. The procession of wagons paraded through the principal thoroughfares, cheered wherever it passed, and then proceeded to the rooms of the Sanitary Commission, where the wagons were unloaded. This was a surprise to all, and helped to keep up the patriotic excitement to the utmost.

After unloading their stores, the farmers proceeded to the Soldiers' Home, where a dinner had been provided expressly for them. Two hundred soldiers on their way to the front dined with them. They made a jolly party. Addresses were delivered after the dinner was ended, the band played its most stirring airs, the best women of the city served them, and poured their tea and coffee, and then the gallant boys, hurrying back to the battle-field from hospitals and furloughs at home, gave cheer upon cheer for the farmers, when they learned of their generosity.

In the midst of the festivities, a sick soldier in the

hospital of the home, to whose dull ear the glad sounds penetrated, inquired the cause. When an explanation was given him, he said, "That is good! God bless the farmers!" and, turning his face to the wall, before the gayety was ended, he yielded his spirit to the God who gave it. With the benedictions of the living and dying resting on them, the farmers climbed to their empty wagons, and returned richer than they came.

Among other donations for which the ladies were unprepared was that of live-stock. Thoroughbred colts, pet bears, Morgan horses, Durham cattle, and a stall-fed ox, which weighed when dressed eighteen hundred pounds, were included in these donations. As we were notified of these novel contributions, advertisements were inserted in the daily papers. A day and hour were appointed for their sale at auction on the sidewalk in front of Bryan Hall. A crowd always collected, and spirited bidding ensued, which resulted in the sale of all the live-stock given to the fair.

# CHAPTER XXII.

LAST DAYS OF THE GREAT FAIR — SOLDIERS' DAY — TOTAL
RECEIPTS NEARLY ONE HUNDRED THOUSAND DOLLARS —
INTERESTING ITEMS AND INCIDENTS.

Dinner given by the Ladies to eight hundred invalid Soldiers in Hospitals
— Lady Managers dined by Gentlemen, who serve the Feast — Mighty
Frolic — " Completely tuckered out!" — Items and Incidents — Afghan
made with Money found in a dead Soldier's Pocket — Contraband's
Gift — Donation of Octogenarians — Mite of the German Woman —
The Luck of the Chickamauga Soldier — Major-General Herron of Iowa
in the Fair — Letters of Gratitude from Soldiers in Hospitals — "Must
see that Fair" — " All I have"— Safe place of Retreat — Pleasant Greetings — "A Soldier's Psalm of Woman" — Cheers for Lincoln — Cheers
for the Soldiers — Cheers for the Ladies of the Sanitary Commission
— Specimen of the Soldiers' Battle-cry — The Dead.

## THE LAST DAY OF THE FAIR.

IT was decided to give a grand dinner on the
closing day of the fair to all the soldiers in
Camp Douglas, the convalescents in the
Marine and City Hospitals, and the Soldiers'
Home. About eight hundred in all were present, but there were many others, too feeble
for the excitement, who remained behind. Public
announcement of the dinner having been made,
donations of refreshments were sent to the hall in
great profusion. Such a furor of preparation as
that morning witnessed! Hot-houses were rifled
of their flowers, — plate-chests of their silver, and
every species of patriotic ornament was devised for

the occasion. Rare fruit, ices, jellies, flowers, and game poured in upon the ladies in the greatest abundance. The best band in the city was engaged for the occasion. The hall was redecorated, and made more attractive than ever. The pretty waiter-girls made their toilets anew, and, taking their places behind the chairs, we saw that we had not merely one Hebe, but scores of them.

Anna Dickinson had agreed to utter the words of cheer and praise and kindly remembrance with which every woman's heart dilated. The ladies felt it was not possible to sufficiently welcome and honor the brave fellows they had invited to dine with them. A more beautifully laid table was never seen. It far surpassed in elegance and sumptuousness that set for the dignitaries of the Northwest the day before, and the dining-hall glowed and glittered with the most brilliant of the combined decorations brought from the other halls of the fair.

At twelve o'clock precisely, all being in readiness, the doors were opened, and the guests of the day marched into the hall. It was a bronzed, scarred, emaciated, halt, blind, deaf, crippled, skeleton corps, some without arms, some without legs, some swinging painfully on crutches, some leaning feebly on those stronger than themselves, all bearing evidence in their persons that they had suffered for their country. "Brave Boys are They!" crashed the band. The ladies waved flags and handkerchiefs, and, according to the programme they had marked out for themselves, essayed a cheer. But it was drowned in audible sobs, as they gazed on the poor boys who were their guests. They were slowly seated at table, and then with eyes humid with tears, and voice

tremulous with emotion, Anna Dickinson, a fair
young girl orator at that time, welcomed them in
eloquent words, in behalf of the managers of the
fair.

Grace was then said by the chaplain of Camp
Douglas, and the waiters darted off for soup, fish,
turkey, game, vegetables, pies, puddings, ices, tea,
coffee, — anything that was called for.   The poor
fellows were served as brothers and sons would have
been at home.   Their food was carved for them, and
their not over vigorous appetites were coaxed and
catered to as though feasting were the supremest joy
of life.   Dinner was soon over, and then came the
after-dinner talk.   Speeches were made by chaplains
and officers who happened to be present.

"Three cheers for Abraham Lincoln! a diamond
in the rough!" proposed a manly voice; and so
mighty a cheer thundered through the hall, that our
guests seemed no longer invalids.   Then "Three
cheers for the ladies of the Northwestern Fair!"
shook the hall again.   The ladies, in their enthusiasm, responded by "Three cheers for the soldiers!"
given with an accompaniment by the band and with
the waving of flags and handkerchiefs.

One of the chaplains proposed that the soldiers
should give the ladies a specimen of their battle cry,
as they charged, double quick, on the enemy — and,
unconsciously to themselves, the men took the attitude, and their faces assumed the determination of
the charge as they uttered so prolonged, unearthly,
and terrific a yell as beggars its description.   We
can imagine its power on the battle-field.

The excitement was now at a white heat, and
there was no vent for it but in music.   The band

played " The Red, White and Blue " — the boys
joining in rousingly with their bass and tenor; the
ladies adding soprano and contralto, and for the
next hour all sang together, until the entire *répertoire* of patriotic and soldier songs was exhausted.
"Let us not forget our dead! " said Chaplain Day.
" They who went out with us to the conflict, but
whose slumbers on the battle-field shall not be
broken until the réveillé of the resurrection morn
shall awaken them.   Let us remember that —

> " ' He who for country dies, dies not ;
> But liveth evermore!' "

All stood in solemn silence, with uncovered heads,
while the band wailed a dirge for those to whom
God had granted a discharge from the conflict, and
promoted to the ranks of the crowned immortals.   A
doxology was the only fitting close to the hour, and
a thousand or more of voices joined in singing
" Praise God, from whom all blessings flow! "   Then
with swelling hearts and quivering voices, with
tremulous clasping of the hands, and broken words
of thanksgiving, the boys slowly returned to the
hospitals.

" We are not worth all this.   We have not earned
this kindness," they said.   " But on our next battle-
field, the memory of this day shall make us braver
and stronger."

Is there but one step from the sublime to the
ridiculous?   I hesitate to give the finale, but, as a
faithful historian, I must tell the truth.   " This is the
soldiers' day!" said a practical woman at the door,
as the boys were making their exit.   " Let us crowd
into it all the good things we can.   Hold on, boys!

Run, John, run round the corner, bring some boxes of fine cigars!" A moment's delay, and the cigars came. And then to every soldier was given, as he went out, cigars and matches. We saw them depart with an aureole of smoke about their brows, if not of glory. To those whose feebleness detained them in the hospitals, boxes of tempting and delicate viands were sent, — such as the surgeons endorsed, — and committees of ladies accompanied them, and served them to the invalids, sometimes in bed. They even spent the larger part of the day in the hospitals, helping the poor fellows to have a veritable gala day.

Now followed a scene. Two hundred young gentlemen from the business circles of the city, had proposed a dinner to the ladies of the dining-hall, and as the boys went out, these gentlemen came in. The girl waiters doffed their white aprons and caps, and the gentlemen begged them to retire to Upper Bryan Hall, while the tables were reset with the help of servants, and the dinner prepared. After an hour or two of waiting, the ladies were escorted to the dining-hall. The gentlemen had attired themselves grotesquely in the uniform of white aprons and caps, which they regarded as the serving-gear of the fair. The motley condition of the tables gave evidence of the handiwork of unskilled men, and not of servants. It was evident they were in for a frolic.

Who that partook of that dinner will ever forget it? Happy she who did not receive a baptism of oyster soup or coffee, as the gentlemen waiters ran hither and thither like demented men, colliding with each other, to the great damage of tureens and coffee urns, and the immense bespattering of the fair ones

waited upon. We saw one city editor industriously
peddling toothpicks before the soup was removed.
Another, presiding at the coffee urn, was so intent
upon a flirtation with his next neighbor, that he
forgot to turn the faucet when the first cup was
filled, and was not reminded of it until the urn was
emptied on the floor, and a river of coffee was running underneath the table, among the feet of the
ladies. For an hour fun and frolic held sway.
Shout after shout of laughter pealed from the merry
girls at the *contretemps* of their servitors. Now and
then came a little shriek at a smash of crockery or
the upsetting of a coffee cup. Faster and faster ran
round the awkward waiters, until, at last, the mas-
culine attendants, whose caps had fallen on their
necks, and whose aprons had got twisted hind-side-
before, gave up in utter despair. They declared
themselves " completely tuckered out," and begged
the ladies to help themselves to anything they liked,
or could find.

In the evening, not satisfied with the fun of the
afternoon, the young people, aided by carpenters,
cleared away the booths, working like Titans, and
wound up the fair with a vigorous dance, that closed
as the clock struck eleven. At the same time, the
German ladies of the fair gave a grand ball at Metropolitan Hall, which was largely attended, and pecuniarily was a great success.

And so ended the Northwestern Fair, whose net
receipts were nearly eighty thousand dollars, with
unsold articles, of sterling value, slowly disposed of
afterwards, to make the sum total nearly a hundred
thousand. Other fairs followed in quick succession —
in Cleveland, Boston, Pittsburg, St. Louis, and finally

in New York and Philadelphia. But none of them were characterized by the enthusiasm, originality, earnestness, and contagious patriotism that glorified this, and made it forever memorable.

### ITEMS AND INCIDENTS.

Several incidents which came to my knowledge during the fair are worthy of record. I will give a few.

In one of the Southwestern hospitals there died a young soldier whose home was in Chicago. He left an only sister to mourn the loss of the strong arm and brave heart necessary to her in the fierce battle of life. After his death there was found in his pockets a small sum of money, all the worldly wealth he had. His sister regarded the money as too sacred to be applied to daily uses. She purchased with it a quantity of worsted, out of which she wrought an afghan, memories of him who died dimming her eyes and saddening her heart as she crocheted. She brought it to the fair, and, modestly donating it, told its history. It was an article of exquisite beauty, and was sold at an early day, for one hundred dollars.

One of the contrabands from Montgomery, Ala., brought an offering to the fair, and, presenting it to the secretary, asked, "Please, missus, may dis yer sheet, what I got wi' my own money, and stitched wi' my own hands, be sold for Massa Linkum's sojers?" She held forth a large bleached cotton sheet, very neatly made. She was a comely woman, and gave her history briefly as follows: "I'se raised in Jones County, Ala. I'se fifty year old, missus. I'se left nine chillen in de land o' bondage. Ten o' my lambs de great Lord took, and dey's done gone home to glory." Out of twenty children she had but one with her. Her touching story, pathetically told, caused a speedy sale of her offering, which brought much more than its actual value.

One of the ladies of the fair was called to the door of Bryan Hall by the doorkeeper, with the statement that " an old man at the ticket office wanted to see her, but dared not come in." She obeyed the summons, and found a white-haired old man, eighty years old and bowed with infirmity. He said: " My wife and I are very poor. We had two sons; both went into the army. One was killed on the 'Hatchie, and the other is still in the service. We want to do something for this fair, but it's so little that we are ashamed to speak of it." On being assured that the smallest gifts were acceptable, he continued: " We keep a few chickens; and, if they will do you any good, I will kill four, and bring them to-morrow all cooked. My wife is as old as I am; but she is a good cook, and will dress and roast them herself." Tickets of admission for himself and wife were given him; and the grateful words of the lady made his withered face glow with pleasure. The next day, at dinner time, he came again, with the nicely roasted fowls, covered with a snowy napkin. " I wish I could do more, lady," he said; " but it's all I have."

An elderly German woman, with toil-hardened hands, came to the managers, and in broken English told her story. She was a widow with two sons, one in the army, and the other a mere lad, whom she supported by taking in washing. She offered fifty cents, and begged the ladies to " please accept that."

A brave fellow from Chickamauga, who had lain for weeks in the hospital, was sent to Illinois on furlough, with the hope that his wounded leg would heal, and his health improve. His wife came to Chicago to meet him, and to help him complete his journey. He was very eager to attend the fair. "Mary, I must see that fair," he said, "if it takes my last dollar!" He was brought in an invalid chair, and carried through Bryan Hall, his wife accompanying him. The brightness of the bazar dazzled him. It was an amazing contrast to the battle-field, hospitals, and barracks he had left behind. A silver cake-basket was being sold in shares at a dollar each. The style was pretty, and the silver was of the value of coin. "I'd like to take a share for you, Mary," said the wounded hero; and a half shadow fell over the face of the wife as she saw his last dollar go. The drawing commenced, and to the wounded brave from Chickamauga was delivered the cake-basket. His ticket had drawn it. There was great delight over his good luck.

"I enjoyed more seeing how glad the ladies were that I was the lucky one," said the happy fellow afterwards, "than I did in getting the cake-basket."

Half a dozen young ladies from Como, Ill., sent five barrels of potatoes to the fair, which they had planted, hoed, and dug, with their own hands. A similar contribution came from Pekin, Ill., from a young lady who "had dedicated a portion of her garden to the soldiers."

A poor contraband mother from Lake Superior sent socks knit by herself for her own son, also a runaway slave, but who went to an early grave while serving in the army of freedom. When the black woman fled from slavery, she went with her baby boy to the cold isolation of the upper lake, feeling safe with him in that remote locality. The war broke out, giving him a chance to strike for the freedom of his downtrodden race; and though he had not attained his majority, the boy enlisted. He was ordered, with his regiment, to the very place of his birth, and in the first engagement he fell a martyr to liberty.

Every day saw large numbers of military men in the fair, many of them officers of high rank, and not a few whose feats of bravery and brilliant daring have given them a place in history. They were always the lions of the hour, and were the recipients of unnumbered courtesies from the ladies. One morning, a tall, slender, fine-looking gentleman, modestly dressed in citizen's clothes, entered the hall, and made the tour of the booths, his numerous questions evincing more than ordinary interest. Soon a soldier who had lost a leg, and walked with a crutch, sprang from his seat, and hobbled towards the young man as fast as his enfeebled condition would allow. Forgetting the military salute in his eagerness, grasping him by the hand, with his face working with emotion, he said, " General, I was with you at Pea Ridge! "

Up came another, with emaciated face and figure, but with the same breathless gladness, " General, I fought under you at Prairie Grove! " Then others: " General, I was with you at Vicksburg! " " I marched with you through Arkansas! " " I have been with you ever since we left Dubuque! "— until, pretty soon, the almost stripling was surrounded with soldiers, all more or less *hors de combat*, and was shaking hands with them, congratulating them, and reciprocating their joy in the heartiest manner.

" Who is he? " was whispered around the hall. " He is certainly a distinguished officer, who is here without shoulder-straps." Soon the Dubuque ladies caught a glimpse of him, and then there was another rush. The soldiers gave way for the ladies from Dubuque and Pittsburg — some of them dear friends of his early life — and for a few minutes he seemed in greater danger from encircling arms, and salutes *not* military, than when at Pea Ridge and Prairie Grove. It was Major-General Frank Herron, whose bravery in the battles of the Southwest made him worthy of honor and warm regard.

A very lively interest was felt in the fair by the soldiers in the Southwestern hospitals, who, since they could do no more, sent innumerable letters and messages to the ladies engaged in it. There were three thousand in the hospitals at Memphis, Tenn., who sent their greetings to the ladies in the following letter, written at their request, and sent by them: —

MEMPHIS, TENN., Oct. 28, 1863.

*To the Managers of the Northwestern Fair:*

LADIES, — The sick and wounded soldiers in the hospitals at Memphis send you greeting, and, through you, return thanks to the women of the Northwest for their efforts to alleviate our wants and sufferings. We are deeply grateful for the sympathy manifested towards us in words and deeds. We are cheered, comforted, and encouraged. Though absent, we are not forgotten by you, nor shall we be, when returned to duty in the field, as we trust we soon may be. We shall be nerved once more to fight on until this unholy rebellion is crushed, and the old flag once more floats over a free, united, and happy people. In the light of your smiles, and in this great earnest of your sympathy, we have an additional incentive never to relax our efforts for our native land, whose women are its brightest ornaments, as well as its truest patriots. May your success be only measured by your love to home and country. In behalf of three thousand soldiers at Memphis,        [Signed]     T. B. ROBB,

*U. S. Sanitary Agent for Illinois.*

A similar letter was sent from the hospitals at Chattanooga, Tenn. It bore the signatures of thousands of the wounded men, traced in every conceivable style of chirography. Many of the autographs indicated the extreme feebleness of the writers. Many of the men who signed it, and were eager to do so, were standing "just on the boundaries of the spirit land"; and some of them passed over the dark river of death before the letter was mailed for Chicago.

The following tribute to the women "whose efforts in behalf of the great fair at Chicago, for the benefit of the Sanitary Commission, accomplished such beneficent results for his sick and wounded comrades," was written by an Illinois soldier at Chattanooga. Has woman ever received a more exquisite tribute?

### A SOLDIER'S PSALM OF WOMAN.

Down all the shining lapse of days,
   That grow and grow forever,
In truer love, and brighter praise,
   Of the Almighty Giver —
Whatever godlike impulses
   Have blossomed in the human,
The most divine and fair of these
   Sprang from the soul of woman.

Her heart it is preserves the flower
   Of sacrificial duty,
Which, blown across the blackest hour,
   Transfigures it to beauty.
Her hands, that streak these solemn years
   With vivifying graces,
And clasp the foreheads of our fears
   With light from higher places.

Oh, wives and mothers, sanctified
   By holy consecrations,

Turning our weariness aside
  With blessèd ministrations!
Oh, maidens, in whose dewy eyes
  Perennial comforts glitter,
Untangling war's dark mysteries,
  And making sweet the bitter —

In desolate paths, or dangerous posts,
  By places which, to-morrow,
Shall be unto these bannered hosts
  Aceldamas of sorrow;
We hear the sound of helping feet —
  We feel your soft caressings —
And all our life starts up to greet
  Your lovingness with blessings!

On cots of pain, on beds of woe,
  Where stricken heroes languish,
Wan faces smile, and sick hearts grow
  Triumphant over anguish.
While souls that starve in lonely gloom,
  Flash green with odorous praises,
And all the lowly pallets bloom
  With gratitude's white daisies.

Oh, lips, that from our wounds have suckea
  The fever and the burning!
Oh, tender fingers, that have plucked
  The madness from our mourning!
Oh, hearts, that beat so loyal true,
  For soothing and for saving!
God send our hopes back unto you,
  Crowned with immortal having!

Thank God! oh, love, whereby we know
  Beyond our little seeing,
And feel serene compassions flow
  Around the ache of being; —
Lo, clear o'er all the pain and dread
  Of our most sore affliction,
The sacred wings of Peace are spread
  In brooding benediction!

# CHAPTER XXIII.

SHERMAN'S MARCH TO THE SEA — DEATH-BLOW TO THE RE-
BELLION — SURRENDER OF LEE — ASSASSINATION OF PRES-
IDENT LINCOLN — THE MARCH OF EVENTS.

The End draws near — Sherman's March to the Sea — He finds the Southern Confederacy a Shell to be easily crushed — Much Anxiety felt at the.
North for the Result — He takes Savannah, with its immense Stores,
and informs the President of his Gift — The South surprised — English
Journals prophesy Failure — Reaches the Atlantic Coast — Co-operates
with Grant and. Lincoln — Richmond evacuated — Lee surrenders —
Delirious Joy of the Nation — Characteristic Procession improvised in
Chicago — Lincoln assassinated — Joy swallowed up in passionate Sorrow — Disbanding of the Army — Motley Treasures brought Home by
Soldiers — Eager to reach Home — Gladness of the Nation at the Return
of Peace.

S the day drew near when the death-blow would be given to the rebellion, a hushed expectancy settled over the country. The return of peace was longed for with an intensity not to be expressed in words; and the movements of the great armies as they drew more closely together for a last, final grapple, were watched with indescribable eagerness. There was no abatement of the iron resolve that the rebellion should be conquered. If it had been necessary to prolong the war another period of four years to accomplish this, the North would have girt itself anew with will and persistence, and matched the

463

emergency. But it was evident that the end was drawing near — that the decisive blow was soon to be struck; and the nervous strain on the people, who waited and listened for this desired consummation, interfered seriously with the ordinary pursuits of business and life.

General Sherman had prepared for his march to the sea. Rome and Atlanta were burned, with their foundries and tanneries, their merchandise and store-houses, their flour-mills and oil refineries, with thousands of bales of cotton, millions of dollars' worth of freight, bridges, turning-tables, freight-sheds, railroad depots, — all were soon in a fierce flame of fire. The few people who remained in Atlanta fled, frightened by the conflagration. In November, Sherman was detached from all his communications, and ready to move. When about to start, he wrote to Admiral Porter, on the Atlantic coast, to " look out for him about Christmas, from Hilton Head to Savannah." To his wife he wrote: " This is my last letter from here. You will hear from me hereafter through rebel sources."

For twenty-four days Sherman's army disappeared from the view of the North, lost in the very heart of the rebellion. About sixty-five thousand men swept over the country, in a track fifty miles wide. General Kilpatrick's cavalry, five thousand strong, moved in front and on each flank; and the advance was from fifteen to twenty miles a day. The holidays found Sherman in Georgia, in possession of Savannah, which he presented to the President in the following terse despatch, —

" I beg to present you, as a Christmas gift, the city of Savannah, with one hundred and fifty guns, plenty of ammunition, and twenty-five thousand bales of cotton."

There proved to be thirty-eight thousand bales. Three steamers were captured, besides locomotives and cars; and eight hundred of the enemy were taken prisoners. The success of this march through the South was not believed in; and, from the middle of November until Sherman was heard of at Savannah, there was great anxiety at the North. The South derided this proposed march to the sea; and English journals, with scarce an exception, prophesied only disastrous results. General Kilpatrick, who made an extensive raid into the South, had declared "the Southern Confederacy to be but a hollow shell, which could be easily crushed"; but his statement was received as the utterance of extreme foolhardiness. Even General Grant, in reply to Sherman's request to be allowed to undertake this enterprise, had written him: "If you were to cut loose from your communications, I do not believe you would meet Hood's army; but you would be bushwhacked by all the old men, little boys, and such railroad guards as are still left at home."

"This march could not have been made through one of the Northern states," says a writer. "And slavery, which the South boasted was an element of strength in war, because it allowed all the whites to enter the army, and yet secured the cultivation of the soil, was found, in an invasion, to be an element of fatal weakness. The working population in a free state would have hung round the flanks of such an invading army like lightning around the edge of a thunder-cloud. But in the South that population was all on the side of the invaders; in short, it was an element of strength to us."

Having rested his army at Savannah, and completed his plans, General Sherman commenced his campaign through the Carolinas. His movements now attracted the attention of the whole country. "What will this wonderful man do next?" was the question in every one's mouth. Some believed that he would strike Augusta. Others were certain that Charleston was the place he wished to capture. But it was his determination to take his army through the heart of the two hostile Carolinas, five hundred miles north, to Goldsboro'. This he did. On the road he pursued such tactics that on the night of the 16th of February, Charleston, S. C., was evacuated, and the Union flag once more floated over Fort Sumter.

Then pushing forward his columns, as though his objective point was Raleigh instead of Goldsboro', he hastened onward, completely befooling the foe. Now he made a feint in one direction, and now in another, wading through boggy marshes and swollen rivers; over inundated lowlands and treacherous quicksands, his route illumined by the conflagrations of property, enkindled by the enemy, in the bitterness of hate and despair. At last he reached Goldsboro'. Then, turning his army over to General Schofield, he hastened to City Point, where he met General Grant and President Lincoln, who gave him a hearty welcome; and the trio consulted together respecting the next move to be made.

Great preparations had been made for the relief of General Sherman's army when it should appear on the Atlantic coast. Hospital supplies of every variety, and in immense quantities, were in readiness at Philadelphia and Washington, with surgeons and nurses to accompany them. Ships were loaded with these sanitary stores, and with food for the men also;

for it was expected that the men who " marched from
Atlanta to the sea" would be famished and exhausted — a skeleton army, requiring medical skill
and careful nursing to save them from death.

But the sanitary supplies and medical skill were
uncalled for. Sherman's men came out from their
long march hale and hearty, having foraged on the
enemy and lived on the fat of the land, but brown
and barefoot, ragged and dirty. It was indeed a tatterdemalion army that invaded the Carolinas. In
a fortnight afterwards, the quartermaster supplied
twenty thousand of the men with shoes, and a hundred thousand with clothing, and everything necessary for entering on another campaign.

The march of events was now very rapid. General Grant wrote to Sheridan, "I now feel like ending the matter, if it is possible to do so before going
back. We will all act together as one army here,
until it is seen what can be done with the enemy."
Sunday, the 2d of April arrived, and all saw the
beginning of the end. A great battle had been
raging near Petersburg for some days, which ended
in the complete rout of the enemy, who fled in confusion, leaving all their guns and a large number of
prisoners in the hands of the Union army. That
night, both Petersburg and Richmond were evacuated.

But as long as General Lee's army had a collective
existence, it could not be said that the war was
ended. This fact was impressed on every mind, and
on no one so strongly as on General Grant. Pre-
caution had been taken to prevent the rebel army
escaping South when it evacuated Richmond. And
now, hemmed in by Sheridan and the Appomattox

River on one side, by Meade on another, by Hancock on a third, and Thomas on the fourth, the destruction of that army was only a question of time. The celerity of General Grant's movements precipitated the surrender of Lee. And on the 9th of April, 1865, General Lee surrendered his sword and the Army of Northern Virginia to the eminent Lieutenant-General commanding the armies of the United States. The rebel army of Johnston, with Sherman in his front and Grant in his rear, must dissolve like the baseless fabric of a vision, or likewise surrender to the victorious armies of the Union. The great rebellion had ended, and the Union remained intact and undivided!

The day for which all loyal souls had prayed and waited for four long years had come at last. The nation was delirious with the intoxication of good news telegraphed from Washington, — "LEE HAS SURRENDERED TO GRANT!" Just as the Sunday evening church services were ended, the bells of Chicago clanged out the glad tidings, and the event they rejoiced in was instinctively understood by heart. All were waiting for it; all knew it could not be long delayed. The iron-throated cannon took up the jubilant tidings, and thundered it from a hundred guns. Bonfires blazed it joyfully in all the streets, rockets flashed it everywhere on the night air, the huzzas and songs of the people rolled out from the heart of the city to the suburbs, and the ordinary quiet of the Sunday night was broken by universal rejoicing.

The next day, the rejoicing was renewed with more *abandon* than ever. Bells pealed afresh, cannon thundered anew, the air was rent with ten thousand

hurrahs. Everybody saluted his neighbor with mingled laughter and tears. Flags floated from steeples
and housetops and windows, — they streamed from
wagons and carriages and car-roofs, — of tiny proportions, men wore them in their button-holes, and
women in their hats. At every street corner one
caught the sound of martial music, mingled with the
ringing bass and tenor of manly voices singing
patriotic songs. Courts adjourned, banks closed,
the post-office was summarily shut up, schools were
dismissed, business was suspended. The people
poured into the streets, frenzied with gladness, until
there seemed to be no men and women in Chicago,—
only crazy, grown-up boys and girls.

A procession was hastily improvised, — the people's procession, — measuring miles in length, and
cheered by the tens of thousands lining the streets
through which it passed. On they came, — the
blue-coated soldiers stepping proudly to glorious
music, — and shouts rent the air, and white handkerchiefs floated from the windows, and gentle
hands waved them welcome. Then followed the
brazen-mouthed cannon, drawn by noble horses, that
arched their necks and stepped loftily, as if conscious
they had the "peace-makers" in their train. On
they came, — men on horseback, men a-foot, six
abreast, led by the Veteran Reserve Corps Band,
thrilling the air with the triumphant strain, "Glory,
Glory, Hallelujah!" The great multitude — tens of
thousands of men, women, and children — caught up
the refrain, and joined in the glorious chorus, singing, with heart and soul and might, "GLORY, GLORY,
HALLELUJAH!"

Still they came. All the drays in the city; all the

steam fire-engines, with the red-costumed firemen; all the express wagons; all the post-office wagons; all the omnibuses, loaded with men, and boys, and soldiers, ringing bells, beating drums, blowing trumpets, and fifes, and every manner of instrument that makes a joyful sound; blossoming with flags, vocal with hurrahs, bearing banners with eloquent mottoes, firing guns and pistols into the air, and in every conceivable manner testifying their unbounded gladness.

As the long procession moved on, fathers pointed out its peculiar features to their sons, and charged them to remember the day, and its history, to tell to their children. Mothers lifted their little daughters, to read the mottoes emblazoned on the banners, and to explain the emblems that thronged the line of march. Were there ever before two such carnival days crowded into one short week? Only a week before, the chords of the national heart were swept by the wildest ecstasy of joy, as tidings of the fall of Richmond flashed over the wires — and now the surrender of Lee made the nation fairly drunken with delight. Peace had returned, —

> "Not like a mourner bowed
> For honor lost, and dear ones wasted;
> But proud, to meet a people proud,
> With eyes that told of triumph tasted!
> Who came, with hand upon the hilt,
> And step, that proved her Victory's daughter —
> Longing for her, our spirits wilt,
> Like shipwrecked men's, on rafts, for water.
>
> Peace, such as mothers prayed for, when
> They kissed their sons, with lips that quivered;
> Which brings fair wages for brave men —
> A nation saved! A race delivered!"

From the height of this exultation the nation was swiftly precipitated to the very depths of despair. On the fourteenth of April, President Lincoln was assassinated, and the great joy of the previous two weeks was drowned in passionate sorrow. Everything was forgotten in the presence of this overwhelming calamity. The air was solemn with the toll of bells. Flags, bordered with crape, floated at half-mast. Minute guns reverberated from vale to hill, from mountain to mountain, and across the continent. Cities and towns and hamlets of the broad land were draped in black. Business was suspended. Men and women wept. At the call of the bells, the churches were thronged with weeping congregations. No attempt at comfort, nor any explanation of the bitter dispensation was given, but all seemed benumbed by the national bereavement. Never was a month so crowded with the conflicting emotions of exultation and despair, as was the month of April, 1865. Richmond fell on the third, General Lee surrendered on the ninth, President Lincoln was assassinated on the fourteenth.

Despite the bitterness of the times, the honesty, simplicity, and kindliness of President Lincoln had greatly endeared him to the national heart, and the people were thrilled with horror at the manner of his death. He had piloted the nation wisely through its stormiest years. Lacking superior mental qualities, and failing of careful educational preparation for his high office, singleness of purpose had guided him, and the wisdom of his presidential life placed him by the side of Washington, as his peer. Enemies, as well as friends, bewailed his death.

The funeral obsequies were celebrated in the Ex-

ecutive Mansion in Washington, and then the body
of the dead ruler was borne to his former home in
Springfield, Ill.    The whole land was draped in
mourning, and the tolling of bells, and the wail of
funereal music accompanied the cortége, as it moved
across the continent on its solemn mission, to the
burial of the coffined corse.

And now began the disbanding of the army.
Regiments returned to their homes on almost every
train.   The army of the Potomac, and the army led
by Sherman, were henceforth only to be known in
history.   Comrades who had shared together the
perils of the picket-line and the storm of the battle;
exposure to the elements, and suffering from wounds;
the fatigue of the march, and the grapple with
swamp fever; the longing for home, and the inexpressible luxury of letters from dear ones left behind, now bade each other adieu.   Scarred and
maimed, these defenders of the Republic exchanged
the discomforts and privations of the camp, for the
solacing influence of their own firesides.   Henceforth, instead of the everlasting drum corps, and the
crack of musketry, they were to hear the voices of
wives and children, parents and friends.

They did not return as they went forth — strong
in numbers, with gleaming guns, stainless uniforms,
and brilliant banners.   But reduced in strength,
dust-stained, battle-scarred, war-worn, with faded
uniforms, tattered flags, sometimes with an empty
coat-sleeve, sometimes swinging on crutches.   Whenever it was possible, as regiments passed through
Chicago on their way home, they were publicly
received.   Addresses were made to them, and dinner
furnished at the Soldiers' Home, where the ladies

were always in readiness to feed two hundred men. Although they bore the unmistakable marks of war in their appearance, they carried themselves proudly, and responded with a will to the cheers that were given them.

So motley a collection of treasures, picked up in the South, as the returning soldiers bore home, one does not often see. One had a yellow puppy, a little barking nuisance, which nestled in his bosom, although he was so sick with chills and fever, as to be almost incapable of taking care of himself. Another had a shrill-voiced, but gay parrot, in a cumbersome cage — another a silken-haired spaniel — another a pet rabbit — another a kitten from Fort Sumter — another a mocking-bird, and the thoughtful fellow had cut off the skirts of his blouse, to wrap around the songster's cage, to keep him warm. They had relics, shells from the Gulf of Mexico, curious insects in boxes, and slips of rare shrubbery, set in potatoes, which they were going to plant at home.

With some, there was a great parade of washing, brushing, and furbishing up, so as to look respectable in their proposed walks about the city, while waiting their departing train. These toilet performances met with every species of comical interference, from their mischievous comrades. Apple, orange, nut, and cake peddlers drove a thriving business among them, every man within reach of the apple woman investing largely in her wares. Hilarious, and full of rough fun, they waited impatiently for the hour when they would leave Chicago. Their conversation was mainly of the campaigns through which they had passed, and the homes to which they were going. Sometimes, as they recounted the changes that had taken place in their absence, a choking sob silenced them, or they dashed into a frolic to conceal their emotions.

" I left four children when I went away," said a middle-aged man; " and now, there is but one left. I shall miss my three little girls."

" My mother has died since I went into the service," said another in a low tone.

" They are going to put me off at Denton," said a third, with an anxious face; " my wife is very low with consumption, and if I should be detained long, I might never see her."

For some, poor fellows! other changes were near at hand. For the labored breath, the incessant cough, the attenuated figure, and the hectic flush predicted a not far distant promotion to the higher ranks, where wars are unknown.

There were enlisted into the service, during the war, 2,850,000 men. By the first of November, 1865, there had been mustered out 1,023,021 men, and the army was reduced to eleven thousand soldiers. There were killed in battle during the war, fifty-six thousand. There died of wounds and disease in the military hospitals, two hundred and nineteen thousand. There died, after discharge, from disease contracted during the service, eighty thousand — making a total loss of about three hundred thousand men. About two hundred thousand were crippled or permanently disabled. One hundred and thirty-four thousand sleep in nameless graves. Of colored troops, one hundred and eighty thousand enlisted, and thirty thousand died. The national debt June 30, 1865, amounted to $2,680,000,000.00. During the war, the

Sanitary Commission disbursed in money and supplies, not less than $25,000,000. The Christian Commission disbursed $4,500,000.

These figures give a better idea of the war of the rebellion, which was gigantic in character, and of the immense sacrifices made by the people, than any elaborate statement in words. The courage of the nation proved equal to the great emergency. Its patriotism never faltered, its faith in the permanency of the undivided Republic grew mightier as the contest was protracted. But never was a nation more profoundly thankful for the cessation of war than were the American people. They turned with infinite gladness to the duties of peace — they sought to forget the dark days of conflict through which they had toiled. Quietly, and without any friction, the vast army was resolved into its original elements, and soldiers became again civilians, members of homes, and components of families. A grateful nation still honors the memories of those who fell in the conflict, cares tenderly for those who were disabled, and cherishes their stricken families.

# CHAPTER XXIV.

MOTHER BICKERDYKE—STORY OF A REMARKABLE WOMAN—
HER MOTHERLY CARE OF THE "BOYS IN BLUE"—HOS-
PITAL SIGHTS AND SCENES—ON THE BATTLE-FIELD AT
NIGHT.

A remarkable Woman — Sent into the Service at Cairo by Ladies of Galesburg, Ill. — Improvises a sick-diet Kitchen — Stratagem to detect the
Thieves who steal her Delicacies — "Peaches don't seem to agree with
you, eh?" — Colonel (now General) Grant removes the dishonest Officials — Mother Bickerdyke after the Battle of Donelson — A Surgeon's
Testimony — She extemporizes a Laundry — Is associated with Mrs.
Porter of Chicago — After the Battle of Shiloh — "I get my Authority
from the Lord God Almighty; have you anything that ranks higher?"—
Her System of foraging — Her "Night-Gowns" as hospital Shirts — "Say
you jerked them from the Secesh, Boys!" — Experiences at Corinth —
Finds a dying Soldier left in a Tent.

AMONG the hundreds of women who devoted
a part or the whole of the years of the war
to the care of the sick and wounded of the
army, "Mother Bickerdyke" stands pre-
eminent. Others were as heroic and consecrated as she, as unwearied in labors, and as
unselfish and self-sacrificing. But she was unique in
method, extraordinary in executive ability, enthusiastic in devotion, and indomitable in will. After her
plans were formed, and her purposes matured, she
carried them through triumphantly, in the teeth of
the most formidable opposition. She gave herself to
the rank and file of the army, — the private soldiers,

476

— for whom she had unbounded tenderness, and developed almost limitless resources of help and comfort.

To them she was strength and sweetness; and for them she exercised sound, practical sense, a ready wit, and a rare intelligence, that made her a power in the hospital, or on the field. There was no peril she would not dare for a sick and wounded man, no official red tape of formality for which she cared more than for a common tow string, if it interfered with her in her work of relief. To their honor be it said, the "boys" reciprocated her affection most heartily. "That homely figure, clad in calico, wrapped in a shawl, and surmounted with a 'Shaker' bonnet, is more to this army than the Madonna to a Catholic!" said an officer, pointing to Mother Bickerdyke, as she emerged from the Sanitary Commission headquarters, in Memphis, laden with an assortment of supplies. Every soldier saluted her as she passed; and those who were at leisure relieved her of her burden, and bore it to its destination. To the entire army of the West she was emphatically "*Mother* Bickerdyke." Nor have the soldiers forgotten her in her poverty and old age. They remember her to-day in many a tender letter, and send her many a small donation to eke out her scanty and irregular income.

I was intimately associated with this remarkable woman during the war. Whenever she came to Chicago, on brief furloughs from army work, my house was her home. Utterly regardless of her own comfort, and ignoring her personal needs, it was absolutely essential that some one should care for her; and this grateful work I took into my own hands.

Whatever were her troubles, hindrances, or liabilities, I persuaded her to entrust them to me; and, with the help of Mrs. Hoge, my inseparable co-worker, she was relieved of them. Little by little, I learned the story of her early life from her own lips, — a story of struggle with poverty, hard fate, and lack of opportunity, but glorified, as were her maturer years, by unselfishness and a spirit of helpfulness, that recognized the claims of every needy creature. Such of the incidents of the following sketch as did not come under my own observation were narrated to me by Mrs. Bickerdyke herself. I only regret my inability to repeat them in her language.

Mary A. Bickerdyke was born in Knox County, Ohio, July 19, 1817. She came of Revolutionary ancestors, and was never happier than when recounting fragments of her grandfather's history, who served under Washington during the whole seven years' struggle. When Washington made the memorable passage across the Delaware, her grandfather was one of those detailed to keep the fires burning on the shore, and crossed in one of the last boats. She married, when about twenty-five, a widower with four or five children, by whom she has been beloved as if she were their natural mother, and between whom and her own two sons she has never seemed to know any difference. The marriage was a happy one, although I suspect that the immense energy and tireless industry of the busy wife proved, sometimes, annoying to the easy-going husband. His death occurred about two years before the breaking out of the war. I have heard her tell married men, in a sort of warning way, and very seriously, that she really believed her husband might have lived twenty years

longer, if he had not worn himself into the grave
trying to boss her. "He wanted me to do everything
in his way," she would say, "and just as he did; but
his way was too slow, I couldn't stand it."

She was living in Galesburg, Ill., and was a member of Rev. Dr. Edward Beecher's church when the
war of the rebellion broke out. Hardly had the
troops reached Cairo, when, from the sudden change
in their habits, their own imprudence, and the ignorance of their commanders on all sanitary points,
sickness broke out among them. At the suggestion
of the ladies of Galesburg, who had organized to do
something for the country — they hardly knew what
at that time — Mrs. Bickerdyke went down among
them. Her well-known skill as a nurse, the fertility
of her resources, her burning patriotism, and her possession of that rare combination of qualities which
we call "common sense," had always enabled her to
face any emergency.

There was at that time little order, system, or discipline anywhere. In company with Mary Safford,
then living in Cairo, she commenced an immediate
systematic work in the camp and regimental hospitals at Cairo and Bird's Point. In the face of obstacles of every kind, she succeeded in working a great
change for the better in the condition of the sick.
The influence of her energetic, resolute, and systematic spirit was felt everywhere; and the loyal
people of Cairo gladly aided her in her voluntary
and unpaid labors. A room was hired for her, and a
cooking-stove set up for her especial use. She improvised a sick-diet kitchen, and carried thence to
the sick in the hospitals the food she had prepared
for them. The first assortment of delicacies for the

sick sent to Cairo by the Chicago Sanitary Commission, were given to her for distribution. Almost all the hospital supplies sent from the local societies of Chicago or Illinois, were, for a time, given to her trustworthy care.

After the battle of Belmont she was appointed matron of the large post hospital at Cairo, which was filled with the wounded. She found time, however, to work for, and to visit daily, every other hospital in the town. The surgeon who appointed her was skilful and competent, but given to drunkenness; and he had little sympathy with his patients. He had filled all the positions in the hospitals with surgeons and officers of his sort, and bacchanalian carousals in the "doctor's room" were of frequent occurrence. In twenty-four hours Mother Bickerdyke and he were at swords' points. She denounced him to his face; and, when the garments and delicacies sent her for the use of the sick and wounded disappeared mysteriously, she charged their theft upon him and his subordinates.

He ordered her out of his hospital, and threatened to put her out if she did not hasten her departure. She replied that "she should stay as long as the men needed her — that if he put her out of one door she should come in at another; and if he barred all the doors against her, she should come in at the windows, and that the patients would help her in. When *anybody* left it would be he, and not she," she assured him, "as she had already lodged complaints against him at headquarters." "Conscience makes cowards of us all"; and he did not proceed to expel her, as he might have done, and probably would, if his cause had been just.

But though *she* was let alone, this was not the case with her supplies for the sick and wounded — they were stolen continually. She caught a ward-master dressed in the shirt, slippers, and socks that had been sent her, and, seizing him by the collar, in his own ward, she disrobed him *sans cérémonie* before the patients. Leaving him nude save his pantaloons, she uttered this parting injunction: " Now, you rascal, let's see what you'll steal next!" To ascertain who were the thieves of the food she prepared, she resorted to a somewhat dangerous *ruse*. Purchasing a quantity of tartar emetic at a drug store, she mixed it with some stewed peaches that she had openly cooked in the kitchen, telling Tom, the cook, that " she wanted to leave them on the kitchen table over night to cool." Then she went to her own room to await results.

She did not wait long. Soon the sounds of suffering from the terribly sick thieves reached her ears, when, like a Nemesis, she stalked in among them. There they were, cooks, table-waiters, stewards, ward-masters, — all save some of the surgeons, — suffering terribly from the emetic, but more from the apprehension that they were poisoned. " Peaches don't seem to agree with you, eh? " she said, looking on the pale, retching, groaning fellows with a sardonic smile. " Well, let me tell you that you will have a worse time than this if you keep on stealing! You may eat something seasoned with ratsbane one of these nights."

Her complaints of theft were so grievous that there was sent her from the Sanitary Commission in Chicago a huge refrigerator with a strong lock. She received it with great joy, and, putting into it the delicacies, sick-diet, milk, and other hospital dainties of which she had especial charge, she locked it in presence of the cook, defying him and his companions. "You have stolen the last morsel from me that you ever will," she said, "for I intend always to carry the key of the refrigerator in my pocket." That very night the lock of the refrigerator was broken, and everything appetizing inside was stolen. The depredation was clearly traced to Tom. This was too much for Mother Bickerdyke. Putting on her Shaker bonnet, she hastened to the provost-marshal, where she told her story so effectively that he sent a guard to the hospital kitchen, arrested the thieving cook, and locked him in the guard-house. The arrest was made so quickly and silently, from the rear of the hospital, that only Mother Bickerdyke and two or three of the patients knew it; and, as she enjoined secrecy, Tom's sudden disappearance was involved in mystery.

Greatly mollified at this riddance of her enemy, Mother Bickerdyke courteously offered to "run the kitchen" until Tom returned; and Dr. —— accepted the proposal.

"I am afraid," said the doctor, as days passed, and no tidings of Tom were received, "I am afraid that Tom went on a spree, and fell off the levee into the river, and is drowned."

"Small loss!" replied sententious Mother Bickerdyke; "I never want to see him again."

Going to the guard-house a week after, on some errand, the doctor discovered the lost cook, and immediately sought his release. He was too late. Mother Bickerdyke had made such charges against him, and the other subordinates of the hospital, that

the provost-marshal investigated them.    Finding
them true, he laid them before General Grant — then
Colonel — who was in command of that department.
He ordered the men sent back to their regiments,
and better officials were detailed in their places.
Their removal was followed shortly after by that of
the surgeon, and Dr. Taggart, one of the noblest
men, was put in his place.    The story of Mother
Bickerdyke's exploits in this hospital preceded her
in the army.    The rank and file learned that she was
in an especial sense their friend, and dishonest and
brutal surgeons and officials, of whom there were not
a few, in the early months of the war, understood, in
advance, that she could neither be bought nor frightened.    Throughout the war, the prestige of her hospital life in Cairo clung to her.

After the battle of Donelson, Mother Bickerdyke
went from Cairo in the first hospital boat, and
assisted in the removal of the wounded to Cairo, St.
Louis, and Louisville, and in nursing those too badly
wounded to be moved.    The Sanitary Commission
had established a depot of stores at Cairo, and on
these she was allowed to make drafts *ad libitum:* for
she was as famous for her economical use of sanitary
stores as she had been before the war for her notable housewifery.    The hospital boats at that time
were poorly equipped for the sad work of transporting the wounded.    But this thoughtful woman, who
made five of the terrible trips from the battle-field of
Donelson to the hospital, put on board the boat with
which she was connected, before it started from
Cairo, an abundance of necessaries.    There was
hardly a want expressed for which she could not
furnish some sort of relief.

On the way to the battle-field, she systematized matters perfectly. The beds were ready for the occupants, tea, coffee, soup and gruel, milk punch and ice water were prepared in large quantities, under her supervision, and sometimes by her own hand. When the wounded were brought on board, — mangled almost out of human shape; the frozen ground from which they had been cut adhering to them; chilled with the intense cold in which some had lain for twenty-four hours; faint with loss of blood, physical agony, and lack of nourishment; racked with a terrible five-mile ride over frozen roads, in ambulances, or common Tennessee farm wagons, without springs; burning with fever; raving in delirium, or in the faintness of death, — Mother Bickerdyke's boat was in readiness for them.

"I never saw anybody like her," said a volunteer surgeon who came on the boat with her. "There was really nothing for us surgeons to do but dress wounds and administer medicines. She drew out clean shirts or drawers from some corner, whenever they were needed. Nourishment was ready for every man as soon as he was brought on board. Every one was sponged from blood and the frozen mire of the battle-field, as far as his condition allowed. His blood-stiffened, and sometimes horribly filthy uniform, was exchanged for soft and clean hospital garments. Incessant cries of "Mother! Mother! Mother!" rang through the boat, in every note of beseeching and anguish. And to every man she turned with a heavenly tenderness, as if he were indeed her son. She moved about with a decisive air, and gave directions in such decided, clarion tones as to ensure prompt obedience. We all had

Engraved by J. J. Cade, New York.

*Copyright, '87.*

A. D. Worthington & Co. Publishers, Hartford, Conn.

## MIDNIGHT ON THE BATTLE FIELD.

"It was Mother Bickerdyke, with a lantern, still groping among the dead. Stooping down, and turning their cold faces towards her, she scrutinized them searchingly, uneasy lest some might be left to die uncared for. She could not rest while she thought any were overlooked who were yet living."

an impression that she held a commission from the Secretary of War, or at least from the Governor of Illinois. To every surgeon who was superior, she held herself subordinate, and was as good at obeying as at commanding." And yet, at that time, she held no position whatever, and was receiving no compensation for her services; not even the beggarly pittance of thirteen dollars per month allowed by government to army nurses.

At last it was believed that all the wounded had been removed from the field, and the relief parties discontinued their work. Looking from his tent at midnight, an officer observed a faint light flitting hither and thither on the abandoned battle-field, and, after puzzling over it for some time, sent his servant to ascertain the cause. It was Mother Bickerdyke, with a lantern, still groping among the dead. Stooping down, and turning their cold faces towards her, she scrutinized them searchingly, uneasy lest some might be left to die uncared for. She could not rest while she thought any were overlooked who were yet living.

Up to this time, no attempt had been made to save the clothing and bedding used by the wounded men on the transports and in the temporary hospitals. Saturated with blood, and the discharges of healing wounds, and sometimes swarming with vermin, it had been collected, and burned or buried. But this involved much waste; and as these articles were in constant need, Mother Bickerdyke conceived the idea of saving them. She sent to the Commission at Chicago for washing-machines, portable kettles, and mangles, and caused all this offensive clothing to be collected. She then obtained from the authorities a full detail of

contrabands, and superintended the laundering of all
these hideously foul garments. Packed in boxes, it
all came again into use at the next battle.

This work once begun, Mother Bickerdyke never
intermitted. Her washing-machines, her portable
kettles, her posse of contrabands, an ambulance or
two, and one or two handy detailed soldiers, were in
her retinue after this, wherever she went. How
much she saved to the government, and to the Sanitary Commission, may be inferred from the fact that
it was no unusual thing for three or four thousand
pieces to pass through her extemporized laundry in a
day. Each piece was returned to the hospital from
which it was taken, or, if it belonged to no place in
particular, was used *in transitu.* She saw it boxed,
and the boxes deposited in some safe place, where
she could easily reach them in time of need.

During a large part of her army life, Mrs Bickerdyke was associated with, and most efficiently supple-
mented by, Mrs. Eliza Porter, wife of a Congregationalist clergyman of Chicago. She entered the
service in the beginning, as did her associate, and
turned not from the work until the war ended. Together they worked in the hospitals, enduring cold
and hunger, dwelling amid constant alarms, breathing the tainted air of wounds and sickness, and fore-
going every species of enjoyment save that which
comes from the consciousness of duties well done.
Unlike in all respects, they harmonized admirably;
and each helped the other. Mrs. Bickerdyke came
less frequently into collision with officials when in
company with Mrs. Porter; and the obstacles in the
way of the latter were more readily overcome when
the energy of Mrs. Bickerdyke opposed them. Mrs.

Porter patiently won her way, and urged her claims mildly but persistently. Mrs. Bickerdyke was heedless of opposition, which only nerved her to a more invincible energy; and she took what she claimed, no matter who opposed. Both were very dear to the soldiers, from each of whom they expected sympathy and pity, as well as courage and help.

After the wounded of Donelson were cared for, Mrs. Bickerdyke left the hospitals, and went back into the army. There was great sickness among our troops at Savannah, Tenn. She had already achieved such a reputation for devotion to the men, for executive ability, and versatility of talent, that the spirits of the sick and wounded revived at the very sound of her voice, and at the sight of her motherly face. While busy here, the battle of Shiloh occurred, nine miles distant by the river, but only six in a direct line. There had been little provision made for the terrible needs of the battle-field in advance of the conflict. The battle occurred unexpectedly, and was a surprise to our men, — who nearly suffered defeat, — and again there was utter destitution and incredible suffering. Three days after the battle, the boats of the Sanitary Commission arrived at the Landing, laden with every species of relief, — condensed food, stimulants, clothing, bedding, medicines, chloroform, surgical instruments, and carefully selected volunteer nurses and surgeons. They were on the ground some days in advance of the government boats.

Here Mother Bickerdyke was found, carrying system, order, and relief wherever she went. One of the surgeons went to the rear with a wounded man, and found her wrapped in the gray overcoat of a rebel officer, for she had disposed of her blanket shawl to some poor fellow who needed it. She was wearing a soft slouch hat, having lost her inevitable Shaker bonnet. Her kettles had been set up, the fire kindled underneath, and she was dispensing hot soup, tea, crackers, panado, whiskey and water, and other refreshments, to the shivering, fainting, wounded men.

"Where did you get these articles?" he inquired; "and under whose authority are you at work?"

She paid no heed to his interrogatories, and, indeed, did not hear them, so completely absorbed was she in her work of compassion. Watching her with admiration for her skill, administrative ability, and intelligence, — for she not only fed the wounded men, but temporarily dressed their wounds in some cases, — he approached her again: —

"Madam, you seem to combine in yourself a sick-diet kitchen and a medical staff. May I inquire under whose authority you are working?"

Without pausing in her work, she answered him, "I have received my authority from the Lord God Almighty; have you anything that ranks higher than that?" The truth was, she held no position whatever at that time. She was only a "volunteer nurse," having received no appointment, and being attached to no corps of relief.

The Chicago boat took down over one hundred boxes of sanitary stores, on which she was allowed to draw. But they were only as a drop in the bucket among the twelve thousand wounded, lying in extemporized hospitals in and around Savannah. Other consignments of sanitary goods were made to her from Chicago and Springfield, Ill. The agents of the St. Louis and Cincinnati Commissions gave to her freely, when she made requisition on them. When every other resource failed, Mother Bickerdyke would take an ambulance, and one of her detailed soldiers as driver, and go out foraging. Never returned she empty-handed. The contrabands were her friends and allies; and she always came back with eggs, milk, butter, and fowls, which were the main objects of her quest. These foraging expeditions sometimes placed her in great peril; but she scorned any thought of danger where the welfare of the boys was concerned.

After she became an agent of the Sanitary Commission, we endeavored to keep her supplied with what she needed. But emergencies were constantly arising which she could not foresee, and for which the Commission could not provide, which would throw her on her own resources; and these never failed her. Sometimes, when opportunities for purchasing hospital supplies came in her way, she would buy largely, and send the bills to the Commission with her endorsement. Again, at other times of great need, she would borrow money, expend it for the boys in her charge, and, sending to Mrs. Hoge and myself vouchers and notes, would leave the affair with us to settle.

The gentlemen of the Commission, while they had no doubt that the good woman made a legitimate use of the money and of the articles purchased, objected to these irregular and unbusiness-like transactions; and they were in the right. Again and again have we taken these bills, notes, and vouchers into our hands, and raised money to pay them outside the Commission, among personal friends who knew Mrs. Bickerdyke through sons, husbands, and brothers.

They believed she should be sustained in her wonderful work, even though she were a little irregular
in her proceedings.

The ladies of the city and country were continually sending Mrs. Bickerdyke boxes of clothing for
her own use.  In her life of hard work, her clothes
were soon worn out; and as she never had time to
bestow on herself, she was greatly in need of such
kindnesses.  Reserving for herself a few articles of
which she had imperative need, she would take the
remainder of the garments in her ambulance to the
Southern women in the neighboring country, and
peddle them for honey, fruit, milk, eggs, and butter,
of which she never could have too much.

Among the articles sent her at one time were two
very elegant long night-dresses, embroidered, and
trimmed with ruffles and lace.  They were the gift
of very dear friends; and she had some scruples
about bartering them away as she did other garments.  Returning with the " plunder " she had received in exchange for her superfluous clothing, she
crossed a railroad track, on which stood a train of
box cars.  Stopping the ambulance, she began to
explore them, according to her usual custom.  Inside
of one were two wounded soldiers going home on
furlough.  Their unhealed wounds were undressed,
and full of vermin; they were weak for lack of food,
were depressed and discouraged, and in all respects
were in a very sorry plight.

" Humph!" said Mother Bickerdyke; " now I see
what them furbelowed night-gowns were sent down
here for.  The Lord meant I should put 'em to a
good use, after all."

The wounds of the poor fellows were washed and

cleansed. Tearing off bandages from the bottom of the night-dresses, she properly dressed and bandaged them. Socks, and drawers, and handkerchiefs were found in the ambulance; but she was entirely destitute of shirts. A happy thought came to her.

" Here, boys," she said; " put on the upper half of these night-gowns; they're just the thing. My sakes! but this *is* lucky!"

But to this the men decidedly objected. " They would wear the dirty, tattered shirts, that had not been changed in two months, rather than go home in a woman's night-gown!"

" Oh, pshaw, boys! don't be fools!" persisted practical Mother Bickerdyke. " Night *gowns*, or night *shirts;* what's the odds? These will be softer to your wounds; and Heaven knows they're enough sight cleaner. Put 'em on, and wear 'em home. If anybody says anything, tell them you've jerked 'em from the secesh, and the folks will think a heap sight more of you for it."

The men were persuaded, and got into the nondescript garments. In passing through Chicago, they halted for a brief rest at the Soldiers' Home, where, when their wounds were dressed, their *outré* shirts were discovered, marked in indelible ink, with Mrs. Bickerdyke's name. We offered to exchange them for genuine hospital shirts; but the men had had such sport already, that they clung to the abbreviated night-gowns, one of which is to-day preserved in a Wisconsin household as a sacred relic.

As the Savannah hospitals were vacated by the transfer of the men farther North, Mother Bickerdyke, still keeping in the immediate rear of the army, was sent to Farmington. Here was one large hospital, of which she was appointed matron. The wounded of the battle of Iuka were brought here, and those disabled in various skirmishes. Here for the two months of July and August, amid incessant alarms from the enemy, Mother Bickerdyke stood at her post, personally superintending the cooking, washing, and nursing of some thousands of sick and wounded men. The hospitals were then removed to Corinth, where the elevated ground gave promise of a healthier situation, and the defences of the town secured perfect safety.

Hardly were the hospitals in running order again, hardly had Mother Bickerdyke again extemporized her laundry and diet kitchens, before the battle of Corinth was fought. On the second day of the fight, to her horror, her hospital came within range of the enemy's artillery, and the fearful missiles of death fell with fatal precision among her helpless men. There was no alternative but to remove the poor fellows again. Worn out with the heat and her unparalleled labors, while shot and shell, and grape and canister were dealing death around her, she bent her energies to this unaccustomed work. They were removed to a beautiful grove within the range of the hostile guns, where shot and shell passed harmlessly over them. After the battle, they were carried back to their hospitals.

This battle greatly increased the labors of Mother Bickerdyke. She had learned how to take care of men brought in from the battle-field, and was always prepared with soups, tea, coffee, milk punch, stimulants, rags, bandages, and whatever else might be needed. The rebel wounded fell into her hands, and, bitterly as our heroine hated the "secesh," all the

Engraved by J.J.Cade, New York.

A REBEL SHELL BURSTING IN A UNION HOSPITAL.

A.D.Worthington & Co.Publishers, Hartford, Conn.

"On the second day of the fight (Corinth) to her horror, her hospital came within range of the enemy's artillery and the fearful missiles of death fell with fatal precision among her helpless men."

bitterness died out of her heart when the wounded in gray uniforms were left to her tender mercies. She became a mother to them, as to the boys in blue. Her work was arduous beyond description. Had she been contented to perform her work as a matter of routine, it would have been easy for her, but this would not suffice her great heart and conscientious nature. Her work was never done. If anything could be suggested to save a man who was dying, to soothe, or inspire, encourage, or strengthen a patient who was anxious or disheartened, her work was not done until this was accomplished. Nowhere in her department was there neglect or suffering, misrule or waste.

Orders had been given to bring the wounded lying in tents into her large hospital, as fast as there was room for them. At last she was informed that the tents were all vacated. With her habit of seeing for herself if the work was done, she went from tent to tent, examining them. Turning from one, she thought she saw a movement under a heap of blankets in a corner. She raised the nauseous, fly-covered blanket, and there lay a man, still breathing, but hardly alive. He had been shot through both cheeks, a part of his tongue had been cut off, which was swollen to bursting in his mouth, and the left shoulder and leg were broken. How long he had been forgotten, no one could tell; but the flies had rioted in his wounds, and he was in a most lamentable condition.

He was brought on a stretcher immediately to her hospital, when she devoted herself to his restoration, fighting grim death inch by inch, hour by hour, until she came off conqueror, and the man recovered. He is living to-day, and is proud to call Mother Bicker-dyke his savior.  It was something to witness the tempest that burst over the heads of the men who had been commissioned to remove the wounded, and had passed by this poor fellow.  Mother Bickerdyke was merciless on such an occasion, and flashed such lightnings of wrath on the offenders as to astonish them into speechlessness.  Nothing so aroused her as carelessness, or neglect of the helpless, the sick, or the wounded.  She would work day and night herself, to relieve suffering, and she was impatient, even to severity, to witness indifference or neglect on the part of others.  Her only thought was to help the poor soldiers; and she did this in a way that secured the favor of man, and the approbation of Heaven.

# CHAPTER XXV.

THRILLING INCIDENTS IN THE LIFE OF MOTHER BICKER-
DYKE—HER HOSPITAL EXPERIENCES—HER FIRST FUR-
LOUGH—RETURN TO THE FRONT—FIGHTING THE DOC-
TORS—A COW-AND-HEN EXPEDITION.

She is much worn down—Extremely Perilous to remain longer without Rest
—Her Health demands a Respite from her Labors for a Time—Comes
to my House on her Furlough—Attends a Wedding—"Have enjoyed
your Wedding as if it were a Prayer-Meeting!"—Calls Meetings to
raise Supplies—Returns to the Front, organizes and regenerates Hospitals—Re-organizes her Laundries in Memphis—Quarrels with the Medical Director—Outgenerals him—"One of us two goes to the Wall, and
*'taint never me!*"—The Storm finally ends in Sunshine—They become
Friends—He sends her North on a Cow-and-Hen Expedition—Returns
with a hundred Cows, and a thousand Hens—Improved Condition of
the Hospitals—Confided in everywhere—Impatient of Red Tape—
Cared little for Sect, but much for the Comfort of the Soldiers.

N November, 1862, Mrs. Bickerdyke was
compelled, for the first time, to take a furlough. She was thoroughly worn out,
although she would not admit it, and was as
indomitable in will, and as Herculean in
energy, as at the first. But the medical director and the surgeons under whose immediate
direction she was then working, and who were noble
men and her personal friends, saw that she had
reached a point of nervous exhaustion when it was
extremely perilous for her to remain longer at her
post. They compelled her to take a furlough. She
came direct to Chicago, and, as I had requested, to

my house. I was not at home when she arrived, but returned that evening. "Norwegian Martha," who had presided in my kitchen for years, and who had never before seen Mother Bickerdyke, informed me of the new arrival in characteristic style.

"Another one more of them nurse woman have come with some carpet-bag," Martha said. (The nurses sent by the Commission into the service had made my house a sort of headquarters as they passed through the city, a proceeding greatly disapproved by Martha.) "This one have no afraid to do anything, and have make herself to take a bath, and have put herself to bed till supper time. She say she have very many hundred miles rode, and very many *all-shot-up*" — shot to pieces — "soldiers to take care of, and she be got awful tired, and, poor woman, she look *seek* (sick). But she have make me to think of my poor mother, what make herself to die in Norway with so much work too hard, before to this country I come. I like this nurse woman what have come more than the rest that stayed away." The influence of Mother Bickerdyke's great maternal heart was felt everywhere.

After tea, I accompanied my family to the wedding of a friend, which was solemnized in a church near by. Wearied as Mother Bickerdyke was, she insisted on making one of the company. She believed it would rest her to see the inside of a meeting-house; it was a sight that had not blessed her eyes for eighteen months, she said. It was an intensely tedious ceremony; for the old clergyman who officiated at the marriage added to a very long prayer, a Scripture reading and a full half-hour's exhortation to good living, with directions for accomplishing it, which he counted off, firstly, secondly, thirdly, and so on. It was a sermon, in fact. After the marriage, the newly wedded halted for a few moments in the church parlor, to take leave of their friends, as they were to proceed directly to the train, *en route* for the distant city of their future residence. Mother Bickerdyke was introduced, at her request; for she had learned that the young husband held the rank of major in one of the Illinois regiments.

"My dear," said our motherly heroine in a *naïve* way to the bride, "I have enjoyed your wedding very much; it has done me as much good as a prayer-meeting. I am very much refreshed by it." (She had slept through the interminable service.) "I am sure you will make your husband a good wife, for you have got the face of a good girl; and I hope you and he will live together a good many years. If he gets wounded in battle, and falls into my hands, I will try to take good care of him for you."

"Why, Mother Bickerdyke! God bless you! I am glad to see you!" burst out the bridegroom, with a mighty welcome. "You have already taken care of me. After the battle of Donelson I was brought up on one of the boats filled with wounded men, and you took care of me, as you did of the rest, like a mother. Don't you remember a lieutenant who had a minie-ball in his leg; and the doctors wanted to amputate the leg, and he fought against their doing it, and how you helped him keep it? I am the man. Here's the old leg, good as new. I have been promoted since." But she could not recall his case among the thousands more seriously wounded whom she had since carefully nursed.

This one wedding, attended on the first evening of

her arrival, was the only recreation of her furlough.
The very next morning she set herself to work to
stimulate the increase of supplies, which were called
for now in greater quantities than ever. A meeting
of the ladies of the city was called in Bryan Hall,
and to them the earnest woman made so eloquent an
appeal, backed by such thrilling statements, that they
consecrated themselves anew to the work of relieving
our brave men. She pursued the same course at
Milwaukee, Springfield, Galesburg, Aurora, and
many other cities. With many of the leading men
of these cities she held interviews, when her devotion,
common sense, pathos, pluck, and energy, so secured
their confidence, and aroused their sympathy, that
they made large donations to the Sanitary Commission, to be repeated quarterly while the war continued.

Rested and recuperated, and having placed her two
sons at boarding-school where she could feel easy
about them, she reported to the medical director at
Memphis, as she had been ordered, in January,
1863. Immense hospitals were being organized in
that city, which was also being made a base of military and medical supplies. She was first set to
organizing the Adams Block Hospital, and, that completed, she was sent to Fort Pickering to re-organize
the "Small-pox Hospital." There had been great
neglect here; and the loathsome place had been left
uncared for until it was fouler and more noisome
than an Augean stable. But Mother Bickerdyke
was just the Hurcules to cleanse it. She raised such
a hurricane about the ears of the officials whose neglect had caused its terrible condition, as took the
heads from some of them, and sent back to their

regiments several private soldiers who had been detailed as nurses.

The storm she raised left the atmosphere and
premises sweeter than she found them. The walls
were whitewashed, the kitchens regenerated, so that
the patients could have the diet necessary to them,
and both they and their beds were supplied with fresh
clothing. Disinfectants were used with a lavish hand,
and then, leaving a matron in charge who was an
abridged edition of herself, she went to the Gayoso
Hospital, to organize and take charge of that.

In the meantime she organized anew her huge
laundries, in which was performed all the washing
of the Memphis hospitals, even when there were
eight and ten thousand patients in them. Washing-
machines, wringers, caldrons, mangles, and any other
needed laundry machinery, were sent her by the
Sanitary Commission. Her old apparatus had been
destroyed at Holly Springs, Miss., when that point
was captured by the enemy, through the incom-
petence of Colonel Murphy, of the Eighth Wisconsin.
About one million dollars' worth of ordnance, sub-
sistence, and quartermasters' stores belonging to
Grant's army was destroyed at Holly Springs at the
time of its capture; and so also was a splendidly
furnished depot of sanitary stores.·

It was some time before the medical authorities
at Memphis were able to understand Mother Bickerdyke. There was perfect harmony between the
military authorities and herself; and she readily obtained from them any co-operation she desired. As
her work increased, she asked for details of more and
more contrabands, and rations for them, until, when I
went down to Memphis, in the spring of 1863, there

were from fifty to seventy men and women in her employ. General Grant had given her a pass anywhere within the lines of his department, into all camps and hospitals, past all pickets, with authority to draw on any quartermaster in his department for army wagons to transport sanitary or hospital stores. This pass, enlarged as his department extended, she held until the end of the war.

The Sanitary Commission authorized her to draw on its depot of stores at Memphis, Cairo, or Chicago, for anything needed for the boys. She was never refused by the Indianapolis, Cincinnati, or St. Louis Commissions. Indeed, the St. Louis Commission supplied her as if she were its own accredited agent; and Mr. Yeatmen, its president, was ever one of her best friends and wisest counsellors. All this power, and authority, and opulence of relief, enlarged her sphere of action, and made her a very important personage in Memphis. She never, in a single instance, abused the trust reposed in her, but, with rigorous and terrible conscientiousness, devoted all she had and was to the cure and comfort of the soldiers in hospital, without favoritism or partiality.

With the medical authorities she was for a time at variance. The medical director at Memphis was a young man belonging to the regular army — able, industrious, skilful, and punctilious. He wished Mrs. Bickerdyke to revolve in an orbit he marked out for her — to recognize *him* as the head, and never to go beyond him, or outside him, for assistance or authority. Moreover, he was a Catholic, and naturally gave the preference to the excellent " Sisters of Mercy " as nurses; nor was he backward in publicly expressing his preference. He disapproved of Mrs. Bickerdyke's laundry; chiefly, it seemed, because he had not organized it. He did not approve of her contraband help, nor of her possessing so much power; nor, if the truth must be told, of Mother Bickerdyke herself. He could not see any excellence in a woman who worked with her own hands, who held no social position, who was as indifferent to the Queen's English as to his red tape, who cared little for the Catholic, but very much for the Congregationalist Church, and who did what she wished, when and as she wished, without consulting him, the medical director.

Mrs. Bickerdyke cared little for what he said or thought, if he did not meddle with her; for she was no more in love with the medical director than he was with her. He inspected her hospital regularly, and never found fault with it; for its perfect management defied criticism. Once, in passing through a ward, he espied some half-dozen eggs under a sick man's pillow. The man was recovering from a fever, and had a great craving for food, that could not be allowed him in his weak condition. Especially, he coveted boiled eggs; and, as the poor fellow was very babyish, Mrs. Bickerdyke had petted him in her motherly way, and tucked half a dozen hard-boiled eggs under his pillow, telling him he should have them to eat when he was well enough. The sick man found a vast deal of comfort in fondling the eggs with his hands. I have seen men in hospitals handling half a dozen potatoes under their pillows in the same way. The medical director espied the eggs, and ordered them to the kitchen, declaring " he would have no hens' nests under the pillows." The man was just weak enough to cry miserably over his loss; and the nurse in charge hastened to report the story to Mother Bickerdyke.

If any unnecessary offence came to her boys, woe to him through whom it came. She would have "shown fight" to Secretary Stanton himself, if he had been the offender. Catching up a large pail filled with eggs, she strode into the ward, her blue eyes blazing, her cheeks glowing: "Dr. ——, will you tell me what harm it does to humor a sick man in an innocent fancy? Let this boy have the eggs where he can see them. There, John, there's a whole pailful of eggs," pushing them under his bed; "and you may keep them there until they hatch, if you've a mind to." And she strode out again. The doctor chose not to hear, and the boy's eggs were not meddled with again.

A few days after, on her return from her regular visit to the Small-pox Hospital, she found that the blow which had been impending had fallen. The medical director had left a written order that all the contrabands detailed to her service should be sent to the contraband camp by nine o'clock the next morning, the hour for hospital inspection. It was night when she returned and received the order, and it was raining hard. Going to the door, she recalled the departing ambulance.

"Here, Andy," she said to the driver, "you and I must have some supper, these mules must be fed, and then we must go to General Hurlburt's headquarters. I'll see if these darkies are going to be sent to the contraband camp. If Dr. —— is going to be ugly, he'll find two can play at that game, and a woman is better at it than a man." The negroes stood around with comically doleful faces, like so many statues in ebony. They liked Mother Bickerdyke and the hospital, and they hated the camp with its forlornness.

"When's we gwine from dis yer hospittle?" they inquired.

"When I tell you to, and not before!" was her laconic answer. "Get yourself ready, Mary Livermore, to go with me!"

I protested against her taking this drive; for the streets had been torn up by the enemy before the city was surrendered, there was no gas, and no street lights, we had not the countersign, the rain poured in torrents, and the project was fraught with danger. She silenced me, "Oh, we'll leave you behind, if you're such a coward; but Andy and I'll go, safe or not safe!" Knowing that I had more prudence than she, I finally accompanied them.

Through the pouring rain, over broken and excavated streets, not a glimmer of light anywhere, save from the one lantern of the ambulance, halted at every few paces by the challenge of the closely set guards, — for Memphis, though conquered, was still a rebellious city, — Mother Bickerdyke and I toiled on to the headquarters of the Post Commander. By and by, we met the officer of the night, making the grand rounds, and he gave us the countersign. Then we proceeded a little more comfortably.

It was hard work to get access to the Commander, for he was in bed. But at last her importunity prevailed, and she was conducted to his presence. She told her story honestly, and with straightforwardness, and asked for written authority to keep her detailed contrabands until he, General Hurlburt, should revoke the order. It was granted; and back through the rain we rode, Mother Bickerdyke triumphant.

The next morning, at nine, the medical director made his appearance at the Gayoso Hospital, according to appointment. The negroes were all at their work in the kitchen, in the laundry, in the wards, everywhere, as if no order had been given for their dismissal. He came to the kitchen, where Mother Bickerdyke was making soup.

"Mrs. Bickerdyke, did you receive an order I left for you Saturday morning?"

"I did, sir!" continuing to season and taste her soup.

"An order for the dismissal of these black people to their camp?"

"Exactly, sir."

"I expected it to be obeyed!" in a positive tone of voice.

"I suppose so, sir!" very nonchalant in manner.

"And why has it not been?" in a louder tone, and with rising anger, menace in his eyes, and a flush of wrath on his cheek.

"Because, sir," turning and facing him, " General Hurlburt has given me an order to keep 'em here until he dismisses them; and, as General Hurlburt happens to outrank you, he must be obeyed before you." And putting her hand in her pocket, she produced General Hurlburt's order.

There was a storm. The doctor was vulgarly angry, and raved in a manner that was very damaging to his dignity. He threatened all sorts of dreadful things, and wound up by telling Mother Bickerdyke that "he would not have her in Memphis" — that "he would send her home before she was a week older."

"But I sha'n't go, doctor!" she answered. "I've

come down here to stay, and I mean to stay until this thing is played out. I've enlisted for the war, as the boys have, and they want me and need me, and can't get on without me; and so I shall stay, doctor, and you'll have to make up your mind to get along with me the best way you can. It's of no use for you to try to tie me up with your red tape. There's too much to be done down here to stop for that. Nor is there any sense in your getting mad because I don't play second fiddle to you; for I tell you I haven't got time for it. And, doctor, I guess you hadn't better get into a row with me, for whenever anybody does one of us two always goes to the wall, and *'tain't never me!*"

The doctor had a keen sense of the ridiculous, and Mother Bickerdyke's novel method of pacification amused him when he got over his short-lived anger. He was really a very superior officer; but like many another clever man he was dominated by the inborn belief that all women were to play " second fiddle " to him. He had the good sense to appreciate blunt Mother Bickerdyke's excellences, and when mutual friends entered on the work of pacification they were successful.

Turning to her one day, in a threatening way, but half jocularly, he said, " Take care, madam; your turn to go to the wall *may* come yet!" "May be so!" was her brief answer; and then she went on with her work. From being at disagreement, they finally came to a perfect understanding, and by and by became the best of friends.

A week after, I was in her hospital about noon, when the wardmaster of the fourth story came to the kitchen, to tell her that the surgeon of that ward

had not made his appearance, the special diet list for
the ward had not yet been made out, and the men
were suffering for their breakfasts.

"Haven't had their breakfasts! Why did'nt you
tell me of this sooner? Here, stop! The poor fellows must be fed immediately." And filling enormous tin pails and trays with coffee, soup, gruel,
toast, and other like food, she sent half a dozen men
ahead with them. Extending to me a six-gallon pail
of hot soup, she bade me follow her, being freighted
herself with a pail of similar size in each hand. I
stood looking on at the distribution, when her clarion
voice rang out to me in tones of authority; "Come,
make yourself alive, Mary Livermore! Try to be
useful! Help these men!" I never knew any one
who deliberately disregarded her orders — I had no
thought but to obey — and so I sat down to feed a
man who was too weak to help himself.

While we were all busy, the surgeon of the ward
came in, looking as if he had just risen from sleeping
off a night's debauch. Instantly there was a change
in the tones of Mother Bickerdyke's voice, and in the
expression of her face. She was no longer a tender,
pitying, sympathizing mother, but Alecto herself.

"You miserable, drunken, heartless scalawag!"
shaking her finger and head at him threateningly,
"What do you mean by leaving these fainting, suffering men to go until noon with nothing to eat, and no
attention? Not a word, sir!" as he undertook to
make an explanation. "Off with your shoulder-
straps, and get out of this hospital! I'll have them
off in three days, sir! This is your fourth spree in a
month, and you shall go where you belong. Off
with your shoulder-straps, I tell you, for they've got

to go." She was as good as her threat, for in less than a week she had made such charges against him that he was dismissed the service, and that by the very medical director with whom she had had weeks' wrangling. The dismissed surgeon went to General Sherman to complain of the injustice done him. "He had been grossly belied, and foul charges had been made against him, which he could prove false," was his declaration. "Who was your accuser?" asked General Sherman; "who made the charges?" "Why — why — I suppose," said the surgeon reluctantly, "it was that spiteful old woman, Mrs. Bickerdyke." "Oh, well, then," said Sherman, "if it was she, I can't help you. She has more power than I — she ranks me."

It was more difficult to supply the hospitals with milk and eggs than with any other necessaries. With the supplies furnished by government, the tea, coffee, sugar, flour, meat, and other like articles, which were usually of good quality, Mother Bickerdyke could work miracles in the culinary line, even when there was a lack of sanitary stores, if she could only have an abundant supply of milk and eggs. But these were very difficult to obtain. They could not be sent from the North, and they could not be purchased in sufficiently large quantities to supply the enormous demand. In the enemy's country, where the hospitals were located, their prices were exorbitant beyond belief. Mother Bickerdyke hit upon a plan to remedy these difficulties. When the medical director came into her hospital one morning, on a tour of inspection, she accosted him thus: —

"Dr. ——, do you know we are paying these Memphis secesh fifty cents for every quart of milk we use? And do you know it's such poor stuff, — two thirds chalk and water, — that if you should pour it into the trough of a respectable pig at home, he would turn up his nose, and run off, squealing in disgust?"

"Well, what can we do about it?" asked the doctor, between whom and herself there was now an excellent understanding.

"If you'll give me thirty days' furlough and transportation, I'll go home, and get all the milk and eggs that the Memphis hospitals can use."

"Get milk and eggs! Why, you could not bring them down here, if the North would give you all it has. A barrel of eggs would spoil, this warm weather, before it could reach us; and how on earth could you bring milk?"

"But I'll bring down the milk and egg producers. I'll get cows and hens, and we'll have milk and eggs of our own. The folks at home, doctor, will give us all the hens and cows we need for the use of these hospitals, and jump at the chance to do it. You needn't laugh, nor shake your head!" as he turned away, amused and incredulous. "I tell you, the people at the North ache to do something for the boys down here, and I can get fifty cows in Illinois alone for just the asking."

"Pshaw! pshaw!" said the doctor, "you would be laughed at from one end of the country to the other, if you should go on so wild an errand."

"Fiddlesticks! Who cares for that? Give me a furlough and transportation, and let me try it!"

So she came North again, and did not stop until she reached St. Louis. She was escorted as far as that city by several hundred cripples, "every one of

whom had lost either a leg or an arm." These she
saw placed in hospitals, and then came on to Chicago.
She secured the cows with little difficulty. Jacob
Strawn, of Jacksonville, one of the wealthy farmers
of Illinois, with a few of his neighbors, gave the
hundred cows without delay. They were sent to
Springfield, Ill., — whence Governor Yates had promised they should be shipped to Memphis, — in herds
of fifteen or twenty, with some one in charge of each
detachment, to take care of the animals.

The hens were sent to the rooms of the Commission in Chicago. In a week after the call, our building was transformed into a huge hennery, and all the
workers therein were completely driven out. The
din of crowing, cackling, and quarrelling was unbearable; and, as the weather was warm, the odor
was yet more insupportable. The fowls were despatched to Memphis in four shipments, in coops
containing about two dozen each.

Before her thirty days' leave of absence was ended,
Mother Bickerdyke was on the return route to her
hospital, forming a part of a bizarre procession of
over one hundred cows and one thousand hens, strung
all along the road from Chicago to Memphis. She
entered the city in triumph, amid immense lowing
and crowing and cackling. She informed the astonished Memphians that, " These are *loyal* cows and
hens; none of your miserable trash that give chalk
and water for milk, and lay loud-smelling eggs."

General Hurlburt, who was then at the head of the
department, hearing of this novel immigration within
his lines, gave up to the noisy new-comers President's Island, lying in the Mississippi opposite Memphis, a stretch of land so elevated that it is above the

highest stage of water. Contrabands were detailed to take charge of them; and as long as Mrs. Bickerdyke remained in Memphis there was an abundance of milk and eggs for the use of the hospitals.

Mrs. Bickerdyke remained at Memphis till after the fall of Vicksburg. During the siege of that defiant stronghold, she went again and again to the hospitals, — a little beyond the reach of the guns, — taking lemons, ice, condensed milk, and portable lemonade. She always left the heroic sufferers more cheerful and comfortable, in their stifling little coops of temporary hospitals, for the good cheer of her visit. After the fall of Vicksburg, she remained at that point, and at Jackson, Miss., until the hospitals were nearly emptied of their severely wounded or sick men. No one ever worked more heroically, unselfishly and untiringly, than did this large-hearted woman for the welfare of sick and suffering soldiers.

# CHAPTER XXVI.

MOTHER BICKERDYKE AND GENERAL SHERMAN — A NIGHT
OF HORROR — HEROIC EFFORTS TO SAVE THE WOUNDED
FROM FREEZING — HEART-RENDING SCENES AND TERRI-
BLE SUFFERING.

Mother Bickerdyke's Idolatry of General Sherman — She becomes an *Attachée* of his Corps — Comes to Chicago and does good Work for Soldiers' Families — Goes to Chattanooga after the Battle, and establishes a
Hospital — Incredible Exertion to save her Patients from Freezing —
Orders Breastworks torn down for Fuel — "All right, Major, I'm arrested! Only don't meddle with me till the Weather moderates!" — General Burnside beleaguered in Knoxville, Tenn. — Sherman marches to
his Relief — Fearful Suffering from Cold and short Rations — Horrors of
the Return Route to Chattanooga — Railroad from Nashville completed
at last — Joyful Welcome of the first Train — All Night in the icy Gale
— She ran from Tent to Tent — She encouraged the shivering Soldiers —
Her Name mentioned only with Tears.

ENERAL SHERMAN was the *beau idéal*
of Mother Bickerdyke. He was her great
man and great soldier. She would always
defend General Grant like a tigress if he
were assailed; but it was clear to every one
that General Sherman was the special object
of her idolatry. And to-day I think she would find
it easy to give her life for Sherman, if the sacrifice
were necessary. She would count it a small thing to
die for him. She rates him higher than Grant,
higher than Lincoln, and altogether superior as a
soldier to Washington or Wellington; and woe to
the luckless wight who would dare lower her ideal!

515

General Sherman on his side fully appreciated Mother Bickerdyke; and when he was curt and repellant to all agents, nurses, and employés of the Sanitary, Christian, and State Commissions, she had the *entrée* to his headquarters, and obtained any favor she chose to ask. There was something in her character akin to his own. Both were restless, impetuous, fiery, hard working, and indomitable. After the fall of Vicksburg, Mother Bickerdyke became a special *attachée* of his corps, the Fifteenth. Ever after, during the war, she considered herself in a special sense under Sherman's direction; and the soldiers of the Fifteenth Corps have always claimed exclusive ownership of her.

When Sherman went to re-enforce Grant at Chattanooga, she came North, by Sherman's direction, and hastened to the same destination by way of Louisville; but, as Sherman's army was to march from the Big Black, across the enemy's country, to Chattanooga, and she was to go round by railroad and steamboat, she had a few days to spare, and came again to Chicago for a brief visit. Her exploits in supplying Memphis with milk and eggs, as well as the grand accounts of her famous nursing, brought home by furloughed soldiers who were scattered through every town in the Northwest, had given her an enviable notoriety. Everybody wanted to see the good woman, and to aid her personally, or assist in her work. Her arrival in Chicago was announced in the papers, when she was overwhelmed with attentions, which she put aside with the utmost indifference. Invitations to visit towns, cities, and societies, poured in upon her like a flood. Receptions were tendered her, ladies offered to make par-

ties for her, and the invitations to lunch came by
dozens. But she declined all, with the stereotyped
rebuke "that the country had a big war on its hands,
and that this was no time for visiting or frolicking."
She made several visits to the families of soldiers
whom she had left in hospital, resident in the vicinity
of Chicago, always carrying aid and comfort with
her.

She found one of these families in great distress
and poverty. The husband and father had been in
positions for ten months that removed him beyond
reach of the paymaster; and his family were in great
need of the money which he failed to receive. They
were owing six months' house rent; and the landlord, a hard man, had served a writ of ejectment
upon them, and was preparing to put them summarily into the street. Mother Bickerdyke paid him a
visit at his office, and sought to turn him from his
purpose with all the peculiar eloquence of which she
was mistress. He could not be moved, but scorned
her and ordered her from his premises. She rose to
go, and, taking a Bible from the shelf, which was
never used except to give legality to oaths, she
opened to the sixteenth chapter of Luke, and, strain-
ing to her full height, with a solemn and almost terrible face, she read these words before an audience
of a dozen or more men, —

"'And it came to pass that the beggar died, and
was carried by angels into Abraham's bosom. The
rich man also died and was buried, and in *hell* —
in HELL — in HELL,'"—increasing the emphasis
each time — "'he lifted up his eyes, being in tor-
ments, and saw Abraham afar off, and Lazarus in
his bosom.' You see what you are coming to,

sir," she added, "and the time may not be far off. May God have mercy on your mean soul! Goodbye." Then the resolute woman sought another house for the soldier's family, and rested not in her humane work until she had raised the money to pay the rent six months in advance.

Her visits always stirred us up at the North. Whenever she needed an extra quantity of sanitary stores, she would write us word to "stir up the aid societies as with a big spoon." And this work was effectually accomplished by one of her visits. Her detailed account of the work done in ministering to our sick and wounded men, the methods employed, together with a recital of events in which she had participated, would quicken our flagging spirits, and incite us all to new labor and sacrifice.

Hardly was the battle of Chattanooga fought, when Mother Bickerdyke was established at the base of Mission Ridge, in a field hospital. Here she was the only woman at work for nearly six weeks. In the very midst of the din and smoke of the carnage, she began to receive the wounded and exhausted, until very nearly two thousand of the worst cases were assigned to her nursing. Never did she render more valuable service. The Sanitary Commission had pushed through from Louisville, with immense trains of wagons, heavily loaded with supplies, and had bountifully provided Mother Bickerdyke with the stores most needed after the battle. The railroad running from Nashville, badly built, with poor material, and for light travel, had been used up long before. But as Chattanooga was to be the base of the army for some time, another road was necessary for heavy army use, and this was now in process of construction. Everything, therefore, needed for the army, — rations and clothing for the men, provender for the horses and mules, hospital supplies for the wounded and sick, — was hauled through in army wagons, while this work was being done.

No pen can depict, and no tongue narrate the sufferings, hardships, and privations of our brave men in southern and eastern Tennessee, during the months of November, December, and January, of 1863 and 1864. Hunger and cold, famine and nakedness were their inseparable companions. Horses and mules starved also, ten thousand animals starving at Chattanooga. The reproachful whinnying complaints of the famishing beasts wrung the hearts of the soldiers, even when they were slowly dying themselves from lack of food.

Mother Bickerdyke's field hospital was on the edge of a forest, five miles from Chattanooga. The weather was as arctic as in New England in the same season. Men were detailed to fell the trees and pile log heaps, which were kept continually burning, to warm the camps and hospitals. These log fires were her only means of cooking; nor could any other be hoped for until the railroad was completed. By these log fires Mother Bickerdyke, with her aids, contrabands, or convalescent soldiers, did all the cooking for her two thousand patients. Here she made tea and coffee, soup and toast. Here she broiled beef and mutton without a gridiron. Here she baked bread by a process of her own invention, blistering her fingers while doing it, and burning her clothing. A dress which she wore at this time came into my hands, and was kept at the rooms of the

Commission for some time as a curiosity. It was burned so full of holes that it would hardly hang together when held up. It looked as if grape and canister had played hide-and-seek through it.

"The boys were all the time putting me out," she said, meaning her dress; "and a dozen of 'em were grabbing me whenever I was cooking by the log fires; for the fire would snap, and my clothes would catch, but I couldn't tell where." After a time men were detailed to tear down some of the store-houses, with the lumber of which they put bunks into other similar buildings, and these served as hospitals. With bricks from the demolished chimneys the men constructed ovens of her design, more convenient for the baking of bread. In one of her foraging expeditions she came across huge potash kettles, and an abandoned mill, where was plenty of flour, cattle, and sheep, which had belonged to General Bragg's discomfited army. All these were laid under contribution for the camp and the hospital.

The last day of the year 1863 was one of memorable coldness, as were the first few days of the year 1864. The rigor of the weather in Chicago at that time actually suspended all outdoor business, and laid an embargo on travel in the streets. It was even severer weather in Mother Bickerdyke's location; for the icy winds swept down Lookout Mountain, where they were re-enforced by currents of air that tore through the valleys of Mission Ridge, creating a furious arctic hurricane that overturned the hospital tents in which the most badly wounded men were located. It hurled the partially recovered patients out into the pouring rain, that became glare-ice as it touched the earth, breaking anew their healing bones, and chilling their attenuated frames with the piercing mountain gale.

The rain fell in torrents in the mountains, and poured down their sides so furiously and suddenly that it made a great flood in the valleys at their base. Before the intense cold could stiffen the headlong current into ice, it swept out into the swollen creeks several of the feeblest of the men under single hospital tents; and they were drowned. Night set in intensely cold, for which the badly fitted up hospitals were wholly unprepared.

All that night Mother Bickerdyke worked like a Titan to save her bloodless, feeble patients from being frozen to death. There were several hundred in hospital tents — all wounded men — all bad cases. The fires were piled higher and higher with logs, new fires were kindled which came nearly to the tents, until they were surrounded by a cordon of immense pyres, that roared and crackled in the stinging atmosphere. But before midnight the fuel gave out. To send men out into the forests to cut more, in the darkness and awful coldness, seemed barbarous. The surgeon in charge dared not order them out, and it is doubtful if the order could have been obeyed had it been given. " We must try and pull through until morning," he said, " for nothing can be done to-night." And he retired to his own quarters, in a helpless mood of mind.

Mother Bickerdyke was equal to the emergency. With her usual disdain of red tape, she appealed to the Pioneer Corps to take their mules, axes, hooks, and chains, and tear down the breastworks near them, made of logs with earth thrown up against them. They were of no value, having served their purpose during the campaign. Nevertheless, an order for their demolition was necessary if they were to be destroyed. There was no officer of sufficiently high rank present to dare give this order; but, after she had refreshed the shivering men with a cup or two of panado, composed of hot water, sugar, crackers, and whiskey, they went to work at her suggestion, without orders from officers. They knew, as did she, that on the continuance of the huge fires through the night, depended the lives of hundreds of their wounded comrades; for there was no bedding for the tents, only a blanket or two for each wounded suffering man.

The men of the corps set to work tearing down the breastworks, and hauling the logs to the fierce fires, while Mother Bickerdyke ordered half a dozen barrels of meal to be broken open, and mixed with warm water, for their mules. Immense caldrons of hot drinks were renewedly made under her direction — hot coffee, panado, and other nourishing potables; and layers of hot bricks were put around every wounded and sick man of the entire fifteen hundred as he lay in his cot. From tent to tent she ran all the night in the icy gale, hot bricks in one hand, and hot drinks in the other, cheering, warming, and encouraging the poor shivering fellows.

Suddenly there was a great cry of horror; and, looking in the direction whence it proceeded, she saw thirteen ambulances filled with wounded men, who had been started for her hospital from Ringgold, in the morning, by order of the authorities. It had become necessary to break up the small outlying post hospitals, and concentrate at Chattanooga. These had been delayed by the rain and the gale, and for hours had been travelling in the darkness and unparalleled coldness, both mules and drivers being nearly exhausted and frozen. On opening the ambulances, what a spectacle met Mother Bickerdyke's eyes! They were filled with wounded men nearly chilled to death. The hands of one were frozen like marble. The feet of another, the face of another, the bowels of a fourth, who afterwards died. Every bandage had stiffened into ice. The kegs of water had become solid crystal; and the men, who were past complaining, almost past suffering, were dropping into the sleep that ends in death. The surgeons of the hospital were all at work through the night with Mrs. Bickerdyke, and came promptly to the relief of these poor men, hardly one of whom escaped amputation of frozen limbs from that night's fearful ride.

As the night was breaking into the cold gray day, the officer in command of the post was informed of Mother Bickerdyke's unauthorized exploits. He hastened down where the demolished breastworks were being rapidly devoured by the fierce flames. He took in the situation immediately, and evidently saw the necessity and wisdom of the course she had pursued. But it was his business to preserve order and maintain discipline; and so he made a show of arresting the irregular proceeding. By no mere order of his could this be done. Not until daydawn, when they could go safely into the woods to cut fuel, were the men disposed to abate their raid on the breastworks, which had served their purpose of defence against the enemy weeks before.

"Madam, consider yourself under arrest!" was the Major's address to ubiquitous Mother Bickerdyke.

To which she replied, as she flew past him with
hot bricks and hot drinks, "All right, Major! I'm
arrested! Only don't meddle with me till the weather
moderates; for my men will freeze to death, if you
do!"

A story got in circulation that she was put in the
guard-house by the Major; but this was not true.
There was some little official hubbub over her
night's exploits, but she defended herself to the
officers who reproved her, with this indisputable
statement, "It's lucky for you, old fellows, that I
did what I did. For if I hadn't, hundreds of men in
the hospital tents would have frozen to death. No
one at the North would have blamed *me*, but there
would have been such a hullabaloo about your heads
for allowing it to happen, that you would have lost
them, whether or no." Some of the officers stood
boldly by her, openly declaring that she had done
right, and advised her to pursue the same course
again, under the same circumstances. This was
needless advice, as she would assuredly have done
so.

The men for whom she labored so indefatigably
could mention her name only with tears and benedictions. And those in camp manifested their approval
of her by hailing her with three times three deafening hurrahs whenever she appeared among them,
until, annoyed, she begged them "for Heaven's
sake to stop their nonsense, and shut up!"

Every form of suffering came at once that winter,
in that section of Tennessee. While the inclement
weather was at its worst, the men were suffering
from short rations, consequent on their distance from
the base of supplies, and the lack of railroad com-

munication. They were in the enemy's country, which had been stripped and peeled for the sustenance of their own troops. It was impossible to keep the large army in that vicinity fully supplied, until the railroad from Nashville was completed — and that was being pushed forward with all possible despatch. Whole brigades were called out to receive as their daily rations three ears of corn to a man, while the horses and mules were served more generously. For the famished beasts had not the spirit of the American soldiers to keep them alive, whether well fed or not. And yet so wild with hunger were many of the men, that a guard stood over the animals while they were feeding, to protect them from the pilfering of the soldiers — and this did not always restrain them.

In the meantime General Burnside, in command of the Ninth and Twenty-third Corps, had crossed the mountains to Eastern Tennessee. Leaving behind his commissary wagons, and subsisting his army on such poor rations as came in their way, avoiding the safe and travelled routes, which were strongly defended by the rebel army, he moved so secretly and rapidly that his approach was not even suspected. The rebel troops were panic-stricken at the appearance of the Union forces, and fled in dismay, leaving behind them in Knoxville a large quantity of quartermaster's stores. So confident was General Bragg of his ability to manage the army under Grant and Sherman at Chattanooga, that he sent Longstreet with his division to recapture Knoxville, of which General Burnside had taken possession. It was the only instance during the war when the Union forces sustained a siege. For three weeks Burnside and his men were locked up in Knoxville, enduring the pangs of hunger, expecting hourly the assaults of the enemy, and ignorant of the fate of the army at Chattanooga.

At last, Burnside managed to send a despatch to General Grant, saying that his supplies would not last a week, and asking for help. Knoxville was ninety miles distant, and to reach it in time to save Burnside would require heavy marching. When Sherman received the order to go to his relief he said: "Seven days before, we left our camps on the other side of the Tennessee with two days' rations, without a change of clothing, stripped for the fight, with but a single blanket or coat per man, from myself to the private, included. We have no provisions but what we have gathered by the road, and are ill-supplied for such a march; but fifteen thousand of our fellow-soldiers are beleaguered in the mountain town of Knoxville; they need relief, and must have it in three days. *That is enough, and it shall be done!*"

His tired troops cheerfully consented to follow their leader on this long march, and started that night. They pressed forward rapidly, at great cost of men and animals, determined to accomplish their errand. But their rapid approach, flushed with victory, was sufficient to drive off the besiegers from Knoxville; and, when they had seen Longstreet decamp with his tatterdemalion troops, they turned and marched back to Chattanooga.

Many of them were in a deplorable condition; for, when the Fifteenth Corps started from the Big Black under General Sherman to re-enforce General Grant, they were clad in summer clothes, light blouses, poor shoes, and thin garments. No distribution of clothing was made to them before they started for Knoxville; for all army supplies were waiting the transportation of the not yet completed railroad. Their insufficient garments were worn out with hard service; and, shivering in summer rags in frigid midwinter, with the smallest amount of food that would keep body and soul together, with worn out shoes, and bruised feet, they came back over the mountains, sometimes tracking their path in blood. No banners waved over them, no martial music inspired them; not even such cheer was theirs as comes from a march in serried columns, where each man seeks to help his comrade onward.

But in squads of twenty, thirty, or fifty, — now in large companies, and then in smaller groups, — sometimes singly and alone, — the weary, famished, shivering, footsore conquerors painfully made their way back. Many sank on the march, and left their bones to bleach on the mountains. Others were so spent with fatigue that they reached Chattanooga only to die. Some live, testimonies to the hardships of that winter, utterly broken in constitution, and doomed to invalidism for the remainder of a reluctant life.

As the poor fellows trooped into Mother Bickerdyke's hospital, she had little to offer them, save sympathy and kind words. She, brave woman, was on short rations with the rest, and often gave up her meagre allowance of food to some wistful, weary soldier less able to fast than herself. But she supplied them with warm water for their swollen and bleeding feet, which had been wrapped by the men in the cut-off skirts of their blouses, on the return march. Sometimes the cloth had festered into the wounded feet, and it required careful nursing to save them from amputation. She taxed her ingenuity to make much out of the little they possessed, and concocted *outré* soups of unusual materials, for which no cook-book has ever given receipts.

Nothing that she did was amiss with them; and the singular preparations of food which she sometimes furnished them from an almost empty larder, were devoured with the keenest relish. "When I get home, boys," she used to tell the men, jocularly, "I shall publish a starvation cook-book, containing receipts for making delicious dishes out of nothing." If any one could prepare such a manual, Mother Bickerdyke is that person.

At last, as the winter was ending, the railroad was completed. One day, when the gloom hung deepest over camp and hospital, a distant and not very distinct sound, as of a steam whistle, aroused the attention of the long-enduring men. Hospital patients sat up, hushed, voiceless, listening for its repetition. It came presently; and as the train rounded the curve to the station, the grateful sound of a long, loud, shrill blast from the whistle of the locomotive smote their ears. It was pleasanter music than any instrument of sweetest note could make.

One mighty shout from camp and hospital answered it; and then a tide of blue-coated humanity surged down to welcome the incoming train. That long-expected train signified to them food, clothing, warmth, comfort, communication with the far-off homes, from which no tidings had reached them for months. They were *not* forgotten — the long-silent North was reaching down to them with hundred-handed bounty.

Up sprang the maimed from their cots, and reached for their rough crutches. Up slowly crept the feeble who had thought themselves done with life, and had turned their faces heavenward. Men who could not walk were led along between those who were stronger, or sometimes borne on the backs of the strongest. And as they saw the long, loaded train halt in their midst, they went wild with joy. They cheered the railroad — the train — the North — the food that had come — the barrels of " Boston crackers," speedily unheaded for them. They patted the giant locomotive, and caressed it as though it were a pet horse. And when three times three cheers were proposed for home, men who were dying, and whose last breath exhaled from their lips a few minutes later, threw up their white wasted hands, and their lips moved in wordless sympathy with the great roar of shouts from manly throats.

# CHAPTER XXVII.

STORY OF MOTHER BICKERDYKE CONCLUDED — FOLLOWING
THE FLAG IN THE ATLANTA CAMPAIGN — HER MOTH-
ERLY MINISTRATIONS IN THE MIDST OF BATTLE — HER
LIFE AND CAREER SINCE THE WAR.

Mother Bickerdyke makes an eloquent Speech — Disregards Sherman's
Orders, and calls on him. Obtains the Favor she seeks — Six Months
in the Rear of Battles — Death of General McPherson — Sherman
begins his March to the Sea — Mother Bickerdyke packs all Hospital
Supplies, and sends to Nashville — Goes to meet Sherman, with a
Steamer loaded with Supplies, as he directed — They are not needed,
and she cares for the Andersonville Prisoners — The War ends, and she
returns to Louisville — Her Life since the War — The Government
grants a pension to her — The Soldiers do not forget her — Her Effort
to keep a Hotel in Kansas not a Success — Unsectarian, but Christian —
Her present Home.

NOW for the first time, and the only time,
Mother Bickerdyke broke down. The
hardships through which she had passed,
her labors, her fastings, her anxieties, had
been sufficient to kill a dozen women. She
was greatly reduced by them; and as soon as
her place could be supplied by another matron, she
came North, a mere shadow of her former self.

The same efforts were made to honor her as on a
previous visit; but, as before, she put aside all invitations. She had rendered great service to the Wisconsin regiments in the Western army; and the
people of Milwaukee, who were just then holding a

fair for the relief of sick and wounded soldiers, would not be denied the pleasure of a visit from her. I accompanied her, for she refused to go anywhere to be lionized unless some one was with her, " to bear the brunt of the nonsense," as she phrased it. She was overwhelmed with attentions. The Milwaukee Chamber of Commerce had made an appropriation of twelve hundred dollars a month for hospital relief, to be continued until the end of the war. And she was invited to their handsome hall, to receive from them a formal expression of gratitude for her care of Wisconsin soldiers. Ladies were invited to occupy the gallery, which they packed to the utmost. A very felicitous address was made her by the President of the Board of Trade, in behalf of the state of Wisconsin, and she was eloquently thanked for her patriotic labors, and informed of the recent pledge of the Board. A reply was expected of her, which I feared she would decline to make; but she answered briefly, simply, and with great power.

"I am much obliged to you, gentlemen," she answered, " for the kind things you have said. I haven't done much, no more than I ought; neither have you. I am glad you are going to give twelve hundred dollars a month for the poor fellows in the hospitals; for it's no more than you ought to do, and it isn't half as much as the soldiers in the hospitals have given for you. Suppose, gentlemen, you had got to give to-night one thousand dollars or your right leg, would it take long to decide which to surrender? Two thousand dollars or your right arm; five thousand dollars or both your eyes; all that you are worth or your life?

" But I have got eighteen hundred boys in my hos-

pital at Chattanooga who have given one arm, and
one leg, and some have given both; and yet they
don't seem to think they have done a great deal for
their country.  And the graveyard behind the hospital, and the battle-field a little farther off, contain the
bodies of thousands who have freely given their lives
to save you and your homes and your country from
ruin.  Oh, gentlemen of Milwaukee, don't let *us* be
telling of what *we* have given, and what *we* have
done!  *We* have done nothing, and given nothing, in
comparison with *them!*  And it's our duty to keep
on giving and doing just as long as there's a soldier
down South fighting or suffering for us."

It would not be easy to match the pathos and eloquence of this untutored speech.

As soon as she had regained health and strength,
Mother Bickerdyke returned to her post.  General
Sherman was pouring supplies, provender, and ammunition into Chattanooga; for it was to be his base
of supplies for the Atlanta campaign.  He had issued
an order absolutely forbidding agents of sanitary
stores, or agents of any description, to go over the
road from Nashville to Chattanooga.  He alleged as
the reason for this prohibition that he wished the
entire ability of the railroad devoted to strictly active
military operations.  There was great distress in the
hospitals below Nashville, in consequence of this
stringent order, and uneasiness and anxiety at the
North, because of its seemingly needless inhumanity.
Mother Bickerdyke found Nashville full of worried
agents, and of sanitary stores that were needed down
the road, and spoiling for lack of transportation.
Her pass from General Grant would take her to
Chattanooga despite General Sherman's prohibition.

Before starting, her fertility of invention manifested itself in a characteristic act. Ambulances with mules in harness were being sent to various points, against the day of need. No barrels were allowed in these ambulances; but all the bags they could hold could be crowded in. Getting such help as she could muster, they made bags, which were filled with dried apples, peaches, potatoes, and any other sanitary articles that could be sent in them as well as in barrels; and the ambulances went away packed with articles for the hospitals. Forty such left for Huntsville, Ala., thirty for Bridgeport, and several for other points. Then Mother Bickerdyke, despite remonstrance and opposition, took the next train for Chattanooga, and made her unexpected *début* at General Sherman's headquarters.

"Halloo! Why, how did you get down here?" asked one of the General's staff officers, as he saw her enter Sherman's headquarters.

"Came down in the cars, of course. There's no other way of getting down here that I know of," replied the matter-of-fact woman. "I want to see General Sherman."

"He is in there, writing," said the officer, pointing to an inner room; "but I guess he won't see you."

"Guess he *will!*" and she pushed into the apartment. "Good morning, General! I want to speak to you a moment. May I come in?"

"I should think you had got in!" answered the General, barely looking up, in great annoyance. "What's up now?"

"Why, General," said the earnest matron, in a perfect torrent of words, "we can't stand this last order of yours, nohow. You'll have to change it, as sure as you live. We can get along without any more nurses and agents, but the supplies we *must* have. The sick and wounded men need them, and you'll have to give permission to bring them down. The fact is, General, after a man is unable to carry a gun, and drops out of the lines, you don't trouble yourself about him, but turn him over to the hospitals, expecting the doctors and nurses to get him well and put back again into the service as soon as possible. But how are we going to make bricks without straw? Tell me that if you can."

"Well, I'm busy to-day, and cannot attend to you. I will see you some other time." But though Sherman kept on writing, and did not look up, Mother Bickerdyke saw a smile lurking in the corner of his mouth, and knew she would carry her point. So she persisted.

"No, General! Don't send me away until you've fixed this thing as it ought to be fixed. You had me assigned to your corps, and told me that you expected me to look after the nursing of the men who needed it. But I should like to know how I can do this if I don't have anything to work with? Have some sense about it now, General!"

There was a hearty laugh at this, and a little badinage ensued, which Mother Bickerdyke ended in her brusque way, with, "Well, I can't stand fooling here all day. Now, General, write an order for two cars a day to be sent down from the Sanitary Commission at Nashville, and I'll be satisfied." The order was written, and for weeks all the sanitary stores sent from Nashville to Chattanooga, and the posts along that road, were sent directly or indirectly through this mediation of Mother Bickerdyke.

When General Sherman was prepared to move on his Atlanta campaign, Mother Bickerdyke with Mrs. Porter accompanied the army on its bloody but victorious march. They were constantly in the immediate rear of the fighting, and made extraordinary exertions to keep the department of special relief at its very highest point of efficiency. In this they were aided by the Sanitary Commission, and by the army officers. It was not unwise for officers to reveal to Mrs. Bickerdyke enough of army plans to enable her to make preparation for coming emergencies, for she always proved a safe depositary of secrets. Those who worked with her most constantly saw that she generally knew when to have prepared in the hospitals, huge kettles of coffee, soup, and mush; when to have rough beds made of pine and hemlock boughs with the large stems cut out, on which were spread blankets; when to order forward teams laden with supplies, following herself in close proximity in an ambulance. They attributed her promptness to intelligent foresight; but it was actual knowledge of coming events, in most cases.

I despair of giving any account of the work accomplished by Mrs. Bickerdyke and Mrs. Porter from April to November of 1864. What it is to "follow an army" when there is no fighting in progress, can only be understood by those who have experienced it. What it was to follow Sherman's army in that Atlanta campaign, when it fought every foot of the way, over rugged mountains, through deep, narrow ravines, through thick, primitive woods, across headlong rivers — to follow with only the one aim of ministering to the exhausted, the suffering, the wounded, the dying — with only a blanket and a pillow for a bed — the roar of artillery, the clash of arms, the cries of distress, and the shout of battle continually resounding — to live night and day in the midst of these horrors, in constant attendance upon the mangled and anguished soldiers brought to them from the rear, or taken to their extemporized hospitals, — this cannot be described.

As they were pushing along in their ambulance on one occasion, packed with battle-stores, they heard the distant sounds of a fierce cannonade — and knew that a battle was in progress ahead of them. On they went, the sounds becoming louder, clearer, and more distinct. Now it was mingled with the crash of musketry, the calls of half a hundred bugles, the thundered commands of officers leading their men to the conflict, the yells of the infuriated soldiers as they hurled themselves on their antagonists with the shock of an avalanche — and sometimes, overtopping all, the awful cries of mortal agony, that came up from the battle-field, from men writhing in every form of ghastly wound. They were in the rear of the battle of Resaca. On one side were heaped the knapsacks, and other *impedimenta,* of which the men had stripped themselves for the fight — on the other the amputating tents of the surgeons, surrounded by an ever-increasing quantity of mangled and dissevered limbs. The field hospitals were in readiness for the wounded, who lay about under trees, and on the grass, awaiting their turn at the amputating table, or to have their wounds dressed.

In a very short time both women were at work. Their portable kettles, with furnaces attached, were set up, their concentrated extract of beef was uncanned, and soon the fainting and famishing men were uttering their thanks for the great refreshment of a palatable soup. In the interim, they dressed wounds, took down memoranda of last messages to be sent North to friends, received and labelled dying gifts to be distributed East, West, and North, encouraged the desponding, and sped the parting soul to Heaven with a brief verse of hymn, a quotation from the words of Christ, or a fervent and tender prayer. This arduous but blessed work they continued at Kingston, Altoona, and Kenesaw Mountain, on to Atlanta.

Never were the services of women more needed; never were soldiers more grateful for their motherly ministrations. The Atlanta campaign was made a success, not alone by the consummate genius and skill of its great commander, but by downright, unflinching, courageous hard fighting, such as the world has never seen surpassed. The whole campaign must forever stand unsurpassed in the annals of history.

Nor were the enemy less daring and wondrously brave than the Union forces. "For half an hour the two armies fought face to face, each side of the same line of intrenchments, with the battle colors of the respective armies flying from the same works." At the battle of Atlanta, General McPherson was killed, an officer beloved by all, civilians, privates, and commanders. General Grant discovered his worth, and depended on him, long before the public had heard of him. He was very able in council, or on the field, and was as noble and pure-minded as he was able. When the tidings of his death reached General Sherman, he turned away from his staff officers, and burst into tears. Nor was General

Grant less afflicted. Always reticent and undemonstrative, he walked away to his headquarters, where, for a long time, he was alone with his sorrow. With her usual thoughtfulness, Mother Bickerdyke took the blouse in which General McPherson met his death, and which was saturated with his blood, washed it, and then forwarded it to the bereaved mother of the dead officer.

After Sherman had taken possession of Atlanta, Mother Bickerdyke went there also, pursuing her unwearied work as the good Samaritan of the soldiers. Not until Sherman stood detached from his communications, with his whole force grouped about Atlanta, ready for his march to the sea, did she prepare for her departure. Then she superintended the packing and boxing of all the hospital supplies, saw them safely and securely on their way to Nashville, and left the doomed city. And then Atlanta was on fire; and, as she looked back, on her road northward, it was enveloped in smoke and flames, like a second Sodom and Gomorrah.

General Sherman had directed her to meet him when he reached the Atlantic coast, and to bring to his troops all the supplies that could be gathered. He gave her orders for transportation on his account to any desired extent. She was in Philadelphia, on the lookout for tidings from him, when he reached Savannah. With his orders, she had obtained a steamboat from the quartermaster; and then she called on the Christian Commission to fill it. Its president, George H. Stuart, did not hesitate to grant Mrs. Bickerdyke's request. The boat was loaded under his direction, with choice dried and canned fruits, clothing, crackers, butter, cheese, tea, sugar, condensed milk, tapioca, extract of beef, corn starch, lemons, oranges, tin cups for drinking, a span of mules, an ambulance for her own use, — everything, in short, suggested by knowledge and experience.

It steamed to Wilmington, S. C., carrying happy Mother Bickerdyke along. Here the Andersonville prisoners were first brought, and again the indefatigable woman set to work, regardless of Sherman and his soldiers, who were well enough without her; for they appeared at Savannah fat and hearty; and if ragged and dirty, the government was able to supply in full their demands for clothing and rations. But the poor Andersonville victims, who had been starved into idiocy and lunacy, now claimed her attention; and not until the last of these were buried, or were able to leave for the North, did she take her departure.

By this time Lee had capitulated, the war was ended, and the whole country was given up to a delirium of thankfulness. Then she followed the stream of blue-coats to Washington, finding daily more work to do than a dozen could perform. She had the great pleasure of witnessing the grand review of the troops at Washington, and then went West, laboring in the hospitals at Louisville and Nashville until they were closed.

While she was at Louisville, some troops left for a distant post in Texas, where scurvy was making sad havoc. As a quantity of anti-scorbutics could be forwarded to the sufferers in the care of these soldiers, Mrs. Bickerdyke decided it should be done. The vegetables could reach their destination without trans-shipment; the captain of the boat promised to delay the departure of the steamer until their arrival on the wharf. Under difficulties that would have thwarted any women less resolute than Mrs. Bickerdyke and Mrs. Porter, wagons were hired, the potatoes loaded, and started for the wharf, both ladies accompanying the shipment. The rain poured in torrents, the mud was almost impassable, and the drivers made slow time. When they reached the landing the boat was far out in the stream.

"It shall come back!" said indomitable Mother Bickerdyke; and, rising in the wagon, while the rain pelted both women piteously, she beckoned energetically to the boat to return. The captain saw her, and seemed to be considering. With yet more emphasis and authority, she waved renewed signals for a return. The boat slackened speed. Now, drivers, bystanders, and both women, by pantomime, that expressed entreaty and command, urged the boat to retrace its course. It rounded to, steamed back to the landing, and took the anti-scorbutics on board.

"I didn't think you could get them down here in this pouring rain, especially as it is Sunday!" explained the captain.

"*Didn't think!*" said Mother Bickerdyke. "Sakes alive! What did you suppose I meant when I told you they *should* be here at the time you appointed? I mean what I say, and I like to have folks do as they agree."

The next morning a caricature appeared in the shop windows of Louisville, representing a woman in a Shaker bonnet ordering a government steamer with a wave of her hand. A copy of it found its way to the rooms of the Commission.

For a year after the war, Mother Bickerdyke

served as house-keeper in the Chicago " Home of the Friendless," where the family averaged one hundred and fifty. Such house-keeping never was known there before. It seemed small business to her, however, and she became discontented and left. She pushed West into Kansas, which was fast filling up with returned soldiers, who were eager to locate the one hundred and sixty acres of land given them by government within the limits of that promising state. She pre-empted her claim with the " boys," taking care to secure it, so that eventually it would become the property of her sons.

Encouraged and aided by the Kansas Pacific Railroad Company, she opened a hotel at Salina, a town of about a thousand inhabitants at that time, lying on the Santa Fé route. Five trains daily passed to and fro through the town, while the " prairie schooners," as the emigrant wagons were called, maintained an almost unbroken procession westward past her doors. She called her house " The Salina Dining-Hall "; but everybody else called it " The Bickerdyke House." In her dining-room, where one hundred and ten persons could be comfortably seated, one was always certain of an excellent meal, well cooked and well served, while the neatness of the whole establishment was proverbial. There were thirty-three sleeping rooms in the house, plainly furnished, but glorified by wonderful cleanliness. When she could pay for the property she was to become its owner. Were Mother Bickerdyke the excellent financier that she is nurse and house-keeper, she would now be in possession of a comfortable home and of a valuable piece of property. It is not often that one woman combines in herself all excellent, or even necessary qualities; and Mother Bickerdyke's hotel passed out of her hands through her lack of financial skill.

When Kansas was ravaged by locusts, and the people were brought to the verge of starvation, she came East to solicit help for them. Carloads of food and clothing were forwarded to various reliable parties for distribution, at her suggestion, while she remained in the field, stimulating continued donations. She went to Washington to plead for seed for the farmers, which was granted in abundance, and only ceased her efforts when the needs of the destitute people were supplied.

She repeated this merciful work when the forest fires of Northern Michigan swept away millions of dollars worth of property, and caused the loss of hundreds of lives. The suffering and destitution of that section of country were inexpressible, and Mother Bickerdyke bent her energies again to the work of relief, distributing in person the supplies she collected. Her executive ability was called into requisition, as, with her customary ubiquity, she was here and there and everywhere, seeking to rebuild homes which had been destroyed, and to gather households dispersed by the merciless conflagration.

At present, she resides in San Francisco, where she has a position in the U. S. Mint. More than eighteen years ago, her friends began to petition Congress to grant her a pension. Their efforts were persistent and earnest, until, a year ago, they were crowned with success, and a monthly pension of $25 was given her. It was a niggardly and tardy recognition of her heroic services. If she had her deserts she would be handsomely provided for by Government. But the Grand Army Posts of the country do not forget her, and her friends will bear her on their hearts, through life.

Last summer she came to Massachusetts for a brief visit with her old friends. She arrived at my home at the close of a dismally rainy day, wet and exhausted. She had spent the day in Boston, searching for an old soldier from Illinois, who had served out three terms in the house of correction, for drunkenness, during the last ten years. I remonstrated. "My dear friend, why do you, at the age of seventy-three, waste yourself on such a worthless creature as B——?" Turning to me with a flash of her blue eyes, she answered: "Mary Livermore, I have a commission from the Lord God Almighty to do all I can for every miserable creature who comes in my way. He's always sure of two friends — God and me!"

Mother Bickerdyke is of medium height, with brown hair, now well sprinkled with white, blue eyes, and a mouth of sweetness and firmness. When young, she must have possessed considerable beauty; for, after more than sixty years' incredible wear and tear of life, she is still a comely woman. Always cheerful, never discouraged, brave, indomitable, witty, shrewd, versatile, clear-headed, unique — she only needed early advantages to have made her a very remarkable woman. Sympathy with the oppressed and feeble, with little children, and with all who are in trouble, is a prominent characteristic of her nature. Although she is a member of the Congregationalist Church, yet in church matters, as in war times, she cuts red tape, and goes where she pleases. She communes now with Methodists, and now with Unitarians, just as she happens to "light on 'em," to use her own phraseology, and nobody can hinder. She is a practical Christian of the most genuine type.

To know the estimation in which she was held by the army, one needs to go West. Many of my engagements are with lecture committees of Grand Army posts in the West. And at the first convenient moment the old veterans look into my face with the inquiries, "How long since you saw Mother Bickerdyke?" or "Isn't it possible to get a pension for Mother Bickerdyke?" Immediately, the members of their households cluster about us, and for a few moments every heart beats faster and kindlier, as her deeds of unselfish heroism are chronicled, or the motherly tenderness of her life in the hospitals is discussed, for the hundredth time.

While this book was in press, I was called to Kansas, a state in which one hundred and eighty thousand soldiers are settled. While I was there, a Soldiers' Convention was held in Topeka, the capital city, which was very largely attended. Mother Bickerdyke came from San Francisco, the invited guest of the Convention, and, just as the veterans were entering on their deliberations, made her appearance in the rear of the house.

In an instant there was a joyful confusion in the neighborhood of the door, a rush, a subdued shout, a repressed cheer. The presiding officer called for order, and rapped vigorously with his gavel. But the hubbub increased, and spread towards the centre of the hall. Again the chairman sought to quell the disturbance, rapping forcibly, and uttering his commands in an authoritative voice: "Gentlemen in the rear of the house must come to order, and take their seats! It is impossible to transact business in this confusion!"

"Mother Bickerdyke is here!" shouted a chorus of voices in explanation, which announcement put an end to all thoughts of business, and brought every man to his feet, and sent a ringing cheer through the hall. All pressed towards the motherly woman, known by all soldiers in the West, many thousands of whom are indebted to her for care, nursing, tenderness, and help, in the direst hours of their lives. Gray-haired and gray-bearded men took her in their arms and kissed her. Others wept over her. Men on crutches and men with empty coat-sleeves stood outside the surging crowd, with shining eyes, waiting their turn to greet their benefactress.

" Why, boys, how you behave!" was Mother Bickerdyke's characteristic exclamation, as, releasing herself from the smothering caresses and the strong imprisoning arms, she wiped away tears of memory and gladness. This raised a shout of laughter. " Oh, mother, your brown hair has grown white as snow," said one; " but I should know you by your speech, if I met you in Africa."

"I should know her by the tender eyes and the kind mouth," said another. " I shall never forget how good they looked to me after the battle of Resaca, where I lost my foot, and gave myself up to die, I was in such pain. I tell you, it seemed as if my own mother was doing for me, she was so gentle. She looked down upon me, and encouraged me, and nursed me, as if I were her son." And he wiped his wet eyes with the back of his hand.

Had Mother Bickerdyke been a queen, she could not have been more royally welcomed. It seemed impossible for the men to pay her sufficient honor. They noted her increasing feebleness, her crippled hands, her snowy hair, her dimming eyes, and said to each other, "It isn't the result of old age; it is what she did for us during the war." Only that Mother Bickerdyke resolutely forbids it, they would surround her with luxury, and she would lack for no comfort, even if they impoverished themselves to obtain them. "The boys have all they can do to make a living for themselves and families," she says, "and they shall not be weighted with the care of me." And so, when the Convention was ended, and the men went back to their farms and shops and offices, she turned her face towards San Francisco, to take up again the burden of her lonely life.

While the Massachusetts State Prison at Charlestown was under the management of Warden Gideon Haynes, I was invited to address the prisoners. At the close of the informal talk, Mr. Haynes gave the convicts who desired to speak with me permission to remain in their seats when the rest marched to their cells. About a dozen accepted the invitation. Of these, three were solicitous to know something concerning Mother Bickerdyke. "Was she living?" "Had she a pension?" "What was her post-office address?" And as each one detailed the circumstances of his personal acquaintance with Mrs. Bickerdyke, I knew enough of his story to be true to believe the whole.

"Ah, if I had had a mother like her," said one, as we parted, "I shouldn't be here to-day. For she was a true mother to me — not only nursing me, but advising me." Similar utterances were made by others.

# CHAPTER XXVIII.

MY REMINISCENCES OF PRESIDENT LINCOLN — EXPERIENCES
IN THE "WIGWAM" — EXCITING SCENES — MY INTER-
VIEWS WITH THE PRESIDENT AT THE WHITE HOUSE.

Early Life of President Lincoln — My first Knowledge of him, in 1858 —
"The Battle of the Giants" — He is nominated in 1860 for the Presi-
dency — My Experience in the "Wigwam" as a Reporter — The memorable Scenes attending the Nomination — My Visit to Washington in
1862 — Gloomy Period of the War — Call on the President — His Depression — Discouraging Statements — Wholesale Desertions from the Army
— " To undertake to fill up the Army is like shovelling Fleas!" — Mrs.
Hoge and I see the President alone — His Suffering during the War —
He contributes the manuscript Proclamation of Emancipation to the
Chicago Sanitary Fair — A Premium sent him as the largest Contributor.

NATURE is not lavish of great men, but dis-
tributes them charily through the centuries.
Often she evolves them from the obscurity
where they have slowly crystallized into
force and clearness only when the crises
appear for whose mastership they were ordained.
Like the stars of evening, they spring not into in-
stantaneous being, but only appear after they have
been slowly formed in dimness and mistiness, after
long revolving, condensing, and gathering pale rays
of light. Then they stand out on the brow of night,
ever after to be the guide and admiration of men.

It was thus with President Lincoln, whose life was

crowned with the glory of martyrdom. The discipline of poverty, and hard wrestling with nature in the blended timber and prairie country of the unsubdued West, matured him to a late but sturdy manhood. The softening culture of the schools was held aloof from him. The civic honors for which in early life he struggled eluded his pursuit, and crowned his rival. The golden stream of Pactolus flowed far away from his feet. And so Nature and circumstance shaped him vigorous, cool-headed, warm-hearted, self-poised, strong-handed. A child-like simplicity remained in him, that ever proved more than a match for the subtleties of political tricksters. Transcendent honesty and clear-sighted goodness stood him in stead of genius and inspiration. For half a century his manhood was built up by gradual accretions of power, strength, and wisdom, and the qualities which inspire trust, and then the great epoch burst upon the country, for which Providence had been shaping him.

The nation was writhing in the agonies of disruption, and the fires of a gigantic civil war were smouldering in her bosom, when Mr. Lincoln took in hand the reins of government. Through Gethsemanes of agony he led the nation steadily, on its sanguinary way to freedom, till the goal was won. Then death claimed him. One moment he was charged with a nation's fate; the next — a shock, a dim, blank pause, and he beheld the King in His glory. One moment the noisy and capricious applause of the people surged around him; the next he heard the Heavenly Voice, " Well done, good and faithful servant! " The nation sobbed its farewell to him, but still reaches out to him in yearning love. It hoards its memories of him as priceless wealth. It exhumes from the past the minutiæ of his daily life, and laughs afresh at his rare humor, and weeps anew over the pathos and tragedy crowded into his history.

I well remember when I first heard of Mr. Lincoln, and the impression made upon me by the first words of his I ever heard. It was in 1858, a year or so after my removal to the West from New England. He had been put forward as a candidate for the seat of Hon. Stephen A. Douglas in the Illinois Senate, whose term of office was soon to expire, and who was himself a candidate for re-election. The two aspirants for the same position "stumped" the state and met in joint debate at seven points of geographical importance. These debates created an intense interest; and everywhere the people flocked to hear them. To this day, that memorable and peculiar discussion is known in Illinois as "the battle of the giants."

Mr. Lincoln had been nominated for State Senator by the Republican Convention at Springfield, Ill., in June, 1858. He addressed the Convention on that occasion, and his speech constituted the platform of the great debate between Mr. Douglas and himself, at which time he made the following prophetic utterance, which has been so often quoted: —

"A house divided against itself cannot stand. I believe this government cannot endure permanently one half slave and one half free. I do not expect the Union to be dissolved — I do not expect the house to fall. But I do expect that it will cease to be divided — it will become all one thing, or all the other." He seemed, even at that early date, to speak with prophetic prevision.

Mr. Lincoln lost the election, and Mr. Douglas won it. But the former gathered to himself the trust of all who hated slavery and loved freedom — while the later forfeited their confidence forever. Mr. Lincoln prepared the way for his triumphant elevation to a higher post of honor — but Mr. Douglas took the initial steps towards a defeat that ended in death.

It was my good fortune to be present at the National Convention in Chicago, in 1860, which nominated Mr. Lincoln to the Presidency. It was held in an immense building erected for the occasion, and known as the " Wigwam." I had undertaken to report the proceedings for an editor friend, and a seat was assigned me near the platform, where the electors from the several states were seated, and where not one word could escape me. My place was in the midst of the great reportorial army collected from all parts of the country. I was fortunate above all women on that occasion, for the far-away gallery was assigned them, and they were strictly forbidden the enclosed and guarded lower floor, which was sacred to men exclusively. From the immensity of the " Wigwam," the proceedings could not be heard in the gallery, and seemed there like gigantic pantomime.

I have never understood the good luck that bestowed me among the reporters at that time, nor how I succeeded in retaining my position when the official attempt was made to remove me. Women reporters were then almost unheard of; and inconspicuous as I had endeavored to make myself by dressing in black, like my brethren of the press, the marshal of the day spied me, after the lower floor was densely packed with masculinity. In stentorian tones that rang through the building, while his extended arm and forefinger pointed me out, and made me the target for thousands of eyes, he ordered me to withdraw my profane womanhood from the sacred enclosure provided for men, and " go up higher," among the women. I rose mechanically to obey, but the crowd rendered this impossible. My husband beside me, reporting for his own paper, undertook to explain, but was not allowed. The reporters about me then took the matter into their own hands, and in a tumult of voices cavalierly bade me " Sit still! " and the marshal " Dry up! " A momentary battle of words was waged over my head, between my husband and the reporters, the police and the marshal, and then I was left in peace. The unconventional West was new to me, and I was a good deal disturbed by this episode, which no one but myself seemed to remember ten minutes later.

I was well repaid for the annoyance, by being a near witness of the electric scenes which followed the nomination of Mr. Lincoln to the Presidency, on the third ballot. Who that saw the tumultuous rapture of that occasion could ever forget it! Men embraced each other, and fell on one another's neck, and wept out their repressed feeling. They threw their hats in air, and almost rent the roof with huzzahs. Thousands and thousands were packed in the streets outside, who stood patiently receiving accounts of the proceedings within, from reporters posted on the roof, listening at the numerous open skylights, and shouting them in detail to the crowd below. Sometimes, messengers ran from these reporters at the skylights to the eaves of the building, thence to vociferate to the remote but patiently waiting crowd outside what had just been said or done. They would then take up the subsiding chorus of shouts within, and re-echo them still more wildly, until they drowned the city's multitudinous roar, and were heard a mile away. The billows of this delirious joy surged around me, as I sat amid the swaying, rocking forms of men who had sprung to their feet and grasped each other by the hand, or had fallen into one another's arms, and were laughing, crying, and talking incoherently.

I confess I was not fully *en rapport* with the insanity of gladness raging around me. It seemed to me these demonstrations were made rather because the anti-slavery principle had triumphed, than because Mr. Lincoln himself was a special favorite. The great majority knew him only as a country lawyer, and not very distinguished at that. But they also knew that he was intensely hostile to human slavery, and had so avowed himself. "Is it *certain* that Mr. Lincoln is an uncompromising anti-slavery man?" I inquired of a Massachusetts reporter next me. "There is no humbug about it? Mr. Lincoln is not anti-slavery just now for the sake of getting votes, is he? Can you inform me?"

For answer, he took from his pocketbook a little fragment of newspaper, which contained this extract from his "Peoria, Ill., speech," made Oct. 16, 1854, and passed it to me with the simple query, "Do you think he can take the back track after saying that?" This is the quotation: —

"Slavery is founded in the selfishness of man's nature — opposition to it, in the love of justice. These principles are in eternal antagonism; and when brought into collision as fiercely as slavery extension brings them, shocks and throes and convulsions must follow ceaselessly. Repeal the Missouri Compromise; repeal all compromises; repeal the Declaration of Independence; repeal all past history; you cannot repeal human nature. It will still be in the abundance of man's heart that slavery extension is wrong, and out of the abundance of the heart his mouth will continue to speak."

When the President-elect left his Illinois home for Washington, to confront an organized and ripened conspiracy against the life of the nation, as he journeyed from city to city, the whole country turned out to look upon the man it had chosen to be its leader.

On a raw February night in 1861, impelled by a like anxious curiosity, I went with the multitude and stood at the edge of an effervescing crowd — that had shouted itself hoarse, and was then gesticulating its frantic delight — that I might look in the rugged, homely face of our future President. Like many others on whose hearts the gradual disruption of the Union that dark winter lay like an agony of personal bereavement, I longed to read in the face of our leader the indications of wisdom and strength that would compel the people to anchor in him and feel safe. His simple, unaffected, but almost solemn words thrilled through and through the hearts of his listeners. Eager lookers-on like myself hung on the skirts of the mercurial crowd, and the comments that trembled from lip to lip indicated their anxiety. "He *seems* like an honest man!" "He is evidently impressed with the solemn responsibilities of the hour!" "*Will* he be equal to this tremendous emergency?"

"There is no spread-eagle nonsense about him — that is one consolation!" "He has taken a big contract — God help him fulfil it!" "He is probably not much of a statesman, nor even a politician; but then he is a Northern man, an anti-slavery man, and he is honest and loyal, and perhaps we could not have done better than to elect 'old Abe' President!" These were the comments made around me, and I saw that all were feeling their way to an anchorage in him, although few found it until a later date.

In November, 1862, I found myself in Washington, whither I had been summoned to attend a council of women connected with the Sanitary Commission. It was a gloomy time all over the country. The heart of the people had grown sick with hope deferred; and the fruitless undertakings and timid, dawdling policy of General McClellan had perplexed and discouraged all loyalists, and strengthened and made bold all traitors. The army was always entrenched or entrenching. Its advance was forbidden by the autumnal rains, and the policy of its commanding general, whatever that might have been. The rebel army was in front, and every day a new crop of rumors was harvested in reference to its purpose. One hour, "Washington was safe!" and "All was quiet on the Potomac!" The next, "The rebels were marching on to Washington!" "They were blocking our river communications!" "They were threatening to overwhelm our forces!" or, "They had already taken our position!" Despondency sat on every face.

"I wonder whether McClellan *means* to do anything!" said Mr. Lincoln one day to a friend. "I should like to borrow the army of him for a day or two."

Those of the women who had come from the loyal and sanguine Northwest, listened in undisguised amazement to the open-mouthed secession of more than one half the people 'we met; for in the Northwest it was hardly safe to talk treason openly; and, despite the discouragements of the military situation in the East, the people bated not one jot of their confidence in the ultimate restoration of the Union, without the loss of a single state. Our hearts died within us; and when the Woman's Council adjourned, we were glad to accept an invitation to call on the President in a body. The President had appointed an early hour for our reception.

I shall never forget the shock which his presence gave us. Not more ghastly or rigid was his dead face, as he lay in his coffin, than on that never-to-be-forgotten night. His introverted look and his half-staggering gait were like those of a man walking in sleep. He seemed literally bending under the weight of his burdens. A deeper gloom rested on his face than on that of any person I had ever seen. He took us each by the hand mechanically, in an awkward, absent way, until my friend Mrs. Hoge, of Chicago, and myself were introduced, when the name of the city of our residence appeared to catch his attention, and he sat down between us.

"So you are from Chicago!" he said, familiarly; "you are not scared by Washington mud, then; for you can beat us all to pieces in that." And then he asked about the weather we had had during the fall, the health of the city, and other matters of local interest, as one to whom the Northwest was home, and dear. It was explained to him that we were all identified with the Sanitary Commission, and that we had

called, before separating to our widely divergent
homes, to obtain from him some word of encouragement — something to cheer and stimulate.  "I have
no word of encouragement to give!" was his sad
and blunt reply.  "The military situation is far from
bright; and the country knows it as well as I do."
There was no attempt at question or answer; but a
momentary deep and painful silence settled on his
auditors.

"The fact is," he continued after a pause, "the
people haven't yet made up their minds that we are
at war with the South.  They haven't buckled down
to the determination to fight this war through; for
they have got the idea into their heads that we are
going to get out of this fix, somehow, by strategy!
That's the word — *strategy!*  General McClellan
thinks he is going to whip the rebels by strategy;
and the army has got the same notion.  They have
no idea that the war is to be carried on and put
through by hard, tough fighting, that will hurt somebody; and no headway is going to be made while
this delusion lasts."

Some one ventured to remonstrate against this, and
reminded the President how hundreds of thousands
had rushed to arms at the call of the country; how
bravely the army and navy had fought at Forts
Henry and Donelson, Pea Ridge, Shiloh, and New
Orleans; and how gloriously they had triumphed.

He admitted this, but returned to his first statement.  "The people *haven't* made up their minds
that we are at war, I tell you!" he repeated, with
great positiveness.  "They think there is a royal
road to peace, and that General McClellan is to find
it.  The army has not settled down into the convic-

tion that we are in a terrible war that has got to be fought out — no; and the officers haven't either. When you came to Washington, ladies, some two weeks ago, but very few soldiers came on the trains with you — that you will all remember. But when you go back you will find the trains and every conveyance crowded with them. You won't find a city on the route, a town, or a village, where soldiers and officers on furlough are not plenty as blackberries. There are whole regiments that have two thirds of their men absent — a great many by desertion, and a great many on leave granted by company officers, which is almost as bad. General McClellan is all the time calling for more troops, more troops; and they are sent to him; but the deserters and furloughed men outnumber the recruits. To fill up the army is like undertaking to shovel fleas. You take up a shovelful," suiting the word with an indescribably comical gesture; "but before you can dump them anywhere they are gone. It is like trying to ride a balky horse. You coax, and cheer, and spur, and lay on the whip; but you don't get ahead an inch — there you stick."

"Do you mean that our men *desert?*" we asked, incredulously; for in our glorifying of the soldiers we had not conceived of *our* men becoming deserters.

"That is *just* what I mean!" replied the President. "And the desertion of the army is just now the most serious evil we have to encounter. At the battle of Antietam, General McClellan had the names of about one hundred and eighty thousand men on the army rolls. Of these, seventy thousand were absent on leave granted by company officers, which, as I said before, is almost as bad as desertion. For the men ought not to ask for furloughs with the enemy drawn up before them, nor ought the officers to grant them. About twenty thousand more were in hospital, or were detailed to other duties, leaving only some ninety thousand to give battle to the enemy. General McClellan went into the fight with this number. But in two hours after the battle commenced thirty thousand had straggled or deserted, and so the battle was fought with sixty thousand — and as the enemy had about the same number, it proved a drawn game. The rebel army had coiled itself up in such a position that if McClellan had only had the seventy thousand absentees, and the thirty thousand deserters, he could have surrounded Lee, captured the whole rebel army, and ended the war at a stroke without a battle.

" We have a Stragglers' Camp out here in Alexandria, in connection with the Convalescent Camp, and from that camp, in three months, General Butler has returned to their regiments seventy-five thousand deserters and stragglers who have been arrested and sent there. Don't you see that the country and the army fail to realize that we are engaged in one of the greatest wars the world has ever seen, and which can only be ended by hard fighting? General McClellan is responsible for the delusion that is untoning the whole army — that the South is to be conquered by strategy." [That very week, General McClellan had been removed from the command of the army, and General Burnside — of whom the President spoke most eulogistically — had been appointed in his place, but none of us knew it that night.]

"Is not death the penalty of desertion?" we inquired.

"Certainly it is."

"And does it not lie with the President to enforce this penalty?"

"Yes."

"Why not enforce it, then? Before many soldiers had suffered death for desertion, this wholesale depletion of the army would be ended."

"Oh, no, no!" replied the President, shaking his head ruefully: "that can't be done; it would be unmerciful, barbarous."

"But is it not more merciful to stop desertions, and to fill up the army, so that when a battle comes off it may be decisive, instead of being a drawn game, as you say Antietam was?"

"It might seem so. But if I should go to shooting men by scores for desertion, I should soon have such a hullabaloo about my ears as I haven't had yet, and I should deserve it. You can't order men shot by dozens or twenties. People won't stand it, and they ought not to stand it. No, we must change the condition of things in some other way. The army must be officered by fighting men. Misery loves company, you know," he added; "and it may give you some consolation to know that it is even worse with the rebel army than it is with ours. I receive their papers daily, and they are running over with complaints of the desertion of their soldiers. We are no worse off than they are, but better; and that is some comfort."

The conversation continued for an hour, the President talking all the while of the country and of the aspect of affairs in the most depressing manner.

When we left him, we agreed among ourselves that it would not be wise to repeat the conversation, so as to have it get into the papers. For, in the then feverish state of the public mind, whatever was reported as coming from the President, no matter how or by whom reported, was eagerly seized upon. The influence of the talk upon ourselves was too dispiriting for us to wish to extend its effect. It cost those of us who belonged to the Northwest a night's sleep. The condition of the country, the unsatisfactory military aspect, the uneasiness of the people, the state of the army, all wore hues of midnight before our interview with the Chief Magistrate, and this had given them such additional gloom that we almost repented our visit to Washington.

The next day my friend Mrs. Hoge, and myself, had another interview with the President, on business entrusted to us. If we were shocked the night before at his haggard face, how much more were we pained when the broad light of day revealed the ravages which care, anxiety, and overwork had wrought. In our despondent condition it was difficult to control our feelings so as not to weep before him. Our unspoken thought ran thus: "Our national affairs must be in the very extremity of hopelessness if they thus prey on the mind and life of the President. The country has been slain by treason — he knows it, and that it cannot recover itself."

Our business ended, before we withdrew we made one more attempt to draw encouraging words from the reluctant head of the nation. "Mr. President," we said timidly, " we find ourselves greatly depressed by the talk of last evening; you do not consider our national affairs hopeless, do you? Our country is not lost?"

"Oh, no!" he said, with great earnestness, "our affairs are by no means hopeless, for we have the right on our side. We did not want this war, and we tried to avoid it. We were forced into it; our cause is a just one, and now it has become the cause of freedom." (The Emancipation Proclamation had just been promulged.) "And let us also hope it is the cause of God, and then we may be sure it must ultimately triumph. But between that time and now there is an amount of agony and suffering and trial for the people that they do not look for, and are not prepared for."

No one can ever estimate the suffering endured by President Lincoln during the war. I saw him several times afterwards, and each time I was impressed anew with the look of pain and weariness stereotyped on his face. "He envied the soldier sleeping in his blanket on the Potomac," he would say, in his torture. And sometimes, when the woes of the country pressed most heavily on him, he envied the dead soldier sleeping in the cemetery.

"Whichever way this war ends," he said to a freind of mine, "I have the impression that *I* shall not last very long after it is over." After the dreadful repulse of our forces at Fredericksburg, when the slaughter was terrific, the agony of the President wrung from him the bitter cry, "Oh, if there is a man out of hell that suffers more than I do, I pity him!"

Mrs. Hoge and I accepted the morsel of hope given us by the President's last words, and went out together. Side by side we walked up Pennsylvania

Avenue, quietly weeping behind our veils, neither trusting herself to speak to the other. But saddening as was this meeting with the President, it was not without its good effect on all of us. We were women, and could not *fight* for the country. But the instinct of patriotism within our hearts, which had lain dormant when our beloved land knew no danger, was now developed into a passion. We returned to our various homes, separated by thousands of miles, more inspired than ever to link ourselves with the hosts of freedom, who were yet to work better and more bravely than they knew.

The women of the Sanitary Commission set themselves to work in the different states of their residence, as their circumstances and localities demanded. We who belonged to the Northwest resolved on a Northwestern Soldiers' Fair, to obtain money for the purchase of comforts and necessaries for the sick and wounded of our army, and immediately began to plan for it. In the projection of this fair there was a double purpose. To obtain money was not its sole aim. We believed it would develop a grateful demonstration of the loyalty of the Northwest to our struggling country; that it would encourage the worn veterans of many a hard-fought field, and strengthen them, as they perilled their lives in defence of their native land; and that it would infuse into the scattered workers for our suffering soldiers an impetus that would last through the war.

The fair came off in about one year after our visit to the President, and yielded the then unprecedented sum of nearly one hundred thousand dollars. It required Herculean effort to conduct this first fair. At first, and for a long time, only two women and no men were interested in it; and this was enough with many to summarily condemn it. It remained throughout a woman's fair. Unlike the East, the West had then few competent and able people of leisure who could work continuously in an enterprise like this. A large fair, pecuniarily successful, had never been held in the West, and was not believed possible. And the public mind was so pre-occupied that it was next to impossible for us to get a hearing for our grand project. But we succeeded; and the fair came off at the appointed time, and was found to have accomplished vastly more than it contemplated.

It attracted the attention of the whole loyal North for weeks, and was the cynosure of all eyes and the theme of all tongues. That it rendered good service to the dear cause of the country was manifest; for disloyalists, from first to last, assailed both it and its managers, publicly and privately, in the most venomous manner. The most malignant falsehoods were put in circulation to its detriment, while the wholesale defamation of its managers, was so coarse and disgusting that it carried with it its own refutation. It was both bane and antidote in one. The spontaneous enthusiasm which the fair enkindled, its electric generosity, its moral earnestness, and its contagious patriotism glorified the occasion, and were of more worth to the country than the money which was raised. Other mammoth fairs, in other large cities, came off after this, largely modelled on its plan, and largely outdoing it in pecuniary results; but by none was its *morale* excelled.

From the first public announcement of this fair, President Lincoln took a lively interest in it. He bore testimony again and again to its moral influence, and inquired concerning its progress of every visitant from the Northwest that found his way to the White House. We wrote with much hesitation — for we never forgot how he was shouldering the woes and cares of the country — asking for some contribution from himself to our fair. The people of the Northwest were idolatrously attached to him; and we knew that any gift from him would be prized above all price. So we urged our petition as earnestly as we knew how, and enlisted Hon. Isaac N. Arnold, of Chicago, a personal friend of Mr. Lincoln, to second our prayers in person.

"Yes," said the President, "I must send something to that fair; but what?"

A happy thought came to Mr. Arnold. "Why not send the ladies the original manuscript Proclamation of Emancipation? They can make a good thing out of it."

The President wished to keep it himself, but finally consented; and it reached Chicago the day after the fair opened. On unlocking my post-office drawer that morning I found the precious document, and carried it triumphantly to Bryan Hall, one of the six halls occupied by the fair, where the package was opened. The manuscript of the Proclamation was accompanied by a characteristic letter, which I have given elsewhere.

Its receipt was announced to the immense throngs crowding the building, who welcomed it with deafening cheers. It was enclosed in an elegant black walnut frame, so arranged that it could be read entirely through the plate glass that protected it from touch, and hung where it could be seen and read by all.

At an early condition of the fair, before a *furor* in

its behalf had been aroused, a patriotic gentleman of Chicago offered the premium of a fine gold watch to the largest single contributor to the fair. The donation of the manuscript Emancipation Proclamation entitled President Lincoln to this watch, which was elegant and valuable, and which, after being properly inscribed, was sent to him. He acknowledged its receipt, in a note written by his own hand. Since his death it is pleasant to know that this watch has fallen into the hands of his son, Robert Lincoln, our late Secretary of War, who holds it sacred as a memento of a touching incident in his father's history.

# CHAPTER XXIX.

REMINISCENCES OF PRESIDENT LINCOLN CONTINUED —
SCENES AT THE WHITE HOUSE — A WIFE'S SAD STORY
AND AFFECTING PETITION — I INTERCEDE WITH THE
PRESIDENT — HIS SYMPATHY AND MERCY.

The President refuses to pardon a Virginia Spy — Wife of the condemned
Illinois Major — Her sad Story — She is too much broken down to plead
for her Husband's Life — " Beg the President not to allow my husband to
be shot! " — I tell her Story — The President's Sympathy — " These Cases
kill me " — He had already commuted the Major's sentence — His Delight
at the Discovery — " I know all about it now " — The grateful Woman
fainted — She is told to go and visit her Husband — The broken-hearted
Wife goes away imploring Blessings on the President — Beautiful Reception of Miss Elizabeth Peabody — Touching Letter to Mrs. Bixby —
Her five Sons were killed in Battle — Humorous Reply to his Advisers —
" Keep Silence, and we'll get you safe across."

HAD an opportunity during the war of
witnessing the reception by the President
of two applications for pardon, which met
with widely different fates. The case of
the first was this: A young man, belonging to
a Virginia family of most treasonable character, remained in Washington when the rest of the
household went with the Confederacy. Though he
took no active part with the loyalists of the capital,
he was so quiet and prudent as to allay their suspicions concerning him, and finally to gain their confidence. He opened a market and kept for sale the
very best quality of meats, supplying many of the

families of prominent officers of the government, and for a time the family at the White House. He even managed to obtain a sort of intimacy in some of these households, through the intrigues of disloyal servants. As afterwards appeared, he possessed himself of information that was valuable to the rebels, and which he imparted to them promptly and unreservedly.

When Lee moved up into Pennsylvania, in the summer of 1863, this young man was suddenly missing from his place of business, and another person was installed in his place. "He was unexpectedly called away by business," was assigned as the reason for his absence. In one of the cavalry fights, or skirmishes, which occurred almost daily in Maryland, or Southern Pennsylvania, during that June raid of Lee's army, the young man was taken prisoner by General Kilpatrick's men, near Winchester, in a "spirited brush" which they had with Stuart's cavalry.

I do not remember all the technicalities of the case, if indeed I ever knew them. But the young man was recognized, was proved to be a spy, and, but for the President's leniency, would have been hanged. Instead of the punishment of death, however, he was sentenced to twenty years' imprisonment. Immediately all the rebels of Washington were moving to his relief. Every wire was pulled that was supposed to have any power to open his prison door. Members of Congress were besought to intercede for him, and at last the President himself was besieged.

It was in the President's room, while waiting my turn for an interview, that I learned the above facts. Two persons were pleading in his behalf — a man

and a woman — the latter elegant, beautiful, and
with a certain air of culture, but the former having
the look of a refined villain. It was a very plausible
story as they told it. " Their truly loyal young kins-
man had gone into Maryland to buy beeves for the
Washington market — was 'gobbled up,' with his
fine, fat kine, by Stuart, who confiscated his property and impressed its owner into his cavalry. And
then, as if that were not calamity enough for one
day, he was captured again by Kilpatrick, who, naturally enough, not understanding the circumstances,
nor the patent loyalty of his prisoner, judged him by
the company in which he was found, and supposed
him to be a rebel like the rest."

The President listened impatiently and with a dark-
ening face. " There is not a word of this true! " he
burst in, abruptly and sternly, " and you know it as
well as I do. He *was* a spy, he has been a spy, he
ought to have been hanged as a spy. From the fuss
you folks are making about him, who are none too
loyal, I am convinced he was more valuable to the
cause of the enemy than we have yet suspected. You
are the third set of persons that has been to me to
get him pardoned. Now I'll tell you what — if any of
you come bothering me any more about his being set
at liberty, that will decide his fate. I will have him
hanged, as he deserves to be. You ought to bless
your stars that he got off with a whole neck; and if
you don't want to see him hanged as high as Haman,
don't you come to me again about him." The peti-
tioners, as may be imagined, " stood not upon the
order of their going, but went at once," and after
their departure the President narrated the facts which
I have given.

The other case was of a different character. I was in the ante-chamber of the President's room, one morning, waiting the exit of Secretary Stanton, who was holding an interview with Mr. Lincoln. Then, as my party was under the escort of a Senator, we were entitled to the next interview. A member of the Cabinet takes precedence of all who wish to enter the presence of the Chief Magistrate. A Senator ranks next, and goes in before any inferior personage. A member of the House is next in order, while persons unattended by any of these officials take their turn among those desiring an audience. As we were waiting the departure of the Secretary of War, who was making a long visit, I looked round upon the crowd who were biding their time to present their claims upon the President's attention.

Standing, sitting, walking, lounging, talking, with hats on, and generally with mouths full of tobacco, there were some fifty men in attendance, and, besides myself, only one woman. She was sitting in a corner of the ante-room, with her face to the wall. Thinking she had shrunk into this place from shamefacedness at being the only woman among so many men, I moved a little towards her to get a peep at her face. I was somewhat curious to look at a woman who feared to face such men as were congregated about her, for they were not of the first order. She was poor looking, shabbily but neatly dressed, middle-aged, sunburned, and careworn. Her hands were tightly clenching a handkerchief, which she held close against her breast, with the evident effort to master the emotion that was shaking her whole frame, and she was weeping. I saw by her manner that she was in trouble, and my heart went out to her.

Putting my arm about her, I stooped and said as kindly as I could, "My poor woman, I am afraid you are in trouble; can I do anything to help you?" She turned a most imploring face towards me, and clutched my hand nervously. "Oh," said she, "I am in great trouble. My husband is to be shot, and if I cannot get him pardoned nobody can comfort me." A kindly appearing man stepped forward, a country neighbor of the poor woman, and told her story.

Her husband was major of an Illinois regiment, and had served two years in the army with honor and fidelity. His colonel, like too many of the same rank, was a hard man, and, when intoxicated, abusive, uncontrollable, and profane. He was, however, a good soldier, and, in the main, popular with his men. While under the influence of strong drink, he had come fiercely in collision with the major, and a most profane and angry altercation ensued in presence of half the regiment. Foul epithets were hurled back and forth until the colonel called the major a "coward," with numerous obscene and profane prefixes which cannot be repeated.

The major was a sober man, reticent, somewhat unpopular, very cool, and slow to anger; but this stung him. "Take that back, colonel!" he demanded, fiercely, drawing his revolver, "or you are a dead man." The colonel repeated the insult, even more offensively. Before the bystanders could interfere, the colonel fell dead by the major's hand. For this he was tried, convicted, sentenced to be shot, and was then lying in jail in Memphis, awaiting his death. He had written his wife a farewell letter, entreating her to be reconciled to the event — a brief epistle, which she gave me to read — full of tenderness for her, and accusation for himself, but evincing great manliness. The Judge-Advocate had also written her, urging her to go immediately to Washington, and in person ask the too-forgiving President to commute her husband's sentence to imprisonment.

A sympathetic neighbor had accompanied her, and they had been in Washington twenty-four hours without having seen the President, simply from their modesty and ignorance of the most expeditious method of getting an audience with him. My expressions of sympathy broke the poor woman completely down. She could not stand, and she sobbed so hysterically that she could not talk. She had been unable to eat or sleep since she had heard her husband's sentence, and, as her townsman expressed it, it seemed as if "she would soon be in her coffin if the President did not take pity on her."

Senator Henderson of Missouri was to introduce my friends and myself to the notice of the President, and we entreated that he would also escort this poor woman, and give her an immediate opportunity to present her petition. He gladly consented. I sought to allay her agitation. "Now you must be calm," I said, "for in a minute or two you are to see the President, and it will be best for you to tell your own story."

"Won't you talk for me?" she entreated; "I am so tired I can't think, and I can't tell all my husband's story; do beg the President not to allow my husband to be shot." I put my arms about the poor creature, and pressed her to my heart as if she had been a sister; for never before or since have I seen a woman so broken down, or one who so awoke my sympathies.

"Don't fear!" I said; "the President does not hang or shoot people when he ought; and he certainly will lighten your husband's sentence when he comes to hear all the facts. While her agitation was at the highest the door opened out into the ante-chamber, and Secretary Stanton came forth with a huge budget of important looking documents. Immediately Senator Henderson ushered us into the apartment the secretary had vacated, two of us leading the trembling wife between us, as if she were a child learning to walk.

The townsman of the woman was first introduced, who then led forth the wife of the condemned major, saying, "This woman, Mr. President, will tell you her story." But instead of telling her story she dropped tremblingly into a chair, only half alive; and, lifting her white face to the President's with a beseeching look, more eloquent than words, her colorless lips moved without emitting any sound. Seeing she was past speech, I spoke quickly in her behalf, stating her case, and urging her prayer for her husband's life with all the earnestness that I felt. All the while the hungry eyes of the woman were riveted on the President's face, and tearless sobs shook her frame. The chair she sat on touched mine, and, with her tremulousness, it beat a tattoo which made me nervous.

The President was troubled. "Oh, dear, dear!" he said, passing his hand over his face and through his hair. "These cases kill me! I wish I didn't have to hear about them! What shall I do? You make the laws," turning to members of Congress in the room, "and then you come with heart-broken women and ask me to set them aside. You have decided that if a soldier raises his hand against his superior officer, as this man has done, he shall die! Then if I leave the laws to be executed, one of these distressing scenes occurs, which almost kills me."

Somebody ventured the remark that "this seemed a case where it was safe to incline to the side of mercy." "I feel that it is always safe," replied the President; "but you know that I am to-day in bad odor all over the country because I don't have as many persons put to death as the laws condemn." The attendant of the wife gave the President an abstract of the case, which had been furnished by the major's counsel, and which the President began gloomily to run over. Now and then he looked up pityingly at the speechless woman, whose white face and beseeching eyes still confronted him, expressive of an intensity of anguish that was almost frightful.

He had turned over some half-dozen pages of the abstract, when he suddenly dropped it, sprang forward in his chair, his face brightened almost into beauty, and he rubbed his hands together joyfully. "Oh," said he, "I know all about it now! I know all about it! This case came before me ten days ago, and I decided it then. The major's crime and sentence were forwarded to me privately, with a recommendation to mercy; and, without any solicitation, I have changed his sentence of death to two years' imprisonment in the penitentiary at Albany. Major —— has been a brave man, and a good man, and a good soldier, and he has had great provocations for a year. Your husband knows all about it before now," he said, addressing the wife; "and when you go back you must go by way of Albany, and see him. Tell him to bear his imprisonment like a man, and take a new start in the world when it is over."

The major's wife did not at first comprehend, but I explained to her. She attempted to rise, and made a motion as if she were going to kneel at the President's feet; but instead she only slid helplessly to the floor before him, and for a long time lay in a dead faint. The President was greatly moved. He helped raise her; and when she was taken from the room, he paced back and forth for a few moments before he could attend to other business. "Poor woman!" he said, "I don't believe she would have lived if her husband had been shot. What a heap of trouble this war has made!"

The expression of the President's face as it dawned upon him that he had already interposed between the major and death will never leave my memory. His swarthy, rugged, homely face was glorified by the delight of his soul, which shone out on his features. He delighted in mercy. It gave him positive happiness to confer a favor.

Once after, I had the pleasure of seeing those sad features light up with holy feeling. It was at a public reception. General Hitchcock had led Miss Elizabeth Peabody, of Boston, to him, the sister-in-law of Hon. Horace Mann, and as such he introduced her. The President shook hands with her cordially, but evidently did not comprehend who she was, nor quite take in what General Hitchcock had said. Reluctantly, and as if she were not satisfied, Miss Peabody moved on with the general, to make way for others who sought the pleasure of an introduction. They had nearly passed from the room, when it could be seen from the quick light that flashed into the

President's face that he had just comprehended what General Hitchcock had said, and who Miss Peabody was. Springing after them, he arrested their progress. "General," said he, "did I understand you to say that this lady is Hon. Horace Mann's sister?"

"Yes," said General Hitchcock, introducing the lady formally once more.

"Allow me to shake hands with you again, Miss Peabody!" said the President, offering both hands, and shaking hers warmly. "When I first came to Washington, Horace Mann was in the zenith of his power, and I was nobody. But he was very kind to me, and I shall never forget it. It gives me great pleasure to take one so near to him by the hand. I thank you for calling on me."

No painter has ever put into the sad face of the President any hint of the beauty that could radiate and completely metamorphose his homely features, when his great soul shone out through them. No sculptor has ever liberated from the imprisoning marble the face that shone like an angel's when the depths of his large heart were reached. "No artist is successful," said Healy, — one of the most successful painters of portraits, — "who does not bring out on the canvas, or in the marble, the best there is in his subject, the loftiest ideal of Nature when she designed the man." If this be true, then neither painter nor sculptor has ever been successful with Mr. Lincoln's face.

President Lincoln had a genius for kindness and sympathy. He travelled out of his way to do good; and, overwhelmed with public affairs, he found time for many exquisite private ministrations. Has anything ever been penned more touching than the following letter, written by him to a mother whom the war had bereaved of five sons?

DEAR MADAM,—I have seen in the files of the War Department a statement of the Adjutant-General of Massachusetts that you are the mother of five sons who died gloriously on the field of battle. I feel how weak and comfortless must be any words of mine which should attempt to beguile you of the grief of a loss so overwhelming. But I cannot refrain from tendering to you the consolation that may be found in the thanks of the Republic they died to save. I pray that our Heavenly Father may assuage the anguish of your bereavement, and leave you only the cherished memory of the loved and lost, and the solemn pride that must be yours to have laid so costly a sacrifice upon the altar of freedom.

Yours very sincerely and respectfully,

A. LINCOLN.

EXECUTIVE MANSION, WASHINGTON, Nov. 21, 1864.

Mrs. Bixby, to whom this letter was written, had a sick son in the hospital at that time, who had been severely wounded in one of Sheridan's battles.

And yet, to this quick and ready sympathy with suffering, which during the war made him " a man of sorrows and acquainted with grief, " he joined an inexhaustible fund of humor that often did him good service. When I was in Washington at one time, people were telling this story of him, and laughing over it with infinite zest.

A delegation of civilians from the North called upon him to tender him some advice concerning the conduct of the war. He was tormented all through his administration with visits from self-appointed and zealous censors and advisers, in whom self-esteem supplanted wisdom, and who made up in presumption for what they lacked in knowledge and experience. They complained that he had gone too fast here, and too slow in another direction. He had not put the right man in the right place, the war was being protracted unbearably, and the people were weary of it. For every mistake, or failure, or shortcoming of the President they had a remedy in the form of advice as impracticable as it was impertinent. He heard them patiently to the end of a half hour, and then not only silenced their complaints, but charmed them into good nature with the following characteristic reply: —

"Gentlemen, suppose all the property you are worth was in gold, and you had put it into the hands of Blondin to carry across the Niagara River on a tight-rope. Would you shake the cable and keep shouting to him, 'Blondin, stand up a little straighter!' 'Blondin, stoop a little more!' 'Blondin, go a little faster!' 'Lean a little more to the North!' 'Bend over a little more to the South!' No, gentlemen, you would hold your breath as well as your tongues, and keep your hands off until he was over. The government is carrying an immense weight. Untold treasure is in its hands. It is doing the very best it can. Do not badger us. Keep silence, and we will get you safe across."

# CHAPTER XXX.

MY LAST INTERVIEW WITH PRESIDENT LINCOLN — SCENES
AT HIS RECEPTIONS — HIS INEXHAUSTIBLE HUMOR — HIS
ASSASSINATION — A NATION IN TEARS.

Chicago projects a second mammoth Sanitary Fair — Attendance of President
and Mrs. Lincoln solicited— His comical Narration of his Experiences at
the Philadelphia Fair — " I couldn't stand another big Fair " — A humorous Inducement — Both promise Attendance — Mrs. Lincoln's Reception
— The President's Manner of Receiving — Crowds in Attendance — Love
for Children — " Stop, my little Man " — " You expect to be President
sometime " — An unexpected Reply — The Humble welcomed — Love
universally manifested for him — The Remains of the martyred President
are received in Chicago — The unfeigned Grief of the Northwest — The
Body lies in State at the Court House — " All is well with him forever ! "

WHEN the second mammoth Sanitary Fair
was planned in Chicago, my friend Mrs.
Hoge and myself were again despatched
to Washington, New York, Philadelphia,
Boston, and other cities, to seek attractions for it; and this time to solicit the attendance of President and Mrs. Lincoln, Generals Grant
and Sherman, with their wives, and other notables.

Once more, and for the last time, we were admitted
to the well-known audience-chamber, and to an interview with the good President. He was already ap-
prised of this second fair, and told us laughingly, as
we entered the room, that "he supposed he knew

what we had come for. This time, ladies, I understand you have come for me." We confessed that no less an ambition was ours than to secure the President of the United States for our fair, and that this alone had drawn us to Washington. He said that he had been to one of these big fairs, and he didn't know as he wanted to go to another. He gave a most laughable account of his visit to the Philadelphia fair.

"Why," said he, "I was nearly pulled to pieces before I reached Philadelphia. The train stopped at every station on the route, and at many places where there were no stations, only people; and my hand was nearly wrung off before I reached the fair. Then from the depot for two miles it was a solid mass of people blocking the way. Everywhere there were people shouting and cheering; and they would reach into the carriage and shake hands, and hold on, until I was afraid they would be killed, or I pulled from the carriage. When we reached the fair it was worse yet. The police tried to open a way through the crowds for me, but they had to give it up; and I didn't know as I was going to get in at all. The people were everywhere; and, if they saw me starting for a place, they rushed there first, and stood shouting, hurrahing, and trying to shake hands. By and by the Committee had worried me along to a side door, which they suddenly opened, pushed me in, and then turned the key; and that gave me a chance to lunch, shake myself, and draw a long breath. That was the only quiet moment I had; for all the time I was in Philadelphia I was crowded, and jostled, and pulled about, and cheered, and serenaded, until I was more used up than I ever remember to have been in my life. I don't believe I could stand another big fair."

"But," we said, "there is no escape from this fair, Mr. Lincoln, and this will probably be the last of them. The Northwest won't listen to your declining; and the ladies of Chicago are circulating a letter of invitation to you, which will have ten thousand signatures of women alone. The whole Northwest proposes to come to Chicago to see you; and the desire is so general and urgent that you must not feel like declining."

"Ten thousand women! What do you suppose my wife will say at ten thousand women coming after me?"

"Oh, the invitation includes her; and we have already seen Mrs. Lincoln and ascertained that she would like to come."

"She would? Well, I suppose that settles the matter, then. I know the people of the Northwest would like to see me, and I want to see them; and, if state duties do not absolutely forbid, — and I hope by that time they will not, — I will try to take a brief tour West at the time of your fair and visit it. I dread it, though."

"We have talked the whole matter over," said Mrs. Hoge; "and the people of Chicago will give you a season of absolute rest when you come. We will put you, except at certain times, where people cannot reach you with their endless shaking hands and making speeches." (Were the words prophetic? This was but five weeks before his assassination.)

"Why, what are you going to do with me? Where do you propose to put me?"

"We will charter a boat to take you out on Lake

Michigan for a trip to Mackinaw, where the affectionate desire of the crowd to shake hands with you cannot be realized."

He rubbed his hands together in a pleased manner, outstretched at arm's length, as he was accustomed to do when specially delighted, and laughed heartily.

"I will come," said he; "I will come! The trip on Lake Michigan will fetch me; you may expect me."

In the afternoon we attended Mrs. Lincoln's reception, at which the President also received calls. We went early, purposely for a private interview with Mrs. Lincoln, when we saw both together. The President playfully accused her of "conspiring to get him into another big fair like that at Philadelphia, when they were both nearly suffocated." She did not deny the charge, but begged that the letter of invitation from the ladies of Chicago might be sent to her to present to her husband. "I told you my wife would be looking after those women!" said the President, with a drollery of tone and gesture.

As the crowds began to throng the lofty, spacious apartments, we passed out and took a stand at one side, where we could watch the steady influx of callers, and the President's reception of them. Some entered the room indifferently, and gazed at him vacantly as if he were a part of the furniture, or gave him simply a mechanical nod of the head. These he allowed to pass with a slight bow in return, as they halted. Others met him with a warm grasp of the hand, a look of genuine friendliness, or grateful recognition, or tearful tenderness, and then the President's look and manner answered their expression entirely. To the lowly, to the humble, the timid colored man or woman, he bent in special kindliness. As soldiers swung themselves past him painfully on crutches, or dangled an empty coat-sleeve at their side, or walked feebly, wan and emaciated from recent sickness in the hospitals, his face took on a look of exquisite tenderness, and brightened into that peculiar beauty which I have often heard mentioned, but never seen depicted.

Not a child was allowed to pass him without a word of kindness. A beautiful bright boy about the size and age of the beloved son he had buried, gazed up reverently at the President, but was going by without speaking.

"Stop, my little man!" said Mr. Lincoln, "aren't you going to speak to me?" The little fellow laid his hand in that of the President, and colored with embarrassment. "You are older than my Tad, I guess."

"I am thirteen, sir!" replied the lad.

"And you go to school, I suppose, and study geography, arithmetic, and history, and all that. One of these days you mean to be President, don't you, and to stand here where I am, shaking hands with everybody?"

"No, sir, I hope not!" replied the boy vehemently; "I never want to be President."

"You may well say that — you may well say you hope not," answered the President; "you have spoken more wisely than you know." And taking the boy's hands in his, he looked lovingly and long in his face.

A poorly dressed, humpbacked woman approached, whose face had that rare spiritual beauty often seen in connection with this deformity. Her lustrous eyes looked up almost adoringly to the Chief Magistrate, but in her humility she forbore to offer her hand. Low bowed the President to her short stature, with that heavenly look in his face, of which I have before spoken, and he said something kindly in low tones to the poor cripple, that called a warm flush of gratitude to her face. It was impossible not to love the President. Awkward, homely, ungraceful, he yet found his way to all hearts, and was the recipient of more affection than any man of the nation.

In the midst of all the attractions of that afternoon, there was but one object of interest. And he was the tall, dark, sad, wan man, who stood in the middle of the room, now kindling with interest in those who accosted him, now sinking back in deep thoughtfulness, unmindful of the procession that filed before 'him, as if occupied with the grave affairs that for four years had rested on his heart and mind. I walked through the magnificent suite of rooms belonging to the Executive Mansion, all thrown open. Everywhere rare and beautiful flowers were exhaling their sweetness — the exquisite strains of the Marine Band were floating on the air — throngs of distinguished and titled people moved though the apartments — and yet the homely President was the nucleus around which all interest and affection clustered. "God bless him!" was the utterance which I heard over and over again, as I loitered an hour or two in the crowd. And if ever a sincere prayer went from my own heart, it was that which trembled on all lips, "God bless the good President!"

Once more I saw the President — and then in Chicago, which opened its arms to receive the hallowed remains of the martyred leader. For two weeks the city had been shrouded in its grief as in a pall. The people of the great metropolis, with tens of thousands from the farms and workshops of the Northwest, went forth to receive the illustrious dead, mingling their tears with the sad wailing of dirges that pulsed through the streets, with the solemn tolling of bells, and the heavy booming of minute guns.

There was none of the hum of business; none of the rush and whirl and hot haste that characterize Chicago, — but closed stores, silent streets, and sadness resting on all faces. Flags bound with crape floated mournfully at half-mast. Black draperies shrouded the buildings. All talk was low and brief. Many wept as they walked, and on the breast or arm of all were mourning badges. All nationalities, creeds, and sects were ranged along the route to be taken by the funeral cortége, or stood amid the solemn pageantry and funereal splendor of the great procession.

At the appointed hour the train arrived at its destination, bearing the corse of the man whom the West loved and delighted to honor. A gun announced its arrival to the solemn crowd. The same order of arrangements was observed as had been planned for the President's reception at the fair, only how heavily shadowed by the atmosphere of death! The sacred remains were removed to the funeral car prepared to receive them, and then they moved sadly and slowly to the Court House, where they lay in state to receive the last visits of affection. Minute guns boomed steadily; bells tolled unceasingly; sad dirges wailed their lamentations; muffled drums beat continuously, and the tears of the people fell as the cortége filed past. As the hallowed dust passed, the stricken throngs uncovered, while audible sobs burst from the bereaved lookers-on.

Not thus had Chicago hoped to receive the beloved President. A month later, and the great Northwest would have prepared for him a brilliant welcome. Then with great shouts rending the air, with salvos of artillery, with thrilling strains of triumphant music, with songs and ovations from old and young, from children and maidens, with flowers and costly gifts, and with overflowing hearts, it had hoped to testify the almost idolatrous love it bore him. God ordered otherwise, and translated him beyond our poor praises — above our earthly offerings.

> " Oh, friend! if thought and sense avail not,
>   To know thee as thou art —
> That all is well with thee forever,
>   I trust the instincts of my heart!"

# CHAPTER XXXI.

HEROISM OF SOLDIERS' WIVES — WHAT THEY ENDURED AT
HOME — A SUNDAY MORNING VISIT TO THEIR FAMILIES —
LEAVES FROM MY JOURNAL — PATHETIC INCIDENTS.

Petition of four hundred and eighty Soldiers in Southern Hospitals — "Ignore us, but look after our suffering Families!" — Heroism of Wives
and Mothers — Visit Soldiers' Families with Chaplain McCabe — Children fierce and wild with Hunger — An underground Room, and great
Wretchedness — The Soldier's Widow dies in the Night — Her Mother,
in the Darkness, defends the Body from Rats — The Baby falls from the
Chamber Window, while the Mother is away washing — A colored
Woman turned out on the Sidewalk, with her dying Child, for unpaid
Rent — Her Husband fighting under Colonel Shaw, in the Fifty-fourth
Massachusetts — Governor Andrew sends me *Carte blanche* in the way
of Relief for Families of that Regiment — The Historian should remem-
ber the Heroism of the Hearthstone.

T a Sanitary Convention held in Des Moines,
Ia., a petition was presented from four hundred and eighty soldiers in the general hospitals at the South, asking, among other
things, that the people of that state would
look after the welfare of their families while
they were in the service of the country. "We are grateful for all kindnesses shown us," was the language
of these veterans. "We appreciate your noble and
thoughtful charity, which reaches us in camp, in the
hospital, and on the battle-field. But we prefer that
you should forget us, and leave us to struggle with
our fate as we may, if you will but look after our

wives and children, our mothers and sisters, who are dependent upon us for support. A severe winter is before them, and we are rent with anxiety as we remember their slender resources, and our meagre and irregular pay. Succor them, and withhold your charity from us."

I often heard the same entreaty from men in the hospital and in camp, from men in health and on the march, and from men just passing into eternity. "Our wives and children, our mothers and sisters, who will take care of them?" Public sympathy was easily awakened for the brave men who went out to fight the battles of the country, and all demands made on the means and money of the loyal North for their relief were promptly met. Money and supplies were poured without stint into the Sanitary Commission; and wherever an opportunity was offered, either by the return of a regiment, or by visits to the hospitals, the people delighted to lavish their bounty directly on the soldiers.

But an immense amount of heroism among the wives of soldiers passed unnoticed, or was taken as a matter of course. For the soldier, he had his comrades about him, shoulder to shoulder. He had excitement. He had praise, if he did well. He had honorable mention, and pitying tears, if he fell nobly striving. But alas for his wife! Even an officer's wife, who had sympathizing friends, who had the comforts and many of the luxuries of life, whose children's future was provided for if their father fell, — what hours of dreadful suspense *she* passed, even under those favorable circumstances!

But for the wife of the poor soldier, who in giving her husband to her country gave everything; who had no friend to say "Well done!" as the lagging weeks of suspense crept on, and she stood bravely at her post keeping want and starvation at bay; whose imagination was busy among the heaps of dead and wounded, or traversing the wretched prison-pens, and shuddering at the thought of their demoniac keepers; who kept down her sobs as her little daughter offered up nightly prayers for "dear papa to come home!" or her son traced slowly with his forefinger the long list of killed and wounded "to see if father's name was there"; who shrouded her eyes from the possible future of her children should her strength give out under the pressure of want and anxiety; compared with her sharp mental torture, the physical suffering of the soldier sinks into insignificance. This silent army of heroines was too often forgotten. They were martyrs who died and made no sign. The shouts of far-off victories drowned their feeble wailings, and the horrors of hospitals overshadowed deeply their unobtruded miseries.

During the progress of one of the sanitary fairs, I called on a man and wife for help in the evening entertainments, when the wife observed, "You are doing a great work in aiding to relieve the sufferings of the soldiers; but there is another class, quite as worthy, that receives but little attention."

"What is that?" I inquired.

"The destitute families of soldiers in the field and of soldiers deceased. My husband enlisted in the beginning of the war. He left a good situation which had yielded us a comfortable living; and I was willing he should, for I was as patriotic as he, and knew that the country needed his services. He was to send me ten dollars of his monthly pay. A man of wealth promised to pay my rent the first year. Another was to furnish the winter's fuel. And another was to supply me with work from his clothing store. I had three children to provide for, the eldest six years, the youngest three months. I expected to live more economically than ever before, and I was willing to do so for the sake of the country. My husband's regiment received marching orders, and, although it was almost like burying him, I bore up under his departure, and put the best foot forward, remembering how much now depended upon me.

"Almost immediately my husband got sick and was sent to the hospital, and there he remained nine months, crippled with rheumatism. All that time not a cent of his pay reached me. My rent was paid the first three months, and then Mr. —— removed to New York, and that was the end of his promise. Mr. ——, who was to help me in the matter of fuel, forgot his promise; and when I went to him to remind him of it, he complained of his own poverty and of the high prices of fuel, and answered me so rudely that I never troubled him afterwards. I only got sewing from the clothing store three months out of twelve. I cannot tell you what I suffered during the first eighteen months. That winter I was in such poverty that I could not obtain food sufficient for us all. The cries of my hungry children almost drove me mad, and to them I carried all the food I obtained, often suffering from hunger myself so that I longed to die.

"Matters went from bad to worse. I was forced to move three times because of unpaid rent, and at last there came a time when I was without money, food, almost without fuel, and utterly without work or the prospect of any. I broke down in utter despair, and one night, after my children got asleep, I rushed down to the lake shore, determined on suicide. At the last moment my courage failed me, as I thought of my three helpless little children left with no one to care for them. I am an Englishwoman, and I had never before known want, and had never begged. But as I went back to my children that night, my pride was humbled, and I resolved to go to the poormaster in the morning and ask that we might be sent to the poorhouse. But in the morning relief came. I received a letter from my husband, with a hundred and thirty dollars in it, and that saved me that time.

" As the months went on the pressure became so terrible that at my entreaty my husband sought his discharge, and obtained it, and came home. You would call the means employed to obtain his discharge dishonorable, and he would not have resorted to them but for the fact that his family was starving. He might have remained in the service a year longer if we had been cared for. I could tell you of other cases harder than mine."

A few weeks later, a slight, delicate, pale-faced woman entered the rooms of the Commission about ten in the morning, whose face told us immediately that she was in suffering. I knew her as a soldier's wife with five small children, for she had been to me before. With a burst of agonized feeling, which no one who witnessed will ever forget, she said, " What shall I do? For God's sake tell me what I shall do! My children have literally, absolutely had not one mouthful to eat since ten o'clock yesterday morning. All yesterday afternoon I tried to get work at washing, scrubbing, or cleaning house. Some did not want me then; others wanted help immediately, but thought me too feeble for their work; others promised me work in a day or two; and I went home as empty-handed as I started. I was going to try again this morning, faint as I am for lack of food; but I have left my children famishing, crying with hunger, and I have come to beg. For God's sake do something for my poor little children!"

A wealthy lady standing by, who had heard the story with streaming eyes, gave the poor mother ten dollars, and hurried her back to buy food for her children. Others interested themselves in her directly, and before night there was sent to the soldier's wife and her children a barrel of flour, two barrels of potatoes, two hams, a bushel of beans, twenty pounds of pork, fifty dollars' worth of groceries, a ton of coal, and a half-cord of wood sawed and split. It was not often, however, that relief came so quickly or in such abundance.

On one occasion the week had been so crowded with work that I was obliged to devote Sunday morning to visiting some half-dozen soldiers' families, concerning whom I was feeling great anxiety. Chaplain McCabe, of the Christian Commission, who had been a chaplain in the army, and was captured at the battle of Bull Run, spending months in Libby Prison, wished to accompany me in these visits. He desired to witness for himself the poverty and distresses of the families of men in the field. With one exception I had visited every family on which we called for a year or longer, and knew their circumstances intimately, so that there was no chance for imposition. I transcribe from my journal the details of the visits made that morning, as they were written out on my return: —

"Visit number one was made to a German woman, whose husband is in the Twenty-fourth Illinois, now before Atlanta, Ga. She has seven children, the two youngest of whom cannot walk,—one from paralysis, and the other from its babyhood. Her husband left her eighteen dollars when he went away, and he has sent her money but once since, as he has been most of the time in the hospital. They own a little house with three rooms, built on leased ground; but the lease expired the first of this month and the land has been sold to an Irishman, who wishes the house moved off. What to do, she is unable to decide. Where she can lease a new lot, or obtain the money for leasing, and for moving the house, she does not know. If her husband were at home, all would be well; for his neighbors with one voice testify to his industry and sobriety. 'He is too much patriot,' they cry; 'he fight too much in the army.' And to prove their assertion they tell you he went into the revolutionary war of Europe in 1848, leaving his family then in distressing circumstances.

"Three times in a year the poor woman has been to me, weeping bitterly because she had not a mouthful of food for herself and children. On one occasion she brought three of her younger children into my kitchen. Ordinarily they are exceedingly quiet and well behaved; but this time they were so hungry that they were fierce and wild, and caught at food like animals, eating so rapidly and voraciously that I had to interfere lest harmful results would follow in the matter of digestion. To feed, clothe, and warm her family this winter, she has only her own labor to depend upon, and the irregular and small remittances from her husband. She washes, cleans house, and picks rags. Both the house and children were scrupulously clean, although indicative of extreme poverty; and the mother, though worn with care and labor, says she does not regret her husband's enlistment. ' It was right,' she says."

"Number two was an American family. The father is in the Ninety-first Illinois, and is in Vicksburg, guarding the prison. He is a carpenter, and could earn two and a half to three dollars per day if he were at home. His wife is a lovely, delicate woman, with three children. The husband is a noble fellow, and has only expended five dollars at the sutler's in two years; and that has been for stationery. He has drawn as little clothing as possible, and sends all his money home. It has reached his wife with unusual regularity. She owns a sewing-machine, gets plenty of work; for she is a most skilful needlewoman, aside from being a good operator on the machine. She is able, with the assistance of her husband's pay, to get along comfortably. But the last hundred dollars from her husband, brought up by one of his discharged lieutenants, was gambled away by the latter when coming up the Mississippi.

"She has lately fallen ill and been confined to her bed by sickness. The loss of this money plunged her into poverty, which, with the instinct of American women, she kept to herself. At last the unpaid rent had accumulated to thirty dollars, and she was in imminent danger of being turned out of doors. Food and fuel were gone, and starvation stared her in the face. All the while she wrote brave, cheerful letters to her husband, hiding the truth from him, and assuring him all was well. She would not distress him with the narration of troubles he could not remedy, she said; and so suffered and kept silence. I learned accidentally of her destitute circumstances. It is needless to say that speedy relief was carried to her and her weeping children.

"Her husband also learned accidentally how sad was the plight of his family, and besought his commander so earnestly for a furlough, that three weeks' leave of absence was given him. That visit brought the wife back from the verge of the grave; and, when her husband returned to his regiment, leaving her the money he had earned at his trade during his furlough, which a few generous people had largely increased by donations that they compelled him to accept, she again took up her burden of life, a little stronger to bear it. She cannot work yet; but she is not forgotten by the generous and patriotic, and will not be.

"Visit number three was to an underground room, in an old tumble-down building, on Wells Street, which is inhabited by nine families, one half of whom live in cellars, below the level of the street. Here, the wife of a soldier in one of the Ohio regiments, an American woman, died some two months since. I only learned of the case after she was dead. I went in the morning to the apartment, and found her aged mother, over seventy, with two children, two and four years of age, her only surviving relatives. They were so poor that they had not even a bit of candle, nor a drop of kerosene, nor a stick of fuel with which to make a light during the night, when the dying woman asked her mother to read some verses from the Scriptures, as she was passing away. The dreadful underground room is infested with rats, and during the remainder of the night the aged mother stood by her daughter's bedside, fighting the rats from the lifeless body.

" A few weeks after the mother's sorrowful death, the youngest child died. There remain now only the aged grandmother and the boy of four years. The husband was killed in the army some eight months before. They have no acquaintances, except among those who are in such abject poverty that affection is killed by it. They have no near relatives. The aged grandmother clings to her little grandson, who is her only tie to life. The sufferings of the dead mother and the entire family have been fearful; and the attenuated figure of the little boy and of the aged woman tell a story of starvation. No one knew them until suffering had done its dreadful work on the young soldier's widow, and laid her at rest from the sorrows of life.

" The poor grandmother is an object of the deepest commiseration. I never go to her comfortless home that I do not surprise her in tears. She is afraid her dead daughter has failed of heaven; and I am always compelled to go over my grounds of assurance that all is well with her. Chaplain McCabe, who listened to the poor woman's story, prayed and sang with her, and bade her be comforted with the confident assertion that her daughter was with the blessed. Arrangements are nearly completed to place the grandmother in the Old Ladies' Home, and to take the little boy into the Home of the Friendless.

" Number four was a soldier's family whose heaviest burdens have been removed by the return of the husband and father to his family. He has been discharged from the service, in consequence of serious injuries received in the left hand, arm, and side, from the bursting of a shell. He has found a little light employment, which, with the work of his energetic American wife, renders them comparatively independent of charity. She has toiled, suffered, and endured patiently, in his long absence, to support herself and child. Since the return of her crippled husband, the pinched look has left her face, and the pallor of death has been supplanted by a healthy hue. 'If I could only get plenty of work,' she says, 'I should be so happy that a queen might envy me!'

"Number five was the wife of one of the men who are forcing their way into Mobile under Admiral Farragut. She is one of the better sort of Irish women; and, though she rarely receives money from her husband, she earns enough to support herself and little daughter. When well, she needs no assistance; but a week's sickness or the loss of a week's work puts her in a tight place.

"Number six is a woman whose husband is in the Seventy-second Illinois. She has three children to maintain, whom she has to neglect in order to earn bread for them. Almost every day, week after week, she leaves the two younger in the care of the older, a little girl of nine years, and goes out to work, washing, scrubbing, and cleaning, from seven in the morning till six in the evening. Last week, when her children were locked up in the room in her absence, the baby, eighteen months old, fell out of the second-story chamber window, and was taken up for dead. It did not kill the child immediately, but he may yet die from the effects of the fall. He was taken to the

PLATE VI.

## FAMOUS UNION BATTLE-FLAGS.

1. Fifth N. H. Reg't.     2. First R. I. Cavalry     3. Sixteenth Conn. Reg't.
4. Fifty fourth (Colored) Mass. Reg't.     5. First Vermont Cavalry.     6. Twentieth Mass. Reg't.

*For Descriptions see pages 47-54.*

PHOTOGRAPHED AND PAINTED FROM THE ORIGINAL FLAGS EXPRESSLY FOR THIS WORK.

A. D. WORTHINGTON & CO. PUPLISHERS. HARTFORD, CONN.

children's ward of the hospital, where he can receive the care and nursing that his mother cannot give him. She is worn to a skeleton with hard work, but rarely complains, or asks for help. These last two women occupy three miserable attic rooms together, paying ten dollars per month for rent; and they render each other all the assistance in their power. Poor as they are, they are very helpful to one another.

"Number seven was a colored woman, whose husband has been in the Fifty-fourth Massachusetts, under Col. Robert G. Shaw, from its organization. Not a cent has yet been paid by government to any colored soldier who has gone from Chicago. This woman was a slave when the war began, — is still, as far as any manumission by her master is concerned. Since her husband's absence, she has passed through hunger, cold, sickness, and bereavement. Her landlord, a rich man of the city, a German, put her out of her house on the sidewalk, in a cold rain storm, because she owed him five dollars for rent, and could not then earn it, as her child was sick unto death with scarlet fever. One of her colored neighbors, as poor as she, took her in; and the baby died on the next Sunday morning. She came to me to get the baby buried, without going to the poormaster. 'It don't seem right for my child to be buried like a pauper,' she said, 'when her father is fighting for the country.' And I agreed with her.

"A way was devised to give the little one decent burial; and the mother's heart is comforted by the thought that her child will never have to pass through what she has. The woman's husband was born a slave in Beaufort, S. C., and thither his regiment was first ordered. He has learned to read and write, and wrote me a most graphic account of the battle in which his heroic colonel, the brave Robert G. Shaw, was killed. I made the poor woman supremely happy by reading to her a letter from Governor Andrew of Massachusetts, giving me *carte blanche* for the relief of the families living in Chicago whose husbands and fathers have enlisted in the Fifty-fourth. I promised to help her to house-keeping again, as soon as she can collect her scattered household goods.

"Number eight was the wife of another colored soldier of the Fifty-fourth Massachusetts. She has four children, and has not received any of her husband's earnings. Government has not paid him. She is lying very sick with typhoid fever. I gladdened her by telling her of Governor Andrew's letter, which will immediately procure her a physician and nurse, medicine, and food for her children. Chaplain McCabe sang her a beautiful hymn, in his melodious and expressive style, and then prayed with her. The colored people in the neighborhood, whom music always attracts, silently flocked into the room, as he sang and prayed; and, as they stood weeping and listening, I found it difficult to repress my own tears for the friendless and feeble wives of the soldiers, of whose sad condition I know so much. They are not remembered, nor ministered to, nor sympathized with, as they should be."

If the history of this war shall ever be written in full, whatever else the historian may forget, he will not fail to chronicle the sublime valor manifested at the hearthstone, all over this struggling land.

# CHAPTER XXXII.

MY FIRST PUBLIC SPEECH — CROSSING THE MISSISSIPPI IN A
ROW-BOAT — "A VOICE FROM THE FRONT" — FACING AN
AUDIENCE FOR THE FIRST TIME — AN EVENTFUL NIGHT.

Return from the Front — Accept Invitation from Dubuque to address the
Ladies — Ferry-boat detained by moving Ice in the Mississippi — Cross
in a Row-boat — The Trip attended with much Danger — The Risk assumed — Many prophesied evil Results — They proved false Prophets —
Crossed the River safely — "All Iowa will hear you to-night" — Appalled at
the Prospect — Am advertised for a Lecture, without being consulted
— "A Voice from the Front!" — Fear to attempt a public Speech —
Hesitation overcome by Colonel Stone's Argument — The Results that
followed — An Iowa Sanitary Fair is planned and carried out — Aggregates nearly $60,000.

CAME up the Mississippi River the last of
April, 1863, where I had been spending
some weeks in work among the hospitals.
I found my desk loaded with invitations to
visit aid societies, or deliver addresses, in
which I should narrate my experiences. All
were eager to hear directly from the army at the
front, which was fighting not the enemy alone, but
swamp fever, malarial diseases, and, worse than all,
scurvy. The invitation which I decided to accept
was one which in the order of date was first given,
and that took me to Dubuque, Ia. The ladies had
written as follows: —

601

"The hall in which we hold our meetings will accommodate about three hundred. We shall pack it for an afternoon meeting. We want you should narrate to the ladies who will be in attendance what you have seen. Explain to them the need of sanitary stores — how it happens that the government does not do everything for the soldiers — and what is the particular kind of relief most necessary. In the evening we shall adjourn to a larger hall, where we shall have music, sell cake, ice cream, hot coffee, and other refreshments, and where we hope the attendance will be doubled. The great attraction will be your presence, and the fact that through you the gentlemen can get such information as they may desire. If we have good weather, we shall clear one hundred dollars."

I started the night before from Chicago, on one of the Pullman sleepers, and reached Dunleith — now East Dubuque — early in the morning. No bridge then spanned the Mississippi at that point — it was only a possibility in the future. A ferry-boat took passengers across. But as we alighted from the train, we saw the boat on the opposite side, with no prospect of being able to steam across immediately. The ice had moved down from the upper river, and was wedged in great masses opposite Dubuque, the broken and ponderous sheets grinding against each other and stretching from shore to shore. All ferriage of freight and passengers had ceased for twenty-four hours, and we only increased the anxious and impatient crowd; most of whom vented their displeasure at this unwelcome blockade in useless imprecations on the railroad officials.

I spent the weary day watching the unmoving ice,

and wondering what was to become of my engagement in the evening. About three in the afternoon, I observed two men, on the Dunleith side, launching a row-boat where the river was open. By dint of earnest entreaty, and promise of handsome payment, I persuaded them to row me over. They assured me that I would be drowned — and one of them declared "if she were *my* wife, she shouldn't go a step!" I was not so certain of that. And I also knew that the boatmen were accustomed to this mode of conveyance, and had no expectation of being drowned themselves. If they dared take the risk, I need not fear to accompany them. My fellow-passengers bade me "good-bye" ruefully, prophesying, with the boatmen, that I should be drowned — or, at least, "handsomely ducked." They all proved false prophets.

It took a long while to cross, for the men were obliged to row up-stream, above the loose ice, into clear water, and then to descend the river on the Dubuque side. I was safely landed, at dark, a mile above the regular wharf. I found my way to the house of my friend, who was to entertain me. A great shout of joy welcomed me as I entered the door. She was the President of the Aid Society, and the ladies had gathered in her parlors to arrange a new programme for the evening, as they despaired of keeping the promise they had made the public. Talking all at once they began to inform me of their grand arrangements for the evening, which my unexpected arrival would enable them to carry out.

So great an interest had been awakened that they had decided to hold their meeting in the evening in the Congregational church, and, to encourage me, they told me that neither Professor Agassiz, nor Bayard Taylor, who had lectured in it that winter, had been able to fill it with their voices. Governor Kirkwood was to preside; the Governor-elect, Colonel Stone, who was at home from the army with a gunshot wound, was to be in attendance; so were the Adjutant-General, the Attorney-General of the state, the leading members of the Legislature of both Houses, the Indian Commissioner, and, in short, almost all the magnates of the state of Iowa.

"You never could have a better opportunity to talk to all Iowa!" said the women, all in one breath. "For every county of the state will be represented in the audience to-night, and everything is auspicious of large results. How immensely fortunate that you were able to cross the river!"

I was appalled and dumbfounded. At that time, I had never attempted a public address to a promiscuous audience. I had only addressed audiences of women, sitting in a chair decorously before them, and trying with all my might to keep my hands folded on my lap. I had no idea whether I had voice to reach an audience such as the ladies had invoked — or courage to bear me through the ordeal. I was sure of one thing — that I had nothing whatever to say to a congregation so imposing in numbers and in character, and I flatly refused to carry out their programme.

"You never should have made these arrangements without consulting me!" was my frightened rejoinder. "I am *not* a public speaker; I have never made a speech in my life, and never have addressed any but companies of women. I had something to say to you, ladies, as the Aid Society, but it is not at all worthy to be presented as an address to the great audience that you have unwisely called together. *I cannot do it!*"

The ladies protested. They had extensively advertised the evening meeting, and the town was gay with colored placards, announcing in letters as large as my hand, not only my name, but "the title of my lecture" — "A VOICE FROM THE FRONT!" — for so they had christened my unborn speech. They knew I could do all they had promised in the bills, if I would only attempt it. They had not supposed it was necessary to consult me — they had taken it for granted that I could talk to three thousand as well as three hundred — and to back down because men were, in part, to compose the audience, why, that was too absurd — I must not think of such a thing. But the more they urged and persuaded, the more cowardly and helpless I became, until, at last, my courage took an utter stampede, and I was hardly able to talk coherently with them in the parlor. No shallop left on the shore by the retreating tide was ever more helpless or inert than I felt myself to be. There was no float in me — and I could not believe there ever would be.

Gentlemen began to arrive — governors, generals home on furlough, colonels, adjutants, and they all joined their entreaties to those of the crestfallen women. But they might as well have entreated a post. The thing was not in me. I dared not attempt it. At last it was settled that Colonel Stone, the Governor-elect, in whose regimental hospital I had spent some days, and with whom I had had an acquaintance at the front, should make my speech for me. I was to tell him what I intended to say to the women — to give him all the points which I wished enforced — to transfer to him such phases of my experience as would be particularly interesting, and, above all, to acquaint him with the sore need of large quantities of sanitary supplies. And especially with the fact that the Army of the Mississippi was suffering extremely from a lack of anti-scorbutics.

The hour for the meeting arrived. The church adjoined my place of entertainment. The gentlemen came in to hurry us, in advance of the advertised hour, for the house was so packed that not another person could enter, nor was an inch of standing room unoccupied. Dreadfully chagrined and depressed — but much less humiliated than I, the innocent cause of their abasement — the ladies of the Aid Society went ahead to the seats reserved for them. Then the dignitaries of the state followed, while Colonel Stone and I brought up the rear. As we passed down from the parlor, he drew me by the arm into the lower reception-room, the door of which stood open as we were passing. Closing the door and turning the key in the lock, he stood with his back to it, and faced me.

"I have no expectation, Mrs. Livermore," he said, "that I can in the least change your decision concerning the evening address, but this has occurred to me. I have seen you at the front, watched your work in the hospitals, and believe you are in earnest, and are honest. When you tell me that you want to be a hand or a foot, an eye or an ear, a voice or an influence in the work of assisting the country in its sad hour of trouble, I believe just what you say; I think you mean it. To-night God has prepared for you an opportunity to speak to all Iowa. You have not wished it. The ladies of the Aid Society have not done it. These eminent gentlemen have *happened* here on various errands, and this opportunity has, in a certain sense, come about providentially. Now, how dare you, when God has given you such an opportunity to do a great work, how dare you refuse, and say, 'I cannot do it'? It is not necessary for you to deliver an oration; it is only necessary to say to the great audience in the church just what you had come prepared to say to the ladies of the Aid Society. It will be more effective than any labored speech, or any carefully prepared address. It is for you to say whether the evening shall be a success for the hospitals of the South — whether the state of Iowa shall commence doing sanitary work, or whether this grand occasion shall prove a failure."

He spoke very impressively, looking me earnestly in the face. For a few moments we stood silently confronting each other. Somehow I felt the full force of all that he had said, and there came over me a complete revulsion of feeling. I felt willing to undertake what I had flatly refused to do while talking with the ladies, and a subtle consciousness stole over me that I should succeed in it. I said, "Very well, Colonel Stone, I will attempt it; only do not allow long preliminaries; and after Governor Kirkwood has opened the meeting, let him introduce you as the orator of the evening. You must explain to the people that I am not a public speaker; that I have never in my life made a public address; that I have only come prepared with a small statement of facts for the Ladies' Aid Society; and then introduce me as quickly as possible, and I will do the best I can."

I followed him down the aisle of the church to the platform, erected in front of the pulpit, where a seat was reserved for me. The ladies of the Aid Society looked their astonishment. As speedily as possible Colonel Stone presented me to the great gathering. I rose by a supreme effort, trembling in every fibre of my being, although outwardly appearing calm. Shutting out all thought of the expectant multitude before me, I concentrated my mind upon what I had to say. For the first ten minutes I talked into utter darkness. It was as if the house was unlighted. I did not even hear the sound of my own voice — only a roaring, as if ten thousand mill-wheels were thundering about me. The knocking of Belshazzar's knees was not a circumstance to the play that mine kept up. The physical tumult into which this effort plunged me was exhausting. It would have prostrated a feebler woman, and it was days before I recovered my usual calmness of nerve and steadiness of poise.

But gradually it began to grow light about me. I began to hear my own voice. I could, after a little, distinguish the faces of people whom I knew. I was aware that I was being heard all over the house. Then I lost all sense of fear, and after the first fifteen minutes I forgot the audience, the fact that I was a novice as a public speaker, and only remembered the destitution, sickness, and suffering I had seen at the front. And the feeling grew strong within me that the people of Iowa, who had, as I knew, contributed but little to the cause of hospital relief, *must* be aroused to do their share of the work. Once I was interrupted by long and loud applause. I was so absorbed that I did not understand it for a moment, and looked around to see what had fallen. I thought some of the seats had given way.

When I closed I supposed I had spoken half an hour; I had in reality talked an hour and a quarter. Governor Kirkwood immediately followed. "Without any attempt at speech-making," he said, "Mrs. Livermore has to-night given us facts. She has told us of the soldiers' needs; she has told us of our duties. It is now our turn to speak, and we must speak in dollars and gifts." And asking Colonel Stone to keep the tally of the contributions, he called for donations.

I cannot describe the scene that followed. More rapidly than two could record it, eight thousand dollars in money were pledged, five hundred barrels of potatoes, eighty-eight barrels of sauer-kraut, one hundred and fifty bushels of onions, which are the very best anti-scorbutics, and five hundred pairs of hospital shirts and drawers.

Attorney-General Bissell now rose, and said: "Mrs. Livermore has told us that it is possible for Iowa to do a great deal through a sanitary fair, and, as the fair epidemic has travelled eastward all over the country, until it has exhausted itself on the Atlantic coast, I think it will be well for us to invoke its re-appearance here in Dubuque. It is now almost eleven o'clock. If those who must leave the house will retire as rapidly as possible, the rest of us will remain; and, if Mrs. Livermore will assist us, we will organize the skeleton of an association for an Iowa Sanitary Fair."

Very few left the church. When the meeting adjourned, at half-past twelve, subject to the call of the President on a future occasion, the organization for a sanitary fair was well formed, and the plans pretty well mapped out. With these results attendant on my first speech, is it surprising that I have accepted the platform as powerful in the advocacy of a good cause, or in advancement of a great reform?

From the beginning of the war Iowa had nobly responded to the call of the country. From her sparse population she had sent forth her sons to assist in the defence of freedom and the subduing of the rebellion, until she was then twenty thousand ahead of her quota. On every battle-field Iowa men had won an imperishable name for the lofty courage with which they had contemned death. From almost every home in Iowa, wives and mothers, sisters and lovers, had surrendered to the exigencies of war those dear to them as their heart's blood. Under the call for men for the " hundred days' service," the colleges and institutions of learning had sent forth their entire senior classes, so that there was not a college Commencement that year in Iowa. And for the same reason the courts had adjourned, and all legal and United States business had been postponed for the present.

But while Iowa had contributed so nobly of her sons to the country, she had not kept pace with the other Northwestern states in the sanitary work for the relief of the sick and wounded. There had been reasons for this. A diversity of opinion as to the best methods of doing this work was probably the most potent. The sanitary supplies had largely been sent through unreliable channels, and so had failed to reach those for whom they were intended. This had brought discouragement throughout the state. But this evening meeting in the Congregational church quickened the whole state into intense activity; and in the furor which followed, she outdid her sister states, which had been longer at work.

After making arrangements at home for my absence, I spent some months in Iowa, riding in " mud-spankers," in stages, " prairie schooners," on railroads, and in every conceivable way. I held meetings, and did whatever was necessary, in connection with the men and women who had organized for this purpose, to make their sanitary fair a great success.

It opened in the last week of June, 1864. I had been kept informed of its steady growth, and was prepared for something creditable, but was surprised by its beauty and magnitude. It was a wonderful fair, when all that pertained to it was fully comprehended. It was held west of the Mississippi, where the refinements and luxuries of civilization were not supposed to exist in large measure. It was held in a new state, where railroads were not numerous, and where prairie stage-coaches were still the principal conveniences for travelling.

At that time more than half the territory of the state was in the hands of Eastern speculators, who refused to open it to immigration. The male population had been so drained by the repeated calls of the country, that women were aiding in the outdoor work of the farms, all through the state, ploughing, reaping, mowing, and threshing. The fair was held in a state not rich, save in the great hearts of its loyal men and women, and its broad acres of virgin prairie, holding uncounted wealth in its bosom. There were no ladies and gentlemen of elegant leisure among her people. Few idlers or listless hangers-on were there, all being engaged in the earnest work of subduing nature,—in building highways and railroads, bridges and steam-boats, school-houses and warehouses, and in bringing the soil under cultivation.

As I entered the spacious City Hall building, three stories high, completely occupied by the fair, and went from one department to another, each filled with articles tasteful, beautiful, and useful, I was astonished at the great variety of wares displayed. This latest born of the great sisterhood of fairs seemed, at a *coup d'œuil*, equal in beauty and general effect to any of its predecessors.

It was intended to hold the fair for one week only. But, finding it impossible to carry out the purpose of the executive committee, it was decided to continue it a week longer. The gross receipts of the first week were sixty thousand dollars. It was a splendid result, and an unparalleled success, when all the circumstances were considered. At the end of the second week the managers of the fair were able to announce their net profits as nearly sixty thousand dollars. In estimating all the disadvantages under which this far-away state labored from the outset, and recalling her patriotism, loyalty, and generosity, one is forced to say, "Many states did excellently; but Iowa excelled them all!"

# CHAPTER XXXIII.

REMINISCENCES OF THE WAR — TOUCHING STORY OF A RING
— THE MAJOR WHO CRIED FOR MILK — CAPTURE OF GEN-
ERAL GRANT — "OLD ABE," THE WISCONSIN WAR EAGLE,
AND HIS WONDERFUL CAREER.

Confronted by one of my own Letters — The widowed Mother tells her
Story — Puts her dead Daughter's Ring on my Finger — Officers' Hospi-
tal at Memphis — Its wretched Condition — Is made comfortable by the
Commission — Incident at the Fabyan House, White Mountains — "Do
you remember the Major who cried for Milk?" — Second Sanitary Fair
in Chicago — Held after the War ended — Regiments, Soldiers, and Offi-
cers received there — An Ovation to General Grant — Executes a flank
Movement on the People — Is captured by young Ladies — "This beats
Vicksburg all out of Sight!" — "Old Abe," the Eagle of the Eighth
Wisconsin — His military Behavior — Children sell his Pictures for the
Soldiers' Fair — Make $16,308.93 by the Sales.

## THE GIFT OF A SOLDIER'S WIDOW AND MOTHER.

SOME few years ago I filled a lecture engagement in Albion, Mich. At the close of the
lecture, I observed, standing outside the
little group of acquaintances who surrounded me, a white-haired, elderly woman, who
approached me with the following inquiry: —

"Do you remember writing a letter for John ——,
of the Twelfth Michigan, when he lay dying in the
Overton Hospital, at Memphis, in the spring of 1863?
After he died, you completed the letter, writing to
his mother and wife; do you remember it?"

I was obliged to tell the sad-faced woman that I
performed so many offices of this kind during the

war, when at the front or in the hospitals, that it was hardly possible for me to recall any individual case.

Drawing from her pocket a letter, that had been worn in pieces where it had been folded, and which was sewed together with fine cotton, she held it up to me.

"Do you remember this letter?"

I recognized my penmanship, and, glancing over the contents of the letter, saw what it was. The first four pages I had written at the dictation of a young man who had been shot through the lungs, and was dying. The language was his, not mine, and I had not amended his phraseology. I had completed the letter after his death, by the addition of three pages, in which I sought to comfort the bereaved survivors.

"I thought John's wife and I would die when we heard he was dead," said the long-bereaved mother. "Your letter saved us. We were both comforted by it, and read it and re-read it, even when we had learned it word for word by much reading. When we heard of other women similarly bereaved, we loaned them the letter, until it was worn in pieces. Then we sewed it together; and then we made copies of it, and sent to our bereaved friends, and kept it in circulation until after the war ended.

"John's death was a great loss to us. He was my only child, and was born after my husband's death, a blessing and a comfort from the day he saw the light. He had been engaged to be married for three years when the war came. He felt that he ought to enlist, but Anna and I could not listen to such a proposal, and we talked it down. At last he felt it was a duty for him to enter the service, and

that he must go. We all three agreed to pray over
it for a week, and to announce our decisions the next
Sunday morning. When we came together at the
end of a week, we had all decided that it was his
duty to serve his country in the field. He enlisted
in the Twelfth Michigan, under good officers, and
the regiment was ordered South immediately.

"Anna insisted that their marriage should take
place before he left, that she might go down and
nurse him if he got sick or was wounded. She
accompanied him as far as Louisville, when she could
go no farther, and was sent homeward. At John's
request we made one family, and she was a true,
loving daughter to me. For eighteen months no ill
tidings were received from my son. He was always
well, never was wounded, and the February before his
death he came home on fourteen days' furlough. We
had received only three letters from him after his return, when your letter came, announcing his death.

"Anna never got over it. She worked and kept
busy, went to church and taught her class in the
Sunday-school, but all the life had gone out of her.
She used to be very gay, and full of frolic and fun,
but she dropped down to a kind of mild sadness, and
I never heard her voice ringing with laughter as in
the old days. She fell into delicate health, and grew
thinner and feebler as the years went by. Eight
years ago she had gastric fever. After the fever was
subdued, she didn't rally, but failed every day, becoming whiter and weaker, until I saw she must die. I
tried hard to persuade her to live, for she was all I
had, and I loved her for her own sake as well as John's.

"One day, when I was bathing her, her wedding
ring rolled off her finger, which had wasted to the

bone, and it was some time before it could be found. I proposed to put it away for safe keeping. 'No,' said Anna, 'let me wear it till I die. Roll a bit of paper on the inside to make it fit my finger. And, mother, when I am gone, if you can learn where Mrs. Livermore lives, send the ring to her, and ask her to wear it for my sake and John's. Tell her it was my dying request.'

"I live eight miles from here," said the worn woman. "And when I saw by the paper that you were going to lecture in Albion, I drove over to see and hear you. The ring has been cleansed this afternoon by a goldsmith, so that no taint of sickness or death clings to it. So please wear it, not only for the sake of John and Anna, but for my sake, for I shall probably never meet you again." And taking my hand, the widowed and childless mother slipped the ring on my finger, from which it has never since been taken. Bidding me "Good-bye," she seated herself in the cutter, and, gathering the reins in her hand, drove away in the moonlight, over the glittering snow, to her desolate home, eight miles away.

Affected as I was by the narrative, I am unable to recall a single circumstance of the event. But for the proof of my own letter I should be half tempted to believe the bereaved woman had confounded me with some other worker in the hospitals, so completely is all memory of the incident effaced from my mind.

## "DO YOU REMEMBER THE MAN WHO CRIED FOR MILK?"

When in Memphis, on one occasion during the war, I heard of an Officers' Hospital in a most pitiable condition. I went over to investigate it. Its wretchedness could not be exaggerated. Government made no provision for the care of officers when they were sick, beyond furnishing medicine and advice. They were better paid than the privates, and were expected to provide themselves with the food and clothing demanded by their situation. But they received their pay at such irregular intervals that, not unfrequently, when they became victims of disease, they suffered for the necessaries of hospital life. which were furnished freely to the rank and file.

There were over a hundred officers in this dreary hospital, many of them gentlemen, and most of them men of intelligence and character. There was not a cot in the wards, nor even an apology for a bed, nor was there an article of hospital clothing. There was an unusual dearth of everything at the Government Purveyor's — so that no remedy for the discomforts of the hospital could be expected from that quarter. A large shipment of hospital furniture, blankets, clothing and food was on its way to Memphis; and when it arrived, I was informed that the Officers' Hospital would be properly fitted up and furnished.

In the meantime, the men were lying in their uniforms, on rubber blankets, or on the bare floor, with their knapsacks for pillows. All were too ill to sit up, and some were sick unto death. Some were accompanied by colored servants, ignorant of any knowledge save what was sufficient for the roughest work, and so stupid and shiftless as to be encumbrances rather then assistants. There were no nurses, not even convalescent soldiers. The poverty and desolation of the hospital were indescribable. The officers did not complain, but expressed satisfaction that the privates were better cared for than they.

I applied to the Sanitary Commission in Memphis, whose shelves and drawers were crowded with clothing, and where large rooms were packed to repletion with cots, tables, bedding, camp-stools, sanitary stores of all kinds, and delicacies. The Commission was not expected to provide for officers, even when they were in hospital — they were popularly believed to be able to care for themselves. Neither was it to allow such mitigable suffering as this to be uncared for, and it moved immediately to the relief of the sick men. I was requested to make out the order for all that was necessary, and wagon-loads of cots, bedding, clothing, and whatever else was needed were immediately despatched, accompanied by relief agents.

There was admirable promptness, and the work of the agents of the Commission was not remitted until every man was relieved of his uniform, bathed, dressed in hospital garments, and placed in a clean, sweet bed. A sick-diet kitchen was established, and four of the women nurses whom I had brought from Chicago were detailed to service in the wards of the hospital. The gratitude of the neglected and helpless officers was unbounded. They could only express their thanks in broken words and sobs.

One morning, the surgeon informed me that all the patients with bowel difficulties might be allowed a specified quantity of milk three times a day — an order which I repeated to the men, as I knew they would welcome it with gratitude, as milk was the article of food they most craved. As I left the ward, I saw one of the officers, a major, bury his face in the pillow, and abandon himself to hysterical weeping. He had been very ill with pneumonia, through which he had barely lived.  His convalescence was slow, and his complete recovery depended on careful nursing and proper diet.

I begged to know the cause of his grief.  After much soothing and coaxing, I drew from him the reason of his tears.  "I want milk too," he sobbed bitterly, "but I haven't had bowel trouble, only pneumonia!" And turning his face to the wall, he broke afresh into violent weeping.  I hastened to the surgeon, and obtained an order for milk to be given patients convalescing from pneumonia, of which I informed the major without delay.  It was with great difficulty I could stanch his tears, for he was so pitifully weak as to be beyond his own control.

Two summers ago, I was at Fabyan's in the White Mountains.  A tall, fine, military looking man sat opposite me at dinner.  Like myself, he was attending the sessions of "The National Institute of Instruction."  The essays and discussions of the morning formed the topic of conversation, in which all joined.  In a lull of the talk, my *vis-à-vis* addressed me personally.

"Pardon me, madam — but were you in Memphis in April, 1863?"

"I was."

"Did you visit the Officers' Hospital at that time, and remain till it was made comfortable, and put on the footing of a first-class institution?"

"I did."

"Do you remember a major who nearly cried himself to death because he wanted milk, which had been prescribed for some of the patients, but not for him, who was recovering from pneumonia?"

"Very well, indeed, sir."

"Allow me to shake hands with you, madam. *I am that man.* I have always believed that I should have died but for the milk diet on which I was then placed. I want to thank you now for the good service you rendered me, as I have never before had an opportunity, and to tell you how ashamed I am when I remember my childishness."

There was no occasion for shame, or a sense of humiliation. For persons of unbending will, and iron control, when in good health, break down into infantile weakness of mind — when surrounded by the tender care of home, and the ministrations of love — if the nerves lose their tone, or disease saps the body of its vigor. How much stronger the tendencies to despondency in a comfortless hospital, where one is left to battle with sickness, uncheered by affection!

### HOW GENERAL GRANT WAS CAPTURED.

A second great sanitary fair was in progress in Chicago when the war ended. At no time were the wants of the soldiers more pressing than then; while the Chicago Soldiers' Home, established for the permanently disabled and indigent soldiers of Illinois, was in suffering need of funds. The profits of the fair were to be divided between the Home and the Commission — and again the Northwest bent its energies to the successful management of a sanitary fair.

The " boys in blue," returning home from service, dropped into the fair continually. Sometimes they came singly, sometimes in companies, and sometimes regiments were received, with pomp and ceremony. To all officers of the army there was accorded a hearty welcome, while the eminent generals, to whose leadership the country owes the preservation of the government and the restoration of peace, were received with ovations.

To General Grant a reception was accorded unequalled in the history of the Northwest. A vast crowd awaited his arrival at the railroad station, and it was with great difficulty that the mounted aids could make a way for him to the fair through the cheering throngs. Inside the bazar, the aid of the police was necessary to enable him to reach the platform. When the bands played "Hail to the Chief," and "The Red, White, and Blue," ten thousand voices sang the words, drowning the instruments. Amid the wildest enthusiasm, he was presented to the people, who received him with tremendous applause, cheer upon cheer, that did not subside for some moments. Addresses were made by generals and governors, poems were read, written for the occasion, and there were music and cheering *ad libitum* — but both General and Mrs. Grant were imprisoned on the platform. They were unable to visit the various departments, to accept the courtesies offered them, nor could they reach the hall where an elegant lunch was awaiting them.

The next day General Grant visited the fair again, accompanied by his wife, and executed the greatest manœuvre of his life. He made a flank movement on the people of Chicago, and visited the bazar in the early morning, when only those were present who were putting the great fancy ware-rooms in order for the day. He had nearly completed the tour of the several departments, both Mrs. Grant and himself had received many handsome gifts prepared especially for them, when the clock struck ten, — the hour for the arrival of the young ladies who were to serve for the day. A volunteer staff of them immediately surrounded the General. He was captured. They accompanied him from booth to booth, and from gallery to gallery, until several hundred of the loveliest girls of the city were in his retinue.

They whisperingly appealed to me, again and again, for permission to kiss the great man, as modest and shy as he was famed, until at last I said to him, —

"General Grant, these girls are very desirous to kiss you, but they have not the courage to propose it themselves."

"Well," said the gallant General, turning towards them, "if they want to kiss me I do not see what there is to hinder. I have been here three days and nobody has kissed me yet but my wife."

Instantly, dozens of charming fairies pounced upon him. He attempted to retreat, but it was in vain. He tried to break through the rosy ranks, but without success. For the first time he confessed himself vanquished, and calmly awaited events. The truth must be told — he gave kiss for kiss. Never was such a man subjected to such an ordeal. On came the maidens, singly, or in file, or by squads. They kissed him on the forehead, they kissed him on the nose, they kissed him on the cheek, chin, or neck. There must have been dozens of kisses lying around loose at the close of this attack, hidden in the General's whiskers. All the while the hero of a hundred battle-fields blushed until his face was crimson.

"Well," said he at the close, "that beats Vicksburg all out of sight!"

It tested the General's courage severely during that visit to show himself anywhere. His appearance on the street was the signal for a furor. A surging sea of humanity set toward him from every point, until the streets were blocked and business interfered with. On the following Sunday he attended the Methodist church on Indiana Avenue. When the service was concluded, the audience filed down one aisle and up the other to grasp the hand of their hero. After streams of people had flowed along for three-quarters of an hour, until it seemed as if half a dozen congregations must have exhausted themselves, it was found that the worshippers of neighboring churches were filing in, and it became necessary to close the church doors.

## THE WISCONSIN WAR EAGLE.

The story of "Old Abe," the Wisconsin war eagle, has been frequently told. The eagle was taken from his nest by an Indian in upper Wisconsin in the summer of 1861. Having been sold by his captor, he was finally presented to Company C, Eighth Wisconsin. A standard was made for him, and he was carried beside the regimental flag. For three years he was in all the marches of the regiment, taking part in twenty-two battles and thirty skirmishes, and was wounded in three of them.

When the regiment was engaged in battle, "Old Abe" manifested delight. At such a time, he would always be found in his proper place, at the head of Company C. When enveloped in the smoke of battle, he spread his pinions, jumped up and down on his perch, uttering such wild and fearful screams as only an eagle can. The fiercer and louder the storm of battle, the fiercer and louder his screams. He seemed always to understand army movements, such as dress parade, and preparation for the march. Before he had been a year in the service, he would give heed directly to "Attention! Battalion!" With his head obliquely to the front, his right eye turned upon the commander, he would listen and obey orders, noting time carefully. After parade had been dismissed, and the ranks were being closed by the sergeant, he would lay aside his soldierly manner, flap his wings, loll about, and make himself at home generally.

When there was an order to form for battle, he and the colors were the first upon the line. His actions upon those occasions were uneasy. He would turn his head anxiously from right to left, looking to see when the line was completed. As soon as the regiment got ready, faced, and began to march, he would assume a steady and quiet demeanor. He could always be seen a little above the heads of the soldiers, close by the flag. That position of honor was never disallowed him.

At the battle of Farmington, May 9, 1862, the men were ordered to lie down on the ground. The instant they did so, "Old Abe" flew from his perch. He insisted on being protected as well as they, and flattened himself on the ground, remaining there until the men rose, when, with outspread wings, he flew back to his place of peril, and held it until the close of the contest. At the battle of Corinth the rebel general Price discovered him, and ordered his men to take him if they could not kill him, adding that "he would rather capture that bird than the whole brigade." The bird was never so excited as

PLATE VII.

## FAMOUS UNION BATTLE-FLAGS:

"Old Abe" War Eagle of the 8th Wis. Reg't. 1. Ninth Iowa Reg't. 2. Second Kansas Battery.
3. Second Wis. Reg't. 4. Seventh Mo. Reg't. 5. Second Kansas Reg't. 6. First Ohio Battery.

*For Descriptions see pages 54-63.*

PHOTOGRAPHED AND PAINTED FROM THE ORIGINAL FLAGS EXPRESSLY FOR THIS WORK.

A. D. WORTHINGTON & CO. PUBLISHERS, HARTFORD, CONN.

during that battle. Flying from his perch to the length of his chain, flapping his wings, with wide-open mouth, his screams could be heard in every lull of the battle.

Mr. Sewell, a Chicago publisher, devised a very original mode of raising money for the sanitary fair, in connection with this war eagle. Pictures of the bird were struck off, and offered for sale. A child that sold one of these pictures for ten cents was to be considered a private in the "Army of the American Eagle." One who sold a dollar's worth was to be commissioned as corporal. Five dollars made one first lieutenant; ten dollars conferred the rank of captain; fifty dollars made a lieutenant-colonel; a hundred dollars a colonel; two hundred dollars brigadier-general; four hundred dollars made a child major-general. The plan took with the children, who were charmed with the ingenious device. All over the country the little folks sold pictures of "Old Abe"— from Maine to Oregon, from upper Minnesota and Lake Superior to points far south which the soldiers had wrested from the enemy.

More than twelve thousand letters were received from boys and girls, which were carefully filed in alphabetical order. The net profits of the children's "Army of the American Eagle" footed up *sixteen thousand three hundred and eight dollars and ninety-three cents.* It was all paid over to the treasury, and cost the fair not one cent for expense. It was more than was paid in by any other department; and all was obtained from the efforts of children. Gold, silver, and bronze medals were presented to the children by Mr. Sewell, through General Sherman, in the fair building, one day near

its close, with all the pomp of speeches, music, hurrahs, and waving of handkerchiefs and flags.

At the close of the war "Old Abe" became the
pensioner of the state, and a room was appointed him
in the State House, at Madison, Wis. An appropriation was made for his care, and for the salary of his
attendant, who took great pride in the warlike bird,
between whom and himself there sprang up an affection that lasted during "Old Abe's" life. In charge
of this attendant, the eagle visited soldiers' re-unions,
became an object of interest and profit at Grand Army
fairs, was borne in procession at the dedication of
soldiers' monuments, and figured at the consecration
of memorial halls. One of these occasions brought
him to Boston, where he excited unusual interest.
He held immense receptions in the "Old South
Meeting-house," where children, as well as adults,
paid him court, all eager to see the imperial bird,
which had been through the fire of scores of battles,
sharing their excitement and danger with the men.
So great was the interest his visit awakened, that
Mrs. Hemmenway, the eminent woman philanthro-
pist of the city, who has assisted in the preservation
of the "Old South" as a historic museum, commissioned an artist to paint "Old Abe's" portrait, which
hangs on the walls, with other pictures of historic
worth.

# CHAPTER XXXIV.

SOLDIERS' LETTERS FROM THE FRONT DURING THE FIRST
YEAR OF THE WAR—VIVID PICTURES OF LIFE IN CAMP
— DESOLATION — AMUSEMENTS — MARCHING — FORAGING
— PICKET DUTY—LETTERS FROM HOME.

Authors of the Letters — Life in Camp — Exploits of the First Iowa — "A
bully Boy" — Hardships of a Chaplain — Fight at Conrad's Ferry —
The Desolation of War — Impatient to be led into Action — "Little
Mack" — President's Reception — The Picture of Weariness and Despair — Amusements — Morals — Without the Comforts of Civilization
— Secession Literature — Hutchinsons sing in Camp — Soldiers wild
with Delight — Dying from Camp Diseases — The poor Horses — Depression of the Men — Picturesque Scenes — Breaking up Camp, and starting
off — Going into Camp for the Night — Foraging — Difficulty of Moving
a large Army — Longing for Letters from Home — Their blessed Influence — "The musty Crackers and rusty Bacon are better" — Fatigues of
Picket Duty — In Pursuit of Something to eat — "Somebody had been
frying Chickens" — Battle of Pea Ridge — As good as Dead the last
half of the Battle.

URING the war I maintained an extensive
correspondence with soldiers in the field
and hospital, and with officers, chaplains,
and nurses. They were mostly personal
acquaintances — men from my own neighborhood; church and Sunday-school associates;
sometimes intimate friends and relatives. In every
instance they were men of a high order, well educated, of a lofty moral character, and who entered
the service from devotion to the imperilled country.
They gave up lucrative positions, withdrew from
their studies in colleges or professional schools, and
all left homes of refinement where they were beloved

and trusted, and where their absence created a sadness, which in some instances was deepened by their death.

I have selected from these epistles some of the most interesting, for the conclusion of this volume. They present phases of life during the war that can be reached in no other way. They give the reader a glimpse of the nobleness of the American soldier, who, trained to the arts of peace, entered into "the hideous business called war" at the behest of duty, but gladly renounced it for the life of the civilian when the bells rang in the joyful tidings of "peace." I doubt if a collection of letters as intelligent and interesting could be gathered from the correspondence of the soldiery of any other nation in the world! I doubt if the general wholesomeness of inner army life, of which one gets hints in these epistles, could be excelled by that of any army ever mustered for battle! I doubt if the American soldiers, the subordinates and privates, were not almost phenomenal in their versatility, patriotism, intelligence, and heroic patience! My interest in them was absorbing during the war; my admiration of and pride in them is limitless since the war ended.

And I never meet the poorest and most desolate of the rank and file in the hospitals and Soldiers' Homes in which the country is sheltering them, that I do not realize anew that the nation owes the soldiers of the last war a debt which it never can pay — a gratitude which it should be proud to manifest.

If the soldiers of the Revolutionary War defended the right of the infant republic to life, and beat back the monarchists that would have strangled it in its cradle, the soldiers of the last war saved it from assassination at the hands of its own children, and cut out by their swords the cancerous evil which was poisoning its whole system and eating away its life. All honor, then, to these last saviors of the republic!

## LIFE IN THE CAMP.

ROLLA, MO., Nov. 23, 1861.

You remember our regiment left Aurora, Ill., on the 24th of September. We have buried two men since we left, although we have had very little sickness. Our commander is General Greusel, an old schoolmate of General Sigel, an officer whom the regiment almost idolizes. Where he leads, the Thirty-sixth Illinois will follow.

We were paid yesterday, and are now well provided with clothes, having two suits throughout, an overcoat, a good oil-cloth blanket, and the best of tents. For all these comforts we are indebted to the untiring energy and perseverance of our officers. We are making quite a reputation as foragers. On the 1st of November, the colonel, with two companies of infantry and two of cavalry, scoured the country for fifty miles round, bringing in a large amount of stock — horses, mules, cattle, sheep, and wagons. Among the prisoners are a rebel colonel and captain. They also captured a drum and flag. The drum is a queer thing. It consists of a hollow log about three feet long, the ends covered with sheepskin. The flag is a piece of white cloth, on which is painted a map of the seceded states. It is a wonderful specimen of Southern ingenuity.

The First Iowa regiment has joined us. It performed various feats, while coming through Missouri, which profoundly disgusted the secessionists. At

Renick the men captured a rebel flag, and ran up the stars and stripes on the same pole. A painter in one of the companies climbed up to the hotel sign in the night, and transformed it from "Yancy House" to "Union House." At Macon they took possession of the office of the *Register*, a hot secession sheet. There are no less than forty printers in the regiment; and before they left the office they had set up, printed, and issued, in its place, a spicy loyal little journal, called "Our Whole Union." When they arrived at Booneville, they entered the office of the *Patriot*, took the place of the editors and compositors, whose secession sentiments had rendered them very unpopular at Booneville, and promptly issued a loyal paper in its stead.

Our chaplain is a capital fellow. The boys call him "a bully boy," which, you know, is their highest praise. On a wearisome march that we made last week, he constantly rode along the line, encouraging the boys with his hearty, cheering laugh. You can have no idea how the men pick up strength after the chaplain speaks to them. He gives us capital sermons, and is very popular, because his discourses never exceed fifteen minutes in length; and as to prayers, there is but one to a service, and that is brief. He is as good a friend to Tom and Dick and Harry, even when he catches them swearing, as he is to an epauletted officer.

We have regular services every Sabbath. The colonel is very strict about our attending Sabbath service; and all must be there who are not on the sick list, or they must go to the guard-house. Religion is compulsory in this regiment. He is very thoughtful about the morals of the men, and so is the chaplain, neither of whom is a man of the preaching sort. But, nevertheless, there will be profanity and other vices. We are expecting a forward movement very soon. For several nights the guards have been doubled, and the men have slept on their arms, ready to start at a moment's warning. At any moment of the day or night our regiment may receive marching orders to start in an hour. We shall be only too glad to go. Yours truly, S. P. S.

## HARDSHIPS OF A CHAPLAIN'S LIFE.

ALEXANDRIA, VA., Nov. 30, 1861.

You seem to think that a chaplain's life must be an easy one. I grant you it may be if a chaplain shirks his duty. But if he is ready to share• the perils of the soldier, a chaplain will find his life full of hardships and exposure. I acknowledge my letters are "light and trifling," as you characterize them; but have you not heard of the boy who whistled to keep up his courage? Let me give you a few facts concerning my life.

I have slept in the open air, with scarcely any covering, so chilled in the morning as to rise with great difficulty. I have slept in a government wagon, with hungry mules foraging around, and snatching the hay which formed my bed. I have slept with crickets, bugs, spiders, centipedes, and snakes crawling about my couch as thick as princes in Germany. For one week I had no food but salt pork, which I detest, and bread which water could not soften. Since I have been in camp, I have not been comfortable the whole of one night, because of cold. I have no abiding-place, nor has the rest of the army. I must be ready to march, rain or shine. Very different this from my life at Hudson, ·N. Y., where I had my books, my study, and home.

Tell H—— [a country clergyman] that he need not come here to see if he likes it, for he can make a few experiments at home. Let him sleep on the floor of the attic a few nights without a pillow or comforter, or in the garden, wrapped in a pair of horse blankets. Let him get a pound or two of the rustiest pork he can buy and some mouldy crackers, and feed on them for a week. Or let him treat himself to a couple of salt herrings, and drink his black coffee without milk or sugar. These will be good preparatory steps before his enlistment. After he has enlisted, tell him he must make up his mind to be a man among •men, cheerful, brave, blameless. He must point out the road, and he must also lead the way. Like Cromwell, he must trust in God, and keep his powder dry.

Dec. 3.—We have just had a battle, that took place at Conrad's Ferry, which resulted disastrously to our troops. A narrow river separated my men, with myself, from the battle-field; and, as we had no means of crossing the deep, swift stream, we could render our companions no assistance. I remained with my comrades during the night, assisting the wounded, and rendering all possible aid to the fugitives. At the conclusion of the fight, our brave fellows were ordered to save themselves as they best could. Many plunged into the water, and swam to an island in the river, and were afterwards conveyed to the Maryland shore. Many of them were nearly naked. All were cold and shivering. I assisted them to the extent of my ability; and not only encouraged the men, but literally drove them to walk to camp without delay. I feared otherwise they would freeze to death.

About midnight the fugitives ceased to arrive, and I sought for rest in a shock of corn beyond the canal. I had scarcely fallen asleep when I was aroused by heavy firing of musketry on the Virginia side of the river. I hastened to the shore, and learned that about four hundred of our soldiers had hidden themselves in the early part of the evening, and had just been discovered. They were slaughtered like sheep. Those that could swim, rushed to the river. Many were drowned. The remainder were butchered on the spot, or made prisoners.

I shall never forget what I saw and heard that night on the banks of the Potomac. It was one of the most dreadful nights of my life. I have passsd many that were sorrowful. I have watched and waited calmly for death amid the chilling blasts of the North and the fearful tornadoes of the torrid zone. I have kept vigil by the bedside of those dear to me as drops of my heart's blood, and have felt that the light had gone out of my life, when the sunrise saw me sitting by my dead. But I have never endured so much of agony and of horror as during that night, when I saw men butchered by the hundreds in cold blood, simply because they wore a different uniform from their murderers.

Yours truly,     G. C.

## THE DESOLATION OF WAR — THE PRESIDENT'S RECEPTION.

FORTRESS MONROE, VA., Dec., 23, 1861.

I take it for granted that you, and all my other friends at home, are desirous to hear from me; so I write as frequently as possible, and am only too thankful if my hastily scrawled epistles keep me in affectionate remembrance, and evoke a reply. The Twentieth Indiana is stationed at Fortress Monroe, perfecting itself in drill, and impatient to be led into action. The prospect of going into winter quarters is very distasteful to us. "We didn't come here to drill and camp, and become veteran soldiers," say the boys. "We came here to fight for our country, and why are we not led into action?" There is a good deal of grumbling over this "masterly inactivity," and the boys are singing much less of the doggerel in praise of McClellan than we heard some few weeks ago.

> "For little Mack,
>     He took the track,
>     And swore to beat the rebels back!
>     Whoop! Whack!
>     Hurrah! for little Mack!"

This has rung through the regiment day after day, until I have almost wished "little Mack" had never been born. We feel the cold weather, and do not perceive much difference between the climate of Virginia and Indiana. The boys have invented all sorts of contrivances for warming their tents, some of which would make you smile. Some answer their purpose, and some are a plague to the inventors. There is one excellent quality in the army. Whatever may be the discomforts of the men, or their hardships, they do not complain, but pass it over with fun and jokes. With a good deal of unemployed time on their hands, and with little to read, and nothing in the way of diversion, they take to fun in a wholesale way. This is better than grumbling or desponding, but we all feel it would be better if we could have full and absorbing employment; such, for instance, as driving the " secesh " down into the Gulf, whose drums we hear within two or three miles of us.

The desolation of war can only be understood by those who behold the country around us despoiled of its grand forests, centuries old. The earth is cast up into fortifications, and trodden into dust by the continuous tramp of three hundred thousand men. The burned village of Hampton, just before us, looks desolate enough. I was over there a few days ago, and brought away as mementoes a fragment of a tombstone bearing date 1701, and recording the death of a man one hundred and twenty-eight years old, and a lump of the melted bell of Hampton church, which was wantonly burned by the rebels. It was more than two centuries old, and was brought to this country from England.

I was sent to Washington with despatches a few days ago; and as I had to stay the night that I might take back answers, I began to look about for diversion. I learned that the President held a levee that evening, and with five other officers I decided to attend it. So, brushing up hats, coats and hair, we started for the White House. No white kids graced our hands, but we thought we had as good a right to see the great " rail-splitter " as anybody. We worked our way to the reception room, through billows of silks and satins, through clouds of lace and feathers, amid spangles and jewelry, epaulets and swords, brass buttons and spurs. The scene was very brilliant, and so was Mrs. Lincoln, the wife of the President. She was all smiles, and decked out in the most fantastic style. But my heart ached for the poor President. He looked the very picture of weariness and despair. While standing listening to the "Hutchinson family," singing patriotic songs, he twice closed his eyes, and partially went to sleep with all that effervescing crowd of office-hunters, contract-seekers, and pleasure-lovers about him. If President Lincoln does not live out his term of office, I, for one, shall not be surprised. I sincerely pity him.

As to any news, you have it and *we* are wholly in the dark; so I shall not undertake to tell you anything. They are making sixteen thousand minie-balls at the Washington Navy Yard, every ten hours. That looks as if this inactivity of the army would end before long. I was very glad to receive your papers and books. They have been read all in pieces. Any donations of that kind will never come amiss.                     Yours truly,               E. G.

## AMUSEMENTS — MORALS — SECESSION LITERATURE.

ROLLA, MO., Jan. 3, 1862.

The holidays are over, and the soldiers are again going through the regular routine of camp life. About three thousand cavalry have gone in search of the much-desired General Price, and I hope they will not return Price-*less*. To-day our mules and wagons have arrived, and the boys have been having sport breaking the wild mules. The whole ground is covered with a sheet of ice and sleet.

Our amusements are various. Ball-playing, pitching quoits, playing dominos and euchre, washing, ironing, cooking, sweeping the street, and last, but not least, writing letters. The fact that a man

belongs to the army, entitles him, we think, to write
*to any one*, so that we are constantly soliciting correspondence, nor do we fail very largely of our
object.

I wish I could give you a description of the country and of the people here. For miles around the
country is dotted with the campfires of the poor
refugees, driven from their homes by the disloyal
bushwhackers. It is a pitiable sight to see these
people, destitute of nearly every comfort of civilization. Hardly one of them has a stove, or other
shelter from the driving storm except a small tent.
The children are barefooted, and their pinched faces
plainly indicate their suffering and starving condition. On an average, I do not find one in fifteen,
among either adults or children, who can read or
write. It is a timber country where we are encamped. The wood is so crooked and knotty that,
when cut and burned, it will not make straight
ashes. The hogs are so thin that they are not discernible to the vision except when viewed by the
left flank (side in front); and the most of the people
in this vicinity have never seen either church or
school-house.

The morals of the soldiers are much better than
could be expected. Only one man has been intoxicated in our company, which is really remarkable
considering the enticement to drunkenness. In the
Fourth Iowa camp, near us, there is a regularly
established Good Templars' Lodge, that holds weekly
meetings. I hope to attend one of them next week,
and will write you if there is anything interesting to
tell. Profanity is very common. It is really a surprise to me, accustomed to it, to hear how easily and

with what originality the men swear. Our chaplain does all in his power, with his mighty persuasion, his never-failing good humor, and his abounding kindliness, to suppress this and every other vice.

Barracks are certainly injurious to the soldiers. The Iowa Fourth have substantial log barracks; and ever since they left their tents and went into them, they have had sickness, one man dying a day on an average. In December they buried thirty men. I attribute much of their sickness to the fact that their camp-ground is in a former burying-ground. This certainly must have something to do with it. Would you like to see one of the recruiting bills of Price's army? Here is a copy of one: —

### SOLDIERS WANTED

In 1th, 6, 7, & 9 Military Districts immediately now is the time to come and join General Price on his march Northeast to drive the abolition hordes from our land your brethren are at work and call for help

By order of    MAJ GENERAL PRICE

(His signature)

Then rally men rally men, around the flag unferld
The gallent deeds of Southern men are ringing through the world
Fall into the Southern ranks form one united band
And we'll drive ABE LINCOLN's armys forever from our land.

This is a *verbatim et literatim et spellatim* copy of a bill stuck up in the land of " secesh." As it is late and I am sleepy, I bid you good night.

Yours truly,      S. P. S.

## HUTCHINSONS SING IN CAMP — SICKNESS OF THE MEN.

FAIRFAX COURT-HOUSE, VA., Jan. 18, 1862.

We have been highly favored lately with concerts given by the "Hutchinson Family." The last one was given in the chapel of Fairfax Seminary. This was occupied before the war by the Episcopal Theological Institute. The buildings are very substantial and beautiful, and of brick, all of which were left with their furniture. The college is used for a hospital. The boarding-houses, and the dwellings of the principals and professors are occupied by the chaplain and surgeon of our regiment, — the First New Jersey, — and by other officers. We have the use of the chapel for meetings, lectures, and concerts. Colonel Farnsworth's Illinois Cavalry is encamped within two miles of us, and the men came up *en masse* to attend the concert. It was very interesting to see with what zest the soldiers crowded around and within the chapel, and how wild they were with delight when some song was sung which met their approbation. There were probably from twenty-five hundred to three thousand jammed into or packed around the chapel. When the Hutchinsons sang "Rock me to sleep, mother," "Do they miss me at home," and other songs which called up recollections of happy days, and of parents and friends, the poor fellows wept, and seemed not to care who saw them.

We are exceedingly tired of the monotonous life we are leading, and of this do-nothing policy. We are willing to go into the jaws of death rather than remain where we are. A scouting party of some two or three hundred cavalry, made up in part of Colonel Farnsworth's and in part from another Illinois regiment near by, commanded just now by Major Beverage, has just started off in high glee. There had been a strife all the morning, often rising into angry and bitter words, among the men, as to who should have the privilege of going off on this dangerous trip. I had hoped to go, for I am as tired as any one of this lazy life. But the lot did not fall on me. We are dying faster from the sicknesses of camp than from the casualties of war. Nearly all the men have bad colds, so that sometimes during a concert the coughing fairly drowns the music. Why should the men not take cold? Many of them lie on the damp ground, with only a blanket under them. Over one hundred and thirty are in the hospital from Colonel Farnsworth's regiment alone. They have buried several men lately; and where the rebels kill one, disease slays ten.

The poor horses look sorry enough, I tell you. They are tied to long poles placed in crotches set in the ground, and extended ten to fifteen rods. On each side are tied the animals. They have no floor or shelter, and are in soft mud six to eight inches deep. An order has just been issued that if any of us poor fellows, standing guard in the wind or storm, wet or cold, tramping through mud and water, drop asleep through fatigue or exhaustion, we are to be shot. Per contra, let a notorious traitor be taken, who has killed and destroyed everything within his reach, and who would murder every loyal man in the Union if he could, and all he has to do is to take the oath, and he is let off. Will you tell me where is the justice of this?　　Yours truly,　T. G. A.

## PICTURESQUE SCENES —FORAGING.

LEBANON, Mo., Jan. 26, 1862.

Since my last, we have met with some changes. We broke camp at Rolla, and marched three days to this location. On the way, we passed a storehouse, in which two thousand barrels of pork and other supplies were stored, intended for Price's army. As we do not intend that he shall visit this locality again, it was loaded on our wagons, and sent ahead, for safe keeping.

At the end of three days we ran short of provisions, and began to be hungry for the despised hardtack which we threw away at Rolla. General Osterhaus, our acting general, did all in his power to protect the hogs and cattle in the way of the moving column. But the boys made a good use of powder and ball, and in some measure supplied our lack of rations. In wonder and amazement I cry, for what purpose was this desolate, unbounded Missouri wilderness created? After travelling four days, we have seen but four houses; and during our sojourn of four months in Missouri we have seen neither church nor school-house. There is a lack of everything here. Yesterday, Sunday, Captain Joslyn sent eight privates and myself in search of meat. We hunted faithfully all day, and at night had found but twelve hogs for a company of eighty men. We shall remember this Sunday for a long time.

Jan. 28. — We broke up camp before daybreak on the 22nd, and were on the road long before sunrise. It is a picturesque scene, this breaking up camp and starting off, and worth an artist's trouble to sketch. At the roll of the drum, we take down our tents, and load them on the wagons. At the second roll we fall into the ranks; then we are ready to march. The smouldering campfires, the hurrying to and fro of the men, the loud word of command, the howl of the teamsters as they get the mules into line, the roll of the drum, and the general bustle and stir, combine to make the occasion lively and interesting.

That afternoon, at one o'clock, we went into camp. We had marched twelve miles. The moment we halt for the night, we stack arms, unsling knapsacks, and break ranks. Then the boys scatter in every direction to get wood, straw, leaves, water, and anything else they can find, with which to make themselves comfortable through the night. By the time we get things ready, our teams have arrived, and we take our tents, pitch them, and make coffee the first thing. This and hard crackers have constituted our supper lately. Still we will not grumble or whine. The next day we marched to Lebanon, where we are now in camp.

We were told this morning that we should be short of meat for the next nine days. Accordingly, two of the boys, with myself, got permission to go foraging. We were not allowed to take our muskets out of camp, and so we took revolvers. After travelling a mile, we overtook a fine large hog. We fired at him — piggy ran. We fired again — he ran again; and so it continued, until we had put twelve balls into this four-footed object of our desire. We skinned the animal, and carried it back in triumph into camp.

We found another treasure. We passed an old storehouse half full of tobacco. You should have seen the way the boys pounced on it. They have been for some days in much need of this filthy weed; and the way they seized it would have done honor to a "half-famished Numidian lion" seizing sheep. The only place we have passed untouched, and from which we have not levied contributions on our

march, has been a graveyard.   The boys did not
even take a slab from that.   Postage stamps are
eight and a third cents apiece, or three for two bits.
I wish you could enclose a few when writing me;
for the paymaster visits us but rarely.   To-night I
go on picket duty, and will not protract my letter.

Yours truly,   S. P. S.

## DIFFICULTY OF MOVING A LARGE ARMY — LONGING FOR LETTERS FROM HOME.

HEADQUARTERS, FORTRESS MONROE, VA., Feb. 3, 1862.

Quietness reigns supreme here at present, and I
doubt if I shall be able to write you even one interesting page.   The weather for some days past has
been rainy, and in consequence we have had no
drills.   We are so near "Dixie" that snow seldom
reaches us, and never in quantities to be anything
but a vexation.   Even our enemies seem to have left
us to amuse ourselves as best we can.   Picket, or
grand guard duty is the only diversion from lazing
in camp these dull, rainy days, and, as the rebels
have deserted us, even that is getting uninteresting.
Tame as it is getting to be, it must be attended to,
as the safety of the entire army depends upon the
grand guard.

The people at home have very imperfect ideas of
the difficulty of moving a large army.   Almost every
paper that we receive from the North criticises our
generals for not exhibiting more energy in sur-
mounting the obstacles that retard the movement
of large bodies of infantry and artillery, with their
army wagons, ambulances, cattle herds, and materials for the building of roads and bridges.   They do
not understand that an army train, upon the most

limited allowance compatible with freedom of operations, for a few days, away from its depots, is an
immense affair. Under the existing allowances in
the Army of the Potomac, says Lieutenant-Colonel
Tolles, a corps of thirty thousand infantry has about
seven hundred wagons, drawn by four thousand two
hundred mules. The horses of officers and of the
artillery will bring the number of animals to be provided for up to about seven thousand.

" On the march, it is calculated that each wagon
will occupy about eighty feet, in bad roads much
more. Consequently, a train of seven hundred
wagons will cover fifty-six thousand feet of road,
or over ten miles. The ambulances of a corps will
occupy about a mile, and the batteries about three
miles. Thirty thousand troops need six miles to
march in, if they form but one column. The total
length of the marching column of a corps of thirty
thousand men is, therefore, *twenty miles*, even without including cattle herds and trains of bridge
material."

In addition to Colonel Tolles' statement, try to
imagine the villanous roads and soil of this country,
its unbridged streams, its forests, and its lack of
railroads. Then remember that in a forward movement not *one* army corps of thirty thousand men is
moved, but four, six, eight, or ten, according to the
magnitude of the proposed operations, and tell me if
the grumblers of the papers ought not to have an
occasional spasm of sense and — silence.

We do not get letters enough. Do the folks at
home write and do the letters miscarry? or do they
forget us? You can have no idea what a blessing
letters from home are to the men in camp. They

make us better men, better soldiers. We get the blues sometimes, and feel like going to the dogs. We are sometimes worn out with duty, wet, and muddy. The coffee is bad, the crackers worse, the bacon worst of all; and we are as hungry as wolves. Just then the mail boy brings in a letter — a good long one from you, or from mother, or from some of the dear girls on the West Side. Immediately all the weariness is gone; the fire has quit smoking; the musty, fusty, rusty crackers and bacon are better; and I am just the happiest fellow in all the world.

One of our men was drunk, and fought and swore so shockingly, day before yesterday, that we had to send him to the guard-house. To-night he is taking a good repenting cry between the blankets. Do you know why? He got a letter this afternoon from his mother, and I have no doubt that she spoke of the Sabbath-school, the church, and the prayer he used to say when a little fellow at home, when his mother tucked him in bed. He instantly made for the blankets; and though he thinks none of us know it, we all know the poor fellow is there sobbing his heart out. *Do* write; long letters; full letters; tell us everything; we want to know particulars.

Yours as ever,      E. G.

## FATIGUES OF PICKET DUTY — BATTLE OF PEA RIDGE.

LEBANON, Mo., Feb. 4, 1862.

My last was broken off rather abruptly because I was detailed to go on picket duty. There is a double row of pickets all the way round this camp, so you can judge of the duty we are required to perform. The inner camp is about twelve miles round. Our squad went out about three miles and camped. We were well provided with cartridges, etc., but had but two hard crackers for twenty-four hours. I was put on the first relief, and as soon as relieved I went with two other men in pursuit of something to eat. Of course we were not allowed to fire a gun, nor could we run down a Missouri hog. We were not foolhardy enough to attempt this, either. I would as soon think of running down a wild horse. I presume you have had little experience with the four-footed sort of animals; you only know the bipeds, and so cannot understand my description of these four-footed Missourians. Why, the sun almost shines through one of them, they are so fearfully thin, and all the boys declare that it takes three of them alongside to make a shadow.

But when the sun went down, three or four suspicious-looking personages might have been seen loitering near the hen-roost of a neighboring plantation. I sha'n't tell you what they did; but whatever the preliminaries were, they were speedily arranged, and before morning the savory smell plainly indicated that somebody had been frying chickens. We were not careful enough, and the feathers betrayed us when the colonel was making the grand round.

I have been again detailed to go out on picket with my company. Our beat extended a mile and a half across a cold and desolate prairie, and cold rain began to fall as soon as we went on guard — characteristic of my luck. It continued to rain and freeze until three o'clock in the morning, and then snowed until we were relieved, at one o'clock next day. We had hardly got back to camp, encased in ice, when the sun burst out in all its splendor. I confess we were a little downhearted when we found only hard crackers. This country is as desolate as Sahara.

PEA RIDGE, ARK., March, 1862.

I am sitting on the battle-ground, and write you a few lines to tell you that a victory has been won besides that at Fort Donelson. Many of our brave boys lie around me, sleeping with the dead. I will not undertake to give you an account of the battle. I could not do it intelligently, and you will have the details before this reaches you. But I have had fighting enough for once. I only wonder that I am alive, for again and again I was covered with earth thrown up by plunging shot. While I lay on the ground at one time, six horses attached to the cannon at our right were killed, and one man in Company E, on my left, was struck in the head with a cannon-ball and killed instantly. I was so sure that I should lose my life, that I really felt no concern about it. I considered myself as good as dead the last half of the battle. Nevertheless, I am still alive and kicking. Our men were very cool and unexcited during the whole battle. Price's army is scattered now in every direction. Many have gone home, and the rest are driven all over the country. The Iowa Fourth and Ninth were terribly cut to pieces. Our regiment, the Thirty-sixth Illinois, lost a few men, and some were wounded. The rebel general Ben McCullough was killed. Generals Mackintosh and Price were wounded. I have not heard from you for weeks. Are you too busy to write?

Yours truly,          S. P. S.

# CHAPTER XXXV.

SOLDIERS' LETTERS FROM THE FRONT DURING THE SECOND YEAR OF THE WAR — HOW A SOLDIER FEELS IN BATTLE — SWAMPS OF THE CHICKAHOMINY — A BABY ON THE BATTLE-FIELD — "OLD ROSY."

Letter from a Nurse on a Hospital Boat — After the Battle of Shiloh — Battle Scenes — "Marching all Day, and fighting all Night" — Fearful Condition of the Sick and Wounded — Intimidating Effect of the howling Shells — Burning commissary Stores — "It is all over! I am to be killed!" — Hard Lot of the Sick — Wading through the villanous Mud of Virginia — General Howard wounded — "Hereafter let's buy our Gloves together!" — Letters from Home — "A Means of Grace" — Negro Friendliness — Splendid Foraging — Surprised at the good-looking Yankees — Life in a Rebel Prison — The Counterpart of Jeffreys and Haynau — Putrid Mule-Beef — Soup swarming with Bugs and Maggots — "A Baby on the Battle-Field" — The Army of the Cumberland — "Old Rosy" — Nationalities represented in the Army — "Schpike dem new Guns! No, Sheneral, it vould schpoil dem!"

## LETTER FROM A NURSE ON THE CITY OF MEMPHIS — AFTER THE BATTLE OF SHILOH.

HOSPITAL BOAT CITY OF MEMPHIS,
PITTSBURG LANDING, TENN., June 6, 1862.

I HAVE not yet become familiar with my new field of labor. It is one where all classes and creeds are reduced to a common equality by the stern leveller, war. You are well versed in the sad story of battle and death connected with this locality. The heart's blood of our sons, fathers, and brothers has been freely poured out on the plains of Shiloh. The common private and the common enemy have been buried where they fell. It was not possible to do otherwise. But I have a kind of heartbreak as I look at the rude and unsightly trenches in which thousands of our soldiers are buried. In one grave

650

within a quarter of a mile of Shiloh church lie forty-seven Union men with their captain. A few rods from them is a long trench in which were buried two hundred and thirty-four secessionists. My post of labor is on the hospital boat City of Memphis. She has taken to the general hospitals at Mound City, Paducah, Cairo, and St. Louis, over five thousand sick and wounded since the battle of Pittsburg Landing. An old, gray-haired man is working with me. He is a nephew of General Winfield Scott. He and three sons are fighting to save the Union; he as a hospital nurse, and they as Union soldiers.

Many incidents of daily occurrence show what strong ties of friendship bind officers and soldiers together. A lieutenant was wounded. We took him on board. When it was time to start, most of his command came to bid him "Good-bye." They took him by the hand, unable to speak a word, but wiped off manly tears from their bronzed cheeks with their coat-sleeves. At last, one who had better control of his feelings than the rest grasped the hand of the lieutenant, and said, "Good-bye, Bob! God bless you! Get well as quick as you can, and write to a fellow as soon you are able!"

Another, whose leg had been amputated, asked me to take the address of his young wife, and, as soon as I could, write her a letter; for he did not wish her to be kept in suspense until he was able to write himself. He seemed disposed to talk; but as he was very weak, and the surgeon insisted upon his being quiet, I sat down beside him, and soothed him by repeating to him fragments of hymns. Twice I went through the whole of that beautiful hymn, "Nearer, my God, to Thee!"

"Oh," said he, "I have heard that sung hundreds of times, but never before did it sound to me so beautiful." He dropped asleep. I went to him two or three times to be sure that all was well with him, and was gratified that his slumbers were so calm. The last time my foot slipped. I brought a shaded night-lamp for examination, and found a large pool of blood coagulating under his cot. I turned the light full upcn the young fellow's face. He was dead. The leg had not been well bandaged after amputation. The artery had slipped, and he had bled to death. I had a very different letter to write the young wife from what I had planned. How thankful I shall be when this stormy night of war is ended, and when the peace bells shall once more announce the beginning of a new day.

Yours as ever, J. S.

## BATTLE SCENES — RETREAT TO HARRISON'S LANDING, VIRGINIA.

CAMP NEAR HARRISON'S LANDING, VA., July 21, 1862.

Of course you have already heard a great deal about our famous retreat — or "*change of front,*" as our commander-in-chief and our newspapers prefer to call it. The scenes through which I passed during that terrible week, seem more like a dream to me than a reality. For seven consecutive days, some part of the army was engaged with the enemy. The men were worn by hardship, and were suffering from the malign influences of an unhealthy climate. But they were obliged to manœuvre before the enemy, or to fight him all day, and then to march all night — carrying knapsacks, guns, and whatever else they needed. This, protracted through a whole week, has been almost unendurable. If ever men merited gratitude at the hand of their country, these poor fellows do.

We were ordered to strike our tents Saturday morning, the 28th of June. It was whispered that we were to fall back from Richmond. Our camp was situated in the timber, some two miles in front of the enemy's lines. We had hardly commenced the business of striking tents, when the enemy's shells began to scream through the air over our heads. Few things have so intimidating an effect upon men as these shells. They howl, shriek, whistle, and sometimes seem to groan, as they pass through the air. And though you cannot see them — so rapid is their flight — unless when they explode, you hear them so distinctly that you think you might see them if you took time and looked sharp. We did not get far from our camping-ground that day. At night, we bivouacked upon the ground.

The next morning I awoke early, not much rested, for my bed was in a swampy pasture, and it had rained. Our sick and wounded had been taken mostly to Savage Station, upon the railroad. A sadder sight I never beheld. I know not how many hundreds of sick and wounded were there, in a condition so unprotected and wretched that a heart of stone would have ached. The number was so large that there were only tents to shelter a few of them. The amount of suffering was so great that to me it seemed absolutely useless to try to do anything to make the poor fellows more comfortable. Their wounds were of every possible description. Some of the gaping wounds were actually flyblown, and covered with larvæ and maggots. Many were without shirts and drawers. Some were entirely nude, and tried to wrap themselves in a ragged blanket.

They were burning commissary stores in the neighborhood, which could not be taken away, and that might fall into the hands of the enemy. In the conflagration there was a constant explosion of shells, that, by accident or otherwise, were mixed with the general mass. The fragments of exploded shells were hurled over among these poor wounded fellows, lacerating and killing them, so that at last all attempts to remove them to a safer place were abandoned, as some of the assistants were themselves killed. All these wounded and sick fell into the hands of the enemy. But as they had more than enough sick and wounded of their own, they sent a flag of truce to General McClellan to come and remove them — and this was done. But in what a plight were they removed!

The day was occupied with marching and countermarching — none of us understanding what was aimed at, and content to blindly obey orders. Again it was night. But after darkness had set in, a battery that the enemy had been getting in position opened upon us. We endured the most fearful shelling, so all confess that heard it, that has been known in the progress of this war. It seemed as though all the fires in the infernal regions had been suddenly let loose upon us. We were in a narrow belt of timber, and the shells flew through like hail, crashing down boughs of trees, and ploughing up the earth where they struck. It was a fearful hour.

Early in the morning, the troops encamped near us, with ourselves, were again in motion. It was a retrograde movement, and we were put nearly at the head of the column. It was a confused, pell-mell march, — infantry, artillery, and cavalry straggling along the road together. Nature was fairly exhausted. Again the flanking guns were opened on us, and for a moment there was a little faltering. I think everybody felt as I did in the first moment, — that we must escape from it. But directly the feeling toned me up, that I *must* go on, though all the batteries of the lower regions should open upon us. On we moved through the trees, balls and shells whistling and howling around us. The fire became so hot that we were ordered to lie down. I expected to be killed. I wondered whether I should be taken off by a minie-ball or a shell. The man next me was torn in a half score of pieces. I was spattered with his blood and rent flesh. Then the splinters of a tree that was struck by a shell covered me, as I lay on the ground. I am amazed now when I recall my mood of mind, for I absolutely grew cheerful and indifferent. "It is all over," I said; "I am to be killed. My body will be so mutilated that it will be buried on the battle-field!" And a great gush of joy stole through me as I remembered that my wife and daughter would not be sickened by the sight of my mangled remains.

There came a momentary lull in the firing, of which advantage was taken. There was a rapid deploying of our troops, a swift unlimbering of the big guns, a terrific cannonading from our side, a fierce charge on our adversaries; and soon by the cheering we knew our men were driving the enemy. I was so utterly exhausted that I remember it all as a dream in a nightmare. Louder and more general became the cheering; the whole muddy, weary, and exhausted army grew wild with delight, and rent the heavens with their cheers. The battle was sharp, but it ended in temporary victory. A few moments' rest was given the men, and then the weary retrograde march was resumed.

Before the head of the column reached Harrison's Landing, it set in to rain, and poured down without stint. In a very few hours, this broad and beautiful plantation, memorable for being the birthplace of General Harrison, was one sea of mud. The sacred soil of Virginia became such a villanous paste that it was all a strong man could do to wade through it. I shall never, throughout eternity, it seems to me, forget the terrible scenes that passed before my eyes on that day. The whole army was worn out, two-thirds suffering from scurvy and malarial diseases, and yet it was obliged to bivouac in this horrible mud, and to be pelted with a drenching rain. The wounded were brought in ambulances by hundreds. The noble mansion of the estate was not a hundredth part large enough to receive them. It was a blessed thing that the river was at hand, and that there were transports upon it to receive these poor fellows, and to bear them to places where they could have better attention.

It fared the worst with the sick. No appeal of theirs was attended to. They lay in thousands around the premises, upon the wet ground, covered only with a bit of gum cloth or a blanket. It was a sight to make a man forever hate the name of war, to see these little mounds of human wretchedness. They gave no signs of life, save a stifled groan, or the motion given to the bit of cloth by the act of breathing. All day and all night they remained in this

PLATE VIII.

## FAMOUS UNION BATTLE-FLAGS.

1. Seventy eighth Ohio Reg't.     2. Seventy eighth Penn. Reg't.     3. Thirty second Ind. Reg't.
4. Ninth Ky. Reg't.     5. One hundred and twenty ninth Ills. Reg't. 6. Eighteenth N.Y. Cavalry.

*For Descriptions see pages 63-65.*

PHOTOGRAPHED AND PAINTED FROM THE ORIGINAL FLAGS EXPRESSLY FOR THIS WORK.

A.D. WORTHINGTON & CO. PUPLISHERS, HARTFORD, CONN.

exposed situation, many of them hurried out of the world by this neglect.  I suppose the surgeons, for the most part, did what they could; but I have a feeling that there is a great fault somewhere.  Everybody declares that the Medical Department, as now organized, is a disgraceful failure.

At the battle of Fair Oaks, General Howard's right arm was shattered by a ball, so that it had to be amputated above the elbow.  Waving the mutilated arm aloft, he cheered on his men, and was borne from the field.  While being carried on a litter, he passed General Kearney, who had lost his left arm in Mexico.  Rising partly on the litter, he called out gayly, "I want to make a bargain with you, General.  Hereafter let's buy our gloves together!"

The estate upon which the army was encamped is called Berkeley on the map.  It is a noble plantation, lying in a bend of the James River.  Every sign of vegetation is trampled out, and its broad acres are as bare and hard beaten as a travelled road.  The house is an ancient brick edifice, quite large, and flanked by two smaller ones.  At a distance are the negro quarters, more comfortable than I have usually found them.  The owner was in Richmond when the army advanced, and had directed the overseer to burn everything that the Yankees could appropriate.  But the order was not carried out.  Most of the elegant furniture was left in the house.  The rich carpets remained upon the floor.  In three hours' time they were completely covered with mud and soaked with human gore.  The genius of destruction is let loose in war.  Soldiers acquire a passion for destruction.  It made my heart ache to see them break mahogany chairs for the fire, and split up a rosewood piano for kindling. But any protest is immediately received by the soldiers with cursing of the rebels and all who sympathize with them.    Yours truly,    z. h. h.


## HEAVY MAILS — NEGRO FRIENDLINESS — SPLENDID FORAGING.

MEMPHIS, TENN., Dec. 20, 1862.

We entered Memphis yesterday afternoon, after a march of eighteen days, when we accomplished one hundred and fifty miles. We were overjoyed to get back, and were no more than comfortably settled when our quartermaster came into camp with one hundred and forty letters for the boys. I was one of the unfortunate ones who received no mail; but I enjoyed the happiness of the rest. A Chicago *Tribune* of Dec. 8 was read from tent to tent, to a tentful at a time. The first notice in the local column was the opening of the new skating park, which seemed incredible to us, as we perspire in our shirt-sleeves, without any fire, as if it were midsummer.

I had gotten over my disappointment when one of the lieutenants came into camp, followed by the captain, the arms of both heaped with letters and papers. They had brought three hundred and ten more letters, and an immense armful of papers. Now, I had fourteen letters and five papers. I read and re-read them, and succeeded in digesting them all by morning. You cannot imagine what a change came over the camp after the men had read their letters.

Sometimes our expeditions and reconnoissances take us away from camp for a month at a time, so

that we neither receive nor send any letters until our
return. The men always become rough and somewhat demoralized on these occasions. They become
profane and boisterous, some of them obscene and
quarrelsome, and there will be bad blood among
them, with the prospect of several fights, as soon as
they can manage them. By and by we get back to
camp, and a big mail awaits us. All the men will
have letters and papers from mothers, wives, sisters,
and friends; and there is a change immediately. A
great quietness falls on the men; they become subdued and gentle in manner; there is a cessation of
vulgarity and profanity, and an indescribable softening and tenderness is *felt*, rather than perceived,
among them. Those who were ready to shoot one
another a few hours before are seen talking with
one another, and walking together, sometimes with
their arms around one another. It is the letters
from home that have changed the atmosphere of the
camp. If the people at home only knew what " a
means of grace " their letters are to the men, they
would write frequently.

The climate is delightful, and as yet we have had
but little weather that could be called chilly. The
December weather has been like that of September
and October in Chicago. Trees are budding, birds
are singing, and the flies are a torment. As we go
farther south I presume the weather will be even
warmer. Almost all the inhabitants left in the
country are old men and women and negroes.
There is any number of the latter. We could have
collected a small army of contrabands if the Emancipation Proclamation had been in effect. Most of the
work in the army is done by negroes. Some regi-

ments have sixty or a hundred of them. They cook, take care of the horses, wash, make roads, build bridges, and do almost all the heavy work. It surprises them to see white men work. " Why," they say, " you can harness a horse as well as any nigger. Our massas could no more harness a horse than they could fly." They constantly ask me why we will not let them fight. Most of them say they will stay with us through thick and thin, if we will only bury them when they are killed. Some of them are very importunate to drill and get ready against they are needed.

You would be surprised to see the amount of provisions the white people have stored away. When our men go to their houses and help themselves to sugar, molasses, meal, or anything, they will beg most pitifully: " Oh, don't take that, it is all I've got! I shall starve!" But an investigation of cellars, sheds, and smoke-houses, reveals immense quantities of supplies. Not a man in ten even pretends to be in favor of the Union; and they say all they dare in favor of the South. They declare that the North has always abused them, and that the time has come for them to rebel. They openly express their surprise to see such good looking men among the Yankees. Our orderly took dinner with a wealthy planter one day, and, while at the table, the lady of the house asked her little daughter, "if that man looked like a Yankee?" pointing to the orderly, who is a very fine looking fellow. " Why, no!" said the young lady; " I don't believe he is." When the orderly asked the reason of her doubt, she answered very frankly, " Why, Yankees are hideous looking creatures!"

Truly yours,        G. T.

### LIFE IN A REBEL PRISON.

WASHINGTON, D. C., Jan. 5, 1863.

It is so long since I have been able to write you, that I feel like saying, in the words of the old Scotch song, —

> " Oh, years have flown since we have met,
> And sorrow has been mine."

I have been learning, with a very ill grace, I fear, a lesson of patience and resignation in the prisons of Dixie. When I enlisted I had no expectation of being covered with glory or crowned with bay leaves; but I confess that I have seen considerably more than I bargained for. I fell into the tender embraces of the " Butternuts " on the 1st of last June, with a score of my comrades of the Ninth Michigan, and we have just been released from their loving hands.

I was taken in a skirmish at Chattanooga, Tenn. My captors conveyed me into the presence of General Kirby Smith. He questioned me very closely as to the number of men we had across the river, if our officers intended to attack the town, etc., — questions which he had no right to ask, and which I had no idea of answering. After evading them for some few minutes, I replied to the august Kirby, as he demanded that I should tell him the truth, that he could easily solve all his own problems by crossing the Tennessee River, and reconnoitring for himself.

" Don't you dare give me any of your Yankee impudence! " was his amiable reply, and then I was dismissed to the camp of the Forty-third Georgia, where I was detained a couple of weeks. With other prisoners, I was marched to Atlanta, Ga., from thence to Macon, and turned in with about thirteen hundred Yankee prisoners, taken at various times and places. The camp consisted of about four acres, and was enclosed by a broad stockade, twenty feet high. I think the location was healthy, and we were well supplied with water; but we lacked almost everything else. The months of my detention there seemed to me like years, life was so desolate.

The infamous Rylander, the "secesh" major in charge of us at Macon, has a counterpart in the bloody-handed Jeffreys of English history, or in the inhuman Haynau of the Hungarian war. He instructed his guards to shoot "the first —— Yankee that came within ten steps of the guard line." I confess that there were days when the wish within me was so strong to murder this tyrant, that it was all I could do to prevent myself rushing upon him, foolhardy as the deed would have been; for I should have fallen before I had reached him. He could have brought a little sunshine into our dreary lives — he could have soothed the dying hours of many of our poor fellows — but he seemed to take a fiendish delight in seeing the men droop and die. Nearly three hundred of our men died in this prison during the four months that I was a prisoner there. Every state in the Union was represented.

Many of the boys were young and not inured to hardships, and they went under rapidly. Fragments of that sad poem, "The Prisoner of Chillon," would cross my memory as I saw palefaced striplings die before my eyes, without the power to help. As true as there is a God in Heaven, many were starved to death, and perished for lack of the bare necessities of life. Some who grew insane with their sufferings, rushed beyond the dead line, and were shot immediately. That was merciful compared to the treatment others received.

Our rations were a half pint of flour and a small piece of bacon per man. Some of the time the bacon was so bad that we had to throw it away. When we did not have bacon, we were sometimes furnished with what we believed was mule beef. At times this was so putrid that it was impossible to eat it. We had no salt, unless we bought it at the rate of two dollars and a half per pound. If we asked for flour, we could have it by paying a dollar for three pints. Sometimes we received beef; but we were never allowed but eighteen pounds of beef, bone included, for one hundred men. Sometimes soup was made with this beef, and with black beans. River water was used in the making of the soup. Part of the time it was without salt; but it always contained plenty of bugs and maggots. Our rubber blankets, canteens, and haversacks were taken from us. Some of us received tents. Some had to lie outdoors; but none of us had anything with which to cover our bodies.

About the middle of September, rumors of a general parole of prisoners reached us, and by the last of October, with as thankful hearts as must have filled the bosoms of those released from the Bastile, we left the hated place. Death on the battle-field, death in the hospital, or death under any circumstances, is preferable to the brutality and starvation of a rebel prison. We were crowded into cattle cars and started for Richmond. At Columbia, S. C., we were stared at like wild animals; and the people appeared surprised and disappointed that we did not have horns, and hoofs. The cultivated and refined ladies amused themselves with walking backwards and forwards, making faces at us, spitting at us, and uttering gibes.

At Charlotte, N. C., we remained four days, awaiting transportation to Raleigh, with only a little rice, bread, and more putrid meat, which lasted us to Raleigh. Here we received crackers that must have been ancient when the war began, to judge from their stoniness, and some raw bacon, which we ate uncooked, for lack of fire. From Raleigh we were sent to Petersburg, and thence to Richmond, where we were paroled.

Ah! you should have seen us when we trod the deck of "Uncle Sam's" transports, if you want to know how men prize liberty. Despite the weak and emaciated condition of the boys, they were wild with enthusiasm. They kissed the flag, hugged the stanchions of the boat, patted its side, and said, "This belongs to Uncle Sam!" I was starving for coffee, and spent most of the first night drinking coffee, until there began to be danger of my becoming water-logged. As we steamed down James River to Fortress Monroe, up Chesapeake Bay, and the Potomac River, to the national capital, I think, despite our worn, ragged, and dirty condition, the sun never shone on a happier set of fellows.

I have some new ideas concerning the Southern soldiers. Hatred of the Northerners seems to be the one absorbing passion of their lives. They have any quantity of brute force, for they have been reared to be hardy physically. But the illiteracy of the Southern army is amazing. Not one in ten can read or write. How the South will get through the winter is a mystery to me, for the corn crop of Georgia and North and South Carolina is exceedingly scanty, and there is a great scarcity of meat. Shoes are worth nineteen dollars a pair. Everything is scarce and expensive. The only means of subduing this rebellion, in camp and in council, is with powder, ball, and bayonet. But will you think me lacking in patriotism when I confess that just now I feel like endorsing Horace Greeley's proposition to "let the wayward sisters depart in peace" — or in *pieces*, as they prefer? Ever yours, J. B. R.

## A BABY ON THE BATTLE-FIELD.

BOLIVAR, TENN., Jan. 10, 1863.

Let me relate a touching little incident that is very affecting. At the battle of 'Hatchie, when the conflict was raging fiercest, midway between the contending forces we found a little blue-eyed baby lying on the cold earth. A tear was on its cheek, which it had wept at finding itself alone, but it was unalarmed amid the awful confusion of the battle. With the missiles of death flying thickly about it, and crowding close upon its life, it lay there in miraculous safety, and by its smiles, and helplessness, and innocence, appealed to us for protection.

Now would you suppose that in the midst of that wild, fierce battle, with the field strewn with the dead, the shrieks of the wounded rending the air with agony, a great army would pause to save a helpless baby? Yet that is just what the Fourteenth Illinois did; and an officer of the regiment ordered the baby carried to headquarters, and tenderly cared for. The next day after the battle, the baby was brought before the Fourteenth and unanimously adopted as "the child of the regiment."

But three or four days later a heart-stricken, poverty-pinched mother came searching the battle-field and the camp in quest of her child. Wild exclamations of thanksgiving burst from her when she learned that her child had been rescued, and cared for with a mother's tenderness. I saw her receive the child, heard her brief prayer for the soldiers who saved it, and, with the blessing of a thousand men following her, she carried away our little laughing, blue-eyed baby.

Always yours,    o.

## THE ARMY OF THE CUMBERLAND — GENERAL ROSE-CRANS — GERMAN OFFICERS.

In Camp near Murfreesboro, Tenn., Jan. 22, 1863.

After so long a silence, I seat myself to write you concerning the Army of the Cumberland. Since the battle of Stone River many changes have taken place with us. Our poor wounded comrades have all been sent North. Not, alas, as they came to us; for then they could carry whatsoever they needed, and now they return unable to carry themselves. But such is the fortune of war.

A large convalescent camp has been established near the fortifications, where the boys are taken as soon as they begin to recover and approach the time when they are fit for duty. This is a noble institution, and reflects credit on our worthy general. Near the camp is a large field or kitchen garden, cultivated by convalescents and details from the army, where will be raised more garden sauce, or "truck," than could possibly be consumed by the entire convalescent corps. This is necessary on account of scurvy.

We are indebted to "Old Rosy" (General Rosecrans) for the great improvement in our bill of fare and general condition. We in the Army of the Cumberland think him almost as big a man as "Old United States" (General Grant) or "Tecumseh" (General Sherman). We have drawn pickles, good ones too; something we have not seen before since we enlisted. They have sharpened our appetites, which, to tell the truth, were keen enough before. We have also received pepper, which you should be deprived of for a time if you wish to know how to appreciate it. We have also received a lot of real "Irish Murphys" (potatoes). These favors cause us to mention the name of "Old Rosy" very gratefully. I think it has never been our good fortune since we went into the service to be situated where there was such general good feeling. We think we have the right man in the right place, and we hope the authorities at Washington will agree with us. We could not lose Rosecrans from this army without serious injury.

A few days ago, one of the boys, in a fit of great wrath, occasioned by a letter he received from his family, who were suffering from want, wrote the following letter to General Rosecrans: —

GENERAL, — I have been in the service eighteen months, and have never received a cent of pay. I desire a furlough for fifteen days that I may go home and remove my family to the poorhouse.

"Old Rosy" gave him his furlough.

In my last I complained about the German officers, did I not? Well, I guess I must take that back.

They are splendid fighters; in fact, all the foreigners are who are with us. I wonder if you know how many nationalities are represented in this army. Sigel is a German, Turchin is a Russian, Stahl a Hungarian, Maggi a Sardinian, De Monteine is a Frenchman, De Courcey an Englishman, Ericsson a Swede, Corcoran and Meagher are Irishmen, and Fidella is an Italian.

There is a German officer in camp concerning whom they tell this story; they say at the battle of Shiloh he rode up to an aide and inquired for Grant. "That's him with the field glass," said the aide, wheeling his horse about. Our Dutchman rode furiously up to the General, and, touching his cap, thus addressed him: —

"Sheneral, I vants to make von report. Schwartz's Battery is took."

"Ah," said the General, "how is that?"

"Vell, you see, Sheneral, de sheshessionists came up to de front of us; de —— sheshessionists flanked us; and de —— sheshessionists came to de rear of us; and Schwartz's Battery vas took."

"Well, sir," said the General, "you, of course, spiked the guns?"

"Vat!" exclaimed the Dutchman, in great astonishment, "Schpike dem guns! Schpike dem new guns! No, Sheneral, it vould schpoil dem."

"Well," said the General, sharply, "what *did* you do?"

"Do, Sheneral? Vy, ve took dem back again from de —— sheshessionists!"

These Germans will fight, and they care as much for this country as we Yankees do. And so, if I have complained of them, forget it.

For several days past, sentence of death has been daily executed upon spies, murderers, and deserters. Spies and murderers are hanged, but deserters are shot. It is a fearful thing for soldiers to shoot their companions in arms, and yet to maintain discipline it has to be done. Two were executed to-day. Thousands flocked to witness the spectacle, but I went as far as possible from the sight of the tragedy. During the last two years I have seen men enough making their unceremonious exit from this vale of tears and "hardtack" not to feel eager to witness any one's deliberate departure.

Cedar rails make excellent firewood, and that is probably the reason why there are no fences in this vicinity. Rail fences disappear like dew before the sun the moment an army camps in their vicinity. Our camp is in close proximity to the battle-ground, and the stench arising from the carcasses of dead horses and mules, which have not been buried, makes our camp anything but agreeable. We are waiting patiently for the fate of Vicksburg to be decided, and then we shall take up a forward march.

Yours truly,                S. P. S.

# CHAPTER XXXVI.

SOLDIERS' LETTERS FROM THE FRONT DURING THE THIRD
YEAR OF THE WAR—HOUSEKEEPING IN CAMP—RIDING
"CRITTER-BACK"—DARING DEEDS—REBEL PICKETS.

Battle of Chickamauga — Remarkable Presentiment — Housekeeping in
Camp — Ignorance of the Enemy — "The walking Regiments" —"Cannon Soldiers" — Wept over his lifeless Body — Ignorance of secesh
Soldiers — Yet they fight bravely — Have plenty of Hay, but no Impunity — Greater Loss by Sickness than on Fields of Battle — Evidence
that the Enemy are near — "Riding Critter-back" — After the Battle
of the Wilderness — "Any Commander but Grant would have retreated" — Recklessness of the Cavalry — Daring of the Soldiers — "Divide
is the word, or you are a dead Johnny!" — Ten thousand Men sing
"Rally round the Flag, Boys!" — "One vast, exultant Roar!" — Talking with rebel Pickets.

## BATTLE OF CHICKAMAUGA.

HEADQUARTERS, FIRST BRIGADE, SECOND DIVISION,
CHATTANOOGA, TENN., Oct. 29, 1863.

THE sounds of booming cannon and retreating musketry have scarcely died away, nor are the effects of the great battle of Chickamauga yet removed from our sight. I see this moment a throng of ambulances wending their way to the pontoon bridge, loaded with our comrades, who, a short time since, were joyous and strong, now carried away minus a leg, without an arm, scarred, gashed, and with a weight of Confederate lead in their bodies.

I shall not undertake to give you any description of the battle. Every prominent paper has its special correspondent down here, and when they write their letters from information obtained by themselves at headquarters — and not from cowardly stragglers — it can be, in the main, depended upon. You at home are probably better acquainted with the details of the battle than we here. My knowledge is properly confined to the part taken by my own brigade. We were not engaged on Saturday at all; but on Sunday, the 20th, we were formed in line of battle, in a strong position. Had we been left there, our loss would not have been what it is, and the loss of the Confederates in their desperate charge upon General Thomas would have been double; for we were in position to attack them with our artillery and infantry, on their left flank.

I think we could not only have checked, but utterly annihilated their massed columns. But no sooner had the troops on our left commenced to give way, than we were moved on the double quick to form a line in the face of a terrible charge, with our troops falling back and breaking through our line, while one section of our battery was unlimbered. Our much-beloved general, William H. Lytle, fell at the head of our column, twice wounded. We could not remove his remains from the field. Our brigade numbered fourteen hundred men, of whom we lost five hundred in killed and wounded. My Company, H, lost eighteen men out of twenty-eight, and two of our officers were killed; but we are in good spirits — have not been whipped, and do not believe while "old Rosy" commands us we can be. We have another idol. It is "little Phil" (General Sheridan). This place is now in such a condition that it is lost to the rebels. They might as well charge up into the heavens to obtain the sun as to waste their time on this place.

I have never come out from any fight with such a sense of loss as from this. Seven of my company are lying side by side in one grave, within four rods of where they fell. My dear messmate, comrade, friend, and bedfellow, Alvin Bunker, from whom I have not been separated one night since we entered the service together, was killed in the act of taking aim. On the night before the battle we lay down together, near where we formed the line in the morning. That was the third night we had been engaged, and so we were obliged to lie down with neither fire nor coffee, although it was very cold and rainy. Alvin and I spread our blankets and lay down together, having on our belts and arms. Holding each other by the hand, we talked for a long night about the possibility of that being the last time we should sleep together. We promised each other that if either fell the other would take charge of his lifeless remains and write home all the particulars. And then — I don't mind telling *you* of it — we repeated together the little prayer, "Now I lay me down to sleep," and, with more solemnity and tenderness than we ever before expressed, we bade each other "Good night."

In the morning, Alvin took out his watch, purse, some photographs, and little keepsakes, directed me what to do with them in case he was killed, and then said, "S——, you will have to go home without me. It is all up with me. I shall be killed in the first hour of the fight." I remonstrated, even with tears, for you know how I loved Alvin; but I could not shake him in the least. Before nine o'clock, as he was standing by me, taking aim, a cannon-ball spattered me with his blood and brains.

All who were alive and not wounded soon retreated,

leaving our wounded for the rebels to rob, and our dead for them to mutilate. But I could not leave my brother, my comrade, and my friend, and I bore his mangled and bleeding body with me a little out of the ranks of the army and wept over it. He was decently buried. If my letter is blue, have I not occasion?        Yours sorrowfully,        S. P. S.

### HOUSE-KEEPING IN CAMP — IGNORANCE OF THE ENEMY.

LITTLE ROCK, ARK., Nov. 20, 1863.

We boys have learned pretty well how to take care of ourselves, and, about as soon as we get into camp, we set up house-keeping, as though we expected to spend our lives in camp. Cosey cabins are fitted up. One will have a fireplace and a chimney, which he plasters with the red earth. Another has "jerked" a crane from some "secesh" house, and swings thereon his three-legged dinner-pot. Tables, stools, and benches are tumbled together in the quickest way possible, and by the roughest of carpenters. Most of us have a bit of looking-glass that hangs on the wall, revealing to us our bronzed faces. Some of the boys have "jerked" a banjo from some quarter, which is strung up on a hook; and before many days the whole camp will have a real homelike air. The spaceways between the tents are cleared and kept smooth, or "policed," as the camp language has it. And in front of the tents there will be always little seats shaded by boughs of trees, where we can take our ease when off parade or duty.

But suddenly there comes some morning an order for striking tents, and then this canvas city vanishes more rapidly than it grew. The regiments march out, the bugles blow, the bands play, the roll of the drum is heard. Then the army wagons stretch along behind, and, at last, where, but a few nights before, all was life and animation, there are only desolation and the various *impedimenta* that a camp always leaves behind.

A more heathenish set of human beings do not exist outside the Orient than the country people of Arkansas; and the soldiers know little more than the civilians. In the parlance of this state, the Arkansas Infantry are "The Walking Regiments"; the artillery are "Cannon Soldiers"; an officer on horseback is "riding critter-back."

We always call our antagonists "Johnny Rebs," and they hail us as "Yanks" and "You-uns." We sometimes have very amusing conversations with the ignorant fellows, which not unfrequently end in practical jokes. Ignorant as they are, they are pretty good fighters, and lead us a lively dance sometimes.

Don't imagine that ignorance is confined wholly to the "secesh." We have a little display of it in our own quarters once in a while. One of the field officers dashed up to headquarters a few weeks ago, his horse reeking with foam from hard riding, dismounted, and threw the reins to his servant, who is, like myself, a Jerseyman.

"Feed him!" said the officer.

"Isn't he too warm to feed now?" inquired the servant.

"No, not at all. You can feed him hay with impunity."

"*Impunity?*" queried old stupid. "We hain't got none. The quartermaster has furnished us hay, but nary a pound of impunity."

We have lost more men by sickness than we have by skirmishes or battles. I imagine that statement is true of the whole army.

Yours very cordially, H. C. L.

## GENERAL GRANT — RECKLESSNESS OF THE CAVALRY — DARING OF THE SOLDIERS.

HEADQUARTERS TWENTIETH INDIANA,
SECOND CORPS, BIRNEY'S DIVISION, June 8, 1864.

We have been resting for two days now, and, after thirty-five days of incessant marching and labor generally, and thirty days of battle, we appreciate it, I assure you. By "rest" I do not mean that we have left the front, and are out of sight and hearing of rebels; for our lines are only five hundred yards apart, and the occasional whirr of a rifle-ball, or the explosion of a shell, is assurance that they still live, full of murderous intent. We commenced the campaign on the 2d of May, and on the 5th were fighting. Every day until the 5th of June our regiment has been under fire, and not a day has passed but that we have lost one or more men before its close. In the charge of the 12th, the flag of the Twentieth Indiana was the first placed upon the rebel works, and its bearer, who had carried it since Gettysburg, was immediately shot down, and fell over among the enemy — dead. He was a noble fellow, and had only planted the flag when he fell.

Again at the crossing of the North Anna we were first, and alone charged the works, protecting the crossing of the others. But I do not like to think or to tell of these honorable deeds; for they always cost us the lives of our comrades, and the spilling of the blood of noble hearts, and their remembrance is painful.

General Grant's tactics are novel, and to us peculiar. Any other commander would have retreated after the battle in the Wilderness, but he does not know how to retreat. He continued the onward movement by flanking General Lee, causing him to seek a new position in haste. This flanking movement has continued until now; and rebel papers say, "Grant is enamoured of his left flank." I hope he will remain so. Confidence is unbounded in him. There is much in the letters of correspondents that is not true in regard to the great general. He never gets in a rage; never goes about cursing and swearing. He is never loud nor swaggering; and as to the stories of his inebriety, they are utterly baseless. He is always cool, self-governed, modest, reticent, quiet, and low-spoken. We are angry in the army, when we read the abominable yarns written concerning the unpretentious Lieutenant-General.

Nor have the stories of his disgusting style of dress a word of truth in them. I have never seen more style at the headquarters of the army than now, and General Grant himself, when I last saw him, was in splendid attire, but almost alone. He is the finest looking man on horseback I ever saw. The "inevitable cigar" is true of him, for he smokes continually. He is so taciturn that when any one comes to us with an account of a talk that he has had, or heard of any one having with General Grant, he is chaffed unmercifully. Not a word that he says is believed.

This is a fine portion of Virginia through which we have passed. War has not, heretofore, laid waste many of these old plantations, and a certain kind of luxury continues here. The people generally have fled at our approach, and, of course, we have appropriated the good things they left behind them, — ice, chickens, pigs, corn meal, etc., — they were luxuries to us. Our mess was so fortunate as to be able to supply itself with lots of corn meal and a cow, so that mush and milk, the best food in the world, has taken the place of the army delicacies, — hardtack and coffee.

A few days ago I met a cavalry man on the road. I was thirsty, and asked him if he had water in his canteen. He replied, "No, not water, but milk." I took the canteen, and laughed at what I supposed was the fellow's joke; for I supposed that the milk had come through the commissary's faucet. But it was indeed milk, not cold.

"Have you found a spring?" said I, laughing.

"Oh, no," replied he, nonchalantly; "there are about forty cows round here, and we just milk them." And so they did. The cavalry men are reckless fellows, under less discipline than the infantry, and have "just everlastingly lived," in army phrase.

When I went ashore at White House, I had not been there an hour before I saw some one coming, leading a cow triumphantly. I followed the man into a farmyard, and there I saw signs of the herd that he told me of, — not forty, but certainly more than twenty.

The daring of our men is to me amazing, as much as I have seen of it. It is reckless foolhardiness at times. But it is not surpassed by that of our enemies. One biting cold morning last winter, when the armies of Meade and Lee were drawn up on opposite sides of a little rivulet, all strung to so high a tension that moments seemed hours, and hours days, the deadly strife was so near at hand, a solitary sheep walked leisurely along the bank of the stream, on the rebel side. A rebel vedette fired and killed the sheep, and, dropping his gun, he rushed forward to secure his prize. In an instant he was covered by a gun in the hands of a Union vedette, who said, in a tone that carried conviction with it, "Divide is the word, or you are a dead Johnny!" "Johnny Reb" assented to the proposition, and there, between the two skirmish lines, the rebel soldier skinned the sheep, took half of it, moved back to his post, and resumed his musket. His challenger in turn dropped his gun, crossed the rivulet, lifted to his shoulder the other half of the sheep, waded back to his line, resumed his gun and the duties of his position amid the hearty cheers of his comrades, who expected to help him eat it.

During one of the eventful nights through which we have been passing, when we lay in line of battle behind our temporary fortifications, and the continuous crack of the sharpshooter's rifle rolled along the front, a solitary, ringing tenor voice struck up the stirring song, "Rally round the flag, boys!" Almost instantly, thousands of men, who seemed to have been waiting for that or something else to dissipate the gloom engendered by the carnage of the day, joined in the melody. The volume of voice with which they rendered the chorus shook the very forests about us: —

"The Union forever, hurrah, boys, hurrah!
Down with the traitor, and up with the star!"

The chorus was repeated, the whole line joining in it, until the refrain swelled into one vast exultant roar, which flung defiance to the enemy, who sent showers of bullets in the direction of the music, but the missiles whizzed harmlessly by. Our men were immensely inspired by the music, and it was very evident that the Johnny Rebs were equally irritated by it.

I have been having a talk with rebel pickets in front. They will trade anything for coffee and sugar, will take greenbacks for tobacco, but decline rebel money, which our boys have taken from their dead. They ask why we do not send back to the South the five thousand Confederate soldiers who have remained in the hospitals in and about Gettysburg, and who are now convalescent. I asked them how they knew this. Their answer was, "We learned by grapevine telegraph." The truth is, these rebels have asked *not* to be sent South, as they will again be forced into the ranks. The pickets express great admiration for General McClellan. They say, "If the South could vote, they would make McClellan President."

Yours sincerely,     E. G.

# CHAPTER XXXVII.

SOLDIERS' LETTERS FROM THE FRONT DURING THE LAST
YEAR OF THE WAR—LIFE IN REBEL PRISONS—DREAD-
FUL SCENES—HORRORS OF ANDERSONVILLE—LAST DAYS
OF THE GREAT REBELLION—PEACE.

A Hospital Picnic—"The Stump Squad"—Strawberries for the Army—
"Virginia a vast Blackberry Field"—"Old Hundred" in Camp—
Hunting Bloodhounds—Letter from a Hospital Nurse in Annapolis
—Thirty thousand Prisoners cooped up at Andersonville, in ten Acres
—Their Hands and Feet rot off—Swarming with Vermin—Bones pro-
trude through the Flesh—The Men become Idiots and Lunatics—Differ-
ent Treatment of Southern Prisoners by the North—"The Yankees take
good Care of us"—Last Days of Sherman's "March to the Sea"—The
Army reaches the Atlantic Coast—Columbia, S. C., is burned—Destitu-
tion of the South—"At the Mercy of a General more powerful than
Grant or Sherman, General Starvation."

## A HOSPITAL PICNIC—"OLD HUNDRED" IN CAMP.

HOSPITAL CAMP NEAR WASHINGTON, D. C., July 26, 1864.

I HAVE been wondering if I could find interesting matter with which to fill a letter to
you. I confess the motive is a selfish one,
for I hope to bring to myself a speedy reply — one of your long spicy letters, full of
news and gossip, and pleasant things about
my negligent friends of the West Side.

I have just witnessed a hospital picnic. It is a
new thing for maimed and sick men to participate in
out-door festivities; but is there any form of kindness, or any manifestation of tenderness, in which
the men and women of the Sanitary Commission fail
to express themselves? If this war has developed

some of the most brutal, bestial and devilish qualities lurking in the human race, it has also shown us how much of the angel there is in the best men and women — has reconvinced me that man, with the propensities of the lower creation still lingering in him, is yet divine, and ordained ultimately to a noble destiny.

The convalescent portion of this large community was out to-day in full force. It was an odd-looking company, I can assure you. For they came to the picnic provided for them with arms in slings, and sometimes with but one arm — sometimes both were lacking. Some on one leg, and others, with scarcely healed wounds, by the aid of friendly hands and crutches, were helped to the place of meeting. But there was a group the like of which, I venture to say, was never before seen at a festive gathering. It was composed of men whose limbs had been recently amputated. "We are the Stump Squad!" said one of the brave fellows facetiously, "and we are determined to see the fun." These were carried in their beds, by nurses and friends, out into the grove, and placed where the shade was densest, and where the breath of heaven could freely kiss their wan faces. New light came into the eyes of these maimed heroes as they looked round on the festive scene. Their stronger comrades made good use of the summer day. Some were engaged in games upon the thick greensward; others were swinging in the great box swings, or trying to amuse themselves in the bowling alleys. They were treated to excellent music, by the fine band of the Fourteenth New Hampshire, who came from their camp to help make the occasion pleasant. Every delicate viand which it was safe for

the poor fellows to eat was furnished them, even to
strawberries and ice-cream. And those were fed who
were unable to help themselves, amid incessant jokes,
witty badinage, and gay repartee.

I suppose you have learned of the efforts of the
ladies to furnish all the sick and wounded men in the
Washington hospitals with strawberries. They distributed this fruit to nearly ten thousand. They
expected to do better than this; but they had difficulty in obtaining strawberries from the Washington
and Baltimore markets, and could not use the money
given them for that purpose. Having a large sum
still unexpended, the ladies determined to use their
own judgment in its expenditure for the men. It is
a great stride from strawberries to tobacco. They
had observed that most of the soldiers desired tobacco, but had not the means for its purchase, and
they consequently distributed tobacco, chewing or
smoking, with pipes, to eleven thousand and sixty-
eight men. The ladies learned very quickly, by
inquiry, that there was nothing, outside of government rations, which the patients in the hospitals more
earnestly desired than this filthy weed.

There is no limit to the thoughtfulness of the
people for the comfort and happiness of the army.
Last Christmas holidays, over five thousand roasted
turkeys, with all the *etceteras*, were sent to the soldiers of the Army of the Potomac, through Adams'
Express and other sources. Blackberries are the
great luxury of the soldier at present. Virginia is
one vast blackberry field. The army was never in
better sanitary condition than now — and it is due,
so the surgeons say, to the free use of blackberries
as a diet. One of the surgeons told me that these

Virginia blackberries would save the government a million dollars in medical and hospital stores.

While I am writing a letter about good times, let me give you another incident. A few nights ago, when the air was perfectly still, and an unusual quiet reigned on the earth and in the heavens, we listened to the singing of " Old Hundred," in which some ten thousand men joined. The air was vocal with the grand old strains. One man had started it, a dozen took it up, and directly the whole camp was singing it. That was the beginning. They went from that to " Sweet Home," " Auld Lang Syne," " America," " The Red, White and Blue," and finally wound up by singing " Coronation." Before they had finished their concert, the blue canopy of evening was studded thickly with stars. I have no doubt the men were not only happier but better for this improvised concert.

One item more, and I am done. One regiment, the Fifty-Second Indiana, has recently been hunting bloodhounds. They have killed between twenty and thirty, valued at a hundred dollars each. They were kept to hunt runaway negroes, and were set upon the track of some of our men; and hence the slaughter. Let me hear from you as soon as you can get leisure to write, and tell me all the news. Not war news, but home news — and all that relates to the old days of peace. Will they ever come again?

Your friend,     E. G.

## LETTER FROM A HOSPITAL NURSE IN ANNAPOLIS, MD. — HORRORS OF ANDERSONVILLE PRISON.

St. John's College Hospital, Annapolis, Md., Dec. 10, 1864.

I had thought that by being detailed to a hospital near where my husband was doing duty, if he were sick or wounded I could be with him in his hour of need. But it was ordered otherwise. I had requested Miss Dix to detail me to these Annapolis hospitals, feeling sure that I should be within reach of him if he should be wounded or should be stricken down with sickness. Not even one of his company or regiment was with him. He was sent to the hospital on the 20th of June, and died the next day among entire strangers, as thousands of our soldiers do. He sleeps among the silent dead, at City Point, Va., on the banks of the James River, where he yielded up his life, a willing sacrifice to the cause of his country and liberty.

I trust some kind woman stood by him to minister to him when dying, as I am daily doing for brave men similarly situated. I believe that the angels of God came down, strengthening him as he passed through the dark valley, and conducted his emancipated spirit to his Father and his God. I am comforted to remember this, and to think of the welcome that he must have received from the near and the dear who had preceded him. I have never so thanked God for the glorious faith of an immortal life beyond the grave as since I have been in these hospitals, witnessing the daily departure of grand and good men to the better world.

Several thousand of our returned prisoners have arrived at Annapolis from Andersonville, Ga., during the last two or three weeks; and more are coming. Over thirty thousand of our men have been held there as prisoners, cooped up like cattle within the space of ten acres, without shelter from the sun, without water, without proper food, and receiving all the while the most brutal treatment. Twelve thousand have been starved into idiocy, lunacy, and death, in that hell of horrors. As the boats containing the poor fellows approach the Landing, a band of music attached to the military post strikes up "The Star-Spangled Banner," or some other national air, which the returning captives who are conscious, welcome with inexpressible delight. The wharf is densely packed with anxious friends, gazing upon the motley group who throng the vessel's deck, most of whom are bareheaded, without shoes, and thinly clad. They are equally anxious, after a captivity, in many cases, of more than two years, to recognize the features of some familiar face from home. Their tears fall in abundance as the poor fellows stand once more upon what they call " God's ground."

Last Monday, the flag of truce boat landed four hundred more men, brought from the prisons of Richmond and Belle Isle. Many were living skeletons, with just the breath of life left in them. The hands and feet of others were dropping off from dry rot. All are completely swarming with vermin, many are insane, and others have been made idiots from the treatment they have received at the South. Over one hundred were carried upon stretchers to the hospitals, only a few rods from the Landing. Oh, to have been treated as they have been! My blood curdles with indignation, and I can hardly endure it. Scores have already passed out of life since last Monday. They died under the stars and stripes, and the flag was laid over their coffins. There has not been a day since their arrival that we have not had eight or ten coffins standing in the chapel, side by side, awaiting funeral services and burial. Sad sights like these must touch the feelings of even the

South; for I know there must be humane men and women among them.

The appearance of many of these poor creatures is very peculiar. Their hair looks dead, sunburned, and faded. Their skins, from long exposure and contact with the pitch-pine smoke of their camp-fires, and a long dearth of soap and water, are like those of the American Indian. Their emaciated forms, with the bones protruding through the skin in many instances, and the idiotic expression of their protruding eyes, tell of unparalleled cruelty and savage barbarity. The strongest land first, and are examined by the surgeon. Those that are able are sent to Camp Parole, a beautiful and well regulated camp, two miles from the hospitals, on the railroad leading to Washington and Baltimore. Then the weaker and more sickly follow, supported by strong men to keep them from falling. Then the stretchers bring after them the sad, large remnant of helpless sufferers, and they are taken to the Naval School Hospitals or to St. John's College Hospital.

Last, and saddest of all, come the martyred dead, who have died on their journey from the prison-pens to this point. There were thirty-eight on one boat, the Baltic, and the same number died after the boat had reached her moorings, before the noon of the next day. The day after the arrival of a recent boat filled with our released men, there was a funeral of forty-three from the Naval School Hospital, who had died on the return voyage. They were buried at one time, with sad and imposing solemnities as such long-tortured martyrs for right and truth should be. As they lay in their coffins, one was struck with the similarity of their appearance, which was that of extreme emaciation, with other indications of death from starvation, exposure, and neglect.

How different this treatment received by our men at the South from that which was given Southern prisoners in the hospitals and camps of the North! A copy of the *Christian Index*, a Baptist paper, published at Macon, Ga., lies before me. Let me give you an extract from a letter published in its columns, written by Captain W. B. Haygood, of Georgia, who was taken prisoner by the Union forces at Gettysburg, in July, 1863. His letter is dated, Hospital at Chester, Pa., Sept. 25, 1863. He says, —

"This is a first-class hospital. Our beds are good, with warm blankets, and all have clean sheets once a week. We have plenty to eat, and it is neatly served. We receive good light bread, beef, pork, ham, mutton, tea, coffee, rice, butter, syrup, and vegetables in abundance. All the prisoners are supplied with good warm clothing. I have a good suit of clothing, and a large woollen shawl. We are all right on the clothing question. We have plenty of reading matter, and I spend a good portion of my time in reading. I am in fine spirits, although I long to be in Dixie. Whatever reports may be in circulation in the South, or if you hear anything that conflicts with what I tell you, don't believe it! The Yankees are taking as good care of us ' rebel prisoners,' as they call us, as of their own men. I confess that my prejudice against the Yankees has died out under their treatment."

It is a significant fact, and a full answer to the charge of cruel treatment of rebel prisoners at the North, that of five hundred who were selected for exchange at Camp Chase, Ohio, two hundred and sixty voted to remain in prison.  And of three thousand two hundred and twenty-three in Camp Douglas, at Chicago at one time, seven hundred and fifteen refused to be exchanged.

Not even are the men in Southern prisons allowed to write letters to their relatives in the North, a privilege which is freely accorded to Southern prisoners in our hands.  Union prisoners at Libby Prison are compelled to limit their letters to six lines.  One of our women nurses, whose husband is detained there in captivity, has just received the following letter from her husband, which has been three months on the way.

DEAR WIFE: — Yours received — In hopes of exchange — Send corn starch — Want socks — No money — Rheumatism in left shoulder — Pickles very good — Send sausages — God bless you — Kiss the baby — Hail Columbia !

Your devoted husband.

Our return soldiers who are able, receive a new set of clothing, two months' back pay, and are sent home on a furlough of thirty days.  Please excuse this imperfectly written letter, written by jerks at odd moments.  My duties as nurse, leave me no leisure.

Yours truly,    M. M. C.

The horrors of southern prisons were well known throughout the North, and desperate chances were often taken by prisoners to escape, and were frequently successful.  The following account of a Union prisoner's escape while on his way to Andersonville is taken from a letter written to the Hon. Samuel P. Bates, LL.D., by a member of a Pennsylvania "Bucktail" regiment.  He says: —

About twenty-five members of the "Bucktails" were captured with me, and we laid a plan for escaping from the cars while on the way to Andersonville. We were to overcome the guard, bind and gag them at a concerted signal, and leap from the car. I had stationed myself near the door, just beside one of the guards, with courage screwed up and nerves strung, ready to do my part. Just after dark it was announced to me that the enterprise had been abandoned.

I then made up my mind to escape alone. The weather was warm, and the guard permitted the door of the car to stand open. His gun rested across it. I stood for more than an hour by his side, just on the point of springing out, but still held back by the dread of what might be the result. I cannot describe my feelings at that time. I knew that in a moment I might be a mangled corpse, or I might be alive and free ; or, what was more likely, I might be disabled from travelling, recaptured, and subjected to the punishment that I knew would follow. I took out my watch, which, through some unaccountable oversight on the part of the rebels, had not been taken from me, and in the darkness felt the hands, and found that it was eleven o'clock. So, waiting for a favorable moment, I suddenly caught hold of the guard's gun, thrust it to one side, and leaped out into the darkness. The next moment I felt myself tumbling and rolling down an embankment. I heard the cry of the guard, trying to raise an alarm, as with a rush and a roar the train swept out of hearing, and I was left alone and free, but far in the heart of the Confederacy. I got upon my feet and felt to see if I was all right. I found that I was slightly bruised, somewhat scratched, and that I was terribly scared ; but, with the exception of breaking open the wound I had received in the Wilderness, I was not much hurt.

Alone, unarmed, I was in the midst of the enemy's country. Above me, to the north, I could see the pole star, which was to be the beacon to guide my footsteps by night. To attempt to go by the seaboard, I knew, would be to invite certain capture. Hence I shaped my course to the north, intending to travel till I had crossed the East Tennessee Railroad, and then strike west till I reached New River, which I meant to follow down to the Kanawha. My first purpose was to get something to eat, for which I felt ready to make any desperate attempt. I travelled through woods and fields for three hours before I came to a house. By that time I was nearly famished, having had nothing to eat for fourteen hours, and then only a small piece of corn-bread. At last I came upon a large Virginia mansion, and, having thought of a plausible story to tell, walked boldly up and knocked at the door. Two large dogs answered my summons by rushing out and barking at me furiously, but I stood my ground; and soon an upper window was thrown open, from which a man asked, "Who's there?" Without answering his question, I said, "Quiet these dogs or I will shoot them." This he did, and then I told him to come to the door, that I was a friend, had command of a scouting party of Confederate soldiers, that we were out of rations and wanted something to eat. He at once came down and proceeded to get what I wanted, all the time talking to me and asking the news. I invented some stories which made him think that the war would soon be over, and that Southern Independence was an accomplished fact. He gave me a large piece of cornbread and about a pound of boiled pork. Thanking him, I bade him good-night and hurried away. Seeing him follow me, I got into the woods as quickly as I could, and in a tone of command I called out, "All right, boys! Fall in! Forward! march!" and, being afraid that my little ruse would be discovered, I was not long in putting a considerable distance between me and that house, after which I sat down and ate a hearty meal, and then, securing a comfortable bed among some dense undergrowth, I lay down and slept till daylight, which was not more than two hours.

During the next five days and nights I travelled as fast as I could in the direction I had determined to pursue, meeting with several very narrow escapes, from capture, and getting my food as best I could, mostly from the negroes, whom I could trust at all times and under every circumstance. On the morning of the sixth day, I heard from a woman, at whose house I had stopped to get something to eat, that the Yankees were at Buckhannon, twenty-five miles across the Blue Ridge. I determined to reach their lines, so I pushed ahead, keeping in the woods as much as possible. During the day I passed over the Great Otter Mountain (Big Peak), and in the evening, about an hour before sundown, I arrived in the valley, and then I knew there was nothing between me and the Union forces but the Blue Ridge, which I determined to cross, if possible, during the night. I cautiously approached a log cabin, knocked at the door, and asked the woman who opened it if I could get something to eat. Being told that I could, I entered and sat down to wait till it was ready. Of course, I had to give an account of myself at every place I stopped, and I was always prepared with some plausible story. Sometimes I was a rebel soldier, going home on furlough; at others I was a scout on important business pertaining to the rebel government. It was only to the negroes that I revealed my true character. To this woman I concluded to tell the truth, so I said I was an escaped prisoner trying to make my way North. While talking and waiting, I was startled to see coming round the corner of the house, with musket in hand, a genuine rebel guerilla. There was no escape. He walked straight up to the door, cocked his musket, and said, " You surrender! " I cannot describe my feelings on hearing that word as he repeated it, " You surrender! " Instead of the bright vision, which had almost come to be a reality, of reaching the Union lines, I saw before me the prospect of probable death by hanging, or, upon the least provocation or pretext, by the hand of my captor; and if I escaped immediate death, then starvation at Andersonville. A heavy weight seemed resting upon my heart. I could feel my lips quiver. I could not control my voice, and for a moment my feelings were those of complete despair. But in another moment I was myself again, and my eyes took in the situation exactly. It did not take me many seconds to make up my mind that, at all hazards, I would escape from my captor or lose my life in the attempt. I determined to take advantage of any chance that should present itself. He directed me to pass out of the door and take the path up the mountain-side leading to the highway. I started, but was stopped by the woman, who said, " Wait till I get you something to eat," and she brought out two pieces of corn-bread, one of which she handed me, which I put in my haversack, and the other to my captor, who was standing with his gun lying across his left arm. Just as he turned his eyes from me, and reached out his right hand, I sprang upon him, seized him by the throat, threw him over upon his back, and with both hands caught hold of his gun, knowing that if I once had possession of it, the tables would be turned. The woman now lent assistance to the rebel, and the only thing for me to do was to beat a retreat and take the chances of a shot. I slipped my hand down the barrel, cocked the piece, and pulled the trigger, thinking I could fire it off and get out of sight before my escort could reload; but it missed fire. So, making a desperate effort, I tore myself from my antagonists and fled. The rebel followed some distance, calling upon me to halt or he would shoot me, and when I was within a few rods of the woods I heard the cap snap; but again the gun missed fire, and in another moment I was over the fence, into the woods, and out of sight. I travelled all night, and in the morning, about daylight, came upon Union pickets, and was soon in camp, safe at last. Yours very truly, C. B. L.


LAST DAYS OF THE "MARCH TO THE SEA."

HEADQUARTERS SECOND BRIGADE, SECOND DIVISION,
FIFTEENTH ARMY CORPS,
CAMDEN, NEAR GOLDSBORO, N. C., March 30, 1865.

I received with great gratitude the package of papers and magazines which you forwarded to me. They were not stale to me, but new and fresh, as I had been out of reading matter for nearly three months. It enlivens the dull monotony of camp life, and makes my tent seem a hundred-fold more like home, with a pile of papers and magazines lying in one corner, waiting perusal.

I believe we were at Beaufort, S. C., when I last wrote you. I dreaded to start out on the road through South Carolina, knowing the settled hate of the soldiers towards the state, and their determination to destroy all they could, as they marched through it. Whether they are right or wrong, they look upon South Carolina as the hot-bed of secession and treason, the prime mover in this cruel war, which has cost so much blood, treasure, and suffering. As I anticipated, fire and smoke and complete destruction marked our pathway.

We arrived at Columbia, the state capital, on the 16th February, with but little fighting and small loss. Our march to the sea had not been hotly contested. Columbia was taken, and the Fifteenth Corps entered the city on the 17th. It was not the intention of our commanding officers that Columbia should be sacked and burned, and stringent orders were given to prevent this. But the saloons and cellars of the city were full of intoxicating drinks. The boys found them, got drunk, and broke from all restraint. A few were shot for disobedience to orders, and many more were arrested; but nothing could stay them. They rushed on in their work of ruin, like the very genius of destruction.

It was a windy night. The city was fired in many places, and as the flames leaped from building to building, all the efforts of officers and sober men were necessary to save families and drunken soldiers from the wrath of the devouring element. In spite of all efforts, some were burned to death. The roaring of the flames, the clouds of black pitchy smoke, the screams of women and children as they fled from burning homes, with the yells of the inebriated and infuriated soldiers, inflamed with whiskey, combined to make that a night of horrors, such as I never before witnessed, and such as I pray God I may never see again. On Saturday morning, the city of Columbia was in ashes. I doubt if a city was ever more completely wiped out in one night.

Camden, the place made memorable in the history of the Revolution by the defeat of General Greene by the British, shared nearly the same fate as Columbia, and from nearly the same cause. The citizens of Camden had taken measures to conceal their liquors in the woods, a mile and a half from town, where they had buried them. But the soldiers found them, got drunk, straggled into Camden, and the night was again lighted up by the fires of burning buildings, which spread their lurid glare over the country for miles.

Cheraw, on the Great Pedee, was the next place of importance we reached. That was pretty well scorched and singed, as was also Fayetteville, on the Cape Fear River. At Columbia much danger attended the burning of the arsenal and the railroad depots, from the bursting of shells. One shell in bursting killed seven men and wounded thirty. Two of the men were never found. The hat of one was found in a tree; all other traces of them were lost.

The country through which we have passed is generally a pine timber, quite level, with light sandy soil, poorly adapted for raising produce, and abounding in swamps and quicksands. In many places where the ground appears to the eye to be dry and firm, a team of mules will break through the crust and go down to their bellies, and the wagon-wheels will sink to the axle-tree or box. We have often found ourselves in such a fix. It has therefore been necessary to corduroy the roads, in some places for miles on a stretch. This has made our march slow, difficult, and laborious.

But the great evil of all is the destitution in which we leave the poorer classes of these people. I have often seen them sitting with rueful countenances as we passed, sometimes weeping. Not a thing has been left to eat in many cases; not a horse, or an ox, or a mule to work with. One of our men who has been out foraging saw a man ploughing with two little boys harnessed into the plough for a team; and a woman told me, with her cheeks wet with tears, that she drew the plough herself while her husband, old and quite decrepit, held it, to prepare the soil for all the corn they raised last year — and now that was gone. It was not the intention of the commanding officers that poor people should be thus mercilessly stripped. But unprincipled stragglers ramble out of the lines, and out of the way of officers, and show no mercy or heart. They are the "bummers" of the army. Those who could, fell into our ranks as refugees, and came through to a point where they could get transportation, fleeing from a general more powerful than General Sherman or Grant — *general starvation*. They were looking for a place where they and their wives and children could live, but did not know where to go.

We passed over the battle-field of the old Revolution, near Camden, and a citizen showed us where General Greene had his headquarters, on a little hill capped by a sugar-loaf-shaped rock. But what were the military operations of that day and age in comparison with the present? I suppose General Greene's whole army would not compare in numbers or efficiency with one of the divisions of our corps.

It is not necessary for me to give accounts of our battles. You receive those by the papers sooner and more complete and correct than I can give them. Suffice it to say, in closing, that men are constantly coming in from the enemy's lines and surrendering. A few came in yesterday, who reported themselves all that were left of one whole division of their army after the battle of the 19th and 20th. They also reported the woods around full of men waiting an opportunity to come into our lines or to return to their homes.

The war is evidently nearing the end. I shall not be surprised any day to learn that Richmond is taken, and that Lee has surrendered. It does not seem to me possible that hostilities can be protracted another three months. The Union forces have overrun the whole South, the country is stripped and peeled, and the rebel soldiers are thoroughly demoralized. The armies of the enemy are melting away like snow in a June sun. Please God, let the day of peace soon dawn! Let war, which is the concentration of everything infernal, end in our republic forever!

Yours for the right,    R. L. T.

Richmond was evacuated, Lee surrendered, and peace declared in two weeks after this letter was written, and a month, nearly, before it reached me. With heartfelt earnestness I repeat the ejaculation of my friend: "In our republic may there be no more war forever!" Slavery, the iniquitous cause of war, is dead, never again to know a resurrection. The nation is entering on a grander work — that of healing, conciliation, and union. A century hence, when these shall have wrought their perfect work, our children's children will justify the fearful expenditure of life and treasure which was the cost of the excision of the hideous serfdom which had become an integral part of the republic. While it remained, there could have been no permanent peace and no certain prosperity. The bravery and sacrifice of the South, worthy of a better cause, could not preserve it. It was already doomed by the advancing civilization of the age, before the North and the South fought across the continent — one for its destruction, the other for its continuance. While we hope that it may know no resurrection here, may we not hope that it will everywhere cease among the nations of the earth?